ESTATE AND GIFT TAXATION

LexisNexis
GRADUATE TAX SERIES

ESTATE AND GIFT TAXATION

Brant J. Hellwig
Professor of Law
University of South Carolina School of Law

Robert T. Danforth
Professor of Law
Washington and Lee University School of Law

 LexisNexis

ISBN: 978-1-4224-2644-9

> NOTE TO USERS
>
> To ensure that you are using the latest materials available in this area, please be sure to periodically check the LexisNexis Law School web site for downloadable updates and supplements at www.lexisnexis.com/lawschool.

Editorial Offices
121 Chanlon Rd., New Providence, NJ 07974 (908) 464-6800
201 Mission St., San Francisco, CA 94105-1831 (415) 908-3200
www.lexisnexis.com

MATTHEW◊BENDER

(2011–Pub.3282)

PREFACE

This text provides teaching materials for a course on the U.S. transfer tax system, as it exists following enactment of the Tax Relief, Unemployment Insurance Reauthorization, and Job Creation Act of 2010. The text is structured through 26 discrete chapters, and the chapter headings supply a reasonable course syllabus. While some of the longer or more complicated chapters may require two class sessions, most chapters are intended to be covered in a single class.

The text opens with an overview of the federal transfer tax regime, one intended to introduce students to the basic structures of the estate tax, gift tax, and generation-skipping transfer (GST) tax at the outset. This chapter closes by summarizing the modern-era legislative developments in the transfer tax context, describing the seminal features of the 2010 legislation while explaining the pre-2001 framework that will return in 2013 if Congress permits the temporary legislation currently in effect to expire. After this introduction, the text proceeds to examine the estate tax and gift tax bases primarily in a context-specific (e.g., life insurance, retained-interest transfers, marital transfers) manner, and the majority of the text is devoted to these topics. The text then transitions to a discussion of the GST tax base and allocation of the GST tax exemption, followed by a discussion of a majority of the special valuation rules under Chapter 14 (apart from § 2702, which is addressed earlier in the context of retained-interest transfers). The text closes with a chapter devoted to the application of the U.S. transfer tax regime in the international setting.

Like other books in the Graduate Tax Series, this text is intended to serve as a complement to the study of the Code and Regulations. Each chapter contains an overview of the subject that is structured around an assignment to these primary authorities. The text differs considerably from the traditional casebook format. Critical passages of important cases or rulings generally are limited to excerpts in the overview, and edited opinions of seminal decisions appear on only a handful of occasions.

Each chapter closes with a set of study problems that students should prepare prior to class. The problems are intended to be realistic; examination of sample trust language followed by a request for suggested revision serves as a frequent theme. Although the text is designed to provide an effective framework for LL.M. study, the text is accessible to J.D. students in an upper-level course.

ACKNOWLEDGMENTS

Brant Hellwig is grateful to the University of South Carolina School of Law for the research support that facilitated this undertaking. Brant wishes to recognize Christopher Hines, whose considerable efforts as research assistant greatly improved the text. Brant thanks Andrew Haile, who mixed useful feedback on a number of chapter drafts with much appreciated encouragement. On a personal level, Brant thanks his daughters, Emily and Molly, for their curiosity about the project and for resisting, to the best of their ability, the urge to ask when he would finally be done. Most importantly, Brant expresses his deepest gratitude to his wife, Tammi, for her love, friendship, and support.

Bob Danforth thanks Washington and Lee University School of Law for its generous support in connection with this project. He also thanks his wife, Lee-Anne, for her patience, love, and understanding in seeing this project through to its completion. Last but not least, he thanks his children, Dinah, Emmy, and Robbie, for making all the hard work worthwhile.

SUMMARY TABLE OF CONTENTS

TABLE OF CONTENTS

TABLE OF CONTENTS

TABLE OF CONTENTS

TABLE OF CONTENTS

TABLE OF CONTENTS

TABLE OF CONTENTS

TABLE OF CONTENTS

TABLE OF CONTENTS

TABLE OF CONTENTS

TABLE OF CONTENTS

TABLE OF CONTENTS

TABLE OF CONTENTS

TABLE OF CONTENTS

TABLE OF CONTENTS

TABLE OF CONTENTS

TABLE OF CONTENTS

TABLE OF CONTENTS

Chapter 1

OVERVIEW OF THE FEDERAL TRANSFER TAX REGIME

The federal transfer tax system consists of three independent albeit related components: the estate tax, the gift tax, and the generation-skipping transfer tax. As a general matter, the estate tax imposes a tax on the transfer of wealth that occurs by reason of an individual's death—to the extent the wealth transferred exceeds a substantial exemption amount. The gift tax prevents easy circumvention of the estate tax by imposing a separate levy on inter vivos gratuitous transfers of property. Broadly speaking, the estate tax and the gift tax operate in tandem to ensure that the gratuitous transfer of an individual's property will be subject to at least one transfer tax levy. Yet because multigenerational transfers in trust can be structured to avoid estate tax inclusion for future generations, the estate tax and the gift tax together would not constitute a comprehensive regime of transfer taxation. Rather, with proper planning, the estate and gift tax regimes could be relegated to a one-time tax on the transfer of property into a trust, where the property could be held indefinitely (subject to state law perpetuities limitations) for the benefit of future generations. As a general matter, the generation-skipping transfer tax negates the ability to exempt transferred property from future transfer taxation by imposing a tax at each generation level—again, to the extent the value of such property exceeds the prevailing exemption amount.

This chapter lays the foundation for the course by providing a brief overview of the three component taxes of the federal transfer tax regime. In addition, the chapter will illustrate how the estate tax and the gift tax operate in tandem while noting the ways in which the two taxes are not fully integrated.

§ 1.01 GENERAL PRINCIPLES OF THE ESTATE TAX

Internal Revenue Code: §§ 2001(a)–(c), 2010, 2031, 2051

With its modern roots reaching back to the Revenue Act of 1916, the federal estate tax imposes a levy "on the *transfer* of the taxable estate of every decedent." IRC § 2001(a) (emphasis added). The framing of the tax has constitutional significance: While Congress may impose excise taxes subject only to the uniformity requirement, any direct tax on property must be apportioned among the States. *See* U.S. Const. art. I, § 8, cl. 1 & § 9, cl. 4. By imposing the tax on the value of the taxable estate that is transferred by reason of the decedent's death (as opposed to the value of the property in the decedent's hands just prior to his death), the estate tax falls comfortably within the excise category. *See* Knowlton v. Moore, 178 U.S. 41, 57 (1900) (interpreting a federal inheritance tax as an indirect excise tax on the transfer of property, stating that "fundamentally considered, it is the power to transmit or the transmission or receipt of property by death which is the subject levied upon by all death duties"); New York Trust Co. v. Eisner, 256 U.S. 345, 349 (1921) (rejecting the argument that the estate tax constitutes an unapportioned direct tax "on the practical and historical ground that this kind

1

of tax always has been regarded as the antithesis of a direct tax"). While this distinction may appear semantic, it colors the determination of what property interests are subject to tax as well as the manner in which that property is valued.

The decedent's "taxable estate" is defined under § 2051 as the decedent's "gross estate" less permissible deductions, and the heart of the estate tax lies in the patchwork definition of the gross estate. Whereas "gross income" for federal income tax purposes is defined expansively under § 61 and subsequently refined through context-specific provisions, no singular baseline definition of the decedent's gross estate exists for estate tax purposes. Rather, § 2031 defines the gross estate by reference to a series of independent inclusionary statutes contained in §§ 2033 through 2044. As one might expect, a decedent's gross estate includes property that is included in his probate estate for state law purposes under § 2033. Yet if that were the end of the matter, the estate tax would be as easy to avoid as the probate process. The gross estate therefore reaches far beyond assets that may be titled in the decedent's individual name at the time of his death, potentially capturing jointly held property (§ 2040), life insurance proceeds (§ 2042), annuities (§ 2039), property over which the decedent possessed a power of appointment (§ 2041), and property the decedent had previously transferred without completely terminating his interest therein (§ 2036 through § 2038). Much of the study of the estate tax is devoted to identifying the beneficial interests in property and the discretionary powers over property that will trigger inclusion in the gross estate.

Once the gross estate is determined, certain deductions are allowed in computing the taxable estate. Many of these deductions are aimed at properly measuring the value of property that passes gratuitously by reason of the decedent's death. For instance, funeral expenses, claims against the decedent's estate, and expenses incurred in administering the decedent's estate are deductible under § 2053. Similarly, casualty losses suffered by the decedent's estate during the administration process are deductible under § 2054. Perhaps the most significant deductions, however, are not aimed at accurately measuring the amount of net transfer. Section 2056, for instance, provides an unlimited deduction for certain transfers of property to the decedent's surviving spouse. This provision reflects congressional intent to treat married couples as a single taxable unit for estate tax purposes. Section 2055 supplies another deduction of potentially unlimited amount for certain transfers of property to charitable or other non-profit organizations. By removing these transfers from the estate tax base, § 2055 can be viewed as a federal matching-gift program of sorts. Lastly, § 2058 provides a deduction for the amount of estate or inheritance taxes paid at the state level, replacing a more generous credit for state death taxes that Congress phased out in 2005.

A decedent's taxable estate is subject to the compressed marginal rate schedule set forth in § 2001(c). As part of the Tax Relief, Unemployment Insurance Reauthorization, and Job Creation Act of 2010,[1] Congress reduced the maximum marginal estate tax rate to 35 percent commencing in 2010. This rate is triggered once the tax base reaches $500,000, and the handful of marginal rates below this amount are largely rendered irrelevant for estate tax purposes due to the operation of the "unified credit." Section 2010 defines the credit as the amount necessary to shield tax on transfers equal to the "applicable exclusion amount." As part of the 2010 legislation, Congress increased the applicable exclusion amount to $5 million commencing in 2010, while providing for this amount to be adjusted on account of increases in the cost of living

---

[1] Pub. L. No. 111-312, 124 Stat. 3296 (2010). As discussed in § 1.07, the changes made to the federal transfer tax regime by the 2010 legislation are effective for years 2010 through 2012 only.

commencing in 2012.[2] The unified credit provided in § 2010 therefore effectively defines a generous zero bracket under the estate tax after which transfers are subject to a 35 percent tax rate.

Liability for the estate tax falls on the executor of the decedent's estate. IRC § 2002. The estate tax return (Form 706) must be filed within nine months of the decedent's date of death. IRC § 6075(a). As a general rule, the due date of the estate tax return also represents the deadline for timely payment of the estate tax. IRC § 6151(a). Absent prior planning, the funds used by the executor to satisfy the estate tax liability will have been included as part of the decedent's taxable estate. Hence, the estate tax is levied on a tax-inclusive basis.

§ 1.02   GENERAL PRINCIPLES OF THE GIFT TAX

Internal Revenue Code: §§ 2501(a), 2502, 2503(a), (b), (e), 2505(a), 2512(a)–(b)

Whereas the federal estate tax was first enacted for the purpose of generating an additional source of revenue, Congress employed the federal gift tax as a defensive measure. Although the gift tax originally stumbled out of the gates (Congress enacted the tax in 1924 only to repeal it in 1926), Congress reinstituted the gift tax in 1932 on a permanent basis to prevent the easy avoidance of a bolstered estate tax.[3] In addition, Congress viewed the gift tax as necessary to protect the income tax base.[4]

Section 2501(a) imposes an annual tax on the "transfer of property by gift." As gratuitous transfers during an individual's lifetime are voluntary, the constitutional characterization of the gift tax as an excise on the act of transferring property is well founded. *See* Bromley v. McCaughn, 280 U.S. 124 (1929) (rejecting claim that the gift tax constitutes an unapportioned direct tax on property). Unlike the estate tax, the gift tax base is structured around a broad general rule. As described in § 2511(a), the gift tax applies to any transfer of property, "whether the transfer is in trust or otherwise, [and] whether the gift is direct or indirect." The receipt of any consideration for a transfer alone is not sufficient to avoid the gift tax. Rather, in situations where the transferor does not receive "an adequate and full consideration in money or money's worth," the difference between the two values constitutes the value of the gift. IRC § 2512(b). To avoid punishing poor negotiators with a gift tax on the value lost in a transaction, the regulations provide a sensible presumption of adequate and full consideration for transfers that occur in the ordinary course of business. *See* Treas. Reg. § 25.2512-8.

Unlike the estate tax, the gift tax provides for certain exclusions from the definition of a gift. Perhaps the most well known is the so-called "annual exclusion" provided under § 2503(b) for present-interest gifts not in excess of $13,000 (based on 2011 inflation-indexed levels). The

---

[2] Additionally, to the extent a predeceased spouse of the decedent did not use his or her unified credit, the unused portion of the predeceasing spouse's credit carries over and is added to the credit otherwise available to the decedent's estate. *Id.* § 303, 124 Stat. at 3302. The new "portability" aspect of the unified credit is addressed in § 19.05.

[3] *See* C. Lowell Harriss, *Legislative History of Federal Gift Taxation*, 18 Taxes 531 (1940), *reproduced in* Paul L. Caron, Grayson M.P. McCouch, & Karen C. Burke, Federal Wealth Taxation Anthology 7–9 (1998).

[4] *See* H.R. Rep. No. 72-708, at 28 (1932) & S. Rep. No. 72-665, at 40 (1932), each of which provides as follows:

The gift tax will supplement both the estate tax and the income tax. It will tend to reduce the incentive to make gifts in order that distribution of future income from the donated property may be to a number of persons with the result that the taxes imposed by the higher brackets of the income tax are avoided. It will also tend to discourage transfers for the purpose of avoiding the estate tax.

exclusion, created to avoid the administrative difficulties of taxing customary transfers between family members such as birthday presents or holiday gifts, presents an unbounded opportunity to transfer wealth without the imposition of any federal transfer tax. A donor can make gifts up to the annual exclusion amount to any number of donees, and that process can be replicated on an annual basis. Thus, for those individuals who are willing to part with a portion of their assets during life (a difficult proposition for some) and who have a sizeable number of would-be beneficiaries, the gift tax annual exclusion can be leveraged into a meaningful source of transfer tax savings. Section 2503(e) provides another exclusion from the definition of a gift, this one unbounded in amount but limited in use. Payments made directly to educational institutions for tuition and to providers of medical care on behalf of other individuals are not treated as transfers of property by gift.

Starting with the value of non-excluded gifts, the base of "taxable gifts" is determined through the allowance of certain deductions. The two available deductions mirror those provided under the estate tax. Section 2523 maintains the treatment of a married couple as a single taxable unit by providing an unlimited deduction for certain transfers of property to the donor's spouse, and § 2522 provides a deduction for transfers of property to charitable or other non-profit organizations.

An individual's taxable gifts are subject to tax at the same rates imposed under the estate tax. *See* IRC § 2502(a) (incorporating the estate tax rate structure provided in IRC § 2001(c)). However, § 2505 provides each individual with a unified credit against the gift tax. This credit, defined by reference to the estate tax unified credit under § 2010, operates to exempt from taxation a combined amount of taxable gifts equal to the applicable exclusion amount under 2010(c). Commencing in 2011, an individual may make $5 million of aggregate taxable gifts without incurring gift tax.[5]

While the estate tax and gift tax share the same nominal rate structure, the obligation to pay the gift tax rests with the donor. IRC § 2502(c). Because the donor's payment of the resulting gift tax is itself not treated as a separate gift, the gift tax generally is levied on a tax-exclusive basis. [For gifts made within three years of a decedent's death, the gift tax is rendered tax-inclusive through the inclusion of the gift tax paid in the decedent's gross estate under § 2035(b)]. In contrast, the estate tax is levied on a tax-inclusive basis, because the funds used by the executor to satisfy the liability typically are included in the decedent's gross estate. In other words, a tax is levied on the amounts used to pay the tax. Due to this distinction between the gift tax and the estate tax, the nominal tax rate structure shared by both yields lower effective rates for gift tax purposes. A marginal tax-exclusive rate of 35 percent translates to a marginal tax-inclusive rate of approximately 26 percent.[6] Hence, for transfers above the amount exempted by the unified credit, a distinct tax preference exists for lifetime transfers that are made sufficiently prior to death.

The gift tax is imposed on an annual basis. As a general rule, a donor who makes gifts in excess of the amounts excluded by § 2503(b) (annual exclusion) or § 2503(e) (exclusion for direct

---

[5] The $5 million figure ignores any increase in the applicable exclusion amount attributable to carryover of the unused portion of unified credit of the individual's predeceased spouse. The "portability" feature of the unified credit is examined in § 19.05.

[6] Assuming a 35 percent rate of tax imposed on the donor without any annual exclusions or unified credit, a $1 million gift would generate a $350,000 gift tax liability for the donor. If this same $350,000 tax were levied in a tax-inclusive manner, the $350,000 tax liability must be added to the $1 million tax base. In this manner, the $350,000 tax liability divided by a $1.35 million tax base yields a tax-inclusive rate of 25.925 percent.

payments of tuition or medical expenses) for which a marital deduction or charitable deduction does not apply must file a gift tax return (Form 709) by April 15th of the year following the calendar year to which the return applies. IRC §§ 6019, 6075(b)(1). The resulting gift tax, if any, generally is due with the return. IRC § 6151(a).

§ 1.03   CALCULATION OF GIFT TAX AND ESTATE TAX LIABILITY

The provisions that govern the computation of the gift tax and the estate tax are designed to subject an individual's cumulative gratuitous transfers of property—whether occurring during life or by reason of death—to a single progression through the marginal rate structure established in § 2001(c). This approach has been maintained even though recent growth in the unified credit under the gift tax and the estate tax and the decreases in the maximum marginal tax rate have effectively eliminated the lower marginal brackets.

The examples below illustrate the mechanics of the gift tax and estate tax liability. For purposes of simplicity, the examples assume that the marginal rate schedule, the inflation-adjusted amount of the annual exclusion, and the unified credit in effect for 2011 apply to all years involved.

[A]   Gift Tax Computation

Calculating the gift tax is a fairly straightforward task. The liability for a given year's taxable gifts is determined by first calculating a tentative tax on all the taxable gifts the donor has ever made—both during the current year and all prior years. A tentative tax on all taxable gifts made in prior years is then subtracted from this amount. Once the incremental tax attributable to the current year's taxable gifts is determined, the individual can apply whatever portion of gift tax unified credit under § 2505 that has not been applied in prior years.

Example 1: In Year 1, *Parent* makes gifts of $1 million to each of her four children. *Parent* has made no prior taxable gifts. Determine *Parent's* gift tax liability for Year 1.

Explanation: Because *Parent* made no taxable gifts prior to Year 1, *Parent's* gift tax liability is determined by applying the marginal rate structure to *Parent's* taxable gifts for that year, and then offsetting this tax with the necessary portion of *Parent's* gift tax unified credit. With respect to each transfer of $1 million to a child of *Parent*, $13,000 is exempted by the § 2503(b) annual exclusion, yielding a gift of $987,000 per child. As no gift tax deductions are implicated under these facts, *Parent's* taxable gifts for Year 1 total $3,948,000.

Under § 2502(a) and, by incorporation, § 2001(c), $3,948,000 of taxable gifts would generate a tax of $1,362,600. Yet because *Parent* has not used any portion of her unified credit under § 2505, $1,362,600 of the $1,730,800 credit is applied to offset the tax liability. Thus, while *Parent* must file a gift tax return for Year 1,[7] she owes no gift tax. In addition, $368,200 of her unified credit remains to be applied toward future gifts.

---

[7] IRC § 6019(a). The gift tax return (Form 709) must be filed by April 15th of the year following the calendar year to which the return applies. IRC § 6075(b)(1). As a general rule, the resulting gift tax will be due with the return. IRC § 6151(a).

Example 2: Building on the facts of Example 1, *Parent* transfers $750,000 to each of her four children in Year 2. Determine *Parent's* gift tax liability for Year 2.

Explanation: The calculation of *Parent's* gift tax liability for Year 2 is somewhat more involved. Again, the starting point is to compute *Parent's* taxable gifts for the current year. Because of the annual gift tax exclusion, *Parent's* transfer of $750,000 to each of her children yields a taxable gift of $737,000 to each. *Parent's* taxable gifts for Year 2 therefore total $2,948,000.

Under § 2502(a), *Parent* first must compute a tentative tax on the sum of the Year 2 taxable gifts ($2,948,000) and the taxable gifts that she has made in all prior years ($3,948,000). The tentative tax on $6,896,000 totals $2,394,400. From this amount, *Parent* must subtract a tentative tax on taxable gifts made in prior years ($1,362,600, as calculated in Example 1). *Parent's* incremental gift tax liability under § 2502(a) for Year 2 therefore totals $1,031,800. After subtracting the portion of *Parent's* § 2505 unified credit that had not been applied in prior years ($368,200), *Parent* is left with a gift tax liability for Year 2 of $663,600.

The graph below illustrates how the gift tax computation under § 2502(a) subjects *Parent's* cumulative taxable gifts to a single progression through the marginal tax rate structure:

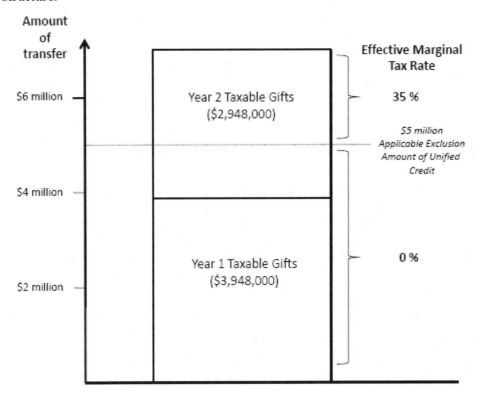

[B]   Estate Tax Computation

Calculation of the estate tax continues the approach of subjecting all of an individual's gratuitous transfers to a single progressive rate structure, although the mechanics of the calculation differ slightly. Under § 2001(b), a tentative tax is computed on the sum of the decedent's taxable estate plus the amount of taxable gifts that the decedent made after 1976 (to the extent those gifts are not independently included in the decedent's gross estate). The amount of the gift tax that would have been payable on the post-1976 gifts under the current tax rates is then subtracted from the tentative tax.[8] The resulting amount is further reduced by the decedent's estate tax unified credit under § 2010, which currently is set at $1,730,800 (sufficient to shield the tax due on a $5 million taxable estate). Note that the entire § 2010 credit will be available at this point, even if the decedent had used all or a portion of the gift tax unified credit. That is because § 2001(b) includes all post-1976 gifts in the tax calculation, not just those in excess of the effective exemption provided by the gift tax unified credit. The example below walks through the calculation required by § 2001(b).

> Example 3: Continuing with the facts of Examples 1 and 2, assume that *Parent* dies in Year 6 owning property worth $6.25 million. After paying $50,000 in funeral expenses and $200,000 in costs of administering the estate, *Parent's* personal representative is left with $6 million to distribute. *Parent's* will directs that $1 million is to be paid to her law school alma mater (a non-profit institution), with the residue of her estate being divided equally among her four children.

> Explanation: The first step in computing *Parent's* estate tax liability is to determine the size of *Parent's* gross estate. Based on the simplified facts, *Parent* has a gross estate under § 2033 of $6.25 million. In computing *Parent's* taxable estate, however, deductions are allowed for the $50,000 of funeral expenses (§ 2053), the $200,000 of administrative expenses (§ 2053), and the $1 million gift to the law school (§ 2055). The taxable estate under § 2051 therefore totals $5 million.

> Once *Parent's* taxable estate is determined, the next step is to compute a tentative tax on *Parent's* taxable estate ($5 million) plus all taxable gifts that *Parent* made after 1976 ($6,896,000) as required by § 2001(b)(1). Applying the § 2001(c) rate schedule to the combined $11,896,000 yields a tentative tax of $4,144,400. Pursuant to § 2001(b)(2), the amount of gift tax payable on the post-1976 gifts computed under the same rates ($663,600) is subtracted, leaving a balance of $3,480,800. Next, the estate may apply the prevailing estate tax unified credit of $1,730,800 (which offsets the tax due on $5 million of transfers). Thus, *Parent's* estate will be liable for an estate tax of $1,750,000.

> The following graph depicts the coordination between the estate tax and the gift tax under the combined fact pattern:

---

[8] If there has been a change in the amount of the unified credit under § 2505 since the year(s) in which the taxable gifts were made and the date of the decedent's death, the unified credit available on the date of the gift is used to determine the gift tax payable for purposes of § 2001(b). *See* Priv. Ltr. Rul. 9250004.

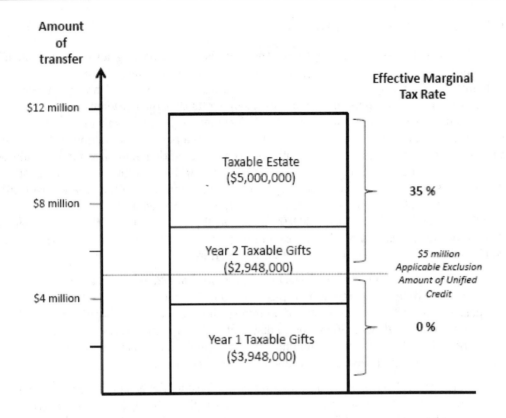

§ 1.04   GENERAL PRINCIPLES OF THE GENERATION-SKIPPING TRANSFER TAX

Internal Revenue Code: §§ 2601, 2602, 2611, 2641, 2613, 2642(a)(1)–(2)

Faced with the estate tax and gift tax bases alone, tax planners had become adept at employing trusts to insulate property from the future imposition of transfer taxes. While the transfer of property into the trust would be subject to estate or gift taxation, these taxes would not be triggered again so long as the property were held in trust for the benefit of future generations. The use of trusts to avoid federal transfer taxation led Congress to introduce the first generation-skipping transfer (GST) tax as part of the Tax Reform Act of 1976, and the current GST tax has its origins in the substantial restructuring of the tax effected by the Tax Reform Act of 1986.

The goal of the GST tax is to ensure that property is subject to federal transfer tax at each generation. With certain exceptions, the GST tax accomplishes this goal by levying a tax on the following three generation-skipping transfers: (1) a direct skip, (2) a taxable distribution, and (3) a taxable termination. *See* IRC § 2611(a). The concept of a "skip person" lies at the heart of the three generation-skipping transfers. As a general matter, a skip person is defined as a natural person who is assigned to a generation two or more generations below that of the transferor. IRC § 2613(a)(1).[9] While generation assignments for close relatives of the transf-

---

[9] In addition, a trust can constitute a skip person if all parties entitled or eligible to receive a current distribution

eror or the transferor's spouse generally are self-explanatory, the Code provides rules for determining the generation to which other individuals will be assigned based on their age in relation to the transferor. *See* IRC § 2651.

A direct skip occurs when a transfer that is subject to estate or gift tax is made to a skip person. A simple example of a direct skip would be a devise from a grandparent (*GP*) to her grandchild (*GC*), who is the daughter of *GP*'s son (*C*). Had *GP* made the devise to *C* instead of skipping over him, the property would have been subject to estate tax in *C's* estate before passing to *GC*. In an attempt to equalize the two scenarios, § 2601 imposes an additional transfer tax on the amount received by *GC* on top of the estate tax that will be due in *GP*'s estate. In the context of a direct skip, liability for the GST tax is imposed on the transferor. IRC § 2603(a)(3). Note that if the direct skip occurs through an inter vivos transfer, the GST tax paid by the donor constitutes an additional gift to the skip person for gift tax purposes. IRC § 2515.

If property is transferred to a trust in which a non-skip person holds an interest, then the GST tax is held in abeyance. For instance, there is no current generation-skipping transfer if *GP* devises property to a trust that provides the trustee with discretion to make distributions to *C* or *GC* during *C's* lifetime. However, if the trustee makes a distribution to *GC* while *C* remains alive, the distribution will constitute a "taxable distribution" that triggers the GST tax. The taxable distribution will be valued by reference to the amount received by the transferee, and the transferee will be responsible for paying the resulting tax. IRC §§ 2621(a), 2603(a)(1).

Assume that, pursuant to the terms of the trust, the trust property will be distributed to *GC* upon *C's* death. Even though the trust assets could have been used to benefit *C* during his lifetime, *C's* beneficial interest in the trust will not cause the trust assets to be included in his gross estate for estate tax purposes. However, the distribution of the trust property to *GC* will constitute a "taxable termination" that triggers imposition of the GST tax. The taxable termination will be measured by reference to the value of the trust assets when the termination occurred, and liability for the resulting tax will rest on the trustee. IRC §§ 2622(a), 2603(a)(2).

The GST tax provides for an exemption that is equal to the amount of transfers exempted from estate taxation by the unified credit. Rather than taking the form of a credit, the GST tax exemption is factored into the rate at which the GST is levied.

The mechanics of applying the GST tax exemption are somewhat labored. Under § 2602, the amount of the generation-skipping transfer is taxed at the "applicable rate." The applicable rate is defined as the maximum estate tax rate (35 percent) multiplied by the "inclusion ratio." IRC § 2641(a). The inclusion ratio, in turn, is defined as the number one less the "applicable fraction," which measures the portion of the transfer that is exempt from GST. In particular, the applicable fraction equals the amount of the GST exemption that is allocated to the transfer divided by the value of the transferred property. IRC § 2642(a)(1), (2). In this manner, a generation-skipping transfer that is fully shielded by an allocation of the available $5 million GST tax exemption (for 2011) will have an applicable fraction of one, which produces an inclusion ratio of zero, which in turn yields an applicable GST tax rate of zero. If the generation-skipping transfer exceeds the amount of the allocated GST tax exemption, then the inclusion ratio will be a fraction between zero and one. From a planning standpoint, generation-skipping transfers are structured to have an inclusion ratio of either zero or one;

---

are skip persons or, if no person is currently entitled or eligible to receive a distribution, then no future distributions could be made to a non-skip person. IRC § 2613(a)(2).

that is, the transfers are structured to be either exempt from the GST tax or fully subject to the 35 percent statutory rate.

§ 1.05 CALCULATION OF GST TAX LIABILITY

The following example will illustrate the calculation of the GST tax liability in the context of a taxable termination.

> Example 4: Grandparent (*GP*) leaves the residue of her estate in trust. The trustee has discretion to distribute income and principal to *GP's* children, *C1* and *C2*, during their lifetimes. Upon the death of the survivor of *C1* and *C2*, the trust assets are to be distributed to *GP's* then-living grandchildren in equal shares.

After satisfying the estate tax liability due in *GP's* estate, the executor funds the testamentary trust with $15 million. Thereafter, the trust assets appreciate in value to $18 million at the time *C1* (who is survived by *C2*) dies. Several years later, *C2* dies when the trust assets are worth $21 million. Pursuant to the trust terms, the remaining trust assets are to be distributed to *GP's* grandchildren.

> Explanation: The death of *C1* does not result in a generation-skipping transfer, because *C2* (a non-skip person) still possesses an interest in the trust. The death of *C2*, however, triggers a taxable termination under § 2612(a). The GST tax would be imposed on the $21 million fair market value of the property then held in trust. In this case, the applicable rate of the GST tax would equal the 35 percent maximum estate tax rate multiplied by the inclusion ratio, which in turn equals one minus the applicable fraction. Assuming all of *GP's* $5 million exemption had been allocated to the trust at *GP's* death, the applicable fraction would be $5 million divided by $15 million, or 1/3. The applicable fraction produces an inclusion ratio of 2/3, which in turn yields an applicable rate for GST tax purposes of 23.33 percent. The trustee therefore will be responsible for paying $4.9 million in GST tax before distributing the remaining $16.1 million of trust assets to *GP's* grandchildren.

§ 1.06 GENERAL STANDARD OF VALUATION

Each of the three taxes that compromise the federal wealth transfer tax system is imposed on the value of transferred property. Property valuation therefore plays a critical role in determining the extent of the transfer tax base. Nonetheless, Congress has not articulated a generally applicable standard for determining the transfer-tax value of transferred property. The Treasury Department has filled this void by regulation, providing a nearly identical standard for determining fair market value under the estate tax and gift tax. *See* Treas. Reg. §§ 20.2031-1(b), 25.2512-1. The estate tax regulation provides as follows:

> The fair market value is the price at which the property would change hands between a willing buyer and a willing seller, neither being under any compulsion to buy or to sell and both having reasonable knowledge of relevant facts.

Hence, value is determined on an objective basis for transfer tax purposes, and any subjective premium or discount the transferor may place on the objective value of the property is irrelevant. As discussed more fully in later chapters, the objective valuation standard has spawned a host of planning techniques aimed at producing an objective value for property that is lower than the subjective value of the property to the actual parties to the transaction.

§ 1.07   MODERN LEGISLATIVE DEVELOPMENTS

The federal transfer tax regime has been set on a mercurial legislative path in recent years. A summary of the primary legislative developments in this arena will provide not only historical perspective, but also guidance on the future of the federal transfer tax system in the event Congress fails to extend temporary legislation currently in effect.

[A]   The Taxpayer Relief Act of 1997

From the standpoint of potential future relevance, the modern history of the federal transfer tax system starts with the Taxpayer Relief Act of 1997.[10] This legislation provided for staggered increases in the applicable exclusion amount of the unified credit to the estate tax and gift tax, which had remained stagnate at $600,000 since 1987. The scheduled increases, largely back-loaded, eventually would have reached a $1 million applicable exclusion amount in 2006. In addition to increasing the amount of the unified credit, the 1997 legislation provided for cost-of-living adjustments to the prevailing $1 million base amount of the GST tax exemption. As a result of these changes, the unified credit reached $675,000 and the inflation-adjusted GST tax exemption stood at $1,060,000 for 2001.

[B]   The Economic Growth and Tax Relief Reconciliation Act of 2001

Although the Economic Growth and Tax Relief Reconciliation Act of 2001 (EGTRRA)[11] is perhaps best known for its across-the-board reduction in the marginal rates of the federal income tax, the legislation prescribed significant structural changes to the federal transfer tax regime. As an initial matter, EGTRRA accelerated the scheduled increases in the amount of the unified credit. Starting in 2002, the unified credit for the estate tax and gift tax shielded $1 million of transfers from taxation. However, commencing in 2004, EGTRRA "decoupled" the unified credit under the gift tax and the estate tax for the first time since 1976. While the applicable exclusion amount of the credit remained at $1 million for gift tax purposes,[12] the applicable exclusion amount for the estate tax was raised to $1.5 million in 2004, $2 million in 2006, and $3.5 million in 2009. The legislation similarly reduced exposure to the GST tax by pegging the GST tax exemption to the applicable exclusion amount of the estate tax unified credit starting in 2004.

---

[10]   Pub. L. No. 105-34, 111 Stat. 788 (1997).

[11]   Pub. L. No. 107-16, 115 Stat. 38 (2001).

[12]   According to reports accompanying EGTRRA, Congress decoupled the unified credit under the gift tax and the estate tax (and maintained the gift tax during the period for which the estate tax was prospectively repealed) over concerns that elimination of the gift tax would promote indiscriminate transfers of appreciated property or income-producing assets to related parties facing a lower marginal income tax rate. In short, the gift tax was retained to protect the integrity of the income tax base. *See, e.g.*, John Buckley, *Estate and Gift Taxes: What Will Congress Do Next?*, 90 Tax Notes 2069, 2070 (June 18, 2001) ("One of the most surprising aspects of the new law is its retention of the gift tax. Retention of the gift tax is an attempt to prevent widespread income tax avoidance. The fact that the new law provides a lower gift tax exemption than estate tax exemption also is a response to potential income tax avoidance."). Mr. Buckley served on the Democratic Staff of the House Ways and Means Committee at the time the 2001 legislation was considered and enacted.

As a result of the considerable increases to the estate tax unified credit and the GST tax exemption, EGTRRA significantly reduced the application of these taxes among the general population. To put these changes in perspective, the number of filed estate tax returns dropped from over 108,000 in 2001 to 33,515 in 2009.[13] However, the tax-reducing provisions of EGTRRA were not limited to increases in the relevant exemption levels. The legislation also reduced the tax rates. Prior to the enactment of EGTRRA, the estate tax and gift tax were levied at a maximum marginal rate of 55 percent.[14] Effective for 2002, EGTRRA reduced the top marginal rate to 50 percent. In addition, the legislation provided for annual 1 percent reductions to this rate until it reached 45 percent in 2007. As the rate of the GST tax is set at the maximum marginal rate of the estate tax, the GST tax experienced concomitant rate reductions.

Although the increases in exemption levels and decreases in the marginal rate structure provided by EGTRRA were significant in their own right, they merely set the stage for the most dramatic aspect of the legislation: repeal of both the estate tax and the GST tax in 2010.[15] Although the gift tax was retained (for the apparent purpose of protecting the income tax base), the maximum marginal rate of the gift tax for 2010 was reduced to match the maximum marginal rate of the federal income tax—35 percent. However, the seminal changes to the federal transfer tax system in 2010 were not legislated to have indefinite effect. Rather, these changes were scheduled to have a one-year shelf life. As a means of avoiding procedural rules that would have required a 60-vote majority in the Senate to pass the legislation,[16] EGTRRA contained a sunset provision that precluded its application to estates of decedents dying, gifts made, and generation-skipping transfers occurring after December 31, 2010. For years following 2010, the Internal Revenue Code was to be applied as if the changes made by EGTRRA "had never been enacted."[17] Accordingly, on January 1, 2011, the federal transfer tax system was scheduled to return in its pre-EGTRRA (that is, pre-2002) form.

Not long after EGTRRA was enacted, the prospective one-year repeal of the estate tax in 2010 garnered its share of ridicule. References to the legislation included the "Throw Momma from the Train" Act. Proponents of estate tax repeal did not regard the sunset provision of the legislation as indicative of a serious intent to reinstate the tax following 2010, but instead dismissed the provision as a mere procedural quirk to be rectified by a future Congress.

---

[13] *See* IRS Statistics of Income, Estate Tax Statistics (2010) (summary data available at http://www.irs.ustreas.gov/pub/irs-soi/10esesttaxsnap.pdf). An estate tax return must be filed if the amount of the decedent's gross estate plus the amount of the decedent's adjusted taxable gifts exceeds the amount of the estate tax unified credit. *See* IRC § 6018(a).

[14] Additionally, § 2001(c)(2) prior to the enactment of EGTRRA imposed a five percent surtax on estates in excess of $10 million to eliminate the benefit of the unified credit and the progressive rate schedule. The surtax therefore applied until the average tax rate faced by the estate equaled the top 55 percent marginal rate, which was accomplished when the tax base equaled $17,184,000. EGTRRA eliminated the five percent surtax commencing in 2002.

[15] *See* EGTTRA § 501, 115 Stat. 38, 69 (2001) (enacting IRC §§ 2210 and 2664). Repeal of the estate tax was coupled with the elimination of the "stepped-up" basis provision of § 1014. In its stead, Congress provided the modified carry-over basis regime of § 1022. *See id.* § 542, 115 Stat. at 76.

[16] The heightened majority voting requirement is attributable to the Congressional Budget Act of 1974. Pursuant to a 1985 amendment to this legislation commonly referred to as the "Byrd Rule" (after its sponsor, the late Senator Robert C. Byrd), proposed legislation that reduces tax receipts beyond the period provided in the Congressional Budget Resolution is out of order in the Senate. Because the 2001 budget resolution covered 10 years, the Byrd Rule rendered revenue-reducing provisions beyond the 10-year window procedurally improper. Suspension of the Byrd Rule requires 60 votes in the Senate, which the proponents of the income tax and transfer tax reductions contained in EGTRRA presumably could not garner.

[17] *Id.* § 901(a)(2), (b), 115 Stat. at 150.

Indeed, most observers on both sides of the estate tax issue assumed Congress eventually would pass legislation resolving the fate of the tax on a non-temporary basis—likely through retention of the tax at 2009 levels, but possibly by making the prospective repeal permanent.

Those observers underestimated the dysfunctional state of Congress. Congress failed to take additional action on the estate tax in 2009 and, as a result, the country awoke on January 1, 2010, to the absence of an estate tax for the first time in roughly a century. Prompt congressional action on the matter promised to occur early in 2010 never materialized, as the executive and legislative branches both focused their attention on other matters. The likelihood of the estate and GST taxes being reinstated on a retroactive basis diminished with time, and the increasing number of decedents reported to have had the "good fortune" of dying during the 2010 estate-tax hiatus did not spur Congress to action. As the close of 2010 drew near, the once improbable scenario of EGTRRA taking effect without modification—that is, one-year repeal of the federal estate tax and GST tax followed by reinstatement of the federal transfer tax regime on pre-EGTRRA terms in 2011—appeared as likely as any.

[C]   The Tax Relief, Unemployment Insurance Reauthorization, and Job Creation Act of 2010

[1]   Deferral of EGTRRA Sunset

Congress finally addressed the expiring tax provisions provided in EGTRRA in the waning days of 2010, following mid-term elections that significantly altered the balance of congressional power among the political parties. The Tax Relief, Unemployment Insurance Reauthorization, and Job Creation Act of 2010 (the "Tax Relief Act of 2010"),[18] passed on December 16, 2010, and signed into law the day after, did so by deferring the sunset provision contained in EGTRRA for two years. Hence, the amendments to the federal transfer tax system made by EGTRRA are now scheduled to expire on December 31, 2012, instead of December 21, 2010.

[2]   Additional Tax Reducing Measures

[a]   Estate Tax Changes

In addition to extending the term of EGTRRA, the 2010 legislation brought a measure of certainty to the federal transfer tax landscape for the 2010 calendar year. As a starting point, the Tax Relief Act of 2010 repealed the portion of EGTRRA that had repealed the estate tax for 2010. The change operated to reinstate the estate tax for decedents dying after December 31, 2009, eliminating the period for which the estate tax had expired (at least as a default matter, as discussed below). Yet rather than reinstating the estate tax at 2009 levels, the Tax Relief Act of 2010 provided for additional tax reductions. The legislation increased the applicable exclusion amount of the estate tax unified credit under § 2010(c) to $5 million, an amount which is to be adjusted commencing in 2012 to account for increases in the cost of living from 2010. *See* IRC § 2010(c)(2), (3).

In addition to considerably increasing the benefit of the unified credit, the Tax Relief Act of 2010 reduced the maximum marginal rate of the estate tax to 35 percent. As the 35 percent bracket commences at $500,000 of transfers, the legislation continued the seriatim dismantling

---

[18] Pub. L. No. 111-312, 124 Stat. 3296 (2010).

of the once prolific progressive rate structure of § 2001(c), which now stands as a shell of its former self.

Even though the Tax Relief Act of 2010 reinstated the estate tax effective January 1, 2010, Congress did not eliminate altogether the benefit of temporary repeal of the estate tax for 2010. Rather, whether due to qualms over the constitutionality of reinstating the estate tax on a retroactive basis or fear of the political ramifications of doing so, the Tax Relief Act of 2010 preserved temporary repeal of the estate tax in elective form. For estates of decedents dying in 2010, the executor could irrevocably elect to apply the provisions of EGTRRA that repealed the estate tax and instituted a system of modified carry-over basis (in lieu of the § 1014 date-of-death value basis). A decedent's executor therefore could compare the estate tax liability that would result from the absence of an election out of the estate tax to the future income tax savings resulting from a stepped-up basis in property received from the decedent under § 1014 as opposed to a basis determined under the modified carry-over basis regime of § 1022. In the majority of cases where the decedent's taxable estate exceeded the decedent's remaining applicable exclusion amount of the unified credit, an election out of the immediate estate tax levy would be preferable.[19]

[b]   GST Tax Changes

On the GST tax front, the Tax Relief Act of 2010 also repealed the portion of EGTRRA that would have repealed the GST tax indefinitely (absent the sunset provision). Yet Congress retained the benefit of GST tax repeal for 2010 by assigning an applicable rate of zero to generation-skipping transfers occurring during that year.[20] Hence, 2010 offered a one-year window for individuals to make direct skip transfers to grandchildren or to make distributions to grandchildren from non-exempt trusts without incurring this additional level of federal transfer tax.

As the statutory rate of the GST tax is pegged to the maximum marginal rate of the estate tax, the Tax Relief Act of 2010 reduced the rate of the GST tax to 35 percent. Similarly, the amount of the GST exemption was increased to $5 million, to be adjusted upward for cost of living commencing in 2012.

[c]   Gift Tax Changes

Whereas EGTRRA had decoupled the unified credit for estate tax and gift tax purposes while providing a lower rate structure for the gift tax commencing in 2010, the Tax Relief of 2010 once again re-unified the gift tax and estate tax on these terms. Commencing in 2011, the legislation increased the applicable exclusion amount of the gift tax unified credit under § 2505 to match that of the estate tax; that is, $5 million to be increased by cost-of-living adjustments starting in 2012. The legislation thus made the "unified" credit label honest once again. The marginal rate schedules of the estate and gift taxes were unified one year earlier in 2010 when the maximum estate tax rate was decreased to match the 35 percent maximum marginal rate of the gift tax for that year forward.

---

[19] Only if the decedent's estate consisted of highly appreciated property (keeping in mind the $1.3 million basis increase available under § 1022) having a value that did not greatly exceed the remaining amount of the decedent's unified credit would it make sense to assent to the imposition of the estate tax.

[20] *Id.* § 302(c), 124 Stat. at 3301.

[d]   Portability of the Unified Credit

Congress not only significantly increased the effective exemptions from the estate tax and gift tax as part of the Tax Relief Act of 2010, it also heeded the repeated recommendations of professional associations to make the unified credit "portable" between spouses. As a result, to the extent a predeceasing spouse did not apply his full unified credit against taxable transfers made during life or by reason of death, the surviving spouse may add the unused portion (the "deceased spousal unused exclusion amount") to the $5 million "basic exclusion amount" in determining the total amount shielded from taxation by the surviving spouse's unified credit.[21] *See* IRC § 2010(c)(4), (5). Portability of the unified credit commences in 2011, and is available only with respect to predeceasing spouses who died after 2010. This feature of the unified credit regime will primarily benefit couples who failed to undertake or choose to forgo the sometimes complicated estate planning necessary to make effective use of the unified credit afforded to the predeceasing spouse while leaving property for the benefit of the surviving spouse.

Portability of the unified credit does not extend to the GST exemption. Rather, an individual's GST exemption is defined by reference to the basic exclusion amount of an individual's unified credit. *See* IRC § 2631(c).

[3]   Sunset Provision

The amendments made to the federal transfer system by the Tax Relief Act of 2010 are temporary in nature. Along with the transfer tax amendments contained in EGTRRA, the changes to the transfer tax system contained in the Tax Relief Act of 2010 are scheduled to expire on December 31, 2012.[22] Hence, in the absence of future congressional action, the federal transfer tax regime will return on pre-EGTRRA terms (that is, with a unified credit shielding only $1 million of combined transfers and with a 55 percent maximum marginal rate) in 2013.

[D]   Summary of Recent Changes

The chart below summarizes the relevant exemption levels and maximum tax rates of all three federal transfer taxes for recent and future years:

---

[21] The details of the portability feature of the unified credit are addressed in § 19.05 as part of the chapter examining the federal transfer tax treatment of the marital unit.

[22] *Id.* § 304, 124 Stat. at 3304.

Year	Gift Tax		Estate Tax		GST Tax	
	Exclusion Amt.	*Max. Rate*	*Exclusion Amt.*	*Max. Rate*	*Exemption*	*Rate*
2009	$1,000,000	45%	$3,500,000	45%	$3,500,000	45%
2010	1,000,000	35%	5,000,000[a]	35%[a]	5,000,000	0%
2011	5,000,000	35%	5,000,000	35%	5,000,000	35%
2012	5,000,000[b]	35%	5,000,000[b]	35%	5,000,000[b]	35%
2013	1,000,000	55%[c]	1,000,000	55%[c]	≈1,400,000[d]	55%[c]

[a] This assumes the decedent's executor does not elect to apply the provisions of EGTRRA calling for repeal of the estate tax in 2010 at the expense of a modified carry-over basis regime under § 1022.

[b] As adjusted for cost of living from 2010.

[c] In addition, a five percent surtax will apply to transfers above $10 million until the benefit of the unified credit and progressive rate structure is exhausted (to produce an average tax rate of 55 percent).

[d] $1 million exemption adjusted for cost of living from 1997.

The chart above takes existing law at face value by assuming that the federal tax regime will return to its pre-EGTRRA state in 2013 as scheduled. However, in light of recent history and for purposes of simplicity, this text proceeds on the assumption that the federal transfer tax provisions contained in the Tax Relief Act of 2010 will be extended indefinitely beyond the current December 31, 2012 expiration date.

§ 1.08   STUDY PROBLEMS

1. Applying the marginal rate schedule, the unified credits levels, and the $13,000 amount of the inflation-adjusted amount of the § 2503(b) annual gift tax exclusion in effect for year 2011 to all years at issue, calculate Frank's gift and estate tax liability resulting from the following transfers:

    - In Year 1, Frank transfers $2 million to each of his two children.

    - In Year 4, Frank transfers to his brother stock in his closely held business having a $3 million appraised value.

    - In Year 8, Frank dies with assets included in his gross estate valued at $7 million. After paying administrative expenses and funeral expenses, $6.5 million remains to be distributed to Frank's children.

2. For purposes of this problem, assume that Frank in problem 1 above (a) did not make the Year 4 gift to his brother, and (b) left the balance of the property included in his gross estate outright to his surviving spouse. As a result of the marital deduction under § 2056, Frank's taxable estate was reduced to zero. In addition to the assets received from Frank, what other benefit does Frank's spouse receive?

3. Approximately five years prior to her death, Barbara created an irrevocable trust for the benefit of her children, naming a local bank to serve as trustee. The trust provides that the trustee may distribute trust income or principal to Barbara's children in the trustee's sole discretion. Upon the death of Barbara's last child, the trust assets are to be distributed to Barbara's then-living grandchildren. Barbara funded the trust with $3

million.

Through her will, Barbara made specific bequests of $2 million to each of her four grandchildren. She left the residue of her estate, valued at $12 million (before reduction for any federal transfer taxes, which were charged against the residue), to her two children in equal shares.

Assuming that 2011 exemption levels apply to all of the transfers, identify which federal transfer taxes will apply (a) when Barbara funds the trust, (b) when Barbara dies, and (c) when the last of Barbara's children die.

Chapter 2

BASIC APPLICATION OF THE ESTATE TAX: PROPERTY OWNED BY THE DECEDENT AT DEATH

Internal Revenue Code:	§§ 2031(a), 2033, 2034
	skim § 2041(a), (b), § 691(a), (c)
Treasury Regulations:	§§ 20.2031-1(a)(1), -5, 20.2033-1, 20.2034-1
	see also § 20.2041-1(b)(1), (2)

The scope of a decedent's gross estate for estate tax purposes is defined in serial fashion by §§ 2033 through 2044. At the most basic level, the estate tax base must include property owned by the decedent at death that passes as part of the decedent's probate estate (whether by will or pursuant to the laws of intestacy). Section 2033 accomplishes this result by including in the gross estate "all property to the extent of the interest therein of the decedent at the time of his death."

Given that the regulations indicate that § 2033 is "concerned mainly with interests in property passing through the decedent's probate estate," *see* Treas. Reg. § 20.2031-1(a)(1), it is tempting to equate the scope of § 2033 with probate property. However, the two are not identical. As discussed in this chapter, § 2033 does not apply to payments that arise by reason of death, even if those amounts are paid into the decedent's probate estate. Inclusion in the probate estate alone thus does not trigger the application of § 2033. On the other hand, the application of § 2033 is not necessarily limited to the probate realm. The original 1916 version of the statute captured property "to the extent of the interest therein of the decedent at the time of his death which after his death is subject to the payment of charges against his estate and the expenses of its administration and is subject to distribution as part of his estate."[1] The Revenue Act of 1926 dropped the descriptive limitations (the phrase starting with "which after his death"), and this amendment could be interpreted as an expansion of the statute to reach non-probate property.[2] In that regard, the focus of § 2033 on the decedent's interest in property "at the time of his death" suggests that the manner in which the property passes upon

---

[1] Revenue Act of 1916, Pub. L. No. 64-271, 39 Stat. 756.

[2] Revenue Act of 1926, Pub. L. No. 69-20, § 302, 44 Stat 9, 77. The legislative history accompanying the Revenue Act of 1926 provides the following explanation for the statutory change: "In the interest of certainty it is recommended that the limiting language above referred to shall be eliminated in the proposed bill, so that the gross estate shall include the entire interest of the decedent at the time of his death in all the property." H.R. Rep. No. 69-1, at 15 (1925). Note that the statutory revision does not necessarily expand the statute into the non-probate arena; rather, the amendment could signal the intention of Congress to capture all property that is capable of descent and devise that is protected from the claims of creditors or that is not brought into the formal probate estate. *See, e.g.,* Treas. Reg. § 20.2033-1(a) (providing that real property owned by the decedent is included under § 2033 "whether it came into the possession and control of the executor or administrator or passed directly to heirs or devisees"); -1(b) (noting that property subject to homestead or other local law exemptions is included in the gross estate).

the decedent's death is irrelevant. Yet despite the literal breadth of the statute, interpretive authorities reveal the following two principles regarding the scope of § 2033: (1) the decedent's interest in the property must have survived the decedent's death; and (2) the decedent must have possessed the right to determine the manner in which his interest would be transmitted. Thus, the potential reach of § 2033 into the non-probate arena is more limited than the text of the statute implies.

§ 2.01 ROUTINE APPLICATION

In the vast majority of cases, the application of § 2033 is straightforward. If the decedent owned property at the time of his death and that property passes according to the decedent's will or pursuant to the laws of intestate succession, § 2033 will include the value of the property in the decedent's gross estate. Therefore, any real property titled in the decedent's individual name that does not pass by a survivorship feature inherent in the property title will be included in the decedent's gross estate under § 2033. Fee simple and tenants-in-common interests thus fall within the scope of § 2033, whereas parcels held as joint tenants with right of survivorship or as tenants-by-the-entirety do not.[3] The regulations indicate that this result holds even if the real estate does not become part of the probate estate, but rather vests immediately upon the decedent's death in his heirs or devisees. *See* Treas. Reg. § 20.2033-1(a).

Personal property is governed by the same rule. Any cash, stocks, bonds, or other investment assets titled in the decedent's individual name will be included in his gross estate under § 2033. If these assets are held on deposit with a bank or brokerage firm, the account balances will be included under § 2033 provided the account was not a joint account with a right of survivorship. If the decedent owned a life insurance policy insuring the life of another (as opposed to his own)[4], the value of the policy will be included under § 2033. Tangible personal property owned by the decedent (such as jewelry, furniture, artwork, clothing, etc.) falls within the scope of § 2033, although the general absence of documentary title to such property may cloud the determination of legal ownership.

By reaching property owned by the decedent that is capable of descent and devise, § 2033 does the heavy lifting in establishing the estate tax base. Indeed, the reach of § 2033 is limited only by the scope of cognizable property interests under state law. For example, in *First Victoria National Bank v. United States*, 620 F.2d 1096 (5th Cir. 1980), the decedent's legal entitlement to continue the production of rice under a government crop control program was held to be property under § 2033 on the basis that the entitlement could have been transferred inter vivos and was capable of transmission at death. In *Estate of Andrews v. United States*, 850 F. Supp. 1279 (E.D. Va. 1994), the district court determined the value to be placed on the decedent's name—more specifically, the ability of the decedent's estate to continue publishing ghostwritten books designating the decedent (a popular writer) as author. Although the case does not specifically address the rationale for including such value in the decedent's gross estate, presumably § 2033 served as the basis for inclusion.

---

[3] However, property held as joint tenants with right of survivorship may be included in the decedent's gross estate under § 2040, addressed in Chapter 7.

[4] Whether the proceeds of a life insurance policy insuring the decedent's life will be included in the decedent's gross estate is governed by § 2042, addressed in Chapter 8.

§ 2.02 TREATMENT OF OUTSTANDING CHECKS

Suppose that an individual has been admitted to the hospital with a terminal illness. Her son, named as her agent under a durable power of attorney, attempts to undertake last-minute tax planning by issuing checks for the available annual gift tax exclusion amount to each of his mother's children and grandchildren. Although the son delivers the checks expeditiously and the checks are promptly deposited by the donees, the individual dies before the checks clear her bank account. Assume that under state law, a stop-payment order may be issued on a check at any time before it has cleared the drawee bank. How much should be included in the decedent's gross estate under § 2033: the actual balance in the bank account as of the decedent's death, or such balance reduced by the amount of issued but uncleared checks (which are honored by the decedent's bank following her death)?

Regulation § 20.2031-5 provides the following guidance on the issue of when the value of a bank account balance may be reduced by issued checks that remain outstanding as of the decedent's death:

> If bank checks outstanding at the time of the decedent's death and given in discharge of bona fide legal obligations of the decedent incurred for an adequate and full consideration in money or money's worth are subsequently honored by the bank and charged to the decedent's account, the balance remaining in the account may be returned, but only if the obligations are not claimed as deductions from the gross estate.

Hence, based on the regulation, a decedent's bank account may be reduced only by outstanding checks that were issued as payment for an item that provided adequate and full consideration to the decedent. This approach is reasonable, as the decedent's gross estate presumably has been augmented by the consideration received or reduced on account of consumption. Additionally, if the amount of the checks were not deducted from the bank account balance, such amounts presumably would give rise to deductions from the gross estate under § 2053. By implication, the regulation does not permit the value of the decedent's bank account to be included in the gross estate under § 2033 to be reduced by outstanding checks that were issued as part of a gratuitous transaction.

Despite the fairly clear guidance in Reg. § 20.2031-5, the Tax Court in *Estate of Belcher v. Commissioner*, 83 T.C. 227 (1984), bowed to practicality and held that checks issued to charitable organizations that remained outstanding as of the decedent's death could be deducted from the account balance required to be included in the decedent's estate. Specifically, the court declared that "upon prompt presentation and actual payment of the checks by the bank," the payment related back to the date the checks were issued. *Id.* at 235. The court relied heavily on its prior decision in *Estate of Spiegel v. Commissioner*, 12 T.C. 524 (1949), which applied the relation-back doctrine to hold that a charitable deduction for income tax purposes could be taken in the year the check was issued even though the check remained outstanding as of year-end.

The Tax Court in *Estate of Belcher* expressly declined to address whether the relation-back doctrine would apply to checks issued to noncharitable donees. And while the Service reluctantly agreed to interpret the *Belcher* decision as creating a "limited, equitable" exception to Reg. § 20.2031-5 for checks issued in good faith to charitable recipients, the Service signaled its intent to enforce the letter of the regulation in the noncharitable context. *See* A.O.D. 1989-014 (Nov. 13, 1989). On that note, the Tax Court in *Newman v. Commissioner*, 111 T.C.

81 (1998), declined to apply the relation-back doctrine for checks issued to individual donees, fearing that such treatment would foster estate-tax avoidance. *See also* Rosano v. United States, 245 F.3d 212 (2d Cir. 2001); McCarthy v. United States, 806 F.2d 129 (7th Cir. 1986); Estate of Gagliardi v. Commissioner, 89 T.C. 1207 (1987) (all declining to apply the relation-back doctrine in this setting). Thus, the last-minute tax planning undertaken by the son in the hypothetical above appears ineffective to reduce the size of the decedent's gross estate.

§ 2.03 PROMISSORY NOTES

Promissory notes issued in favor of the decedent are included in the gross estate under § 2033. This result is not affected by any provision in the decedent's will directing that the note be cancelled or the amounts owed forgiven. *See* Treas. Reg. § 20.2033-1(b). Rather, the value of the note is included in the decedent's gross estate, and the cancellation occurring by way of the decedent's will is treated as a bequest of the note to the obligor.

A more favorable estate tax result can be achieved if the cancellation is not the product of unilateral, discretionary action on the part of the decedent, but rather is required by the parties' underlying contractual arrangement. Promissory notes that call for amounts owed to be cancelled upon the obligee's death are commonly referred to as self-cancelling installment notes or SCINs.[5] If the debt cancellation feature is respected for estate tax purposes, nothing will be included in the decedent-obligee's gross estate under § 2033 on account of the note because the decedent-obligee possesses no contractual rights that are capable of transfer. Rather, the payment obligations in his favor terminate by reason of his death.

For the SCIN technique to be respected for estate tax purposes, the obligor must pay a premium for the cancellation feature, either in the form of an increased face amount of the obligation or through an enhanced interest rate (both of which increase the rate of return to the lender). *See* Estate of Moss v. Commissioner, 74 T.C. 1239 (1980) (holding that property sold to a corporation for notes that would be cancelled upon the seller's death were not treated as bequests of the cancelled amounts because of parties' stipulation that the notes supplied adequate and full consideration for the cancellation component). Given the potential for self-cancelling installment notes to foster estate tax avoidance when issued between family members, one can expect the Service to scrutinize these arrangements closely to determine if they are commercially reasonable. Courts may find these arrangements dubious as well. *See* Estate of Musgrove v. United States, 33 Fed. Cl. 657 (1995) (refusing to respect a self-cancelling feature of an interest-free demand note issued in favor of the decedent one month prior to his death). *But see* Estate of Costanza v. Commissioner, 320 F.3d 595 (6th Cir. 2003) (finding that the taxpayer had rebutted presumption against enforceability of an intra-family SCIN based on the decedent's "real expectation of repayment").

---

[5] These instruments often are employed with sales of property to an intentionally defective grantor trust (IDGT), an irrevocable trust that is treated as a grantor trust for income tax purposes.

§ 2.04   ACCRUED INCOME PAYMENTS

[A]   Accrued Salary and Investment Income

The cash method of accounting commonly used by individuals for purposes of income tax reporting does not apply in the estate tax context. Rather, in addition to including in the gross estate the underlying investment property in the form of stocks, bonds, notes, and rental real estate, § 2033 also captures investment income that has accrued as of the decedent's death. Hence, a decedent's gross estate includes accrued interest on bonds, bank accounts, or promissory notes; dividends payable to the decedent or his estate (provided the decedent was alive as of the dividend record date); and accrued rent. *See* Treas. Reg. § 20.2033-1(b). The same rule applies to the return on the decedent's labor. Any wages, salary, or other compensation to which the decedent was entitled at the time of his death but had yet to be paid is included under § 2033. *See, e.g.*, Rev. Rul. 55-123, 1955-1 C.B. 443 (right of decedent's estate to receive payment for legal services performed on a contingent fee basis included in gross estate under predecessor of § 2033). The preceding examples are specific illustrations of the general rule that any account receivable owned by the decedent in his individual capacity that can be collected by his estate or transmitted by descent or devise constitutes property under § 2033.

[B]   Deferred Compensation

Determining the proper application of § 2033 is perhaps most challenging in the context of deferred compensation arrangements. Deferred compensation is one of the few instances in which § 2033 can reach into the non-probate arena, as payments following the decedent's death under these plans are made directly to the plan beneficiaries by way of contract. As the authorities discussed below reveal, courts have placed a significant emphasis on whether the decedent's rights to payments under the deferred compensation plan are indefeasibly vested as of the decedent's death.

The decedent in *Estate of Garber v. Commissioner*, 271 F.2d 97 (3d Cir. 1959), served as the president of two related companies. Each corporation had established a qualified retirement trust that benefitted the decedent. The trusts were funded solely with contributions from the corporations, and the trust funds were held exclusively for the benefit of the participating employees or their beneficiaries. In other words, no portion of the trust funds could revert to the employer corporations or be used to satisfy the corporation's creditors. Pursuant to the plan, the decedent could have taken his benefits as a lump-sum payment upon retirement. However, the decedent worked past his retirement age and until the time of his death. Pursuant to directions filed with the employer, the decedent's benefits under the plan were paid to his children.

In finding that the retirement trust benefits paid to the decedent's children were included in his gross estate under the predecessor to § 2033, the Third Circuit stressed that the primary issue in determining inclusion under the statute was the extent of the decedent's control over the funds that gave rise to the death benefits at issue. As reflected in the excerpt below, the court found that the decedent possessed sufficient control over the death benefits to warrant inclusion under § 2033:

> Garber chose not to receive pension benefits. He was president of both corporations at the time of his death. . . . Garber's benefits under the plans must be regarded as being

based on indefeasible rights growing out of his employment by the corporations, akin to deferred compensation payments and as constituting "property" within the meaning of [§ 2033]. . . . This property, acquired by Garber in consideration of his services as president of the corporations and under the terms of the plans and the trust agreements, became fixed when the corporations made their contributions to the [trusts]. At these times Garber's aliquot portions of the [trusts] were credited to and earmarked for him. Garber possessed the right to receive the entire sum of his interests in the [trusts] by way of lump sum payments if he quitted the companies at the retirement ages applicable to him under the respective plans, or upon the contingencies relating to the funds, hereinbefore set out. He also possessed the right . . . to receive the lump sum payments and . . . he directed the pension boards to pay to certain classes of beneficiaries related to him by blood or marriage the credits accrued to him at the time of his death. His children as beneficiaries in fact received the whole of the lump sum payments on his death by direction of the pension boards. We conclude that Garber had a sufficient degree of control over those portions of the [trusts] which had accrued to him to render the lump sum payments made to his children . . . includible in his gross estate under [§ 2033].

Id. at 103–04; *see also* Rosenberg v. United States, 309 F.2d 724 (7th Cir. 1962) (following *Estate of Garber*). *Compare* Glenn v. Hanner, 212 F.2d 483 (6th Cir. 1954) (holding that retirement plan amounts that could be withdrawn by the decedent only upon retirement or termination of employment were not included in his gross estate where the decedent died prior to attaining retirement age and while still employed).

The Third Circuit's decision in *Estate of Garber* should be contrasted with the Tax Court's later decision in *Estate of Wadewitz v. Commissioner*, 39 T.C. 925 (1963), *aff'd*, 339 F.2d 980 (7th Cir. 1964). The decedent in *Estate of Wadewitz* participated in an unfunded nonqualified deferred compensation plan; that is, his employer merely promised to make certain payments to the decedent upon his retirement without irrevocably setting aside assets to fund the payment obligations. If the decedent died prior to receiving all of the installment payments, the plan provided that remaining amounts would be paid to his children in equal shares. The Tax Court distinguished *Estate of Garber* primarily on the basis that the decedent in *Estate of Wadewitz* never possessed the ability to receive his retirement benefits through a lump-sum payment during his lifetime. In holding that the benefits paid to the decedent's children were not includible under § 2033, the Tax Court reasoned that the decedent's interest in the retirement benefits terminated upon his death:

Under the contract here in question Wadewitz acquired the right to receive monthly payments for a fixed 15-year term following his retirement or the termination of his employment. In the event of his death prior to the expiration of the 15-year period, the balance of the payments due under the contract was to be paid to certain beneficiaries named in the contract who were jointly designated by Wadewitz and [employer]. Consequently, his death prior to the expiration of the 15-year term terminated his own interest under the contract and also caused the remainder interests of the designated beneficiaries to become fixed. These beneficiaries were in the position of third party beneficiaries under the contract with [employer]. Their interests under the contract clearly were not derived from the estate of Wadewitz. No interest in the contract which the decedent possessed during his life was transferrable through his estate either by will or by intestacy. The situation here, in our opinion, is essentially the same as if the decedent had received under the will of another a right to receive certain monthly payments for 15 years or until his death and, in the event of his death prior to the end of the 15-year period, the remaining payments due were payable to certain designated beneficiaries. If Wadewitz' interest had been so created, it clearly would represent a terminable interest and as such would not constitute property includable in his gross estate under the general provisions of § 2033.

Id. at 934–35.[6]

The Tax Court's comparison of the deferred compensation arrangement in *Estate of Wadewitz* to a devise of a life estate in favor of the decedent followed by a distribution to designated remainder beneficiaries is not entirely satisfying. It implies that the employer insisted on paying a portion of the decedent's compensation in this manner, as opposed to the decedent seeking the tax benefits of deferring receipt of a portion of his compensation through the retirement plan. Had decedent instead taken all of his compensation currently, his gross estate under § 2033 presumably would have been enhanced by the amounts in question (assuming decedent had not consumed those amounts before his death). In short, the Tax Court's analogy assumes that the decedent had no input into the structure of the compensation arrangement.[7] Nonetheless, the Tax Court's refusal in *Estate of Wadewitz* to apply § 2033 to benefits that the decedent was not capable of receiving during his lifetime was followed by the First Circuit in *Estate of Porter v. Commissioner*, 442 F.2d 915 (1st Cir. 1971).

To the extent a unifying principle can be distilled concerning the application of § 2033 to amounts paid by a decedent's employer to the decedent's estate or to certain of the decedent's relatives (whether or not selected by the decedent), it is the following: Section 2033 will not apply to amounts that the decedent was not in some manner capable of receiving during his lifetime. *See, e.g.*, Commissioner v. Estate of Albright, 356 F.2d 319 (2d Cir. 1966) (payment right present); Harris v. United States, 72-1 U.S. Tax Cas. (CCH) 12,845, 1972 U.S. Dist. LEXIS 13992 (C.D. Cal. Apr. 27, 1972) (payment right absent); Hinze v. United States, 72-1 U.S. Tax Cas. (CCH) 12,842, 1972 U.S. Dist. LEXIS 13991 (C.D. Cal. Apr. 27, 1972) (payment right absent); Worthen v. United States, 192 F. Supp. 727 (D. Mass. 1961) (payment right absent).

[C] Treatment as IRD

Accrued income payments do not lose their status as gross income just because the decedent did not live long enough to collect them. Rather, such payments are characterized as income in respect of a decedent (IRD) under § 691(a) to be included in the gross income of the person who collects it. To ensure that these amounts do not escape taxation as a result of the decedent's death, § 1014(c) denies a step-up in basis for IRD items.

Inclusion of the value of IRD items in a decedent's gross estate at their full value for estate tax purposes appears excessive. Had the decedent simply survived to the point of collection,

---

[6] Although the Tax Court found § 2033 inapplicable, it went on to hold that the amounts paid to the decedent's children were included in his gross estate under § 2039. The application of § 2039 to annuities payable to the decedent is discussed in Chapter 14.

[7] While perhaps not entirely consistent with reality, the Tax Court's analogy in *Estate of Wadewitz* is consistent with the general reluctance to apply the constructive receipt doctrine to deferred compensation arrangements based on speculation concerning what the employee could have negotiated in the way of current compensation. *See, e.g.*, Rev. Rul. 60-31, 1960-1 C.B. 174, 178 (constructive receipt doctrine cannot be applied based on speculation concerning whether the employer would have been willing to make earlier payment of compensation).

the estate tax would have been imposed only on the after-income-tax proceeds. While one approach to alleviate this discrepancy would be to "tax-effect" the value of the IRD item for estate tax purposes (that is, to reduce the value of the IRD item by the lurking income tax liability), such an approach would lack precision because the income tax liability turns on the attributes of the party that collects the payment—attributes that likely will not be known when the estate tax return is filed. Section 691(c) therefore approaches the problem from the opposite angle by permitting the party who includes the IRD item in gross income to deduct the marginal estate tax attributable to the inclusion of the IRD item in the decedent's gross estate.[8]

§ 2.05 PROPERTY INTERESTS THAT ARISE UPON DEATH

As indicated by the Tax Court in *Estate of Wadewitz*, an interest in property that terminates by reason of the decedent's death (frequently referred to as a terminable interest) is not included in the decedent's gross estate under § 2033 because such interest is not capable of transmission by the decedent. The corollary of this proposition holds true as well. That is, if the decedent never possessed an interest in property during his lifetime but the property interest arose as a result of his death, § 2033 does not operate to capture the property even if the property is payable to the decedent's estate (and therefore subject to descent and devise). The foundational case of *Connecticut Bank & Trust Co. v. United States*, 465 F.2d 760 (2d Cir. 1972) illustrates this latter point.

The *Connecticut Bank & Trust* case addressed whether the proceeds of a wrongful death claim were subject to inclusion in the decedent's estate under § 2033. Whereas most wrongful death statutes provide that proceeds of the claim are to be paid to certain statutory beneficiaries, the Connecticut statute at issue provided that such proceeds would be paid into the decedent's estate. Hence, although the decedent could not enjoy these amounts during his lifetime by definition, he could direct their disposition by will. The Second Circuit rejected the government's invocation of § 2033 on the following basis:

> Simple logic mandates the conclusion that an action for wrongful death cannot exist until the decedent has died, at which point, he is no longer a person capable of owning any property interests. The Government's reply to this is that at the very instant of death the right of action arose which the decedent was then capable of owning at death. The only authorities cited for this position, however, are cases where *preexisting* property interests were *valued* as of the instant of death, but valuation at time of death of prior existing interests is a far different concern from that in this case where the property interest has sprung from the fact that the death has taken place.
>
> . . . . Where, as here, there was no property interest in the decedent which passed by virtue of his death, but rather one which arose only after his death, such an interest is not property owned at death and not part of the gross estate under § 2033.

Id. at 763 (emphasis in original). The Service ultimately acquiesced to the result in *Connecticut Bank & Trust* in Revenue Ruling 75-127, 1975-1 C.B. 297.

---

[8] The availability of § 691(c) relief, however, has not stopped taxpayers from attempting to tax-effect the value of IRD items. *See* Estate of Kahn v. Commissioner, 125 T.C. 227 (2005) (rejecting the estate's attempt to reduce value of IRA by expected federal income tax liability of beneficiaries).

The combination of the terminable-interest rule and the arising-at-death corollary can produce curious results. For example, suppose a decedent devised property in trust that designated A as the lifetime beneficiary; upon A's death, the trust property is to be distributed to A's probate estate. Analyzing the lifetime and remainder interests separately yields no inclusion under § 2033, so perhaps the combination of the two should not alter the result. On the other hand, when the two interests are joined, the hallmarks of § 2033 appear satisfied: A possesses the beneficial enjoyment of property during his lifetime along with the power (through direction in his will) to determine the manner in which the property will be transmitted at death. The only possible deficiency is that the power to transmit the property at death does not emanate from the interest that A possesses in the property during his lifetime.

The Seventh Circuit in *Second National Bank of Danville v. Dallman*, 209 F.2d 321 (7th Cir. 1954) addressed a scenario similar to the hypothetical above. The decedent in *Dallman* was entitled to receive annual payments equal to three percent of the principal amount retained by the insurance company from the proceeds of a policy insuring the decedent's father. The decedent was not entitled to withdraw any portion of the principal during her lifetime. The decedent possessed the right to designate a contingent beneficiary to succeed to her interest in the policy proceeds; in default of such designation, the policy proceeds were to be paid to the decedent's probate estate upon her death. The decedent failed to designate a contingent beneficiary, and, accordingly, the insurance company paid the proceeds to the decedent's estate to be distributed according to the terms of her will.

In addition to other theories,[9] the government contended that the predecessor of § 2033 operated to include the principal held by the insurance company in the decedent's gross estate. The Seventh Circuit rejected this position, citing the inability of the decedent to access the principal amount during her lifetime. *Id.* at 324. Hence, the decedent did not possess ownership of the property at the time of her death. Additionally, the court did not believe that the decedent's ability to direct the transmission of the principal amount at her death—whether through the appointment of a contingent beneficiary or through the terms of her will—was sufficient to warrant application of the predecessor of § 2033. Although the court's analysis is somewhat difficult to follow, the court stressed that any such power flowed from the terms of the contract between the decedent's father and the insurance company as opposed to an interest in the property that the decedent possessed during her lifetime. *See id.* at 326. Hence, under the rationale employed by the Seventh Circuit in *Dallman*, the power to determine the transmission of property at death must constitute an aspect of the decedent's lifetime interest in property in order to implicate § 2033.

---

[9] The government also contended that the principal retained by the insurance company was included in the decedent's gross estate based on the decedent's possession of a power of appointment over such amount. The court rejected this basis for inclusion, apparently reasoning that the prerequisites to the appointment of a contingent beneficiary precluded the decedent from possessing a power of appointment at the time of her death. *See id.* at 324. Additionally, the court concluded that the power to direct the distribution of property paid into a decedent's probate estate does not rise to the level of a power of appointment, instead insisting that the power must emanate from the initial transferor of the property (in this case, the decedent's father). *Id.* The Fifth Circuit later rejected the *Dallman* court's analysis on this point, concluding that the ability to dispose of property by will constituted a general power of appointment. *See* Keeter v. United States, 461 F.2d 714 (5th Cir. 1972) (holding remainder payable to estate includible under § 2041); *see also* Rev. Rul. 55-277, 1955-1 C.B. 456 (rejecting the *Dallman* court's holding on the power of appointment issue). The relationship between § 2033 and § 2041 is discussed in § 2.06.

The Service has indicated that it will not follow the Seventh Circuit's decision in *Dallman*. In that regard, regulations promulgated under § 2041 (addressing inclusion in the gross estate based on the possession of a power of appointment over property) provide that if a decedent possesses a lifetime interest in a trust that calls for the remainder to be paid to the decedent's probate estate, the trust remainder is captured in the decedent's gross estate under § 2033 notwithstanding the potential application of § 2041. *See* Treas. Reg. § 20.2041-1(b)(2) (explaining the relation of § 2041 to other sections).

§ 2.06   EFFECT OF POWER OF APPOINTMENT OVER PROPERTY

Returning to the hypothetical trust created for *A*'s lifetime benefit in § 2.05 above, suppose that the remainder is not directed to be paid into *A*'s estate but rather is to be distributed to the person or persons *A* designates through a provision in his will. If *A* does not exercise his testamentary power of appointment, the trust property will be distributed to *A*'s issue as takers in default.

Under the hypothetical trust as modified, the trust remainder will not become part of *A*'s probate estate. Nonetheless, *A* possesses the ability to determine the manner in which the trust property will be distributed upon his death. Does *A*'s lifetime interest in the property, when coupled with the ability to direct its transmission at his death, cause the trust property to be included in § 2033?

The Supreme Court addressed this question in *Helvering v. Safe Deposit & Trust Co.*, 316 U.S. 56 (1942). The *Safe Deposit & Trust* case concerned trusts established for the lifetime benefit of tobacco heir Z. Smith Reynolds. With minor variations, the trusts called for certain income payments to be made to the decedent until he attained age 28, at which time the trust assets would be distributed to him outright. In the event the decedent died prior to distribution, the trust assets were to be distributed pursuant to his general testamentary power of appointment—meaning the decedent could appoint the property by will as he saw fit, including to his estate or to his creditors. If the power of appointment was not exercised, the trust remainder would pass to his siblings. The decedent passed away at the age of 20 without having validly exercised his powers of appointment.

Contending that (a) the decedent's lifetime interest in the trust, (b) his ability to obtain distribution of the trust principal at age 28, and (c) his unilateral ability to designate the beneficiaries of the property at his death collectively were "substantially equivalent to fee simple title," the government sought to include the trust property under the predecessor of § 2033. *Id.* at 58. The Supreme Court was not persuaded:

> [E]ven if we assume with the Government that the restrictions upon the decedent's use and enjoyment of the trust properties may be dismissed as negligible and that he had the capacity to exercise a testamentary power of appointment, the question still remains: Did the decedent have "at the time of his death" such an "interest" as Congress intended to be included in the gross estate under [§ 2033]? It is not contended that the benefits during life which the trusts provided for the decedent, terminating as they did at his death, made the trust properties part of his gross estate under the statute. And viewing [§ 2033] in its background of legislative, judicial, and administrative history, we cannot reach the conclusion that the words "interest . . . of the decedent at the time of his death" were intended by Congress to include property subject to a general testamentary power of appointment unexercised by the decedent.

Id. at 58–59. The Court bolstered its decision by referring to the predecessor of § 2041 (which at the time included in the gross estate property that passes pursuant to general power of appointment only if the power was exercised by the decedent), noting that such provision would be unnecessary if the existence of a general power of appointment—regardless of exercise—were sufficient to warrant inclusion under § 2033.[10]

The *Safe Deposit & Trust* case makes clear that the combination of a lifetime interest in property coupled with the legal ability to direct the manner in which the property will be transmitted at death does not automatically trigger application of § 2033. Rather, for property to be included under § 2033, the decedent's lifetime interest in the property must be capable of transmission by death. The decision also sheds light on the nature of § 2033. Despite its rather broad language, § 2033 is not designed to be a default, catch-all description of property to be included in the decedent's gross estate; rather, it serves merely as one of several independent grounds for inclusion. Section 2033 just so happens to be the section that picks up the most routine of property transfers that occur by reason of death.

§ 2.07 EXPECTANCIES AND FUTURE INTERESTS

While the scope of what constitutes an "interest" in property for purposes of § 2033 is a matter of federal tax law, the requisite interest must lie in "property" that is recognized for state law purposes. Hence, as in many other areas of federal tax law, the scope of § 2033 cannot be divorced from state law, but rather depends on it. In that regard, the outer bounds of cognizable state-law property interests cannot be precisely defined. As noted in *First Victoria National Bank v. United States*, 620 F.2d 1096, 1102 (5th Cir. 1980):

> The attempt to define property is an elusive task. There is no cosmic synoptic definiens that can encompass its range. The word is at times more cognizable than recognizable. It is not capable of anatomical or lexicographical definition or proof.

Despite the general uncertainty regarding the scope of property under state law, one principle from the first-year property course remains clear: A mere expectancy of receiving property in the future does not rise to the level of a property interest. Thus, if a decedent is named as devisee under the will of an individual alive at the time of the decedent's death, the possibility that property may be paid to the decedent's estate pursuant to the individual's will does not implicate § 2033.[11] In a similar vein, payments that are made to the decedent's estate or to certain of the decedent's relatives at the discretion of the decedent's employer—rather than pursuant to a binding legal obligation—fall outside the scope of § 2033 for want of an enforceable property interest. *See* Estate of Barr v. Commissioner, 40 T.C. 227 (1963).

While the principle that mere expectancies do not constitute property appears simple on its face, its application becomes somewhat difficult in the context of future interests. A future interest constitutes a present property interest, even though possession of the underlying property is postponed. For example, assume that *T* devises property in trust for the lifetime benefit of *A*, remainder to *B*. At the moment of *T*'s death, *B* possesses a vested remainder in

---

[10] As discussed in Chapter 14, the mere possession of a general power of appointment over property (regardless of whether the power is exercised) now is sufficient to cause the subject property to be included in the power holder's gross estate under § 2041(a)(2).

[11] This example is more illustrative than real, as the possibility of property being paid into the decedent's estate is likely non-existent due to the general rule that devises in favor of deceased individuals lapse.

the trust. Even if B were to die prior to the remainder becoming possessory, the remainder would be included in B's gross estate under § 2033. *See* Estate of Hamilton v. Commissioner, T.C. Memo. 1976-354, 35 T.C.M. (CCH) 1609; *see also* Treas. Reg. § 20.2031-7(d)(2)(ii) (providing for actuarial valuation of remainder).[12] On the other hand, if the trust had provided that the remainder was to be distributed to B if he was then living, otherwise to B's then-living issue, then upon B's death prior to A nothing would be included in B's gross estate under § 2033. The survivorship condition operates to extinguish B's interest in the trust upon his death. *See* Rev. Rul. 55-438, 1955-2 C.B. 601. As one final illustration of the application of § 2033 to future interests, assume that the trust remainder is to be paid to C if C is then living, otherwise to B. Assuming that B survives T but predeceases both A and C, is anything included in B's gross estate under § 2033? Yes. B possesses a contingent remainder in the trust principal and this remainder interest is not extinguished upon his death. However, the value of B's contingent remainder necessarily will depend on the likelihood of C surviving A. *See* Rev. Rul. 61-88, 1961-1 C.B. 417 (providing that decedent's right to receive distribution of trust principal upon death of the life tenant without surviving issue should be valued under general valuation principles).

With these principles concerning the application of § 2033 to future interests in mind, the notion of an expectancy returns when a party is given discretionary authority to distribute trust principal. Suppose that in the first trust (A is lifetime beneficiary, remainder to B), the trustee is afforded full discretion to distribute all or a portion of the trust principal to A for any reason. Because there is no guarantee that there will be any trust principal remaining at A's death, it may be tempting to dismiss B's interest in the trust as a mere expectancy. Yet that conclusion is not proper. Despite the trustee's invasion power, B nonetheless possesses a vested remainder in the trust principal—a recognized property interest under state law. Of course, the prospect of principal being distributed to A would weigh on the valuation of the remainder interest.

To come even closer to the expectancy line, assume that S establishes an inter vivos trust for his lifetime benefit, over which he retains an unqualified right of revocation. The trust provides that upon S's death, all remaining trust property shall be distributed to B. Note that, from a practical perspective, B's interest in the trust is not materially different from that of a named devisee under a will. Yet because revocable trusts have current legal effect (as opposed to wills, which operate only upon the death of the testator), B's interest in the trust could be described as a vested remainder subject to divestment through the exercise by S of the right of revocation—a long label, but a present property interest nonetheless. In the event B were to predecease S, should B's interest in the trust be included under § 2033? According to the government, yes. In Revenue Ruling 67-370, 1967-2 C.B. 324, the Service held that B's interest would be included in the gross estate under § 2033 on the basis that it was descendible, devisable, and alienable under state law. While the ruling declared that the possibility of divestment of the remainder following the decedent's death did not warrant the assignment of a nominal value to the interest, it is difficult to imagine how such an interest could be valued.

---

[12] Given the liquidity burdens an estate could face as a result of the inclusion of the value of a future interest in the decedent's gross estate, a decedent's executor may elect under § 6163(a) to defer payment of the estate tax attributable to a reversionary or remainder interest in property until six months following termination of the prior possessory interest in the property.

§ 2.08   INCHOATE SPOUSAL INTERESTS IN PROPERTY

Because the hallmarks of inclusion under § 2033 include (a) an interest in property during life that (b) the decedent is capable of transmitting at death, an issue arises concerning the effect of a surviving spouse's inchoate interest in property owned by a deceased spouse that arises upon the predeceasing spouse's death. Taking a surviving wife's common-law dower interest in real property as an example, the wife is entitled to a life estate in one-third of the deceased husband's real estate. Because of this inchoate property interest, the deceased husband is not entitled to transmit fee simple ownership of the property at death. Should the wife's dower interest affect the property interest that is included in the deceased husband's estate under § 2033, perhaps limiting the inclusion to the remaining interest in real property that the decedent is capable of transmitting? Although this would appear to be a plausible interpretation of the statute, Congress enacted § 2034 to fill any such gap left in § 2033.

Section 2034 provides that a decedent's gross estate includes the value of all property "to the extent of any interest therein of the surviving spouse, existing at the time of the decedent's death as dower or curtesy, or by virtue of a statute creating an estate in lieu of dower or curtesy." The regulations under § 2034 indicate that the intent of the statute is to ensure that the full value of the property owned by the decedent at the time of his death is included in his gross estate, notwithstanding any inchoate spousal interest in the property that ripens upon the death of the predeceasing spouse. "Thus, the full value of property is included in the decedent's gross estate, without deduction of such an interest of the surviving husband or wife, and without regard to when the right to such an interest arose." Treas. Reg. § 20.2034-1. Accordingly, forced transfers to spouses pursuant to state law do not serve to reduce the decedent's gross estate.

§ 2.09   STUDY PROBLEMS

1.   Janice recently predeceased her husband, Mark. In connection with the administration of Janice's estate, Mark has prepared a list of all of his wife's assets. Identify which of these assets, if any, would be included in Janice's gross estate under § 2033:

  a.   Joint bank account with Mark. The account provides for a right of survivorship.

  b.   Ownership of a life insurance policy on Janice's life.

  c.   Ownership of a life insurance policy on Mark's life.

  d.   Residence owned by Janice and Mark as tenants-by-the-entirety.

  e.   A brokerage account titled in Janice's individual name.

  f.   A beneficial interest in an LLC that has title to the family beach house.

  g.   Securities held in a UGMA account for the benefit of Janice's daughter of which Janice was named as the custodian.

  h.   A tenants-in-common interest in timberland held by Janice. Janice's siblings held the remaining interests in the real property.

  i.   A vehicle titled in Janice's name.

  j.   A paycheck that was deposited to Janice's account one week after her death.

2. With respect to any of the assets above that are included in Janice's probate estate, does Mark's state-law right to receive an elective share of Janice's estate affect the amount included in Janice's gross estate?

3. An actor was named to receive an Academy Award posthumously. Suppose the voting members of the Academy of Motion Picture Arts and Sciences met on November 1 of Year 1 to determine the winner. On December 1 of Year 1, the winning actor passed away. On February 1 of Year 2, the awards ceremony takes place, and the actor's family receives the statuette along with a cash prize. Is anything included in the actor's gross estate under § 2033?

4. Dan loaned $100,000 to his son, Sam. The loan, evidenced through a promissory note, called for Sam to make regular payments at seven percent interest compounded annually.

    As an estate planning technique, Dan also sold some undeveloped beach property to an irrevocable grantor trust. The trust did not pay cash for the property; rather, the trust issued Dan a promissory note calling for the future payment of the $2 million value of the property. The promissory note issued by the trust also called for regular payments at seven percent interest compounded annually.

    At Dan's death, assume that $80,000 remains outstanding on the note from Sam and $1.6 million remains outstanding on the installment obligation issued by the trust. Dan's will provides that any balance on Sam's note is to be cancelled upon his death. Dan's will is silent as to the installment note issued by the trust; however, the promissory note itself provides that any remaining principal obligation will be cancelled upon Dan's death.

    What amounts, if any, will be included in Dan's estate on account of these promissory notes? If you need additional information, what questions would you like to have answered?

5. Candace is the owner of what is referred to as a payable on death ("POD") bank account. Pursuant to the account agreement, withdrawals can be made only by Candace during her lifetime. Yet upon her death, the account balance does not become part of her probate estate; rather, it is paid to the "POD payee" on the account, which Candace designates to be her niece. Upon Candace's death, is the balance in the account included in her gross estate under § 2033?

6. How would your answer to Question 5 above change, if at all, had Candace *irrevocably* designated her niece as the POD payee of the account?

7. You represent Bob in connection with drafting his estate-planning documents, and you have asked him to provide a detailed inventory of his assets. After going through the standard items, Bob mentions to you, "Oh yeah, I think I may be a beneficiary under my uncle's trust." You ask Bob to get a copy of the trust document for you to review. He does so, and the trust provides as follows:

    Upon my death, the Trustee shall retain the property in trust, and pay the net income therefrom to my wife in regular installments but not less frequently than annually. The Trustee may also distribute as much of the trust principal to my wife as the Trustee deems necessary for her health, maintenance, and support in her accustomed manner of living. Upon my wife's death, the trust assets shall be distributed one-half to my nephew Bob and one-half to my niece Betty.

Bob's uncle passed away years ago, but Bob's aunt is still living. After producing the trust document, Bob says "I shouldn't have to worry about this from an estate tax standpoint should I? I mean, I haven't seen one dime from this trust yet, and I'm not sure I ever will." What is your advice?

8. Return to the hypothetical provided at the beginning of § 2.02. Pursuant to the Tax Court's decision in *Newman v. Commissioner*, the amount of the checks written and delivered to the family members would not be deducted from the decedent's bank account in determining the amount included in his gross estate under § 2033. What, if anything, could be done to achieve the desired result?

Chapter 3

GENERAL SCOPE OF THE GIFT TAX: GRATUITOUS TRANSFERS OF PROPERTY

Internal Revenue Code:	§§ 2501(a)(1), 2511(a), 2512(a)-(b)
	§§ 2503(g), 2035(b)
	skim § 7872(a)–(e), (f)(1)–(7)
Treasury Regulations:	§ 25.2511-1(a), (c)(1), (d)–(e), (g), (h)(1)–(3), (6)–(8)
	§§ 25.2511-2(a), (f), 25.2512-8

Whereas a decedent's gross estate for federal estate tax purposes is defined as the sum of property that is captured through a series of specific, independent inclusionary provisions (§§ 2033 through 2044), the federal gift tax base is structured around a single broad, general rule of inclusion. Section 2501(a)(1) imposes an annual excise tax on "the transfer of property by gift." While Congress has not undertaken to affirmatively define a gift for this purpose, it has indicated its intention that the term not be defined narrowly: "[T]he tax imposed by section 2501 shall apply whether the transfer is in trust or otherwise, whether the gift is direct or indirect, and whether the property is real or personal, tangible or intangible." IRC § 2511(a). The legislative history accompanying the permanent enactment of the federal gift tax indicated that the tax base was to be broadly construed:

> The terms "property," "transfer," "gift," and "indirectly" are used in the broadest and most comprehensive sense; the term "property" reaching every species of right or interest protected by law and having an exchangeable value.

> The words "transfer . . . by gift" and "whether . . . direct or indirect" are designed to cover and comprehend all transactions . . . whereby, and to the extent . . . that property, or a property right is donatively passed to or conferred upon another, regardless of the means or the devise employed in its accomplishment.

H.R. Rep. No. 72-708, at 27–28 (1932) & S. Rep. No. 72-665, at 39 (1932), both quoted in *Dickman v. Commissioner*, 465 U.S. 330, 348 (1984). With little statutory guidance apart from these general directives, the task of delineating the boundaries of a transfer subject to the federal gift tax has been left to administrative guidance and judicial resolution.

§ 3.01 RELEVANCE OF DONATIVE INTENT AND CONSIDERATION RECEIVED

Recall that in the landmark case of *Commissioner v. Duberstein*, 363 U.S. 278 (1960), the Supreme Court addressed the circumstances under which a transfer of property would constitute a gift for purposes of the § 102(a) exclusion from gross income. Among other hallmarks, the Court noted that a gift for income tax purposes "proceeds from a 'detached and disinterested generosity,'" and the Court stressed that the transferor's intention in making the transfer was critical to the inquiry. *Id.* at 285 (quoting Commissioner v. Lo Bue, 351 U.S. 243, 246 (1956)). These principles for defining a gift for purposes of the income tax do not carry over to the federal gift tax. In fact, the regulatory guidance to § 2511 expressly disclaims the relevance of the transferor's subjective motivations: "Donative intent on the part of the transferor is not an essential element in the application of the gift tax to the transfer. The application of the tax is based on the objective facts of the transfer and the circumstances under which it is made, rather than on the subjective motives of the donor." Treas. Reg. § 25.2511-1(g)(1).

One of the primary roles of the federal gift tax is to prevent the estate tax from being easily avoided through lifetime gratuitous transfers that serve to deplete the transferor's future gross estate. Accordingly, the most important objective factors in determining whether a gift has occurred are (1) whether the transferor received consideration for the transfer and, if so (2) the value of the consideration received. Although § 2512 provides authority for determining the value of a gift, the statute serves a definitional role as well. It provides as follows:

> Where property is transferred for less than an adequate and full consideration in money or money's worth, then the amount by which the value of the property exceeded the value of the consideration shall be deemed a gift, and shall be included in computing the amount of gifts made during the calendar year.

IRC § 2512(b).

By implication, a transfer of property that is made for an adequate and full consideration in money or money's worth does not constitute a gift for federal gift tax purposes. No gift tax would be needed in that instance, as such a transfer would not deplete the individual's future transfer tax base but instead would simply preserve it in a different form. Only where the value of the transferred property exceeds the value of the consideration will a gift arise, and the values of both items are to be determined under the objective willing-buyer, willing-seller standard.[1] *See* Treas. Reg. § 25.2512-8 (noting that a gift will arise if the value of the transferred property "exceeds the value in money or money's worth of the consideration given therefor"); *see also* Wheeler v. United States, 116 F.3d 749, 766 (5th Cir. 1997) (noting that the transfer tax scheme "eschews subjective requirements in favor of the objective requirements set forth in the statutes"). Hence, the presence of common-law consideration that may render the transfer non-gratuitous from the perspective of state law alone will not preclude the application of the gift tax. *See* Treas. Reg. § 25.2512-8 ("A consideration not reducible to a value in money or money's worth, as love and affection, promise of marriage, etc., is to be wholly disregarded. . . ."). Rather, consideration received is relevant only to the extent it prevents depletion of the transferor's estate.

The Supreme Court addressed the relevance of donative intent and common-law consideration through its decision in *Commissioner v. Wemyss*, 324 U.S. 303 (1945). In *Wemyss*, the taxpayer proposed marriage to a widow who was reluctant to accept because any remarriage on her part would terminate her beneficial interest in a trust created by her late husband

---

[1] Treas. Reg. § 25.2512-1 defines the value of property as "the price at which such property would change hands between a willing buyer and a willing seller, neither being under any compulsion to buy or to sell, and both having reasonable knowledge of relevant facts." The critical role that valuation plays in the federal transfer tax system is discussed in Chapter 7.

(under which she received substantial distributions of annual income). In order to hold his would-be bride harmless from this consequence, the taxpayer transferred to her stock worth approximately $150,000. Shortly after this transfer, the two married. Even though the transfer at issue could be styled as a bargained-for exchange, the Supreme Court in *Wemyss* upheld the government's imposition of a gift tax. The Court first rejected the notion that the absence of donative intent precluded the finding of a gift—the position taken by the appellate court below—by noting that considerations for determining whether a transfer constitutes a gift under common law had not been imported into the federal gift tax. *Id.* at 306. The Court next rejected the contention that the absence of financial gain to the transferee precluded the transfer from constituting a gift. While the widow surrendered her beneficial interest in the trust in exchange for the $150,000 of stock that accompanied her agreement to re-marry, that consideration did not flow to the transferor. As the Court explained, "[t]o allow detriment to the donee to satisfy the requirement of 'adequate and full consideration' would violate the purpose of the statute and open wide the door for evasion of the gift tax." *Id.* at 307–08. Hence, consideration given by the transferee of property is relevant to the determination of whether a transfer constitutes a gift for gift tax purposes (and, if so, the amount of the gift) only to the extent it augments the transferor's future gross estate.

If the determination of whether a transfer of property is subject to the federal gift tax is based solely on whether the transferor received adequate and full consideration in money or money's worth as required under § 2512(b), then the gift tax potentially could apply to poorly negotiated commercial transactions—that is, those in which the taxpayer received a bad bargain. Yet the regulations provide a safe harbor that avoids adding insult to injury in this setting. Under Reg. § 25.2512-8, a sale, exchange, or other transfer that takes place "in the ordinary course of business" will be treated as having been made for an adequate and full consideration in money or money's worth. A transfer in the ordinary course of business is parenthetically defined as one that is bona fide, at arm's length, and free from donative intent.

The safe harbor provided in Reg. § 25.2512-8 for transfers in the ordinary course of business is grounded in terms of administrability. There is no reason for the government to scrutinize transfers where the transferor's economic self interest operates to protect his future transfer tax base. The situation changes altogether, however, when the transferee is a member of the transferor's family. Intrafamily transfers are subject to heightened scrutiny, and transfers to family members are presumed to constitute gifts. *See* Kimbell v. United States, 371 F.3d 257, 265 (5th Cir. 2004) (imposition of heightened scrutiny); Estate of Muhammad v. Commissioner, 965 F.2d 520, 521 (7th Cir. 1992) (presumption of gift). Furthermore, in order for the transfer to escape gift tax scrutiny under Reg. § 25.2512-8, the transferor essentially must prove a negative—the absence of donative intent.[2] Doing so is no simple task, particularly when the transferee is a natural beneficiary of the transferor's estate. *See* Beveridge v. Commissioner, 10 T.C. 915 (1948) (citing testimony of taxpayer's advisors and attorneys to support its finding that the taxpayer's payment to estranged daughter in settlement of property dispute was made for adequate and full consideration).

---

[2] In an unpublished decision, the Ninth Circuit Court of Appeals determined that a transfer of real property from a grandmother to her grandchildren in exchange for a private annuity did not qualify for the Reg. § 25.2512-8 safe harbor of presumed adequate consideration in part on the absence of evidence demonstrating a lack of donative intent. *See* Estate of Cullison v. Commissioner, 221 F.3d 1347, 85 A.F.T.R.2d 2000-1908 (9th Cir. 2000) (unpublished opinion).

§ 3.02 NECESSITY OF A TRANSFER OF PROPERTY

Although the scope of the gift tax is intended to be broadly interpreted, there is one prominent limitation suggested by the statute: the necessity of a transfer of *property*. *See* IRC § 2501(a); *see also* Treas. Reg. § 25.2511-1(g)(1) (stating that the gift tax "is applicable only to a transfer of a beneficial interest in property"). The statutory requirement of a conveyance of property naturally places a premium on how broadly that concept is defined.[3]

[A] Gratuitous Provision of Services

One of the first cases to address the necessity of a transfer of property was *Commissioner v. Hogle*, 165 F.2d 352 (10th Cir. 1947). The taxpayer in *Hogle* established irrevocable trusts for the benefit of his children. Pursuant to the arrangement, the taxpayer managed a securities trading account for the benefit of the trusts, and the trusts were entitled to any profits generated on the account. In this manner, the taxpayer irrevocably assigned the future net profits of his trading activities to the trust. Bolstered by its success in taxing the trading profits to the taxpayer for income tax purposes on assignment-of-income principles,[4] the Commissioner asserted that the trading profits constituted a gift from the taxpayer to the trust. With the issue framed in this manner, the Tenth Circuit had little difficulty ruling in favor of the taxpayer. The court explained that, while the gift tax was to be broadly construed, the tax could not be sustained unless there existed "an effective transfer of title or other economic interest or benefit in property having the quality of a gift." *Id.* at 353. Because the trading profits had been irrevocably assigned to the trust, the trust owned the profits the moment they were created. Accordingly, the court concluded that "[t]here was no transfer directly or indirectly from Hogle to the trusts of title to, or other economic interest in, the income from trading on margin." *Id.* at 353–54. The government's victory on the income tax front thus did not translate to success in subjecting the arrangement to the gift tax.

Instead of arguing that the taxpayer transferred the trading profits to the trusts, the government in *Hogle* could have argued that the value of the taxpayer's services constituted the subject of the taxable transfer. Indeed, the Tenth Circuit highlighted that the essence of the transaction was a donation of services: "What, in fact and in reality, Hogle gave the trusts . . . was his expert services in carrying on the trading, personal services in the management of the trusts." *Id.* at 353. While the court did not address whether the rendition of services free of compensation carried gift tax consequences, the result of the cases implied that services were not to be equated with property. In that vein, the government concedes that the gratuitous rendition of services falls outside the scope of the gift tax, as long as the waiver of compensation (express or implied) occurs within a reasonable time of commencing the provision of services. *See* Rev. Rul. 66-167, 1966-1 C.B. 20 (estate fiduciary's waiver of statutory commissions within six months of appointment did not give rise to taxable gift); *cf.* Rev. Rul. 64-225, 1964-2 C.B. 15 (trustee's waiver of statutory commissions executed after close of taxable years in which services were rendered constituted a taxable gift).

One justification for not taxing the gratuitous rendition of services is that doing so is not necessary to protect the transfer tax base. As individuals are not required to provide services for compensation but rather are free to choose leisure (subject to practical constraints), the

---

[3] A similar inquiry is raised by § 2033 in the estate tax context. *See* Chapter 2.01, *supra*.

[4] *See* Hogle v. Commissioner, 132 F.2d 66 (10th Cir. 1942).

gratis provision of services does not necessarily deplete the provider's future estate tax base. Of course, to the extent an individual compensates a third party to provide services to another, the payment of compensation depletes the transferor's estate and the transaction constitutes a gift to the service recipient. *See* Treas. Reg. § 25.2511-1(h)(3) ("The payment of money or the transfer of property to B in consideration of B's promise to render a service to C is a gift to C. . . .").

[B]   Interest-Free Loans and Rent-Free Use of Property

A natural extension of the issue of whether the gratuitous rendition of services implicates the federal gift tax is whether the interest-free use of money or the rent-free use of other property similarly escapes gift tax scrutiny. The two contexts are analogous. Just as the provision of services without compensation does not deplete the transferor's estate given the absence of a legal obligation to work, no legal obligation exists to make property productive of income. Accordingly, perhaps the gratuitous provision of the use of money or property on a temporal basis should be free of gift tax consequences.

Despite any parallels to the gratuitous provision of services, the argument for excluding the uncompensated use of money or property from the scope of the gift tax is more difficult to sustain statutorily. The gift tax applies to a transfer of property, and the right to use money or property for a term constitutes a recognized property interest under state law. The government advanced this argument in Revenue Ruling 73-61, 1973-1 C.B. 408, stating that "[t]he right to use property . . . is itself an interest in property." The ruling announced the government's position not to follow the district court decision in *Johnson v. United States*, 254 F. Supp. 73 (N.D. Tex. 1966), which held that the gift tax had no application to interest-free loans on grounds that these arrangements did not lead to estate depletion. The Tax Court, affirmed by the Seventh Circuit, advanced the *Johnson* approach by holding that the benefit of an interest-free loan of $18 million fell outside the scope of the gift tax. *See* Crown v. Commissioner, 67 T.C. 1060 (1977), *aff'd*, 585 F.2d 234 (7th Cir. 1978). The government nonetheless maintained its stance that the uncompensated transfer of the use of money or property was subject to the gift tax, and this persistence paid off when the issue reached the Supreme Court in *Dickman v. Commissioner*, 465 U.S. 330 (1984).

[1]   *Dickman v. Commissioner*

The *Dickman* case involved a husband and wife who lent over $1 million to their son and to a family-owned corporation. The loans were evidenced by promissory notes payable on demand and bearing no interest. The Supreme Court sustained the government's imposition of a gift tax, as reflected in the principal portions of the majority opinion excerpted below:

DICKMAN v. COMMISSIONER
United States Supreme Court
465 U.S. 330 (1984)

II

A

The statutory language of the federal gift tax provisions purports to reach any gratuitous transfer of any interest in property. Section 2501(a)(1) of the Code imposes a tax upon "the transfer of property by gift." Section 2511(a) highlights the broad sweep of the tax imposed by § 2501 providing in pertinent part:

"Subject to the limitations contained in this chapter, the tax imposed by section 2501 shall apply whether the transfer is in trust or otherwise, whether the gift is direct or indirect, and whether the property is real or personal, tangible or intangible. . . ."

The language of these statutes is clear and admits of but one reasonable interpretation: transfers of property by gift, by whatever means effected, are subject to the federal gift tax.

The Committee Reports accompanying the Revenue Act of 1932, ch. 209, 47 Stat. 169, which established the present scheme of federal gift taxation, make plain that Congress intended the gift tax statute to reach all gratuitous transfers of any valuable interest in property. Among other things, these Reports state:

"The terms 'property,' 'transfer,' 'gift,' and 'indirectly' are used in the broadest and most comprehensive sense; the term 'property' reaching every species of right or interest protected by law and having an exchangeable value.

"The words 'transfer . . . by gift' and 'whether . . . direct or indirect' are designed to cover and comprehend all transactions . . . whereby, and to the extent . . . that, property or a property right is donatively passed to or conferred upon another, regardless of the means or the device employed in its accomplishment." H.R. Rep. No. 708, 72d Cong., 1st Sess., 27-28 (1932); S. Rep. No. 665, 72d Cong., 1st Sess., 39 (1932).

The plain language of the statute reflects this legislative history; the gift tax was designed to encompass all transfers of property and property *rights* having significant value.[5]

On several prior occasions, this Court has acknowledged the expansive sweep of the gift tax provisions. In *Commissioner v. Wemyss*, 324 U.S. 303, 306, 65 S. Ct. 652, 654, 89 L. Ed. 958 (1945), the Court explained that

---

[5] [4] The comprehensive scope of the gift tax, reflected by its statutory language and legislative history, is analogous to that of § 61 of the Code, 26 U.S.C. § 61, which defines gross income as "all income from whatever source derived." Section 61 has long been interpreted to include all forms of income except those specifically excluded from its reach. See, *e.g., Commissioner v. Glenshaw Glass Co.*, 348 U.S. 426, 75 S. Ct. 473, 99 L. Ed. 483 (1955). Similarly, the gift tax applies to any "transfer of property by gift," Code § 2501(a)(1), "[s]ubject to the limitations contained in this chapter," Code § 2511(a). Accordingly, absent an express exclusion from its provisions, any transfer meeting the statutory requirements must be held subject to the gift tax.

"Congress intended to use the term 'gifts' in its broadest and most comprehensive sense . . . [in order] to hit all the protean arrangements which the wit of man can devise that are not business transactions within the meaning of ordinary speech."

The Court has also noted that the language of the gift tax statute "is broad enough to include property, however conceptual or contingent," *Smith v. Shaughnessy*, 318 U.S. 176, 180, 63 S. Ct. 545, 547, 87 L. Ed. 690 (1943), so as "to reach every kind and type of transfer by gift," *Robinette v. Helvering*, 318 U.S. 184, 187, 63 S. Ct. 540, 542, 87 L. Ed. 700 (1943). Thus, the decisions of this Court reinforce the view that the gift tax should be applied broadly to effectuate the clear intent of Congress.

B

In asserting that interest-free demand loans give rise to taxable gifts, the Commissioner does not seek to impose the gift tax upon the principal amount of the loan, but only upon the reasonable value of the use of the money lent. The taxable gift that assertedly results from an interest-free demand loan is the value of receiving and using the money without incurring a corresponding obligation to pay interest along with the loan's repayment.[6] Is such a gratuitous transfer of the right to use money a "transfer of property" within the intendment of § 2501(a)(1)?

We have little difficulty accepting the theory that the use of valuable property—in this case money—is a legally protectible property interest. Of the aggregate rights associated with any property interest, the right of use of property is perhaps of the highest order. One court put it succinctly:

> " 'Property' is more than just the physical thing—the land, the bricks, the mortar—it is also the sum of all the rights and powers incident to ownership of the physical thing. It is the tangible and the intangible. Property is composed of constituent elements and of these elements the right to *use* the physical thing to the exclusion of others is the most essential and beneficial. Without this right all other elements would be of little value. . . ." *Passailaigue v. United States*, 224 F.Supp. 682, 686 (MD Ga. 1963) (emphasis in original).

What was transferred here was the use of a substantial amount of cash for an indefinite period of time. An analogous interest in real property, the use under a tenancy at will, has long been recognized as a property right. * * * For example, a parent who grants to a child the rent-free, indefinite use of commercial property having a reasonable rental value of $8,000 a month has clearly transferred a valuable property right. The transfer of $100,000 in cash, interest-free and repayable on demand, is similarly a grant of the use of valuable property. Its uncertain tenure may reduce its value, but it does not undermine its status as property. In either instance, when the property owner transfers to another the right to use the object, an identifiable property interest has clearly changed hands.

The right to the use of $100,000 without charge is a valuable interest in the money lent, as

---

[6] [5] The Commissioner's tax treatment of interest-free demand loans may perhaps be best understood as a two-step approach to such transactions. Under this theory, such a loan has two basic economic components: an arm's-length loan from the lender to the borrower, on which the borrower pays the lender a fair rate of interest, followed by a gift from the lender to the borrower in the amount of that interest. See *Crown v. Commissioner*, 585 F.2d 234, 240 (CA7 1978).

much so as the rent-free use of property consisting of land and buildings. In either case, there is a measurable economic value associated with the use of the property transferred. The value of the use of money is found in what it can produce; the measure of that value is interest—"rent" for the use of the funds. We can assume that an interest-free loan for a fixed period, especially for a prolonged period, may have greater value than such a loan made payable on demand, but it would defy common human experience to say that an intrafamily loan payable on demand is not subject to accommodation; its value may be reduced by virtue of its demand status, but that value is surely not eliminated.

This Court has noted in another context that the making of an interest-free loan results in the transfer of a valuable economic right:

> "It is virtually self-evident that extending interest-free credit for a period of time is equivalent to giving a discount equal to the value of the use of the purchase price for that period of time." * * *.

Against this background, the gift tax statutes clearly encompass within their broad sweep the gratuitous transfer of the use of money. Just as a tenancy at will in real property is an estate or interest in land, so also is the right to use money a cognizable interest in personal property. The right to use money is plainly a valuable right, readily measurable by reference to current interest rates; the vast banking industry is positive evidence of this reality. Accordingly, we conclude that the interest-free loan of funds is a "transfer of property by gift" within the contemplation of the federal gift tax statutes.

C

Our holding that an interest-free demand loan results in a taxable gift of the use of the transferred funds is fully consistent with one of the major purposes of the federal gift tax statute: protection of the estate tax and the income tax. The legislative history of the gift tax provisions reflects that Congress enacted a tax on gifts to supplement existing estate and income tax laws. H.R. Rep. No. 708, at 28; S. Rep. No. 665, at 40; see also 65 Cong. Rec. 3119–3120, 8095–8096 (1924); Harriss, Legislative History of Federal Gift Taxation, 18 Taxes 531, 536 (1940). Failure to impose the gift tax on interest-free loans would seriously undermine this estate and income tax protection goal.

A substantial no-interest loan from parent to child creates significant tax benefits for the lender quite apart from the economic advantages to the borrower. This is especially so when an individual in a high income tax bracket transfers income-producing property to an individual in a lower income tax bracket, thereby reducing the taxable income of the high-bracket taxpayer at the expense, ultimately, of all other taxpayers and the Government. Subjecting interest-free loans to gift taxation minimizes the potential loss to the federal fisc generated by the use of such loans as an income tax avoidance mechanism for the transferor. Gift taxation of interest-free loans also effectuates Congress' desire to supplement the estate tax provisions. A gratuitous transfer of income-producing property may enable the transferor to avoid the future estate tax liability that would result if the earnings generated by the property—rent, interest, or dividends—became a part of the transferor's estate. Imposing the gift tax upon interest-free loans bolsters the estate tax by preventing the diminution of the transferor's estate in this fashion.

III

Petitioners contend that administrative and equitable considerations require a holding that no gift tax consequences result from the making of interest-free demand loans. In support of this position, petitioners advance several policy arguments; none withstands studied analysis.

A

Petitioners first advance an argument accepted by the Tax Court in *Crown v. Commissioner*:

> "[O]ur income tax system does not recognize unrealized earnings or accumulations of wealth and no taxpayer is under any obligation to continuously invest his money for a profit. The opportunity cost of either letting one's money remain idle or suffering a loss from an unwise investment is not taxable merely because a profit *could have been made* from a wise investment." 67 T.C. at 1063–1064.

Thus, petitioners argue, an interest-free loan should not be made subject to the gift tax simply because of the possibility that the money lent *might* have enhanced the transferor's taxable income or gross estate had the loan never been made.

This contention misses the mark. It is certainly true that no law requires an individual to invest his property in an income-producing fashion, just as no law demands that a transferor charge interest or rent for the use of money or other property. An individual may, without incurring the gift tax, squander money, conceal it under a mattress, or otherwise waste its use value by failing to invest it. Such acts of consumption have nothing to do with lending money at no interest. The gift tax is an excise tax on *transfers* of property; allowing dollars to lie idle involves no transfer. If the taxpayer chooses not to waste the use value of money, however, but instead transfers the use to someone else, a taxable event has occurred. That the transferor himself could have consumed or wasted the use value of the money without incurring the gift tax does not change this result. Contrary to petitioners' assertion, a holding in favor of the taxability of interest-free loans does not impose upon the transferor a duty profitably to invest; rather, it merely recognizes that certain tax consequences inevitably flow from a decision to make a "transfer of property by gift." 26 U.S.C. § 2501(a)(1).

B

Petitioners next attack the breadth of the Commissioner's view that interest-free demand loans give rise to taxable gifts. Carried to its logical extreme, petitioners argue, the Commissioner's rationale would elevate to the status of taxable gifts such commonplace transactions as a loan of the proverbial cup of sugar to a neighbor or a loan of lunch money to a colleague. Petitioners urge that such a result is an untenable intrusion by the Government into cherished zones of privacy, particularly where intrafamily transactions are involved.

Our laws require parents to provide their minor offspring with the necessities and conveniences of life; questions under the tax law often arise, however, when parents provide more than the necessities, and in quantities significant enough to attract the attention of the taxing authorities. Generally, the legal obligation of support terminates when the offspring reach majority. Nonetheless, it is not uncommon for parents to provide their adult children with such things as the use of cars or vacation cottages, simply on the basis of the family relationship. We assume that the focus of the Internal Revenue Service is not on such traditional familial matters. When the Government levies a gift tax on routine neighborly or familial gifts, there will be time enough to deal with such a case.

Moreover, the tax law provides liberally for gifts to both family members and others; within the limits of the prescribed statutory exemptions, even substantial gifts may be entirely tax free. First, under § 2503(e) of the Code, 26 U.S.C. § 2503(e) (1982 ed.), amounts paid on behalf of an individual for tuition at a qualified educational institution or for medical care are not considered "transfer[s] of property by gift" for purposes of the gift tax statutes. More significantly, § 2503(b) of the Code provides an annual exclusion from the computation of taxable gifts of $10,000 per year, per donee; this provision allows a taxpayer to give up to $10,000 annually to each of any number of persons, without incurring any gift tax liability. The "split gift" provision of Code § 2513(a), which effectively enables a husband and wife to give each object of their bounty $20,000 per year without liability for gift tax, further enhances the ability to transfer significant amounts of money and property free of gift tax consequences. Finally, should a taxpayer make gifts during one year that exceed the § 2503(b) annual gift tax exclusion, no gift tax liability will result until the unified credit of Code § 2505 has been exhausted. These generous exclusions, exceptions, and credits clearly absorb the sorts of *de minimis* gifts petitioners envision and render illusory the administrative problems that petitioners perceive in their "parade of horribles."

*   *   *

IV

As we have noted [in Section III.B.], Congress has provided generous exclusions and credits designed to reduce the gift tax liability of the great majority of taxpayers. Congress clearly has the power to provide a similar exclusion for the gifts that result from interest-free demand loans. Any change in the gift tax consequences of such loans, however, is a legislative responsibility, not a judicial one. Until such a change occurs, we are bound to effectuate Congress' intent to protect the estate and income tax systems with a broad and comprehensive tax upon all "transfer[s] of property by gift." Cf. *Diedrich v. Commissioner*, 457 U.S. 191, 199, 102 S. Ct. 2414, 2419, 72 L. Ed.2d 777 (1982).

We hold, therefore, that the interest-free demand loans shown by this record resulted in taxable gifts of the reasonable value of the use of the money lent. Accordingly, the judgment of the United States Court of Appeals for the Eleventh Circuit is * * * *Affirmed.*

Although the holding of *Dickman* is limited to the interest-free loan context, the reasoning of the decision reaches beyond the unrecompensed use of money. In stating that it had "little difficulty accepting the theory that the use of valuable property—in this case money—is a legally protectable property interest," the Court indicated that the gift tax potentially applies to the gratuitous provision of the use of *any* property. The majority specifically noted that parents may provide their adult children with use of vehicles or vacation homes, but ultimately dismissed any concerns about the gift tax reaching into such areas on the basis that (a) the government likely would not be interested in examining such transfers, and (b) that any such transfers likely would be shielded from gift tax scrutiny by the available annual gift tax exclusion under § 2503(b) or through the use of a portion of the individual's unified credit under § 2505.

Are these responses to what the majority tagged the "parade of horribles" satisfying? As reflected in his dissent, Justice Powell was not persuaded. He pointed out that the annual gift tax exclusion would not obviate the need to identify and value *de minimis* transfers of the use of property in situations where the donor already made substantial cash gifts to the donee. *Id.* at 351–52 (Powell, J., dissenting). Furthermore, use of the donor's unified credit against the gift tax is not painless. First, the donor would be required to file a gift tax return to disclose the transfer, the value of the gift, and the application of the unified credit to absorb the tax otherwise due. *See id.* at 352. This is no small administrative hurdle. Furthermore, as demonstrated in Chapter 1, any lifetime use of the credit reduces the amount of property that can be transferred at death free of the estate tax. *See id.* Hence, the consequences of the gift tax applying to the uncompensated use of property cannot be readily dismissed. On the other hand, administrative difficulties in applying the gift tax in this context are relevant in interpreting the statute, if at all, only to the extent the statutory directive is ambiguous. If the statutory language is clear (as the majority believed), then any resulting administrative concerns are matters to be raised with Congress.

If the use of a vacation home by an adult child can trigger gift tax consequences, then should the provision of food and shelter to a minor child be subject to the same treatment? After all, an uncompensated transfer of property or the use of property takes place in each setting. The idea of subjecting the expenditures of child rearing to the gift tax would strike most as noxious, and the basis for this intuition lies in the legal duty of support that a parent owes a child. Although no explicit authority exists in this area, expenditures in the nature of support of a minor child or other dependent are not regarded as gratuitous. This approach is consistent with the holding of Revenue Ruling 68-379, 1968-2 C.B. 414, which analyzed a transfer from a husband to his wife that served to discharge the husband's support obligations. The ruling held that the value of the wife's support rights constituted consideration for the transfer under § 2512(b), so that the transfer resulted in a taxable gift only to the extent the value of the property transferred exceeded the value of the support rights surrendered.

[2] Statutory Responses to *Dickman*

[a] Section 7872

Congress responded to the holding of the *Dickman* case by enacting § 7872 to address the range of tax consequences stemming from loans that do not call for the payment of interest at market rates (below-market loans). *See* Deficit Reduction Act of 1984, Pub. L. No. 98-369, § 172(a). Among other arrangements, § 7872 applies to "gift loans," defined as a below-market loan where the forgoing of interest is in the nature of a gift. IRC § 7872(f)(3). Gift loans are divided into two categories: (1) demand loans that, as the name suggests, are payable at the demand of the lender, and (2) terms loans, which refers to any loan other than a demand loan. IRC § 7872(f)(5), (6). A demand loan is below market if the interest payable on the loan is less than the federal short-term rate under § 1274(d) for the period in which the interest is being determined. IRC § 7872(e)(1)(A), (f)(2)(B). A term loan, on the other hand, is below market if the amount loaned exceeds the present value of all payments due under the loan—computed using a discount factor equal to the applicable federal rate (compounded semiannually) for the term of the loan in effect on the day the loan was made. IRC § 7872(e)(1)(B), (f)(2)(A).

From an estate-planning perspective, demand gift loans are preferable to gift loans that have a stated term. If the loan is payable upon the demand of the lender, the difference between the amount of interest paid under the loan and the interest that should have been charged (computed at the short-term federal rate) in a given year is treated as having been transferred from the lender to the borrower on the last day of the calendar year. IRC § 7872(a). As the benefit of the below-market loan is calculated and treated as transferred on an annual basis, the annual gift tax exclusion under § 2503(b) is available to shield all or a portion of this transfer from gift tax consequences. However, the gift that occurs through lending money at below-market rates for a defined term is treated as occurring at the outset of the loan. In this context, the borrower is treated as receiving an upfront payment equal to the difference between the amount loaned and the present value of all payments to be made over the term of the loan. IRC § 7872(b)(1), (d)(2). Hence, only one year's annual exclusion will be available to shield the deemed transfer from gift tax consequences. The comparative treatment of demand gift loans versus term gift loans is illustrated through the examples below.

Example 1: *Parent* lends *Child* $250,000 on an interest-free basis. *Child* executes a promissory note in favor of *Parent*, and the note provides that *Parent* may demand full payment of the outstanding loan balance at any time. The loan remains outstanding for 3 years. Assume that the federal short-term rate for each year at issue is 4 percent.[7]

Because the loan is payable on demand, each year *Parent* is treated as transferring the difference between (a) interest computed on the loan balance at 4 percent compounded semiannually ($10,100), and (b) the interest that *Child* paid on the loan (zero). This produces an annual gift of $10,100, which can be fully excluded under § 2503(b) assuming no other gifts in excess of the remaining annual exclusion amount from *Parent* to *Child* during the calendar year.

Example 2: Assume the same loan between *Parent* and *Child*, except the loan cannot be called upon the demand of *Parent*. Rather, *Child* is obligated to pay the $250,000 principal three years from the date the loan was made.

Assuming a short-term federal rate of four percent compounded semi-annually, the present value of the balloon-payment three years out is $221,993. Thus, when the loan is issued, *Parent* is treated as making a present gift to *Child* of $28,007. A significant portion of this gift is excluded under § 2503(b), but the annual exclusion is not sufficient to shield the entire transfer from gift taxation.

Section 7872 provides a *de minimis* exception for gift loans. The statutory regime does not apply when the aggregate amount of all loans—whether below market or not—between individuals does not exceed $10,000. IRC § 7872(c)(2)(A). However, this exception is not to the extent the proceeds of the loan are used to purchase stocks, bonds, rental property, or other income-producing assets. IRC § 7872(c)(2)(B); Prop. Treas. Reg. § 1.7872-8(b)(4) (treating stock as income-producing property, regardless of dividend stream). Furthermore, the exception is available only for loans between natural persons. Loans between individuals and trusts do not qualify for the exception because the trust—as opposed to the trust beneficiary—is regarded as the relevant party. Prop. Treas. Reg. § 1.7872-8(a)(2)(i). On the other hand, a loan between an individual and a custodian of a UGMA account for the benefit

---

[7] Under Prop. Treas. Reg. § 1.7872-13(a), the appropriate federal short-term rate to be used on a demand loan that remains outstanding for the full calendar year is the blended short-term rate, which is the average of the short-term rate outstanding on January 1 and the rate outstanding on July 1.

of minor is treated as occurring between the individual and the minor, rendering the *de minimis* available in this context. *Id.*

Pursuant to § 7872(f)(7), a husband and wife are treated as one person. Thus, not only are loans between husband and wife disregarded for purposes of § 7872, but a husband and wife cannot attempt to maximize the § 7872(c)(2) exception by each making loans of $10,000 to a child or other beneficiary. Any such arrangement would be treated as a single loan of $20,000, rendering the entire loan (as opposed to just the $10,000 excess) subject to the § 7872 regime.

[b] Section 2503(g)

Section 2503(g), enacted 4 years after the Supreme Court's decision in *Dickman*,[8] clarifies that a loan of a "qualified work of art" to a § 501(c)(3) organization will not be treated as a transfer for gift tax purposes so long as the use of the artwork is related to the purpose or function of the entity's tax exemption. IRC § 2503(g)(1). For this purpose, a qualified work of art is defined broadly as any archeological, historic, or other "creative tangible personal property." IRC § 2503(g)(2). While the enactment of the § 2503(g) exclusion can be interpreted as confirming the potential reach of the gift tax to the gratuitous provision of the use of property (consistent with the reasoning in *Dickman*), the gift tax exclusion also can be explained as part of the overall statutory scheme to ignore such transactions altogether for transfer tax purposes. *See* IRC § 2503(g)(1) (providing that the loan of artwork is not treated as a transfer for *all* transfer tax purposes, and further directing that the value of the artwork shall be determined as if the loan had not been made). Thus, if the existence of the loan of artwork will not diminish the value of the property included in the owner's gross estate, there is no need to protect the estate tax base by subjecting the loan to gift tax.[9]

[C] Transfer Requirement

To this point, the discussion has focused on whether the object of a particular gratuitous transfer constitutes a sufficiently cognizable property interest to implicate the federal gift tax. In addition to necessitating the conveyance of a property interest, § 2501(a) requires a transfer of that property interest during the donor's lifetime. Although the existence of a transfer will be clear in the vast majority of cases, the government has advanced an expansive interpretation of the concept in its continued struggle to subject deferred compensation benefits to federal transfer taxation. The Tax Court decision in *DiMarco v. Commissioner*, 87 T.C. 653 (1986), provides the leading examination of the lifetime transfer predicate to the gift tax.

The decedent in *Estate of DiMarco* was employed at IBM from 1950 until his death in 1979. The decedent was survived by a spouse, whom he married in 1953. As an employee of IBM, the decedent automatically was subject to a survivor's income benefit plan that had been established by IBM prior to his joining the company. Under this plan, IBM would pay three times the employee's annual compensation to the employee's surviving spouse, minor or dependent children, or dependent parents. Payments were to be made out of IBM's general assets on a periodic basis until the benefit was exhausted or no eligible survivors remained. If

---

[8] Section 2503(g) was added by the Technical and Miscellaneous Revenue Act of 1988, Pub. L. No. 100-647, § 1018(s)(2)(B).

[9] *See* Joseph M. Dodge, *Are Gift Demand Loans of Tangible Property Subject to the Gift Tax?*, 30 Va. Tax Rev. 181, 227–30 (2010) (making this point).

the employee was not survived by a spouse or dependent covered by the plan, then no benefit would be paid. The decedent retained no powers over the plan—that is, he could not select beneficiaries of the income benefit, he could not modify the terms of the benefit plan, and he could not terminate his participation in the plan apart from terminating his employment.

In examining the decedent's estate tax return, the Service determined that the decedent made a completed gift when he commenced employment with IBM. However, the Service argued that the gift should be held in abeyance under an open-transaction theory until it was capable of valuation (which did not occur until the time of his death). As the Tax Court explained, at times the government appeared to advance a related theory for the same result. Instead of making a completed gift that would be valued at a later point, the decedent made an incomplete gift of the death benefit upon commencing employment that the decedent later completed upon his death. As reflected in the excerpt below, the Tax Court rejected both theories.

ESTATE OF DIMARCO v. COMMISSIONER
United States Tax Court
87 T.C. 653 (1986)

Respondent argues that decedent transferred a property interest in the survivors income benefit for gift tax purposes on January 9, 1950. This transfer was either complete or incomplete for gift tax purposes. If the transfer was complete, we have little difficulty in disposing of this case because a completed transfer would have been a taxable gift that was made by decedent before December 31, 1976, and section 2001 expressly defines an adjusted taxable gift as a taxable gift that was made after December 31, 1976. On the other hand, if the transfer was incomplete for gift tax purposes, we do not believe that it became complete or that we can deem that it became complete at the time of decedent's death. Section 25.2511-2(f), Gift Tax Regs., provides that—

> [t]he relinquishment or termination of a power to change the beneficiaries of transferred property, *occurring otherwise than by the death of the donor (the statute being confined to transfers by living donors)*, is regarded as the event that completes the gift and causes the tax to apply. * * * [Emphasis added.]

We believe that this regulation precludes our finding in this case that the alleged transfer of property by decedent on January 9, 1950, became complete for gift tax purposes by reason of decedent's death.

We recognize, of course, that respondent does not assert in this case that the alleged transfer on January 9, 1950, became complete and subject to the gift tax because decedent's death terminated a power to change the beneficiaries of the transferred property. Even so, in view of the fact that a transfer of property that becomes complete because the donor's death terminates a power to change the beneficiaries of the transferred property is not subject to the gift tax, we decline to hold that a transfer of property that becomes complete because the donor's death makes it possible for the first time to value the transferred property is subject to the gift tax. We perceive nothing in the gift tax statute or the regulations that would justify such a result.

In addition, we believe that respondent has confused the issues of completion and valuation in this case. Respondent appears to argue that, because the value of the survivors income benefit could not be determined on January 9, 1950, when the alleged transfer occurred, the transfer should be treated as incomplete for gift tax purposes until the survivors income benefit became susceptible of valuation, when decedent died, at which time the transfer became complete and subject to the gift tax. For the reasons stated above, we have already held that transfers of property do not become complete for gift tax purposes by reason of the death of the donor. We also question, however, whether the fact that the value of transferred property cannot be readily determined at the time of transfer is relevant in determining whether the transfer is complete for gift tax purposes. We have noted above that transfers of property are complete and subject to the gift tax at the time the donor relinquishes dominion and control over the transferred property. Nothing in the statute or the regulations suggests that, even if a donor relinquishes dominion and control over transferred property, the transfer is or can be considered to be incomplete for gift tax purposes if the value of the property is uncertain. To the contrary, in *Smith v. Shaughnessy*, 318 U.S. 176, 180 (1943), the Supreme Court appears to have considered and expressly rejected this argument in the following language:

> The government argues that for gift tax purposes the taxpayer has abandoned control of the remainder and that it is therefore taxable, while the taxpayer contends that no realistic value can be placed on the contingent remainder and that it therefore should not be classed as a gift.

> We cannot accept any suggestion that the complexity of a property interest * * * can serve to defeat a tax. * * * Even though these concepts of property and value may be slippery and elusive they can not escape taxation so long as they are used in the world of business. The language of the gift tax statute, 'property * * * real or personal, tangible or intangible,' is broad enough to include property, however conceptual or contingent.* * *

Accordingly, we reject any suggestion by respondent either that transfers of property are incomplete for gift tax purposes simply because 'no realistic value can be placed' on the property at the time the transfer occurs, or that transfers of property become complete for gift tax purposes only when the value of the transferred property can be easily ascertained.

Respondent also argues that completed transfers of property for gift tax purposes can and should be treated as open transactions in those cases where the transferred property is difficult to value, and that valuation of the transferred property and the imposition of the gift tax should be postponed until the value of the property can be readily determined. We reject this contention. The clear language of the statute and the regulations requires that transferred property be valued for gift tax purposes at the time the transfer becomes complete. Section 2512(a) provides that, in the case of a gift, "the value thereof at the *date of the gift* shall be considered the amount of the gift." (Emphasis added.) In addition, section 25.2511-2(a), Gift Tax Regs., states as follows:

> The gift tax is not imposed upon the receipt of the property by the donee, nor is it necessarily determined by the measure of enrichment resulting to the donee from the transfer * * *. On the contrary, the tax is a primary and personal liability of the donor, is an excise upon his *act of making the transfer*, [and] *is measured by the value of the property passing from the donor* * * *. [Emphasis added.]

As a result, property must be valued and the gift tax imposed at the time a completed transfer of the property occurs.

We also agree with petitioner that decedent never made a taxable gift of any property interest in the survivors income benefit because we find no act by decedent that qualifies as an act of 'transfer' of an interest in property. His participation in the plan was involuntary, he had no power to select or change the beneficiaries of the survivors income benefit, no power to alter the amount or timing of the payment of the benefit, and no power to substitute other benefits for those prescribed by the plan.

* * *

Respondent argues, however, that decedent's simple act of going to work for IBM on January 9, 1950, constituted an act of transfer by decedent for gift tax purposes. We disagree. None of the cases cited by respondent hold that, without more, the simple act of going to work for an employer that has an automatic, non-elective, company-wide survivors income benefit plan similar to the one at issue in this case constitutes a 'transfer' of an interest in the benefit for either estate or gift tax purposes. Moreover, we doubt that it can be maintained seriously that decedent began his employment with IBM on January 9, 1950 (when he was 24, unmarried, and without dependents), for the purpose or with any intention of transferring property rights in the survivors income benefit. While we agree with respondent that a taxable event may occur without a volitional act by the donor, as in a case where an incomplete transfer of property becomes complete because of the occurrence of an event outside the donor's control, we do not believe that a taxable event can occur for gift tax purposes unless there is first and in fact an act of transfer by the donor; and there can be no act of transfer unless the act is voluntary and the transferor has some awareness that he is in fact making a transfer of property, that is, he must intend to do so. * * * It is apparent to us that decedent never intended and never voluntarily acted to transfer any interest that he may have owned in the survivors income benefit. There being no act of transfer by decedent, there can be no transfer of property by gift.

Following the Tax Court's decision in *Estate of DiMarco*, the Service acquiesced in the result. *See* 1990-2 C.B. 1 n.3. In the process, the Service abandoned its attempt to subject unfunded employee death benefits of this sort to transfer taxation under an open-transaction gift theory. *See* Rev. Rul. 92-68, 1992-2 C.B. 257, *revoking* Rev. Rul. 81-31, 1981-1 C.B. 475.

§ 3.03 TREATMENT OF BINDING AGREEMENTS TO MAKE FUTURE TRANSFERS

Suppose that *Mother*, seeking to provide *Son* with an incentive to finish his education, promises to pay *Son* $100,000 upon his graduation from college. The promise is made in Year 1 and *Son* graduates from college in Year 4. Upon *Son's* performance, *Mother's* promise becomes enforceable under state law. Yet due to financial constraints, *Mother* pays *Son* only $40,000 at the graduation ceremony in Year 4. She pays the remaining $60,000 in equal installments in Years 5 and 6, respectively.

Clearly *Mother* has made a gift to *Son* at some point; the question is when the gift takes place. Resolution of this issue has significant practical consequences. The gift tax is assessed annually on all taxable gifts made in a given calendar year. Furthermore, the gift tax exclusion under § 2503(b) (discussed in detail in Chapter 5) is renewed on an annual basis. Hence, the determination of when the gift takes place drives not only the proper reporting of the transaction, but also the determination of how much of the transfer is subject to tax.

Given that § 2501(a) imposes the tax on the "transfer of property by gift during such calendar year" while Reg. § 25.2511-2(a) explains that the gift tax is "an excise upon [the taxpayer's] act of making the transfer," a textual interpretation suggests that the gift tax should be assessed on a cash-method basis. That is, the gift would not occur until a literal transfer of property pursuant to the binding commitment takes place. At one point, the Service adopted this approach in determining when a taxable transfer occurred. Yet as reflected in the landmark case of *Commissioner v. Estate of Copley*, 194 F.2d 364 (7th Cir. 1952), discussed below, the cash-method approach has not prevailed.

Like many prominent cases in the gift tax arena, *Estate of Copley* involved a transfer of property in contemplation of marriage. In 1931, the taxpayer entered into an prenuptial agreement with his future wife under which he agreed to pay her $1 million. Under the agreement, which was to become effective upon marriage, the $1 million amount was "to become and to be her sole and separate property." *Id.* at 364. While the couple was married roughly a week after executing the agreement, the required transfers from the husband were anything but timely. The husband first transferred property worth $500,000 to his wife in 1936, and the second $500,000 transfer of property did not occur until 1944. Given that the federal gift tax was not enacted until 1932, the Service determined that no taxable gift occurred until the literal transfer of property pursuant to the agreement. The Seventh Circuit disagreed:

> Under the law of Copley's residence and domicile (Illinois), there is no question but that the agreement of the parties, upon their marriage, became a binding and legally enforceable obligation. . . . . Copley's obligation to pay his wife one million dollars the next day after their marriage was a debt and possessed all the indicia of a promissory note payable on demand. She could have assigned and conveyed good title to the instrument which evidenced his obligation to pay, and either Mrs. Copley or her assignee could have maintained an action against Copley and recovered a judgment. And it can hardly be questioned but that Copley by the obligation thus assumed depleted the net worth of his estate and that the net worth of his wife's estate was augmented, each to the extent of one million dollars.

> Thus, the rights and obligations of Copley and his wife had become definitely fixed more than one year prior to the enactment of the gift tax act of 1932. True, at that time Copley had not discharged the contractual debt or obligation which he owed to his wife and, so far as the record discloses, she had made no effort to enforce payment. And any reason why discharge of the obligation was delayed we think immaterial. The point is that his wife in 1936 and 1944 agreed to and did accept on each occasion $500,000 in securities in discharge of Copley's obligation and in lieu of the money which he was obligated to pay her. It is contrary to reason and common sense to say that the delivery of such property by Copley in 1936 and 1944, and its acceptance by his wife, was other than a discharge of the 1931 obligation.

Id. at 365–66. Not long after the *Estate of Copley* decision was issued, the Second Circuit followed its holding in stating that "a binding promise to make a gift becomes subject to the gift taxation in the year the obligation is undertaken and not when the discharging payments are made." *Rosenthal v. Commissioner*, 205 F.2d 505, 509 (2d Cir. 1953).[10]

---

[10] *But see* Bradford v. Commissioner, 34 T.C. 1059 (1960) (holding the taxpayer's assumption of her husband's payment obligations did not constitute a gift to the husband and distinguishing the decisions in *Estate of Copley* and *Rosenthal* based on the practical improbability of the taxpayer actually making the assumed payments).

Some time after the *Estate of Copley* and *Rosenthal* decisions, the Service finally accepted the view that a taxable gift tax takes place when the uncompensated commitment to make future transfers becomes legally binding. Thirteen years after the *Estate of Copley* decision, the Service signaled its acquiescence. *See* 1965-2 C.B. 4 (reversing prior non-acquiescence). Through Revenue Ruling 79-384, 1979-2 C.B. 344, the Service interpreted the hypothetical at the outset of this discussion as yielding a taxable gift when *Mother's* promise to pay became enforceable upon *Son's* graduation. Furthermore, in Revenue Ruling 84-25, 1984-1 C.B. 191, the Service clarified that an individual's transfer of a legally enforceable promissory note for less than an adequate and full consideration in money or money's worth gives rise to a taxable gift under § 2511 in the year in which the note becomes "binding and determinable in value rather than when the promised payment is actually made."

The rule that a gift occurs upon the creation of a binding commitment to make future payments is subject to one qualifier: the commitment must be unconditional. In *City Bank Farmers Trust Co. v. Hoey*, 101 F.2d 9 (2d Cir. 1939), for instance, the Second Circuit determined that a court-imposed obligation to make future payments did not give rise to a taxable gift on the theory that the court order was subject to modification at any time. Similarly, a condition on a payment obligation proved determinative in Revenue Ruling 75-71, 1975-1 C.B. 309. The ruling concerned three sisters, each named as beneficiaries under another living sister's will, who mutually agreed to transfer a portion of their future devise to the children of any sister who did not survive the testator. Because the uncertainty over whether the sisters would receive any devise (even if they survived the testator) was not eliminated until the testator's death, the ruling held that the contractual obligation of the surviving sister to make payments under the agreement did not become definite and enforceable until such time.[11]

§ 3.04 STUDY PROBLEMS

1. Franklin sends his son Charles to the finest private school in town. Tuition costs $20,000 per year. When Charles turned 16, Franklin purchased a new car for him (titled in Charles' name) costing $30,000. During the summer, Franklin allows Charles to stay at his summer cottage on the Maine coast with Charles' older sister, Ann, who is 25. What are the gift tax consequences, if any, of these events?

2. Mother is a molecular biologist who has developed a compound that she believes will be useful in combating cancer cells. At an early stage of development, she transfers title to the technology to Daughter. While the value of the compound at this stage is difficult to determine, assume that the unproven technology would trade hands between a willing buyer and willing seller for $1 million. Mother continues to work on the compound in her lab periodically for three years. While she is doing so, Father provides the necessary legal work in connection with obtaining FDA approval for the treatment. After the treatment receives FDA approval, a multinational pharmaceutical company purchases the rights to the technology for $200 million. What are the gift tax consequences, if any, of these events?

---

[11] Revenue Ruling 75-71 should be compared with Revenue Ruling 79-238, 1979-2 C.B. 339, which involved a similar agreement among beneficiaries of an irrevocable trust. In Revenue Ruling 79-238, the Service held that each beneficiary made a gift to his or her children upon entering into the compact, reasoning that the agreement operated as a present transfer of one-half of each sibling's contingent remainder interest in the trust.

3. Ellis is an executive with a software corporation who received restricted stock from her employer in Year 1. Ellis must surrender the stock to the employer if she terminates her employment for any reason prior to Year 7, at which point the restriction lapses. In Year 2, Ellis promises to convey the stock to her daughter Diane if Diane is accepted to medical school. In Year 4, Diane receives her acceptance letter. A couple weeks later but now in Year 5, Ellis formally assigns the stock certificates. Ellis continues to work for the company through Year 7, when the restrictions on the stock lapse.

   In what year did Ellis make a gift to Diane? Base your answer on the principles discussed in the chapter, and then compare your answer to the holding of Rev. Rul. 98-21, 1998-1 C.B. 975.

4. Darla and her husband recently divorced. As part of the property settlement, Darla received fee title to the couple's former residence. Darla cannot step foot in the house, however, because memories of her former husband that she associates with the house make her nauseated. She therefore sells the house to her son for $300,000, even though comparable houses in the neighborhood have recently sold for around $400,000. Darla is happy to sell the house for $300,000 though; in fact, she would be willing to sell the house to a stranger for $250,000 just to get rid of it.

   Has Darla made a gift to her son?

5. Anthony's grandmother wants to help him with the rising cost of law school, but she does not want to pay for it outright. So she agrees to lend him $20,000 each year interest free. No promissory note is executed. Rather, Anthony promises to pay his grandmother $1,000 per month when he starts his job following graduation until the loan is repaid. Three years after Anthony graduated from law school, his grandmother told him that she was forgiving payment of the remaining balance. In general terms, discuss the gift tax consequences, if any, of these transactions.

Chapter 4

SELECTED GIFT TAX PLANNING TECHNIQUES AND GOVERNMENT CHALLENGES

Internal Revenue Code: § 2035(b)

§ 4.01 IDENTIFYING THE RELEVANT PROPERTY INTEREST BEING TRANSFERRED

Family-owned business entities such as partnerships and limited liability companies have become prominent estate-planning vehicles, largely because of the promise of valuation discounts available in this setting. By first transferring property to the entity and then assigning a beneficial interest in the entity to the donee, the donor is able to value the transferred property interest (that is, the beneficial interest in the entity) by applying discounts for lack of marketability and lack of control that are traditionally associated with non-controlling interests in closely held entities.[1] In order to obtain this valuation benefit, however, the subject of the gratuitous transfer must constitute the equity interest in the entity as opposed to the property that is transferred to the business entity by the donor. While this principle may seem simple enough, the notion of indirect gifts of property and the possible application of the step-transaction doctrine muddy the waters.

[A] Indirect Gifts Through Business Entities

As a general rule, a business entity does not constitute a potential donee for transfer tax purposes; rather, an uncompensated transfer to a business entity constitutes an indirect gift to the equity owners. The regulations provide specific guidance on this point in the context of a transfer to a corporation for less than an adequate and full consideration in money or money's worth: "A transfer of property by B to a corporation generally represents gifts by B to the other individual shareholders of the corporation to the extent of their proportionate interests in the corporation." Section 25.2511-1(h)(1). This principle was applied by the Fifth Circuit in *Kincaid v. United States*, 682 F.2d 1220 (5th Cir. 1982). The taxpayer in *Kincaid* contributed ranch property to a corporation of which the taxpayer and her two sons owned the voting stock. In exchange for the transfer of the property, the taxpayer received additional shares of stock; however, the value of the additional shares did not rise to the level of adequate and full consideration. Accordingly, the court determined that the $463,000 difference between the value of the ranch and the value of the stock she received in the entity constituted a gift to the shareholders. Because the taxpayer as a 34 percent shareholder could not make a gift to

---

[1] Principles of valuation in general, and the valuation benefits of closely held entities in particular, are addressed in Chapter 7.

herself, the court held that 33 percent of the difference (approximately $150,000) constituted an indirect gift to each of her two sons.

[1] *Shepherd v. Commissioner*

The Tax Court had reason to consider Reg. § 25.2511-1(h)(1) and the *Kincaid* decision in the partnership context through the court-reviewed decision in *Shepherd v. Commissioner*, 115 T.C. 376 (2000), *aff'd*, 283 F.3d 1258 (11th Cir. 2002). The taxpayer in *Shepherd* transferred title to timberland along with minority stock ownership of several banks to a partnership in which he owned a 50 percent beneficial interest. The taxpayer's sons owned the remaining beneficial interests equally, 25 percent each. The partnership agreement provided that any capital contribution would be allocated pro-rata among the existing partners' capital accounts. Accordingly, the property contributions enhanced each son's partnership capital accounts by 25 percent of the value of the contributed properties.

In valuing the gratuitous transfers to his sons, the taxpayer applied entity-related valuation discounts associated with the transfer of family-owned partnership interests. The taxpayer argued that, in substance, the enhancement of the sons' capital account balances amounted to an assignment of partnership interests. The problem for the taxpayer, however, was that the chosen form of the transaction did not match the claimed substance. The father did not make assignments of partnership interests; rather, he transferred ownership of the real estate and the bank stock to the partnership. As indicated in the regulations, the gift tax focuses on the transfer that emanates from the donor:

> The gift tax is not imposed upon the receipt of the property by the donee, nor is it necessarily determined by the measure of enrichment resulting to the donee from the transfer, nor is it conditioned upon ability to identify the donee at the time of the transfer. On the contrary, the tax is a primary and personal liability of the donor, is an excise upon his act of making the transfer, *is measured by the value of the property passing from the donor*, and attaches regardless of the fact that the identity of the donee may not then be known or ascertainable.

Treas. Reg. § 25.2511-2(a) (emphasis added).

Citing this regulation, the Tax Court dismissed the taxpayer's argument that the transaction should be characterized as a transfer of partnership interests from the taxpayer to his sons. Instead, the Tax Court cited Reg. § 25.2511-1(h)(1) and the *Kincaid* decision to hold that the transfer constituted an indirect gift of the timberland and bank stock from the taxpayer to his two sons to the extent of the sons' beneficial interests in the partnership. 115 T.C. at 388–89. The source of disagreement in the court-reviewed opinion stemmed from how these indirect transfers were further characterized and valued. Instead of valuing the gifts by starting with the value of the property that the taxpayer transferred to the partnership, subtracting the value of the enhanced partnership interest received by the transferor as consideration, and then equally dividing the difference on account of the sons' 25 percent partnership interests (which would have matched the process followed by the Fifth Circuit in *Kincaid*), the majority characterized the transactions as an indirect transfer of a 25 percent undivided interest in the timberland and the bank stock to each son. *Id.* at 389–90. In effect, the majority of the Tax Court gave the taxpayer the benefit of a transfer that did not occur—the taxpayer's direct transfer of an undivided fractional interest in the timberland and stock to the sons followed by the son's contribution of this property to the partnership. As a result, the taxpayer was able to apply a fractional-interest discount in valuing the real property that he indirectly transferred to the sons.[2]

This characterization of the transaction charitably afforded by the majority in *Shepherd* is suspect. As noted by Judge Ruwe and Judge Beghe in separate dissents, the subject of the property transferred by the taxpayer was his undivided ownership of the real property and the bank stock. Under Reg. § 25.2511-2(a), the gift tax is levied on the value of the property transferred by the donor, not on the value of the property received by the donee. In the view of the dissents, the value of the gift would be measured by the value of the property actually transferred by the taxpayer (undivided ownership of the land and stock), reduced by the value of the consideration received, pursuant to § 2512(b). *See id.* at 413 (Ruwe, J., dissenting) & 415–16 (Beghe, J., dissenting).[3] Despite these credible objections, the Eleventh Circuit affirmed the decision of the Tax Court majority. *See* 283 F.3d 1258 (11th Cir. 2002).

[2] *Pierre v. Commissioner*

The Tax Court in *Pierre v. Commissioner*, 133 T.C. 24 (2009), again wrestled with the issue of what property interest served as the subject of the transfer for gift tax purposes. The donor in *Pierre* originally capitalized a single-member LLC with cash and publicly traded securities. In forming the LLC, the donor did not elect for the entity to be classified as an association that would be taxed as a corporation. Instead, she relied on the default classification of such entity to be "disregarded as an entity separate from its owner." Treas. Reg. § 301.7701-3(b)(1)(ii). The classification as a disregarded entity applies "for federal tax purposes . . . and does not depend on whether the organization is recognized as an entity under local law." Treas. Reg. § 301.7701-1(a)(1). Twelve days after capitalizing the LLC, the donor transferred a 50 percent LLC interest to each of two trusts established for the benefit of her son and granddaughter, respectively. The taxpayer treated the transfer of a 9.5 percent LLC interest to each trust as a gift to utilize her available unified credit and GST exemption. The transfer of the remaining 40.5 percent LLC interest to each trust was structured as a sale for which the taxpayer received promissory notes secured by the transferred interests.[4]

The Tax Court in *Pierre* first was tasked with determining whether the relevant property interest to be analyzed from a federal gift tax perspective constituted the actual state-law LLC interests that the donor transferred (as contended by the donor) or a pro-rata portion of the disregarded entity's assets (as contended by the Service).[5] Resolution of this issue would determine whether valuation discounts traditionally associated with the transfer of a minority

---

[2] Apart from the minority-interest discount associated with the combined blocks of stock transferred by the taxpayer in the partnerships, no further discount was triggered by the deemed transfer of a 25 percent undivided interest in these stock holdings to the sons. Thus, while the taxpayer in *Shepherd* missed out on the entity-related valuation discounts, the fractional-interest discount allowed on the real estate mitigated much of the damage.

[3] While Judge Ruwe and Judge Beghe shared the same approach of starting with the value of the real estate and bank stock transferred by the taxpayer, Judge Ruwe advocated subtracting 50 percent of such value in measuring the taxable gift. However, Judge Beghe was not as forgiving. He would have subtracted only the discounted value of the taxpayer's enhanced partnership interest. *See Shepherd*, 115 T.C. at 416 (Beghe, J., dissenting).

[4] The face amount of the promissory note was equal to the value of the transferred LLC interests as determined under an appraisal obtained by the taxpayer. The LLC made distributions to the trusts to enable the trusts to make the required interest payments; no payments of principal had been made on the notes at the time the gift tax case was litigated.

[5] The Tax Court addressed the Service's invocation of the step transaction doctrine in a subsequent opinion. This aspect of the *Pierre* case is discussed in § 4.01[B] below.

interests in a closely held entity would be available in valuing the gifts. The entity classification regulations promulgated under § 301.7701 appeared to favor the government's position. As a default matter, the entity-classification regulations in effect at the time provided that a single-member LLC was disregarded as an entity separate from its owner "for federal tax purposes."[6] Treas. Reg. § 301.7701-3(a). The creation of a multiple-member LLC resulting from the taxpayer's transfer of LLC interests to the two trusts caused the LLC to be classified as a partnership for federal tax purposes only from that point forward. *See* Treas. Reg. § 301.7701-3(f)(2).

In a divided court-reviewed decision, the Tax Court majority concluded that the entity-classification regulations simply did not speak to the issue of the property interest being transferred. 133 T.C. at 32. ("The question before us . . . is not the question addressed by the check-the-box regulations.") Even though those regulations by their terms treat a single-member LLC as a disregarded entity "for federal tax purposes," the majority interpreted the regulations as being limited to determining how *the entity itself* would be taxed. *See id.* at 35. The concurrence made this point more explicit, claiming that the entity classification regulations apply "for federal tax purposes," not "for *all* federal tax purposes." *Id.* at 38 (Cohen, J., concurring) (emphasis in original). In this manner, the Tax Court determined that the property interest to be analyzed from a gift tax perspective consisted of state-law LLC interests, thereby presumably providing the donor with the benefit of valuation discounts. The holding of the Tax Court majority in *Pierre* rests on dubious ground, however, as it depends on rejecting the interpretation of the regulations advanced and previously employed by the issuing agency. *See* Rev. Rul. 99-5, 1999-1 C.B. 434 (holding that a second member's purchase of a 50 percent interest in an LLC from the previous single member constituted a purchase of a 50 percent interest in each of the LLC's underlying assets, followed by a contribution of those assets to the entity).

[B] The Step Transaction Doctrine

Taxpayers who introduce a partnership or LLC layer into their gratuitous transfers must be mindful of the potential application of the step transaction doctrine. For example, an individual may transfer marketable securities to a partnership (with the value of such securities being credited to his capital account balance) and, subsequent to the contribution, make formal assignments of partnership interests in hopes of claiming entity-related discounts in valuing the gifts. If the steps are viewed as a single, integrated transaction, however, the government could invoke the step transaction doctrine to characterize the transaction as an indirect gift of the property contributed to the partnership. If successful in changing the subject of the gratuitous transfer in this manner, valuation discounts traditionally associated with the transfer of minority interests in closely held entities would fall by the wayside. The Tax Court in *Senda v. Commissioner*, T.C. Memo. 2004-160, 88 T.C.M. (CCH) 8, upheld the government's application of the step transaction doctrine in this context.

The *Senda* case involved two separate capitalizations of partnerships with marketable securities that allegedly were followed by assignments of partnership interests to the taxpayers' children. With respect to the first partnership, husband and wife transferred stock

---

[6] The owner of a single-member LLC can elect to have the entity classified as an association, which is taxed as a corporation for federal tax purposes. *See* Treas. Reg. § 301.7701-3(a). Following the tax years at issue in *Pierre*, the entity classification regulations were amended to provide that a single-member LLC would be treated as a separate entity in all cases for federal excise tax and employment tax purposes. *See* Treas. Reg. § 301.7701-2(c)(2)(iv), (v).

in a publicly traded corporation to a partnership and, on the same day, assigned limited partnership interests in the entity to their children. With respect to the second partnership, the taxpayers transferred additional shares of stock to the partnership and, 42 days later, assigned limited partnership interests to their children. The Service argued that each of these transactions constituted indirect gifts of the stock to the children rather than direct gifts of partnership interests. The Tax Court agreed, finding the case sufficiently similar to the facts of *Shepherd* to warrant characterizing the transfer as an indirect gift of the property contributed to the partnership. The *Senda* court cited the unreliability of the evidence concerning the actual order of the transactions and concluded that "[a]t best, the transactions were integrated . . . and, in effect, simultaneous." *Id.* The Eighth Circuit affirmed. *See* 433 F.3d 1044, 1048–49 (8th Cir. 2006).

In *Linton v. United States*, 638 F. Supp. 2d 1277 (W.D. Wash. 2009), the federal district court faced a scenario similar to that in *Senda*—that is, the court determined that the taxpayers' transfer of property to the LLC and the taxpayers' gifts of LLC interest occurred simultaneously. However, in determining that the taxpayers made indirect gifts of the property they conveyed to the LLC (which would not warrant the same valuation discounts), the district court did not rely on the taxpayer's failure to properly sequence the transactions. *See id.* at 1287. Instead, the court explained that it would reach the same holding under the step transaction doctrine:

> Regardless of which [articulation of the step transaction doctrine] is applied, plaintiffs made "stepped" indirect gifts to their children's Trusts of the assets they contributed to [the LLC]. The binding commitment test is met because plaintiffs executed binding Trust Agreements and Gift Documents at the same time they took the first step of contributing property to the LLC; as counsel for plaintiffs conceded during oral argument, these documents would have been valid after signing had they never been dated. The end result test is likewise satisfied because plaintiffs undisputedly had a subjective intent to convey as much property as possible to their children while minimizing their gift tax liability, pursuant to which they crafted, with the aid of an attorney and a tax advisor, a scheme consisting of "pre-arranged parts of a single transaction." . . . In addition, the interdependence test is met because the undisputed evidence demonstrates that plaintiffs would not have undertaken one or more of the steps at issue absent their "contemplation of the other integrating acts." But for the anticipated 40% to 49% discount in calculating gift taxes, premised on the low market appeal of [the LLC's] structure, plaintiffs would not have contributed assets to the LLC. Indeed, the quantum of property transferred to [the LLC] was determined solely on the basis of maximizing the tax advantages of the transaction. Because the events here satisfy all three of the step transaction tests, the Court need not choose among the different standards, and the Court holds as a matter of law that, under the step transaction doctrine, plaintiffs made gifts to their children's Trusts of pro rata shares of the assets they contributed to [the LLC.]

Id. at 1288–89.

While the application of the step doctrine in *Senda* and *Linton* constitutes an ominous development to planners who use closely held entities primarily as vehicles through which to transfer wealth, courts are not always sympathetic to the government's invocation of the step transaction doctrine in this setting. For instance, in *Holman v. Commissioner*, 130 T.C. 170 (2008), the court refused to collapse the funding of a partnership with subsequent gifts of partnership interests. The taxpayers in *Holman* first transferred stock in a publicly traded corporation to a family-owned partnership. Only six days later, the taxpayers made assignments of partnership interests for the benefit of their children. Each of these two steps was appropriately documented. Despite the close proximity of these two transactions, the court reasoned that "the passage of time may be indicative of a change in circumstances that gives independent significance to a partner's transfer of property to a partnership and the subsequent gift of an interest in that partnership to another." *Id.* at 189. Given that the value of the securities held by the partnership lost 1.316 percent of their value between the formation of the partnership and the gift of partnership interests, the court determined that the taxpayers bore "real economic risk" during this interim period that warranted respecting the separate transactions for gift tax purposes. *Id.* at 190–91; *see also* Gross v. Commissioner, T.C. Memo. 2008-221, 96 T.C.M. (CCH) 187 (refusing to collapse the formation of a partnership and gifts of partnership interests under the step transaction doctrine when the transactions were separated by 11 days).

In a subsequent opinion in the *Pierre* case, the Tax Court applied the step transaction doctrine in a slightly different manner in the family limited partnership context. *See* Pierre v. Commissioner, T.C. Memo. 2010-106, 99 T.C.M. (CCH) 1436. Recall that the taxpayer in *Pierre*, as the sole member of an LLC that she had capitalized with cash and marketable securities, transferred a 50 percent interest in the LLC to each of two trusts established for the benefit of family members. The combined transfer, which occurred on the same day, consisted of a gift of a 9.5 percent LLC interest and a sale of a 40.5 percent interest in exchange for a secured promissory note. Whereas the taxpayer valued the gift of the 9.5 percent interest in isolation, the Service contended that the gift and sale components of the transfer to each trust should be collapsed under the step transaction doctrine. In this manner, the value of the gift would be determined by first determining the value of a 50 percent LLC interest and then subtracting the value of the promissory note the taxpayer received in exchange. [This latter approach would necessarily result in a smaller minority-interest discount in valuing the gift.] The Tax Court agreed, noting that "nothing of tax significance" occurred between the gift transactions and sale transactions and finding that the two steps "were planned as a single transaction" that was broken into multiple steps "solely for tax purposes."[7] *Id.* at 1440.

§ 4.02 TRANSFER PROVISIONS DESIGNED TO AVOID GIFT TAX

[A] Conditions Subsequent

In *Commissioner v. Procter*, 142 F.2d 824 (4th Cir. 1944), the taxpayer possessed remainder interests in two trusts that were to become possessory upon his mother's death. He assigned these remainder interests to a separate trust, which obligated the trustees to use trust property to satisfy the balance due on loans to the taxpayer by the taxpayer's mother. The taxpayer retained an income interest in any funds that remained after repayment of the loans, and the principal of the trust was to be distributed to the taxpayer's children upon his death. In an attempt to insulate the transfer from gift tax consequences, the taxpayer inserted a savings clause into the transfer document. This provision instructed that, in the event of a

---

[7] Because of the government's failure to offer expert testimony to value the combined transfer of a 50 percent LLC interest, the result for the taxpayer in *Pierre* was not as bad as one might expect. In the end, application of the step transaction doctrine in the case yielded only a slight reduction in the minority-interest discount employed to value the transferred interest, from 10 percent to 8 percent.

final order or judgment determining that any portion of the transfer constituted a gift, then that portion of the property would "automatically be deemed not to be included in the conveyance in trust hereunder and shall remain the sole property of [the taxpayer]." *Id.* at 827. The Fourth Circuit refused to enforce this provision on policy grounds:

> This is clearly a condition subsequent and void because contrary to public policy. A contrary holding would mean that upon a decision that the gift was subject to tax, the court making such decision must hold it not a gift and therefore not subject to tax. . . . It is manifest that a condition which involves this sort of trifling with the judicial process cannot be sustained.

Id. The court justified its holding on three grounds: (1) the provision had a tendency to discourage the collection of tax; (2) the condition would obstruct the administration of justice by forcing courts to pass on a moot issue; and (3) the condition itself was illogical—a final order of judgment of a tax liability could not be reversed by a subsequent transfer. *Id.* at 827–28.

The *Procter* case has come to stand for the proposition that conditions subsequent to the initial gratuitous transfer that are introduced for the purpose of avoiding the imposition of the gift tax violate public policy. The Service in Revenue Ruling 86-41, 1986-1 C.B. 300, provided examples of two other provisions that it viewed as unenforceable under the *Procter* doctrine. The first example consisted of conveyance of an undivided fractional interest in real property with the following adjustment clause: If the value of the conveyance exceeded the prevailing annual exclusion amount, then the fractional amount of the conveyed property would be reduced so that the value of the gift would be fully shielded by the exclusion amount. The second example achieved the same result, albeit through a different route. Instead of reducing the portion of the conveyed property in hindsight, the transfer obligated the transferee to return to the transferor the dollar amount by which the value of the real property exceeded the annual exclusion. In short order, the ruling determined that both adjustment clauses would be disregarded for gift tax purposes. *See also* Ward v. Commissioner, 87 T.C. 78 (1986) (transfer of stock in which a savings clause similar to the first example of Rev. Rul. 86-41 was held unenforceable); Harwood v. Commissioner, 82 T.C. 239 (1984) (transfer of partnership interests in which a savings clause similar to the second example of Rev. Rul. 86-41 was held ineffective because conditions for adjustment not satisfied).

[B] Defined Value Transfers

With savings clauses or other conditions subsequent to an initial gratuitous transfer being unenforceable under *Procter* and its progeny, taxpayers recently have turned their sights to so-called "defined value" transfers as a way of avoiding the condition-subsequent label. The first case litigated in this area was *McCord v. Commissioner*, 120 T.C. 358 (2003), *rev'd*, 461 F.3d 614 (5th Cir. 2006). In *McCord*, a husband and wife made irrevocable transfers of all of their limited partnership interests in a family-owned partnership to four donees, two of which were tax-exempt entities. However, the assignment agreement did not specify the respective percentages of partnership interests that were to be transferred to each donee. Instead, the assignment agreement specified only the *value* of partnership interests that each donee was to receive.

Simplifying the facts somewhat,[8] the assignment agreement instructed that the assigned partnership interests would be allocated among the donees in following cascading order: (1) generation skipping transfer trusts (GST trusts) were to receive partnership interests equal to the amount of the taxpayers' remaining GST tax exemption; (2) the taxpayers' sons were to receive partnership interests worth approximately $7 million, reduced by the value of the interests conveyed to the GST trusts under the first allocation; (3) a non-profit symphony was to receive the lesser of $134,000 worth of partnership interests or the amount of any partnership interests that remained after the first two allocations; and (4) a tax-exempt community foundation was to receive the value of any partnership interests not allocated under the prior provisions.[9] *Id.* at 364–65. The taxpayers retained no control over how the assigned partnership interests would be allocated among the donees. Rather, the donees made this determination several months after the assignment by having the assigned partnership interests appraised and allocating those interests in accordance with the defined-value instructions. Only at this point were the precise percentage partnership interests transferred to each donee established. A few months after the donees executed the confirmation agreement, the partnership redeemed the limited partnership interests held by the tax-exempt organizations.

The taxpayers reported the value of their gifts based on the per-unit value reflected in the appraisal, which incorporated a variety of entity-related valuation discounts. The Service determined that the per-unit value of the assigned partnership interests was almost double the amount claimed by the taxpayers, and therefore increased the value of the gifts to the GST trusts and to the taxpayers' sons. The taxpayers, however, were not particularly concerned with the government's valuation objection. They argued that, pursuant to the formula clause in the assignment agreement, the government's increased valuation of the assigned partnership interests simply meant that more of the partnership interests should have been allocated to the tax-exempt community foundation as the residual-value donee. *Id.* at 369. This adjustment would have produced no additional revenue; the increased gift to the community foundation would have been offset by an increased charitable deduction. [Keep in mind, however, that the percentage partnership interest received by the foundation was set by the donees' confirmation agreement, and that the foundation's interest had been redeemed shortly thereafter.] The government, in turn, responded that any transfer that systematically protected a revaluation of the transferred property from generating additional tax revenue was void on public policy grounds.

The Tax Court issued a sharply divided court-reviewed decision in the case. The majority opinion approached the matter by starting with the percentage partnership interests that ultimately were received by each donee—in effect, treating the taxpayers' assignment agreement and the donees' confirmation agreement as components of a single transaction. *Id.* at 396–97. After determining the proper per-unit value of the assigned partnership interests through a painstaking analysis, the majority then applied this value to the percentage partnership interests that were actually received by the donees to determine the resulting gift tax consequences. The majority refused to treat the revaluation of the partnership interests as

---

[8] The description ignores the reduction in the value of the gifts to the GST trusts and to the taxpayers' sons based on the donees' agreement to assume any contingent estate tax liability that would have resulted under IRC § 2035(b) had the donees died within three years of the transfer.

[9] The value of the partnership interests to be used in executing the defined-value conveyance was defined in a manner identical to the willing-buyer/willing-seller definition of value for transfer tax purposes set forth in Reg. § 25.2512-1.

allocating additional interests to the tax-exempt foundation, noting that the community foundation was not entitled an additional share of the transferred partnership interests under state law.[10] Having undermined the taxpayers' attempt to bullet-proof the gift from valuation challenge in this manner, the majority did not need to address the public policy challenge. However, other judges of the Tax Court would have utilized the public policy doctrine articulated in *Procter* and *Ward* to deny any increase in the charitable deduction for amounts the charitable organizations would never receive. *See id.* at 427–30 (Laro, J., dissenting, joined by Vasquez, J.).

On appeal to the Fifth Circuit, the government dropped its public policy argument and, instead, advanced the theory endorsed by the Tax Court majority. In a fairly indignant opinion, the Fifth Circuit emphatically reversed in the taxpayers' favor.[11] McCord v. Commissioner, 461 F.3d 614, 632 (5th Cir. 2006). As reflected below, the Fifth Circuit disapproved of the majority's consideration of the manner in which the donees allocated the percentage partnership interests among themselves:

> It is clear beyond cavil that the Majority should have stopped with the Assignment Agreement's plain wording. By not doing so, however, and instead continuing on to the post-gift Confirmation Agreement's intra-donee concurrence on the equivalency of dollars to percentage of interests in [the partnership], the Majority violated the firmly-established maxim that a gift is valued as of the date that is complete; the flip side of that maxim is that subsequent occurrences are off limits.

Id. at 626. Without explaining how the property interests transferred to each donee could be determined without reference to the donees' confirmation agreement, the Fifth Circuit viewed the transfer of value that occurred under the assignment agreement as completing the gift. Accordingly, any increase in the per-unit valuation of the partnership interests could not increase the taxpayers' gift tax liability. *Id.* at 628.

Defined-value transfers understandably have become quite popular in the estate-planning community since the Fifth Circuit's reversal in *McCord*. Although the appellate court in *McCord* did not address challenges to defined value transfers based on *Procter*-like public policy objections because the government did not advance these arguments on appeal,[12] the Tax Court's subsequent decision in *Estate of Petter v. Commissioner*, T.C. Memo. 2009-280, 98 T.C.M. (CCH) 534, has mitigated any lingering public policy concerns.

The taxpayer in *Petter* first transferred stock in United Parcel Service (UPS) to an LLC, and then made gratuitous assignments of LLC units. Each assignment concerned a specified number of LLC units, with a defined value being transferred to an irrevocable trust with the remaining value passing to a community foundation. The transfer agreements provided that if the value of the units transferred to the trust as finally determined for gift tax purposes

---

[10] The majority rejected the taxpayers' claim that the defined-value formula used in the assignment agreement operated to increase the percentage interest received by the community foundation, noting that the assignment agreement directed that determinations of value be based on the willing-buyer/willing-seller standard contained in the gift tax regulations instead of basing valuation determinations of such value "as finally determined for Federal gift tax purposes." *Id.* at 397.

[11] The Fifth Circuit went so far as to direct the Tax Court to assess all costs to the government. McCord v. Commissioner, 461 F.3d 614, 632 (5th Cir. 2006).

[12] Nonetheless, the overall tone of the Fifth Circuit's decision in *McCord* suggests that the court would have rejected a public policy challenge out of hand.

exceeded the amount of the defined value transfers, then the trust would make corrective transfers of LLC units to the charitable beneficiary. The Service challenged the per-unit value of the transferred LLC interests and further argued that any purported re-allocation of units from the trust to the charitable beneficiary should be disregarded under *Procter* as a subsequent transfer. The Tax Court disagreed, finding that the taxpayer's transfer was one of a formula amount instead of an absolute number of LLC units. The court found this distinction meaningful, noting that "savings clauses are void, but formula clauses are fine." *Id.* at 542. In addition to distinguishing the *Procter* decision, the Tax Court went on to dismiss other public policy arguments against the technique, noting that a redetermination of the value of the transferred parties would have economic consequences to the transferees and relying on the fiduciary obligations of the charitable organizations to enforce its rights under the gift agreements. In short, the court was not willing to treat the charities as serving a mere accommodation role in the taxpayer's estate planning.

§ 4.03   EFFECT OF LIABILITY ASSUMPTION BY DONEE

[A]   Assumption of Gift Tax Liability

Liability for payment of the federal gift tax imposed by § 2501(a) rests upon the donor. IRC § 2502(c). However, if the donor conditions the gift upon the donee's agreement to pay the resulting gift tax, the tax liability assumed by the donee is deducted from the amount of the taxable transfer.[13] *See* Rev. Rul. 75-72, 1975-1 C.B. 310. In many respects, this result simply follows from the instruction provided in § 2512(b) that the gift tax applies to transfers of property only to the extent the value of the transferred property exceeds the value in money or money's worth of the consideration received by the transferor.

Where the gratuitous transfer consists of appreciated property, however, the donor must be mindful of the potential adverse income tax consequences of this technique. As explained in *Diedrich v. Commissioner*, 457 U.S. 191, 198–99 (1982), the donee's assumption of the donor's tax liability transforms a purely gratuitous transaction into a part-sale, part-gift. The donor will realize gain on the transaction to the extent the liability assumed by the donee exceeds the donor's basis in the transferred property. *See* IRC § 1001(a); Treas. Reg. § 1.1001-1(e).

When a donee assumes the donor's liability for payment of gift tax attributable to the transfer, a textual issue arises under § 2035(b). Recall that, to prevent donors from exploiting the tax-exclusive nature of the gift tax by making taxable gifts when death appears on the horizon, Congress enacted § 2035(b) to gross-up the decedent's estate tax base by the amount of any gift tax paid "by the decedent or his estate" on gifts made by the decedent within the three-year period preceding the death. If the obligation to pay the gift tax is assumed by the donee of the transfer, does the donee's payment of gift tax (rather than the decedent or the decedent's estate) negate the possible application of § 2035(b)? The taxpayer-estate in *Estate of Sachs v. Commissioner*, 88 T.C. 769 (1987), advanced this interpretation to no avail. In a court-reviewed decision, the Tax Court reasoned that the donees' payment of gift tax represented a constructive payment by the decedent because the payment discharged the decedent's statutory obligation. The Eighth Circuit affirmed. *See* Estate of Sachs v.

---

[13] Because the amount of the taxable transfer depends on the tax liability, the tax liability is computed through the following circular computation: $tax = rate \, (transfer - tax)$. Under this formula, the tax liability is equal to $[(transfer \times rate) / (1 + rate)]$.

Commissioner, 856 F.2d 1158 (8th Cir. 1988). Accordingly, while the net gift technique reduces the value of the transfer and, consequently, the gift tax liability, the technique does not serve to inoculate a transfer from the potential reach of § 2035(b).

[B] Assumption of Contingent Estate Tax Liability

While the gift tax generally is levied on a tax-exclusive basis because the gift tax paid by the donor is not itself treated as a taxable gift, § 2035(b) provides a limited exception to the tax-exclusive norm. Under this provision, any gift tax paid by a decedent or a decedent's spouse on gifts made by the decedent or the decedent's spouse within three years of the decedent's death must be included in the decedent's gross estate for estate-tax purposes. In this narrow context, gift tax paid by the donor would itself be subject to an additional transfer tax. Thus, the gift tax for transfers made within three years of death is retroactively converted into a tax-inclusive transfer tax (like the estate tax).

Returning to the *McCord* decision, the children assumed the gift tax liability that resulted from the assignment of partnership interests in their favor. Alone, this simply rendered the transactions a traditional "net gift" to the donees. But the children in *McCord* assumed an additional potential liability in hopes of further reducing the amount of the taxable transfers: the potential increased estate tax liability that would result under § 2035(b) if either of their parents died within three years of making the gifts of partnership interests. McCord v. Commissioner, 120 T.C. 358, 399 (2003). The children estimated the amount of this contingent liability through a present-value calculation of a mortality-adjusted computation of the estate tax liability.

The Tax Court rejected the taxpayers' attempt to reduce the value of the gifts by the children's assumption of the taxpayers' potential increased estate tax liability attributable to § 2035(b). In addition to determining that the computation of this liability assumption was too speculative, the court also relied on the "estate depletion" theory of the gift tax. The court noted that the parents did not receive any present benefit in money or money's worth (as required under § 2512(b)) on account of the children's assumption of the contingent estate tax liability. Rather, any pecuniary benefit from the arrangement could be realized only by the donor's estate. *Id.* at 403. Note that this benefit would not be subject to estate taxation in the decedent's estate, because the benefit would come into existence by definition only after the decedent's death.

The Fifth Circuit reversed the Tax Court on this issue as well. Conceding that the calculation of this assumed liability was speculative, the Fifth Circuit nonetheless concluded that the obligation was "sufficiently determinable" on the date the gifts were made to be taken into account by a willing buyer and willing seller in valuing the transfer. McCord v. Commissioner, 461 F.3d 614, 631 (5th Cir. 2006). The Fifth Circuit never addressed the Tax Court's estate-depletion rationale.

§ 4.04 STUDY PROBLEMS

1. Nancy owns undeveloped beachfront property worth $2 million. [She inherited the property from her father 20 years ago, when the property was worth $250,000.] Nancy transfers the property to her son for no consideration. As a condition to the transfer,

the son agrees to pay any gift tax imposed on Nancy.

Ignoring any annual gift tax exclusion and assuming that Nancy has made prior transfers that have exhausted her unified credit, what are the gift tax consequences of the transfer? Are there any other consequences to Nancy that must be considered?

2.   Mildred wants to consolidate ownership of her marketable securities into a family-owned LLC. She is considering transferring $2 million of stock to each of her four children, and then having the children make capitalizing transfers to the LLC. Each child would receive a 10 percent interest in the LLC. Mildred would contribute another $12 million for a 60 percent interest. Mildred also is considering transferring the full $20 million to the LLC first, and later making assignments of 10 percent LLC interest to each of her children. Which approach is preferable? What steps can Mildred take to ensure that her chosen form of the transaction is respected?

3.   Darby transfers a 90 percent limited partnership interest to a trust established for the benefit of her children. Pursuant to an appraisal obtained by Darby at the time of the transfer, the 90 percent interest was worth $10 million. Concerned that the government may challenge the discounts employed in the appraisal, the transfer document provides that in the event the value of the transferred interest exceeded the $10 million value, the appropriate percentage interest as limited partner would be re-transferred to Darby. The government challenges the valuation, and successfully asserts that the value of the 90 percent interest is $18 million. As a result of this revaluation, Darby then contends that limited partnership interests valued at $8 million must be re-conveyed to her, negating any additional gift tax. Does this technique work?

    a.   What if the transfer agreement provided that a limited partnership interest representing the value in excess of $10 million would be transferred to Darby's law school alma mater?

    b.   What if the transfer agreement instead provided for the transfer of a 90 percent limited partnership interest, to be allocated first to the trust to the extent of partnership interests having a value of $10 million (as finally determined for gift tax purposes) with the excess passing to Darby's law school alma mater?

Chapter 5

TRANSFERS EXCLUDED FROM THE GIFT TAX BASE

Internal Revenue Code: § 2503(b), (c), (e)
                                  §§ 529(c)(2)(B), 2501(a)(4)
Treasury Regulations: §§ 25.2503–2(a), 25.2503–3, 25.2503–4, 25.2503–6

§ 5.01 THE ANNUAL EXCLUSION

Section 2503(b) provides a per-donee exclusion of gratuitous transfers from the "total amount of gifts" for each taxable year. This annual exclusion was a feature of the gift tax when it was permanently enacted in 1932. The Senate Finance Committee explained the purpose of the annual exclusion as follows:

> Such exemption, on the one hand, is to obviate the necessity of keeping an account of and reporting numerous small gifts, and, on the other, to fix the amount sufficiently large to cover in most cases wedding and Christmas gifts and occasional gifts of relatively small amounts.

S. Rep. No. 72-665, at 41.

The annual exclusion initially was set at $5,000, a fairly generous amount at the time. Indexed for inflation based on the Consumer Price Index, the $5,000 exemption translates to approximately $82,400 in 2011 dollars. Of course, the annual exclusion has not kept pace with inflation. In fact, the first reaction of Congress was to lower it. Viewing the exclusion level as posing an excessive threat to the transfer tax base, Congress decreased the exemption to $4,000 through the Revenue Act of 1938 and then further lowered it to $3,000 through the Revenue Act of 1942.[1] The exemption remained at this level until the Economic Tax Recovery Act of 1981, through which Congress increased the exemption to $10,000 after noting that inflation had significantly eroded the benefit of the exclusion.[2] While the $10,000 amount of the exclusion remains fixed in the minds of many laypeople, Congress provided for inflation indexing of the annual exclusion in $1,000 increments through the Taxpayer Relief Act of 1997. *See* IRC § 2503(b)(2). The first such adjustment occurred in 2002 when the exemption

---

[1] In 1938, the House of Representatives expressed its concern as follows:

> As there is no limitation upon the number of such exemptions which may be availed of annually, a donor may, over a period of years, dispose of a large amount of property free of tax. In view of the frequency with which donors are induced by the exemption to build up estates of considerable size for members of their families, the present amount of the exemption is regarded as unreasonably large.

H.R. Rep. No. 75-1860, at 61 (1938). Despite the reduction to $4,000, the House expressed the same concern in 1942. *See* H.R. Rep. No. 77-2333, at 37 (1942).

[2] *See* S. Rep. No. 97-144, at 129 (1981).

increased to $11,000. As of 2011, the inflation-adjusted level of the exclusion is $13,000.

Although the origins of the annual exclusion rest in administrative convenience, the exclusion provides a formidable vehicle for transferring substantial amounts of wealth without federal transfer tax consequence. As an example, assume that *Grandfather* has two children and four grandchildren, and that he fully utilizes the exclusion by making total gifts of $13,000 (including the value of traditional occasion-associated gifts[3]) to each such descendant annually. Over the course of a 10-year period, *Grandfather* will have reduced his future gross estate by $780,000. If *Grandfather* faces the highest 35 percent marginal estate tax rate, these annual exclusion transfers will yield an estate tax savings of $273,000. And this figure does not take into consideration any appreciation in the transferred property or income it generates prior to *Grandfather's* death. Given the potential for the annual exclusion to exempt substantial transfers of wealth from the gift tax, the exclusion under § 2503(b) has garnered considerable administrative and judicial attention.

[A] Necessity of a Present Interest in Property

The gift tax annual exclusion under § 2503(b) is not available for all transfers that otherwise would constitute gifts under § 2501(a). Rather, the statute provides a parenthetical exception for "gifts of future interests in property." The regulations under § 2503(b) indicate that a future interest for this purpose is a legal concept grounded in state property law:

> "Future interest" is a legal term, and includes reversions, remainders, and other interests or estates, whether vested or contingent, and whether or not supported by a particular interest or estate, which are limited to commence in use, possession, or enjoyment at some future date or time.

Treas. Reg. § 25.2503-3(a). Hence, the transfer of a vested remainder in property is not entitled to be excluded from the total amount of gifts under § 2503(b). As explained by the Supreme Court in *Fondren v. Commissioner*, 324 U.S. 18, 20–21 (1945),

> [I]t is not enough to bring the exclusion into force that the donee has vested rights. In addition he must have the right presently to use, possess or enjoy the property. These terms are not words of art, like "fee" in the law of seizin, . . . but connote the right to substantial present economic benefit. The question is of time, not when title vests, but when enjoyment begins. Whatever puts the barrier of a substantial period between the will of the beneficiary or donee now to enjoy what has been given him and that enjoyment makes the gift one of a future interest within the meaning of the regulation.

See also Rev. Rul. 54-401, 1954-2 C.B. 320 (transfer of vested remainder interest in property not entitled to annual exclusion). *But see* Rev. Rul. 78-168, 1978-1 C.B. 298 (transfer of remainder interest to the income beneficiary constitutes a present interest gift where the two interests are merged into fee simple title pursuant to state law).

---

[3] The original justification for the annual exclusion at times appears lost on estate planners, many of whom treat the exclusion amount under § 2503(b) as applying *in addition to* any transfers that take place in traditional gift-giving contexts. Perhaps the latter are viewed as being outside the feasible administrative bounds of the gift tax. However, this interpretation of the § 2503(b) exclusion is dubious at best.

[1] Identification of Donee

Although the imposition of the federal gift tax does not depend on the ability to identify the specific donee of a transfer of property, *see* Treas. Reg. § 25.2511-2(a), the application of the annual exclusion on a per-donee basis requires donee identification. In that regard, the justification for the blanket denial of the annual exclusion for transfers of future interests in property rests in the potential difficulty of identifying the ultimate recipients of such transfers and the values of their interests: "The exemption being available only in so far as the donees are ascertainable, the denial of the exemption in the case of gifts of future interests is dictated by the apprehended difficulty, in many instances, of determining the number of eventual donees and values of their respective gifts." H.R. Rep. No. 72-708, at 29; S. Rep. No. 72-665, at 41, both quoted in *United States v. Pelzer*, 312 U.S. 399, 403 (1941).

The disallowance of the annual exclusion to gifts of future interests in property would have little if any application if a trust as an entity (or, perhaps, the trustee on behalf of a trust) constituted the "person" to whom gifts are made for purposes of § 2503(b). In light of this potential anomaly, the Supreme Court in *Helvering v. Hutchings*, 312 U.S. 393 (1941), held that a transfer in trust is to be treated as a transfer to the trust beneficiaries for purposes of evaluating the availability of the annual exclusion.[4] Corporations and other business entities similarly are disregarded as donees for purposes of the exclusion; instead, the transfer is treated as a gift to the owners of the entity. *See* Treas. Reg. § 25.2511-1(h)(1) ("A transfer of property by B to a corporation generally represents gifts by B to the other individual shareholders of the corporation to the extent of their proportionate interests in the corporation."). Such look-through treatment, however, does not mean that the imposition of the entity layer is irrelevant. Because the donee's ability to presently enjoy the property transferred to the entity generally depends on some action taken by the entity (e.g., the declaration of dividends or liquidation of the entity), courts have characterized the transfer as constituting a future interest in property. *See, e.g.*, Heringer v. Commissioner, 235 F.2d 149, *cert. denied*, 352 U.S. 927 (1956); Chanin v. United States, 393 F.2d 972 (Ct. Cl. 1968) (each involving transfers to a corporation); *see also* Rev. Rul. 71-443, 1971-2 C.B. 337 (same). *But see* Wooley v. United States, 736 F. Supp. 1506 (S.D. Ind. 1990) (transfers of partnership capital held not to be gifts of future interests because the donee-partners possessed the right under state partnership law to demand distribution of the balance of their capital accounts).

Although transfers to trusts or business entities are analyzed on a look-through basis, the regulations recognize one possible exception to this rule: a transfer to a "charitable, public, political or similar organization which may constitute a gift to the organization as a single entity, depending on the facts and circumstances." Treas. Reg. § 25.2511-1(h)(1); *see also Hutchings*, 312 U.S. at 398 (raising the possibility of treating these entities as the relevant donee due to the inability to identify the ultimate beneficiaries of such transfers). The Service provided guidance on when it would treat a political organization as an independent donee for purposes of applying the annual exclusion in Revenue Ruling 72-355, 1972-2 C.B. 532.[5]

---

[4] As an additional justification, the Court in *Hutchings* noted that treating the trust as the donee would permit individuals to unilaterally expand the application of the annual exclusion through the "simple expedient" of creating additional trusts to serve as donees. 312 U.S. at 397.

[5] As a result of the enactment of § 2501(a)(4), discussed in infra § 5.03, certain transfers to political organizations now are exempt from the gift tax.

[2] Potential Qualification of Income Interest in Trust

Just because a gift is made to a trust does not mean that all hope is lost for application of the annual exclusion. As explained in the regulations, "[a]n unrestricted right to the immediate use, possession, or enjoyment of property or the income from property (such as a life estate or term certain) is a present interest in property." Treas. Reg. § 25.2503-3(b); *see also Fondren*, 324 U.S. at 21 ("if the income of a trust is required to be distributed periodically, as annually, . . . the gift of the income is one of a present interest. . . ."). Thus, even though an income interest in a trust necessarily constitutes a stream of payments to be received in the future, the "future interest" characterization is avoided because the income beneficiary is currently entitled to the periodic benefit. However, the donor bears the burden of establishing not only that an interest in property constitutes a present interest, but also that the value of such interest is capable of determination. *See* Rev. Rul. 55-678, 1955-2 C.B. 389.

[a] Deferral or Contingencies Relating to Income Payments

Unconditional present entitlement to the use of transferred property or the income it generates is crucial to the availability of the annual exclusion in this context. Any gap between the transfer of property and the beneficiary's entitlement to income distributions can render the beneficiary's interest in the trust a future interest. For example, in *Hessenbruch v. Commissioner*, 178 F.2d 785 (3d Cir. 1950), a trustee's ability to accumulate the income of a trust until the beneficiary attained the age of majority (at which point income distributions became mandatory) was sufficient to negate application of the annual exclusion—even though the beneficiary was only *three months* away from attaining majority when the trust was funded. *See also* Jardell v. Commissioner, 24 T.C. 652 (1955) (oil and gas royalty interest to commence less than three months from conveyance held to be future interest). Contingencies relating to an income interest also may trigger the future interest prohibition. Revenue Ruling 75-506, 1975-2 C.B. 375, concerned a trust created for two beneficiaries. The trust income was to be distributed in equal shares to the beneficiaries until the first to die, at which point all income would be distributed to the survivor. Upon the death of the surviving beneficiary, the trust principal would be distributed to the donor or the donor's estate. Although each beneficiary's right to one-half of the trust income constituted a present interest in property, the potential to receive distributions of all of the trust income was held to constitute a future interest due to the contingency of survival. The value placed on this contingent income interest therefore was not subject to exclusion under § 2503(b), even though the contingency, by definition, would be resolved in favor of one of the beneficiaries.

[b] Trustee Discretion to Accumulate Income

Subjecting income distributions to the discretion of the trustee generally precludes the availability of the annual exclusion—even if the discretion must be exercised in accordance with an ascertainable standard. In *Commissioner v. Disston*, 325 U.S. 442 (1945), the trustees were directed to accumulate income for the minor trust beneficiary until majority; however, a later provision in the trust directed the trustees to currently distribute as much income "as may be necessary for the education, comfort and support" of the trust beneficiary. *Id.* at 444. In rejecting the donor's invocation of the annual exclusion with respect to the beneficiary's interest in the trust income, the Court explained that, "[i]n the absence of some indication from the face of the trust or surrounding circumstances that a steady flow of some ascertainable portion of income to the minor would be required, there is no basis for a conclusion that there is a gift of anything other than for the future." *Id.* at 449.

[c]   Trustee Discretion to Distribute Principal

The ability of the trustee to make discretionary distributions of trust principal to one other than the income beneficiary generally proves fatal to the availability of the annual exclusion, because the trustee's ability to undermine the future income stream in this manner prevents the assignment of an ascertainable value to the interest. *See* Prejean v. Commissioner, 354 F.2d 995 (5th Cir. 1966) (trustee possessed discretion to distribute trust income to various beneficiaries according to their needs); Hockman v. United States, 327 F. Supp. 332 (D. Md. 1971) (trustee possessed ability to invade principal for the income beneficiary or any member of his or her "immediate family"). However, in *Jones v. Commissioner*, 29 T.C. 200 (1957), the Tax Court determined that the trustee's ability to distribute principal to the donor's children for their maintenance, education and support, or for any emergency occasioned by sickness or casualty, was "so remote as to be negligible." *Id.* at 215. Note that the holding in *Jones* is fairly lenient. Only by disregarding the trustee's ability to distribute principal altogether were the income interests capable of valuation and, thus, subject to the benefit of the annual exclusion.

The discretionary authority to distribute principal does not jeopardize the annual exclusion if such distributions are limited to the income beneficiary. That stands to reason, because a principal distribution would not undermine the beneficiary's right to the income stream; rather, the beneficiary would continue to receive the income from the property owned in her individual capacity. Hence, if an income beneficiary otherwise possesses a present interest in property, the possibility that such interest will be diminished by the exercise of a discretionary power to distribute principal is disregarded for annual exclusion purposes so long as "no part of such interest will at any time pass to any other person." IRC § 2503(b); *see also* Treas. Reg. § 25.2503-3(b).

[d]   Potential Effect of Broad Administrative Powers

Even the elimination of all express contingencies on the distribution of income to the beneficiary does not guarantee availability of the annual exclusion for the income interest. Broad trustee powers to manipulate the amount of the income stream have been found to preclude the annual exclusion, either because the present interest was not capable of valuation or because the income interest did not meet the present interest threshold. In *Fischer v. Commissioner*, 288 F.2d 574 (3d Cir. 1961), the trust beneficiaries were entitled to distributions of "net income," which was defined as the rental income from the transferred properties "over and above disbursement and operating expenses and monies paid for amortization of any mortgages involved." *Id.* at 575. Although the government conceded that the beneficiaries' right to distributions of net income constituted present interests in the transferred property, the Third Circuit affirmed the Tax Court's finding that the donor failed to establish the amount, if any, by which the rental income would exceed the anticipated expenditures. *Id.* at 576–77; *see also* Hamilton v. United States, 553 F.2d 1216 (9th Cir. 1977) ("The instrument leaves too much control in the trustees, both in the management of the farm and in the distribution of income. Under the agreement, no beneficiary can be said to have a present interest in either principal or income."); Van Den Wymelenberg v. United States, 397 F.2d 443 (7th Cir. 1968) (broad administrative powers capable of significantly affecting income stream from trust; value of income interest not ascertainable); Rev. Rul. 77-358, 1977-2 C.B. 342 (requirement that all losses on the sale of trust property be allocated to income rendered income interest incapable of valuation). However, standard fiduciary discretion to allocate receipts and disbursements between income and principal does not render a beneficiary's right to income a future interest in property. *See* Mercantile-Safe Deposit & Trust Co. v. United States, 311 F. Supp. 670 (D. Md. 1970) (holding that standard fiduciary discretion to apportion receipts and disbursements between income and principal does not render right to trust income a future interest); *see also* Swetland v. Commissioner, T.C. Memo. 1978-47, 37 T.C.M. (CCH) 249 (standard administrative powers do not render income interests incapable of valuation).

[e]   Transfer of Unproductive Property

If the grant of broad administrative powers that can be employed by a trustee to diminish the value of the income stream payable to a beneficiary threatens the availability of the annual exclusion, then the transfer of unproductive property in trust is even more problematic. The trust will produce little or no income as a default matter, and trustee action through reinvestment of the trust property—which may be prohibited under the governing document—will be necessary to ensure a meaningful income stream.

The Fourth Circuit decision in *Maryland Nat'l Bank v. United States*, 609 F.2d 1078 (4th Cir. 1979), serves as the leading authority on whether a beneficiary's income interest in trust property that does not produce income nonetheless constitutes a present interest in property. The donor in *Maryland National Bank* transferred a one-half interest in a partnership to a trust for the benefit of her family members. The partnership held real estate that had been in the donor's family for 70 years. For the most part, the partnership operated at a loss. Only once in a 13-year period did the partnership generate net income and, even then, such income was not distributed by the entity.

The trust instrument required the net income of the trust to be distributed to the beneficiaries in set proportions at least annually. However, the trustees were expressly authorized to invest in or retain nonproductive assets, and the trust required that the proceeds of any sale of partnership property be distributed to the trust beneficiaries only if the trustees did not apply the proceeds toward the purchase of a greater interest in the original partnership property.

The taxpayer pointed to the absolute right of the trust beneficiaries to receive distributions of income under the trust instrument, and contended that this right alone was sufficient to satisfy the present interest requirement. The value of the income interest could then be valued through the use of actuarial tables. As reflected in the excerpt below, the Fourth Circuit was not persuaded by this formalistic approach:

> The absence of a steady flow of ascertainable income to the beneficiary can result just as surely from a lack of any prospect of income as it can from restrictions on the trustees' power to disburse income. In either event the result is the same, and the exclusion should be denied because no present interest was conveyed. *Disston* places a dual burden on the taxpayer[:] the first is implicit, the second explicit. The taxpayer must show that the trust will receive income, and, second, that some ascertainable portion of the income will flow steadily to the beneficiary.

> Application of these principles to the facts of this case presents little difficulty. The executor has failed to prove that the partnership has produced any income for distribution to the beneficiaries, that steps have been taken to eliminate the losses it

has sustained annually, or that there will be any income in the foreseeable future. Moreover, the trust authorizes the trustees to hold this unproductive property, and it bars them from reinvesting for more than three years the proceeds from the sale of partnership real estate, which is the trust's only significant asset, into stocks, bonds, or other real estate to generate income. In sum, neither the circumstances of the case nor the provisions of the trust realistically establish that the beneficiaries actually will receive a steady flow of income.

The executor, however, urges that this hiatus in the proof can be filled by use of the actuarial tables, which calculate the present value of an estate for a term of years by assuming a prescribed rate of return on the corpus. *See* Treas. Reg. § 25.2512-9(f) (1970). It is undisputed that if use of the tables is permissible, the present worth of each beneficiary's interest would exceed $3,000.

The tables are appropriate only when there is proof that some income will be received by the trust beneficiaries. "Where the property may yield no income at all . . . the tables are not applicable." *Morgan v. Commissioner*, 42 T.C. 1080, 1088 (1964), *aff'd*, 353 F.2d 209 (4th Cir. 1965). The tables are designed to calculate the value of a present interest, not create it. Indeed, even if it is assumed that the disbursal clause of the trust standing alone is facially sufficient to create a present interest, the uncertainty that the beneficiaries will receive income precludes exclusion, whether or not resort is had to the tables. *See Berzon v. Commissioner*, 534 F.2d 528 (2d Cir. 1976); *Stark v. United States*, 477 F.2d 131 (8th Cir. 1973); *Fischer v. Commissioner*, 288 F.2d 574 (3d Cir. 1961). Although the Willis trust gave the beneficiaries an unconditional right to receive income, bestowing this right did not of itself create a present interest. Without any prospect of income, the bare right to receive income was illusory, and all that characterized the gift was the future enjoyment of the corpus.

The burden the Fourth Circuit placed on the donor in *Maryland National Bank* to establish that the trust beneficiaries would receive a predictable income stream stands in sharp contrast to the prior decision of the Sixth Circuit in *Gilmore v. Commissioner*, 213 F.2d 520 (1954). The government in *Gilmore* argued that the ability of the trustees to invest the trust principal in non-income producing property precluded the beneficial interest in the trust from constituting a present interest. The Sixth Circuit disagreed, holding that the legal right to receive whatever income existed was sufficient:

> [T]he trust gives the donee the absolute right to all income. The fact that there may not be income during a year is not a contingency imposed by the donor. It is the right of a donee to the income, rather than the accident of whether there is income at any given time, that is the criterion of present interest. That the corpus of a trust may consist of non-interest bearing notes, payable at a future date, does not prevent a gift from being one of present interest.

Id. at 522 (citing Commissioner v. Kempner, 126 F.2d 853 (5th Cir. 1942) (transfer of non-interest bearing notes in trust did not compel a finding that the gift was of a future interest)).

[3] Contractual Rights to Future Payment

The form through which a transfer occurs is crucial to the determination of whether an interest in property avoids the "future interest" prohibition. As discussed above, the bar for establishing that an income interest in property transferred in trust constitutes a present interest in property is high. Yet outside of the trust context, the transfer of a contractual right to future payments receives far more permissive treatment. In fact, as explained in the regulations, a contractual deferral in payment does not even implicate the future interest analysis: "The term has no reference to such contractual rights as exist in a bond, note (though bearing no interest until maturity), or in a policy of life insurance, the obligations of which are to be discharged by payments in the future." Treas. Reg. § 25.2503-3(a). Hence, the payment by A of premiums on a life insurance policy on his life but which is owned by B will constitute present interest gifts. However, if A instead transferred the insurance policy to a trust in which B possessed the right to all distributions of income, the transfer in trust would constitute a future interest in property because no income stream would exist until A's death. Compare Treas. Reg. § 25.2503-3(c), Exs. 2 & 6. The Service has explained that the basis for the disparate treatment of the two transfers rests in the ability of the donee who receives outright ownership of the policy to exercise all legal incidents of ownership—including the right to surrender the policy for whatever cash value exists. See Rev. Rul. 55-408, 1955-1 C.B. 113.

The distinction between outright transfers of property and transfers in trust for purposes of determining whether the transfer constitutes a future interest for annual exclusion purposes may be showing signs of erosion. For example, in Hackl v. Commissioner, 335 F.3d 664 (7th Cir. 2003), the Seventh Circuit upheld the Tax Court's determination that a transfer of a restricted beneficial interest in a family-owned LLC constituted a gift of a future interest.

The donors in Hackl were a husband and wife who had formed an LLC through the contribution of two tree farms worth $4.5 million together with $8 million of cash and securities. The husband served as the initial manager of the LLC and, in that capacity, controlled distributions from the entity. A member of the LLC could not withdraw from the entity or sell his or her interest without the manager's approval, and any non-sanctioned sale conveyed only the seller's rights to distributions from the entity. Shortly after forming the LLC, the husband and wife began transferring interests in the LLC to their children and other family members.

Standing alone, the transferred LLC interest constituted a property interest under state law, and the donors transferred the percentage interests in the LLC outright—that is, free of any trust restrictions. In short, whatever economic benefit that an ownership interest in the entity represented was transferred to the donee. Although the taxpayers argued that the outright transfer was sufficient to satisfy the present interest requirement, the Seventh Circuit (affirming the Tax Court) was not persuaded. The court found the restrictions on the LLC interests contained in the operating agreement determinative:

> In this case, [the LLC's] operating agreement clearly foreclosed the donees' ability to realize any substantial present economic benefit. Although the voting shares that the Hackls gave away had the same legal rights as those that they retained, [the LLC's] restrictions on the transferability of the shares meant that they were essentially without immediate value to the donees. Granted, [the LLC's] operating agreement did address the possibility that a shareholder might violate the agreement and sell his or her shares without the manager's approval. But, as the Tax Court found, the possibility that a shareholder might violate the operating agreement and sell his or her shares to a transferee who would then not have any membership or voting

rights can hardly be called a substantial economic benefit. Thus, the Hackls' gifts—while outright—were not gifts of present interests.

335 F.3d at 667–68; *see also* Price v. Commissioner, T.C. Memo. 2010-2, 99 T.C.M. (CCH) 1005 (declining invitation to reconsider decision in *Hackl* and, instead, following it); Fisher v. United States, 105 A.F.T.R.2d 1347 (S.D. Ind. 2010) (also following *Hackl*); Hutchinson v. Commissioner, 47 T.C. 680 (1967) (ten-year restriction on the transfer of stock in a closely held corporation rendered the transfer one of a future interest in property). Thus, while the failure of property to produce a current income stream alone may not implicate the future interest rule, restrictions on the sale or disposition of such property likely will be sufficient to place the transfer into the future interest category.

[B]   Use of Withdrawal Rights to Create Present Interest

Given the restrictions on qualifying a transfer in trust for the § 2503(b) annual exclusion through use of an income interest, many taxpayers shun this approach. Recall that all income must be currently payable to the beneficiary, the trustee generally cannot possess discretion to accumulate income or to distribute principal to other beneficiaries, and concerns arise if the trust is to hold non-productive property. On top of these numerous restrictions, the annual exclusion will not shield the entire transfer from gift taxation because some portion of the value of the transferred property will be allocated to the trust remainder. Hence, despite the numerous cases and rulings examining when an income interest in a trust avoids future interest characterization under § 2503(b), few estate planning transactions are structured to maximize the annual exclusion in this manner.

Rather, taxpayers have turned to the use of lapsing rights of withdrawal over property contributed in trust (the income of which may be accumulated, and the principal of which the trustee may possess discretion to distribute) to qualify the entire transfer for the § 2503(b) exclusion. The leading case in this area is *Crummey v. Commissioner*, 397 F.2d 82 (9th Cir. 1968). In fact, the case has become so ubiquitous in the estate planning arena that trusts employing the withdrawal power technique frequently are referred to as "Crummey trusts" and such withdrawal rights as "Crummey powers." The case concerned an irrevocable trust created for the benefit of the donors' children, two of whom were minors during the years at issue. With respect to any addition that was made to the trust, the trust instrument provided that each child could demand in writing payment of the lesser of $4,000 or the child's share of the addition. The demand power lapsed at the end of the calendar year in which the addition was made. For any child that was a minor, the trust provided that "the child's guardian may make such demand on behalf of the child." *Id.* at 83.

The Ninth Circuit held that the children's demand rights over trust contributions rendered the transfers present interests so as to qualify for the annual exclusion. In doing so, the court emphasized the beneficiaries' legal right to exercise the withdrawal right, even if such exercise was not likely as a practical matter:

> As we visualize the hypothetical situation, the child would inform the trustee that he demanded his share of the additions up to $4,000. The trustee would petition the court for the appointment of a legal guardian and then turn the funds over to the guardian. It would also seem possible for the parent to make the demand as natural guardian. This would involve the acquisition of property for the child rather than the management of the property. It would then be necessary for a legal guardian to be appointed

to take charge of the funds. The only time when the disability to sue would come into play, would be if the trustee disregarded the demand and committed a breach of trust. That would not, however, vitiate the demand.

All this is admittedly speculative since it is highly unlikely that a demand will ever be made or that if one is made, it would be made in this fashion. However, as a technical matter, we think a minor could make the demand.

* * * As a practical matter, it is likely that some, if not all, of the beneficiaries did not even know that they had any right to demand funds from the trust. They probably did not know when contributions were made to the trust or in what amounts. Even had they known, the substantial contributions were made toward the end of the year so that the time to make a demand was severely limited. Nobody had made a demand under the provision, and no distributions had been made. We think it unlikely that any demand ever would have been made.

All exclusions should be allowed under the *Perkins* test or the 'right to enjoy' test in *Gilmore*. Under *Perkins*, all that is necessary is to find that the demand could not be resisted. We interpret that to mean legally resisted and, going on that basis, we do not think the trustee would have any choice but to have a guardian appointed to take the property demanded.

* * *

Under the circumstances suggested in our case, it is doubtful that any demands will be made against the trust—yet the Commissioner always allowed the exclusion as to adult beneficiaries. There is nothing to indicate that it is any more likely that [adult child] will demand funds than that any other beneficiary will do so. The only distinction is that it might be easier for him to make such a demand. Since we conclude that the demand can be made by the others, it follows that the exclusion should also apply to them.

Id. at 87–88. The Service acquiesced to the Ninth Circuit decision. *See* Action on Dec., 1972 AOD LEXIS 112 (Jan. 14, 1972). Additionally, the Service later formally abandoned its position of disallowing the annual exclusion if no guardian had been appointed for a minor beneficiary and, instead, sanctioned application of the annual exclusion so long as (a) there existed no legal impediment to the appointment of a guardian and (b) the minor beneficiary could exercise the withdrawal right. *See* Rev. Rul. 73-405, 1973-2 C.B. 321.

In rulings following the *Crummey* decision, the Service emphasized the need for the beneficiary possessing a withdrawal right to have a meaningful opportunity to exercise it. In Revenue Ruling 81-7, 1981-1 C.B. 474, the Service disallowed the annual exclusion based on a beneficiary's withdrawal right over a contribution to a trust, where the right lapsed just two days after the contribution of which the beneficiary was provided no notice. The Service examined a more reasonable withdrawal right in Revenue Ruling 83-108, 1983-2 C.B. 167, one that lapsed 45 days after the contribution of which the trustee was required to provide notice within 10 days of the contribution. The Service allowed the annual exclusion for a transfer to the trust just two days prior to year end, even though the beneficiary was not provided notice of the withdrawal right until shortly after the new year. Thus, while the Ninth Circuit in *Crummey* did not appear overly concerned that the beneficiaries likely were not aware of their withdrawal rights, the conservative approach is to ensure that the beneficiaries are informed of each withdrawal right when it is created and that they are afforded a reasonable period to exercise their rights.[6]

The *Crummey* decision represented a powerful victory for taxpayers, who naturally sought to expand its reach. In *Estate of Cristofani v. Commissioner*, 97 T.C. 74 (1991), the taxpayers attempted to multiply the number of annual exclusions available to shield a transfer in trust from gift tax by providing withdrawal rights not only to the current trust beneficiaries (the donor's children), but also to those possessing only a contingent remainder interest in the trust (the donor's grandchildren). The Tax Court held in favor of the taxpayer, reasoning that the *Crummey* decision did not require the trust beneficiaries to possess a vested present interest or vested remainder interest in the trust in order for a withdrawal right to give rise to a present interest gift. *Id.* at 83. Rather, the court stressed that the contingent beneficiaries possessed the same legal rights to withdraw amounts from the trust as did the current trust beneficiaries:

> As discussed in *Crummey*, the likelihood that the beneficiary will actually receive present enjoyment of the property is not the test for determining whether a present interest was received. Rather, we must examine the ability of the beneficiaries, in a legal sense, to exercise their right to withdraw trust corpus, and the trustee's right to legally resist a beneficiary's demand for payment. *Crummey v. Commissioner*, 397 F.2d at 88. Based upon the language of the trust instrument and stipulations of the parties, we believe that each grandchild possessed the legal right to withdraw trust corpus and that the trustees would be unable to legally resist a grandchild's withdrawal demand. We note that there was no agreement or understanding between the decedent, the trustees, and the beneficiaries that the grandchildren would not exercise their withdrawal rights following a contribution to the Children's Trust.

Id; see also Estate of Kohlsaat v. Commissioner, T.C. Memo. 1997-212, 73 T.C.M. (CCH) 2732 (following *Estate of Cristofani* and permitting annual exclusions for withdrawal rights afforded to 16 contingent beneficiaries of transfer in trust).

The Service declined to appeal the *Cristofani* decision, and it issued a measured acquiescence to the result of the case only. *See* A.O.D. CC-1992-08, 1992 AOD LEXIS 9 (Mar. 23, 1992); A.O.D. CC-1996-010, 1996 AOD LEXIS 4 (July 15, 1996). Nonetheless, the Service signaled its intention to continue litigating cases "whose facts indicate that the substance of the transfers was merely to obtain annual exclusions and that no bona fide gift of a present interest was intended." A.O.D. CC-1996-010, 1996 AOD LEXIS 4 (July 15, 1996).

The *Crummey* and *Cristofani* decisions have rendered the future interest prohibition under § 2503(b) something of a farce. The withdrawal-right technique sanctioned by these decisions has functionally eliminated the impediment for the well advised, at the expense of the transaction costs of providing notice of withdrawal rights to beneficiaries and the minute risk that a beneficiary might actually exercise the right. Restricting the use of withdrawal rights to qualify transfers in trust for the annual exclusion has been a frequent topic of proposed legislative reform, with the latest recommendation coming from the Joint Committee on Taxation.[7]

---

[6] That said, courts have proven rather forgiving on these fronts. In *Estate of Cristofani v. Commissioner*, 97 T.C. 74 (1991), the Tax Court found a 15-day exercise period sufficient. And in *Estate of Holland v. Commissioner*, T.C. Memo. 1997-302, 73 T.C.M. (CCH) 3236, the Tax Court held that failure to provide the beneficiaries with written notice of their withdrawal rights was not fatal to the availability of the annual exclusion.

[7] *See* Joint Committee on Taxation, *Taxation of Wealth Transfers Within a Family: A Discussion of Selected Areas*

[C]   Transfers to Minors—§ 2503(c)

At a theoretical level, a transfer of property to a minor raises some concern as to whether the minor's legal inability to contract with respect to the property threatens the present interest requirement of § 2503(b). However, the Service dispelled any notion that an outright transfer of property to a minor constitutes the transfer of a future interest. "An unqualified and unrestricted gift to a minor, with or without the appointment of a legal guardian, is a gift of a present interest. . . ." Rev. Rul. 54-400, 1954-2 C.B. 319. This assurance notwithstanding, most donors do not find outright transfers to minors desirable for perhaps obvious reasons. Rather, donors often prefer some type of custodial arrangement, one that provides a third party with discretion over the use of the transferred property for the minor's benefit. Under the general principles of § 2503(b), such third-party discretion would render the transfer one of a future interest.

Yielding to the practical considerations motivating custodial transfers to minors, Congress enacted § 2503(c) as part of the 1954 Code.[8] This subsection provides that future interest characterization will not apply if a transfer to an individual under the age of 21 meets the following two conditions: (1) the property or the income it generates may be expended by or for the benefit of the donee prior to the donee attaining age 21, and (2) any portion of the property or income that is not so expended will pass to the donee upon attaining age 21 or, if the donee dies prior to that age, will be paid into the donee's estate or as the donee may appoint under a general power of appointment. If these requirements are satisfied, the annual exclusion is available to shield from taxation the entire amount of the transfer (opposed to only the value of a mandatory income interest under § 2503(b)). The thrust of § 2503(c) is to replicate an outright transfer of property to an adult while allowing a third party to control the funds until the donee attains age 21.

[1]   Expenditure Requirement

The expenditure requirement of § 2503(c) clearly permits a third party to exercise discretion in distributing funds to or for the benefit of the donee. However, the regulations warn that there can be "no substantial restrictions" on the exercise of such discretion. Treas. Reg. § 25.2503-4(b)(1). Limiting distributions to be made for the "support, care, education, comfort, and welfare," of the donee does not impose a substantial restriction on the exercise of discretion, due to the lack of objective limitations on the scope of "welfare" and similar terms. See Rev. Rul. 67-270, 1967-2 C.B. 349. Yet requiring the custodian or trustee to consider the resources otherwise available to the donee before making distributions runs afoul of the substantial restriction prohibition. See Rev. Rul. 69-345, 1969-1 C.B. 226. Furthermore, restricting distributions to defined purposes that are limited in scope, such as health care or education alone, violates the expenditure requirement of § 2503(c). See, e.g., Pettus v. Commissioner, 54 T.C. 112 (1970) (expenditures limited to "accident, illness, or other emergency").

for Possible Reform, JCX-23-08, at 46–49 (2008) (offering three separate proposals aimed at restricting the use of _Crummey_ withdrawal powers to exploit the annual exclusion).

[8] The Senate Report accompanying the legislation explained that "[g]ifts to minors are often hindered by the fact that it is not clear how such a gift can be made in trust or through a guardian for a minor's benefit other than as a future interest, and for future interests the [annual] exclusion is not available." S. Rep. No. 83-1622, at 127 (1954).

[2]   Distribution Requirement

Consistent with the theme of placing a custodial transfer on par with that of an outright gift to an adult, § 2503(c)(1) requires that the transferred property and its income pass to the donee at age 21. However, this requirement does not mean that the custodial or trust arrangement must terminate at that time. Rather, the donee only must be afforded the opportunity to withdraw the transferred funds at that point. In *Heidrich v. Commissioner*, 55 T.C. 746 (1971), the Tax Court determined that a beneficiary's continuing right to withdraw funds from the trust after attaining age 21 through a written demand satisfied the § 2503(c)(2)(A) requirement. Following the *Heidrich* decision, the Service announced that the distribution requirement would be satisfied even if the donee's right to withdraw the trust property lapsed after a defined period following the donee's attaining age 21. *See* Rev. Rul. 74-43, 1974-1 C.B. 285.

If the donee were to die prior to age 21, § 2503(c)(2) requires the property to be distributed to the donee's probate estate or pass pursuant to the donee's general power of appointment (the latter of which avoids subjecting the property to probate administration). Either option ensures that the transferred property will be included in the donee's gross estate for estate tax purposes.[9] If the terms of the transfer seek to qualify for § 2503(c) treatment through the granting of a general power of appointment to the minor, the power may be one exercisable during life or by will, and any state law limitation on the donee's legal ability to exercise the power will be disregarded. Treas. Reg. § 25.2503-4(b).

[3]   Treatment of Income Interests

Suppose a trust is created for the benefit of a minor permitting the trustee to expend the trust property or its income for the donee's benefit until attaining age 21, at which point any accumulated income remaining in the trust would be distributed to her outright. The trust corpus would continue to be held in trust until the donee attained age 30. Does the transfer comply with the distribution requirement under § 2503(c)(2)(A)? In other words, can an income interest in transferred property be treated as an independent property interest for purposes of the § 2503(c) present-interest safe harbor, when the statute refers to "property and the income therefrom"? The Third Circuit in *Commissioner v. Herr*, 303 F.2d 780 (3d Cir. 1962) concluded that it could, and thus permitted an annual exclusion under § 2503(c) in a trust similar to the hypothetical above as to the income interest only. The Service acquiesced to the approach of the *Herr* decision through Revenue Ruling 68-670, 1968-2 C.B. 413, and the Regulations now reflect this approach. *See* Treas. Reg. § 25.2503-4(c).

The taxpayer in *Estate of Levine*, 526 F.2d 717 (2d Cir. 1975), attempted to bootstrap a pre-21 discretionary income interest (which qualifies as a present interest in property under *Herr*) with a post-21 mandatory income interest in trust property (which, had it commenced immediately, would have constituted a present interest under § 2503(b)) in order to claim an annual exclusion for the entire income interest. The Second Circuit rejected this attempted combination of income interests, and instead evaluated the post-21 mandatory income stream in isolation. Because the latter income interest, by definition, would not commence until years after the transfer, the court determined that the interest constituted a future interest in property for which the annual exclusion was not available.

---

[9] Inclusion of property in a decedent's gross estate on account of the decedent's possession of a power of appointment is addressed in Chapter 14.

[4]   Facilitation of UGMA/UTMA Accounts

Section 2503(c) has shaped the Uniform Gift to Minors Act and the Uniform Transfers to Minors Act, some version of which has been enacted in each state. While these statutory custodial arrangements simplify annual-exclusion transfers to minors, they can create estate tax pitfalls if the donor names herself as custodian.[10] The primary drawback of these transfers is the requirement that the property be made available outright to the donee upon attaining age 21. Donors who desire for the donee to reach a more mature age prior to receiving property outright but who nonetheless desire to exclude the transfer in full under § 2503(b) thus are left with the withdrawal-right technique sanctioned in the *Crummey* case.

[D]   Leveraging the Annual Exclusion

Given that the annual exclusion under § 2503(b) offers an avenue to transfer wealth free of estate and gift taxation, taxpayers naturally have sought to employ the exclusion as expansively as possible. These attempts follow two routes: (1) multiplying the number of exclusions in a given year through the use of intermediaries or (2) front-loading multiple years' exclusions into one transfer.

[1]   Intentional Use of Intermediaries

Suppose *Parent* wishes to transfer $130,000 to *Child* this year. Armed with the knowledge that she can transfer $13,000 to any number of donees each year without gift tax consequence, *Parent* suggests making $13,000 transfers to nine of her friends, who can then turn around and transfer such amount to *Child* (in addition to *Parent's* $13,000 gift to *Child*). Hopefully, you would discourage *Parent* from following this approach. In *Heyen v. United States*, 945 F.2d 359 (10th Cir. 1991), the taxpayer transferred bank stock (valued at less than the then-available $10,000 annual exclusion) to 29 individuals, some of whom were employees of the bank. All but two of 29 then endorsed blank stock certificates permitting the stock to be reissued to members of the taxpayer's family. The Tenth Circuit affirmed the district court's treatment of 27 of the 29 transfers as indirect gifts to the members of the taxpayer's family who ultimately received the stock. In addition, the Court of Appeals affirmed the imposition of a civil fraud penalty due to the taxpayer's intent to evade gift tax by not disclosing the purported annual exclusion transfers on her gift tax return.

[2]   Front-Loading of Multiple Years' Exclusions

[a]   Use of Loans That Are Later Forgiven

Suppose that *Parent* opts for a different approach. She transfers $13,000 outright to *Child* and, in addition, loans *Child* $117,000. The loan is memorialized in a promissory note, which calls for the payment of adequate interest so as to avoid § 7872. In each of the next nine years, *Parent* forgives $13,000 of the principal balance until the loan is satisfied. If the loan is respected, then *Parent* has effectively transferred $130,000 to *Child* in one year without gift tax consequence.

The critical issue is whether the loan will be respected. Assuming that the parties have

---

[10]   In that situation, the property likely will be included in the donor's gross estate under § 2036(a)(2) or § 2038. This possibility is discussed in Chapter 11.

created a bona fide debt instrument, there appears to be nothing abusive about the arrangement. If *Parent* were to die before the note is satisfied, then the value of the debt obligation would be included in her gross estate under § 2033. On the other hand, if *Parent* never possessed an intention to have *Child* make payments pursuant to the promissory note, then the debt obligation may be disregarded for transfer tax purposes.

An instructive case on this point is the Second Circuit's decision in *Estate of Maxwell v. Commissioner*, 3 F.3d 591 (2d Cir. 1993). The decedent in that case sold her residence to her son and daughter-in-law for a stated price of $270,000, which the court accepted as the fair market value of the property. No cash changed hands, however. The son and daughter-in-law executed a $250,000 promissory note secured by the residence in favor of the decedent, and the decedent forgave the remaining $20,000 (twice the prevailing annual gift tax exclusion) owed on the sale price. The decedent continued to occupy the residence under lease, and her purported rent payments largely cancelled out the interest due on the promissory note. The decedent's son and daughter-in-law never actually made a payment of principal; rather, the decedent forgave $20,000 of the principal each year, and then cancelled the remaining balance through her will. While the precise issue in the case was whether the decedent had received adequate and full consideration for the transfer so as to avoid the application of § 2036(a)(1),[11] this issue turned in part on whether the promissory note that she received on the transfer constituted consideration of any kind. The Second Circuit phrased the relevant inquiry as follows: "The question is whether [the note] is actually what it purports to be—a bona fide instrument of indebtedness—or whether it is a facade." *Id.* at 595. Relying on the Tax Court's finding of an understanding between the parties that the loan would never be repaid, the Second Circuit determined that the note did not provide the decedent with consideration.

The Service has taken the position that a pre-arranged plan to forgive notes received upon the transfer of property renders the transaction a gift. *See* Rev. Rul. 77-299, 1977-2 C.B. 343; *see also* Deal v. Commissioner, 29 T.C. 730 (1958) (finding that promissory notes were not intended to be enforced and therefore did not provide consideration for the transfer). However, other cases have held that the transferor's intention to forgive the balance on a loan does not automatically disqualify the promissory note from constituting consideration for the transfer. *See* Haygood v. Commissioner, 42 T.C. 936 (1964); Estate of Kelley v. Commissioner, 63 T.C. 321 (1974).

[b] Section 529 Plans

In the context of § 529 pre-paid college tuition plans or college savings accounts (which receive preferential income tax treatment), Congress has expressly authorized front-loading of annual exclusion transfers. Section 529(c)(2)(B) provides that a donor can elect to treat aggregate contributions to such a plan or account in a given year as being made ratably over a five-year period. [Of course, a contribution to 529 plan normally would be disqualified from the annual exclusion as a future interest in property, but § 529(c)(2)(A)(i) suspends the future interest rule in this context.] In this manner, a parent may contribute $65,000 to a § 529 plan in one year without gift tax consequence. However, in doing so, the donor has exhausted her annual exclusion for the next five years.

---

[11] Inclusion of transferred property in the decedent's gross estate based on retained beneficial enjoyment under § 2036(a)(1) is addressed in Chapter 10.

[E]   A Note on Uncleared Checks

In order to take advantage of the annual exclusion under § 2503(b) for a given calendar year, it is critical that the gift be completed before year end. Taxpayers often find themselves scrambling to complete their annual exclusion gifts before the end of the calendar year, and a frequent issue that arises in this context is whether the delivery of a check will suffice.

Recall that if a donor makes a gift by way of check prior to her death, such amount nonetheless will be included in the donor's gross estate under § 2033 if the check did not clear the donor's bank account prior to her death.[12] The justification for inclusion rests in the donor's ability to revoke the transfer prior to the check being honored by the drawee bank. In *Metzger v. Commissioner*, 38 F.3d 118 (4th Cir. 1994), the Fourth Circuit addressed a similar issue in the gift tax setting. The Fourth Circuit determined that a check delivered to the donee prior to the year end and deposited by the donee before such time, but which did not clear the donor's bank until the following year, would relate back to the date the check was deposited so long as: (1) the donor intended to make a gift; (2) delivery of the check was unconditional; and (3) the donee presented the check for deposit within a reasonable time of issuance. *Id.* at 123. The Service indicated its intention to follow the *Metzger* decision in Revenue Ruling 96-56, 1996-2 C.B. 161. Hence, if annual exclusion gifts are made through the issuance of standard checks, the donees must deposit the checks prior to the end of the calendar year in order to not waste the donor's annual exclusion for that year (or, perhaps more practically, in order to preserve their ability to receive another annual exclusion gift in the following year).

§ 5.02   PAYMENT OF TUITION AND MEDICAL EXPENSES

Concern over the potential gift tax consequences resulting from the payment of tuition for a child who had attained the age of majority or the payment of medical expenses on behalf of elderly family members spurned Congress to enact § 2503(e) as part of the Economic Recovery Tax Act of 1981.[13] The section provides that a "qualified transfer" shall not be treated as a transfer of property by gift,[14] and a "qualified transfer" is defined to include (1) a payment of tuition to an educational organization and (2) a payment to a medical care provider. *See* IRC § 2503(e)(2). The exclusion for payments of tuition or medical care expenses applies in addition to the annual exclusion under § 2503(b), and is not limited in amount. Furthermore, the excluded payments can be made by anyone for the benefit of any other—that is, the relationship between the donor and the donee is irrelevant. *See* Treas. Reg. § 25.2503-6(a). Indeed, apart from the definition of a qualified transfer, the most significant limitation prescribed in § 2503(e) is the method of payment. To avoid problems of tracing in ensuring that the transfer was made for the intended purpose, § 2503(e)(2) requires that the payment be made directly to the educational institution or the medical care provider. A reimbursement provided to an individual who has paid or will pay the same expenses does not qualify for the exclusion. *See* Treas. Reg. § 25.2503-6(c), Ex. 4.

---

[12] See discussion in § 2.02.

[13] *See* H.R. Rep. No. 97-201, at 193 (1981) (stating that "such payments should be exempt from gift taxes without regard to the amount paid for such purposes").

[14] In addition, such payments if made to a "skip person" are exempt from the imposition of GST tax. *See* IRC § 2642(c)(1), (c)(3)(B) (which provides the exemption through the assignment of a zero inclusion ratio for such transfers). The GST tax base is discussed in Chapter 21.

The exclusion for payments of tuition is available for full-time or part-time students at an educational organization as defined in § 170(b)(1)(A)(ii). The exclusion is limited to tuition only; related costs of education such as books, supplies, and housing are not covered. *See* Treas. Reg. § 25.2503-6(b)(2). Note, however, that payments of such ancillary expenses may be excluded if they fall within the transferor's state-law obligation to support the transferee.

The exclusion for the payment of medical care expenses is limited to payments for medical care as defined in § 213(d), but includes amounts paid for medical insurance on behalf of a donee. *See* Treas. Reg. § 25.2503-6(b)(3). However, the exclusion is not available for the payment of medical expenses that are reimbursed by the donee's insurance. This creates the curious possibility of an excluded transfer retroactively losing its exemption if a later insurance reimbursement is received by the donee. To avoid complications relating to the annual reporting requirement of the gift tax in this setting, the gift is treated as occurring on the date the reimbursement is received by the donee. *Id.*

§ 5.03   POLITICAL CONTRIBUTIONS

Following years of controversy over whether transfers to political organizations constituted gifts under § 2511[15] and, if so, the application of the annual exclusion to such transfers,[16] Congress enacted § 2501(a)(4) in 1975 to exclude from the gift tax base transfers to and for the use of a political organization as defined in § 527(e)(1). The motivation for the express exclusion was the congressional belief that "the tax system should not be used to reduce or restrict political contributions." H.R. Rep. No. 93-1502, at 110 (1974). That purpose notwithstanding, Congress failed to legislate a parallel exemption under the estate tax. Hence, only lifetime transfers to political organizations avoid federal transfer taxation.

§ 5.04   STUDY PROBLEMS

1. A client calls you on December 31, seeking confirmation that he can complete his annual exclusion gifts to his children by mailing all of them checks for $13,000. What is your advice? Is there any additional information you would like to request from your client?

2. *Parent* purchases for *Child* a $20,000 single-premium annuity that cannot be assigned or surrendered for value. The annuity provides for payments to commence when *Child*,

---

[15] *See, e.g.*, Stern v. United States, 436 F.2d 1327 (5th Cir. 1971) (holding that transfers to political organizations did not constitute taxable gifts on the basis that they were made for adequate and full consideration under Reg. § 25.2512-8 because they furthered the personal and property interests of the transferor); Carson v. Commissioner, 71 T.C. 252 (1978), *aff'd*, 641 F.2d 864 (10th Cir. 1981) (divided Tax Court found that gift tax was not intended to apply to political contributions because the contribution was made to further the contributor's own social or political interests); Du Pont v. United States, 97 F. Supp. 944 (D. Del. 1951) (finding that contributions to political organization constituted taxable gifts because the purported benefit of the contribution was not shared by the contributor alone); Rev. Rul. 72-583, 1972-2 C.B. 534 (Service announcing its intention not to follow the *Stern* case outside of the Fifth Circuit).

[16] *See, e.g.*, Rev. Rul. 77-131, 1977-1 C.B. 295 (contributions to several political committees supporting the same candidates were not to separate donees for purposes of the annual exclusion); Rev. Rul. 74-199, 1974-1 C.B. 285 (detailing evidentiary standard for establishing when political organizations will be regarded as separate donees for purposes of the annual exclusion); Rev. Rul. 72-355, 1972-2 C.B. 532 (illustrating the circumstances under which political organizations will be regarded as separate donees for purposes of the annual exclusion).

now age 16, attains age 35. Does the annual exclusion apply to *Parent*'s purchase of the annuity?

3. *Parent* transfers $20,000 in trust for the benefit of *Child*. The trust terms provide that all income is to be accumulated and added to principal, until *Child* attains age 35. At that point, regular payments of income and, if necessary, principal will be made to *Child* for his lifetime. Upon *Child's* death, the trust is to distribute to *Child's* then-living issue. Does the annual exclusion apply to *Parent's* funding of the trust?

4. Same as Problem 3, except *Parent* funds the trust with $100,000 and the trust provides that *Child*, *Child's* two children, and *Child's* spouse each may withdraw up to $13,000 within 30 days of *Parent's* transfer.

5. Following *Parent's* contribution in Problem 4, the 30-day period expires with no one having exercised his or her withdrawal right. Should the inaction on the part of the beneficiaries trigger any transfer tax consequence?

6. Your client wants to create a trust for his two daughters, ages six and eight respectively. He proposes the following provisions: (1) the trust income shall be distributed to them or expended for their benefit in equal shares; (2) principal may not be invaded until the youngest daughter attains age 21, at which time the trustee is authorized to make distributions of principal to either daughter for the recipient's health, education, support, and maintenance; (3) when the youngest child attains age 35, the remaining trust property is to be distributed to them in equal shares.

    Does any portion of the transfer qualify for the annual exclusion? If your client wanted to qualify the entire transfer in trust for the annual exclusion, what changes would be necessary?

7. *Godmother* makes the following payments to or for the benefit of *Godson*:

    -   $40,000 tuition to his college (paying the invoice directly);

    -   $10,000 payment to college student housing;

    -   $6,000 to *Godson* to cover his medical insurance premiums;

    -   $15,000 for living expenses.

    Which, if any, of these payments may be excluded from the gift tax base?

8. *Grandfather* wants to give *Granddaughter* $100,000 this year for her to start a fashion design business. He is not interested in investing in the business, but rather wants this amount to represent *Granddaughter's* own equity. At the same time, *Grandfather* does not want the transaction to trigger gift tax consequences. Do you have any advice?

Chapter 6

TRANSFERS IN SATISFACTION OF MARITAL OR SUPPORT OBLIGATIONS

Internal Revenue Code: §§ 2043(b), 2053(a)(3), (c)(1)(A), 2512(b), 2516
Treasury Regulations: § 25.2512-8

The treatment of transfers for consideration is crucial in determining the scope of the transfer tax base. Although couched in terms of a valuation provision, § 2512(b) serves a definitional role by providing that a transfer constitutes a gift only to the extent that the property was transferred for "less than an adequate and full consideration in money or money's worth."[1] A similar operative rule applies under the estate tax. Section 2053(a)(3) affords a deduction from the gross estate for claims against the decedent's probate estate. When such claims are based upon "a promise made or entered into by the decedent," the deduction is limited to the amount attributable to a bona fide contract "for an adequate and full consideration in money or money's worth." IRC § 2053(c)(1)(A). Transfers for consideration under the estate tax and gift tax therefore share a common approach: only transfers that do not operate to deplete the transferor's transfer tax base are exempt from taxation.[2] Consistent with this principle, intangible benefits received as consideration for a lifetime transfer do not insulate the transfer from gift taxation, even though such benefits may render the transfer enforceable by the transferee as a matter of state law. *See* Treas. Reg. § 25.2512-8 ("A consideration not reducible to a value in money or money's worth, as love and affection, promise of marriage, etc., is to be wholly disregarded, and the entire value of the property transferred constitutes the amount of the gift.").

With these foundational principles in mind, this chapter examines the tax treatment of transfers made in exchange for the release of marital rights and legal obligations of support. From a doctrinal standpoint, the heart of this inquiry lies in determining when the release of

---

[1] Both the transferred property and the consideration received are to be determined according to the willing-buyer, willing-seller standard. *See* Treas. Reg. § 25.2512-8 (noting that a gift will arise if the value of the transferred property "exceeds the value in money or money's worth of the consideration given therefor"). As a general rule, the property is valued for gift tax purposes at "the price at which such property would change hands between a willing buyer and a willing seller, neither being under any compulsion to buy or to sell, and both having reasonable knowledge of relevant facts." Treas. Reg. § 25.2512-1.

[2] The main exception to this general rule can be found in Reg. § 25.2512-8, which presumes that transfers made "in the ordinary course of business" are exempt from gift tax consequences. So long as the transfer was "bona fide, at arm's length, and free from any donative intent," the regulations presume the transferor received adequate and full consideration in money or money's worth, notwithstanding any actual deficiency in the objective value of the consideration received. In this manner, a transferor who receives the bad end of a bargain in an arm's length transaction does not have to suffer the additional indignity of having to pay gift tax on the amount of lost value.

such legal rights will supply "adequate and full consideration in money or money's worth" for estate and gift tax purposes.

§ 6.01   TRANSFERS IN DISCHARGE OF MARITAL RIGHTS

[A]   Estate Tax Treatment

Section 2034 confirms that a decedent's estate is not entitled to exclude from the gross estate property owned by the decedent to the extent of a surviving spouse's dower or curtesy interest (or statutory rights in lieu of such common-law interests) in such property. In order to prevent spouses from circumventing the application of § 2034 through contractual arrangements, § 2043(b)(1) provides that the relinquishment of (a) dower or curtesy interests in the decedent's property, (b) statutory rights created in lieu of dower or curtesy, or (c) "other marital rights" in the decedent's property or estate, shall not be considered to have provided the decedent with consideration in money or money's worth "to any extent." An unfulfilled contractual obligation to transfer property in exchange for the release of marital rights therefore will not give rise to a deduction from a decedent's gross estate, as deductible claims based on a promise or agreement must be supported by an adequate and full consideration in money or money's worth.[3] IRC § 2053(a)(3), (c)(1)(A). Taken together, §§ 2034 and 2043(b)(1) ensure that post-mortem transfers in satisfaction of the transferee spouse's marital rights—whether pursuant to state law or private agreement—are not excluded from the transfer tax base.

[B]   Gift Tax Treatment

One approach to resolving the gift tax treatment of transfers in satisfaction of an individual's inchoate marital rights in property of his spouse is to focus on whether the transfer augments the transferor spouse's future gross estate. From this estate-depletion perspective, the transaction cannot be treated as having been made for consideration. When spouses marry and one spouse acquires inchoate rights in the property of the other, the creation of such inchoate rights is not accompanied by any additional consideration supplied to the propertied spouse. Rather, the marriage simply creates the prospect of certain transfers being made to the other spouse upon dissolution of the marriage, whether by reason of death or divorce. Thus, the creation of inchoate spousal rights in property can be seen as a contingent estate-depleting event. A transfer of property in exchange for the release of such marital property rights therefore serves only to accelerate or solidify the resulting estate depletion. *See* Estate of Herrmann v. Commissioner, 85 F.3d 1032, 1041 (2d Cir. 1996) (addressing transfer in exchange for release of right to equitable distribution upon divorce, and observing that "[w]hat [the transferee] gave up added nothing to her husband's estate; what [the transferee] received depleted it").

While the estate-depletion rationale focuses on interpreting the estate and gift taxes in a uniform structural manner, courts have stressed textual consistency in reconciling the two tax bases. *See* Estate of Sanford v. Commissioner, 308 U.S. 39, 44 (1939) (noting the role of the gift

---

[3] While the availability of the marital deduction may moot the issue in certain instances, it will not do so categorically. Such transfers may be made incident to divorce, in which case the marital deduction is no longer available. Even if transfers are made to a surviving spouse, such transfers may not qualify for the marital deduction due to the terminable interest rule of § 2056(b)(1). The marital deduction is addressed in Chapter 19.

tax to supplement the estate tax, and instructing that "[t]he two are in pari materia and must be construed together"). The importance of interpreting "adequate and full consideration in money or money's worth" consistently under the estate tax and gift tax proved determinative to the Supreme Court's examination of the gift tax consequences of property transferred pursuant to an antenuptial agreement in *Merrill v. Fahs*, 324 U.S. 308 (1945).

In *Merrill*, a husband funded a trust for the benefit of his wife in exchange for the wife's agreement to release her marital rights in the husband's property. In addressing whether the wife's release supplied adequate and full consideration in money or money's worth for the transfer under the predecessor of § 2512(b), the Court concluded that the gift tax treatment of the release of marital rights should match that under the estate tax. That is, the release of such rights supplied no consideration for gift tax purposes:

> We believe that there is every reason for giving the same words in the gift tax the same reading. Correlation of the gift tax and the estate tax still requires legislative intervention. But to interpret the same phrases in the two taxes concerning the same subject matter in different ways where obvious reasons do not compel divergent treatment is to introduce another and needless complexity into this already irksome situation. Here strong reasons urge identical construction. To hold otherwise would encourage tax avoidance. And it would not fulfill the purpose of the gift tax in discouraging family settlements so as to avoid high income surtaxes. There is thus every reason in this case to construe the provisions of both taxes harmoniously.

Id. at 313 (citations and footnote omitted).

The Supreme Court's holding in *Merrill* has been incorporated into regulatory guidance, which now provides that "a relinquishment or promised relinquishment of dower or curtesy, or of a statutory estate created in lieu of dower or curtesy, or of other marital rights in the spouse's property or estate, shall not be considered to any extent a consideration 'in money or money's worth.'" Treas. Reg. § 25.2512-8. Hence, § 2512(b), as amplified through the regulations, supplies a rule identical to that of § 2043(b)(1) under the estate tax.

[C] Scope of "Marital Rights" Precluded from Supplying Consideration

The scope of marital rights in property that are precluded from constituting consideration for a transfer for purposes of §§ 2512(b) and 2043(b)(1) does not extend to a vested or presently enforceable right that one spouse has in the property of another. *See* Estate of Carli v. Commissioner, 84 T.C. 649 (1985) (explaining that the phrase "other marital rights" as employed in § 2043(b)(1) extends only to those rights conferred to a surviving spouse by local law upon the death of his or her spouse, and does not apply to enforceable rights to property during the spouse's joint lifetimes); *see also* Glen v. Commissioner, 45 T.C. 323 (1966) (holding that § 2043(b) does not apply to the relinquishment of a presently enforceable claim to an outright portion of a spouse's property upon divorce). As community property titled in the name of one spouse is beneficially owned by both spouses equally for transfer tax purposes, a spouse's release of his interest in community property will supply consideration for transfer tax purposes. *See Estate of Carli*, 84 T.C. at 658 (holding that wife's relinquishment of her community property rights in husband's future earnings constituted consideration for transfer in her favor).

In addition, the scope of "marital rights" that are precluded from supplying consideration under §§ 2512(b) and 2043(b)(1) is limited to inchoate rights in the other spouse's property. Although not readily clear from a textual standpoint, the term does not extend to a legal obligation of support owed by one spouse to another. *See* Rev. Rul. 68-379, 1968-2 C.B. 414 (explaining that a release of support rights does not constitute a release of "other marital rights" for purposes of Reg. § 25.2512-8). Rather, as discussed in § 6.04 below, the release of support rights constitutes consideration for transfer tax purposes to the extent of their commuted value.

§ 6.02   TRANSFERS EXTINGUISHING MARITAL RIGHTS INCIDENT TO SEPARATION OR DIVORCE

[A]   The *Harris* Decision

In *Harris v. Commissioner*, 340 U.S. 106 (1950), the Supreme Court took up the question of whether its holding in *Merrill* extended to transfers made between spouses in settlement of their property rights occasioned by reason of their divorce. The property settlement agreement the spouses executed called for transfers from each spouse to the other, with the result being an approximate net transfer of $100,000 from wife to husband. However, the transfers under the agreement were conditioned on the issuance of a divorce decree, and the agreement provided that its terms had to be submitted to the court for approval.

The Court in *Harris* resolved the issue of whether the net transfer from the wife was supported by consideration under § 2512(b) again by reference to the treatment of such transfers under the estate tax. In particular, the Court noted that a deduction for a claim against the estate under § 2053(a)(3) required that it be supported by "adequate and full consideration in money or money's worth"—which the release of marital rights could not provide under § 2043(b)(1)—only when the claim was founded upon a "promise or agreement." *See* IRC § 2053(c)(1)(A). Conceding that the transaction therefore would have given rise to a taxable gift from the wife if based on the property settlement agreement alone, *see Harris*, 340 U.S. at 109, the Court determined that the transaction fell outside of the "promise or agreement" realm because the transfers ultimately were founded upon the judicial decree of divorce. *See id.* at 111–12 ("If 'the transfer' is effected by court decree, no 'promise or agreement' of the parties is the operative fact. In no realistic sense is a court decree a 'promise or agreement' between the parties to a litigation."). In emphasizing this distinction, the Court appeared to place considerable weight on the possibility that a reviewing court might modify the terms of the property settlement before incorporating the terms of the agreement into the divorce decree. *See id.* at 110.

The reasoning of the *Harris* decision is suspect. Whether the release of marital rights in property constitutes consideration under § 2512(b) should focus on the nature of the property interest relinquished, not the means by which the relinquishment took place. Perhaps what motivated the Court to endorse the dubious distinction between court-decreed transfers and those pursuant to private agreement was the belief that the triggering circumstance of divorce tempered concerns over such transfers being employed to undermine the transfer tax base. *See* Estate of Herrmann v. Commissioner, 85 F.3d 1032, 1040 (2d Cir. 1996) (noting that the prospect of tax avoidance is "rendered negligible by the arms-length nature of the unhappy context"). After all, divorce is a rather drastic means of achieving a gift or estate tax advantage.

[B] Section 2516(1)

Not long after the Supreme Court's decision in *Harris*, Congress enacted § 2516 as part of the Internal Revenue Code of 1954 to eliminate the distinction between property settlements effected pursuant to court decree or private agreement. In its current form, § 2516 provides that if (a) spouses enter into a written agreement concerning their marital and property rights and (b) divorce occurs within a three-year window beginning one year prior to the agreement's execution and ending two years thereafter, any transfer made pursuant to the agreement in settlement of the transferee spouse's marital or property rights will be considered to have been made for an adequate and full consideration in money or money's worth.[4] IRC § 2516(1). Whether the agreement is approved or incorporated into a divorce decree is expressly declared irrelevant. Hence, if a transfer complies with the terms of § 2516, it will have no gift tax consequence.

In 1984, Congress amended § 2043(b) to supply a parallel rule for the estate tax. While the release of marital rights does not supply consideration for estate tax purposes as a general rule, § 2043(b)(2) provides that transfers that comply with § 2516(1) will be treated as made for an adequate and full consideration in money or money's worth for purposes of § 2053(a)(3). Accordingly, post-mortem transfers made pursuant to an agreement that satisfies § 2516(1) can be deducted from the decedent-spouse's gross estate—a provision that is critical given that the estate tax marital deduction will not be available when the marriage ends in divorce.

[C] The Lasting Relevance of *Harris*

While the enactment of § 2516(1) supersedes the holding of the *Harris* decision in the vast majority of cases concerning settlements of property rights pursuant to divorce, the statute does not overrule the *Harris* case entirely. Rather, in instances in which § 2516(1) does not apply—perhaps because the couple's divorce is not finalized within the three-year window of the agreement as dictated by the statute or because the property settlement agreement is not reduced to writing—the *Harris* precedent will remain available to potentially shield such transfers from gift tax consequence. The Service has indicated that it will follow *Harris* outside the § 2516(1) context, but only in situations where the divorce court has the power to decree a settlement of all property rights or to vary the terms of the parties' prior settlement agreement. Rev. Rul. 60-160, 1960-1 C.B. 374. Courts have confirmed this limitation on the backstop relief offered by the *Harris* decision. *See, e.g.*, Estate of Barrett v. Commissioner, 56 T.C. 1312 (1971) (finding *Harris* inapplicable because the divorce court did not have the power to approve, disapprove, or modify the property settlement agreement absent evidence of fraud or other extreme circumstances).

§ 6.03 TRANSFERS IN DISCHARGE OF SUPPORT OBLIGATIONS

[A] General Principles

The transfer tax treatment of payments made pursuant to a legal obligation of support highlights the limits of the estate-depletion approach to evaluating transfers for consideration. When an individual legally obligates himself to support another—whether by reason of

---

[4] As discussed in § 6.03 below, § 2516 provides a similar rule for transfers providing a reasonable allowance for the support of issue of the marriage during minority.

marriage, procreation, or adoption—that act does not serve to augment his future gross estate. Nonetheless, payments made pursuant to the support obligation are not subject to the gift tax. The gift tax does not reach personal consumption, and transfers made for the benefit of an individual whom the transferor is legally obligated to support can be reasonably viewed as falling within the personal consumption realm.

Because expenditures made pursuant to a support obligation do not implicate the gift tax, transfers of property made in exchange for a release of the legal obligation of support should be afforded the same treatment. In effect, transfers made to discharge a support obligation represent nothing more than an acceleration of payments that would have been exempt from the gift tax when made. *See* E.T. 19, 1946-2 C.B. 166, 168 (characterizing payments made in lieu of support rights as "merely . . . the liquidation of a presently existing obligation"). From a structural standpoint, transfers in discharge of support obligations will avoid gift taxation only if the transferee's release of his support rights is regarded as providing the transferor with consideration in money or money's worth under § 2512(b). The Service confirmed this result in Revenue Ruling 68-379, 1968-2 C.B. 414, by holding that a wife's release of her husband's support obligation in exchange for a transfer of property supplied consideration under § 2512(b) to the extent of the value of her support rights. *See also* Estate of Herrmann v. Commissioner, 85 F.3d 1032 (2d Cir. 1996) (recognizing that the release of spousal support rights can constitute consideration for purposes of the estate and gift taxes); Estate of Kosow v. Commissioner, 45 F.3d 1524 (11th Cir. 1995) (holding that the release of support rights supplied adequate and full consideration in money or money's worth under § 2053). Valuation of the released support rights assumes critical importance in this context, as any transfer in excess of the value of the support obligation will constitute a gift. *See* Rev. Rul. 77-314, 1977-2 C.B. 349 (providing examples of transfers in trust to discharge support rights owed to a spouse).

[B]   Section 2516(2)

As applied to transfers made in discharge of support obligations owed to minors, § 2516 confirms the general rule that transfers in exchange for the release of support obligations are supported by consideration. In particular, § 2516(2) provides that transfers made pursuant to a written agreement relating to marital and property rights (where divorce occurs within the requisite three-year window of such agreement) will be presumed to have been made for an adequate and full consideration in money or money's worth to the extent made to provide a "reasonable allowance" for the support of issue of the marriage during minority.

While § 2516(2) provides a safe harbor of presumed consideration for transfers in discharge of support obligations owed to minor children that are made incident to separation or divorce, the safe harbor applies for gift tax purposes only. The safe harbor of presumed sufficient consideration offered by § 2043(b)(2) extends only to transfers that satisfy the terms of § 2516(1) relating to transfers to a spouse in settlement of marital or property rights. The § 2043(b)(2) safe harbor does not extend to transfers in discharge of support that comply with § 2516(2).[5]

---

[5] This limitation can be explained in terms of the structure of § 2043(b). Section 2043(b)(1) provides as a general rule that transfers of dower or curtesy interests, or other statutory rights created in lieu of such interests, or other marital rights in the decedent's estate or property, will not be regarded as providing consideration for estate tax purposes. Hence, the exception to this general rule provided by § 2043(b)(2) naturally would be limited to transfers in discharge

However, the safe harbor for payments in discharge of support obligations likely is not necessary, as such a transfer is supported by consideration in money or money's worth under general principles. Hence, to the extent a decedent became presently obligated to make payments in discharge of a legal support obligation, transfers made in satisfaction of that agreement following the decedent's death should be entitled to the deduction for enforceable claims under § 2053(a)(3). *See* Estate of Hundley v. Commissioner, 52 T.C. 495 (1969), *aff'd*, 435 F.2d 1311 (4th Cir. 1971) (deduction under § 2053(a)(3) allowed for payments to be made in exchange for wife's release of then-existing support rights); Rev. Rul. 71-67, 1971-1 C.B. 271 (commuted value of support rights relinquished per separation agreement allowed as a deduction for claim against the estate).

§ 6.04   TRANSFERS TO ADULT CHILDREN INCIDENT TO DIVORCE

Transfers to adult children cannot be supported by consideration in the form of a release of support rights, as a parent's support obligation terminates upon the child's attaining the age of majority. Hence, a spouse's transfer to an adult child made pursuant to a property settlement agreement will trigger the estate tax. Can this result be avoided through an expansive application of the *Harris* decision? For example, suppose that a property settlement agreement submitted to a divorce court for its approval and potential modification requires one spouse to create trusts for the benefit of the couple's adult children. Does the transfer avoid gift taxation (or estate taxation if satisfied after the spouse's death) on the basis that it was made pursuant to the judicial decree as opposed to a "promise or agreement" as contemplated under § 2053(c)(1)(A)? Stated differently, does the *Harris* decision provide a carte-blanche opportunity for individuals to shield transfers from gift and estate taxation by rendering them subject to court approval and modification?

Not surprisingly, courts have soundly rejected an expansive interpretation of the *Harris* decision. The Tax Court in *Hooker v. Commissioner*, 10 T.C. 388, 392 (1948), explained that the gift tax could not be sidestepped "by the clever process of entering into an agreement to make a transfer, supported by an inadequate money consideration, and then making the transfer to satisfy a judgment on the agreement." The Fifth Circuit affirmed, and several other courts have followed suit. *See* Hooker v. Commissioner, 174 F.2d 863 (5th Cir. 1949); Rosenthal v. Commissioner, 205 F.2d 505 (2d Cir. 1953); Wiedemann v. Commissioner, 26 T.C. 565 (1956).

There exists one limited avenue through which a transfer for the benefit of an adult child will be exempt from gift tax or, if satisfied after death, will be deductible from the decedent's gross estate. If the transfer was made in exchange for a spouse's voluntary reduction in payments made in discharge of marital rights or support obligations, the transfer will be supported by consideration to the extent of such reduction. *See* Glen v. Commissioner, 45 T.C. 323 (1966) (creation of trust for adult child in exchange for wife's relinquishment of support rights held to be supported by consideration); Rev. Rul. 77-314, 1977-2 C.B. 349 (holding in *Situation 2* that a transfer of an interest in trust income to an adult child was not a taxable gift to the extent of the reduced income interest accepted by spouse in satisfaction of support rights); Rev. Rul. 79-363, 1979-2 C.B. 345 (holding that § 2516(1) applies to transfers to a third person to the extent spouse "specifically and deliberately" released support rights to obtain the transfer); *see*

---

of marital rights addressed in § 2516(1)—not to the discharge of support obligations which are not considered as marital rights in property in the first place.

also Spruance v. Commissioner, 60 T.C. 141 (1973), *aff'd*, 505 F.2d 731 (3d Cir. 1974) (finding that taxpayer had failed to produce sufficient evidence that taxpayer's former spouse had bargained away a portion of support rights in exchange for transfer to adult children). However, the gift tax is not avoided in this context entirely. Rather, the spouse who negotiates for the transfer to the adult child through acceptance of a reduced benefit is viewed as making a gift to the child to the extent of the reduction. *See* Rev. Rul. 77-314, 1977-2 C.B. 349; Rev. Rul. 79-363, 1979-2 C.B. 345. Accordingly, the issue is not whether the transfer to the adult child will be subject to gift tax but instead the proper identity of the donor.

§ 6.05   STUDY PROBLEMS

1. Maya and Jeff are married and reside in a separate property state. Maya owns title to real property, and she has just received an unsolicited offer to purchase the property at a premium value. Even though Jeff's name does not appear on the title, Jeff possesses an inchoate dower-like interest in the property that could ripen into a life estate upon Maya's death. Accordingly, the transaction will close only if Jeff executes the deed. At closing, Jeff refuses to sign the deed unless Maya agrees to allow him to use $50,000 of the sale proceeds to purchase a new truck and a wide screen television. Maya shakes her head, but reluctantly agrees. Has Maya made a gift to Jeff? [To confirm that you answered the question correctly, see Rev. Rul. 79-312, 1979-2 C.B. 29.]

2. Richard and Stephanie are in the process of obtaining a divorce. The couple has two children: Chandler, age 16, and Connie, age 20. The agreement calls for Richard to make the following transfers:

   - $500,000 to Stephanie in satisfaction of her equitable distribution rights.

   - $800,000 in trust for the lifetime benefit of Stephanie, in satisfaction of her rights to alimony. The trust provides that a unitrust amount of five percent of the trust assets will be made to Stephanie for her lifetime, with the remainder being paid to Richard's then living issue. Assume that the actuarial value of Stephanie's interest in the trust is $600,000. Further assume that an independent appraisal of Stephanie's support rights values them at $550,000.

   - $300,000 in trust for the benefit of Chandler. The transfer is made in satisfaction of Richard's support obligation to Chandler, which is valued at $75,000. The agreement provides that Richard will have no further obligations for Chandler's college education.

   - $300,000 in trust for the benefit of Connie. The agreement provides that Richard will have no further obligations for Connie's college education.

   The agreement requires the approval of the divorce court, and will be operative only upon the issuance of a judicial decree of divorce. The divorce court issues the decree eight months after the agreement was executed, and the decree incorporates the agreement without modification.

   a. Discuss the gift tax consequences of the transfers to Richard.

   b. Same as (a), except the judicial decree of divorce is not issued until three years after the settlement agreement was executed.

c. Same as (b), except the divorce court did not possess the authority to modify the parties' agreement.

d. Same as (a), except that Richard dies shortly after the divorce decree was entered and prior to making any of the required transfers. To what extent will Richard's estate be entitled to a deduction under § 2053(a)(3) assuming his estate is required to fulfill his obligations under the decree?

Chapter 7

GENERAL PRINCIPLES OF TRANSFER TAX VALUATION

Study of the federal transfer tax system largely focuses on the scope of the gift, estate, and GST tax bases. However, equally important to the practical incidence of the federal transfer tax system is the amount at which property included in these tax bases is valued. With the three taxes applying at a 35 percent marginal rate after available exemptions are exhausted, considerable tax savings can be achieved through the assertion and defense of a low valuation of transferred property. The potential tax savings explains the abundance of litigation concerning the transfer tax value of property, as well as the prominence of estate planning techniques that exploit weaknesses in the valuation regime.

§ 7.01 REFERENCE POINT FOR VALUATION

Internal Revenue Code: §§ 2031, 2512(a)

Before examining the principals that guide the determination of the value of property for purposes of the federal transfer tax system, it is necessary to identify the precise point at which the transferred property is to be valued and in whose hands ownership of the property should be evaluated. For instance, should the property be valued in the hands of the transferor (whether decedent or donor) immediately prior to the transfer, in the hands of the transferee immediately after the transfer, or in isolation between the two? While resolution of this issue may not affect the valuation of transferred property in the majority of cases, it can prove determinative where the property is subject to a restriction in the hands of the transferor but not the transferee. Another related question is whether the transferred property should be valued with reference to all property owned or transferred by the transferor, or should property transfers to separate transferees be valued in isolation? As discussed below, resolution of this second question turns on whether the property is transferred inter vivos or by reason of death.

[A] Estate Tax Value

[1] Pre-Distribution Transformations of Property

Property included in the gross estate is to be valued "at the time of [the decedent's] death." IRC § 2031. While this pronouncement appears straightforward, it does not expressly address whether changes in the bundle of property rights that are triggered by reason of the decedent's death should be considered in the determination of estate tax value. Drawing on the excise nature of the estate tax as taxing the privilege of transmitting property at death,[1] the Fifth

---

[1] The excise nature of the estate tax is critical to the constitutionality of the tax. *See* Knowlton v. Moore, 178 U.S. 41 (1900) (upholding federal inheritance tax as an indirect excise tax on the transmission of property); New York Trust Co. v. Eisner, 256 U.S. 345 (1921) (holding federal estate tax constitutional on same grounds). If the estate tax instead

Circuit in *United States v. Land*, 303 F.2d 170 (5th Cir. 1962), sought to clarify this point:

> Brief as is the instant of death, the court must pinpoint its valuation at this instant—the moment of truth, when the ownership of the decedent ends and the ownership of the successors begins. It is a fallacy, therefore, to argue value before—or—after death on the notion that valuation must be determined by the value either of the interest that ceases, or of the interest that begins. Instead, the valuation is determined by *the interest that passes*, and the value of the interest before or after death is pertinent only as it serves to indicate the value *at* death. In the usual case, death brings no change in the value of property. It is only in the few cases where death alters value, as well as ownership, that it is necessary to determine whether the value at the time of death reflects the change caused by death, for example, loss of services of a valuable partner to a small business.

> * * *

> Underlying the determination in these instances that the valuation of property passing at death reflects the changes wrought by death is a basic economic fact: value looks ahead. To find the fair market value of a property interest at the decedent's death we put ourselves in the position of a potential purchaser of the interest at that time. Such a person would not be influenced in his calculations by past risks that had failed to materialize or by restrictions that had ended. Death tolls the bell for risks, contingencies, or restrictions which exist only during the life of the decedent. A potential buyer focuses on the value the property has in the present or will have in the future. He attributes full value to any right that vests or matures at death, and he reduces his valuation to account for any risk or deprivation that death brings into effect, such as the effect of the death on the brains of a small, close corporation. These are factors that would affect his enjoyment of the property should he purchase it, and on which he bases his valuation. The sense of the situation suggests that we follow suit.

Id. at 172–73 (emphasis in original). The decedent in *Land* owned a partnership interest that could be purchased for two-thirds of its value by the remaining partners if he withdrew during his life. However, if the decedent remained a partner until his death (which he did), the surviving partners were obligated to purchase the interest at its full fair market value in order to avoid dissolution. In accordance with its framing of the valuation inquiry, the Fifth Circuit determined that the right of the other partners to purchase the decedent's interest at a discount was not relevant to the estate tax value of the property, because the decedent's death extinguished the right. *Id.* at 175; *see also* Goodman v. Granger, 243 F.2d 264 (3d Cir. 1957) (valuing annual payments to former employee conditioned on employee's agreement not to compete without regard to the risk of forfeiture, which was foreclosed by employee's death). *But see* Estate of McClatchy v. Commissioner, 147 F.3d 1089 (9th Cir. 1998) (reversing the Tax Court and holding that the decedent's stock interest was to be valued based on federal securities law restrictions existing prior to, but not after, the decedent's death).

---

were simply a wealth tax administered on property owned at the time of death, the tax would constitute a direct tax on property in violation of Article I, Section 9 of the Constitution.

[2] Emphasis on Amount Passing from Decedent

In addition to clarifying that changes in value occasioned by reason of the decedent's death (whether value enhancing or value diminishing) are to be considered in determining the estate tax value of property, the Fifth Circuit's opinion in *Land* also instructs that the valuation inquiry must focus on the value of property passing from the decedent as opposed to the value of property received by the successor. Indeed, this is a fundamental distinction between an estate tax and an inheritance tax. *See* Ithaca Trust Co. v. United States, 279 U.S. 151, 155 (1929) ("The tax is on the act of the testator not on the receipt of property by the legatees.").

The Ninth Circuit stressed this point in *Ahmanson Foundation v. United States*, 674 F.2d 761 (9th Cir. 1981). At the time of his death, the decedent in *Ahmanson* owned a controlling interest in a holding company that owned several successful operating businesses. The decedent also owned all of the stock (99 nonvoting shares and 1 voting share) of a shell corporation formed to undertake a postmortem recapitalization of his stock holdings. The decedent's estate planning documents directed that ownership of his holding company stock be transferred to the shell corporation. The nonvoting shares of the shell corporation were devised to charity, and the single voting share was devised to the decedent's son.

Because the decedent's stock in the holding company was required to be contributed to the shell corporation by reason of the decedent's death, the Ninth Circuit determined that the relevant asset to be valued for estate tax purposes was the decedent's ownership of the shell corporation, enhanced by the contribution of the holding company stock. *Id.* at 767. However, the court rejected the estate's argument that the nonvoting shares were to be valued separately from the voting share because the respective stock interests passed to different parties:

> In its brief, the Foundation argues forcefully that the [shell company] shares should be partitioned into two blocks prior to valuation. That is, the 99 shares going to the Foundation should be valued separately from the 1 share that had a private destination. The Foundation argues that because the estate tax is imposed upon the transfer of property, the valuation of property in the gross estate must take into account any changes in value brought about by the fact of the distribution itself. It is undisputed that the valuation must take into account changes brought about by the death of the testator. Ordinarily death itself does not alter the value of property owned by the decedent. However, in a few instances such as when a small business loses the services of a valuable partner, death does change the value of property. The valuation should also take into account transformations brought about by those aspects of the estate plan which go into effect logically prior to the distribution of property in the gross estate to the beneficiaries. . . .

> We must distinguish, however, the effect of "predistribution" transformations and changes in value brought about by the testator's death from changes in value resulting from the fact that under the decedent's estate plan the assets in the gross estate ultimately come to rest in the hands of different beneficiaries. The estate tax is a tax upon a transfer as the Foundation contends. However, it is a tax on the privilege of passing on property, not a tax on the privilege of receiving property. . . . There is nothing in the statutes or in the case law that suggests that valuation of the gross estate should take into account that the assets will come to rest in several hands rather than one.

Id. at 768 (citations omitted). Accordingly, because the decedent owned all shares at the time of his death, the estate tax value was to be based on his unitary ownership interest.[2] Viewing the holding of the *Ahmanson* case positively, the identity of the recipient of the decedent's property (and, in particular, any property holdings of the recipient) is not relevant to valuing the interest passing from the decedent. *See* Estate of Bright v. United States, 658 F.2d 999 (5th Cir. 1981) (holding that decedent-spouse's 27.5 percent community property interest in stock was to be valued in isolation, without regard to its transfer to a trust of which her husband, who held the remaining 27.5 percent interest, served as trustee).

[B]   Gift Tax Value

If property is transferred gratuitously, the amount of the gift is the value of the property on the date of the transfer. IRC § 2512(a). The regulations elaborate on this standard, instructing that the tax "is measured by the value of the property passing from the donor." Treas. Reg. § 25.2511-2(a). In this sense, the valuation inquiry under the gift tax parallels that under the estate tax. Yet whereas a decedent has only one gross estate the value of which must be determined, each gift from a donor is valued in isolation.

For example, in Revenue Ruling 93-12, 1993-1 C.B. 202, the Service addressed the gift tax consequences to a donor who, holding all of the stock of a corporation, transferred a 20 percent interest to each of his five children. The ruling held that each gift was to be valued separately and that a minority-interest discount with respect to each gift would not be disallowed simply because the ownership of a controlling interest remained within the family unit. Because the transfers operated to eliminate voting control of the corporation, the sum of the five gifts would not reach the value of the donor's ownership interest prior to making the gifts. By contrast, had the donor retained sole ownership of the corporation until his death and made the same transfers under his will, the value included in his gross estate would have been the fair market value of his 100 percent interest.

With the distinction between estate tax valuation and gift tax valuation in mind, consider the following scenario: An individual who owns 51 percent of the outstanding stock of a corporation learns she has a terminal illness. She transfers a 1 percent interest to each of her two children, and then dies weeks later. The individual devises her remaining 49 percent interest to her children in equal shares. In the normal course, the two lifetime transfers would be valued in isolation, as would the block of stock passing by way of the decedent's death. However, in *Estate of Murphy v. Commissioner*, T.C. Memo. 1990-472, 60 T.C.M. (CCH) 645, the Tax Court held that it was not appropriate to value stock holdings of the decedent at death through the application of a minority-interest discount, on grounds that the "explicit purpose and effect of fragmenting the control block of stock was solely to reduce Federal tax." *Id.* at 658. Additionally, the court determined that the decedent, together with her daughters who received the 1 percent stock interests by inter vivos transfer, "continually exercised control powers" over the corporation. *Id.*

---

[2] This is not to say that the value of the property passing to a particular beneficiary is irrelevant. Because the charitable deduction is based on the amount of transfers to charitable recipients, the charitable deduction was limited to the separate value of the 99 nonvoting shares that passed to the charitable foundation. This aspect of the *Ahmanson* case is discussed in Chapter 18.03[A].

§ 7.02   THE WILLING BUYER-WILLING SELLER STANDARD

Treasury Regulations: §§ 20.2031-1(b), 25.2512-1

Despite the practical importance of valuation in the federal transfer tax regime, the general standard by which value is to be determined is not articulated by statute. Rather, the default definition of fair market value for transfer tax purposes is supplied in the regulations:

> The fair market value [of property] is the price at which the property would change hands between a willing buyer and a willing seller, neither being under any compulsion to buy or to sell and both having reasonable knowledge of relevant facts. The fair market value of a particular item of property includible in the decedent's gross estate is not to be determined by a forced sales price. Nor is the fair market value of an item of property to be determined by the sale price of the item in a market other than that in which such item is most commonly sold to the public, taking into account the location of the item wherever appropriate.

Treas. Reg. § 20.2031-1(b) (valuation for estate tax purposes); *see also* Treas. Reg. § 25.2512-1 (nearly identical definition of value for gift tax purposes). As noted by the Supreme Court, the willing buyer-willing seller standard for determining fair market value "is nearly as old as the federal income, estate, and gift taxes themselves." United States v. Cartwright, 411 U.S. 546, 551 (1973).

The regulatory definition of fair market value seeks to identify the objective market value of property. Judicial interpretations of the valuation standard have clarified that the relevant "willing buyer" and "willing seller" of the subject property are hypothetical persons who do not necessarily possess the same characteristics as the actual transferor and transferee. *See* Estate of Mellinger v. Commissioner, 112 T.C. 26 (1999); *see also* Propstra v. United States, 680 F.2d 1248 (9th Cir. 1982); Estate of Bright v. United States, 658 F.2d 999 (5th Cir. 1981). The hypothetical willing buyer and willing seller are dedicated to achieving the maximum economic advantage. *See* Estate of Davis v. Commissioner, 110 T.C. 530 (1998).

By focusing on the objective value of the transferred property to hypothetical third persons, the transfer tax system fails to reach what may be considered the owner's consumer surplus in the property—that is, the value the owner places on the property in excess of the value at which the property would trade on the relevant market. This potential spread between the objective value of transferred property to a third party and the subjective value of property to the transferees serves as the cornerstone of many estate planning strategies.

§ 7.03   NATURE OF INQUIRY

[A]   An Inexact Science

The fair market value of transferred property is a question of fact, and this factual determination often is not straightforward. As stated by the Tax Court, "[v]aluation is not an exact science and each case necessarily turns on its own particular facts." Estate of Spruill v. Commissioner, 88 T.C. 1197, 1228 (1987). Litigants, however, often are adamantly convinced of the correctness of their valuation. The Tax Court in *Messing v. Commissioner*, 48 T.C. 502 (1967), issued the following oft-repeated admonition:

> Too often in valuation disputes the parties have convinced themselves of the unalter-
> able correctness of their positions and have consequently failed successfully to

conclude settlement negotiations—a process clearly more conducive to the proper disposition of disputes such as this. The result is an overzealous effort, during the course of the ensuing litigation, to infuse a talismanic precision into an issue which should frankly be recognized as inherently imprecise and capable of resolution only by a Solomon-like pronouncement.

Id. at 512; *see also* Henry v. Commissioner, 4 T.C. 423, 447 (1944) ("Valuation of real estate, like many questions of fact, can never be completely rationalized.").

Justifying a particular valuation of property can prove to be an exhausting use of judicial resources. Courts therefore frequently implore parties to resolve valuation disputes by private agreement. *See* Symington v. Commissioner, 87 T.C. 892, 904–05 (1986) ("The bottom line is that we are more than ever convinced that valuation cases should be disposed of by the parties by way of settlement or other procedures short of court proceedings."). Nonetheless, parties may perceive an incentive to assert and defend extreme valuations if reviewing courts are likely to resolve the dispute by compromising the competing positions.[3] The Tax Court in *Buffalo Tool & Die Mfg. Co. v. Commissioner*, 74 T.C. 441 (1980), sought to dispel this perception by attacking its premise:

> The parties should keep in mind that, in the final analysis, the Court may find the evidence of valuation by one of the parties sufficiently more convincing than that of the other party, so that the final result will produce a significant financial defeat for one or the other, rather than a middle-of-the-road compromise which we suspect each of the parties expects the Court to reach.

Id. at 452. Despite this admonition, courts have proven reluctant to adopt a winner-take-all approach that would incentivize parties to moderate their positions. Instead, courts often reach valuation determinations that fall somewhere within the range of valuations asserted by the parties.

[B]   Use of Expert Testimony

In cases of disputed valuation, parties frequently seek to bolster their positions through the testimony of expert witnesses. While expert testimony may prove useful to a court in making its determination, the court is not bound by an expert's opinion. The Tax Court has outlined the relevance and permissible use of expert testimony concerning matters of valuation as follows:

> We evaluate the opinions of experts in light of the demonstrated qualifications of each expert and all other evidence in the record. We have broad discretion to evaluate " 'the overall cogency of each expert's analysis.' " We are not bound by the formulae and opinions proffered by expert witnesses, especially when they are contrary to our judgment. Instead, we may reach a determination of value based on our own examination of the evidence in the record. The persuasiveness of an expert's opinion depends largely upon the disclosed facts on which it is based. Where experts offer

---

[3] The prospect of penalties may provide a deterrent to taxpayers on this front. Section 6662 imposes an accuracy-related penalty equal to 20 percent of the tax deficiency in cases of a "substantial estate or gift tax valuation understatement," which occurs if the value of property as claimed on the appropriate return is 65 percent or less than the amount determined to be the correct value of the transferred property. IRC § 6662(a), (b)(5), (g)(1). The penalty increases to 40 percent in the case of a "gross valuation misstatements," which occurs if the reported value of the property is equal to or less than 40 percent of the amount later determined to be the correct value. IRC § 6662(h)(2)(C).

divergent estimates of fair market value, we shall decide what weight to give those estimates by examining the factors used by those experts to arrive at their conclusions. While we may accept the opinion of an expert in its entirety, we may be selective in the use of any part of such an opinion. We also may reject the opinion of an expert witness in its entirety.

Estate of Davis v. Commissioner, 110 T.C. 530, 538 (1998) (citations omitted). Trial courts increasingly have conveyed their frustration with the absence of credible support for the conclusions of expert witnesses. *See, e.g.,* Estate of Kaufman v. Commissioner, T.C. Memo. 1999-119, 77 T.C.M. (CCH) 1779, *rev'd,* 243 F.3d 1145 (9th Cir. 2001). Additionally, the Tax Court has warned that "experts may lose their usefulness and credibility when they merely become advocates for one side." Estate of Halas v. Commissioner, 94 T.C. 570, 577 (1990).

[C]   Relevance of Hindsight

Suppose a decedent owned illiquid property that the estate valued at $100x as of the date of the decedent's death. Ten months after the decedent's death (shortly after the decedent's estate tax return was filed), the estate sold the property for $130x. To what extent is the price at which the property later sold relevant in determining the property's value for estate tax purposes? "In general, property is valued as of the valuation date on the basis of market conditions and facts available on that date *without regard to hindsight.*" Estate of Gilford v. Commissioner, 88 T.C. 38, 52 (1987) (emphasis in original). However, a court may consider postmortem events solely for the "limited purpose" of determining the expectations of a willing buyer and willing seller on the valuation date and whether those expectations were "reasonable and intelligent." Estate of Jephson v. Commissioner, 81 T.C. 999, 1002 (1983); *see also* First Nat'l Bank v. United States, 763 F.2d 891, 894 (7th Cir. 1985) (subsequent events may be considered if the evidence "would make more or less probable the proposition that the property had a certain fair market value on a given date"). Due to the inherent difficulty of cordoning information gained with the benefit of hindsight, the limited purpose for which hindsight is relevant may prove to be of considerable practical breadth.

§ 7.04   PUBLICLY TRADED SECURITIES

Treasury Regulations: § 20.2031-2(a), (b)(1), (c), (e), (f), (h)
                              § 25.2512-2(a), (b)(1), (c), (e), (f)

In addition to the general willing buyer-willing seller standard for determining fair market value of property for transfer tax purposes, the regulations provide a number of valuation rules or guidelines that are particular to the type of property being transferred. One such area is publicly traded stocks or bonds.

Publicly traded securities are to be valued on a per-share or per-bond basis on the applicable valuation date of the transfer.[4] To account for fluctuations in trading value occurring over the course of a day, the per-share or the per-bond value generally is equivalent to the average of the highest and lowest quoted selling prices on the valuation date. Treas. Reg. §§ 20.2031-

---

[4] For gift tax purposes, the applicable valuation date is the date of the gift. The applicable valuation date for estate tax purposes generally is the date of the decedent's death; however, if the decedent's estate elects to value property on the alternate valuation date pursuant to § 2032, the applicable valuation date is the earlier of the date the property is disposed of by the estate or six months after the date of the decedent's death. Alternate valuation under § 2032 is discussed in § 7.09.

2(b)(1), 25.2512-2(b)(1). If the markets are not open on the relevant date of transfer, the value is determined by a weighted average of the values determined on the trading days before and after the date of transfer. *Id.* If actual sales are not available during a reasonable period before and after the applicable valuation date, then the fair market value may be determined by taking the average of the bona fide bid and asked prices on the valuation date. Treas. Reg. §§ 20.2031-2(c), 25.2512-2(c).

The regulations recognize that, in certain cases, the fair market value of publicly traded securities may not be reflected by the appropriate selling prices or bid and asked prices. If the transferor establishes that these valuation methods, standing alone, are not indicative of fair market value, either a "reasonable modification" to the valuation methods will be permitted or "other relevant facts and elements of value" will be considered in determining fair market value. Treas. Reg. §§ 20.2031-2(e), 25.2512-2(e).

[A] Blockage Discounts

The most common type of adjustment to fair market value in this setting is a "blockage discount," reflecting the inability to liquidate a disproportionately large block of stock at prevailing market prices. As explained by the Tenth Circuit in *Maytag v. Commissioner*:

> Sales of small lots of stock on an exchange on which it is listed may not afford a reliable yardstick for fixing the fair market value of large blocks which if disposed of rapidly might overtax the market and depress the price. The capacity of the market to absorb a large offering of a particular stock is a factor for appropriate consideration along with other factors in arriving at the fair market value of such stock at the critical time.

187 F.2d 962, 966 (10th Cir. 1951). A blockage discount is not presumed by the sheer size of stock holdings; rather, the transferor must establish that a liquidation of the stock could not be accomplished within a "reasonable time by skilled brokers following prudent practices for liquidation" to claim the discount.[5] Helvering v. Maytag, 125 F.2d 55, 63 (8th Cir. 1942).

The necessity and extent of a blockage discount generally is established by expert testimony. While testimony may warrant a percentage discount from the prevailing market price, the regulations note that the fair market value of the stock may be determined by other means in this context—in particular, by reference to the price at which the stock could be sold through an underwriter. Treas. Reg. §§ 20.2031-2(e), 25.2512-2(e).

The application of the blockage discount for estate tax purposes is based on the volume of stock owned or controlled by the decedent at death. However, in the gift tax setting, application of the blockage discount can be more complicated. Should the extent of the discount be based on the total amount of stock transferred at the same time to any number of donees, or should each gift be valued in isolation? Consistent with the general rule that separate gifts are to be independently valued for gift tax purposes, the regulations confirm that the relevant block of stock to be valued is determined "with reference to each separate gift." Treas. Reg. § 25.2512-2(e). The Tax Court upheld the validity of the regulation in *Rushton v. Commissioner*, 60 T.C. 272 (1973), reasoning that "[i]t is illogical to determine the value of each gift

---

[5] Note that the circumstances necessary to justify a blockage discount may have the opposite effect on the fair market value of the stock. If the size of the block of stock to be valued would supply a would-be purchaser with outright or effective control over the corporation, a control premium to the prevailing market price may be warranted. Control premiums are addressed in § 7.07.

separately and yet take into account the effect of all gifts of shares upon the market. The two concepts are irreconcilable." *Id.* at 278. The Fifth Circuit affirmed. 498 F.2d 88 (5th Cir. 1974).

[B] Selling Expenses

The proceeds realized from the disposition of stock generally will be reduced by broker's commissions and other associated expenses of the disposition. However, the fair market value of the stock is not reduced by the associated costs of disposition. Rather, to the extent an estate incurs expenses in disposing of the stock, those expenses will be allowed as a deduction from the gross estate under § 2053(a)(2).[6] *See* Rev. Rul. 83-30, 1983-1 C.B. 224 (underwriting fees necessary in marketing large block of stock are not to be considered in blockage discount; such fees instead are deductible as administration expenses).

[C] Mutual Fund Shares

Valuation of shares in an open-end investment company (mutual fund) presents a challenge under the willing buyer-willing seller standard for valuation. The shares do not change hands between investors; rather, purchases and redemptions of fund shares must occur with the fund itself. In particular, a purchaser of fund shares typically must pay a sales charge in addition to the pro-rata value of the fund assets represented by the shares, whereas a redemption of shares by the fund will be at pro-rata value only. Hence, the price at which the shares can be acquired from the fund always differs from the price at which the shares can be sold to the fund.

The government originally resolved the impasse under the willing buyer-willing seller standard in this context by setting fair market value at the price a disinterested investor would have to pay to acquire the shares from the fund. However, the Supreme Court rejected this approach in *United States v. Cartwright*, 411 U.S. 546 (1973). Noting that the estate held no hope of receiving the price asked by the fund and that the fund—the only possible buyer—would not pay this amount, the Court concluded that the regulatory pronouncement that the asked price determined fair market value was "unrealistic and unreasonable." *Id.* at 550. Following the *Cartwright* decision, the regulations were reissued to comply with its holding that fair market value in this context is to be determined by reference to the redemption price of the fund shares. *See* Treas. Reg. §§ 20.2031-8(b), 25.2512-6(b).

§ 7.05 REAL PROPERTY

Valuation of real property for transfer tax purposes is determined under the generally applicable willing buyer-willing seller standard. As explained by the Service in Revenue Procedure 79-24, 1979-1 C.B. 565, unimproved real property is valued by reference to comparable sales:

> When the property to be appraised has not recently been the subject of an arm's-length transaction, the best method of estimating the value of unimproved real property is by use of the market data or comparable sales approach. . . .

　　　* * *

---

[6] The deduction for expenses incurred in the administration of a decedent's estate is addressed in Chapter 17.

Detailed analyses of the comparable property sales should include considerations of similarity of highest and best use legally permissible, the time interval between sale date and valuation date, economic similarities and trends affecting the neighborhoods. . . .

Comparable property sales may be used only after the sales prices have been adjusted for differences between the properties. In making adjustments the appraiser should adjust to the property being appraised. . . . Adjustments are a judgmental conclusion of the appraiser and are usually shown as a percentage change.

Id. at 565–66. Reliance on comparable sales also serves as the primary approach to valuing noncommercial, residential real property.

Real property that is productive of income, such as an apartment complex or an office building, generally is valued on the basis of the property's income stream. Under the income based approach to valuation, the estimate of a single year's stabilized net income is divided by the capitalization rate to determine the fair value of the property. For obvious reasons, the determination of the capitalization rate is crucial to this method of valuation. The appropriate capitalization rate generally is determined based on the relationship between net operating income and sales prices of comparable assets. *See* Learner v. Commissioner, T.C. Memo. 1983-122, 45 T.C.M. (CCH) 922 (applying capitalization of income approach in valuing commercial realty).

[A]   Fractional-Interest Discount

Transfers of undivided interests in real property, titled as tenants in common, typically are valued at less than the interest's pro-rata value of the property valued as a whole. A "fractional-interest discount" from pro-rata value is justified on the following deficiencies in the nature of these property interests: the absence of unilateral control over the property; the limited market for disposing of fractional interests in real property; the potential costs of partition to realize undivided ownership; and the potential incurrence of other legal fees to resolve disputes between co-owners. *See* Estate of Bonner v. United States, 84 F.3d 196 (5th Cir. 1996).

While the Service has recognized the general propriety of a fractional-interest discount in this context, it has taken the position that the discount should reflect only the costs of partitioning the subject property. The Service has justified this limitation on grounds that the deficiencies inherent in a fractional interest in real property can be unilaterally removed through a proceeding to partition the property in kind. *See* Tech. Adv. Mem. 9336002 (Sept. 10, 1993); *see also* Estate of Baird v. Commissioner, T.C. Memo. 2002-299, 84 T.C.M. (CCH) 620 (describing the Service's position that the only discount in determining fair market value was the cost of partition). The Fifth Circuit resoundingly rejected such a blanket limitation on the fractional-interest discount. *See* Estate of Baird v. Commissioner, 416 F.3d 442 (5th Cir. 2005). Given the Tax Court's determination that a 60 percent discount from pro-rata value was warranted in valuing the fractional interests, the appellate court determined that the limitation advanced by the Service lacked substantial justification and, accordingly, awarded litigation costs to the estate.

Despite the Fifth Circuit's rejection of the cost-of-partition approach, the Tax Court has continued to recognize this approach to valuing fractional interests in realty. In *Ludwick v. Commissioner*, T.C. Memo. 2010-104, 99 T.C.M. (CCH) 1424, the Tax Court valued a 50 percent interest in a Hawaii vacation home based on the fair market value of 50 percent of the property in question discounted by the costs of (a) maintaining the property and (b) selling the property, the latter of which would include the costs of a possible partition. The costs associated with a partition action, in turn, were reduced by the relative likelihood that a partition action would be required to dispose of the co-tenancy interest (with the court determining that a partition action would be necessary 10 percent of the time). This process led the court to approve a discount from proportionate value of slightly less than 15 percent, significantly less than that sought by the taxpayer.

For estate tax purposes, fractional-interest discounts are available for the transfer of tenancy in common interests only. As later discussed in Chapter 8, § 2040 governs not only the inclusion of jointly owned property in a decedent's gross estate but also the manner of valuing the included portion of the property. Because the value to be included starts at the property valued as a whole and permits proportionate exclusions based on the relative contributions to the purchase price made by surviving co-owners, § 2040 effectively precludes fractional-interest discounts.[7]

[B] Highest and Best Use

Suppose a decedent died owning a family manor in a once bucolic area that, at the time of the decedent's death, rests at the edge of an expanding suburban community. The decedent's heirs would like to preserve the property as a family estate. Should the family's decision to not fully exploit the economic benefit of the property be binding for estate tax purposes?

As a general rule, no. Property is to be valued with reference to the "highest and best use" of the property on the date of valuation, which is defined as the "reasonable and probable use that supports the highest present value." Symington v. Commissioner, 87 T.C. 892, 897 (1986). In determining the highest and best use of the property, only realistic, potential uses of the property may be considered. Hence, to value property at a use different from that actually employed by the parties, the alternative more profitable use of the property must be reasonably obtainable.

The Tax Court applied the "highest and best use" rule to real property in *Frazee v. Commissioner*, 98 T.C. 554 (1992). The case involved lifetime gifts of property that the donor valued according to the property's agricultural use. The government, on the other hand, based its valuation on the potential use of the property for industrial or commercial purposes. Declaring the donor's use of the property irrelevant, the court determined that the property should be valued based on its potential for industrial use if demand for industrial property existed at the time of the transfer and if it were feasible to rezone the property to accommodate such use. *Id.* at 563–64. The court ultimately valued the property at its industrial use after finding that a willing buyer would have considered purchasing the property as a site for industrial development.

[C] Section 2032A Special Use Valuation

Internal Revenue Code: § 2032A(a), (b)(1)–(3), (c)(1)–(2)(A), (c)(6),
(d)(1)–(2), (e)(1)–(8), 2035(c)(1)(B)

---

[7] The valuation of property held as joint tenants with right of survivorship is discussed in § 8.03[A].

Through the introduction of § 2032A in 1976, Congress abrogated the "highest and best use" approach to valuing real estate under a narrow set of circumstances. The congressional motivation behind the enactment of § 2032A was to reduce the tax burden on family farms or closely held businesses by valuing the property at its existing use if the decedent's family members desired to continue the operation. As explained by the Joint Committee on Taxation:

> Congress believed that, when land is actually used for farming purposes or in other closely held businesses (both before and after the decedent's death), it is inappropriate to value the land on the basis of its potential "highest and best use" especially since it is desirable to encourage the continued use of property for farming and other small business purposes. Valuation on the basis of highest and best use, rather than actual use, may result in the imposition of substantially higher estate taxes. In some cases, the greater estate tax burden makes continuation of farming, or the closely held business activities, not feasible because the income potential from these activities is insufficient to service extended tax payments or loans obtained to pay the tax.

Staff of Joint Comm. on Tax'n, General Explanation of the Tax Reform Act of 1976, at 537 (1976), *reprinted in* 1976-3 C.B. (vol. 2) 1, 549.

The statute, which has been periodically expanded since its enactment, permits a decedent's executor to elect to value "qualified real property" on the basis of its actual use. The scope of qualified real property is defined by a host of conditions, summarized below:

1. *Ownership of Domestic Property*: The decedent must be a United States citizen, and the subject property must be located in the United States. IRC § 2032A(b)(1). The real property may be owned by the decedent either directly or indirectly through ownership of an interest in a corporation, partnership, or trust that holds title to the real property. Treas. Reg. § 20.2032A-3(b)(1). However, in the case of indirect ownership of real property through an entity, the decedent's interest in the entity must qualify as an interest in a closely held business under § 6166(b)(1).[8] *Id.*

2. *Qualified Use of Property*: The property must have been used by the decedent or a member of his family for a "qualified use" at the time of the decedent's death, which includes use of the property as a farm or for farming operations, or in another form of a trade or business. IRC § 2032A(b)(2). A member of an individual's family for this purpose includes a spouse, an ancestor, a lineal descendant, a lineal descendant of a spouse, a lineal descendant of a parent (or spouse's parent), and the spouse of any of the aforementioned lineal descendants. IRC § 2032A(e)(2).

3. *Pre-Death Participation*: For periods aggregating five years during the eight-year period prior to the decedent's death, the decedent or a member of his family must have owned the property, used it for a qualified use, and materially participated in the operation of the farm or other business. IRC § 2032A(b)(1)(C).

4. *Acquisition from Decedent*: The property must have been acquired or must have passed from the decedent to a "qualified heir" of the decedent. IRC § 2032A(b)(1). A qualified heir refers to a member of the decedent's family. IRC § 2032A(e)(1).

---

[8] In general terms, an interest in a closely held business for purposes of § 6166(b) requires the decedent to possess a 20 percent voting interest in the entity or to be one of 45 or fewer owners.

5. *Concentration Test*: The combined personal property and real property acquired from the decedent used for a qualified use must equal or exceed 50 percent of the adjusted value of the decedent's gross estate. IRC § 2032A(b)(1)(A). Additionally, the adjusted value of the real estate acquired from the decedent that satisfies the qualified use and material participation test under § 2032A(b)(1)(C) must equal or exceed 25 percent of the adjusted value of the decedent's gross estate. IRC § 2032A(b)(1)(B). Lifetime transfers of other assets made by the decedent to permit his estate to meet these two percentage tests may not be effective, as the value of the gross estate for § 2032A purposes includes the value of all transfers made within three years of death. *See* IRC § 2035(c)(1)(B).

6. *Postmortem Use of Property*: The individuals who receive an interest (whether or not possessory) in the property must file an agreement with the estate tax return consenting to the imposition of an additional tax if, within 10 years following the decedent's death, the qualified heir either (a) disposes of the property other than by a disposition to a member of the qualified heir's family, or (b) ceases to use the property for the qualified use to which the property was put when acquired from the decedent. *See* IRC § 2032A(b)(1)(D), (c)(1)–(2), (d)(2). The additional tax is designed to recapture the estate tax benefit provided by the § 2032A special-use valuation regime when the decedent's family members do not continue to operate the farm or small business.

If these various conditions are satisfied, the decedent's estate may value farmland based on a capitalization of average rental income for comparable property in the vicinity under § 2032A(e)(7). All other qualified real property, in addition to farmland if the estate so elects, may be valued under a "complex and relatively subjective" five-factor test set out in § 2032A(e)(8). Estate of Klosterman v. Commissioner, 99 T.C. 313, 317 n.4 (1992). The extent of the valuation reduction, however, may not exceed $750,000, as adjusted for inflation from 1997. *See* IRC § 2032A(a)(2)–(3). For 2011, the limitation as adjusted for inflation equaled $1,020,000.

§ 7.06   TANGIBLE PERSONAL PROPERTY

Treasury Regulations: § 20.2031-6(b)

Items of tangible personal property having significant artistic or intrinsic value, such as paintings, jewelry, and antiques, must be valued by an expert appraisal in a sworn statement to be filed with the estate tax return. Treas. Reg. § 20.2031-6(b). In addition, the executor must submit a statement signed under penalties of perjury concerning the qualification and disinterested character of the appraiser. *Id.*

As in the context of transfers of undivided fractional interests in real property, taxpayers have claimed that the transfer of co-tenancy interests in personal property should be valued through the application of fractional-interest discounts. However, courts appear less willing to accept the mere assertion of such discounts in the tangible personal property setting. *See, e.g.*, Estate of Pillsbury v. Commissioner, T.C. Memo. 1992-425, 64 T.C.M. (CCH) 284 (rejecting fractional interest discount in furnishings as not supported by evidence). Additionally, the discounts recognized by courts tend to be far less generous in this context. For example, in *Stone v. United States*, 103 A.F.T.R.2d 1379 (9th Cir. 2009) (unpublished opinion), the Ninth Circuit sustained a trial court decision to allow only a five percent fractional-interest discount for the estate's tenants-in-common interest in a collection of paintings. The court rejected the estate's claimed discount of 44 percent, noting the dissimilarities between the art market and the real estate or limited partnership interest markets upon which the estate's appraiser relied in calculating the discount.

A blockage discount generally arising in the valuation of significant concentrations of publicly traded stock also may be appropriate in the context of artwork collections. In *Estate of Smith v. Commissioner*, 57 T.C. 650 (1972), *aff'd*, 510 F.2d 479 (2d Cir. 1975), the Tax Court explained the relevance of a blockage discount in valuing 425 metal sculptures created by the decedent as follows:

> We think that, at the very least, each willing buyer in the retail art market would take into account, in determining the price he would be willing to pay for any given item, the fact that 424 other items were being offered for sale at the same time. The impact of such simultaneous availability of an extremely large number of items of the same general category is a significant circumstance which should be taken into account. In this connection, the so-called blockage rule utilized in connection with the sale of a large number of securities furnishes a useful analogy.

Id. at 658. As another example, the Tax Court permitted a combined blockage discount of 50 percent in valuing the paintings of Georgia O'Keeffe, which had the effect of reducing the estate tax value of her retained works from $72 million to $36 million. *See* Estate of O'Keeffe v. Commissioner, T.C. Memo. 1992-210, 63 T.C.M. (CCH) 2699.

§ 7.07 CLOSELY HELD BUSINESSES INTERESTS

Treasury Regulations: §§ 20.2031-3, 25.2512-3

The valuation of beneficial interests in closely held business entities has risen to the forefront of the estate-planning community, as individuals increasingly use entities traditionally associated with the conduct of a business as vehicles to facilitate the transmission of family assets. While these entities offer advantages typically associated with trusts (such as consolidation of management and asset protection), these entities offer transfer tax benefits that trusts do not—namely, the prospect of a variety of valuation discounts.

[A] Factors in Determining Value

The regulations provide limited additional guidance on the valuation of equity interests in closely held entities beyond a restatement of the willing buyer-willing seller standard. *See* Treas. Reg. §§ 20.2031-3, 25.2512-3. The regulations note that relevant factors to be considered are the appraised fair market value of the entity's assets, including goodwill, as well as the demonstrated earning capacity of the business.

The Service has provided extensive additional guidance on the valuation of closely held business interests in Revenue Ruling 59-60, 1959-1 C.B. 237. In addition to providing concrete factors to be considered in the valuation process,[9] the ruling notes that closely held business

---

[9] The ruling provides the following nonexclusive list of factors relevant to valuation of a business interest:
    a. The nature of the business and the history of the enterprise from its inception.
    b. The economic outlook in general and the condition and outlook of the specific industry in particular.
    c. The book value of the stock and the financial condition of the business.
    d. The earning capacity of the company.
    e. The dividend-paying capacity.
    f. Whether or not the enterprise has goodwill or other intangible value.

interests generally are valued with reference to the net assets of the entity, through a capitalization of earnings, or some combination of the two. The relative weight to be afforded to each valuation method depends on the nature of the business. Businesses engaged in the sale of goods or services to the public tend to be valued on the basis of earnings, whereas entities that serve primarily as holding companies tend to be valued with reference to the value of their net assets. *Id.* § 5, 1959-1 C.B. at 242–43.

For valuations based on a capitalization of earnings, the most critical factor in valuing the entity is the selection of the capitalization rate. Recognizing the absence of standardized capitalization rates, Revenue Ruling 59-60 designates the following as important factors to be considered in selecting the rate: (1) the nature of the business, (2) the risk involved, and (3) the stability of past earnings. *Id.* § 6, 1959-1 C.B. at 243.

For valuations based on net asset value, the most difficult determination concerns the existence and extent of the goodwill of the business. Goodwill is based on the earning capacity of the business. *Id.* § 4.02(f), 1959-1 C.B. at 241. However, high earnings of a business alone do not conclusively establish the existence of goodwill. Rather, the earning capacity of a business may be attributable to the personal services or skills of the owners, which is not an entity asset. *See* Wilmont Fleming Engineering Co. v. Commissioner, 65 T.C. 847 (1976); *see also* Brandt v. Commissioner, 8 T.C.M. (CCH) 820 (1949) (finding that no goodwill survived the decedent's death because earning capacity of business was attributable to the decedent's personal efforts); Rev. Rul. 59-60, § 4.02, 1959-1 C.B. at 239 (acknowledging that loss of manager of a "so-called 'one-man' business" may depress the value of the stock of the entity).

[B] Discounts and Premiums

Once the value of a business as a whole has been determined, the proportionate value of the entity represented by the transferred interest could be valued accordingly—that is, at its pro-rata value as a whole. Pro-rata valuation, however, is a rarity. Taxpayers frequently invoke discounts from pro-rata value to reflect disabilities associated with the ownership of closely held entities. For its part, the Service contends that premiums to pro-rata value are appropriate in certain situations.

[1] Minority-Interest Discount

If the equity interest to be valued does not provide the transferee with a controlling interest in the entity, the interest generally is valued through application of a "minority-interest" discount. *See* Ward v. Commissioner, 87 T.C. 78, 106 (1986) ("The courts have long recognized that the shares of stock of a corporation which represent a minority interest are usually worth less than a proportionate share of the value of the assets of the corporation."). The discount recognizes that a hypothetical purchaser would take into consideration the following disabilities inherent in a minority interest: (1) the inability to control the management of the enterprise or the investment of the entity's assets; (2) the inability to influence the entity's distribution policy, so as to ensure a current return on investment; and (3) the inability to liquidate his investment by causing the entity to redeem his interest or liquidate entirely.

---

g. Sales of the stock and the size of the block of stock to be valued.

h. The market price of stocks of corporations engaged in the same or a similar line of business having their stocks actively traded in a free and open market, either on an exchange or over-the-counter.

Rev. Rul. 59-60, § 4.01, 1959-1 C.B. at 238–39.

Experts often use closed-end mutual funds (that is, funds that do not provide a right of redemption) to approximate the extent of the minority-interest discount. *See* Holman v. Commissioner, 130 T.C. 170, 203 (2008) (explaining that, because the fund shares are highly marketable, any discount from net asset value must be attributable to the holder's lack of control).

The owner of corporate stock representing a voting interest greater than 50 percent possesses the ability to transfer voting control in the entity. For this reason, estate planning with respect to minority interest discounts tends to utilize partnerships or limited liability companies instead of corporations. As a general rule, the transfer of an interest in a partnership or limited liability company does not entitle the transferee to become a member of the entity possessing full voting rights—much less controlling voting rights. *See* Unif. Ltd. P'ship Act, § 702, 6A U.L.A. 461–62 (2001) (rights of transferee of a partner's transferable interest is limited to distributions paid in respect of interest); Rev. Unif. Ltd. Liab. Co. Act § 502, 6B U.L.A. 496–97 (2006) (nearly identical provision in the LLC context). Accordingly, the estate of a decedent who served as the general partner of a limited partnership and possessed a 99 percent economic interest in the entity may still assert a minority-interest discount in valuing the decedent's interest.

[2] Control Premium

Just as a taxpayer will seek to discount the pro-rata value of an interest in a closely held business that does not afford the holder the right to exercise control over the entity, the Service will assert that a controlling interest in an entity should be valued at a premium over pro-rata value. The value of the control premium is the percentage by which the amount paid for a controlling block of shares exceeds the amount that otherwise would have been paid for the shares if sold separately as minority interests. *See* Estate of Salsbury v. Commissioner, T.C. Memo. 1975-333, 34 T.C.M. (CCH) 1441 (upholding a 38 percent control premium). As explained by the Tax Court in *Newhouse v. Commissioner*, 94 T.C. 193 (1990), the justification for valuing a controlling shareholder's interest at a premium includes the shareholder's ability to "unilaterally direct corporation action, select management, decide the amount of distribution, rearrange the corporation's capital structure, and decide whether to liquidate, merge, or sell assets." *Id.* at 251–52. However, the ability of a controlling shareholder to exploit corporate assets for a personal advantage does not serve as a solid basis for the control premium. *See* Ahmanson Foundation v. United States, 674 F.2d 761 (9th Cir. 1981) (rejecting control premium based on opportunity of controlling shareholder to exploit corporate assets for personal advantage); Estate of Salsbury v. Commissioner, 34 T.C.M. (CCH) at 1451 (characterizing the ability of a dominant shareholder to draw excessive salary as "too speculative to be afforded much weight" while recognizing that the ability to control investment of corporate assets warrants a premium).

Even an interest in an entity that constitutes a minority interest may be valued through application of a control premium if the owner of the minority interest possesses a swing vote sufficient to constitute majority action. The premium above the pro-rata value of the minority interest reflects the practical influence that the holder of the interest possesses over corporate action. *See* Estate of Winkler v. Commissioner, T.C. Memo. 1989-231, 57 T.C.M. (CCH) 373 (ascribing a 10 percent premium to a 10 percent stock interest where remaining stock held by two shareholders).

[3]   Marketability Discount

Equity interests in closely held businesses—whether a minority interest or a controlling interest—often are valued at a discount from pro-rata value to reflect the lack of a market on which these interests can be readily liquidated. Simply put, one cannot dispose of an interest in a closely held business through the mere expedient of placing a sell order with a broker. Rather, the interest must be actively marketed in some fashion, and there exists little assurance regarding the time it will take to sell the interest. *See* Estate of Andrews v. Commissioner, 79 T.C. 938 (1982) (recognizing that even a controlling interest in a closely held business may be discounted to reflect absence of a ready private placement market).

[4]   Discount for Built-In Gains

Following repeal of the *General Utilities* doctrine as part of the Tax Reform Act of 1986,[10] shareholders could not liquidate a corporation without triggering the recognition of gain at the corporate level on appreciated assets. *See* IRC § 311(a), (b). As a result, taxpayers owning interests in corporations that are valued on a net-asset basis have claimed discounts for the income tax liability that would be triggered if their stock were to be redeemed through a corporate distribution of property or through a liquidation of the corporation altogether.

The Tax Court originally was reluctant to accept a discount for the lurking income tax liability in corporate assets without some indication that a liquidation of the entity was planned or even contemplated. *See* Ward v. Commissioner, 87 T.C. 78 (1986). Due to the speculative nature of the tax, the potential liability did not have any reliable present value. *See* Estate of Luton v. Commissioner, T.C. Memo. 1994-539, 68 T.C.M. (CCH) 1044. However, the Tax Court began to relax its rejection of the built-in gains discount in *Estate of Davis v. Commissioner*, 110 T.C. 530 (1998). For the first time, the court recognized that a hypothetical willing buyer and hypothetical willing seller of the stock interest would not agree to a price that made no adjustment for the lurking income tax liability—even if no liquidation or sale of corporate assets was contemplated on the valuation date. *Id.* at 546–47. Yet, rather than recognizing this adjustment as an independent basis for discounting the value of the transferred stock, the court viewed the contingent liability as a component of the marketability discount.

The appellate courts have proven more receptive to the taxpayers' argument for a separate discount for a corporation's built-in gain liability. In *Eisenberg v. Commissioner*, 155 F.3d 50 (2d Cir. 1998), the Second Circuit concluded that a separate discount for the lurking income tax liability in corporate assets was warranted in valuing transferred stock, even if no liquidation of the corporation was imminent. However, the court intimated that the discount should not reflect the full amount of the tax liability. *See id.* at 58 n.15. The Fifth Circuit in *Estate of Dunn v. Commissioner*, 301 F.3d 339 (5th Cir. 2002), rejected even this limitation on the extent of the discount. The court reasoned that, for corporations valued on a net-asset basis, a hypothetical buyer of the stock interest must be assumed to acquire the interest solely for the purpose of acquiring the corporation's assets. In other words, a corporate liquidation must be assumed for valuation purposes. *See id.* at 352–53. Accordingly, the Fifth Circuit permitted a dollar-for-

---

[10] In *General Utils. & Operating Co. v. Helvering*, 296 U.S. 200 (1935), the Supreme Court held that a corporation did not recognize taxable income at the corporate level on the distribution of appreciated property. Congress adopted the holding of the case through the nonrecognition provision of § 311(a). However, through the enactment of § 311(b) as part of the Tax Reform Act of 1986, Congress reversed the nonrecognition rule as it applied to appreciated property. *See* Pub. L. No. 99-514, § 631(c), 100 Stat. 2085, 2272 (1986). This legislative change is commonly referred to as the repeal of the *General Utilities* doctrine.

dollar discount for the amount of the built-in corporate capital gain tax liability attributable to the valued interest, even though the parties did not contemplate liquidating the entity.[11] Attracted to the simplicity and certainty surrounding the Fifth Circuit's allowance of a dollar-for-dollar reduction for the built-in capital gains tax liability, the Eleventh Circuit endorsed this approach in *Estate of Jelke v. Commissioner*, 507 F.3d 1317 (11th Cir. 2007). The more receptive approach of the appellate courts to the built-in gains discount appears to have softened the Tax Court's position. *See* Estate of Jensen v. Commissioner, T.C. Memo. 2010-182, 100 T.C.M. (CCH) 138 (upholding the estate's claim to discount based on 100 percent of lurking long-term capital gain in corporate property).

[C] Attempts to Combat Entity-Associated Valuation Discounts

Given the established judicial recognition of discounts for lack of control and lack of marketability in valuing interests in a closely held entity associated with the conduct of a business, these entities have become a staple in the estate planner's arsenal. Trusts traditionally served as the vehicle of choice for transferring beneficial ownership of property to future generations while consolidating authority over the investment management and distributional decisions in a trustee. However, the estate tax consequences of retained beneficial interests in trust property or retained discretionary authority over the beneficial enjoyment of trust property are unfavorable, to put it mildly.[12] Business entities therefore have been employed as trust substitutes for purposes of circumventing the unfavorable estate tax provisions applicable to trusts, while at the same time generating considerable transfer tax savings through the exploitation of valuation discounts.

Because transfer tax valuation is based on the objective value of property as determined by a hypothetical transaction between a willing buyer and willing seller, individuals may seek to drive a wedge between the subjective value they ascribe to property and the objective value to others by transferring assets capable of ready valuation (such as marketable securities) to a family-owned partnership or LLC. The transferred interests will be subject to practical deficiencies in the hands of a hypothetical transferee. The disabilities are real, and they may operate to the detriment of the actual transferee of the property. However, where assets in a business entity are held by individuals who may be viewed as a single economic unit (such as a family), the potential for these deficiencies in value to be actually realized is minimized. Hence, the subjective value of the transferred business interest to the transferee likely will be considerably more valuable to the actual transferee than the property's objective value to a hypothetical third party.

Understandably, the Service has not been content to simply sit back and witness the destruction of transfer tax value through the deliberate exploitation of valuation discounts associated with closely held business entities. Rather, it has advanced a number of theories to

---

[11] In *Smith v. United States*, 391 F.3d 621 (5th Cir. 2004), the Fifth Circuit refused to extend its holding in *Estate of Dunn* to discount the value of an IRA included in a decedent's estate by the income tax liability that would be incurred by the beneficiaries upon liquidation of the account. Instead, the court reasoned that the asset would not constitute an item of income in respect of a decedent (IRD) in the hands of a hypothetical willing buyer, who would not necessarily be one of the parties designated under § 691(a). *See* 391 F.3d at 629. Additionally, the court noted that Congress had accounted for the lurking income tax liability in this context by providing the beneficiaries with an income tax deduction for the amount of the estate tax attributable to the IRD item by way of § 691(c).

[12] The potentially adverse estate tax consequences associated with transfers in trust are discussed in Chapters 10 and 11.

combat or eliminate the discounts altogether. As discussed below, the Service's efforts on this front have not been particularly fruitful.[13]

[1] "Unity of Ownership" Argument

The Service has attempted to combat the prevalent use of discounts to value beneficial interests in closely held entities by contending that a "relevant fact" to be considered in the valuation calculus is that a willing seller would seek to maximize the value of his interest by selling only in conjunction with other owners who, together, could convey at least a controlling interest in the entity. In this manner, any valuation detriment attributable to the ownership of a minority interest in such an entity would be negated.[14]

The Service advanced this "unity of ownership" theory in *Estate of Bright v. United States*, 658 F.2d 999 (5th Cir. 1981). As mentioned above, the decedent in *Estate of Bright* owned a 55 percent interest in corporate stock with her husband as community property. The decedent's death severed the community, and the decedent devised her resulting 27.5 percent interest to a trust of which her husband served as trustee. The government argued that, in effect, the decedent's husband would not be foolish enough to sell the decedent's 27.5 percent interest in isolation. Rather, in order to maximize the value of the estate's interest, the husband would sell it together with the 27.5 percent interest that he owned in his individual capacity. The government therefore argued that the value of the decedent's 27.5 percent interest should equal one-half of the value of a 55 percent interest valued as a controlling block. Characterizing the government's argument as one of attempted family attribution,[15] the Fifth Circuit rejected it as "logically inconsistent" with the willing buyer-willing seller standard set out in the regulations. *Id.* at 1005. The court explained that, because the value of transferred property is to be measured by the value that passes from the decedent as opposed the value received by the transferee, the "willing seller" cannot be identified with either the actual transferor or transferee. *Id.* at 1005–06. The Ninth Circuit in *Propstra v. United States*, 680 F.2d 1248 (9th Cir. 1982), endorsed the rejection of the "unity of ownership" theory in *Estate of Bright*, and further justified its rejection of the argument in terms of administrability:

> The use of an objective standard avoids the uncertainties that would otherwise be inherent if valuation methods attempted to account for the likelihood that estates, legatees, or heirs would sell their interests together with others who hold undivided interests in property. Executors will not have to make delicate inquiries into the feelings, attitudes, and anticipated behavior of those holding undivided interest in the property in question. Without an explicit directive from Congress we cannot require executors to make such inquiries.

Id. at 1252 (footnotes omitted).

---

[13] One of the few arguments that has proven successful for the government in this context is the application of § 2036(a) to the property transferred by a decedent to the entity, as discussed in § 11.06. However, due to the expansive interpretation of the statutory exception to § 2036(a) for transfers made for full and adequate consideration, the government's argument under § 2036 essentially has been reduced to a trap for the unwary. *See* § 13.04.

[14] The same theory could be employed to negate a fractional-interest discount in property owned as tenants in common.

[15] The "family attribution" characterization is misleading, as the government's argument did not depend on the parties being related. Rather, the argument was predicated on the likelihood that parties having separate but similar economic interests in the entity would act in concert to maximize the value of their holdings.

To the extent the government's unity of ownership argument is interpreted to be one of family attribution of property holdings, the Service signaled in Revenue Ruling 93-12, 1993-1 C.B. 202, that it would no longer assume "that all voting power held by family members may be aggregated" in valuing transferred stock for transfer tax purposes. *Id.* at 203. In a circumscribed holding, the Service announced that "a minority discount will not be disallowed solely because a transferred interest, when aggregated with interests held by family members, would be a part of a controlling interest." *Id.* While this may stop short of an endorsement of the *Estate of Bright* decision, it has been interpreted as such. Indeed, estate planners often restructure ownership of property from a form in which the subjective value of property matches its objective value (e.g., marketable securities) to a form where the subjective and objective values intentionally diverge (e.g., by contributing property to closely held business entities), without concern that the remaining interests in the transferred property are held by related parties.

[2] Economic Substance Doctrine

The circumstances of certain cases make clear that property was transferred to an entity solely for the highly touted transfer tax benefits associated with the transfer of interests in closely held business entities. In the income tax setting, courts have demonstrated a willingness to disregard transactions that have no purpose or meaningful economic impact apart from the tax benefits the transaction purports to create. However, courts have been far more reluctant to employ similar judicial doctrines in the transfer tax context. For instance, in *Estate of Strangi v. Commissioner*, 115 T.C. 478 (2000), a terminally ill decedent transferred the bulk of his assets to a family limited partnership. The Tax Court examined a variety of non-tax justifications that purportedly motivated the decedent to capitalize the entity and systematically rejected each one. However, in a somewhat baffling fashion, the court nonetheless refused to disregard the existence of the partnership for tax purposes as lacking economic substance. Instead, the court reasoned as follows:

> The formalities were followed, and the proverbial "i's were dotted" and "t's were crossed". The partnership, as a legal matter, changed the relationships between decedent and his heirs and decedent and actual and potential creditors. Regardless of subjective intentions, the partnership had sufficient substance to be recognized for tax purposes. Its existence would not be disregarded by potential purchasers of decedent's assets, and we do not disregard it in this case.

Id. at 486–87; *see also* Knight v. Commissioner, 115 T.C. 506 (2000) (refusing to disregard partnership for gift tax purposes because partnership formation would be taken into account by willing buyer). In light of this pronouncement, the transfer tax setting appears to be one context in which form enjoys a preference over substance.[16]

---

[16] As part of the Health Care and Education Reconciliation Act of 2010, Congress added § 7701(o) to legislatively affirm the common law economic substance doctrine and to clarify its application. *See* Pub. L. No. 111-152, § 1409, 124 Stat. 1029 (2010). As a general rule, the statute provides that, in any transaction to which the economic substance doctrine is relevant, the transaction will be treated as having economic substance only if, (a) the transaction meaningfully changes the taxpayer's economic position apart from tax effects and (b) the taxpayer has a substantial non-tax purpose for entering the transaction. IRC § 7701(o)(1). For purposes of the statute, the economic substance doctrine refers to the common law doctrine which disallows tax benefits "under subtitle A" (that is, the federal income tax) with respect to transactions that lack economic substance or a business purpose. IRC § 7701(o)(5). Accordingly, the codified version of the economic substance doctrine does not apply in the federal transfer tax context. While the legislation may be interpreted as implicitly limiting the common law economic substance doctrine to the income tax

[3] Defects in Forming and Capitalizing Entity

The allegiance to form announced by the Tax Court in *Estate of Strangi* notwithstanding, courts have proven remarkably forgiving with respect to defects in the form of transactions in the family limited partnership setting. For example, in *Church v. United States*, 85 A.F.T.R.2d (RIA) 804 (W.D. Tex. 2000) (unreported decision), the decedent signed a partnership agreement two days prior to her death. However, the certificate of limited partnership was not filed until two days after her death. Additionally, the corporate general partner of the partnership was not formed until five months after the decedent's death, and the re-titling of the decedent's brokerage account was similarly delayed. Notwithstanding these defects, the district court held that the partnership was in substantial compliance with the state partnership act prior to the decedent's death, and that the decedent had effectively transferred her interest in the securities to the partnership upon her execution of the partnership agreement. Accordingly, the decedent was deemed to have owned and transferred partnership interests by reason of her death even though major aspects of the partnership formation were not completed until well after the decedent's death.

Similarly, in *Keller v. United States*, 104 A.F.T.R.2d 6015 (S.D. Tex. 2009) (unreported decision), the decedent executed a partnership agreement six days prior to the date of her death. Yet the partnership was not formally funded prior to the decedent's death, nor was the corporate general partner formally capitalized. Believing that the attempt to utilize the family partnership technique had escaped them, the decedent's advisors failed to proceed with the partnership transactions. However, upon learning of the holding of the *Church* case, the advisors "sprang into action" and completed the formalities of the partnership formation roughly a year after the decedent's death. The district court determined that the decedent's execution of the partnership agreement was sufficient to form the partnership for estate tax purposes, because the executor of the decedent's estate had a fiduciary obligation to complete the partnership formation transactions. Accordingly, the decedent was determined to own partnership interests as of her death, and these interests were valued through the application of minority-interest and marketability discounts.

[4] Step Transaction Doctrine

Although the broad-based economic substance doctrine thus far has failed to gain a foothold in the transfer tax setting, courts have demonstrated a willingness to employ a more narrow substance-over-form remedy: the step-transaction doctrine. In *Senda v. Commissioner*, T.C. Memo. 2004-160, 88 T.C.M. (CCH) 8, the taxpayers transferred shares of stock to two family limited partnerships and, on the same day, assigned limited partnership interests to their children. Citing the lack of credible evidence that the taxpayers in fact funded the partnership prior to transferring the partnership interests to their children, the Tax Court concluded that "[a]t best, the transactions were integrated . . . and, in effect, simultaneous." *Id.* at 11. The Tax Court determined that the transactions constituted indirect gifts of the corporate stock to the taxpayers' children. The Eighth Circuit affirmed, explaining that "[i]n some situations, formally distinct steps are considered as an integrated whole, rather than in isolation, so federal tax liability is based on a realistic view of the entire transaction." 433 F.3d 1044, 1048 (8th Cir. 2006). Accordingly, the valuation inquiry focused on the marketable securities, and the claimed valuation discounts fell by the wayside. A similar approach was adopted in *Linton v. United*

---

setting, nothing in the statute precludes a court from extending the judicial doctrine to the estate and gift tax.

States, 638 F. Supp. 2d 1277 (W.D. Wash. 2009), in which the district court determined that transfers of LLC interests that were effected prior to or simultaneous with transfers of property to the LLC should be valued as indirect gifts of the LLC property.

Despite its application in the *Senda* and *Linton* cases, the step-transaction doctrine does not appear to pose much of an obstacle in the family limited partnership context. In *Holman v. Commissioner*, 130 T.C. 170 (2008), the taxpayers' assignment of partnership interests occurred on the fifth day following the transfer of stock to the partnership. Citing the economic risk borne by the taxpayers in this time period, the Tax Court refused to treat the transactions as an indirect gift of the transferred stock. *Id.* at 190; *see also* Gross v. Commissioner, T.C. Memo. 2008-221, 96 T.C.M. (CCH) 187 (step-transaction doctrine not applied where gift of partnership interests occurred 11 days after last capitalizing transfer).

§ 7.08   ANNUITIES AND TEMPORAL INTERESTS IN PROPERTY

Internal Revenue Code:	§§ 7520(a), (c), 2702(a)
Treasury Regulations:	§§ 20.7520-1(b)(1)–(2), 25.7520-1(b)(1)–(2)
	§§ 20.7520-3(b), 25.7520-3(b)
	§§ 20.2031-7(a) to (d)(iv)
	§§ 20.2031-8(a); 25.2512-6(a)

Section 7520 directs that fair market value of temporal interests in property be determined pursuant to actuarial tables issued by the Service. *See* IRC § 7520(a), (c). Such temporal interests in property include income interests in property for life or for a term of years, remainder interests in property in favor of third parties, and reversionary interests in property in favor of the transferor. On its face, § 7520 also governs the valuation of annuities; however, the regulations clarify that commercially issued annuities are to be valued by reference to the price at which the issuing company would sell the same or "comparable contracts." *See* Treas. Reg. §§ 20.2031-8(a), 25.2512-6(a).

The actuarial valuation method prescribed by § 7520 estimates the present value of a future payment stream associated with the transferred interest. Both the annual rates of return to be earned on the transferred property as well as the discount factor to be applied in reducing future payment streams to present value are determined by reference to an interest rate component. *See* Treas. Reg. §§ 20.7520-1(b)(1), 25.7520-1(b)(1). By statute, the interest rate component equals 120 percent of the Federal midterm rate (rounded to the nearest 2/10 of 1 percent) in effect under § 1274(d)(1) for the month in which the valuation date falls. IRC § 7520(a)(2). In addition to the interest rate component, possessory interests in property that are defined in terms of an individual's lifetime necessitate the application of a mortality component. *See* Treas. Reg. §§ 20.7520-1(b)(2), 25.7520-1(b)(2). The mortality tables are based on information gained from the United States Census, and are required to be updated every 10 years. IRC § 7520(c)(3). Single-life mortality components for transfers with valuation dates after May 1, 2009 (Table 2000CM), are reproduced in Reg. § 20.2031-7T(d)(7).

[A] Examples

As an example, assume a donor transfers property worth property $500,000 in trust for the lifetime benefit of his long-term girlfriend.[17] The trust provides that the trust beneficiary is to receive the net income generated by the transferred property for life. Upon the beneficiary's death, the trust property is to revert to the donor or the donor's estate. At the time the trust is funded, the donor's girlfriend is age 38, and the applicable Federal midterm rate is 4.8 percent. The interest-rate component to be used for § 7520 purposes therefore equals 5.8 percent (5.76 percent rounded to the nearest 2/10 of 1 percent).

Regulation § 20.2031-7T(d)(1) provides the actuarial component to be used in determining the remainder interest following a life estate measured by the lifetime of a single individual. *See* Treas. Reg. § 25.2512-5(a) (providing that actuarial tables from estate tax regulations apply for gift tax valuation as well). Applying the table, the remainder factor following a life estate of a 38-year-old assuming a 5.8 percent rate of return is 0.13661. Applying this factor to the transfer, the donor's reversion is valued at $68,305. The life estate is valued at the balance of the transferred property, or $431,695. Note that the actuarial components assigned to the remainder interest in transferred property bear a direct relationship to the age of the life tenant and an inverse relationship to the discount rate.

Now suppose that instead of providing his girlfriend with an income interest in the transferred property, the donor directs the trustee to make annual payments of $50,000 to his girlfriend at the close of each year. Pursuant to Reg. § 20.2031-7T(d)(2)(iv), the present value of a right to receive an annuity payable at the end of each year for a term of years is determined by multiplying the annual payment by the appropriate annuity actuarial factor.[18] The annuity actuarial factor is determined by subtracting the actuarial component attributable to a remainder interest following a term of years reproduced in Reg. § 20.2031-7(d)(6) from the number 1.00 (to arrive at the component attributable to the term interest) and then dividing the resulting figure by the applicable § 7520 interest rate. The annuity actuarial component is then multiplied by the annual annuity payment to determine the value of the annuity.

Applying these rules to the example, the actuarial component attributable to a remainder interest following a 10-year term certain assuming a § 7520 rate of 5.8 percent is 0.569041. The factor attributable to the annuity therefore is 0.430959. Dividing this amount by 5.8 percent yields an annuity actuarial factor of 7.4303. Multiplying this amount by the $50,000 annual annuity payment yields a value of $371,515 for the transferred annuity.

[B] Effect of Uncertain Events

The actuarial valuation regime prescribed by § 7520 does not translate well to interests that are conditioned on events other than an individual's death. In Revenue Ruling 61-88, 1961-1 C.B. 417, the Service addressed the valuation of a contingent remainder interest in a trust that would become possessory only if the lifetime beneficiary of the trust, a married 44-year-old woman who had never had children, died without issue. The ruling concluded that the

---

[17] The example uses a non-relative to avoid § 2702, which creates a special valuation regime for transfers in trust to members of the transferor's family. *See* § 10.05[B].

[18] Adjustments for annuity payments made at other intervals during the year are provided in Table J, which also is reproduced in Reg. § 20.2031-7(d)(6).

valuation of the remainder interest "by the mere mechanical application of actuarial formulas is not supportable." *Id.* at 417. However, the ruling was quick to note that this determination did not mean the remainder interest was valueless.[19] Rather, recognizing that the contingent remainder interest in these circumstances could be "of considerable value," the ruling concluded that the remainder had to be valued under the general willing buyer-willing seller standard of Reg. § 20.2031-1(b), giving consideration to all known circumstances relating to the particular life tenant. *Id.* at 418; *see also* Treas. Reg. § 20.7520-3(b)(1)(iii) (if § 7520 valuation not appropriate, determination of fair market value to be made based on all facts and circumstances). Although death without issue may not be capable of actuarial approximation, the prospects of an individual remarrying are sufficiently definite to resort to actuarial tables. For example, in Revenue Ruling 71-67, 1971-1 C.B. 271, the decedent was obligated to make support payments to his surviving spouse for her lifetime or until her subsequent remarriage. In determining the commuted value of these payments, the Service sanctioned the use of actuarial figures drawn from the American Remarriage Table to discount the value of the spouse's interest based on the prospect of her remarriage.

[C]   Departures from Tables

The mortality component of the § 7520 valuation tables may not be used if the individual who serves as the measuring life is terminally ill at the time the transfer is completed. Treas. Reg. §§ 20.7520-3(b)(3)(i), 25.7520-3(b)(3). The purpose of this limitation is to prevent parties from exploiting the actuarial tables when the parties know that the portion of the property attributable to the measuring life is overvalued. For purposes of this exception, an individual known to have an incurable illness or other deteriorating physical condition will be considered terminally ill if there is at least a 50 percent probability that the individual will die within one year. *See id.* However, if the individual survives for 18 months after the date of the transfer, the individual shall be presumed to have not been terminally ill. This later presumption can be rebutted only through the provision of clear and convincing evidence to the contrary. *See id.*

[D]   Potential Effect of § 2702

The actuarial approximations of value provided by the § 7520 regime are just that—approximations. In any particular case, the discount rate and the mortality components embedded in the actuarial valuation may understate or overstate the value of the transferred property interest. Any imprecision resulting from the use of actuarial tables is justified by the resulting ease of administration. No experts are needed to determine the fair market value of the temporal property interest at issue, and courts need not intervene to reconcile conflicting valuations. However, because the actuarial valuations are binding on both the taxpayer and the government, one can expect that taxpayers will exploit the valuation tables when the underlying assumptions operate to the taxpayers' advantage.

As an example, assume that a donor transfers stock in a closely held corporation to a trust for the ultimate benefit of his children, but the donor retains the right to the income from the trust property for a period of 10 years. The donor values the gift of the remainder by

---

[19] However, in certain instances, a court may determine that restrictions imposed on a future interest render it incapable of reasonable valuation. For example, in *Robinette v. Helvering*, 318 U.S. 184 (1943), the Court determined that a lifetime gift could not be reduced by the value of the donor's reversionary interest where the reversion was conditioned on the absence of the surviving issue of the donor at the death of the life tenants.

subtracting the actuarial value of his term interest, which presumes that the trust property will earn a rate of return equal to 120 percent of the applicable Federal mid-term rate. However, the donor fully intends that the corporation will never pay a dividend. If use of the § 7520 tables were permissible in this context, the donor effectively will receive a tax-free reduction to the value of the gift to his children.

Concerned with the exploitation of the actuarial tables in this manner, Congress enacted § 2702 to govern the valuation of transfers in trust for the benefit of family members where the donor retains an interest in the property. Section 2702 adopts a harsh general rule: any interest retained by the donor in this context will be assigned a value of zero. IRC § 2702(a)(2)(A). Therefore, the remainder interest will be valued at the full amount of the transfer, regardless of its actual fair market value. Only if the donor's interest takes the form of a "qualified interest" sanctioned by the statute—which provides a more reliable payment stream to the donor—will use of the § 7520 tables in this context be permitted. The details of § 2702 are discussed in the context of retained interest transfers in Chapter 10.

§ 7.09   SECTION 2032 ALTERNATE VALUATION

Internal Revenue Code:	§ 2032
Treasury Regulations:	§ 20.2032-1(b)(2), (c)(1), (d), (f)(1)
	§ 20.7520-1(b)(1)

As a general rule, property is to be valued for estate tax purposes as of the date of the decedent's death. However, pursuant to § 2032, a decedent's executor may elect to value the property included in the gross estate as of the "alternate valuation date"—generally six months following the decedent's death. *See* IRC § 2032(a)(2). The provision, enacted in 1935 following the stock market crash of 1929, was intended to ameliorate the potentially drastic increase in the effective estate tax rate that could be occasioned by a precipitous drop in property values.

To elect the alternate valuation regime, both the value of the decedent's gross estate and the amount of the estate tax and GST tax liability must be reduced by its application. IRC § 2032(c). This requirement prevents parties from exploiting the alternate valuation regime to obtain a greater step-up in basis under § 1014 in situations where there would be no resulting estate tax cost (because the estate is fully shielded from tax by available deductions or credits). If elected, the alternate valuation system applies across-the-board in valuing the decedent's gross estate. In other words, the decedent's executor cannot apply alternate valuation selectively with respect to depreciated assets only. *See* Treas. Reg. § 20.2032-1(b)(1).

While property included in the gross estate generally is valued as of six months following the decedent's death, two exceptions exist to this general approach. First, if property included in the decedent's gross estate is distributed, sold, exchanged, or otherwise disposed of by the estate, the property is valued as of the date of such transfer.[20] IRC § 2032(a)(1). Although this exception "comprehends all possible ways by which property ceases to form a part of the gross estate," Treas. Reg. § 20.2032-1(c)(1), the provision does not apply to real property that vests immediately in the decedent's heirs or devisees. Rather, to the extent the realty remains subject to the claims of the decedent's creditors, no distribution for purposes of § 2032 occurs.

---

[20] Thus, if property is sold at its fair market value during the six-month window from an estate that elects the alternate valuation regime, the sale will not result in the realization of gain or loss, as the fair market value of the property on that date becomes the estate's basis in the property under § 1014. *See* IRC § 1014(a)(2).

See Rev. Rul. 78-378, 1978-2 C.B. 229. If the rule were otherwise, the alternate valuation would be unavailable with respect to real property as a practical matter.

The second exception pertains to property that is "affected by mere lapse of time." IRC § 2032(a)(3). Such interests shall be included in the gross estate at their date of death value, with any adjustment in value between then and the alternate valuation date that is not attributable to the mere lapse of time. As an example, suppose a decedent died owning a remainder interest in a trust that will become possessory after a relative's death. The remaining life expectancy of the relative will be determined as of the decedent's death, even if the decedent's estate elects to value the gross estate under the alternate valuation regime. Any enhancement in the actuarial value of the decedent's remainder resulting from the relative being six months older is attributable to the mere passage of time and, accordingly, is disregarded. However, the fair market value of the trust property to which the § 7520 actuarial values apply will be determined as of the date six months following the decedent's death, as this factor is not affected by the mere passage of time. *See* Treas. Reg. §§ 20.2032-1(f)(1), 20.7520-1(b)(1).

The alternate valuation regime is not intended to expand the scope of property subject to taxation in the decedent's estate. Rather, alternate valuation applies only to property included in the decedent's gross estate as of the date of death, and property earned or accrued thereafter remains exempt from estate taxation even if alternate valuation is elected. *See* Treas. Reg. § 20.2032-1(d). Interest paid on bonds, dividends paid on stock, and rent received from the lease of property that accrues after the date of the decedent's death will not be swept into the estate tax base by operation of the alternate valuation regime. Only in situations where the payment received represents a replacement for property included in the gross estate—as opposed to an investment return thereon—will the amount received be treated as "included property" for alternate valuation purposes. *See* Treas. Reg. § 20.2032-1(d)(4) (addressing distributions in partial liquidation of corporate stock).

§ 7.10   STUDY PROBLEMS

1.   Annette received stock of her corporate employer as part of an employee retention program. The terms of the stock grant provided that if Annette terminated her employment within five years for any reason other than death or disability, the stock would be forfeited back to the employer. Annette died four years after receiving the stock. Discuss how the stock will be valued in Annette's gross estate.

2.   Bart purchased two vacant lots in a development several years ago as an investment. He is contemplating making gifts of the realty to his two children who he wants to benefit equally. Bart figures the simplest approach is to transfer one lot to each. Do have any suggestions on restructuring the gifts?

3.   Ellen owns a 60 percent interest in the stock of a corporation; the remaining 40 percent is owned by her brother. Ellen transfers a 15 percent interest to her son. Two years later, Ellen dies owning a 45 percent interest in the corporation. Ellen's will devised a 36 percent interest to her son, and the remaining 9 percent interest is devised in equal shares to her nephews and nieces (9 total).

     a.   Comment on Ellen's proposed gift of a 15 percent interest to her son. In particular, what factors will be relevant to the valuation of the stock?

b. Suppose that the government asserts that the 36 percent interest Ellen devised to her son should be valued through the application of a control premium, because the devise when added to the son's 15 percent interest affords him majority ownership. Comment on the government's argument.

c. Ellen's executor asserts a minimal value on the one percent stock interest left to each niece and nephew. Comment on the estate's argument.

d. If Ellen desired to retain the right to vote the stock during her lifetime but wanted to make transfers of the economic rights to the stock, how could Ellen have accomplished her goals? [Note that the straightforward approach of transferring the stock while retaining the legal right to vote the stock is effectively precluded by § 2036(b).]

4. Randolph dies on March 1, Year 1, owning the following assets:

Asset	Date of death value
Mutual fund shares	3,000,000
Corporate bonds	1,000,000
Real estate	2,000,000
Treasury bills	250,000

The stock market experiences a stark "correction" in June of Year 1, and the value of the mutual fund shares held by the estate declines to $1.8 million. The executor believes that the stock market dip represents an overreaction to economic data, and that the market will rebound significantly in the near future. All other asset values are relatively constant. Do you have any suggestions for the executor to minimize the decedent's estate tax liability?

5. Assume the facts of problem (4), except that Randolph also owned a $3 million life insurance policy insuring the life of his wife. The replacement value of the policy is $750,000 as of Randolph's death. In August of Year 1, Randolph's wife dies unexpectedly in a car accident. What effect, if any, will the death of Randolph's wife have on Randolph's estate tax liability?

6. Your friend Bette was raised on a farm owned and operated by her parents. She now works on Wall Street for an investment banking firm. Her mother (who survived her father) recently died. In discussing her mother's estate with you over lunch, Bette quotes the estate's lawyer as saying, "Looks like we will get a $1 million break on valuing the real property because your parents operated it as a farm." She asks you if this is true. What is your response?

7. Pursuant to a property settlement agreement, Victor transfers $1 million in trust for the benefit of his former wife. The trust provides that the income of the trust is to be paid to his former wife for her lifetime, with the remainder passing to Victor or his probate estate. Assuming Victor's former wife is age 40 at the time of the trust funding, what is the actuarial value of her life estate? Assume, alternatively, that the prevailing Federal midterm rate is 3.6 percent and 5.6 percent.

Chapter 8

JOINT INTERESTS IN PROPERTY

Internal Revenue Code: § 2040
Treasury Regulations: §§ 25.2511-1(h)(4), (5), 20.2041-1

§ 8.01   CREATION OF A JOINT INTEREST

[A]   Standard Approach

As a general rule, if an individual purchases property titled in his name and that of another—whether as tenants in common, joint tenants with right of survivorship, or tenants by the entirety—the purchaser has made a gift to the co-tenant of his undivided fractional interest in the property. *See* Treas. Reg. § 25.2511-1(h)(5). Where more than one donee is designated as a co-tenant of the property, the transfer constitutes a separate gift to each donee (which, in turn, allows for the application of multiple annual exclusions to the transfer). In *Buder v. Commissioner*, 25 T.C. 1012 (1956), the Tax Court allowed two annual exclusions for the donor's transfer of bonds to his son and daughter-in-law as tenants by the entirety, but predictably rejected the donor's creative invocation of a third exclusion attributable to the entirety as a separate legal entity under state law.

If title to the property does not provide for a right of survivorship in the surviving joint tenant (as is the case with tenancies in common) or if the right of survivorship inherent in the title can be defeated through unilateral severance of the tenancy (as is the case with joint tenancies), the amount transferred to each donee equals his fractional interest of the purchase price. The rationale for this treatment is that each donee has the potential to realize outright ownership of his fractional interest in the property through a partition proceeding. On the other hand, if the right of survivorship cannot be defeated through the unilateral action of any joint tenant (as is the case with tenancies by the entirety), then the amount transferred to each donee is not based on their percentage interest in the property alone. The likelihood of each spouse surviving the other and thereby receiving outright ownership of the property also must be considered in valuing the separate gifts.[1] Transfers of property to spouses as tenants by the entirety therefore will constitute equal gifts to each spouse only by coincidence.

The Service illustrated the tax consequences resulting from the purchase of property in the joint names of others in Revenue Ruling 78-362, 1978-2 C.B. 248. Under the hypothetical facts of the ruling, *D* paid $30x as a down payment on real property that *D* caused to be titled in the

---

[1] *See* Stephens, Maxfield, Lind, Calfee & Smith, Federal Estate and Gift Taxation ¶ 9.04[1] (8th ed. 2002) (citing regulations issued under former § 2515 addressing the creation of tenancies by the entirety prior to that section's repeal in 1981).

names of *D*, *A*, and *B*, as joint tenants with right of survivorship. The property was subject to a mortgage of $120x, which *D* paid in regular monthly installments. The ruling summarized the tax consequences as follows:

> In the present situation, *D*, *A*, and *B* owned equal interests in the jointly owned property that could be unilaterally severed. Since *D* provided the funds for the down payment and received no consideration from *A* and *B*, *D* made taxable gifts of the one-third interests to *A* and *B* when the property was purchased and placed in joint ownership. Inasmuch as the expenses of the property were the obligations of *D*, *A*, and *B* in equal shares, *D*'s monthly payments of the mortgage were gifts to *A* and *B* when *D* paid their respective one-third shares of the obligations without the expectation of reimbursement from *A* and *B*.

[B] Exception for Revocable Transfers

While the creation of joint interests in property generally carries immediate gift tax consequences, that approach does not hold if the interest of a party holding joint title can be revoked by the donor. Take a standard joint bank account with right of survivorship as an example. *Mother* opens the account and is the source of all deposits; *Son* is listed as a joint account holder primarily to permit him to write checks on *Mother's* behalf. Pursuant to the terms of the account, *Mother* can withdraw the entire account balance and thereby defeat *Son's* interest. Hence, the mere creation of the joint account does not guarantee that *Son* will benefit from the account. The gift tax consequences therefore are deferred until *Son* withdraws funds for his individual benefit without objection from *Mother*.[2] *See* Treas. Reg. § 25.2511-1(h)(4). This wait-and-see approach applies in any situation where the transferor can reclaim the subject property without the consent of other joint account holders. *Id.*

§ 8.02 INCLUSION OF JOINTLY HELD PROPERTY IN GROSS ESTATE

Whereas the gift tax treatment of the creation of joint interests in property is fairly straightforward, no singular approach governs the estate tax consequences of owning property jointly with others. Rather, the appropriate inclusionary statute turns on whether the decedent's interest in the property survives or is extinguished by the decedent's death. Recall that if the decedent possesses an interest in the property that is capable of descent and devise (such as an interest as tenant in common), the value of the decedent's co-tenancy interest will be included in his gross estate under § 2033. Yet if the decedent's interest in the property is terminated upon his death through a right of survivorship in favor of the other joint owners, § 2033 has no application. Joint interests in property that provide a right of survivorship in the remaining co-owners therefore must be included in the decedent's gross estate under another section, less the estate tax be easily circumvented through this common non-probate transfer. Section 2040 serves that role.

---

[2] *See* Unif. Probate Code §§ 6-221, 6-222 (1989) (authorizing a financial institution to disburse funds in a joint account to any account holder without inquiry into the source of deposits to the account). *But see id.* § 6-211 (providing that, as between joint account holders, the account balance belongs to the parties in proportion to the net contribution of each to the account).

[A] General Framework—Proportionate Inclusion Based on Financial Contribution

Section 2040(a) provides two inclusionary regimes for property held by the decedent with others as joint tenants with right of survivorship or as tenants by the entirety. One governs property acquired by purchase, while the other addresses property acquired through gift, devise, bequest, or inheritance.

[1] Property Acquired by Purchase

With respect to property acquired by purchase, the starting point under § 2040(a) is to include in the decedent's gross estate the *full value* of property in which the decedent owned a joint interest providing for rights of survivorship. Similarly, *all sums* on deposit in a bank account titled jointly in the names of the decedent and another with rights of survivorship are included in the decedent's gross estate as an initial matter.[3] The decedent's estate can mitigate the potentially overbroad default rule of full inclusion by establishing that the surviving joint tenant supplied consideration for the property or was the source of amounts deposited to the relevant account.[4] *See* Treas. Reg. § 20.2040-1(a) (clarifying that the executor bears the burden of proof); *see also* Heidt v. Commissioner, 8 T.C. 969 (1947), *aff'd per curiam*, 170 F.2d 1021 (9th Cir. 1948). If a surviving joint tenant made his own contributions toward the purchase price of the property or to the balance of the joint account, then the fraction of the property's value or the account balance attributable to such contributions is subtracted from the amount included in the decedent's gross estate. IRC § 2040(a) ("except" clause).

> Example 1: *A* purchased property with his sister, *S*, as joint tenants with right of survivorship. The property costs $500,000. *A* provided $450,000 of the purchase price, *S* the remaining $50,000. If *A* were to predecease *S*, 90 percent of the then fair market value of the property will be included in his gross estate under § 2040(a). *See* Treas. Reg. § 20.2040-1(c)(1). However, if *S* were to predecease *A*, only 10 percent of the property's value will be included in her gross estate. *See* Treas. Reg. § 20.2040-1(c)(3). In both cases, it is assumed that the decedent's estate can sufficiently establish the contributions to the purchase price supplied by the surviving co-tenant.

[2] Property Transferred Gratuitously

The approach of including property in a joint-owner's gross estate based on relative financial contributions to the property's purchase price is inapposite where no co-owner purchases the property. Hence, a different rule is needed if the jointly owned property was acquired by the co-owners through gift, devise, bequest, or inheritance from another. In that context, the amount included in a deceased joint tenant's gross estate is equal to the decedent's fractional interest of the property's fair market value. IRC § 2040(a) (second "provided" clause). Reconciling this rule with the application of § 2040(a) to purchased property, the statute

---

[3] The regulations make clear that this aspect of § 2040(a) is not limited literally to bank accounts, but extends to "a bond or other instrument" titled in the name of the decedent and any other person, payable to either or to the survivor. Treas. Reg. § 20.2040-1(b).

[4] If a surviving joint tenant supplied consideration for the property that was acquired from the decedent for less than adequate and full consideration in money or money's worth, then the exclusion is limited to the portion of the property attributable to the consideration supplied by the surviving joint tenant. IRC § 2040(a) (first "provided" clause).

effectively treats each joint tenant as having purchased his gratuitously received portion of the property for value.

> Example 2: *Father* devised an undivided tract of real estate to *C1*, *C2*, and *C3* as joint tenants with right of survivorship. Years later, *C1* predeceases *C2* and *C3*. Under § 2040(a), one-third of the value of the property will be included in *C1's* gross estate. *See* Treas. Reg. § 20.2040-1(c)(8).

[B]   Simplified Treatment of Spousal Property

If property is jointly owned by spouses with rights of survivorship, § 2040(b) supplies a simplifying convention: One-half of the value of the property will be included in the decedent's gross estate.[5] The spouses' relative contributions toward the purchase price of the property are irrelevant. The simplified convention applies only if the joint ownership is limited to the decedent and his spouse, either as tenants by the entirety or as joint tenants with right of survivorship. If a non-spouse is included on the title, then the general rules of § 2040(a) will govern the interests of all parties. Given that the majority of jointly held property is owned between spouses, the simplified approach of § 2040(b) in practice operates as the general rule.

[C]   Relative Contributions of Property Owners—Tracing and Measurement Problems

Returning to property jointly owned by individuals who are not spouses, the approach of § 2040(a) as it applies to purchased property appears fairly straightforward. Simply start with the full value of the property as of the decedent's death, and then subtract the portion of such value attributable to the contributions of other joint owners of the property. Yet determining the relative contributions made by the surviving joint tenants that warrant an exclusion from the decedent's gross estate can be complicated in practice. Specific rules relating to the determination of contributions from other joint tenants are discussed below.

[1]   Financed Acquisition Costs

Suppose *A* and *B*, who are not married, acquire jointly owned property for $100,000. The two each supply $5,000 at closing, and they finance the remaining $90,000 of the purchase price. Both *A* and *B* sign the promissory note as obligors. Consistent with the treatment of debt for income tax purposes, *A* and *B* are treated as having made equal contributions to the acquisition of the property for purposes of § 2040(a). That remains the case even if only one party makes the monthly mortgage payments out of separate funds. Rather than altering the relative contributions toward the purchase price, one-half of each mortgage payment will constitute a gift to the non-paying obligor. *See* Rev. Rul. 78-362, 1978-2 C.B. 248 (citing Estate v. Woody v. Commissioner, 36 T.C. 900 (1961)).

---

[5]   This convention does not apply if the surviving spouse is not a citizen of the United States. IRC § 2056(d)(1)(B). Under these circumstances, the relative-contribution rule of § 2040(a) applies instead. Selected transfer tax issues arising in the international context are addressed in Chapter 26.

[2] Subsequent Investments in Property

Recall that for income tax purposes, capital improvements to property are treated as subsequent acquisition costs that increase the property's basis. IRC § 1016(a)(1). The same treatment applies in the context of § 2040(a), as the regulations include the cost of "capital additions" in the value of the denominator under the exclusionary rule. Treas. Reg. § 20.2040-1(a)(2). Complications arise, however, if the property has fluctuated in value between its acquisition and the later investments in the property. For instance, returning to the example above where *A* and *B* purchased property for $100,000, assume that the property subsequently appreciated in value to $400,000. At that point, *A* expended $50,000 of his own funds toward capital improvements of the property. *A* later predeceased *B* when the property was valued at $600,000. What portion of the property should be included in *A's* gross estate under § 2040(a)?

Applying the terms of § 2040(a) literally would lead to including two-thirds of the value of the property, or $400,000, in *A's* gross estate. Of the total $150,000 in acquisition costs and capital improvements, *A* provided $100,000. This approach, however, does not accurately measure the relative contributions of the parties. Namely, it undervalues *B's* contribution to the property by not taking into account the increase in the property's value between the cash outlays. A more reasoned approach would treat the interim appreciation in the property as a cash contribution made by *A* and *B* together. Hence, the total contributions would equal $450,000, consisting of $100,000 (initial purchase price), $300,000 (appreciation allocable to *A* and *B* in equal shares), and $50,000 (capital improvements paid for by *A*). Employing this method, *A's* relative contribution to the purchase price would be $250,000 divided by $450,000, or 5/9. As a result, only $333,333 would be included in *A's* gross estate under § 2040(a). Whether this approach would be accepted by the Service or endorsed by courts is not clear, although the Tax Court has indicated that a formulaic approach may be necessary in such a situation (which was not then before the court due to the lack of appreciation in the property). *See* Peters v. Commissioner, 46 T.C. 407, 415 n.4 (1966). Note that implementing the more accurate method of determining the relative contributions of the joint tenants in this context necessitates determining the value of the property at the time the subsequent improvements were made—a determination that can prove difficult in hindsight.

[3] Contributions Attributable to Income or Appreciation in Gifted Property

In order for a contribution to the purchase price of property by a surviving joint tenant to be considered under the exclusionary formula of § 2040(a), the contribution cannot be attributable to a gratuitous transfer from the decedent. In terms of the statute, the consideration supplied by the other joint tenant must be shown "to have originally belonged to such other person and never to have been received or acquired by the latter from the decedent for less than an adequate and full consideration in money or money's worth." IRC § 2040(a) ("except" clause). The purpose of this condition on the contribution provided by the surviving joint tenant is to prevent the easy manipulation of the general rule of § 2040(a) by funneling funds used to acquire property through the other joint tenants prior to purchase.

While cash or other property gratuitously provided to the surviving joint tenant by the decedent is ignored as a contribution by the joint tenant under § 2040(a), a more cumbersome issue is whether the prohibition extends to income derived from gifted property or amounts attributable to post-gift appreciation. With respect to interest or dividend payments received on gifted property, § 2040(a) follows the storied distinction between property and income under the federal income tax. That is, payments of income severable from the underlying property are treated as the surviving joint tenant's individual property. *See* Treas. Reg. § 20.2040-1(c)(5); *see also* Howard v. Commissioner, 9 T.C. 1192 (1947) (dividends received on gifted stock treated as donee's separate property). Similarly, if property previously conveyed gratuitously by the decedent to the other joint tenant is later sold by the joint tenant who then applies the sale proceeds toward the purchase of jointly owned property, the portion of the sale proceeds attributable to post-gift appreciation in the property is treated as a contribution of the other joint tenant's separate funds. *See* Rev. Rul. 79-372, 1979-2 C.B. 330; *see also* Harvey v. United States, 185 F.2d 463 (7th Cir. 1950). Yet if the other joint tenant does not sell property received from the decedent by gift but instead exchanges such property for his interest in replacement property jointly held with the decedent as of the decedent's death, then the entire purchase price is deemed to have been supplied by the decedent. *See* Treas. Reg. § 20.2040-1(c)(4). Hence, where the surviving joint tenant has previously received property from the deceased joint tenant by gift, the post-gift appreciation in the property will not be regarded as a contribution toward the purchase of the jointly owned property unless it is first reduced to cash.[6]

The treatment of post-gift appreciation in property previously transferred by the decedent to the other joint tenant under the § 2040(a) exclusionary rule becomes even more difficult when the previously transferred property was itself jointly held. For instance, assume that a decedent (*D*) conveys *Blackacre* to himself and his brother (*B*) when *Blackacre* has a value of $100,000. After *Blackacre* increases in value to $300,000, the parties exchange it for *Whiteacre*, again taking title as joint tenants with right of survivorship. *D* then dies. The regulations indicate that the entire purchase price for *Whiteacre* will be treated as being provided by *D*, so that the entire value of the property will be included in *D's* gross estate under § 2040(a). *See id.* Can this result be avoided by first liquidating *Blackacre* and then using the cash proceeds to purchase *Whiteacre* (adverse income tax consequences notwithstanding)? Revenue Ruling 79-372 and *Harvey v. United States* referenced above would suggest that a conversion of appreciation to cash is sufficient to treat a portion of the post-gift appreciation as a contribution from the surviving joint tenant's separate funds. However, the district court in *Endicott Trust Co. v. United States*, 305 F. Supp. 943 (N.D.N.Y. 1969), concluded otherwise by attributing the entire purchase price of the replacement property in this context to the decedent. Hence, the liquidation of jointly held property followed by the reinvestment of the proceeds in the same manner is not sufficient to treat a portion of the purchase cost (namely, the surviving tenant's share of post-gift appreciation) as having been supplied by the surviving joint tenant.

[4] Consideration Provided Through Services or Use of Property

The exclusionary rule under § 2040(a) presumes that the relative contributions toward the acquisition cost of the jointly owned property will be made in cash or property. Yet what if the surviving joint tenant provided services to the decedent or afforded the decedent use of property in exchange for his interest? Should the value of services or the rental value of property constitute property received from the decedent for adequate and full consideration in money or money's worth so as to treat the surviving joint tenant as having contributed to the cost of the property? Case law addressing this issue remains unclear.

---

[6] Note that a sale for cash will trigger recognition of the gain for income tax purposes. IRC § 1001(a), (c).

In *Spaeder v. United States*, 478 F. Supp. 73 (W.D. Pa. 1978), the decedent supplied funds for his long-time friends (a married couple) to purchase a new home. The property was titled in the names of the decedent and his friends as joint tenants with right of survivorship, with the decedent possessing an undivided one-half interest in the property. As part of the transaction, the decedent's friends promised to provide the decedent with "care, comfort, and support" by residing with him. *Id.* at 79. The decedent's estate took the position that the friends' agreement to provide care to the decedent amounted to consideration for the purchase of their interest in the house. The district court disagreed, explaining that the consideration provided by the decedent's friends in the form of services to the decedent did not constitute consideration "in money or money's worth" as required by the statute. *Id.*

The district court's holding in *Spaeder* on this front is questionable at best. If services rendered to a transferor did not amount to the provision of consideration in money or money's worth, then every payment for a service would amount to a gift under § 2512(b)—an absurd result. Indeed, the Tax Court has held that a transferee's agreement to provide care and support to a transferor for the remainder of her life constitutes consideration in money or money's worth under § 2512 to the extent of the present value of the future services. *See* Bergan v. Commissioner, 1 T.C. 543 (1943). The statutory basis for the district court's holding in *Spaeder* is therefore flawed.

The estate tax consequences of consideration supplied by the surviving joint tenant through the provision of services can be more rationally determined by isolating the component aspects of the arrangement.[7] Rather than providing the *entire* purchase price of the property, the decedent essentially pre-pays the present fair market value of the future services through a cash payment to the service provider. The service provider, in turn, contributes that amount of cash toward the purchase of his interest in the property. When the relevant cash flows of the arrangement are segregated in this manner, the financial contribution of the surviving joint tenant that invokes the exclusionary rule under § 2040(a) is unmistakable.

The Tax Court in *Estate of Concordia v. Commissioner*, T.C. Memo. 2002-216, 84 T.C.M. (CCH) 254, equivocated on whether the provision of services could amount to consideration paid by a joint tenant for § 2040 purposes in addressing whether the provision of the use of other property constituted consideration under the statute. The decedent in *Concordia* conveyed property that she owned individually to herself and her niece as joint tenants with right of survivorship. In exchange for the conveyance, the niece agreed to allow the decedent to live with her and to manage rental property owned by the decedent. The decedent's estate included only one-half the value of the jointly held property under § 2040(a), contending that the niece supplied consideration for her one-half interest. The Tax Court agreed, finding that the fair rental value of the decedent's use of the niece's residence exceeded one-half of the value of the transferred property. Hence, the court had no need to consider whether the niece's property management services constituted additional consideration supplied by the niece toward the purchase price. Nonetheless, the Tax Court in *Concordia* did not recite the blanket disallowance of services as consideration articulated in *Spaeder*. If anything, the opinion suggests that the court would have taken the value of the services into consideration if necessary. *Id.* at 258 (noting that if the value of the services "should be included in the numerator of the formula for exclusion," the portion excluded would further exceed the one-half amount claimed by the estate).

---

[7] Unfortunately, doing so also highlights the income tax consequences of the arrangement to the service provider.

[5] Tracing Difficulties with Bank Accounts

The burden placed on the estate to establish the amount of funds contributed by the surviving joint tenant (and never acquired gratuitously from the decedent) under the exclusionary rule of § 2040(a) is intensified in the context of joint bank accounts. Given the fluidity of funds in that context, the estate not only must identify the deposits made by the surviving joint tenant, but also must establish that the joint tenant did not subsequently withdraw those amounts. As illustrated in *Drazen v. Commissioner*, 48 T.C. 1 (1967), this task can prove onerous. Accordingly, for clients with meaningful exposure to the estate tax, joint bank accounts between non-spouses should be avoided unless the parties intend for only one account holder to supply the deposits.

§ 8.03 COMPARATIVE TREATMENT OF TENANCY IN COMMON INTERESTS

The creation of joint interests in property carries the same gift tax consequences regardless of whether the property is titled as a tenancy in common or a joint tenancy with right of survivorship. However, the estate tax ramifications of these state-law interests can differ significantly. These potential discrepancies are described below.

[A] Valuation Discrepancies

If a decedent dies owning a fractional interest in property as a tenant-in-common, his interest is included in his gross estate under § 2033 and is valued under the willing buyer-willing seller general standard of valuation set forth in Reg. § 20.2031-1(b). As previously described in Chapter 7, a co-tenant's lack of unilateral control over the subject property and the resulting limited market for joint interests support meaningful discounts from the pro-rata value of the tenants in common interest.[8] Of course, a co-tenancy interest in property as a joint tenant with right of survivorship is subject to the same practical detriments of undivided fractional ownership of property. Yet if a decedent provided half the total consideration for his joint tenancy interest, then half of the property's total value will be included in his estate under § 2040(a). Because § 2040 values the joint tenancy interest as a portion of the property's total, unfractionalized value, no discounts to reflect the inherent detriments of co-ownership are available. In *Estate of Young v. Commissioner*, 110 T.C. 297 (1998), the Tax Court clarified that § 2040 provides not only a rule of inclusion, but also a case-specific method of valuation. In the process, the court rejected the taxpayer's attempts in employing the general standards of § 2031 in valuing the decedent's joint interest in property. Property co-owned as joint tenants with right of survivorship therefore suffers a relative valuation disadvantage when compared to property co-owned as tenants in common.

[B] Severance of Joint Tenancy as Means of Reducing Estate Tax

Suppose that *Mother* purchased property that she caused to be titled in her name and that of *Daughter* as joint tenants with right of survivorship. Since the purchase, the property has increased in value three fold. If nothing were to change, the entire value of the property will be included in *Mother's* gross estate under § 2040(a) when she dies. Yet note that if *Mother*

---

[8] For discussion of fractional interest discounts available in valuing tenants in common interests, see § 7.05[A].

and *Daughter* were to sever the joint tenancy and instead hold title as tenants in common, only a one-half interest in the property would be included in *Mother's* gross estate under § 2033.[9] [In addition, fractional interest discounts will be available in valuing the one-half undivided interest.] Note that the estate tax savings from this move come at the expense of a full step-up in the property's income tax basis under § 1014 and the potential detriment of subjecting *Mother's* interest in the property to the vagaries of probate administration. Yet for a client whose assets will be subject to the highest marginal estate tax rate, the spread between estate tax rates and capital gain rates (not to mention *Daughter's* ability to defer recognition of the income tax by continuing to hold the property) counsel in favor of severing the joint tenancy.

§ 8.04 RECONCILING THE ESTATE AND GIFT TAX CONSEQUENCES

In the example above, note the apparent over-taxation of *Mother's* transfers to *Daughter*. *Mother* was treated as transferring one-half of the purchase price of the property to *Daughter* upon creation of the joint tenancy. Then, if the joint tenancy remains intact, the full value of the property will be included in *Mother's* gross estate when she dies. While it appears that more than 100 percent of the property's value is being subject to federal transfer taxation, the reduction to the tentative estate tax liability afforded for gift tax payable on gifts made by the decedent under § 2001(b) prevents this result. Through this computation, the date-of-death value of the property—but no more—is subject to federal transfer taxation.

§ 8.05 STUDY PROBLEMS

1. Brandon purchases a tract of timberland for $750,000. At closing, he directs that title be issued in his name and that of Emma and Smith (his children) each as one-third joint tenants with right of survivorship. Several years later, timber on the property is cut and sold for $300,000. The owners use the proceeds to purchase an undeveloped lot at the coast, again taking title as joint tenants with right of survivorship. At Brandon's death 10 years later, the timberland is worth $900,000 and the coastal lot is worth $480,000.

   a. What are the gift tax consequences of these transactions?

   b. What amounts will be included in Brandon's gross estate on account of these properties?

2. Assume that several years after Brandon's death, the coastal lot has skyrocketed in value to $1.2 million. Emma and Smith continue to hold the property as joint tenants with right of survivorship. What estate-tax exposure does each face on account of the property? Is there anything they could do to reduce such exposure?

3. Betsy opens a brokerage account in her name and that of her husband, Jason, and makes an initial contribution of $1 million to the account. Jason later contributes $200,000 of his separate funds. When the securities in the account have appreciated in value to $1.8 million, Jason dies.

---

[9] This is the case even if the elimination of survivorship rights occurs within three years of death, as the claw-back rule of § 2035(a) does not apply to property that would have been included in the decedent's gross estate under § 2040.

    a.   What are the gift tax consequences of these transactions?

    b.   How much of the account balance will be included in Jason's gross estate?

4.   Mildred purchases a mountain home with her granddaughter, Michelle, for $400,000. Mildred pays $100,000 at closing, and takes out a loan in her individual name for the $300,000 balance of the purchase price. Michelle, however, agrees to provide considerable services in renovating the cabin on the property. After the cabin is renovated, the property is appraised at $600,000. Mildred then dies. Theoretically, what portion of the property's value should be included in Mildred's gross estate? State any additional information you may need to answer the question.

Chapter 9

LIFE INSURANCE

Internal Revenue Code:	§ 2042
	see also § 2035
Treasury Regulations:	§§ 20.2042-1, 25.2511-1(h)(8), (9)
	see also §§ 20.2031-2(f), -8(a), 25.2512-6(a)

In its most basic form, life insurance represents a contractual obligation of an insurer to pay a stated amount to a beneficiary designated by the owner of the policy upon the death of the insured. Life insurance is widely used in the estate planning context, with multiple variations existing on this basic theme. The popularity of life insurance is attributable in no small measure to the preferential treatment it receives under the federal income tax. Amounts invested through a life insurance policy grow on a tax-deferred basis,[1] and such deferral turns into an outright tax exemption when the policy proceeds are payable by reason of the insured's death. *See* IRC § 101(a). In addition to exempting investment yields, the exclusion from gross income afforded to life insurance proceeds exempts any mortality gain realized through the arrangement.[2] Yet income tax advantages alone do not account for the popularity of life insurance in the estate-planning context. Individuals often turn to life insurance to provide a source of liquidity to finance anticipated estate tax obligations of their estates, particularly where the estate will consist of closely held business interests or other illiquid assets. Planning with life insurance therefore can prevent the dreaded tax-driven fracture of the family business or family farm.[3] As discussed in this chapter, life insurance arrangements may be structured so that the proceeds of the policy will escape inclusion in the decedent-insured's estate. Hence, the skillful use of life insurance can convert the federal estate tax from a tax-inclusive levy to a tax-exclusive one.

Given the widespread use of life insurance as a vehicle to transfer wealth, a comprehensive estate tax must reach these arrangements. The federal estate tax in its original form, however, did not expressly address life insurance. The Service was forced to rely on the predecessor of § 2033 in its attempts to subject life insurance proceeds to estate taxation. While this proved sufficient to capture policy proceeds that were paid into the decedent's estate,[4] concerns arose

---

[1] As a general rule, amounts invested through a life insurance policy grow free of current tax, and withdrawals will be included in gross income only to the extent they exceed the premiums paid for the policy. *See* IRC § 72(e)(5), (6).

[2] Mortality gain can be described as the financial gain realized by the decedent from "winning" his bet with the life insurance company by failing to meet his actuarially determined life expectancy.

[3] Life insurance is prevalent in the closely held business context apart from estate tax considerations, as policies often are employed to provide the corporation or surviving shareholders with sufficient liquidity to meet their obligations under buy-sell agreements that are triggered by reason of an owner's death.

[4] *See, e.g.*, Mimnaugh v. United States, 66 Ct. Cl. 411 (1928) (holding that the proceeds of life insurance policies paid

that proceeds paid directly to designated beneficiaries would escape inclusion.[5] Congress was not long in correcting this legislative deficiency, enacting the predecessor to § 2042 as part of the Revenue Act of 1918.[6] In its current form, § 2042 includes the proceeds of insurance on the life of the decedent in the decedent's gross estate in two instances: (1) when the proceeds are receivable by the decedent's executor; and (2) when the proceeds are receivable by other beneficiaries if the decedent possessed an incident of ownership over the policy. As the first ground for inclusion constitutes something of a trap for the unwary, the majority of estate tax planning with life insurance centers on the second ground—that is, structuring life insurance arrangements so as to leave the decedent devoid of incidents of ownership.

§ 9.01 INSURANCE ON THE LIFE OF THE DECEDENT

As a preliminary matter, § 2042 applies only to amounts received as "insurance under policies on the life of the decedent." IRC § 2042(1), (2). If the decedent died owning insurance on the life of another, the policy would be treated as would any other asset for estate tax purposes. Inclusion of such policies generally is governed by § 2033.

Section 2042 does not provide an express definition of "insurance." While the vast majority of cases fail to implicate this definitional question, the issue has been raised in non-conventional arrangements. The regulations connote a broad interpretation of the statute, stating that insurance for purposes of the statute "refers to life insurance of every description, including death benefits paid by fraternal beneficial societies operating under the lodge system." Treas. Reg. § 20.2042-1(a)(1). Apart from indicating its potential to reach arrangements outside of conventional insurance contracts, this circular definition is unavailing. Courts therefore have articulated common law characteristics of insurance. In *Helvering v. Le Gierse*, 312 U.S. 531 (1941), the Supreme Court noted that the primary characteristics of insurance are the shifting of risk of the decedent's premature death and the spreading of that risk by the party paying the death benefit. Death benefits paid by the surviving members of a group or club therefore constitute insurance, as the risk of a member's premature death is borne by the survivors. *See* Commissioner v. Treganowan, 183 F.2d 288 (2d Cir. 1950) (death benefit paid by surviving members of NYSE found to be insurance governed by predecessor of § 2042); *see also* Rev. Rul. 65-222, 1965-2 C.B. 374 (following *Treganowan*). If payment of the death benefit operates as a release for potential tort claims, however, the payment does not constitute insurance for purposes of § 2042. *See* Rev. Rul. 57-54, 1957-1 C.B. 298. Rather, payment must be conditioned only upon the death of the insured.

Concerned that parties were exploiting the tax deferral afforded to investments in life insurance policies by structuring investment vehicles with relatively insignificant insurance

---

into the decedent's probate estate were included in his gross estate under the predecessor of § 2033); *see also* H. Rep. No. 65-767, at 22 (1918), 1939-1 C.B. (Part 2) 86, 101 (noting the prevailing understanding that insurance payable to the executor of the decedent's estate was included in the gross estate under predecessor of § 2033).

[5] The House report accompanying the Revenue Act of 1918 concluded that amounts passing directly from the insurance company to a designated beneficiary fell outside the reach of the predecessor of § 2033 on the basis that such amounts were not subject to the debts of the decedent or to the administrative expenses incurred in the decedent's probate estate. *See* H. Rep. No. 65-767, at 22, 1939-1 C.B. (Part 2) at 101–02. The report expressed concern that "[a]gents of insurance companies have openly urged persons of wealth to take out additional insurance payable to specific beneficiaries for the reason that such insurance would not be included in the gross estate." *Id.* at 22, 1939-1 C.B. (Part 2) at 102.

[6] Revenue Act of 1918, Pub. L. No. 65-254, § 402(f), 40 Stat. 1057, 1098.

components, Congress enacted § 7702 as part of the Tax Reform Act of 1984 to define a "life insurance contract" for all purposes of the Internal Revenue Code. The statute defines the term by reference to disjunctive statutory tests aimed at identifying arrangements with an excessive investment component. If a policy is treated as life insurance under pre-existing judicial norms but fails to meet the statutory definition of a life insurance contract under § 7702(a), the policy proceeds payable upon the decedent's death are treated as insurance only to the extent they exceed the net surrender value of the policy. IRC § 7702(g)(2). In that narrow instance, the application of § 2042 would be limited to the proceeds in excess of the net surrender value.[7]

§ 9.02   PROCEEDS RECEIVABLE BY EXECUTOR

Under § 2042(1), life insurance proceeds on the life of the decedent will be included in the decedent's gross estate to the extent they are "receivable by the executor." Whether the payment of proceeds into the decedent's probate estate was intended by the decedent is irrelevant: "It makes no difference whether or not the estate is specifically named as the beneficiary under the terms of the policy." Treas. Reg. § 20.2042-1(b)(1). For example, proceeds that are paid into the decedent's estate because the designated beneficiary forfeited his interest in the policy proceeds by killing the testator are captured by § 2042(1). *See* First Kentucky Trust Co. v. United States, 737 F.2d 557 (6th Cir. 1984).

Inclusion under § 2042(1) cannot necessarily be avoided through the generous provision of primary and contingent beneficiaries. Insurance proceeds "receivable" by the executor includes not only those literally paid into the probate estate but also amounts paid to third parties for the benefit of the estate. For instance, insurance proceeds payable to third parties will be considered receivable by the executor under § 2042(1) if the recipient is legally obligated to apply the funds toward the payment of the decedent's debts or the administrative expenses of the probate estate. *See* Treas. Reg. § 20.2042-1(b)(1). Accordingly, if a policy were purchased to secure the decedent's personal obligations under a commercial loan, the proceeds will be captured in the decedent's gross estate under § 2042(1). *Id.*

Life insurance trusts are often created to provide a source of liquidity for the payment of the decedent's estate tax liability. Given that such liability is a legal obligation of the decedent's estate, attention must be paid in the drafting process to avoiding inclusion under § 2042(1). In particular, the terms of a trust designed to receive life insurance proceeds should not obligate the trustee to satisfy the decedent's estate tax liability. Instead, the trustee should be afforded discretion to make loans to the decedent's probate estate or to purchase estate assets as a means of supplying the decedent's estate with the desired liquidity.

§ 9.03   INCIDENTS OF OWNERSHIP POSSESSED BY THE DECEDENT

The second basis for inclusion under § 2042 focuses on the powers over the policy retained by the decedent as opposed to the recipient of the proceeds. Under § 2042(2), proceeds payable to beneficiaries other than the executor will be included in the decedent's gross estate if the decedent possessed "any of the incidents of ownership" of the policy at the time of his death.

---

[7] Other inclusionary provisions presumably would govern whether the net surrender value of the policy is included in the gross estate.

Noting that the range of incidents of ownership is not capable of exhaustive cataloging, the legislative history nonetheless provided the following examples: the right of the insured to the economic benefits of the policy, the power to change the beneficiary, the power to surrender or cancel the policy, the power to assign the policy or to revoke an assignment, and the power to pledge the policy as collateral or to borrow from the insurer against the policy. *See* H.R. Rep. No. 77-2333, at 163 (1942); S. Rep. No. 77-1631, at 235 (1942). This congressional guidance resurfaced to a large degree in Reg. § 20.2042-1(c)(2).

[A]   Framing the Relevant Inquiry

Before exploring what rights over a life insurance policy rise to the level of an incident of ownership for purposes of § 2042(2), it is important to understand how the incident-of-ownership inquiry is framed as a general matter. The determination of whether the decedent possessed an incident of ownership over a life insurance policy under § 2042(2) at the time of his death turns on the legal rights retained by the decedent over the policy, regardless of the practical likelihood of those rights being exercised. For instance, the father of the decedent in *United States v. Rhode Island Hospital Trust Co.*, 355 F.2d 7 (1st Cir. 1966), maintained physical possession of a life insurance policy that he purchased on the life of his son, the decedent. The terms of the policy afforded the decedent certain rights over assignment of the policy and designation of the beneficiary. However, the decedent exercised those rights only at the direction of his father, who viewed himself as possessing absolute control over the policy regardless of its terms. The decedent's estate claimed that the father's dominance left the decedent without incidents of ownership over the policy. The First Circuit was unmoved:

> Viewed against this background, what power did decedent possess? That is the relevant question—not how did he feel or act. Did he have a capacity to do something to affect the disposition of the policy if he had wanted to? Without gaining possession of the policy itself, he could have borrowed on the policy. He could have changed the method of using dividends. He could have assigned the policy. He could have revoked the assignment. Should he have gained possession of the policy by trick . . . force, or chance, he could have changed the beneficiary, and made the change of record irrevocable. Other such possibilities might be imagined. We cite these only to evidence the existence of some power in decedent to affect the disposition of the policy proceeds. In addition, he always possessed a negative power. His signature was necessary to a change in beneficiary, to a surrender for cash value, to an alternation in the policy, to a change in dividend options. Even with this most limited power, he would be exercising an incident of ownership "in conjunction with" another person.

Id. at 11 (citations omitted). Similarly, in *Commissioner v. Estate of Noel*, 380 U.S. 678 (1965), the Supreme Court rejected the notion that the decedent's inability to effectuate any change over a flight insurance policy while aboard a flight (that ended in a fatal crash) precluded him from possessing incidents of ownership over the policy. Convinced that Congress did not intend for an individual's estate tax liability to turn on the momentary capacity to dispose of property, the Court concluded that the incidents-of-ownership inquiry under § 2042(2) should turn on "a general, legal power to exercise ownership."[8] *Id.* at 684.

---

[8] Even though § 2042(2) generally turns on the decedent's legal entitlement to exercise incidents of ownership over a policy, legal rights that are afforded to the decedent by way of an insurance agent's mistake will not implicate the statute. *See* National Metropolitan Bank v. United States, 87 F. Supp. 773 (Ct. Cl. 1950); Schongalla v. Hickey, 149 F.2d

In certain instances, the irrelevance of practical control over an insurance policy can work to the taxpayer's advantage. For example, in *Estate of Bloch v. Commissioner*, 78 T.C. 850 (1982), the decedent caused a trust of which he served as trustee to take out three policies insuring his life. The decedent later pledged these policies as collateral loans in which he had a personal interest. Noting that the decedent's actions constituted a breach of his fiduciary duty as trustee, the Tax Court held that his misappropriation of the policies did not leave him with an incident of ownership over the policy for purposes of § 2042(2).

[B]   Jointly Held Powers

Incidents of ownership need not be solely held by the decedent in order to implicate § 2042(2). As the statute indicates, the prohibited incident of ownership may be exercisable by the decedent "either alone or in conjunction with any other person." IRC § 2042(2). This rule applies even if the co-holder of the incident of ownership possesses an interest adverse to the exercise of the power. *See* Gesner v. United States, 600 F.2d 1349 (Ct. Cl. 1979) (noting irrelevancy of adversity of interest).

Similarly, the manner in which the decedent may exercise an incident of ownership with another is immaterial. Section 2042(2) applies to joint powers that (a) afford the decedent the ability to initiate action, (b) require the decedent to consent to action initiated by another, or (c) provide the decedent the opportunity to veto action taken by another. In *Commissioner v. Estate of Karagheusian*, 233 F.2d 197 (2d Cir. 1956), the decedent's wife had transferred an insurance policy on his life to a trust which she could amend or revoke only with the consent of the decedent and their daughter. The Second Circuit held that the consent requirement amounted to an incident of ownership over the policy held by the trust, explaining that "[i]t makes no difference whether under the trust instrument the decedent may initiate changes or whether he must merely consent to them." *Id.* at 199; *see also* Schwager v. Commissioner, 64 T.C. 781 (1975) (necessity of decedent's consent to change of beneficiary on policy owned by employer held to be incident of ownership).

[C]   Contingent Rights

The potential effect of a contingency upon the exercise of an incident of ownership is not addressed in § 2042(2) or the regulations thereunder. The statutory and regulatory silence on the issue could be interpreted as indicating that contingencies on the exercise of a power are irrelevant for purposes of § 2042. However, a number of cases suggest otherwise.

In *Estate of Smith v. Commissioner*, 73 T.C. 307 (1979), the decedent possessed the right to purchase a policy on his life owned by his employer if the employer surrendered the policy or otherwise failed to maintain the coverage. The Service argued that the decedent's ability to preclude the employer from exercising an incident of ownership over the policy—namely, the right to surrender or cancel it—itself constituted an incident of ownership in the decedent, relying on its holding in Revenue Ruling 79-46, 1979-1 C.B. 303, to that effect. The Tax Court was not persuaded. The court rejected the Service's argument on the basis that the decedent's rights were subject to a condition precedent over which he lacked control.[9]

---

687 (2d Cir. 1945). This approach is not so much an exception to the general rule as it is a clarification, as contracts that are the product of a mistake generally are not enforceable.

[9] Note that, under this reasoning, the mere ability to veto the exercise of an incident of ownership would not

The Tax Court employed similar reasoning in *Estate of Beauregard v. Commissioner*, 74 T.C. 603 (1980). Pursuant to a property settlement agreement and local court order, the decedent was obligated to name his minor children as beneficiaries of his life insurance policy. Despite the potential for the decedent to regain the right to designate the beneficiary of the policy once his children attained majority, the court determined that the decedent did not possess an incident of ownership at the time of his death because the condition precedent had not been satisfied. In short, the court viewed the decedent's potential future rights over the policy as too remote to implicate § 2042(2). *See also* Estate of Margrave v. Commissioner, 618 F.2d 34 (8th Cir. 1980) (wife's designation of decedent's revocable trust as beneficiary of policy on decedent's life did not provide decedent with an incident of ownership over policy; court held that decedent possessed a power over only an expectancy given wife's ability to change beneficiary of policy); Rev. Rul. 81-166, 1981-1 C.B. 477 (acquiescing to *Margrave*).

In the context of employer-provided group life insurance, the Service sensibly ruled that an individual's ability to terminate coverage by quitting his job did not rise to the level of an incident of ownership. *See* Rev. Rul. 72-307, 1972-1 C.B. 307. Nonetheless, the Service contended that an individual's ability to convert the group coverage into an individual policy upon the cessation of employment satisfied the incident-of-ownership standard. Following its decisions in *Estate of Smith* and *Estate of Beauregard*, the Tax Court rejected the Service's position in *Estate of Smead v. Commissioner*, 78 T.C. 43 (1982). The court characterized the decedent's ability to convert the policy to individual coverage by leaving his job as "entirely too contingent and too remote" to implicate § 2042(2). *Id.* at 52. The Service acquiesced to the *Estate of Smead* decision through Revenue Ruling 84-130, 1984-2 C.B. 194.

[D] Necessity of Economic Benefit

A certain level of confusion exists as to whether an incident of ownership must provide some economic benefit to the decedent and, if so, the scope of what constitutes an economic benefit in this context. The source of this uncertainty lies in the wording of Reg. § 20.2042-1(c)(2). The legislative history introducing the "incidents of ownership" standard cited as merely one example of an incident of ownership the insured's rights to the economic benefit of the policy. *See* H.R. Rep. No. 77-2333, at 163 (1942); S. Rep. No. 77-1631, at 235 (1942). While the regulation recites the legislative guidance on incidents of ownership almost verbatim, it opens with the following summation: "Generally speaking, the term [incidents of ownership] has reference to the right of the insured or his estate to the economic benefits of the policy." Through this formulation, what started as a mere example of an incident of ownership could be interpreted as a defining element of all such incidents. *See, e.g.*, Estate of Rockwell v. Commissioner, 779 F.2d 931 (3d Cir. 1985) (holding that decedent's right to veto designation of beneficiaries of policies held in trust did not constitute an incident of ownership because decedent could not employ the veto right to his own economic benefit). On the other hand, Reg. § 20.2042-1(c)(2) cites the power to change the policy beneficiary as an incident of ownership, and this power does not inure to the economic benefit of the decedent.[10] Thus, if economic benefit to the decedent does constitute the *sine qua non* of an incident of ownership, the concept must be broadly interpreted.

---

implicate § 2042(2) if the action capable of veto were never initiated. The application of § 2042(2) to veto powers, however, is well settled.

[10] Unless the decedent names his estate as beneficiary, in which case the proceeds would be captured under § 2042(1).

The issue of whether an incident of ownership must confer an economic benefit upon the decedent has been highlighted in cases analyzing the decedent's right to select the manner in which death benefits will be paid to beneficiaries. In *Estate of Lumpkin v. Commissioner*, 474 F.2d 1092 (5th Cir. 1973), the decedent held no powers under a group term policy on his life other than the ability to select among different payout options. Noting that the right to alter the timing of enjoyment of transferred property generally implicates the retained-power provisions of § 2036(a)(2) and § 2038,[11] the Fifth Circuit determined that a similar right over insurance proceeds constituted an incident of ownership for purposes of § 2042. However, addressing the same factual scenario, the Third Circuit in *Estate of Connelly v. United States*, 551 F.2d 545 (3d Cir. 1977), found § 2042(2) inapplicable because the right to select payout options did not confer an economic benefit upon the decedent. Not surprisingly, the Service has expressed its disapproval of the *Estate of Connelly* decision.[12] *See* Rev. Rul. 81-128, 1981-1 C.B. 469. Therefore, from a planning perspective, the benefit of offering settlement options to those covered by group term insurance likely is not worth the estate tax risk.

[E] Powers Held in Fiduciary Capacity

Estate tax planning with respect to life insurance commonly involves the use of irrevocable trusts to own policies as a means of separating the incidents of ownership from the insured. If successful, the policy proceeds will not be included in the decedent's gross estate but nonetheless will be administered according to the terms of the trust as established by the decedent.

Simply transferring legal title to the policy to the trust is not sufficient to avoid § 2042, as incidents of ownership can be held in a fiduciary capacity. *See* Treas. Reg. § 20.2042-1(c)(4). In particular, if the decedent in his capacity as trustee possesses the power (individually or in conjunction with another) to change the beneficial ownership of the policy or its proceeds, the policy proceeds will be included in his gross estate under § 2042(2). The same result holds even if the decedent's power is limited to affecting the time and manner in which the policy or its proceeds will be enjoyed by fixed beneficiaries. *Id.* Additionally, the decedent may possess an incident of ownership over the policy in this setting even if he lacks a beneficial interest in the trust.

Given the breadth of Reg. § 20.2042-1(c)(4), naming the insured as a trustee of a trust structured to own the policy is not advisable.[13] Yet the designation of a third-party trustee does not avoid the application of Reg. § 20.2042-1(c)(4) in all cases. If the decedent possessed the ability to remove the trustee and to name a replacement, the decedent can be treated as possessing the trustee's powers due to his considerable leverage over the trustee's decisions. After years of litigation over whether a decedent should be treated as possessing the powers of a trustee he could remove as an across-the-board rule,[14] the government articulated a safe

---

[11] Inclusion under these statutes based on the decedent's control over the timing of enjoyment of transferred property is addressed in Chapter 11.

[12] Note that if the policy were held in a trust of which the decedent served as trustee, the decedent's ability to determine the time or manner in which the policy proceeds would be enjoyed by others would constitute an incident of ownership. Treas. Reg. § 20.2042-1(c)(4). Given that this indirect power is sufficient to trigger inclusion of the policy proceeds under § 2042(2), it is puzzling that the same power held directly would be treated differently.

[13] If the insured is named as a fiduciary, the rights the insured can exercise in that capacity are severely constrained in order to avoid inclusion under § 2042(2). *See, e.g.*, Priv. Ltr. Rul. 9111028 (Dec. 17, 1990).

[14] This issue was litigated in the context of §§ 2036 and 2038, as they apply to transfers of property over which the

harbor in Revenue Ruling 95-58, 1995-2 C.B. 191. So long as the decedent cannot appoint as successor trustee himself or any party related or subordinate to him within the meaning of § 672(c), the trustee's powers will not be attributed to the decedent by way of the removal power. While the ruling technically related to the retained-interest provisions of §§ 2036 and 2038, the holding and the analysis on which it relies appear equally applicable in the § 2042 context.

[F] Powers Obtained Through Devolution

The critical inquiry under § 2042(2) is whether the decedent possessed an incident of ownership over the policy at the time of his death. From a textual standpoint, the manner in which the decedent acquired those incidents appears irrelevant. Nonetheless, a circuit court split emerged over whether § 2042(2) should reach incidents of ownership that the decedent held in a fiduciary capacity as the result of a transfer from a third party. In *Estate of Skifter v. Commissioner*, 468 F.2d 699 (2d Cir. 1972), the decedent was named as trustee of a trust created under his wife's will to which she transferred various policies insuring the decedent's life. The Second Circuit held that the decedent did not possess incidents of ownership over the policies, in large measure because he did not create the trust nor transfer the policies to it. However, the Fifth Circuit rejected this approach in *Rose v. United States*, 511 F.2d 259 (5th Cir. 1975), instead interpreting the statute as reaching powers acquired through retention and devolution equally. Somewhat surprisingly, the Service abandoned its victory in *Rose* and endorsed the approach of *Estate of Skifter* through the issuance of Revenue Ruling 84-179, 1984-2 C.B. 195:

> An insured decedent who transferred all incidents of ownership in a policy to another person, who in an unrelated transaction transferred powers over the policy in trust to the decedent, will not be considered to possess incidents of ownership in the policy for purposes of § 2042(2) of the Code, provided that the decedent did not furnish consideration for maintaining the policy and could not exercise the powers for personal benefit. The result is the same where the decedent, as trustee, purchased the policy with trust assets, did not contribute assets to the trust or maintain the policy with personal assets, and could not exercise the powers for personal benefit.

Id. at 196. Hence, if the decedent did not transfer the policy to the trust of which he serves as trustee nor the consideration for purchasing the policy, § 2042(2) will apply only if the decedent could exercise the incidents of ownership for his personal benefit.

[G] Incidents of Ownership Held Through Entities

In addition to trusts being structured to possess the incidents of ownership of life insurance so as to remove the proceeds from the insured's estate, it is not uncommon for insurance to be owned by closely held corporations, partnerships, or LLCs. Oftentimes an entity purchases insurance in order to finance its redemption obligations upon an owner's death, or simply to compensate for the loss of a critical participant in the enterprise. In such cases—where the proceeds of the insurance policy are payable to or for the benefit of the entity—the estate tax treatment of the proceeds will be determined outside of § 2042. In that case, the proceeds

---

decedent retained or possessed continued control. *See* Estate of Wall v. Commissioner, 101 T.C. 300 (1993); *see also* Estate of Vak v. Commissioner, 973 F.2d 1409 (8th Cir. 1992) (holding that the right to remove and replace with independent trustee did not render transfer incomplete for gift tax purposes).

payable to the corporation by way of the decedent's death will be taken into account in valuing the decedent's beneficial interest in the entity under § 2033. *See* Treas. Reg. § 20.2042-1(c)(6); *see also* Rev. Rul. 83-147, 1983-2 C.B. 158 (applying same rule in the partnership context).

If the closely held entity functions more in the nature of a trust, § 2042 is potentially applicable. In particular, if the entity possesses all incidents of ownership over the policy but designates as beneficiary an individual or individuals whom the decedent-insured intends to benefit at his death, the entity's incidents of ownership can be attributed to the decedent. When Reg. § 20.2042-1(c)(2) was first promulgated in 1958, the last sentence provided that an incident of ownership included "a power to change the beneficiary reserved to a corporation of which the decedent is the *sole stockholder*." T.D. 6296, 23 Fed. Reg. 4,529, 4,565 (June 24, 1958) (emphasis added). In 1974, this brief treatment of corporate-held incidents of ownership was dropped in favor of the more expansive treatment contained in Reg. § 20.2042-1(c)(6). *See* T.D. 7312, 1974-1 C.B. 277. Under the existing regulatory framework, a corporation's incidents of ownership will be attributed to the decedent through his stock ownership where the decedent "is the sole *or controlling* shareholder." Treas. Reg. § 20.2042-1(c)(6) (emphasis added). A controlling shareholder for this purpose is one who possesses more than 50 percent of the combined voting power of the entity.[15] *Id.* The Tax Court rebuffed a challenge to the validity of Reg. § 20.2042-1(c)(6) as applied outside the context of a wholly owned corporation in *Estate of Levy v. Commissioner*, 70 T.C. 873 (1978).

By its terms, Reg. § 20.2042-1(c)(6) provides for the attribution of incidents of ownership only in the context of corporate-owned policies. Partnerships and LLCs, however, are the business entities that are more frequently used as trust substitutes. Revenue Ruling 83-147, 1983-2 C.B. 158, addresses the regulatory gap by employing the aggregate theory of partnerships for tax purposes. That is, each partner is treated as individually owning an incident of ownership that literally is held by the entity. Attribution of incidents of ownership in the partnership context therefore is not limited to owners who possess a controlling interest. Yet, as in the case of corporate-owned insurance, the ruling provides that § 2042 will not apply to partnership-owned insurance to the extent the proceeds are payable to or for the benefit of the entity. *See also* Knipp v. Commissioner, 25 T.C. 153 (1955) (incidents of ownership of partnership-owned policies payable to the entity not attributed to decedent-insured).

[H]   Split-Dollar Insurance

So-called "split-dollar" life insurance refers to arrangements under which two parties contribute to the payment of premiums and divide the economic rights in the policy. Traditional split-dollar arrangements arose in the employment context as a means of providing deferred compensation to corporate executives. However, individuals and related parties may enter into similar "private" split-dollar arrangements outside the employment context.

In a traditional split-dollar arrangement, a trust created by an executive takes out a policy on the executive's life. The executive and the corporate employer then enter into a contractual

---

[15] The regulations further provide that, in addition to stock individually owned by the decedent, the decedent will be treated as owning all stock held (a) jointly, but only to the extent of the decedent's proportionate contributions to the purchase of the stock, (b) by a voting trust to the extent of the decedent's beneficiary interest therein, and (c) by a trust with respect to which the decedent was treated as the owner under §§ 671–679. Treas. Reg. § 20.2042-1(c)(6).

agreement under which the corporation pays a portion of the premium attributable to the increase in the policy's cash surrender value. The trust supplies the balance of the premium, which generally is attributable to the pure term coverage. Upon the insured's death, the corporation is entitled to the greater of the cash surrender value of the policy immediately prior to the insured's death or the total premiums it provided; the remaining proceeds of the policy are paid to the trust.

Addressing an arrangement similar to that described above, the Service has ruled that the insured will not possess incidents of ownership over the portion of the policy paid to the trust so long as the corporation's rights in the policy are limited to receiving future payment of the policy's cash surrender value. *See* Rev. Rul. 76-274, 1976-2 C.B. 278, *as modified by* Rev. Rul. 82-145, 1982-2 C.B. 213. Recall that even if the insured is a controlling shareholder of the corporation, the corporation's incidents of ownership over the remaining portion of the policy are not attributed to the decedent because those proceeds are paid to the entity. *See* Treas. Reg. § 20.2042-1(c)(6). Hence, the arrangement will have estate tax consequences to the insured only to the extent the amounts actually paid to the corporation pursuant to the arrangement increase the value of the decedent-insured's stock in the corporation.

Slight modifications to the arrangement can lead to drastically different estate tax results. Suppose that in addition to the right to receive payment of the cash surrender value of the policy upon termination of the agreement or the insured's death, the corporation was entitled to borrow against the policy's cash value while the split-dollar arrangement remained in force. The right to borrow against an insurance policy constitutes an incident of ownership. Even if the right to borrow against the policy is limited to the policy's cash value, the incident of ownership subjects the entire proceeds to inclusion under § 2042(2). *See* Rev. Rul. 79-129, 1979-1 C.B. 306; Rev. Rul. 82-145, 1982-2 C.B. 213. Thus, if the insured is a controlling shareholder of the corporation, the death benefit payable to the trust will be included in the insured's gross estate through the application of Reg. § 20.2042-1(c)(6).[16]

[I] Reversionary Interests

The text of § 2042(2) expressly addresses only one type of incident of ownership: a reversionary interest in the policy. Such an interest includes the possibility that the policy or the proceeds of the policy may return to the decedent or his estate or become subject to a power of disposition by him. Only reversionary interests that exceed five percent of the value of the policy immediately before the death of the decedent rise to the level of an incident of ownership. This aspect of § 2042(2), which can be avoided through proper drafting of trust instruments, will be discussed in connection with § 2037 (governing reversionary interests in general) in Chapter 12.

---

[16] In 2003, the Service issued final regulations addressing the income tax, gift tax, employment tax, and self-employment tax consequences of split-dollar life insurance arrangements. *See* T.D. 9092 (Sept. 17, 2003). Although the particulars of the detailed regulatory scheme are not addressed in this text, the regulations categorize split-dollar arrangements into two camps: (1) the loan regime addressed in Reg. § 1.7872-15 and (2) the equity regime governed by § 1.61-22. The "collateral assignment" arrangement described in this setting is governed by Reg. § 1.7872-15, and § 7872 governs the arrangement represents a below-market loan between the employer and the insured. On the other hand, if the employer is designated as the owner of the life insurance policy, then the tax consequences of the arrangement are governed by the economic benefit regime of Reg. § 1.61-22.

§ 9.04   TRANSFERS WITHIN THREE YEARS OF DEATH

Section 2042(2) looks to whether the decedent possessed incidents of ownership over the policy at the moment of the decedent's death. When considered in connection with § 2035(a), the relevant time period is expanded to three years prior to the decedent's death. Section 2035(a) operates to include the proceeds of life insurance in the decedent's gross estate if (1) the decedent made a transfer of property or relinquished a power within three years of his death, and (2) but for the transfer of property or relinquishment of power, the insurance proceeds would have been included in the decedent's gross estate under § 2042. Hence, if a decedent transfers ownership of a policy on his life and dies within the three-year period, the policy proceeds will be captured in his gross estate through a combination of §§ 2035(a) and 2042(2). In contrast, the decedent's transfer of funds to another (whether it be a family member or a life insurance trust) to facilitate the acquisition of the policy or the maintenance of premiums does not implicate § 2035(a), even if the decedent transferred those funds within three years of death.[17] *See* Estate of Perry v. Commissioner, 927 F.2d 209 (5th Cir. 1991); Estate of Headrick v. Commissioner, 918 F.2d 1263 (6th Cir. 1990); Estate of Leder v. Commissioner, 893 F.2d 237 (10th Cir. 1989). From the standpoint of planning with a new life insurance policy, it therefore is critical to ensure that ownership of the policy rests in the third party from the moment the policy is issued.

Section 2035(a) is not limited to transfers of property or relinquishments of powers undertaken by the decedent directly. Recall that incidents of ownership possessed by a corporation will be attributed to a decedent for purposes of § 2042(2) if the decedent possesses a controlling interest in the entity (and the proceeds are not payable to or for the benefit of the corporation) under Reg. § 20.2042-1(c)(6). Accordingly, if a corporation transfers an incident of ownership within the three-year period, that transfer implicates § 2035(a). *See* Rev. Rul. 82-141, 1982-2 C.B. 209 (reasoning that such result is mandated by the principles under the attribution rules of Reg. § 20.2042-1(c)(6)). Yet what if the relevant transfer is an additional step removed from the policy? That is, the corporation maintains its incidents of ownership over the policy, but the decedent gratuitously transfers a sufficient portion of his stock to avoid controlling shareholder status. The Service has ruled that § 2035 is triggered in this context as well. *See* Rev. Rul. 90-21, 1990-1 C.B. 172 (expanding the logic of Rev. Rul. 82-141).

The application of § 2035(a) to life insurance policies that are transferred within three years of the decedent's death can raise questions regarding the proper amount to be recaptured. Suppose the decedent transferred the policy within the three-year period, and the donee paid the premiums from that point forward. Section 2035(a) on its face will include the entire policy

---

[17] Prior to its amendment as part of the Tax Reform Act of 1976, § 2035(a) generally reached transfers that were made "in contemplation of death." The 1976 legislation dropped this subjective approach, and instead captured all property transferred by the decedent within three years of death. *See* Tax Reform Act of 1976, Pub. L. No. 94-455, § 2001(a)(5), 90 Stat. 1519, 1848. Under these prior versions of the statute, courts had little difficulty treating the transfer of funds to a third party to acquire a policy on the insured's life in the same manner as a transfer of the policy itself—capturing the policy proceeds in the decedent's gross estate in both cases. *See, e.g.*, Bel v. United States 452 F.2d 683 (5th Cir. 1971) (holding that the decedent's acquisition of a policy in the names of his children constituted an act of transfer to which § 2035 applied). Congress again amended § 2035 in 1981, enumerating the predicate bases for inclusion under § 2035 had the relevant transfer or relinquishment of power not taken place. *See* Economic Recovery Tax Act of 1981, Pub. L. No. 97-34, § 424(a), 95 Stat. 172, 317. As § 2033 is not among the predicates so designated, § 2035 does not operate to recapture outright transfers within three years of death. Hence, the transfer of cash to a third party—whether applied toward insurance premiums or otherwise—within the three-year period no longer implicates § 2035.

proceeds in the decedent's gross estate. However, at least a portion of those proceeds are attributable to donee's post-transfer investment in the policy. Courts have resolved this incongruity by including only the portion of the policy proceeds equal to the ratio of the decedent's premium payments to the total premiums paid on the policy. *See* Estate of Silverman v. Commissioner, 61 T.C. 338 (1973), *aff'd*, 521 F.2d 574 (2d Cir. 1975); Estate of Friedberg v. Commissioner, T.C. Memo. 1992-310, 63 T.C.M. (CCH) 3080.

§ 9.05   GIFT TAX CONSEQUENCES OF LIFE INSURANCE

[A]   Transfer of Policy

The gift tax treatment of lifetime transfers of life insurance policies parallels the estate tax treatment through its emphasis on the relinquishment of incidents of ownership over the policy. By way of implication, Reg. § 25.2511-1(h)(8) provides that the insured's transfer of a life insurance policy to another or the insured's payment of a premium on a policy owned by another will not constitute a completed gift unless the insured retains no reversionary interest in the policy, no power to revest the economic benefits of the policy in himself or his estate, and no power to change the policy beneficiaries or their proportionate benefits. Hence, if an individual transfers a life insurance policy to his children but retains the right to borrow against the policy, the transfer is held in abeyance for tax purposes. If the children exercise their ownership rights to withdraw a portion of the cash value of the policy or surrender the policy altogether, the transfer will be rendered complete at that point to the extent of the withdrawn amounts. The withdrawal completes the gift, as it extinguishes the donor's incident of ownership over the policy. Note that, although the approach of Reg. § 25.2511-1(h)(8) harmonizes the estate and gift tax treatment of life insurance, it has the unfortunate consequence of potentially leaving events that fix the gift tax liability of the donor at the discretion of others.

[B]   Payment of Premiums

In one sense, the gift tax consequences surrounding the payment of premiums on a life insurance policy are relatively straightforward. If the insured pays a premium on a policy owned by a third party (and over which the insured retains no incidents of ownership), the insured has made a gift equal to the premium amount. However, what if the premium is paid by a third party other than the insured? That too would constitute a gift by the party supplying the premium payment to the owner of the policy, unless the payor did so to protect his own unconditional interest in the policy. For instance, if a life insurance policy were owned by an irrevocable trust that called for the distribution of trust assets to the insured's two children upon his death, a premium payment by one of the insured's children would constitute a gift of one-half of the premium amount only. *See* Commissioner v. Berger, 201 F.2d 171 (2d Cir. 1953) (premium payments by insured spouse on policy owned by irrevocable trust and in which spouse possessed a secondary lifetime income interest held not a gift to the extent of spouse's actuarial interest in trust). This result will not hold, however, if the beneficiary's interest in the life insurance policy is not unconditional. *See* Harris v. Commissioner, 10 T.C. 741 (1948) (wife's payment of premiums on husband's life determined to be gifts because wife was not guaranteed to receive policy proceeds upon husband's death).

[C]   Availability of Gift Tax Annual Exclusion

Given the primary benefit of life insurance lies in the payment of the proceeds upon the insured's death, transfers of life insurance raise the prospect of the future interest prohibition under the annual gift tax exclusion. However, Reg. § 25.2503-3(a) dispels any such concerns by plainly stating that a "future interest" for annual exclusion purposes does not encompass the contractual rights in a life insurance policy which are discharged through future payments. Nonetheless, if the policy is transferred in trust, restrictions on the beneficiaries' interests in the trust may be grounds for annual exclusion disallowance. In that event, the annual exclusion can be salvaged through other means, such as providing the beneficiaries with *Crummey* withdrawal rights over amounts periodically transferred to the trust (typically in the form of premium payments).[18]

§ 9.06   EFFECT OF COMMUNITY PROPERTY LAWS

The regulations under § 2042(2) contemplate the effect of state-law community property regimes on the application of the statute. The effect of community property law on inclusion under § 2042(1) is perhaps easiest to conceptualize. If the proceeds of a policy that are paid into the decedent's gross estate represent community property, only the decedent's beneficial interest in one-half of the funds will be included in his gross estate. *See* Treas. Reg. § 20.2042-1(b)(2). As a corollary, the surviving spouse's relinquishment of his beneficial interest in the funds in favor of the decedent's estate presumably would carry gift tax consequences.

The effect of community property law on inclusion under § 2042(2) is slightly more complicated. When Congress adopted the incidents-of-ownership test for inclusion under § 2042(2), it eliminated any reliance on who supplied payment of the policy premiums. Yet through Reg. § 20.2042-1(c)(5), the source of premium payments resurfaces as a relevant consideration for married individuals residing in community property states. As a general matter of state law, the proceeds of insurance policies acquired with community funds retain their character as community property. In that case, only half of the policy proceeds will be included under § 2042(2). Treas. Reg. § 20.2042-1(c)(5); *see also* Rev. Rul. 94-69, 1994-2 C.B. 241. This result holds even where the deceased spouse's incidents of ownership—such as the right to designate the beneficiary—pertain to the policy as a whole. The regulations reach this result by treating the decedent as possessing the relevant incident of ownership as agent for his spouse with respect to one-half of the policy. *See* Treas. Reg. § 20.2042-1(c)(5).

The treatment of policies acquired with community funds as beneficially owned by both spouses for estate tax purposes has implications for the non-insured spouse. First, if the non-insured spouse were to predecease his spouse, one-half of the fair market value of the policy would be included in his gross estate under § 2033. *See* Rev. Rul. 75-100, 1975-1 C.B. 303 (addressing valuation of the policy in that instance). Second, if the non-insured spouse survives and at least one-half of the proceeds are not payable to him, he has made a gift of his beneficial interest in the policy to the designated beneficiary. *See* Treas. Reg. § 25.2511-1(h)(9); Kaufman v. United States, 462 F.2d 439 (5th Cir. 1972) (surviving spouse makes taxable gift only if he receives less than his one-half share of proceeds; other half payable to third party is attributed to insured spouse).

---

[18] For a discussion of the use of withdrawal rights to qualify transfers in trust for the gift tax annual exclusion pursuant to the Ninth Circuit's decision in *Crummey v. Commissioner*, 397 F.2d 82 (9th Cir. 1968), see § 5.01[B].

§ 9.07 VALUATION

[A] Gift Tax Valuation

The transfer of an existing life insurance policy can present challenges with respect to valuation. The cash surrender value of the policy does not provide an accurate reflection of the value of the transfer, as it does not capture the benefit of being able to maintain the existing insurance arrangement. This point is best illustrated by assuming that the insured is terminally ill at the time of the transfer. Consequently, the Supreme Court in *United States v. Ryerson*, 312 U.S. 260 (1941), held that the transfer of single-premium life insurance policies had to be valued by reference to the replacement cost of the policies rather than their cash value.

The holding of *Ryerson* is reflected in the regulations, which require that the transfer of paid-up insurance policies be determined by reference to the replacement cost of the existing coverage. Treas. Reg. § 25.2512-6(a), Exs. 1 & 3. However, the regulations adopt a different valuation approach for policies on which further premium payments are required. In that case, the value of the transferred policy may be estimated by reference to the interpolated terminal reserve value of the policy, increased by the unearned portion of the last premium payment made on the policy. Treas. Reg. § 25.2512-6(a). The mechanics of this computation are illustrated in Example 4 of Reg. § 25.2512-6(a). Through its use of the policy's terminal reserve value—a figure maintained by the insurer to estimate its financial exposure on the contract—to estimate the amount of the gift, the regulation favors administrability over accuracy.

[B] Estate Tax Valuation

Valuation of insurance on the life of the insured for estate tax purposes is fairly straightforward. If either prong of § 2042 is satisfied with respect to insurance on the life of the decedent, the policy proceeds are included in the gross estate. Estate tax valuation becomes more interesting when the decedent owned a policy insuring the life of another. In that case, estate tax valuation mirrors that under the gift tax. As a general rule, the policy is included in the decedent's gross estate under § 2033 at its replacement value. Treas. Reg. § 20.2031-8(a)(1). However, if the replacement value cannot be readily determined by reference to the cost of comparable contracts because further premiums are to be paid on the policy, the value of the policy can be estimated by adding the unearned portion of the latest premium to the policy's interpolated terminal reserve value as of the decedent's death. Treas. Reg. § 20.2031-8(a)(2), (a)(3), Ex. 3.

§ 9.08 ESTATE TAX APPORTIONMENT

Recall that, as a general rule, liability for the federal estate tax liability rests on the decedent's estate. *See* IRC § 2002. Section 2206 provides an exception to this rule with respect to life insurance proceeds that are received by a beneficiary other than the executor. In that instance, the statute provides the decedent's executor with a right to recover the average (as opposed to marginal) estate tax attributable to the inclusion of proceeds in the decedent's gross estate. The decedent can waive this § 2206 right of recovery by so directing in his will; however, careful consideration should be given to the potential burden placed on the beneficiaries of the decedent's probate assets before including such a waiver.

§ 9.09 STUDY PROBLEMS

1. Janet owned a $1 million paid-up life insurance policy on her husband, Steve. A few weeks after receiving news that Steve had been diagnosed with a terminal illness, Janet died in an accident. Discuss the estate tax consequences of the life insurance policy to Janet's estate.

2. Herb transfers a life insurance policy on his life to a Uniform Gifts to Minors Act account for the benefit of his granddaughter, and Herb names himself as custodian. In that capacity, Herb can make discretionary distributions of the UGMA funds to or for the benefit of the granddaughter until she attains age 21, at which point the granddaughter can demand distribution of the remaining property. Herb cannot use the UGMA funds for his own benefit.

    a. If Herb dies while the policy remains titled in his name as custodian, will the proceeds be included in his gross estates under § 2042?

    b. How would your answer to (a) change if Herb were one of two co-custodians of the account?

    c. How would the answer change if Herb's wife originally owned the policy and she transfers it to the UGMA account (of which Herb still serves as custodian)?

3. Cecilia recently purchased a $2 million policy on her life. A few weeks later, after Cecilia's attorney completed drafting an irrevocable trust to hold the policy and receive the proceeds upon her death, Cecilia assigned ownership of the policy to the trust. The terms of the trust provide that the trustee may make distributions of trust income or principal to or for the benefit of Cecilia's children and grandchildren until her death, at which point the property will be divided into separate shares for each of Cecilia's two children. Cecilia's brother is designated as trustee. In each of the two years after creating the trust, Cecilia paid the $20,000 annual premium on the policy. A few weeks after making the second annual premium payment, Cecilia died.

    a. Discuss the estate and gift tax consequences of these transactions.

    b. What, if anything, would you change from a tax planning standpoint?

4. Frank owns a $500,000 life insurance policy on his wife Tonya. Frank's son, Sam, is designated as the beneficiary of the policy. Within nine months of Tonya's death, Sam disclaims his interest in the policy. No contingent beneficiary is named. Pursuant to the terms of the policy, the policy is paid to Tonya's estate. Discuss the estate tax consequences to Tonya's estate of these events.

5. Zack and Leah live in a community property state. Zack owned a policy on his life, the proceeds of which were paid to his daughter from a prior marriage. Zack and Leah used community funds to purchase and maintain the policy. Discuss the estate and gift tax consequences of this arrangement.

6. Susan owns 60 percent of the stock of a corporation, and her brother owns the remaining 40 percent interest. The corporation owns a life insurance policy on Susan's life, the beneficiary of which is her husband.

    a. Will the policy proceeds be included in Susan's gross estate?

    b. Same as (a), except that the corporation is the beneficiary of the policy.

c. Same as (a), except that the corporation transferred the policy to an irrevocable trust for the benefit of Susan's husband two years prior to her death.

d. Same as (a), except that Susan transferred a 20 percent interest in the corporation to her husband five years prior to her death.

e. Same as (d), except that the entity is an LLC instead of a corporation.

7. Roger enters into a split-dollar arrangement with his employer. The employer agrees to pay a portion of the premium attributable to the increase in the cash surrender value, and it is entitled to receive the cash value of the policy upon Roger's death. An irrevocable trust created by Roger owns the policy, and the trust is entitled to the policy proceeds in excess of the cash surrender value that must be paid to the corporation. In reviewing the split-dollar agreement on behalf of Roger from an estate-tax planning standpoint, what red flags should you look for? Assume Roger is a controlling shareholder in the corporation.

Chapter 10

TRANSFERS WITH RETAINED BENEFICIAL ENJOYMENT

Internal Revenue Code:	§§ 2035, 2036(a)(1), (b), 2702
Treasury Regulations:	§ 20.2036-1(a), (b)(1)–(2), -1(c)(1) to (2)(i)
	Prop. Treas. Reg. § 20.2036-2(a), (b), (e)(1), (2)
	§§ 25.2511-1(e), 25.2512-2(b), (c)
	§§ 25.2702-3, -4, *skim* § 25.2702-5

Congress enacted § 2036 to prevent easy circumvention of the estate tax through the creation of temporal interests in property. Recall that § 2033 does not reach property in which the decedent's interest is extinguished by reason of his death. Hence, if the decedent transferred title to his residence to his children but retained a life estate in the property, the residence would not be captured in his gross estate under § 2033. Although the life estate technique would not be devoid of federal transfer tax consequence absent § 2036 (as the transfer of the remainder interest would constitute a taxable gift), the technique would permit individuals to remove post-transfer appreciation in the property from the transfer tax base without relinquishing beneficial ownership of the property.

Recognizing the need for the estate tax to reach property beneficially owned by the decedent until the point of death, the estate tax in its original form applied to property "[t]o the extent of any interest therein of which the decedent has at any time made a transfer . . . intended to take effect in possession or enjoyment at or after his death."[1] That provision serves as the precursor to § 2036, which now frames the grounds for inclusion in terms of the rights retained by the decedent over the transferred property. With respect to property in which the decedent retained a beneficial interest,[2] § 2036 captures property transferred by the decedent if he retained the "possession or enjoyment of, or the right to income from" the property for his life, for a period not ascertainable without reference to his death, or for a period which in fact does not end before his death. IRC § 2036(a)(1). Through the application of § 2036(a)(1), the transferred property will be included in the decedent's gross estate at its date-of-death value—the same result that would have been reached had the decedent retained outright ownership of the property until his death. As explained in this chapter, § 2036 applies to retained-interest transfers beyond those involving traditional life estates in property.

---

[1] Revenue Act of 1916, Pub. L. No. 64-271, § 202(b), 39 Stat. 756, 777–78.

[2] Section 2036 also applies to property over which the decedent retained the right to affect the beneficial interests of others. *See* IRC § 2036(a)(2). This aspect of § 2036 is addressed in Chapter 11 alongside § 2038.

§ 10.01   SECTION 2036(a)(1)

[A]   Retained Beneficial Interest Predicates

Section 2036(a)(1) retained-interest transfers fall into two categories: (1) transfers in which the decedent has retained the possession or enjoyment of the transferred property, and (2) transfers in which the decedent has retained the right to the income from the transferred property. The distinction between these two formulations lies in the nature of the transferred property. The "possession or enjoyment" of property refers to personal use property or other property that is used in-kind; by contrast, the "right to income" from property relates to financial assets that generate a cash flow return. *See* H.R. Rep. No. 81-1412, at 11 (1949) (Conf. Rep.) (describing the predecessor of § 2036(a)(1) as reaching "reserved rights to the income from transferred property and rights to possess or enjoy non-income-producing property").

[1]   Possession or Enjoyment of Property

Inclusion under § 2036(a)(1) on grounds that the decedent retained possession or enjoyment over the transferred property typically arises in the context of transferred real estate. Although its application is fairly clear in the context of a life estate in property, the decedent need not possess a legally enforceable right to occupy the premises. *See* Estate of Abraham v. Commissioner, 408 F.3d 26 (1st Cir. 2005). Rather, this prong is implicated if the decedent's ability to continue his use of the transferred property results from an informal agreement among the parties that can be implied from the circumstances of the transfer. *See* Guynn v. United States, 437 F.2d 1148 (4th Cir. 1971); Estate of McNichol v. Commissioner, 265 F.2d 667 (3d Cir. 1959). Furthermore, possession or enjoyment of transferred property need not be literal in order to implicate § 2036(a)(1); the transferor's continued ability to use the property if he so chooses is sufficient. *See* Estate of Linderme v. Commissioner, 52 T.C. 305 (1969) (decedent moved to nursing home prior to death; § 2036(a)(1) applied based on parties' implied agreement that decedent retained right to occupy transferred residence).

[a]   Continued Possession or Occupancy

Not all instances in which the decedent continued to use or possess transferred property will trigger inclusion of the property under § 2036(a)(1). For instance, taxpayers have successfully avoided the application of § 2036(a)(1) to transfers of business property of which the transferor retains possession through an arm's-length lease. In *Estate of Barlow v. Commissioner*, 55 T.C. 666 (1971), the decedent and his spouse transferred title to farmland to their sons and contemporaneously leased the property from their sons at its fair rental value. Finding that the decedent's continued use of the property was not retained under the transfer but instead purchased through the lease, the Tax Court found the transaction to be outside of § 2036(a)(1). The Service subsequently acquiesced. 1972-2 C.B. 1. En route to its holding in *Estate of Barlow*, the Tax Court noted the potential applicability of substance-over-form arguments in the sale-leaseback context, and similar transactions involving personal use property appear prone to challenge on such grounds. In *Estate of Maxwell v. Commissioner*, 3 F.3d 591 (2d Cir. 1993), the decedent purported to sell her residence to her son and daughter-in-law for $270,000 and then to lease the property back from them. However, the transaction was designed so that little, if any, cash would change hands. The decedent accepted the transferees' promissory note as payment, forgiving twice the annual exclusion amount on an annual basis and then cancelling the remaining loan balance through her will. The interest payments owed to the decedent under the promissory note were largely offset by her rental obligation under the lease.[3] Affirming the Tax Court's decision, the Second Circuit regarded the purported sale-leaseback transactions as shams and instead determined that the substance of the arrangement satisfied the elements of § 2036(a)(1). Yet even in instances where the lease is not disregarded as a sham, § 2036(a)(1) can rear its head. If the lease does not call for the payment of fair rental value or if the parties fail to adhere to their obligations under the lease, § 2036(a)(1) can apply on grounds that some portion of the use of the transferred property was retained by the decedent as opposed to purchased. *See* Estate of Disbrow v. Commissioner, T.C. Memo. 2006-34, 91 T.C.M. (CCH) 794.

The continued use of transferred property for no consideration generally evidences an implied understanding among the parties regarding the decedent's retained beneficial use of the property. *See* Rev. Rul. 78-409, 1978-2 C.B. 234. However, if the transferee is the spouse of the transferor, courts have regarded the transferor's continued occupancy as a natural consequence of the marital relationship as opposed to an economic benefit retained on the transfer. *See* Union Planters Nat'l Bank v. United States, 361 F.2d 662 (6th Cir. 1966) (describing co-occupancy in this context as an incident of the marital relationship); Gutchess v. Commissioner, 46 T.C. 554 (1966) (declaring that joint occupancy of a residence by spouses alone is insufficient to indicate an implied agreement concerning retained enjoyment of the property); *see also* Rev. Rul. 70-155, 1970-1 C.B. 189 (endorsing the Tax Court's reasoning in *Gutchess* in the context of spousal co-occupancy). Even instances of co-occupancy between the decedent and his child can escape application of § 2036(a)(1), although the case against § 2036(a)(1) in those instances is strengthened by the transferee's payment of property taxes and other expenses of the property. *See* Diehl v. United States, 21 A.F.T.R.2d 1607 (W.D. Tenn. 1967) (decedent's co-occupancy with son and daughter-in-law determined not to be pursuant to implied agreement but rather to the transferee's familial obligation to care for decedent in his elder years); Estate of Spruill v. Commissioner, 88 T.C. 1197 (1987) (decedent's occupancy of home with son and daughter-in-law held not pursuant to implied agreement; testimony indicated that decedent would have been asked to leave if he could not get along with daughter-in-law). *But see* Rev. Rul. 78-409, 1978-2 C.B. 234 (rejecting the result in *Diehl* and signaling the Service's intention to apply § 2036(a)(1) when the decedent's possession and enjoyment of the property continued without limitation).

The Second Circuit in *Estate of Stewart v. Commissioner*, 617 F.3d 148 (2d Cir. 2010), issued a remarkably forgiving opinion in this context. The decedent in *Estate of Stewart* owned title to her residence, where she lived with her son. After being diagnosed with cancer and upon the advice of her estate planning attorney, the decedent transferred to her son a 49 percent interest in the property as tenants in common. Following the transfer, the parties' use of the residence continued unaltered. Reversing the Tax Court, the Second Circuit held that mere co-occupancy of residential property by donor and donee as tenants in common alone did not support the existence of an implied agreement among the parties that the donor would retain the beneficial enjoyment of the transferred property. Although not expressly stated in the opinion, the Second Circuit appeared to base its holding on the right of a co-tenant under state law to use the entire property, so long as he does not exclude other co-tenants. Although

---

[3] Note that even if the sale-leaseback arrangement were respected, the transaction produces adverse income tax consequences in the context of personal use property. Because the rental income to the transferees is not offset by a rental deduction to the transferor, the preferential tax treatment of imputed income is lost.

the reasoning of the *Estate of Stewart* is scant and the result suspect, the decision may create a significant exception to § 2036(a)(1) for transfers of fractional interests in personal use property.

[b]   Enjoyment of Property

While the continued possession of property is an objective inquiry, the notion of when a transferor retains "enjoyment" of property is a more nebulous matter. As explained by the Third Circuit, enjoyment for purposes of § 2036(a)(1) "is not a term of art, but is synonymous with substantial present economic benefit." Estate of McNichol, 265 F.2d at 671 (citing Commissioner v. Estate of Holmes, 326 U.S. 480 (1946)).

The bounds of what constitutes enjoyment of retained property was one of the many issues addressed by the Supreme Court in *United States v. Byrum*, 408 U.S. 125 (1972), a seminal decision in the § 2036 arena. The decedent in *Byrum* created irrevocable trusts for the benefit of his children and funded them with interests in three closely held corporations through which he conducted an operating business. Although an independent party served as trustee, the decedent retained the right to vote the transferred stock. The transfers left the decedent with voting control over all three corporations.

As one of its theories for including the transferred stock in the decedent's gross estate under § 2036,[4] the Service argued that the decedent retained enjoyment of the transferred shares through his ability to exercise control over the corporation to his pecuniary benefit—namely, the ability to guarantee himself employment and to determine his compensation. The Court rejected this expansive interpretation of § 2036(a)(1), explaining that the statutory text "plainly contemplates retention of an attribute of the property transferred—such as a right to income, use of the property itself, or a power of appointment with respect either to income or principal." *Id.* at 149. From this standpoint, the decedent had transferred all possible pecuniary benefit flowing from the transferred stock (e.g., right to dividends and proceeds of sale) to the trust.

Soon after the Supreme Court clarified that the "enjoyment" of transferred property under § 2036 was limited to an economic attribute of the transferred property, Congress stepped in to restore ambiguity. As part of the Tax Reform Act of 1976, Congress legislatively reversed the result in *Byrum* by amending § 2036(a) to provide that the retention of voting rights over transferred stock "shall be considered to be a retention of the enjoyment of such stock."[5] Pub. L. No. 94-455, § 2009(a), 90 Stat. 1520, 1893 (1976). The corrective legislation has been restated and refined in § 2036(b), which continues to equate the retention of voting rights in controlled corporations with the enjoyment of the transferred stock.[6] In the view of the authors, § 2036(b) is most appropriately viewed as a result-oriented provision. That is, rather than representing an intentional legislative expansion of the concept of "enjoyment" for

---

[4] The Service's primary argument was that the decedent retained the right to designate the persons who shall possess or enjoy the property or the income therefrom under § 2036(a)(2) through his ability to control the corporations' dividend policies. The Court's interpretation of § 2036(a)(2) in this context is discussed in Chapter 11.

[5] The amendment mistakenly referred to voting rights "in retained stock," but the intention of the statute to apply to voting rights in transferred stock was clear. *See* H.R. Rep. No. 94-1380, at 65 (1976) (referring to voting rights "in transferred stock").

[6] The specifics of § 2036(b) are addressed in § 10.02.

purposes of § 2036(a)(1), the legislation simply is intended to achieve inclusion by referencing a basis for inclusion under § 2036(a).[7]

Given the congressional imprecision with the concept of "enjoyment" in § 2036(b), the Tax Court's questionable application of the term in *Estate of Bongard v. Commissioner*, 124 T.C. 95 (2005), was not surprising. The decedent in *Estate of Bongard* transferred stock in a closely held corporation to a closely held LLC, and he later transferred certain of his LLC units to a closely held limited partnership. Analyzing the second transfer—that is, the transfer of LLC units to the partnership—the Tax Court included the LLC units in the decedent's gross estate under § 2036(a)(1). The court explained that the decedent retained the enjoyment of the transferred LLC units through his practical ability to control whether those units would ever be redeemed for cash. *Id.* at 130–31. Hence, "enjoyment" for purposes of § 2036(a)(1) was predicated on the decedent's control over the transferred property, not a retained economic benefit in the property. This analysis cannot be reconciled with the Supreme Court's guidance in *Byrum*, a point not lost on the dissent. *Id.* at 150–51 (Chiechi, J., concurring in part and dissenting in part).

[2] Right to Income

Inclusion of income-producing property under § 2036(a)(1) is predicated on the retention of the right to income payments. Whereas this aspect of § 2036(a)(1) employs the concept of a "right" to income, this term is not intended to limit the statute's application to legally enforceable rights. Congress inserted the phrase "right to" into the statute to clarify its application when a transferor is entitled to income payments even if he chooses not to receive them. *See* H.R. Rep. No. 72-708, at 46–47 (1932); S. Rep. No. 72-665, at 49–50 (1932). Because the phrase is intended to broaden the scope of § 2036(a)(1) rather than limit its application, *see Estate of McNichol*, 265 F.2d at 671, § 2036(a)(1) cannot be avoided simply by pointing to the absence of a legal right to income payments received by the transferor. As found by the Tax Court in *Estate of Paxton v. Commissioner*, 86 T.C. 785 (1986), an implied agreement between the decedent and a third-party trustee that distributions would be made to the decedent as requested is sufficient to trigger inclusion of trust assets under § 2036(a)(1).

[a] Retained Interest in Trust

Assets transferred to a self-settled irrevocable trust permitting discretionary distributions to the settlor will be captured in the settlor's gross estate under § 2036(a)(1) if the settlor serves as a trustee. In that case, the settlor retains the ability to influence distributions of income to himself. However, if the settlor names a third party to serve as trustee, the ability of the settlor to receive discretionary distributions may not rise to the level of a § 2036(a)(1) interest. The argument for avoiding § 2036(a)(1) is that any distributions of income to the settlor emanate from the beneficial exercise of the trustee's discretion rather than from the settlor's retained interest in the trust.[8]

Notwithstanding the analytical distinction, arrangements of this sort remain precarious

---

[7] In truth, § 2036(b) would have been better framed as an amendment to § 2036(a)(2)—that is, to treat the retention of voting rights in controlled corporations as a right to determine the timing and amount of distributions with respect to the transferred stock. This point is explored further in Chapter 11.

[8] *See* Joseph M. Dodge, Transfers with Retained Interests and Powers, 50-5th Tax Mgmt. Port. (BNA), at A-23 (offering this explanation).

from a planning standpoint. *See* Priv. Ltr. Rul. 200944002 (refusing to rule on whether assets contributed to a self-settled asset protection trust would be included in the settlor's gross estate under § 2036(a)(1) based on the third-party trustee's ability to make discretionary distributions to settlor). If, in hindsight, the trustee exercised its discretion to distribute most or all of the income from the trust to the settlor, courts may find that the distributions were made pursuant to an implied agreement among the parties from the outset. *See* Estate of Skinner v. United States, 316 F.2d 517, 520 (3d Cir. 1963) ("[E]very case of this sort must stand on its own facts and . . . the practice of assuming that a trustee, corporate or otherwise, is necessarily independent of the cestui whom he represents, need not be followed invariably but may be rebutted by circumstances."); *see also* Rev. Rul. 2004-64, 2004-2 C.B. 7 (warning that an exercise of discretion in favor of the decedent, combined with an understanding between the decedent and the trustee concerning the trustee's exercise of discretion, "may cause" inclusion of the trust assets in the decedent's gross estate under § 2036(a)(1)).

[b]   Rights to Income Held Indirectly

A right to income under § 2036(a)(1) can be retained directly or indirectly. If income payments can be applied toward the legal obligations of the decedent, the result is the same as if the decedent had received the payments himself. Treas. Reg. § 20.2036-1(b)(2). With this in mind, transfers in trust for the benefit of a transferor's spouse or children warrant close scrutiny. If the trust directs the trustee to make distributions that fall within the scope of the transferor's legal support obligation, the trust assets will be captured under § 2036(a)(1).[9] *See* Commissioner v. Estate of Dwight, 205 F.2d 298 (2d Cir. 1953) (portion of trust included in gross estate under predecessor of § 2036(a)(1) based on percentage of trust income to be paid for the maintenance and support of the decedent's spouse); Estate of Richards v. Commissioner, T.C. Memo. 1965-263, 24 T.C.M. (CCH) 1436, *aff'd*, 375 F.2d 997 (10th Cir. 1967) (§ 2036(a)(1) held applicable on grounds that decedent retained enforceable right to have trust income applied to discharge his legal obligation to support wife). A discretionary ability to distribute trust income to satisfy the legal obligations of the grantor will be treated in the same manner when the grantor serves as trustee. *See* Estate of Prudowsky v. Commissioner, 55 T.C. 890 (1971), *aff'd*, 465 F.2d 62 (7th Cir. 1972) (property of UGMA account included in decedent's gross estate under § 2036(a)(1) based on decedent's ability, as custodian of account, to distribute property to satisfy his legal obligation to support minor child).[10]

However, § 2036(a)(1) generally is not implicated if the discretionary ability to distribute trust income to beneficiaries to whom the decedent owes an obligation of support rests with a third-party trustee—regardless of whether the discretion is in fact exercised. The justification is that no right to the income had been retained, as neither the decedent nor the beneficiary who owed the support obligation could compel a distribution in the beneficiary's favor. *See* Commissioner v. Estate of Douglass, 143 F.2d 961 (3d Cir. 1944); Estate of Mitchell v. Commissioner, 55 T.C. 576, *acq.* 1971-2 C.B. 3. Perhaps the most assured way of avoiding § 2036(a)(1) in this context is simply to eliminate the standard of distribution altogether, as

---

[9] However, if the transfer of property to the trust operates to discharge the settlor's legal obligations, then the settlor retains no interest in the trust. In that case, the transaction is one for consideration, the gift tax consequences of which must be determined under § 2512(b). Transfers for consideration are addressed in Chapter 13.

[10] The Uniform Transfers to Minors Act attempted to avoid this result through the insertion of the following language: "A delivery, payment, or expenditure under this section is in addition to, and not in substitution for, and does not affect any obligation of a person to support the minor." Uniform Transfers to Minors Act § 14(c) (1986).

amounts distributed to the beneficiary for no stated purpose will not reduce the transferor's support obligation.[11] *See* Colonial-American Nat'l Bank v. United States, 243 F.2d 312 (4th Cir. 1957).

[c]   Annuities

The § 2036(a)(1) paradigm is not ideally suited for application to property transferred in exchange for a contractual commitment to make regular annuity payments. To start, the annuity payments represent a partial return of principal coupled with an investment yield, which generates problems of tracing payments to income or principal. Furthermore, the annuity payments may not represent a retained interest in the transferred property, particularly when paid from the issuer's general assets. [This latter discrepancy is not implicated, however, where the trustee is required to make annuity payments from trust assets.] The estate tax treatment of annuities—including the limited application of § 2036(a)(1)—is addressed in Chapter 15.

[B]   Period for Which Beneficial Interest Must Be Retained

While § 2036(a)(1) is aimed at transfers through which the decedent retained a beneficial interest in property for the remainder of his lifetime (so that the transfer of beneficial ownership would take effect at his death), the statute would be easily circumvented if it applied only to retained temporal interests equal to the transferor's remaining lifetime. For instance, the transferor's beneficial interest could be drafted to terminate a short time before his death, or the retained term could avoid any reference to the decedent's lifetime while being set at a sufficient length to likely accomplish the same result. For these reasons, § 2036(a)(1) applies if the interest in transferred property is retained not only (1) for the decedent's life, but also (2) for any period not ascertainable without reference to the decedent's death or (3) for any period which does not in fact end before the decedent's death.

The second expression of the retained interest term is sufficient to capture a secondary life estate under § 2036(a)(1). For example, suppose A transferred property in trust requiring the payment of income to B for life, then to A for life, remainder to C. Section 2036(a)(1) applies to the arrangement—even if A predeceases B—because A retained a beneficial interest in the property the termination of which cannot be determined without reference to A's death. Treas. Reg. § 20.2036-1(b)(1)(ii). In that case, the full value of the trust property less the actuarial value of B's remaining lifetime income interest will be included in A's gross estate. Treas. Reg. § 20.2036-1(c)(1)(i).

Although the third formulation of the retained interest term was intended to prevent the avoidance of § 2036(a)(1) through term interests approximating the decedent's lifetime, the statute applies regardless of the term length. The only issue is whether the decedent died prior to expiration of the retained term.

---

[11] However, as discussed in Chapter 14, the elimination of an ascertainable standard on discretionary distributions could create adverse transfer tax consequences for the party holding the power if the party is a permissible beneficiary of such distributions.

[C]   Necessity of a Transfer by Decedent

Section 2036 operates only to recapture property that has been the subject of a transfer by the decedent. Transfers by others that provide the decedent with beneficial enjoyment of property therefore fall outside the statute's scope. Thus, if *Parent* transfers property in trust requiring income to be paid to *Child* for life, remainder to *Grandchild*, the trust property will escape estate taxation at *Child's* death. Again, in order to prevent circumvention of the statute, § 2036(a) is not limited to literal transfers by the decedent. Rather, property transferred by the decedent for purposes of § 2036 includes constructive transfers made on his behalf.

The Tax Court decision in *Estate of Morton v. Commissioner*, 12 T.C. 380 (1949), provides a straightforward example of a constructive transfer to which § 2036(a)(1) applies. The decedent in *Estate of Morton* survived her husband and thereby became entitled to a lump-sum payment of insurance proceeds on his life. Rather than receiving this payment, the decedent elected to have the insurer retain the proceeds and pay her interest on such amount for her lifetime. Any amounts remaining at the decedent's death were to be paid to her daughters. The court held that the decedent's election amounted to a transfer on her part, declaring that the failure of the decedent to take literal possession of the funds "advances [the estate's] position not at all." *Id.* at 384.

[1]   Reciprocal Trust Doctrine

Reciprocal trusts are one type of constructive transfer under § 2036(a) that has received a measure of notoriety, in part because the Supreme Court addressed the arrangement in *United States v. Estate of Grace*, 395 U.S. 316 (1969). The technique involves two individuals who, rather than creating a trust for their own lifetime benefit, fund trusts for the lifetime benefit of the other in an attempt to fail the transfer requirement of § 2036(a)(1). In cases where the evidence revealed that each trust was established as a quid pro quo for the other, courts have had little difficulty "un-crossing" the arrangement to treat each beneficiary as funding his own trust. *See* Lehman v. Commissioner, 109 F.2d 99 (2d Cir.), *cert. denied*, 310 U.S. 637 (1940). Based on this evidentiary standard, however, the doctrine would apply only in the most egregious of cases (or, perhaps more aptly, to the most poorly advised of taxpayers). When the Supreme Court weighed in on the technique in *Estate of Grace*, it lowered the evidentiary bar to application of the doctrine significantly:

> [W]e hold that application of the reciprocal trust doctrine is not dependent upon a finding that each trust was created as a *quid pro quo* for the other. Such a "consideration" requirement necessarily involves a difficult inquiry into the subjective intent of the settlers. Nor do we think it necessary to prove the existence of a tax-avoidance motive. . . . [S]tandards of this sort, which rely on subjective factors, are rarely workable under the federal estate tax laws. Rather, we hold that application of the reciprocal trust doctrine requires only that the trusts be interrelated, and that the arrangement, to the extent of mutual value, leaves the settlers in approximately the same economic position as they would have been in had they created trusts naming themselves as life beneficiaries.

395 U.S. at 324 (footnotes omitted).

The elimination of the subjective quid-pro-quo standard in lieu of an objective albeit vague standard of interrelatedness has significantly enhanced the government's litigating position in this context. Furthermore, the lack of precise boundaries for determining whether two trusts are "interrelated" under the *Estate of Grace* standard advances desirable policy objectives, as it discourages use of the technique for the risk-adverse. Although a variety of factors may be relevant to the interrelatedness inquiry, the timing of the respective transfers and the uniformity of the trust terms are among the most critical.

[2] Surviving Spouse Elections

The so-called "widow's election trust"—historically employed by testators in community property jurisdictions—provides another interesting example of a constructive transfer under § 2036(a). Under the technique, a predeceasing spouse transfers his interest in the couple's community property to a trust for the lifetime benefit of the surviving spouse, but only if the surviving spouse consents to the transfer of her interest in the community property in the same manner. If the election is not made, the surviving spouse receives nothing under the predeceasing spouse's will. If the surviving spouse makes the election, the trust that receives the couple's community property interest will have two grantors who presumably make equal contributions to the trust. While the portion of the trust attributable to the contributions of the predeceased spouse will be exempt from the surviving spouse's estate, the surviving spouse has made a transfer to which § 2036(a)(1) applies.[12]

[D] Adequate and Full Consideration Exception

Section 2036(a) is expressly inapplicable to a transfer that constitutes a "bona fide sale for an adequate and full consideration in money or money's worth." The purpose of the statutory exception is relatively straightforward: There is no need for the estate tax to apply to transfers for which the decedent had been fully compensated. As the exception exists under a number of retained-interest sections and has emerged at the forefront of certain estate-planning techniques, it is separately addressed in Chapter 13.

[E] Family Limited Partnerships

Section 2036(a) recently has experienced a resurgence in the context of closely held limited partnerships or limited liability companies that fall under the generic label of "family limited partnerships." Family limited partnerships have proven immensely popular as estate-planning vehicles, largely due to the judicial acceptance of significant discounts in valuing transfers of beneficial interests in these entities. Yet this technique offers the added advantage of permitting transferors to retain an economic interest in the property transferred to the partnership or control over same.

The government has mounted a concerted litigation campaign challenging the claimed transfer tax benefits of family limited partnerships, to relatively little success. However, one bright spot for the Service has been its ability to recapture property transferred to the

---

[12] There exists at least the potential for the transfer from the surviving spouse to be excluded from the application of § 2036(a)(1) on the basis that the income interest received by the surviving spouse in the property transferred by the predeceased spouse supplies "adequate and full consideration in money or money's worth." As discussed in Chapter 13, however, courts are split on whether the property interest against which consideration must be measured in this context is the full value of the property transferred to the trust or only the value of the remainder interest in the trust (that is, the full value of the property transferred by the surviving spouse less the value of her income interest). *See* § 13.03.

partnership under § 2036(a)(1) based on the existence of an implied understanding among the parties that the transferor would retain the economic benefit of the partnership property.[13] Circumstances that support the finding of such an implied agreement include: (a) the transferor's continued rent-free use of property contributed to the entity (such as a residence); (b) the transferor's use of partnership funds to pay personal expenses[14] or to make gifts to family members; (c) the ability of the transferor to pledge partnership property as collateral for personal loans; (d) the transferor's contribution of the bulk of his assets to the entity; and (e) the transferor's elderly age. While it is generally believed that § 2036(a)(1) applies only to family limited partnerships involving the most egregious of taxpayer conduct, such cases do not appear in short supply. *See, e.g.*, Estate of Bigelow v. Commissioner, 503 F.3d 955 (9th Cir. 2007); Estate of Korby v. Commissioner, 471 F.3d 848 (8th Cir. 2006); Estate of Strangi v. Commissioner, 417 F.3d 468 (5th Cir. 2005); Estate of Malkin v. Commissioner, T.C. Memo. 2009-212, 98 T.C.M. (CCH) 57938; Estate of Jorgensen v. Commissioner, T.C. Memo. 2009-66, 97 T.C.M. (CCH) 1328; Estate of Hurford v. Commissioner, T.C. Memo. 2008-278, 96 T.C.M. (CCH) 422; Estate of Concetta H. Rector v. Commissioner, T.C. Memo. 2007-367, 94 T.C.M. (CCH) 567.

§ 10.02   RETAINED VOTING RIGHTS OVER TRANSFERRED STOCK

Reacting to the taxpayer's victory in *United States v. Byrum*, Congress originally amended § 2036(a)(1) to provide that the retention of voting rights over transferred stock constituted the retention of the "enjoyment" of the transferred stock so as to invoke § 2036(a)(1).[15] Congress modified this so-called "anti-*Byrum*" rule in 1978 to limit its application to the retention of voting rights in controlled corporations.[16] The legislation as revised is now contained in § 2036(b).

Under § 2036(b)(1), a decedent is treated as having retained the enjoyment of transferred stock if (1) the decedent retained the right to vote the transferred shares, and (2) the corporation whose stock was transferred is a "controlled corporation."[17] The voting-interest threshold for triggering controlled corporation status is fairly low: the decedent need only own or possess the right to vote 20 percent of the total combined voting power of the corporation. IRC § 2036(b)(2). Ownership for this purpose includes direct and indirect ownership, with

---

[13] The Service has experienced limited success in including partnership property in the decedent's gross estate under § 2036(a)(2) based on the decedent's retained control over partnership distributions. This broader application of § 2036(a) is discussed in § 11.07.

[14] In this regard, many cases have determined that partnership distributions made to or for the benefit of the decedent's probate estate provide evidence of the decedent's retained beneficial enjoyment of the transferred property. *See* Estate of Strangi v. Commissioner, 417 F.3d 468, 477 (5th Cir. 2005) ("[P]art of the 'possession or enjoyment' of one's assets is the assurance that they will be available to pay various debts and expenses upon one's death."); *see also* Estate of Jorgensen v. Commissioner, T.C. Memo. 2009-66, 97 T.C.M. (CCH) 1328; Estate of Rosen v. Commissioner, T.C. Memo. 2006-115, 91 T.C.M. (CCH) 1220. *But see* Estate of Anna Mirowski v. Commissioner, 1290, T.C. Memo. 2008-74 n.49, 95 T.C.M. (CCH) 1277 (dismissing relevance of post-mortem distributions from family-owned LLC to decedent's estate to finance payment of estate tax, reasoning that the decedent's estate tax obligation could not be viewed as her personal obligation given that it could arise only after her death).

[15] Tax Reform Act of 1976, Pub. L. No. 94-455, § 2009(a), 90 Stat. 1520, 1893.

[16] Revenue Act of 1978, Pub. L. No. 95-600, § 702(i)(1), 92 Stat. 2763, 2931.

[17] Perhaps an implicit third requirement is that the relevant transfer was of corporate stock. For this purpose, a transfer of cash or property to a trust which the trust uses to finance the purchase of corporate stock will be treated as a transfer of stock by the decedent. *See* Prop. Treas. Reg. § 20.2036-2(e)(2).

attribution rules borrowed from corporate taxation determining the latter. *Id.* (incorporating § 318 stock ownership attribution regime). Even if the decedent dropped below the 20 percent voting power threshold prior to his death, the corporation will still be considered to be controlled by him for purposes of § 2036(b) if the threshold were satisfied at any point after the stock transfer and within three years of his death.

In determining whether the decedent possessed the right to vote stock for purposes of § 2036(b), it is immaterial whether the decedent could vote the stock alone or in conjunction with another. Furthermore, the capacity in which the decedent possessed the right to vote the transferred stock is irrelevant as a general matter. Voting rights are counted toward the 20 percent threshold whether the decedent could vote the stock in his individual capacity, as trustee of a voting trust, or as trustee of a trust to which the stock is transferred.[18]

The requirement that the decedent retain the voting rights over transferred stock as a condition to the application of § 2036(b) undermines the purpose of the legislation significantly. For example, if a 60 percent shareholder transfers a five percent stock interest outright to a trust of which a third party serves as trustee, the transfer does not trigger § 2036(b). That is the case even though the decedent possesses effective voting control over the corporation, rendering the right to vote the five percent transferred interest largely irrelevant.[19] *See* Prop. Treas. Reg. § 20.2036-2(a). On the other hand, if the decedent had retained the right to vote the transferred stock (perhaps by serving as trustee of the trust), the transferred stock interest would be captured under § 2036(a)(1) by way of § 2036(b). Notwithstanding the dramatically different estate tax results, the transfers are virtually indistinguishable as a practical matter.

Similarly, § 2036(b) has no application to the transfer of shares of non-voting stock. The Senate report accompanying the enactment of § 2036(b) acknowledged this limitation, which the Service has endorsed. *See* Rev. Rul. 81-15, 1981-1 C.B. 457; Prop. Treas. Reg. § 20.2036-2(a).[20] This limitation significantly undermines the remedial purpose of § 2036(b) by supplying a safe-harbor to accomplish the very estate planning objective that § 2036(b) was intended to curtail. Section 2036(b) therefore has been reduced primarily to a trap for the unwary.

§ 10.03 AMOUNT INCLUDED

If § 2036(a)(1) applies to property transferred by the decedent, the date-of-death value of the transferred property is brought back into the decedent's gross estate. Assuming that the original transfer gave rise to a taxable gift, the primary effect of § 2036(a)(1) is to subject

---

[18] The only possible distinction between voting rights held individually and those held as trustee relates to contingent voting rights. As explained in the proposed regulations, rights to vote stock that are conditioned on an event that has not yet occurred are counted toward the 20 percent threshold if held individually; contingent rights in a fiduciary capacity are taken into consideration only if and when the contingency is removed. *See* Prop. Treas. Reg. § 20.2036-2(a) (flush paragraph).

[19] The legislative history accompanying § 2036(b) confirms this limitation on the statute:

The rule would not apply to the transfer of stock in a controlled corporation where the decedent could not vote the transferred stock. For example, where a decedent transfers stock in a controlled corporation to his son and does not have the power to vote the stock any time during the 3-year period before his death, the rule does not apply even where the decedent owned, or could vote, a majority of the stock.

S. Rep. No. 95-745, at 91 (1978), *quoted in* Rev. Rul. 81-15, 1981-1 C.B. 457.

[20] Hence, the tax-free recapitalization of a corporation into voting and non-voting shares followed by the transfer of non-voting stock could circumvent § 2036(b); however, that technique remains susceptible to challenge on step-transaction grounds.

post-transfer appreciation in the property to federal transfer taxation (as well as subjecting the entire transfer to tax on a tax-inclusive basis). *See* IRC § 2001(b)(2) (reducing tentative estate tax by gift tax payable on prior transfer).

The application of § 2036(a)(1) to recapture the transferred property in the decedent's gross estate explains the primary advantage to the government of invoking the statute in the family limited partnership context. As a general matter, only the value of the decedent's remaining beneficial interests in a family limited partnership will be included in his gross estate under § 2033. These interests often are valued through the application of significant discounts to the decedent's pro-rata portion of the entity valued as a whole.[21] Yet if the government is successful in applying § 2036(a)(1) to the property contributed to the partnership, valuation discounts associated with closely held business interests fall by the wayside. Additionally, the application of § 2036(a)(1) in this context negates any benefit from prior transfers of beneficial interests in the entity; the property transferred to the partnership is included in the gross estate regardless of who owns the beneficial interests in the entity.[22]

In limited circumstances, § 2036(a)(1) will apply to recapture only a portion of the transferred property. For instance, if the decedent transferred income-producing property to a trust and retained the right to 25 percent of the net income of the trust, § 2036(a)(1) will apply to the corresponding percentage of the transferred property. Treas. Reg. § 20.2036-1(c)(1)(i). Furthermore, if the decedent's retained beneficial interest was subject to an intervening life estate, the amount included under § 2036(a)(1) is the date-of-death value of the transferred property less the remaining value of the intervening life estate. *Id.*

§ 10.04   TRANSFERS WITHIN THREE YEARS OF DEATH

Section 2036 is precise in its description of the term of the beneficial interest that the decedent must retain in transferred property in order to trigger inclusion under the statute. Although the retention of beneficial enjoyment of the property for the decedent's life, for a period not ascertainable without reference to his death, or for a period that does not end before his death triggers § 2036(a)(1), a transfer with a retained life estate that the decedent renounces prior to his death does not. However, through the application of § 2035(a), the termination of the decedent's retained beneficial interest will prevent the property from being included in his gross estate only if made more than three years prior to his death.

Turning back to the application of § 2036(a)(1) through the retention of voting rights in stock of a controlled corporation pursuant to § 2036(b), the relinquishment or cessation of a right to vote stock will be treated as a transfer of property for purposes of § 2035. Thus, if a decedent retained the right to vote transferred stock, the retained voting rights must be terminated more than three years prior to death in order to avoid inclusion of the transferred stock under § 2035(a).

---

[21] For a discussion of valuation discounts typically associated with non-controlling interests in closely held entities, see § 7.07.

[22] As prior transfers often are designed to benefit from the § 2503(b) annual exclusion from the gift tax, the application of § 2036(a)(1) in this context effectively eliminates any benefit of the § 2503(b) exclusion.

§ 10.05   GIFT TAX CONSEQUENCES

[A]   Potential to Render Gift Incomplete or to Reduce Value of Gift

As is the case in many instances under the federal gift tax, the relevant guidance concerning the gift tax consequences of retained beneficial interests in property is provided through the regulations rather than the statute. As a general matter, a completed gift requires that the donor part with dominion and control over the transferred property so as to leave him no power to change its disposition, whether for the donor's own benefit or for the benefit of another. Treas. Reg. § 25.2511-2(b). Consistent with this principle, a donor's ability to revest beneficial title to transferred property in himself renders a gift incomplete. Treas. Reg. § 25.2511-2(c). If the donor retains no ability to cause the transferred property to be transferred back to him but the donor retains a beneficial interest in the transferred property, the amount of the gift will be reduced by the donor's interest only if it is "susceptible of measurement on the basis of generally accepted valuation principles." Treas. Reg. § 25.2511-1(e).

While these authorities easily absolve the funding of a revocable inter vivos trust from gift tax consequences, they shield the funding of many irrevocable trusts from gift tax as well. For example, suppose a settlor funds an irrevocable trust under which the trustee is authorized to make discretionary distributions of income and principal to the settlor and members of his family. If the settlor serves as a trustee, the settlor's ability to distribute the trust principal to himself renders the transfer incomplete. Treas. Reg. § 25.2511-2(c). The gift tax consequences of the trust funding are less clear, however, if the settlor designates a third-party trustee. In Revenue Ruling 77-378, 1977-2 C.B. 347, the Service explained that the transaction generally would constitute a completed gift, as the transferor did not retain any enforceable rights in the trust but instead only a mere expectancy of future distributions that was not capable of reliable valuation. Yet the ruling mentioned one avenue under which the trust funding could nonetheless remain an incomplete gift: If the settlor "could utilize the trust assets by going into debt and relegating [his] creditors to the trust." 1977-2 C.B. at 348–49 (citing Paolozzi v. Commissioner, 23 T.C. 182 (1954)). Note that the justification for characterizing the gift as incomplete in this context is that the settlor has retained the ability to revest (albeit indirectly) beneficial title in the property in himself. See Treas. Reg. § 25.2511-2(c). Accordingly, the gift tax consequences of establishing the trust turn on governing state law. If the trust assets are exempt from the claims of the settlor's creditor—that is, the relevant jurisdiction recognizes self-settled asset protection trusts—the funding of the trust completes the gift. However, if the relevant state law subjects the trust assets to the payment of the settlor's claims, the gift will not be completed until and to the extent distributions are made to third-party beneficiaries. Treas. Reg. § 25.2511-2(f).

The Supreme Court decision in Robinette v. Helvering, 318 U.S. 184 (1943), provides a succinct illustration of the gift tax treatment of retained interests in trust. In Robinette, the taxpayer transferred property in trust, reserving a life estate in her favor. Upon her death, the trust property was to be held for the benefit of her mother and stepfather if either survived, with the remainder being distributed to those of the taxpayer's issue who attained the age of 21. The taxpayer first argued that the absence of such issue at the moment the trust was funded precluded a completed gift of the remainder, a point the Court properly rejected by observing that a taxable gift does not depend on the ability to presently identify the donee. Id. at 186–87; see also Treas. Reg. § 25.2511-2(a). The taxpayer further argued that the transfer of the remainder interest should have been reduced by the value of her retained reversionary interest in the trust. Citing the numerous contingencies to which the reversion was subject, the Court concluded that the value of the reversion was not capable of reasonable approximation:

> The petitioner does not refer us to any recognized method by which it would be possible to determine the value of such a contingent reversionary remainder. It may be true as the petitioner argues that trust instruments such as these before us frequently create "a complex aggregate of rights, privileges, powers and immunities and that in certain instances all these rights, privileges, powers and immunities are not transferred or released simultaneously." But before one who gives this property away by this method is entitled to deduction from his gift tax on the basis that he had retained some of these complex strands it is necessary that he at least establish the possibility of approximating what value he holds. Factors to be considered in fixing the value of this contingent reservation as of the date of the gift would have included consideration of whether or not the daughter would marry; whether she would have children; whether they would reach the age of 21; etc. Actuarial science may have made great strides in appraising the value of that which seems to be unappraisable, but we have no reason to believe from this record that even the actuarial art could do more than guess at the value here in question.

Id. at 188–89 (distinguishing Smith v. Shaughnessy, 318 U.S. 176 (1943), in which the grantor's reversion depended only upon surviving his wife).

At one point, the ability to reduce the amount of a taxable gift through the retention of a beneficial interest in the transferred property that was capable of reasonable valuation presented significant planning opportunities. For instance, if a grantor funded a trust and reserved the right to the income from the trust assets for 20 years, the transfer would constitute a gift only to the extent of the actuarial value of the remainder interest. *See* IRC § 7520(a); Treas. Reg. § 25.2511-5(a), (d). The actuarial value of a remainder interest decreases as the presumed interest rate increases. Accordingly, in a high interest rate environment, a grantor could exploit the actuarial presumptions by funding the trust with property that does not produce a steady income stream. Instead, the trust assets could be invested primarily for capital appreciation. So long as the grantor survived the term of the retained interest, the appreciation in the trust property would not be captured in his estate under § 2036(a)(1). This planning technique, commonly referred to as the grantor retained income trust (GRIT), ultimately proved too good to be true. As discussed below, Congress has provided specific valuation rules for intra-family transfers of this sort through the enactment of § 2702.[23]

---

[23] Congress originally attempted to address the use of GRITs and similar techniques that exempt future appreciation in property from federal transfer taxation through an expansion of § 2036. In 1987, Congress enacted § 2036(c), which in general terms adopted a back-end approach of including the transferred property in the decedent's gross estate or subjecting the transferred property to gift taxation when the retained interest terminated. *See* Omnibus Budget Reconciliation Act of 1987, Pub. L. No. 100-203, § 10402(a), 101 Stat. 1330, 1330-431. However, § 2036(c) proved unwieldy in application and was short lived. Congress repealed it in 1990 when it adopted the special valuation provisions of §§ 2701–2704. *See* Omnibus Budget Reconciliation Act of 1990, Pub. L. No. 101-508, § 11601, 104 Stat. 1388, 1388-490 to -491.

[B]　Section 2702

In 1990, Congress introduced Chapter 14 (§§ 2701 to 2704) to the federal transfer tax regime. These provisions represent the legislative response to planning techniques that undermined the transfer tax base through the manipulation of general valuation principles. Congress explained the need for § 2702, applicable to retained-interest transfers, as follows:

> [T]he committee is concerned about the undervaluation of gifts valued pursuant to Treasury tables. Based on average rates of return and life expectancy, those tables are seldom accurate in a particular case, and therefore, may be the subject of adverse selection. Because the taxpayer decides what property to give, when to give it, and often controls the return on the property, use of Treasury tables undervalues the transferred interests in the aggregate, more often than not.

136 Cong. Rec. 30,538 (1990), *quoted in* Walton v. Commissioner, 115 T.C. 589, 599 (2000).

Congressional response to the problem was fairly heavy handed. As a general rule, a retained interest to which § 2702 applies is assigned a value of zero. Accordingly, the gift of the remainder interest will be valued at the entire amount of the transferred property. The retained interest will avoid this zero-value presumption only if it constitutes a "qualified interest," which the statute permits to be valued under the § 7520 actuarial tables. As described below, the terms of a qualified interest reduce the potential for taxpayers to exploit the assumptions on which the actuarial tables rely.

[1]　Scope of the Statute

Section 2702 does not apply to all retained-interest transfers. Rather, the statute reaches only those transfers in which a member of the transferor's family receives an interest. IRC § 2702(a)(1). A transferor's family for this purpose includes (a) the transferor's spouse, (b) an ancestor or lineal descendant of the transferor or his spouse, (c) a sibling of the transferor, and (d) spouses of the individuals in (b) and (c). IRC §§ 2702(e), 2704(c)(2). Transfers to a non-spouse cohabitant therefore are not subject to the punitive § 2702 valuation regime.

Although § 2702 is couched in terms of a transfer in trust, the concept reaches a variety of non-trust transfers. For instance, if property is transferred in a manner to create one or more successive term interests in the property—including life estates and interests for a term of years—the transfer is treated as a transfer in trust for § 2702 purposes.[24] IRC § 2702(c)(1). Hence, if *Parent* transfers undeveloped real property to *Child* while retaining a life estate, *Parent's* gift of the remainder interest will be valued at the full value of the transferred property. If *Child* pays *Parent* the actuarial value of his remainder interest, *Parent* nonetheless has made a gift of the full value of the property less the consideration received. *See* Treas. Reg. § 25.2702-4(d), Ex. 2.

Section 2702 cannot be sidestepped by avoiding a literal transfer of property to a family member. Rather, the statute applies if term interests in property are created upon the property's acquisition. In particular, if two or more members of a family acquire successive interests in the property, the person receiving the term interest is treated as acquiring the entire property and then transferring the remainder interest to the family member. IRC

---

[24] A leasehold interest in property is not treated as a term interest in property so as to implicate § 2702 so long as the lease is for adequate and full consideration. Treas. Reg. § 25.2702-4(b).

§ 2702(c)(2). In this manner, the acquisition of the property will constitute a gift to the family member acquiring the remainder interest, measured by the full value of the property less any consideration supplied by the family member.

[2] Qualified Interests

By identifying certain qualified interests that will be spared the draconian zero-valuation fate, § 2702 essentially channels retained-interest transfers into legislatively sanctioned forms. In terms of a lead (as opposed to remainder[25]) retained interest, two types of qualified transfers exist: (1) an annuity interest—that is, an interest which consists of the right to receive a fixed amount payable at least annually; and (2) a unitrust interest—that is, an interest which consists of the right to receive at least annually a fixed percentage of the fair market value of the trust assets (determined annually). IRC § 2702(b)(1), (2).

Following the enactment of § 2702, tax planning with retained interests generally centers on transfers of property that will outperform the § 7520 discount rate used to value the retained interest. If successful, appreciation in excess of the § 7520 rate will pass to the remainder beneficiary free of gift tax and, if the grantor survives the term of the retained interest, free of estate tax as well.[26] Because retained unitrust interests return a portion of this excess appreciation to the grantor, unitrusts generally are not the qualified interest of choice. Rather, most planning in this area takes the form of grantor retained annuity trusts (GRATs) that satisfy the § 2702(b)(1) definition of a qualified interest.

Treasury has provided detailed guidance on a "qualified annuity interest" in Reg. § 25.2702-3(b). As explained in the regulations, a qualified annuity interest need not provide level payments to the grantor over the trust term. Rather, the payments can vary, so long as a given year's payment does not exceed 120 percent of that paid in the preceding year. Treas. Reg. § 25.2702-3(b)(1)(ii). Furthermore, the annual payment need not be expressed as a fixed dollar amount. Instead, the annuity payment can be expressed as a fixed percentage of the initial fair market value of the trust property. Treas. Reg. § 25.2702-3(b)(1)(ii)(B). In significant concession to the taxpayer, the regulations provide that the baseline fair market value of the trust property can be that "as finally determined for federal tax purposes." *Id.* Thus, if the Service were to challenge the valuation of the property transferred in trust, a portion (and perhaps all) of the increased value will be attributed to the interest retained by the grantor. Qualified annuity trusts defined in this manner therefore provide a measure of insurance against valuation disputes.

A prevalent planning technique involves the use of qualified annuity interests that are designed to equal the entire value of the trust property, so that the gift of the remainder interest in the property is valued at zero. This technique, referred to as the zeroed-out GRAT, was approved by the Tax Court in *Walton v. Commissioner*, 115 T.C. 589 (2000), and the Service acquiesced to the *Walton* decision through 2003-2 C.B. 964, Notice 2003-72. In order for a zero value to be assigned to the remainder interest, the qualified annuity interest payments must

---

[25] A noncontingent remainder interest in a trust can constitute a qualified interest, but only if the prior interests in the trust are annuity interests or unitrust interests as described in § 2702(b)(1) and (2), respectively. IRC § 2702(b)(3).

[26] If the transferor does not survive the term of the retained interest, the portion of the trust property included in the transferor's gross estate will be the amount necessary to generate a return equal to the payment stream the transferor was receiving at the time of his death (capped at the date-of-death fair market value of the trust property). Treas. Reg. § 20.2036-1(c). The cap will be realized in the majority of cases.

be made to the grantor's estate if the grantor dies within the trust term—otherwise, the possibility of the remainder interest receiving the unpaid amounts will be of some value.[27] A GRAT that generates no immediate gift tax consequence provides the grantor with the opportunity to transfer future appreciation free of gift and estate tax. To succeed, the trust property must appreciate in excess of the § 7520 rate used to structure the annuity interest and the grantor must survive the trust term. If unsuccessful on either ground, the grantor likely will be in the same position from a transfer tax standpoint as if he had not engaged in the transaction. Hence, the downside of the technique is limited to the costs of implementation.

[3] Special Treatment for Personal Residences

As is often the case in matters of federal taxation, personal residences are afforded preferential treatment under § 2702. Namely, the statute is expressly inapplicable to a transfer in trust if the trust property consists solely of a residence to be used as a personal residence by persons holding a term interest in the trust. IRC § 2702(a)(3)(iii). The regulations identify two types of trust that will satisfy the personal residence exception: a "personal residence trust" under Reg. § 25.2702-5(b), and a "qualified personal residence trust" under Reg. § 25.2702-5(c). The restrictions on a personal residence trust are fairly severe. In particular, the trust must prohibit the sale of the residence during the original trust term, and the trust can hold no asset other than the residence. Treas. Reg. § 25.2702-5(b)(1). Hence, the prospect of the trust holding cash to pay expenses of the property is out of the question. The terms of a qualified personal residence trust (QPRT) are more permissive. A QPRT is permitted to hold cash to be applied toward expenses of the property (including mortgage payments) or improvements to the property. Treas. Reg. § 25.2702-5(c)(5)(ii)(A). Additionally, a QPRT is permitted to sell the residence and apply the proceeds toward a replacement property. Treas. Reg. § 25.2702-5(c)(5)(ii)(C). Given the more liberal parameters of the QPRT, it is the planning vehicle of choice in this arena. In that regard, the Service has provided a sample QPRT agreement in Rev. Proc. 2003-42, 2003-1 C.B. 993, making it easier for taxpayers to successfully navigate the numerous regulatory requirements en route to exempting future appreciation in the property from estate or gift tax.

Recall that, from a tax planning standpoint, QPRTs are successful only if the grantor survives the term of the retained interest. The grantor's survival of the trust term, however, leads to another set of complications. If the grantor wishes to continue residing in the property, the continued possession generally must be purchased through the payment of fair market value rent to the trust or to the remainder beneficiaries—a prospect many transferors may find displeasing. [However, if a grantor can get over the prospect of having to rent what he may view as his own house, the payment of rent provides an additional opportunity to reduce the grantor's future gross estate.] The ability of a grantor to avoid this problem by repurchasing the property is constrained. The trust instrument must prohibit the sale or transfer of the residence to the grantor, the grantor's spouse, or an entity controlled by either during the term of the retained interest. Treas. Reg. § 25.2702-5(c)(9). The prohibition on such sales extends past the retained interest term for as long as the trust constitutes a grantor trust for income tax purposes. *Id.* Thus, a sale of the residence following the term of a QPRT is permitted only

---

[27] The critical aspect of the Tax Court's decision in *Walton* was its determination that a qualified annuity interest included the right of the grantor's estate to receive the remaining annuity payments in the event of the grantor's death—contrary to the guidance then provided in Example 5 of Treas. Reg. § 25.2702-3(e). The regulation has since been modified to reflect the Service's acquiescence to the *Walton* decision.

in situations where the transaction will constitute a taxable exchange.

§ 10.06 STUDY PROBLEMS

1. Dave irrevocably transfers $1 million of marketable securities to a trust under which the trustee is permitted to distribute income and/or principal to or among Dave and his children in such amounts as the trustee deems advisable. Upon Dave's death, the trust assets will be distributed to Dave's living issue.

    a. Dave and his sister serve as co-trustees of the trust. Discuss the gift tax consequences to Dave upon funding the trust and the estate tax consequences to Dave's estate upon his death.

    b. How would your answer change, if at all, if Dave did not serve as trustee?

2. Kate lives in a house close to a local university, and she traditionally has rented a garage apartment in the back of her property to students for $750 per month. Kate wants to transfer title to the property to her daughter and son-in-law, but she also would like to move into the garage apartment so that she can remain close to her family.

    a. Assume that Kate does so without paying any rent to her daughter and son-in-law. What will be the estate tax consequences upon Kate's death?

    b. Is there a way the arrangement can be structured so as to avoid the application of § 2036(a)(1) altogether?

3. Several years ago, Bonita started a clothing boutique which she structured as a wholly-owned corporation. The business took off after her clothes were touted by a popular actress on national TV. Concerned about the size of her potential gross estate at that point, Bonita established two trusts, one for the benefit of her niece and another for the benefit of her nephew, and she funded each trust with a 20 percent interest in the clothing corporation. Bonita designated herself to serve as trustee together with her brother.

    a. What are the potential estate tax consequences to Bonita's estate upon her death?

    b. Would your answer change if Bonita's business were structured as an LLC?

    c. When advised of the answer in (a), Bonita immediately resigns as trustee. Will her resignation be sufficient to avoid adverse estate tax consequences?

4. Catherine is a woman of significant means, and her financial advisor has recently informed her that she can reduce her future estate tax liability significantly by transferring her assets to a family limited partnership. Upon hearing this fantastic news, Catherine directs her attorney to form the partnership to which Catherine and her children will make contributions. Catherine contributes the bulk of the partnership property, assigning her residence, her entire marketable securities portfolio, and all of her municipal bonds to the entity in exchange for her interest therein. The only thing she retains in her name is her vehicle and a checking account with a few thousand dollars. Catherine continues to reside in the residence, and she uses a debit card on the account she transferred to the partnership to pay her personal expenses. Discuss the future estate tax consequences of the arrangement.

5. In order to prepare his children to handle the significant sums they stand to inherit at his death, Gerald forms a separate LLC with each of his three children and capitalizes each with $10 million of securities (representing a combined 25 percent of Gerald's holdings). Each child serves as the manager of his or her LLC, actively managing the property in that capacity. Gerald and his children all respect the LLCs as separate and distinct from their personal affairs. In reviewing the LLC agreements, however, you stumble across the following sentence in each: "In the event Gerald should require funds for his care and maintenance, or in the event Gerald's estate requires funds to discharge expenses and claims, [Child] shall direct the LLC to distribute one-third of the amounts so required." Is this sentence anything to worry about from an estate tax standpoint?

6. Mark dies survived by his wife, Marie. Mark's will was drafted some 30 years before his death. It provides for a $500,000 conditional devise to a trust that provides for income distributions to Marie for her lifetime, remainder to the couple's children. The condition on the devise is that Marie must contribute an equal amount of her own funds to the trust. Marie, who is 78 years old at the time, accepts the conditional devise by contributing $500,000 of her separate property to the trust. Marie complies with the conditional devise in her favor, and the entire value of the trust grows to $1.4 million at Marie's death.

   In general terms, describe the gift tax consequences to Marie upon funding the trust and the estate tax consequences to Marie upon her death.

7. Louise purchases a parcel of timberland with her younger sister, Barbara. The deed to the property creates a legal life estate in Louise, remainder to Barbara. Louise and Barbara split the purchase price equally. Assume that, based on the actuarial tables, Barbara's remainder interest is worth 40 percent of the property's value. Discuss the gift tax consequences of the purchase.

Chapter 11

TRANSFERS WITH RETAINED POWERS OVER BENEFICIAL ENJOYMENT

Internal Revenue Code:	§§ 2035, 2036(a)(2), 2038(a)(1), (b)
Treasury Regulations:	§§ 20.2036-1, 20.2038-1
	§§ 25.2511-1(g)(2), 25.2511-2(b) to (g)

Many individuals of sufficient means are willing to pursue the transfer tax benefits of lifetime gifts (e.g., effective rate reduction through the tax-exclusive levy, removal of future appreciation from the transfer tax base) by parting completely with the economic benefit of transferred property. The tougher pill to swallow often proves to be the prospect of relinquishing control over the manner in which the transferred property is used or enjoyed by others.[1]

This chapter explores the tax treatment of transfers that leave the transferor with some measure of control over the use or enjoyment of transferred property, a subject dominated by nuance as much as any transfer tax topic. Mastering the intricacies of this field is critical for estate planners, given the natural desire of their clients to reduce exposure to the estate tax without parting with property on an absolute basis. In this regard, the admonition of the First Circuit is worth noting at the outset: "[T]he cost of holding onto the strings may prove to be a rope burn." Old Colony Trust Co. v. United States, 423 F.2d 601, 605 (1st Cir. 1970).

As a general rule, an individual's ability to control the beneficial enjoyment of transferred property will render the transfer incomplete from an estate tax perspective. Two largely overlapping provisions under the estate tax—§§ 2036(a)(2) and 2038(a)(1)—operate to capture in the decedent's gross estate property over which the decedent possessed an impermissible level of control. Section 2036(a)(2) looks forward from the point of the lifetime transfer to determine if the decedent retained the "right . . . to designate" the individuals who would enjoy the transferred property or the income it generates, while § 2038(a)(1) examines in hindsight whether the transferred property was subject to any change through the decedent's power to "alter, amend, revoke, or terminate" the transfer at the time of his death.[2] Taken together, the two provisions apply to a surprisingly wide range of retained powers. On the other hand, the two sections share broad exceptions that render them avoidable as a practical matter.

---

[1] As once succinctly explained by an estate-planning practitioner at a conference attended by one of the authors, "Clients don't mind making gifts to their kids. They just don't want them to enjoy the money." Lee A. Sheppard, *NYU/Tax Analysts Seminar: News Analysis—How Can We Hold On to the Estate Tax?*, 86 Tax Notes 1051, 1052 (Feb. 21, 2000).

[2] As § 2038(a)(2) applies only to transfers made prior to 1936, the minor differences between subsections (a)(1) and (a)(2) will not be addressed.

The gift tax consequences of transfers involving retained control over beneficial enjoyment largely parallel those under the estate tax in that such transfers generally are treated as incomplete gifts. That being said, the two regimes are not entirely consistent in this context. In particular, it is possible for property that had been transferred as part of a completed gift nonetheless to be captured in the transferor's gross estate under the retained-power provisions.

§ 11.01   RETAINED CONTROL OVER BENEFICIAL ENJOYMENT OF TRANSFERRED PROPERTY

[A]   The § 2036(a)(2) Right to Designate

In addition to applying to transfers through which the decedent retained the beneficial enjoyment of the transferred property, § 2036 captures property if the decedent retained "the right, either alone or in conjunction with any person, to designate the persons who shall possess or enjoy the property or the income therefrom." IRC § 2036(a)(2). As with § 2036(a)(1), the right to determine the beneficial enjoyment of others under § 2036(a)(2) must be retained for the decedent's life, for a period not ascertainable without reference to his death, or for a period which does not in fact end before his death. Thus, from an estate tax standpoint, a transferor's retention of the right to control the beneficial enjoyment of property transferred to others has the same consequence as a transferor's retention of the economic benefit of the transferred property—in both instances, the transferred property is brought back into the transferor's gross estate at its date-of-death value.

A so-called "spray" or "sprinkling" trust of which the transferor serves as trustee provides a classic example of a transfer that implicates § 2036(a)(2). Suppose a settlor contributes property to a trust for the benefit of his children, the terms of which provide the trustee with discretion to make distributions of income or principal to the trustee's children as the trustee deems necessary and appropriate. If the settlor serves as trustee or as a co-trustee with others, he has retained the power to determine how the income from the transferred property will be distributed, if at all, among his children. This discretionary power to determine who will receive the income from transferred property constitutes the linchpin of § 2036(a)(2). See Treas. Reg. § 20.2036-1(b)(3) (describing § 2036(a)(2) as including a "reserved power to designate the person or persons to receive the income from the transferred property").

While the prospect of capturing property in the decedent's gross estate under § 2036(a)(2) generally arises in the context of transfers in trust, the statute has potential application outside of the trust context. See IRC § 2036(a) (referencing transfers "by trust or otherwise"). For example, suppose that *Parent* transferred vacation property to each of her three children as tenants-in-common. In order to avoid disputes among the children regarding use of the property, *Parent* conditioned the transfer on each child signing a co-tenancy agreement whereby use of the property will be determined by *Parent* for her lifetime. Through this arrangement, *Parent* has retained the right to designate the persons "who shall possess or enjoy" the property under § 2036(a)(2). See Treas. Reg. § 20.2036-1(b)(3) (stating that § 2036(a)(2) is implicated by the power to designate the persons "to possess or enjoy nonincome-producing property").

[1]   Power to Accumulate Income

The text of § 2036(a)(2) suggests that it applies only where the decedent retained the ability to determine the identity of the person who would receive the income from transferred property. Suppose then that a trust is established for the benefit of a single individual, with the trustee possessing the discretionary ability to accumulate the income of the trust as he saw fit. To eliminate the prospect of another possible beneficiary, the trust provides for the principal and any accumulated income to be distributed to the beneficiary upon the beneficiary's attaining a certain age or to the beneficiary's probate estate if he died prior to that point. Hence, the trustee's discretion relates only to the timing of the income distributions, not the identity of the party who ultimately receives them. As explained by the Tax Court in *Estate of O'Connor v. Commissioner*, 54 T.C. 969 (1970), the power over the timing of income distributions alone is sufficient to implicate § 2036(a)(2) if held by the transferor:

> It is well settled that section 2036(a)(2) requires inclusion of both the original principal and the accumulated income of an irrevocable trust in the settlor's gross estate where at the time of his death the settlor retains the discretionary power either to distribute trust income to income beneficiaries or to accumulate such income and add it to principal; the power to deny to the trust beneficiaries the privilege of immediate enjoyment and to condition their enjoyment upon their surviving the termination of the trust has been considered to be of sufficient substance to qualify as a power to "designate" within the meaning of section 2036(a)(2).

Id. at 973 (citations omitted); *see also* United States v. O'Malley, 383 U.S. 627 (1966) (reaching same result under predecessor of § 2036(a)(2)); Estate of Alexander v. Commissioner, 81 T.C. 757 (1983) (reiterating the holding of *Estate of O'Connor*). Hence, the power to deny a beneficiary the current enjoyment of income from transferred property alone is sufficient to trigger the application of § 2036(a)(2).

[2]   Power to Accelerate Distribution of Principal

The regulations make clear that a § 2036(a)(2) right to designate extends only to powers over the income generated by transferred property. "The phrase . . . does not include a power over the transferred property itself which does not affect the enjoyment of the income received or earned during the decedent's life." Treas. Reg. § 20.2036-1(b)(3). In light of this limitation, suppose a settlor funds a trust for the benefit of his children that requires the trustee to distribute trust income to the settlor's children on an annual basis. In addition, the trustee possesses the discretionary authority to distribute trust principal to any of the settlor's children as the trustee sees fit. If the settlor designates himself as trustee, will his discretion over distributions of principal implicate § 2036(a)(2)? Note that a distribution of trust principal to one of the settlor's children would ensure that all the future income from the distributed principal would be received by that child alone, rather than being divided among all of the settlor's living children as required by the trust instrument. The discretionary ability to distribute principal in this context therefore amounts to the ability to alter the recipients of the income from the transferred property. However, if a trust is established for the benefit of a single individual with the remainder to be later distributed to the individual outright or to his probate estate, the ability to accelerate the distribution of trust principal does not implicate § 2036(a)(2).[3] In that case, only one individual can ever receive the income from the transferred

---

[3] As suggested by the § 2036 regulations, however, the power to accelerate distribution of principal will implicate

property—the difference lies in whether the income is received directly through ownership of the underlying property or indirectly through the trust.

[B] Necessity of Retained Right

By its terms, § 2036(a)(2) applies only to a retained "right" to determine the beneficial enjoyment of transferred property. However, the regulations refer to § 2036(a)(2) as including a "reserved power" to designate the parties who will receive the income from transferred property or who will possess or enjoy non-income producing property. Treas. Reg. § 20.2036-1(b)(3). The issue of whether § 2036(a)(2) necessitates a legally enforceable right as opposed to a practical power over beneficial enjoyment was addressed by the Supreme Court in *United States v. Byrum*, 408 U.S. 125 (1972), a case first mentioned in the context of § 2036(a)(1).[4]

Recall that the decedent in *Byrum* created irrevocable trusts for the benefit of his children, funding them with interests in three closely held corporations through which he conducted an operating business. Although an independent party served as trustee, the decedent retained the right to vote the stock conveyed to the trusts. The transfers left the decedent with voting control over all three corporations.[5] The Service relied primarily on § 2036(a)(2) in its attempt to include the transferred stock in the decedent's gross estate. The Service contended that the decedent's retention of the right to vote the transferred stock effectively amounted to a reserved right to accumulate income by stopping the flow of income into the trust. The foundation for the government's contention was that the decedent's status as majority shareholder afforded him the ability to elect the corporate boards, which in turn afforded him indirect control over the corporations' dividend policies. By directing the board to withhold dividends, the decedent possessed the power to eliminate the income stream payable to the trust.

The Service's theory was not well received by the Supreme Court. The Court determined that the decedent's influence over the makeup of the corporate boards did not leave him with a § 2036(a)(2) power over the beneficial enjoyment of the transferred stock, in part because the decedent did not possess a legally enforceable right to direct the corporations' dividend policies:

> It must be conceded that Byrum reserved no such "right" in the trust instrument or otherwise. The term "right," certainly when used in a tax statute, must be given its normal and customary meaning. It connotes an ascertainable and legally enforceable power, such as that involved in *O'Malley*. Here, the right ascribed to Byrum was the power to use his majority position and influence over the corporate directors to "regulate the flow of dividends" to the trust. That "right" was neither ascertainable nor legally enforceable and hence was not a right in any normal sense of that term.

> Byrum did retain the legal right to vote shares held by the trust and to veto investments and reinvestments. But the corporate trustee alone, not Byrum, had the right to pay out or withhold income and thereby to designate who among the beneficiaries enjoyed such income. Whatever power Byrum may have possessed with

---

§ 2038(a)(1). *See* Treas. Reg. § 20.2036-1(b)(3). The application of § 2038(a)(1) in this context is addressed in § 11.02[C].

[4] *See* § 10.01[A][1][b].

[5] In two of the three corporations, the decedent's retention of the right to vote the transferred stock was necessary to maintain his voting control over the entity. With respect to third, however, the decedent continued to possess voting control through the 59 percent stock interest he owned following the transfer.

respect to the flow of income into the trust was derived not from an enforceable legal right specified in the trust instrument, but from the fact that he could elect a majority of the directors of the three corporations. The power to elect the directors conferred no legal right to command them to pay or not to pay dividends. A majority shareholder has a fiduciary duty not to misuse his power by promoting his personal interests at the expense of corporate interests. Moreover, the directors also have a fiduciary duty to promote the interests of the corporation. However great Byrum's influence may have been with the corporate directors, their responsibilities were to all stockholders and were enforceable according to legal standards entirely unrelated to the needs of the trust or to Byrum's desires with respect thereto.

The Government seeks to equate the *de facto* position of a controlling stockholder with the legally enforceable "right" specified by the statute. Retention of corporate control (through the right to vote the shares) is said to be "tantamount to the power to accumulate income" in the trust which resulted in estate-tax consequences in *O'Malley*. The Government goes on to assert that "(t)hrough exercise of that retained power, (Byrum) could increase or decrease corporate dividends . . . and thereby shift or defer the beneficial enjoyment of trust income." This approach seems to us not only to depart from the specific statutory language, but also to misconceive the realities of corporate life.

Id. at 136–139 (footnotes omitted).[6]

The Supreme Court's interpretation of § 2036(a)(2) as requiring an "ascertainable and legally enforceable power" in *Byrum* stands in sharp contrast to the legal standard necessary to satisfy § 2036(a)(1), which may be implicated by an implied agreement among the parties established through circumstantial evidence. The discrepancy between the application of § 2036(a)(1) and § 2036(a)(2) is perhaps best illustrated by the Tax Court case of *Estate of Goodwyn v. Commissioner*, T.C. Memo. 1973-153, 32 T.C.M. (CCH) 740. The decedent in *Estate of Goodwyn* transferred property to an irrevocable trust for the benefit of his sons. Under the trust instruments, the trustees possessed the discretionary power to accumulate or distribute trust income. Although independent parties were designated as trustees, the court found that the decedent exercised "complete control" over the investment of the trust property and the determination of the amounts to be distributed to the trust beneficiaries. *Id.* at 752. Notwithstanding this finding, the Tax Court determined that the arrangement failed to implicate § 2036(a)(2), based solely on the fact that the decedent's control did not emanate from a legally enforceable power as required by *Byrum*. *Id.* at 754. Hence, legal rights as opposed to de facto practice determine the application of § 2036(a)(2).

---

[6] Query whether the Supreme Court focused on the wrong capacity through which the decedent in *Byrum* could have influenced the dividends paid with respect to the transferred stock. While the decedent's status as majority shareholder did not provide him with an ascertainable and legally enforceable power over the corporations' dividend policies, the decedent continued to serve as a director of each corporation. In that capacity, he possessed the right to vote, together with the other directors, on the amount of dividends, if any, to be paid. Because this right was ascertainable and legally enforceable, it would have satisfied the Court's preliminary standard. Furthermore, the decedent's capacity as majority shareholder ensured his ability to continue serving on the board if he so chose.

§ 11.02   POWER TO ALTER, AMEND, REVOKE OR TERMINATE

Section 2038(a)(1) operates to include in the decedent's gross estate any property that the decedent has previously transferred, to the extent of any interest the enjoyment of which was subject to change through a power to alter, amend, revoke, or terminate held by the decedent at the time of his death.[7] While § 2038(a)(1) shares the same general focus as § 2036(a)(2)—that is, the decedent's ability to affect the beneficial enjoyment of transferred property—important structural differences exist between the two statutes. Whereas § 2036(a)(2) applies only to powers that the decedent retained through the transfer for the requisite § 2036 term, § 2038 does not require the power to have been retained as part of the original transfer. Rather, the decedent simply must possess the § 2038(a)(1) power at the time of his death. Furthermore, even if both statutes are implicated, the effect of the two may differ. Section 2038 operates to include only that portion of the property that remains subject to the decedent's prohibited power at the time of his death. Section 2036(a)(2), on the other hand, operates to include the entire amount of transferred property, even though only a portion of such property (namely, the income interest) is subject to the decedent's retained power. In situations where both sections are implicated, the government will invoke the one that results in the largest inclusion in the gross estate. *See* Estate of Farrel v. United States, 553 F.2d 637 (Ct. Cl. 1977).

[A]   Revocable Transfers

Section 2038(a)(1) is most commonly applied to revocable transfers. The revocable inter vivos trust has become a popular estate-planning vehicle, as it permits individuals to avoid the costs and publicity associated with probate administration while also providing a vehicle for the transfer of property management in the event of the settlor's incapacity. However, the technique offers no estate tax advantages. Powers commonly retained by grantors in this context to alter or amend the trust terms, or to revoke the trust altogether, cause the entire trust property to be included in the gross estate under § 2038(a)(1).[8]

The application of § 2038(a)(1) is not limited to express powers of revocation. For instance, if a settlor transfers property to an irrevocable trust having a third-party trustee, the trust assets nonetheless will be included in the settlor's gross estate under § 2038(a)(1) to the extent the trust property could be reached by the settlor's creditors. As explained by the Service, the power to subject the trust property to the payment of claims effectively constitutes a power to terminate the trust. *See* Rev. Rul. 76-103, 1976-1 C.B. 293. The operation of state trust law therefore will be critical in this context. On that note, the Uniform Trust Code provides that the creditor of a settlor of an irrevocable trust may reach the maximum amount that the trustee is capable of distributing to or for the settlor's benefit. Unif. Trust Code § 505(a)(2), 7C U.L.A. 535 (2006). Section 2038(a)(1) therefore has broad potential application in the context of irrevocable transfers, so long as the settlor remains a discretionary beneficiary of the trust.

---

[7] It is worth noting that when Congress expanded the description of the § 2038 predicate powers in 1936 to expressly include a power to "terminate," it intended merely to clarify the scope of the statute rather than expand its application. *See* Commissioner v. Estate of Hofheimer, 149 F.2d 733 (2d Cir. 1945); *see also* H.R. Rep. No. 74-2818, at 10 (1936) ("Since in substance a power to terminate is the equivalent of a power to revoke, this question should be set to rest. Express provision to that effect has been made and it is believed that it is declaratory of existing law.").

[8] Note that the power to revoke a transfer altogether would cause the transferred property to be included in the decedent's gross estate under § 2036(a)(1) based on the decedent's right to enjoy the income from the transferred property.

Gifts made on behalf of a decedent by an agent acting under a power of attorney have proven to be a focal point of litigation concerning § 2038(a)(1). Seeking to unwind the transfer tax benefits attributable to the often last-minute use of the gift tax annual exclusion, the government has challenged gifts in this context as falling outside of the scope of the agent's general authority to manage the principal's property (and possibility as contrary to the principal's fiduciary obligations). As such, the transfers would have been revocable by the principal, and § 2038(a)(1) therefore would apply to capture the transferred amounts in the decedent's gross estate. *See, e.g.*, Estate of Casey v. Commissioner, 948 F.2d 895 (4th Cir. 1991). The application of § 2038(a)(1) in this context can be avoided by expressly granting the agent the power to make gratuitous transfers on behalf of the principal, although careful consideration should be given to the practical ramifications of authorizing an agent to deplete the principal's resources in this manner.[9]

[B]　Power to Alter or Amend

Section 2038(a)(1) applies not only to a power to revoke the trust and return the trust assets to the settlor, but also to the less drastic powers to alter or amend the beneficial interests of others. *See* Porter v. Commissioner, 288 U.S. 436 (1933) (explaining that the terms "alter" and "amend" under predecessor of § 2038 were not intended to be merely duplicative of "revoke"). In particular, the power to alter the interests of defined beneficiaries or to change the beneficiaries of transferred property implicates § 2038(a)(1). *See id.*; Florida Nat'l Bank v. United States, 336 F.2d 598 (3d Cir. 1964); Commissioner v. Chase Nat'l Bank, 82 F.2d 157 (2d Cir. 1936). This result holds even where the power may be exercised by the decedent only by way of will. *See* Adriance v. Higgins, 113 F.2d 1013, 1015 (2d Cir. 1940) ("It can make no difference whether a trust deed reserves a power to amend the trust by an inter vivos instrument, or by a will, or by both.").

[C]　Power to Accelerate Distribution

The regulations under § 2038 indicate that the statute can be implicated in instances where the beneficiary of the property cannot be changed. The ability to affect the time and manner in which the transferred property may be enjoyed is sufficient. *See* Treas. Reg. § 20.2038-1(a) (flush paragraph). The limits of § 2038(a)(1) in this regard were addressed by the Supreme Court in *Lober v. United States*, 346 U.S. 335 (1953).

The decedent in *Lober* created separate trusts for the individual benefit of his children, the terms of which permitted the decedent to accumulate or distribute income until the child attained age 21. The principal of the trust was to be distributed to the child at age 25 or, in the event of the child's death prior to such age, to the child's probate estate. In addition to his rights over trust income, the decedent possessed the right to distribute trust principal to the child as he saw fit. Although the child for whom the trust was created possessed a vested remainder in the trust principal, the Court nonetheless relied on its prior decision in *Commissioner v. Estate of Holmes*, 326 U.S. 480 (1946), to include the trust property in the decedent's gross estate under the predecessor of § 2038(a)(2):

---

[9] For example, it may be advisable to limit the amount of gifts that can be made to the then available gift tax annual exclusion, and further to require that any gifts must be made equally to a class of beneficiaries (i.e., the principal's children) in order to prevent a self-serving exercise of the power.

The trust instrument here gave none of [the decedent's] children full "enjoyment" of the trust property, whether it "vested" in them or not. To get this full enjoyment they had to wait until they reached the age of twenty-five unless their father sooner gave them the money and stocks by terminating the trust under the power of change he kept to the very date of his death. This father could have given property to his children without reserving in himself any power to change the terms as to the date his gift would be wholly effective, but he did not. What we said in the *Holmes* case fits this situation too: "A donor who keeps so strong a hold over the actual and immediate enjoyment of what he puts beyond his own power to retake has not divested himself of that degree of control which [the predecessor of § 2038(a)(2)] requires in order to avoid the tax."

Lober, 346 U.S. at 337 (quoting *Holmes*, 326 U.S. at 487); *see also* Rev. Rul. 70-513, 1970-2 C.B. 194.

Assuming the decedent possessed no rights over the income generated by property transferred in trust but instead only the right to accelerate the distribution of trust principal, § 2038 would operate to include only the value of the remainder interest as of the decedent's death. *See* Treas. Reg. § 20.2038-1(a) (flush paragraph) ("[O]nly the value of an interest in property subject to a power to which section 2038 applies is included in the decedent's gross estate under section 2038."). Hence, rather than including the entire value of the transferred property as is typically the case under § 2036(a)(2), § 2038 in this instance would not apply to the portion of the transferred property attributable to the outstanding income interest of the beneficiaries.

[D]   Qualitative Nature of Power

The Court of Claims in *Estate of Tully*, 528 F.2d 1401 (Ct. Cl. 1976), explored the bounds of what influence held by the decedent rises to the level of a power to alter, amend, revoke, or terminate under § 2038(a)(1). The decedent in that case was one of two equal shareholders in a corporation which had contractually agreed to pay a death benefit to the shareholders' widows. The government first argued that the decedent could exercise his power as 50 percent shareholder to cause the corporation to change the contractual death benefit as he saw fit. The Court of Claims disagreed. Noting that any action by the decedent could have been blocked by the other 50 percent shareholder, the court explained that the power must be "*demonstrable, real, apparent and evident*, not speculative" in order to implicate § 2038(a)(1). *Id.* at 1404 (emphasis in original).

The government next argued that the decedent possessed the requisite § 2038(a)(1) power over the death benefit in conjunction with the corporation and its other shareholder. Recognizing the § 2038 powers can be held jointly, the court nonetheless rejected the government's alternate theory on grounds that the concept of a "power" under § 2038 "does not extend to *powers of persuasion*." *Id.* (emphasis in original). The government's theories for invoking § 2038 did not stop there. It argued that a § 2038(a)(1) power could be found in the decedent's ability to renegotiate his employment contract to alter the amount of the death benefit. Predictably, the court found the prospect of bilateral contract renegotiation too speculative to implicate § 2038. Finally, the court rejected the government's argument that the decedent could effectively terminate the death benefit by obtaining a divorce. Citing the independent significance of such action, the court characterized the last argument as "approach[ing] the absurd." *Id.* at 1406.

[E]   Superseded Transfers

Unlike § 2036(a)(2), the power to alter, amend, revoke, or terminate a previous transfer need not be retained by the decedent in order to invoke § 2038(a)(1). Instead, the statute focuses only on whether the decedent possessed the requisite power at the time of his death. Suppose then that *Husband* gratuitously transfers property to *Wife*, who subsequently devises that property to a trust created under her will. The trust provides the trustee with discretion to distribute trust income and principal among the couple's children as the trustee sees fit, and *Wife's* will designates *Husband* to serve as trustee. Assuming that *Husband* continues serving in this capacity until his death, will the trust property be brought into his gross estate under § 2038(a)(1)? Or should the prior transfer by *Husband* effectively be extinguished for § 2038 purposes by *Wife's* intervening devise?

As a general rule, the decedent must have created the relevant powers through his transfer in order to implicate § 2038(a)(1), even if those powers need not be retained as part of the transfer. As explained by the district court in *Estate of Reed v. United States*, 75-1 U.S.T.C. (CCH) ¶ 13,073, at 87,477 (M.D. Fla. 1975):

> Section 2038(a)(1) . . . seems to be designed to apply to situations where the transferor-decedent himself sets the machinery in motion that purposefully allows fiduciary powers over the property interest to subsequently return to him, such as by an incomplete transfer. Section 2038(a)(1) does not seem to be intended to reach the value of a property interest of which the decedent, prior to his death, made a complete, absolute disposition simply because, at the time of his death, by a totally unrelated and fortuitous reconveyance, he had some degree of fiduciary power or control over the interest.

Id. at 87,480 (citations omitted). Thus, § 2038 would not apply to capture the trust property in *Husband's* estate in the hypothetical above, as the relevant powers were created by *Wife* through her testamentary transfer. On the other hand, had *Husband* originally transferred the property to the trust and named *Wife* as trustee, with *Husband* later assuming the trusteeship upon *Wife's* death, § 2038(a)(1) would capture the trust property in *Husband's* gross estate. *See* Rev. Rul. 70-348, 1970-2 C.B. 193 (reaching this result in the context of a UGMA account).

[F]   Contingent Powers

The significance of prerequisites to the exercise of a discretionary power is another topic on which §§ 2036(a)(2) and 2038(a)(1) differ. A § 2036(a)(2) right to designate exists even if the exercise of such power was subject to a contingency beyond the decedent's control and which did not in fact occur prior to the decedent's death. Treas. Reg. § 20.2036-1(b)(3). Hence, if a decedent transferred property to a discretionary trust for the benefit of his children, the decedent's ability to serve as a substitute trustee only in the event of the named trustee's death or mental incapacity will cause the trust property to be included in the decedent's gross estate in full. Section 2038(a)(1), however, is more forgiving in this regard. While § 2038(b) makes clear that merely subjecting a power to a notice requirement is not sufficient to avoid the statute, the statute does not apply if the power was subject to a contingency beyond the decedent's control that did not occur prior to the decedent's death. Treas. Reg. § 20.2038-1(b). The concession for contingent powers under § 2038 often will prove hollow, however. Given that identical powers over the beneficial enjoyment of transferred property frequently implicate both § 2036(a)(2) and § 2038(a)(1), the government simply will advance § 2036(a)(2) in such circumstances.

§ 11.03   EXCLUDED POWERS

Powers over the beneficial enjoyment of transferred property that otherwise would implicate §§ 2036(a)(2) or 2038(a)(1) are subject to two significant exceptions, both having a common-law origin: (1) powers that relate to the administration or management of trust property, and (2) powers that are limited by an ascertainable standard. These exceptions have considerable breadth as a practical standpoint, and their existence provides taxpayers with a roadmap to accomplish the very objective that §§ 2036(a)(2) and 2038(a)(1) were intended to prevent.

[A]   Administrative or Managerial Powers

Suppose a trust provides for the net income of the trust to be distributed to the beneficiaries at regular intervals, with the principal to be distributed at a defined point in the future. The arrangement leaves the trustee with no express discretion concerning distributions from the trust. On the other hand, the trustee generally possesses both the authority and obligation to invest the trust property, and the manner in which the property is invested can affect significantly the relative interests of the trust beneficiaries. For instance, the trustee could invest in high-yield, high-risk corporate bonds to increase the income payments to the current trust beneficiaries. Or the trustee could reduce significantly the mandatory income distributions by investing primarily for future appreciation. Despite the practical significance of discretion over the investment of trust property, powers held in an administrative or managerial capacity generally fall outside the scope of §§ 2036 and 2038.

The exclusion for administrative powers has its origins in the case of *Reinecke v. Northern Trust Co.*, 278 U.S. 339, 346 (1929), in which the Supreme Court simply declared that reserved powers of management did not provide the decedent with "any control" over the beneficial enjoyment of the trust property. The Tax Court expanded on this point in *King v. Commissioner*, 37 T.C. 973 (1962), holding that the decedent's reservation of the widest discretion over investment decisions did not implicate §§ 2036(a)(2) or 2038(a)(1) given the trustee's fiduciary obligation to exercise such discretion evenhandedly:

> [W]e think that although the decedent, under his broad discretionary powers with respect to investment, might invest in properties producing either a high or low return of income, such powers would have to be exercised in good faith in accordance with his fiduciary responsibility and could not be used for the purpose of attempting to favor any beneficiary or class of beneficiaries to the detriment of the other beneficiaries.

Id. at 980. This principle has been so oft-repeated as to become settled law. *See* Old Colony Trust Co. v. United States, 423 F.2d 601 (1st Cir. 1970) (stating that "no aggregation of purely administrative powers" can be equated with ownership for estate tax purposes); United States v. Powell, 307 F.2d 821 (10th Cir. 1962) (reasoning that investment power was subject to judicially enforceable external standards); Budd v. Commissioner, 49 T.C. 468 (1968) (characterizing managerial powers as "hardly broad enough" to implicate § 2038).

[B] Powers Subject to Ascertainable Standard

Even powers that affect the beneficial enjoyment of transferred property directly—as opposed to indirectly through investment allocation determinations—nonetheless may fall outside the scope of §§ 2036 and 2038. If a transferor's exercise of discretion over distributions is limited by an ascertainable standard, then the transferor will be treated as simply carrying out the directive of the trust instrument as opposed to acting according to personal whim. The theory behind this exception was explained by the Second Circuit in *Jennings v. Smith*, 161 F.2d 74 (2d Cir. 1947). In that case, the decedent served together with his sons as trustees of two separate trusts created for the individual benefit of each son. The trusts provided that income was to be accumulated and added to principal, unless the trustees determined in their absolute discretion that the disbursement of income was "reasonably necessary to enable the beneficiary . . . to maintain himself and his family, if any, in comfort and in accordance with the station in life to which he belongs." *Id.* at 75–76. The Second Circuit concluded that the decedent had not thereby retained the right to designate the beneficial enjoyment of the transferred property under the predecessor of § 2036(a)(2),[10] reasoning as follows:

> [W]e think the decedent effectively put that "right" beyond his own control or retention by imposing conditions upon the exercise of it. A "right" so qualified that it becomes a duty enforceable in a court of equity on petition by the beneficiaries does not circumvent the obvious purpose of [the predecessor of § 2036(a)(2)] to prevent transfers akin to testamentary dispositions from escaping taxation.

Id. at 78–79. Hence, the justification for the ascertainable standard exception is the same as that underlying the exception of administrative powers—both are subject to judicial review and enforcement by a court acting in equity.

Not surprisingly, a wealth of litigation has centered on what standards for distribution are sufficiently definite to benefit from the ascertainable standard exception. Standards for distribution expressed in terms of the beneficiary's health, education, or maintenance receive favorable treatment. *See, e.g.*, Leopold v. United States, 510 F.2d 617 (9th Cir. 1975) ("support, education, maintenance and general welfare"); Wier v. Commissioner, 17 T.C. 409 (1951) ("support, maintenance and education"). Standards expressed in these terms benefit from the analogy to § 2041, which excepts from the definition of a general power of appointment one that is limited "by an ascertainable standard relating to the health, education, support, or maintenance" of the decedent.[11] IRC § 2041(b)(1)(A). Authorizing the trustee to determine in its sole discretion whether the standard for distribution has been satisfied does not alter the result, on the theory that grants of discretion cannot remove judicial review of a trustee's actions entirely. *See* Budd v. Commissioner, 49 T.C. 468 (1968) (finding that external standard would operate to constrain the "sole" or "uncontrolled" discretion of the trustee); *see also* Treas. Reg. § 25.2511-1(g)(2) (providing that "the fact that the governing instrument is phrased in discretionary terms is not in itself an indication that no such standard [for distribution] exists").

---

[10] In a prior portion of the opinion, the court held the predecessor of § 2038 inapplicable on the basis that the condition for disbursement of income—financial need of the beneficiary or his family—was not implicated prior to the decedent's death. Jennings v. Smith, 161 F.2d 74, 77–78 (2d Cir. 1947).

[11] Inclusion in the gross estate based on a decedent's power of appointment over property is discussed in Chapter 14.

On the other hand, standards for distribution expressed in terms of the beneficiary's "happiness" or "best interests" generally are found to be impermissibly vague. *See* Old Colony Trust Co. v. United States, 423 F.2d 601 (1st Cir. 1970) (no ascertainable standard for distributions in the "best interests" of beneficiary); *see also* Treas. Reg. § 25.2511-1(g)(2) (rejecting "pleasure, desire, or happiness" of beneficiary as an ascertainable standard). The same can be said of distributions that the trustee determines to be "necessary." *See* Leopold v. United States, 510 F.2d 617 (9th Cir. 1975) (no ascertainable standard in distributions that were "necessary and proper"); Estate of Cutter v. Commissioner, 62 T.C. 351 (1974) (no ascertainable standard in distributions "necessary for the benefit" of beneficiary). However, in certain instances, courts have interpreted apparently overbroad standards of distribution as imposing an ascertainable standard by relying on the context of the trust instrument as a whole. For example, in *Estate of Ford v. Commissioner*, 53 T.C. 114 (1969), the trust document permitted distributions for the "support, maintenance, education, welfare, and happiness" of the beneficiary. *Id.* at 125. While the standard of "happiness" generally would be impermissibly broad, the court interpreted this and all other grounds for distribution as being conditioned on a finding of the beneficiary's financial need. This overarching requirement rendered the standard sufficiently objective to be enforced by a court of equity. *Id.* at 126.

The exception to §§ 2036(a)(2) and 2038(a)(1) for discretionary distributions that are subject to an ascertainable standard provides taxpayers with a broad safe harbor through which to retain control over the beneficial enjoyment of transferred property. A provision limiting discretionary distributions to the recipient's "health, education, support or maintenance," even where support is expressly defined to encompass the recipient's accustomed manner of living, fits comfortably within the ascertainable-standard safe harbor. *See* Treas. Reg. § 25.2511-1(g)(2) (distributions to enable the beneficiary to "maintain his accustomed standard of living" constitutes ascertainable standard). Yet from a practical standpoint, the limitation is anything but constraining; the vast majority of distributions to or for the benefit of an individual can be justified on one of those grounds. To the extent there is a downside from including such a standard,[12] it may make it more difficult for the settlor-trustee to defend a decision to forgo distributions altogether. But even this potential drawback can be mitigated by directing the trustee to consider the other resources available to the beneficiary in exercising its discretion. In this manner, the exception to §§ 2036(a)(2) and 2038(a)(1) for powers subject to an ascertainable standard can be employed to significantly undermine the fundamental purpose of those statutes.

[C] UGMA Accounts and Section 529 Plans

Individuals making gifts to minors frequently do so through the Uniform Gifts to Minors Act or similar legislation, seeking the benefits of a standardized custodial arrangement that qualifies for the gift tax annual exclusion under § 2503(c). From an estate tax planning standpoint, the transferor to a UGMA account should designate as custodian someone other than himself. Because the custodian can distribute the principal or income of a UGMA account for the support, maintenance, education, or *benefit* of the minor, the custodian's discretion is not limited by an ascertainable standard. The account balance therefore will be included in the transferor-custodian's gross estate under §§ 2036(a)(2) and 2038(a)(1). *See* Rev. Rul. 59-357, 1959-2 C.B. 212; Rev. Rul. 57-366, 1957-2 C.B. 618; Estate of Prudowsky v. Commissioner, 55

---

[12] On the other hand, including such a standard may cause the trust assets to be included in the settlor's gross estate under § 2036(a)(1) if the settlor-trustee remained legally obligated to support the beneficiary.

T.C. 890 (1971), *aff'd per curiam*, 465 F.2d 62 (7th Cir. 1972). By way of statutory exclusion, however, amounts transferred to a § 529 qualified tuition program or to a Coverdell educational savings account will not be included in the transferor's gross estate, even where the transferor continues to control the beneficial enjoyment of such amounts as account owner. IRC §§ 529(c)(4)(A), 530(d)(3).

[D] Power to Substitute Property of Equivalent Value

In the current estate planning environment, trusts often are structured to achieve "grantor trust" status under subchapter J, so that the grantor of the trust is treated as the owner of the trust assets for income tax purposes. Grantor trust status is desirable because it permits the grantor to sell property to the trust without triggering a realization event for income tax purposes (as one cannot make a sale to oneself). Additionally, grantor trust status permits the grantor to pay the income tax liability of the trust without gift tax consequence,[13] permitting the trust to realize a pre-tax rate of investment return.

One of the more popular means of ensuring that a trust will achieve grantor trust status under subchapter J without causing the trust assets to be recaptured in the grantor's gross estate at death is for a person to be afforded the power, in a non-fiduciary capacity, to reacquire trust property by substituting property of equivalent value. *See* IRC § 675(4)(C); Treas. Reg. § 1.675-1(b)(4). The estate tax consequences of the grantor retaining such a power at one point were of some concern. In *Estate of Jordahl v. Commissioner*, 65 T.C. 92 (1975), the Service argued that the grantor's power as trustee to substitute property of equal value for that originally transferred to the trust constituted a power to "alter, amend, or revoke" the trust under § 2038(a). The Tax Court rejected this argument on the basis that such a power presented the decedent no greater ability to alter the trust than traditional managerial powers held not to implicate § 2038(a)(1).

While the Service later acquiesced to the decision in *Estate of Jordahl*, the case concerned a power of substitution held in a fiduciary capacity. Indeed, the Tax Court seemed moved by the fiduciary obligations the decedent had to observe in exercising the substitution power. *Id.* at 97 ("[D]ecedent was bound by fiduciary standards. Even if decedent were not a trustee, he would have been accountable to the succeeding income beneficiary and remaindermen, in equity, especially since the requirement of 'equal value' indicates that the power was held in trust."). However, the power of substitution necessary to trigger grantor trust status under § 675(4)(C) must be held in a *nonfiduciary* capacity. Doubts existed as to whether beneficial estate tax treatment of powers of substitution was conditioned on such powers being held in a fiduciary capacity. The Service largely dispelled any such concerns, however, through the issuance of Revenue Ruling 2008-22, 2008-1 C.B. 796. The ruling held that a grantor's retained power to reacquire trust property by substituting other property of equivalent value did not cause the trust assets to be recaptured under §§ 2036 or 2038, even where the power was held in a non-fiduciary capacity. The ruling reasoned that the requirement that the substituted properties be of equivalent value precluded any alteration of the beneficial enjoyment of the trust assets, and that the trustee had a fiduciary obligation to ensure that the valuation standard was satisfied. In this manner, Revenue Ruling 2008-22 cleared an estate tax path for a § 675(4)(C) power of substitution to be used to trigger grantor trust status.

---

[13] Because the grantor is primarily liable for the income tax liability generated by the trust, the grantor's payment of the tax does not give rise to a taxable gift. *See* Rev. Rul. 2004-64, 2004-2 C.B. 7.

§ 11.04   CAPACITY IN WHICH POWER IS HELD

[A]   Jointly Held Powers

Section 2036(a)(2) and § 2038(a)(1) powers can be held in a wide range of capacities, with both statutes possibly being implicated in situations where the decedent-transferor could exercise little control as a practical matter. The text of each statute makes clear that a power held in conjunction with another is sufficient. In this regard, the fact that the joint holder of the power may possess an interest adverse to its exercise is immaterial. Treas. Reg. § 20.2036-1(b)(3), § 20.2038-1(a) (flush paragraph). Similarly immaterial is the manner in which the joint power may be exercised. Sections 2036(a)(2) and 2038(a)(1) apply whether the power authorized the decedent to initiate action, required the decedent's consent for action to be taken, or simply afforded the decedent with the opportunity to veto proposed action. *See* Grossman v. Commissioner, 27 T.C. 707 (1957) (declaring that "it is irrelevant whether the decedent's participation initiates the termination, or, as here, is in the nature of a consent after others have set the machinery in motion, it being sufficient under [the predecessor of § 2038] merely that she act 'in conjunction' with the others"); *see also* Rev. Rul. 70-513, 1970-2 C.B. 194 (applying § 2038 based on grantor's veto power).

[B]   Ability to Terminate Trust Under State Law

In certain extreme instances, jointly held powers to terminate a trust will be exempt from estate tax consequence. As provided in Reg. § 20.2038-1(a)(2), a decedent's power to terminate a trust with the consent of all other parties possessing an interest in the trust will not implicate § 2038 so long as the power adds nothing to the rights of the parties under state law. *See also* Helvering v. Helmholz, 296 U.S. 93 (1935) (holding that right to join with all trust beneficiaries to terminate trust does not render the transfer one intended to take effect in possession or enjoyment at the time of the transferor's death under predecessor of § 2038). While Reg. § 20.2038-1(a)(2) and the *Helmholz* decision originate in the context of § 2038, the same result should hold under § 2036(a)(2). The theory of this exception is fairly straightforward: the decedent's power emanates from default state law rather than the decedent's intentionally incomplete transfer.

[C]   Power to Remove and Replace Trustee

Powers that implicate §§ 2036 and 2038 can exist via attribution. As a general rule, a decedent will be regarded as holding all powers actually held by a third-party trustee whom the decedent could remove and appoint himself as a successor. *See* Treas. Reg. § 20.2036-1(b)(3); § 20.2038-1(a)(3). While subjecting the removal and replacement power to a condition beyond the decedent's control that did not occur prior to the decedent's death will preclude the attribution of powers for purposes of § 2038, *see* Treas. Reg. § 20.2038-1(b), the same cannot be said of § 2036. *See* Rev. Rul. 73-21, 1973-1 C.B. 405 (declaring contingencies on removal power irrelevant for § 2036 purposes); *see also* Estate of Farrel v. United States, 553 F.2d 637 (Ct. Cl. 1977) (attributing trustee powers to decedent where the decedent could not remove trustee but only could name herself as a replacement if a vacancy arose). In order to permit grantors some discretion to remove and replace third-party trustees without triggering severe estate tax consequences, the Service announced a safe harbor through Revenue Ruling 95-58, 1995-2 C.B. 191. Under the ruling, a decedent-grantor will not be treated as possessing the powers of a trustee he could remove so long as the decedent was limited to appointing as a replacement trustee someone other than himself or a party related or subordinate to the decedent within the meaning of § 672(c).

§ 11.05 TRANSFER REQUIREMENT

[A] Treatment of Accumulated Income

Both §§ 2036 and 2038 apply only to property that was previously transferred by a decedent. Suppose then that a decedent transferred $100,000 of corporate bonds to a trust that provided him, in his capacity as trustee, with complete discretion to distribute income and principal as he saw fit. Instead of distributing the interest income, the decedent instead reinvested the proceeds so that the trust grew to $250,000 by the time of his death. Although the value of the property originally contributed to the trust will certainly be captured in the gross estate under either §§ 2036(a)(2) or 2038(a)(1), do those sections also reach amounts attributable to accumulated income? After all, the decedent never literally transferred such amounts; they simply were paid into the trust by reason of the trust's ownership of the underlying bonds. The Supreme Court in *United States v. O'Malley*, 383 U.S. 627 (1966), refused to limit the reach of § 2036(a)(2) in this manner:

> All income increments to trust principal are . . . traceable to [the decedent] himself, by virtue of the original transfer and the exercise of the power to accumulate. . . . With respect to each addition to trust principal from accumulated income, [the decedent] had clearly made a "transfer" as required by [the statute]. Under that section, the power over income retained by [the decedent] is sufficient to require the inclusion of the original corpus of the trust in his gross estate. The accumulated income added to principal is subject to the same power and is likewise includible.

Id. at 632–33 (citations omitted).

[B] Constructive Transfers

Recall that in *United States v. Grace Estate*, 395 U.S. 316 (1969), the Supreme Court applied the reciprocal trust doctrine where grantors established trusts for the lifetime benefit of the other, provided the trusts were interrelated and left the grantors in approximately the same economic position had they created the trusts for their own benefit.[14] The articulation of the Court's holding in *Estate of Grace* raised a question concerning whether the grantor's retention of an economic benefit from the transferred property was a necessary condition to the doctrine's application. In other words, could the doctrine apply in the context of reciprocal trusts that were interrelated and left the grantors with §§ 2036(a)(2) or 2038(a)(1) powers over the trust naming them as trustee, or was the reciprocal trust doctrine limited to the § 2036(a)(1) context?

In *Estate of Bischoff v. Commissioner*, 69 T.C. 32 (1977), the Tax Court determined that the reciprocal trust doctrine had equal application in the context of crossed powers over the beneficial enjoyment of transferred property: "In *Grace* the two trusts were uncrossed because they were 'interrelated' *and not*, as petitioners urge, because the decedent therein held a direct economic interest in the property." *Id.* at 46 (emphasis in original). The court

---

[14] The *Estate of Grace* decision and the reciprocal trust doctrine are discussed in § 10.01[C][1].

later expressed incredulity at the thought that the Supreme Court in *Estate of Grace* intended to close a loophole under § 2036(a)(1) while permitting the same loophole to flourish under §§ 2036(a)(2) and 2038(a)(1). The Tax Court's application of the reciprocal trust doctrine in the context of retained powers over beneficial enjoyment of transferred property was followed by the Federal Circuit in *Exchange Bank & Trust Co. v. United States*, 694 F.2d 1261 (Fed. Cir. 1982), but rejected by the Sixth Circuit in *Estate of Green v. United States*, 68 F.3d 151 (6th Cir. 1995).

Outside of the reciprocal trust setting, other instances of constructive transfers discussed in the context of § 2036(a)(1) (generally based on substance-over-form principles)[15] are equally applicable to determining whether the transfer requirement of §§ 2036(a)(2) and 2038 is satisfied.

[C]   Split-Gift Elections

Section 2513 permits spouses to elect to treat a transfer literally made by one spouse as if the transfer had been one-half by each. The primary benefit of the so-called "split-gift" election is that it creates the possibility for two annual exclusions to reduce the amount of the taxable gift instead of one. However, the election creates the potential for problems under §§ 2036(a)(2) and 2038(a)(1). For instance, assume that *Wife* transfers $26,000 to a UGMA account established for the benefit of her daughter, designating *Husband* as custodian of the account. In order to exempt the entire transfer from gift taxation, *Husband* makes the § 2513 election. For gift tax purposes, *Husband* therefore is treated as contributing one-half of the account balance. If *Husband* dies prior to the account being distributed, does this split-gift election render *Husband* as the transferor of one-half of the account balance for estate tax purposes? In Revenue Ruling 74-556, 1974-2 C.B. 300, the Service ruled that one merely considered to be a transferor by the operation of § 2513 is not treated as a transferor for purposes of the retained power provisions. Accordingly, §§ 2036(a)(2) and 2038(a)(1) would have no application to *Husband's* estate in the above hypothetical. The corollary to the generally taxpayer-friendly rule is that, had *Wife* designated herself as custodian, the entire account balance would have been included in her gross estate notwithstanding the § 2513 election.

[D]   Adequate and Full Consideration Exception

Both §§ 2036 and 2038 are expressly inapplicable to a transfer that constitutes a "bona fide sale for an adequate and full consideration in money or money's worth." The scope of this critical statutory exclusion is separately addressed in Chapter 13.

§ 11.06   FAMILY LIMITED PARTNERSHIPS

The rise of family limited partnerships as an estate planning vehicle is most commonly attributed to the significant discounts that courts have sustained in valuing the transfer of beneficial interests in such entities. Yet another compelling if not equally attractive feature of the family limited partnership technique is the ability of transferors to retain some measure of control over the beneficial enjoyment of the property transferred to the entity. For example, an individual who contributes property to a partnership in exchange for an interest in the

---

[15] *See* § 10.01[C].

entity as general partner (typically a senior family member) will possess the ability to determine the timing and amount of distributions of partnership income or the partnership property itself. While such powers held in the context of a trust would generally implicate §§ 2036(a)(2) and 2038(a)(1), estate planners took the position that such powers held as a fiduciary of an entity typically associated with the conduct of a business were exempt from estate tax consequence. This position relied primarily on the Supreme Court's decision in *United States v. Byrum*, 408 U.S. 125 (1972).

Recall that the Supreme Court in *Byrum* held that the decedent, in his capacity as majority shareholder of the three corporations in which he had transferred stock, did not possess an ascertainable and legally enforceable right over the corporations' dividend policies. Rather, the majority shareholder owed fiduciary duties to the minority shareholders and, likewise, the corporate directors owed fiduciary duties to all shareholders. Hence, the board of directors could not subordinate its fiduciary duties to the majority shareholder's personal desires concerning the corporate dividend policies.[16] Yet the Court did not base its rejection of the government's § 2036(a)(2) argument on the absence of a legal right alone. It went on to further debunk the government's contention that the decedent possessed a practical power over the flow of the income on the transferred stock:

> There is no reason to suppose that the three corporations controlled by Byrum were other than typical small businesses. The customary vicissitudes of such enterprises—bad years; product obsolescence; new competition; disastrous litigation; new, inhibiting Government regulations; even bankruptcy—prevent any certainty or predictability as to earnings or dividends. There is no assurance that a small corporation will have a flow of net earnings or that income earned will in fact be available for dividends. Thus, Byrum's alleged *de facto* "power to control the flow of dividends" to the trust was subject to business and economic variables over which he had little or no control.

> Even where there are corporate earnings, the legal power to declare dividends is vested solely in the corporate board. In making decisions with respect to dividends, the board must consider a number of factors. It must balance the expectation of stockholders to reasonable dividends when earned against corporate needs for retention of earnings. The first responsibility of the board is to safeguard corporate financial viability for the long term. This means, among other things, the retention of sufficient earnings to assure adequate working capital as well as resources for retirement of debt, for replacement and modernization of plant and equipment, and for growth and expansion. The nature of a corporation's business, as well as the policies and long-range plans of management, are also relevant to dividend payment decisions. Directors of a closely held, small corporation must bear in mind the relatively limited access of such an enterprise to capital markets. This may require a more conservative policy with respect to dividends than would [be] expected of an established corporation with securities listed on national exchanges.

---

[16] This aspect of the *Byrum* decision is discussed in § 11.01[B]. The credence the Court afforded to fiduciary duties held in the context of closely held entities was belied by its prior decision in *Commissioner v. Sunnen*, 333 U.S. 591 (1948), an assignment-of-income case in which the Court observed the following about a majority shareholder's ability to procure the cancellation of a contract on behalf of the corporation: "Should a majority of the directors prove unamenable to his desires, the frustration would last no longer than the date of the next annual election of directors by the stockholders, an election which the taxpayer could control by reason of his extensive stock holdings." *Id.* at 608–09.

Nor do small corporations have the flexibility or the opportunity available to national concerns in the utilization of retained earnings. When earnings are substantial, a decision not to pay dividends may result only in the accumulation of surplus rather than growth through internal or external expansion. The accumulated earnings may result in the imposition of a penalty tax.

These various economic considerations are ignored at the directors' peril. Although vested with broad discretion in determining whether, when, and what amount of dividends shall be paid, that discretion is subject to legal restraints. If, in obedience to the will of the majority stockholder, corporate directors disregard the interests of shareholders by accumulating earnings to an unreasonable extent, they are vulnerable to a derivative suit. They are similarly vulnerable if they make an unlawful payment of dividends in the absence of net earnings or available surplus, or if they fail to exercise the requisite degree of care in discharging their duty to act only in the best interest of the corporation and its stockholders.

Id. at 139–42 (footnotes omitted).

As indicated by a series of private letter rulings and internal legal memoranda issued over the course of the 1990s, the Service appeared to accept that the *Byrum* decision precluded the application of §§ 2036(a)(2) and 2038(a)(1) to discretionary powers over distributions in the partnership context. *See, e.g.*, Priv. Ltr. Rul. 9710021 (Mar. 7, 1997); Priv. Ltr. Rul. 9415007 (Apr. 15, 1994); Priv. Ltr. Rul. 9310039 (Mar. 12, 1993); Tech. Adv. Mem. 9131006 (Aug. 2, 1991). The government reconsidered this non-binding position, however, as part of its litigation campaign against the use of family limited partnerships to undermine the transfer tax base. The government's invocation of the retained power provisions of §§ 2036(a)(2) and 2038(a)(1) was accepted by the Tax Court in *Estate of Strangi v. Commissioner*, T.C. Memo. 2003-145, 85 T.C.M. (CCH) 1331, a pivotal decision in the transfer tax arena notwithstanding its designation as a memorandum decision.

Like most family limited partnership cases, the decision in *Estate of Strangi* was fact intensive. Acting through his son-in-law [Mr. Gulig] as his agent under a durable power of attorney, the decedent formed a family partnership [SFLP] two months before he died of cancer at the age of 81. He transferred approximately $10 million of property to the entity, mostly in the form of cash and marketable securities, in exchange for a 99 percent interest in the entity as limited partner. A corporation [Stranco] in which the decedent was a 47 percent shareholder was formed to serve as the 1 percent general partner of the partnership. The decedent's children purchased the remaining 53 percent interest in the corporate general partner. The decedent's son-in-law was hired to manage the day-to-day affairs of the corporate general partner, which possessed managerial authority over the partnership. In this manner, the decedent's son-in-law (who also happened to be his agent) possessed discretionary authority over distributions from the partnership.

In addition to the traditional claim that the decedent retained the economic benefit of the property transferred to the partnership pursuant to an implied agreement among the parties sufficient to trigger inclusion under § 2036(a)(1), the Service alternatively argued that the decedent retained the right to designate the beneficial enjoyment of the trust property under § 2036(a)(2). Although the Tax Court accepted the government's § 2036(a)(1) argument regarding the implied retention of the economic benefit of the transferred property, the court went on to address the § 2036(a)(2) argument—apparently because the parties argued it so extensively in their briefs. *Id.* at 1340. As reflected in the excerpt below, the Tax Court found

§ 2036(a)(2) applicable and rejected the contention that the *Byrum* decision precluded such a result.

ESTATE OF STRANGI v. COMMISSIONER
United States Tax Court
T.C. Memo. 2003-145, 85 T.C.M. (CCH) 1331

To summarize, review of the documentary evidence discussed above reveals that decedent here retained rights of a far different genre from those at issue in *United States v. Byrum*, *supra*. Rather than mere "control", management, or influence, there are traceable to decedent through the explicit provisions of the governing instruments ascertainable and legally enforceable rights to designate persons who shall enjoy the transferred property and its income. The estate's reliance on a limited partner's lack under [state partnership law] of participation in control and under the SFLP agreement of management authority is thus misplaced. The alleged absence of such powers cannot negate the dispositive rights granted in the instant case. The SFLP/Stranco arrangement placed decedent in a position to act, alone or in conjunction with others, through his attorney in fact, to cause distributions of property previously transferred to the entities or of income therefrom. Decedent's powers, absent sufficient limitation as discussed *infra*, therefore fall within the purview of section 2036(a)(2).

The Supreme Court in *United States v. Byrum*, *supra*, relied upon several impediments to the exercise of powers held by Mr. Byrum in concluding that such powers did not warrant inclusion under section 2036(a)(2). Here, the rights held by decedent are of a different nature and were not accompanied by comparable constraints. In our view, the constraints alleged by the estate are illusory.

One circumstance highlighted by the Supreme Court was the existence of an independent trustee with the sole authority ultimately to pay or withhold income from the trust. Here, in contrast, no similar layer of independence was interposed. Rather, decisions with respect to distributions were placed in Stranco, of which decedent owned 47 percent and was the largest shareholder. All decisions ultimately were made by Mr. Gulig, who continued to act as decedent's attorney in fact.

Another element stressed by the Supreme Court was the manner in which the flow of funds allegedly under Mr. Byrum's control would be subject to economic and business realities consequent upon the status of the relevant corporations as typical small operating enterprises. Earnings and dividends of a small operating company could be affected by, inter alia, changes in products, in competition, or in industry regulation and outlook; use of funds for replacement of plant and equipment or for growth and expansion; and the need to retain sufficient earnings for working capital. These complexities do not apply to SFLP or Stranco, which held only monetary or investment assets.

Yet another constraining factor cited by the Supreme Court was the presence of fiduciary duties held by directors and shareholders, and it is upon this aspect of the Supreme Court's opinion that the estate focuses. The Supreme Court emphasized that corporate directors and shareholders have a fiduciary duty to promote the best interests of the entity, as opposed to their personal interests. The Supreme Court further pointed to a substantial number of unrelated minority shareholders who could enforce these duties by suit.

The fiduciary duties present in *United States v. Byrum* . . . ran to a significant number of unrelated parties and had their genesis in operating businesses that would lend meaning to the standard of acting in the best interests of the entity. As a result, there existed both a realistic possibility for enforcement and an objective business environment against which to judge potential dereliction. Given the emphasis that the Supreme Court laid on these factual realities, *Byrum* simply does not require blind application of its holding to scenarios where the purported fiduciary duties have no comparable substance. We therefore analyze the situation before us to determine whether the fiduciary duties relied upon by the estate would genuinely circumscribe use of powers to designate.

* * *

None of the foregoing obligations cited by the estate is sufficiently on par with those detailed in *United States v. Byrum, supra*, to bring the present case within the Supreme Court's rationale.

Concerning Mr. Gulig, any fiduciary duties that Mr. Gulig might have had in his role as manager of Stranco (and thereby of SFLP) are entitled to comparatively little weight on these facts. Prior to his instigation of the SFLP/Stranco arrangement, Mr. Gulig stood in a confidential relationship, and owed fiduciary duties, to decedent personally as his attorney in fact. Thus, to the extent that Stranco or SFLP's interests might diverge from those of decedent, we do not believe that Mr. Gulig would disregard his preexisting obligation to decedent.

As regards fiduciary obligations of Stranco and its directors, these duties, too, have little significance in the present context. Although Stranco would owe a fiduciary duty to SFLP and to the limited partners, decedent owned the sole, 99-percent limited partnership interest. The rights to designate traceable to decedent through Stranco cannot be characterized as limited in any meaningful way by duties owed essentially to himself. Nor do the obligations of Stranco directors to the corporation itself warrant any different conclusion. Decedent held 47 percent of Stranco, and his own children held 52 of the remaining 53 percent. Intrafamily fiduciary duties within an investment vehicle simply are not equivalent in nature to the obligations created by the *United States v. Byrum, supra*, scenario.

* * *

In sum, the estate's averment that decedent's " 'rights' . . . were severely limited by the fiduciary duties of other people who (according to *Byrum*) presumably could be counted on . . . [to] observe those restraints" rests on a faulty legal premise and ignores factual realities. First, the Supreme Court's opinion in *United States v. Byrum, supra*, provides no basis for "presuming" that fiduciary obligations will be enforced in circumstances divorced from the safeguards of business operations and meaningful independent interests or oversight. Second, the facts of this case belie the existence of any genuine fiduciary impediments to decedent's rights. We conclude that the value of assets transferred to SFLP and Stranco is includable in decedent's gross estate under section 2036(a)(2).

While the Fifth Circuit affirmed the result in *Estate of Strangi*, it did so only by holding that the Tax Court's finding of an implied agreement concerning the retention of the economic benefit of the transferred property was not clearly erroneous. *See* Estate of Strangi v. Commissioner, 417 F.3d 468 (5th Cir. 2005). Unlike the Tax Court, the Fifth Circuit declined to delve into the § 2036(a)(2) thicket.[17] *Id.* at 478 n.7. The application of § 2036(a)(2) in the family limited partnership context therefore remains something of an unresolved issue. Yet if nothing else, the Tax Court's decision in *Estate of Strangi* indicates that courts will not blindly accept *Byrum* as precluding the application of § 2036(a)(2) merely because property was transferred to a partnership or LLC in lieu of a trust.

§ 11.07   TRANSFERS WITHIN THREE YEARS OF DEATH

A transferor cannot avoid the application of §§ 2036(a)(2) and 2038(a)(1) simply by relinquishing the prohibited power shortly before death. Rather, unless the power is relinquished more than three years prior to the decedent's death, § 2035 will include the amount of property that would have been captured by §§ 2036 and 2038 had the power not been relinquished. Note that § 2035(a) is redundant as it applies to powers under § 2038(a)(1)—the latter of which contains its own three-year recapture provision.

Section 2035(e) provides an important practical concession to taxpayers who employ revocable inter vivos trusts for estate planning purposes. In order to place transfers from such trusts on par with transfers of property titled in the transferor's individual name, § 2035(e) provides that any transfer from a grantor trust for income tax purposes will be considered as having been made by the decedent directly for purposes of §§ 2036 and 2038. Accordingly, transfers of property from a revocable trust within three years of the decedent's death will not be brought back into the decedent's gross estate.

§ 11.08   GIFT TAX CONSEQUENCES OF RETAINED POWERS

The thrust of the gift tax treatment of transfers with retained powers over the beneficial enjoyment of transferred property is largely consistent with that under the estate tax, in that such transfers will be considered incomplete in many instances. However, the two regimes are not completely unified in this context; a transfer that is captured in the decedent's gross estate under §§ 2036(a)(2) or 2038(a)(1) can be the product of a completed gift.

As a starting point, a donor who retains no power to alter the disposition of transferred property has made a completed transfer for gift tax purposes. Treas. Reg. § 25.2511-2(b). However, the corollary is not necessarily true. That is, the retention of certain powers over the beneficial enjoyment may render the gift incomplete, but it does not do so categorically.

[A]   Revocable Transfers

Perhaps the most obvious instance of a transfer of property not viewed as complete for gift tax purposes is one which the donor reserves the right to revoke. Treas. Reg. § 25.2511-2(c). If the donor can cause the property to be returned to him, nothing definite has occurred from a transfer tax standpoint.

---

[17] In its prior decision in *Kimbell v. United States*, 371 F.3d 257 (5th Cir. 2004), the Fifth Circuit addressed the potential application of § 2036(a)(2) in brief terms only. The court determined that the decedent in that case did not possess the right to enjoy or designate the persons who would enjoy property she transferred to an LLC (which served as the 1 percent general partner of a family limited partnership), because the decedent owned only a 50 percent interest in the LLC of which her son was designated the sole manager. *Id.* at 270.

As discussed in the context of § 2038, a transfer to an irrevocable trust can be treated as effectively revocable for gift tax purposes. If a creditor of a settlor can reach the assets of a trust in which the settlor retains a discretionary beneficial interest, the creation of the trust will constitute an incomplete gift to that extent. In effect, the transferor has not relinquished dominion and control over property that he could cause to be paid for his benefit. *See* Outwin v. Commissioner, 76 T.C. 153 (1981); Paolozzi v. Commissioner, 23 T.C. 182 (1954); Rev. Rul. 76-103, 1976-1 C.B. 293. The scope of a creditor's state-law rights to reach trust assets therefore is critical to determining the gift tax consequences of funding irrevocable trusts.

[B] Powers to Alter Interests of Others

A transfer can be rendered incomplete without the retention of the economic benefit of transferred property. A donor's reservation of a right to alter the beneficial interests in transferred property—through the ability either to alter the relative interests of existing beneficiaries or to add new ones—generally renders the gift incomplete as well. Treas. Reg. § 25.2511-2(c); *see also* Estate of Sanford v. Commissioner, 308 U.S. 39 (1939) (holding that grantor's power to designate new trust beneficiaries other than himself rendered the transfer incomplete under the gift tax).

By way of example, suppose a donor transfers property to a trust for the benefit of his children under which the trustee is authorized to distribute amounts of income and principal among the children as the trustee sees fit. Upon the death of the last child, the trust property is to be distributed to the donor's then living descendants. If the donor serves as the sole trustee, the funding of the trust does not constitute a completed gift of the children's interests due to the donor's continued ability to alter their relative interests. Instead, gifts to the donor's children will be completed only to the extent the donor relinquishes all control by making a distribution in their favor. Treas. Reg. § 25.2511-2(f). Note that while the funding of the trust does not constitute a completed gift of the children's interests, the same cannot be said of the remainder interest in favor of the donor's descendants. As the donor retains no ability to alter the disposition of the remainder, that portion of the transfer constitutes a completed gift.

As under the estate tax, the general rule that powers over the beneficial enjoyment of transferred property render a transfer incomplete from a gift tax standpoint is subject to a significant exception. Discretionary powers held in a fiduciary capacity that are limited by a fixed and ascertainable standard will not cause the transfer to be incomplete from a gift tax perspective. Treas. Reg. § 25.2511-2(c). In this regard, the regulations provide useful guidance on what constitutes a sufficiently definite standard for this purpose:

> A clearly measurable standard under which the holder of a power is legally accountable is such a standard for this purpose. For instance, a power to distribute corpus for the education, support, maintenance, or health of the beneficiary; for his reasonable support and comfort; to enable him to maintain his accustomed standard of living; or to meet an emergency, would be such a standard. However, a power to distribute corpus for the pleasure, desire, or happiness of a beneficiary is not such a standard. The entire context of a provision of a trust instrument granting a power must be considered in determining whether the power is limited by a reasonably definite standard. For example, if a trust instrument provides that the determination of the trustee shall be conclusive with respect to the exercise or nonexercise of a power,

the power is not limited by a reasonably definite standard. However, the fact that the governing instrument is phrased in discretionary terms is not in itself an indication that no such standard exists.

Treas. Reg. § 25.2511-1(g)(2). Therefore, had the donor in the hypothetical above sought to avoid the future application of §§ 2036(a)(2) and 2038(a)(1) by limiting distributions to his children for the recipient's "health, education, support or maintenance," the entire transfer would have been currently taxable for gift tax purposes.

[C] Powers over Timing and Manner of Enjoyment

Transfers through which a transferor retains the mere ability to affect the timing and manner in which the transferred property is enjoyed by defined beneficiaries is one area in which the resulting gift tax treatment differs markedly from that of the estate tax. A power that is limited to the timing and manner of enjoyment of transferred property has no gift tax consequence. Treas. Reg. § 25.2511-2(d). Therefore, a transfer akin to the trust at issue in *Lober*, where there existed only one possible beneficiary of the trust and the trustee possessed the power to accelerate distribution of trust principal, would constitute a completed gift notwithstanding the future application of § 2038(a)(1). Similarly, the power to defer distributions of income to a beneficiary as seen in *Estate of O'Connor* would not render the gift incomplete, the looming application of § 2036(a)(2) notwithstanding. Rather, a reserved power must permit the donor to alter the amount received by the transferees or the identity thereof in order to render the transfer incomplete for gift tax purposes.

[D] Joint Powers

Jointly held powers is another area in which the gift tax and estate tax treatment of transfers with retained powers diverge. Whereas the existence of a joint holder of a power possessing an interest adverse to the exercise of the power does not preclude the application of §§ 2036(a)(2) or 2038(a)(1), the gift tax takes a more practical approach to the issue. A donor is treated as possessing a power that is exercisable by him in conjunction with another not having an interest substantially adverse to its exercise. Treas. Reg. § 25.2511-2(e). By way of corollary, the existence of an adverse party will prevent a donor's jointly held power from rendering a gift incomplete.

The downside of this approach is that the gift tax consequences turn on the factual determination of whether the joint power holder possesses a sufficiently adverse interest in the property. In making this determination, the interests of power holders in the transferred property are assessed at face value. In other words, the likely compliance by a power holder who is related to the grantor as a practical matter will not alone preclude the power holder from being treated as an adverse party. *See* Commissioner v. Prouty, 115 F.2d 331 (1st Cir. 1940). In the same vein, a power held by a party who may be described as truly adverse to the grantor (such as a divorced spouse) does not provide the power holder with an *interest* in the transferred property that is substantially adverse to the exercise of the power for purposes of Reg. § 25.2511-2(e). *See* Latta v. Commissioner, 212 F.2d 164 (3d Cir. 1954).

[E]   Release or Termination of Power

If a transfer is rendered incomplete because the donor retained a power to alter the respective interests of the beneficiaries of transferred property, the relinquishment or termination of such a power will complete the gift. Treas. Reg. § 25.2511-2(f). However, if the donor reserves the power for the remainder of his lifetime, the termination of such power does not complete the gift; rather, application of the gift tax is limited to living donors. *Id.* In that case, the transferred property will be captured in the decedent's gross estate under §§ 2036 or 2038.

§ 11.09   STUDY PROBLEMS

1.   Nate transfers property to Mega Bank Trust Co. as trustee under a trust instrument that contains the following provisions:

The trustee shall distribute as much of the trust income or principal to such one or more of the settlor, the settlor's spouse, or the settlor's children in such amounts and at such intervals as the trustee, in its sole discretion, determines necessary or appropriate.

Upon settlor's death, the trust property shall be distributed to the settlor's then living descendants per stirpes.

Settlor hereby retains the right to revoke or amend the terms of the trust through a written declaration delivered to the trustee.

    a.   Discuss the gift tax consequences upon the funding of the trust and the estate tax consequences of the trust upon Nate's death.

    b.   Same as (a), except that two years prior to his death, Nate exercised his right to amend the trust by revising the first paragraph to read as follows:

The trustee shall distribute as much of the trust income or principal to such one or more of settlor's spouse or the settlor's children in such amounts and at such intervals as the trustee, in its sole discretion, determines necessary or appropriate.

After making this alteration, Nate relinquished his power to revoke or amend the trust.

Discuss the gift tax consequences of these changes, as well as the estate tax consequences upon Nate's death.

    c.   How would your answer to (b) change, if at all, had the revisions to the trust in (b) been made four years prior to Nate's death?

2.   Claire establishes a trust for the benefit of her son, Ike, and funds the trust with $5 million of marketable securities. The trust calls for the net income of the trust to be distributed to Ike on an annual basis until he attains age 50, at which time the trust will be distributed to him outright. Should Ike die prior to attaining such age, the trust property will be paid into his probate estate. Local Trust Co. is designated to serve as trustee. However, Claire reserves for her lifetime the right to direct the trustee to withhold a given year's income and add it to principal. In addition, Claire can direct the

trustee to make distributions of principal to Ike.

Claire dies while Ike is age 43. The trust property is valued at $8 million at the time; assume that the actuarial value of Ike's remaining income interest is $500,000.

    a.   Discuss the gift tax and estate tax consequences of the arrangement for Claire.

    b.   How would your answer to (a) change if, five years prior to her death, Claire relinquished the power to direct the trustee to withhold income payments?

3.   Rob and Bob are brothers. Rob contributes $400,000 to a trust containing the following language:

The trustee shall distribute as much of the trust income or principal to Bob's children in such amounts and at such intervals as the trustee, in its sole discretion, determines necessary or appropriate. Upon Bob's death, the trust assets shall be distributed to Bob's then living descendants per stirpes.

Rob designates Bob to serve as trustee. At the same time, Bob transfers $500,000 to an irrevocable trust for the benefit of Rob's children containing the same terms, and designates Rob to serve as trustee.

    a.   When Rob dies, the assets of the trust that Bob funded (of which Rob serves as trustee) are valued at $800,000. Discuss the estate tax consequences of the arrangement to Rob.

    b.   Assume now that the provision in the trust established by Rob reads as follows:

The trustee shall distribute as much of the trust income or principal to Bob's children in such amounts and at such intervals as the trustee, in its sole discretion, determines necessary or appropriate for the recipient's health, education, support in his or her accustomed manner of living, or maintenance. Upon Bob's death, the trust assets shall be distributed to the Bob's then living descendants per stirpes.

The trust established by Bob contains the same provisions. How does this change affect your answers to (a), if at all?

4.   Howard creates a trust for the benefit of his grandchildren. The trust instrument provides for annual income payments to be made to the grandchildren until the youngest attains age 25, at which time the trust will be distributed in equal shares to the grandchildren then living. The trust also provides for the trustee to make distributions to one or more of the grandchildren as the trustee sees fit. The trust is irrevocable.

    a.   Assume that Howard designates himself to serve as trustee. Discuss the gift tax consequences upon funding the trust, and the estate tax consequences upon Howard's death.

    b.   How would your answer to (a) change if Howard merely served as co-trustee with Private Bank & Trust Co.?

    c.   How would your answer to (a) change if Howard designated Private Bank & Trust Co. to serve as the sole trustee?

d. How would your answer to (c) change if Private Bank & Trust Co. took discretionary action only when Howard called it with instructions, which Private Bank & Trust Co. routinely followed.

e. How would your answer to (c) change if Howard reserved the right to remove and replace Private Bank & Trust Co. as trustee?

5. Elaine owns an oceanfront condominium. For the past 10 years, Elaine has permitted each of her three children to take their families to the condo for one week each month. Elaine takes the remaining week.

Looking for ways to reduce her estate tax exposure, Elaine first transfers the condo to a wholly owned, manager-managed LLC and later assigns a 25 percent LLC interest to each child. As manager of the LLC, Elaine technically controls who may use the condo and when. She and her children continue to use the property as they have in the past.

Discuss the likely estate tax consequences if Elaine dies owning her 25 percent LLC interest while serving as manager of the LLC.

Chapter 12

TRANSFERS WITH RETAINED REVERSIONARY INTERESTS

Internal Revenue Code:	§§ 2037, 2042(a)(2)
Treasury Regulations:	§§ 20.2037-1(a) to (e), 20.2042-1(c)(3), 20.7520-3(b)(ii)

In its original form, the estate tax attempted to reach incomplete lifetime transfers by expanding the gross estate to include transfers "in contemplation of or intended to take effect in possession or enjoyment only at or after death."[1] This broad, subjective standard evolved into the retained interest provisions contained in §§ 2036 through 2038. The middle installment of this trilogy often is overlooked because of its limited scope and application. Section 2037 can be conceptualized as the corollary to § 2036: Whereas § 2036(a)(1) concerns the retention of the beneficial enjoyment of transferred property, § 2037 is aimed at transfers that leave open the possibility of the transferred property itself returning to the decedent.[2] Because transfers with retained reversions are rarely intentionally employed in the estate planning context, § 2037 has been relegated to something of a legislative footnote. In keeping with its prominence in the current transfer tax regime, the discussion of § 2037 in this chapter will be brief.

§ 12.01 OVERVIEW OF § 2037

Like §§ 2036 and 2038, § 2037 is limited to instances in which the decedent has made a lifetime transfer of property that does not constitute a bona fide sale for an adequate and full consideration in money or money's worth.[3] Within this context, § 2037 applies to transferred property if the following requirements are satisfied: (1) a third party's interest in the property can be possessed or enjoyed, through ownership of such interest, only by surviving the decedent; (2) the decedent retained a reversionary interest in the transferred property; and (3) the value of the decedent's reversionary interest exceeds a *de minimis* threshold of five percent of the value of the transferred property. IRC § 2037(a); Treas. Reg. § 20.2037-1(a). If these requirements are satisfied, § 2037 operates to include in the decedent's gross estate the value of the transferred property that is conditioned upon surviving the decedent, with the value of that interest being determined immediately after D's death. *See* Treas. Reg. § 20.2037-1(d) & (e), Ex. 4.

---

[1] Revenue Act of 1916, Pub. L. No. 64-271, § 202(b), 39 Stat. 756, 778.

[2] The regulations highlight this dichotomy by indicating that § 2037 does not apply to retained rights to the income from transferred property. *See* Treas. Reg. § 20.2037-1(c)(2) (excluding income rights from the definition of a reversionary interest to which § 2037 potentially applies).

[3] The statutory exclusion for a bona fide sale for an adequate and full consideration in money or money's worth is separately addressed in Chapter 13.

The basic application of § 2037 can be illustrated through the following example: D transfers property in trust for the lifetime benefit of his wife, W; upon W's death, the trust property is to be distributed to D if he is then living, otherwise to D's then living descendants. The transfer creates three separate interests: (1) the beneficial life estate in favor of W; (2) a reversion in D; and (3) a contingent remainder in D's descendants. Note that of the two interests created in favor of third parties, only the contingent remainder held by D's descendants could possibly trigger application of § 2037. As W receives her interest immediately and thus need not survive D, her interest does not satisfy the survivorship requirement. The same cannot be said of the contingent remainder in favor of D's then living descendants. That class will not be determined until W's death, and the class will take nothing unless D is not living at the point. Hence, the interest of D's descendants is contingent upon surviving D. Section 2037 will operate in this context to capture in D's gross estate the entire date-of-death value of the trust property less the value of W's outstanding life estate.[4] *See* Treas. Reg. § 20.2037-1(e), Ex. 3. Note that this conclusion rests on the reasonable assumption that the value of D's reversionary interest exceeds five percent of the value of the trust property.

§ 12.02   SURVIVORSHIP REQUIREMENT

As a preliminary matter, the inclusion of transferred property in the decedent's gross estate under § 2037 is limited to interests the possession or enjoyment of which can be realized only by surviving the decedent. IRC § 2037(a)(1); Treas. Reg. § 20.2037-1(b). Section 2037 therefore necessitates a counterfactual inquiry: At the time of the transfer, was it possible for the transferee to obtain possession or enjoyment of the transferred property through ownership of such interest while the decedent was still living? If so, § 2037 has no application.

As an example, assume D created a grantor retained annuity trust (GRAT) that terminated after a five-year term or upon D's earlier death, with the trust assets being distributed to A if then living, otherwise to D's probate estate.[5] Further assume that D died four years after funding the GRAT. While A thereby received distribution of the trust property upon D's death, A's interest in the transferred property was not conditioned upon surviving D; rather, it was possible for A to receive distribution of the trust property after five years had D survived the GRAT term. Hence, the transferred property is not recaptured in D's gross estate by reason of § 2037.[6] *See* Treas. Reg. § 20.2037-1(b).

In determining whether possession or enjoyment of transferred property is conditioned upon surviving the decedent, § 2037 does not check reality at the door. Rather, a transfer that makes no explicit reference to the decedent's life can implicate the § 2037 survivorship requirement as long as the natural consequence of the transfer is to delay possession or enjoyment of the property until the decedent's death. Returning to the GRAT hypothetical above, assume that D, age 65, retained an annuity interest for a 40-year term. While it is theoretically possible for A to receive distribution of the trust property during D's lifetime, it

---

[4] There is no need to address the application of § 2037 in the event D survived W; in that case, D's reversion would ripen into possession and the property would be included in his gross estate under § 2033.

[5] The reversion in favor of D's probate estate is provided in the hypothetical only to satisfy the remaining requirements of § 2037(a). No such reversion would be intentionally used in practice, as it would thwart (if it became possessory) the intended transfer tax benefits of the technique.

[6] Nonetheless, the entire amount of assets held in the GRAT likely will be included in D's gross estate under § 2036(a)(1). *See* Treas. Reg. § 20.2036-1(c)(2), discussed in § 15.01[D].

is highly improbable. The regulations warn that if the means by which the transferee can receive possession of the transferred property other than by reason of surviving the decedent is "unreal" *and* if the decedent in fact died before this alternate event, the survivorship condition to § 2037 will be presumed satisfied. Treas. Reg. § 20.2037-1(b) & (e), Ex. 5.

The Tax Court decision in *Thacher v. Commissioner*, 20 T.C. 474 (1953), endorsed an expansive interpretation of the survivorship requirement as applied to present beneficial interests in property that are subject to divestment during the decedent's lifetime. The decedent in *Estate of Thacher* created a trust for the lifetime benefit of his wife. However, the trust instrument provided that the trust would be terminated upon the couple's divorce or legal separation, with the trust assets being returned to the decedent in that event. The Service contended that the value of the wife's lifetime beneficial interest in the trust was included in the decedent's gross estate under the predecessor of § 2037(a), on the basis that the interest was one "intended to take effect in possession or enjoyment at or after his death." *Id.* at 482. Based on the relevant legislative history, this characterization would be implicated only if the beneficiary had to survive the decedent to possess or enjoy the property—the standard now incorporated in the statutory text. *See id.* at 484 (citing H.R. Rep. No. 81-1482 (1942)). The estate understandably argued that the decedent's wife need not survive the decedent to possession or enjoy her beneficial interest in the trust, as it commenced immediately upon the trust funding. The court, however, accepted the government's argument to the contrary: "Only upon the death of the decedent was [the] possible termination of the wife's life estate removed. Only then did the wife's interest in the income of the trust estate ripen into an absolute, unconditional life estate. . . ." *Id.* at 483. Accordingly, current beneficial interests in trust can be subject to inclusion under § 2037(a) if subject to divestment in favor of the decedent during the decedent's lifetime.

§ 12.03 NECESSITY OF A RETAINED REVERSIONARY INTEREST

The second principal condition to the application of § 2037 requires the decedent to have retained a "reversionary interest" in the transferred property. IRC § 2037(a)(2). As provided in § 2037(b), such an interest includes not only the possibility that the transferred property may return to the decedent or his probate estate, but also the possibility that the transferred property may become subject to a power of disposition held by the decedent.

Note that the application of § 2037 does not require the decedent's reversionary interest to become possessory or, in the case of a power of disposition, actionable. Indeed, in many transfers implicating § 2037, the decedent's reversionary interest will be extinguished by reason of his death. The reversionary interest requirement is satisfied if such interest remained outstanding as of the moment prior to the decedent's death, when the relative value of such interest will be measured against the five percent *de minimis* threshold.

[A] Conventional Reversions

By defining a reversionary interest to include any possibility that the transferred property may return to the decedent or to his probate estate, § 2037(b)(1) covers conventional notions of a reversion in property. However, the application of § 2037 does not require a primer on the state-law characterization of future interests, as the term "reversionary interest" is not employed in a technical manner. *See* Treas. Reg. § 20.2037-1(c)(2). Rather, the concept turns on the possible result—that is, property being returned to the decedent or to the decedent's estate—not the label placed on the interest by which that result may be achieved. In *Helvering v. Hallock*, 309 U.S. 106 (1940), the Supreme Court explained why the application of the predecessor of § 2037 should not be driven by the finer points of state-law conveyancing, overriding prior authority to the contrary:[7]

> The law of contingent and vested remainders is full of casuistries. . . . The importa-
> tion of these distinctions and controversies from the law of property into the
> administration of the estate tax precludes a fair and a workable tax system. . . .
> Distinctions which originated under a feudal economy when land dominated social
> relations are peculiarly irrelevant in the application of tax measures now so largely
> directed toward intangible wealth.

Id. at 117–18 (footnotes omitted).

[B] Powers of Disposition

In addition to applying to reversions in a conventional sense, a reversionary interest for purposes of § 2037 also includes a possibility that the transferred property may become subject to a power of disposition by the decedent. IRC § 2037(b)(2). In *Estate of Tarver v. Commissioner*, 255 F.2d 913 (4th Cir. 1958), the Fourth Circuit interpreted this aspect of the § 2037 reversionary interest as encompassing a contingent distribution of property to a trust created under the terms of the decedent's will, on the theory that the decedent retained the right to alter his will until his death. In addition, the lifetime ability of a decedent to allocate the remainder interests among a designated group of individuals (other than himself) or to distribute principal in favor of a lifetime beneficiary constitutes the requisite power of disposition. *See* Costin v. Cripe, 235 F.2d 162 (7th Cir. 1956); Klauber v. Commissioner, 34 T.C. 968 (1960). While these latter powers may implicate § 2037(a) where the survivorship condition is also satisfied, such powers often will trigger inclusion in the decedent's gross estate on other grounds, namely §§ 2036 or 2038. Determining whether § 2037 reaches transferred property based on the decedent's potential power of disposition therefore often amounts to an unnecessary exercise.

[C] Retention Requirement

The reversionary interest necessary to satisfy § 2037(a)(2) must have been retained by the decedent through the transfer. However, the retention can occur not only pursuant to the express terms of the transfer but also by operation of law.[8] Treas. Reg. § 20.2037-1(c)(2). That stands to reason, as a transfer in trust "to A for life, remainder to A's then living issue" under which state law implies a reversion in favor of the grantor should not be treated differently than if the conveyance had spelled out the reversion by continuing ". . . or, in default thereof, to D or D's estate."

---

[7] In *Klein v. United States*, 283 U.S. 231 (1931), the Court determined that a future interest payable to the donor if living at the death of the lifetime trust beneficiary triggered the statute. However, shortly after issuing the *Klein* decision, the Court in *Helvering v. St. Louis Union Trust Co.*, 296 U.S. 39 (1935), determined that the statute was not implicated by a vested remainder following the death of the lifetime beneficiary that could have been divested in favor of the decedent if the decedent were then living.

[8] Section 2037(a)(2) contains a parenthetical exception for transfers occurring prior to October 8, 1949, reflecting the requirement under prior law that the reversionary interest be expressly retained.

Apart from instances in which state law implies a reversion, it is difficult to imagine an instance in which a reversion would be retained by operation of law.[9] The regulations make clear that the mere possibility that a transferor may receive the transferred property by way of devise or inheritance from the transferee does not constitute the retention of an interest. *Id.* The same goes for the transferor's potential to receive the property through spousal inheritance protections under state law. *Id.* These exceptions simply confirm that an outright, unconditional transfer of property will not implicate § 2037 due to state-law possibilities of a subsequent transfer in favor of the decedent. Therefore, in order for a reversionary interest to implicate § 2037, the grounds for the reversion must arise from the terms of the decedent's transfer.

§ 12.04 POWER OF APPOINTMENT EXCLUSION

Even if a transferee's interest in property is conditioned upon surviving the decedent and the decedent retains a non-*de minimis* reversionary interest, the application of § 2037 can be negated by the existence of a power of appointment over the transferred property. Specifically, if any beneficiary could have obtained possession or enjoyment of the transferred property during the decedent's lifetime through the exercise of a power of general power of appointment (as defined in § 2041) that was exercisable immediately at the time of the decedent's death,[10] § 2037 has no application to the transferred property. IRC § 2037(b).

It is tempting to view the power-of-appointment exception as a mere clarification of the survivorship condition. *See* Treas. Reg. § 20.2037-1(b) (addressing the exception in the context of the survivorship condition). That is, the existence of the power of appointment provides an alternate means by which the beneficiary could have obtained possession or enjoyment of the property other than by reason of surviving the decedent. Yet note that the same can be said of the ability to receive property under any power of appointment (whether a general power of appointment or otherwise), but the statutory exception applies to general powers of appointment only. Furthermore, the power of appointment need not be exercised in favor of the transferee whose interest is subject to the survivorship condition. *See* Treas. Reg. § 20.2037-1(e), Ex. 6 (decedent transferred remainder interest in trust to his children; decedent's wife possessed general power of appointment in her favor). Hence, the exception for property subject to a general power of appointment outstanding as of the decedent's death—whether held by the decedent or a third party—constitutes a stand-alone exclusion under § 2037, one limited to situations in which the property will be subject to transfer taxation by reason of the power.

---

[9] The case of *Commissioner v. Estate of Marshall*, 203 F.2d 534 (3d Cir. 1953), provides a possible illustration. The decedent in *Estate of Marshall* conveyed property in trust for the lifetime benefit of his wife, with the remainder to be distributed to her intestate heirs. Because the decedent was included as an intestate heir of his wife under the relevant state law, one could characterize this as the retention of a reversion by operation of law. However, in substance, the reversion was retained through the express terms of the transfer, with the decedent's reversion being articulated by reference to state law. The Third Circuit resolved the case in favor of the estate on a dubious determination that the other intestate heirs could have received the state law interest afforded to the surviving spouse without surviving the decedent.

[10] The definition of a general power of appointment and the transfer tax consequences that attend such a power are discussed in Chapter 14.

§ 12.05 *DE MINIMIS* THRESHOLD

At one point in the history of § 2037, a remote reversionary interest of miniscule value was sufficient to cause the recapture of transferred property in the decedent's gross estate. In *Estate of Spiegel v. Commissioner*, 335 U.S. 701 (1949), the Court addressed the application of the predecessor to § 2037 to a trust the decedent had created for the benefit of his three children. Upon the decedent's death, the trust property essentially was to be distributed among his children in equal shares, with the share created for any predeceased child passing to that child's issue or, if none, being added to the shares created for the decedent's other children. Noting that the trust property would be returned to the decedent's estate if he was not survived by any of his children or grandchildren, the Court determined that the decedent retained the requisite reversionary interest. The Court was not moved by the remote nature of the reversion, which was valued at only .007 of one percent of the trust property. *Id.* at 733–34 (Burton, J. dissenting) (detailing the approximate value placed on the reversion). Instead, the Court dismissed the value of the reversion as irrelevant, stressing that the mere existence of *any* such interest prevented the transfer from becoming fully complete until the decedent's death. *Id.* at 707. In this manner, a reversion valued at less than $100 before the decedent's death triggered inclusion of trust assets worth over $1.1 million, generating an estate tax liability in the neighborhood of $450,000.

Responding to the Court's decision in *Estate of Spiegel*, Congress enacted a valuation threshold for reversionary interests to implicate the predecessor of § 2037.[11] That threshold now is reflected in § 2037(a)(2), which requires the value of the reversionary interest to exceed five percent of the value of the transferred property.[12] If the decedent's reversionary interest rests in his potential power of disposition over transferred property, that interest is to be valued as if the property would return to the decedent under the same conditions. Treas. Reg. § 20.2037-1(c)(3).

[A] Determining the Numerator

For purposes of testing the reversionary interest against the *de minimis* threshold, the value of the reversion is to be determined as of the moment immediately prior to the decedent's death, through the use of "usual methods of valuation." IRC § 2037(b). Such methods specifically include the use of mortality and actuarial tables published in the regulations. *Id.* Returning to the hypothetical introduced at the outset of the chapter—*D*'s transfer of property in trust to *W* for life; remainder to *D* if he is then living, other to *D*'s then living descendants—the value of *D*'s reversionary interest would be equal to the actuarial value of the remainder interest in the trust multiplied by the relative probability that *D* would survive *W*. Each of these determinations are made immediately prior to *D*'s death. For perhaps obvious reasons, the actual health of the decedent immediately prior to his death is not taken into consideration in determining the likelihood that *D* would survive *W*. *See* Treas. Reg. § 20.7520-3(b)(3)(ii). If the case were otherwise, § 2037 would apply only to reversionary interests retained by decedents who died unexpectedly. *See* Roy v. Commissioner, 54 T.C. 1317 (1970) (making this point). *But see* Hall v. United States, 353 F.2d 500 (7th Cir. 1965) (holding

---

[11] *See* Technical Changes Act of 1949, Pub. L. No. 81-378, § 7(a), 63 Stat. 891, 895.

[12] The five percent value for a reversion has relevance for income tax purposes as well. If the value of the reversion at the time trust is created (as opposed to the moment prior to the decedent's death as under § 2037) exceeds five percent of the trust property, the trust is treated as a grantor trust pursuant to § 673(a).

it improper to disregard decedent's declining physical health in valuing reversion).

The above example assumed that the decedent's reversionary interest was capable of being valued according to pertinent actuarial tables. However, if the condition to the decedent's reversionary interest is not subject to actuarial valuation, then the general valuation standard of Reg. § 20.2031-1 must be employed in valuing the decedent's reversionary interest. *See* Treas. Reg. § 20.2037-1(b)(3). For example, assume *D* transferred property in trust to *W* for life; remainder to *W's* issue then living. If *W* dies without surviving issue, the remainder is to be paid to *D* if then living, otherwise to *C*. Under this somewhat strained example, *D's* reversionary interest must be determined by reference to the prospect of *D* not only surviving *W*, but also *W* dying without surviving issue. The second condition falls outside the scope of the actuarial valuation tables. In that case, the default "willing buyer-willing seller" standard of Reg. § 20.2031-1(b) controls.

Note that the five percent threshold imposed under § 2037(a)(2) assumes that the decedent's reversionary interest is capable of valuation. If the interest cannot be valued in accordance with recognized principles, should its value be presumed to be zero or in excess of the five percent threshold? Authorities on this point are mixed. In *Graham v. Commissioner*, 46 T.C. 415 (1966), the decedent retained a power of disposition over trust assets that was exercisable only in the event his daughters elected to terminate the trust. The Tax Court concluded that the inability to value the reversionary interest according to conventional means necessitated treating the reversion as having no value at all. *Id.* at 427 (citing Estate of Cardeza v. United States, 261 F.2d 423 (3d Cir. 1958)). On the other hand, the Tax Court in *Thacher v. Commissioner*, 20 T.C. 474 (1953), presumed that the prospect of property returning to the decedent in the event he and his wife divorced or legally separated exceeded the five percent threshold absent evidence to the contrary. *Id.* at 483. Perhaps the key to reconciling these cases lies in the Senate Report accompanying the Internal Revenue Code of 1954, which instructs as follows:

> Where it is apparent from the facts that property could have reverted to the decedent under contingencies that were not remote, the reversionary interest is not to be necessarily regarded as having no value merely because the value thereof cannot be measured precisely.

S. Rep. No. 83-1622, at 469 (1954). Hence, for reversions not capable of valuation through conventional means, the presumption of which side of the five percent line the reversion will fall turns on whether the court finds the contingencies to be sufficiently "remote." The decisions in *Estate of Graham* and *Estate of Thacher* can be reconciled on grounds that the prospects of a couple divorcing are far more likely than individuals exercising their power to terminate a trust that was established for their benefit.

[B] The Relevant Denominator

The value against which the decedent's reversion is measured for purposes of § 2037 is the entire value of the transferred property—not just the value of the interest that is contingent upon surviving the decedent. *See* Treas. Reg. § 20.2037-1(c)(4). Hence, the baseline for evaluating the five percent threshold will not necessarily equal the value of property to be captured in the decedent's gross estate if the threshold is cleared. Namely, the baseline will exceed the inclusion amount where others possess interests in the property not contingent upon surviving the decedent.

§ 12.06 REFERENCE POINT FOR DETERMINING AMOUNT INCLUDED

While the decedent's reversionary interest in transferred property must exceed the five percent threshold under § 2037(a)(2) in order to implicate § 2037, the pre-death value of the decedent's reversionary interest in the property does not also represent the amount included in the decedent's gross estate by operation of § 2037. Rather, the amount captured in the decedent's gross estate under § 2037 is the value of the interests in the transferred property the possession or enjoyment of which were conditioned upon surviving the decedent, and the value of such interests are determined immediately *after* the decedent's death. Example 4 of Reg. § 20.2037-1(e) illustrates this point. Under this example, *D* transferred property in trust with income payable to *Wife* for life; remainder to *Son* if then living, otherwise to *D* if then living, otherwise to *X* or *X*'s estate. Assuming that the value of the remainder interest in the trust when multiplied by the relative likelihood of *D* surviving both *Wife* and *Son* exceeded five percent of the value of the trust property immediately prior to *D*'s death (hence satisfying the five percent *de minimis* threshold), § 2037(a) captures the value of *X*'s contingent remainder in the trust in *D*'s gross estate. As expressly stated in the example, *X*'s interest in the property is valued for this purpose as of the time immediately *after D*'s death.

§ 12.07 APPLICATION OF § 2035

Section 2037 cannot be avoided through the simple relinquishment of the would-be predicate reversionary interest shortly before death. Like its retained-interest counterparts, § 2037 is subject to the 3-year recapture provision of § 2035. Thus, any amount that would have been included under § 2037 had the decedent not relinquished the reversionary interest within three years of his death will be included in his gross estate under § 2035(a). In order to determine whether the reversion would have caused transferred property to be included under § 2037 in the absence of its relinquishment, the hypothetical reversion must be reconstructed and valued as of the moment prior to the decedent's death. *See* Rev. Rul. 79-62, 1979-1 C.B. 295.

§ 12.08 REVERSIONARY INTERESTS IN LIFE INSURANCE PROCEEDS

The estate tax consequences of a reversionary interest in property are not limited to § 2037. Rather, the decedent's possession of a reversionary interest in a life insurance policy or its proceeds may constitute an incident of ownership that will trigger inclusion of the policy proceeds under § 2042(2). This aspect of § 2042 in large part replicates the scope of a reversionary interest under § 2037. As an initial matter, the decedent's reversionary interest in the life insurance policy or its proceeds must exceed five percent of the value of the policy, to be determined immediately prior to the decedent's death according to established valuation principles. IRC § 2042(2). In valuing the interest, however, the incidents of ownership held by others must be taken into consideration. Treas. Reg. § 20.2042-1(c)(3). Tracking somewhat the general power of appointment exclusion provided in § 2037(b), the regulations under § 2042 provide that a decedent will not be considered to possess a reversionary interest exceeding the five percent threshold if another person possesses the unilateral ability to withdraw the cash value of the policy. Treas. Reg. § 20.2042-1(c)(3). Similarly, the Service has ruled that the ability of another person to revoke a reversionary interest held by the decedent will preclude the reversion from clearing the five percent threshold. *See* Rev. Rul. 79-117, 1979-1 C.B. 305. As is the case under § 2037, a reversionary interest in the life insurance context does not extend to the prospect of inheriting a policy or its proceeds from another, or receiving such amounts pursuant to spousal inheritance protections under state law. Treas. Reg. § 20.2042-1(c)(3).

§ 12.09 POSSIBLE INCLUSION UNDER § 2033

A reversion in property that fails to implicate § 2037—perhaps because no party's interest is contingent upon surviving the decedent or because the reversion fails the five percent threshold—can nonetheless be included in the decedent's gross estate under § 2033. *See* Adriance v. Higgins, 113 F.2d 1013 (2d Cir. 1940); Henry v. Commissioner, 4 T.C. 423 (1944), *aff'd*, 161 F.2d 574 (3d Cir. 1947). However, for § 2033 to apply, the reversion cannot be extinguished by reason of the decedent's death but instead must remain outstanding in favor of the decedent's estate. If that is the case, the amount included under § 2033 will be limited to the actual value of the reversion, which is often far less than the value of the transferred property to which § 2037 otherwise would apply.

§ 12.10 STUDY PROBLEMS

1. Kathleen is married to Paul, and they have two teenage children. Kathleen transfers $1 million of securities to an irrevocable trust, designating a third-party trust company to serve as trustee. The trust provides for discretionary distributions of income and principal to Paul for his lifetime. Upon Paul's death, the trust assets will be distributed to Kathleen if she is still living, otherwise to Kathleen's then-living issue per stirpes.

   Evaluate Kathleen's estate tax exposure under § 2037, stating any assumptions you may find necessary.

2. Same as (1), except Paul can withdraw the trust principal upon written notice delivered to the trustee.

3. Same as (1), except the trust is to be distributed upon Paul's death to Kathleen's then living issue, per stirpes.

4. Same as (3), except the trust provides that if Paul and Kathleen divorce or legally separate, the trust shall terminate and be paid over to Kathleen.

5. Tripp funds an irrevocable trust for the lifetime benefit of his nephew, Bart. Upon Bart's death, the trust assets are to be distributed to Bart's then living issue. The trust says nothing more. Evaluate the potential estate tax consequences of the trust to Tripp.

6. Colleen established a trust for the benefit of her son, Liam, for his lifetime. Upon Liam's death, the trust property is to be distributed among Liam's children in such amounts and proportions as Colleen shall direct if she is then living; otherwise, the property will be distributed to Liam's then living issue or, in default thereof, to the American Cancer Society.

   a. Identify the reversionary interest retained by Colleen for purposes of § 2037.

   b. Assume the value of the trust property as of Colleen's death is $10 million. Explain the different results if Colleen's reversionary interest is valued at $400,000 instead of $550,000.

Chapter 13

THE ADEQUATE AND FULL CONSIDERATION EXCEPTION

Internal Revenue Code:	§§ 2035(a)(1), (d), 2036(a), 2037(a), 2038(a)(1), 2043(a)
Treasury Regulations:	§§ 20.2036-1(a), 20.2038-1(a)(1), 20.2037-1(a), 20.2043-1(a), 25.2512-8

The retained interest provisions contained in §§ 2036 through 2038 all except from their reach transfers that constitute a "bona fide sale for an adequate and full consideration in money or money's worth."[1] [For purposes of brevity, this exception at times will be referred to as the "statutory exception."] The theory of the statutory exception is relatively straightforward: There is no need to navigate the labyrinth of the retained-interest and retained-power provisions of the estate tax if a transaction does not serve to deplete the transferor's future gross estate. The Tax Court in *Estate of Frothingham v. Commissioner*, 60 T.C. 211 (1973), explained this rationale in the following terms:

> [W]here the transferred property is replaced by other property of equal value received in exchange, there is no reason to impose an estate tax in respect of the transferred property, for it is reasonable to assume that the property acquired in exchange will find its way into the decedent's gross estate at his death unless consumed or otherwise disposed of in a nontestamentary transaction in much the same manner as would the transferred property itself had the transfer not taken place.

Id. at 215. Yet despite the apparent simplicity of the statutory exception, its application has proven to be one of the more vexing issues in the transfer tax arena. As illustrated in a number of cases discussed in this chapter, a textual application of the statutory exception often conflicts with the intended purpose of the statute as a whole.

§ 13.01 STRUCTURAL FRAMEWORK

The adequate and full consideration exception to the retained-interest provisions of §§ 2036, 2037, and 2038 appears in each instance by way of parenthetical. By its terms, the statutory exception is satisfied only if the transfer arose from a bona fide sale that supplied the decedent with adequate and full consideration in money or money's worth. In instances where the

---

[1] Transfers for consideration also have potential relevance in determining the amount of jointly owned property to be included in the decedent's gross estate under § 2040(a). Recall that the decedent's estate is entitled to exclude a proportionate amount of the value of jointly owned property from the gross estate equal to the portion of the purchase price supplied by the surviving joint tenant, but only to the extent the consideration supplied by the surviving joint tenant was not acquired from the decedent for less than an adequate and full consideration in money or money's worth.

decedent received consideration for the transfer that fell short of the "adequate and full . . . in money or money's worth" standard, § 2043(a) steps in to limit the amount included in the decedent's gross estate. Under § 2043(a), the amount that otherwise would be included in the gross estate by reason of the retained-interest or retained-power provision is reduced by the value of the consideration received by the decedent. However, the relevant points of valuation for this purpose are not the same. The property otherwise to be included in the decedent's gross estate is determined as of the decedent's death, whereas the consideration received by the decedent is determined as of the time of the transfer. Thus, assuming positive rates of investment return, § 2043 overvalues the gross estate by not accounting for the appreciation in the consideration received.

[A]   Sufficiency of Consideration

A finding that a transfer provides the transferor with adequate and full consideration in money or money's worth serves to exempt the transfer from the gift tax and the estate tax.[2] For gift tax purposes, the consideration received is valued according to the same objective standard employed to value the transferred property. Any difference between these two values constitutes a gift under § 2512(b). *See* Treas. Reg. § 25.2512-8 (providing that the gift tax reaches sales or exchanges for consideration "to the extent that the value of the property transferred . . . exceeds the value in money or money's worth of the consideration given therefor"). The only exception from this absolute rule is if the transfer occurs in the "ordinary course of business," in which case the sufficiency of consideration is presumed. *See id.*

The Supreme Court has declared on a number of instances that the phrase "adequate and full consideration" is to be afforded the same construction under the gift tax and estate tax. *See* Estate of Sanford v. Commissioner, 308 U.S. 39, 44 (1939) (noting the supplementary nature of the gift tax to the estate tax, and directing that "[t]he two are in pari materia and must be construed together"); Merrill v. Fahs, 324 U.S. 308, 313 (1945) ("We believe that there is every reason for giving the same words in the gift tax the same reading."). In keeping with this approach, the regulations under § 2043 impose a strict standard for testing the sufficiency of consideration in the context of retained-interest transfers: The "price" paid for transfer "must have been an adequate and full equivalent reducible to a money value." Treas. Reg. § 20.2043-1. The necessity of monetarily equivalent consideration was confirmed by the Fifth Circuit in *Wheeler v. United States*, 116 F.3d 749 (5th Cir. 1997), when it instructed that "unless a transfer that depletes the transferor's estate is joined with a transfer that augments the estate by a commensurate (monetary) amount, there is no 'adequate and full consideration' for the purposes of either the estate or gift tax."[3] *Id.* at 762. In this manner, the statutory exception to the retained-interest provisions of the estate tax guards against the use of lifetime transfers to deplete the transferor's future gross estate.

---

[2] This may not be entirely accurate, as the transfer must also constitute a bona fide sale in order to satisfy the estate tax exemption. *See* § 13.01[B]. However, in the vast majority of cases, a transfer that meets the consideration standard will satisfy the bona fide sale requirement as well.

[3] With no explanation, the Fifth Circuit relaxed this standard significantly in *Kimbell v. United States*, 371 F.3d 257 (5th Cir. 2004), when it restated its instruction from *Wheeler* as follows: "In other words, the asset the estate receives must be *roughly equivalent* to the asset it gave up." *Id.* at 262 (emphasis added). The *Kimbell* decision is discussed in the context of family limited partnership cases in § 12.03.

[B] Role of "Bona Fide Sale" Condition

If the purpose of the adequate and full consideration exception to the retained interest provisions is to guard against estate depletion, the requirement of adequate and full consideration "in money or money's worth" would appear sufficient for the task. What, then, is the purpose of requiring the transaction to constitute a "bona fide sale"? This aspect of the statutory exception could plausibly be viewed as redundant, particularly given that the regulations interpreting these sections make no mention of a bona fide sale when describing the exception. *See* Treas. Reg. § 20.2036-1(a) (stating that the statute does not apply "to the extent that the transfer was for an adequate and full consideration in money or money's worth"); *see also* Treas. Reg. §§ 20.2037-1(a)(1), 20.2038-1 (same). On the other hand, the regulations under § 2043 refer to the exception in its full statutory form and elaborate on the exception as follows:

> To constitute a bona fide sale for an adequate and full consideration in money or money's worth, the transfer must have been made in good faith, and the price must have been an adequate and full equivalent reducible to a money value.

Treas. Reg. § 20.2043-1(a). In this manner, the bona fide sale qualifier imposes a subjective litmus test to the objective requirement of monetarily equivalent consideration.

The Second Circuit in *Estate of Maxwell v. Commissioner*, 3 F.3d 591 (2d Cir. 1993), addressed the bona fides of a transaction between related parties structured as a sale. The decedent in *Estate of Maxwell* sold her residence to her son and daughter-in-law in exchange for its approximate fair market value. However, no cash changed hands at closing or, for that matter, ever. The decedent forgave $20,000 (twice the then available annual exclusion), and then took a promissory note for the balance. The decedent continued to occupy the residence under a lease, but her rental payments were largely offset by the interest payments due to her under the note. The decedent forgave $20,000 of the loan principal each year, and the loan balance outstanding as of her death was cancelled through the terms of her will. The Service sought to include the value of the residence in the decedent's gross estate under § 2036(a)(1), but the estate claimed that the transaction satisfied the statutory exception. In its decision affirming the Tax Court, the Second Circuit framed the issue as follows: "The question is whether [the note] is actually what it purports to be—a bona fide instrument of indebtedness—or whether it is a facade." *Id.* at 595. Finding the decedent's intent germane to the "bona fide" inquiry, the court concluded that the note should not be respected as supplying consideration to the decedent for the transfer.[4]

Consistent with the Second Circuit's approach in *Estate of Maxwell*, the Fifth Circuit in *Wheeler v. United States* described the role of the "bona fide sale" qualifier as ensuring that the relevant transactions were not illusory or sham. *See* 116 F.3d at 763. The court then posited a more expansive purpose of the bona fide sale component of the statutory exception, suggesting that it could operate to shield "legitimate, negotiated commercial transfers" from the reach of the retained-interest provisions. *Id.* at 763–64. Viewed from this perspective, the "bona fide sale" qualifier would operate in a manner analogous to the safe harbor under the gift tax for transfers in the ordinary course of business, which presumes that transfers that are "bona fide, at arm's length, and free from any donative intent" provide the transferor with monetarily

---

[4] Note that the effect of the holding in *Estate of Maxwell* is to include post-transfer appreciation in the property in the decedent's gross estate, and to deny the decedent the benefit of her attempted use of the gift tax annual exclusion in the years including and following the transfer.

equivalent consideration. Treas. Reg. § 25.2512-8. Yet if the phrase "adequate and full consideration in money or money's worth" is to be interpreted in a uniform manner under the estate and gift taxes, the implied safe-harbor for commercial transactions would fall under the "adequate and full consideration" aspect of the statutory exception—not the "bona fide sale" component. Hence, the Fifth Circuit's suggestion in *Wheeler* of a safe harbor for commercial transactions is likely correct as a practical matter but imprecise in suggesting that the safe harbor falls under the "bona fide sale" heading.

Regulations promulgated in 2008 under § 2036 raise the prospect of the bona fide sale qualifier supplying a meaningful restriction on the scope of the statutory exception. Responding to claims that assets transferred to a Grantor Retained Annuity Trust (GRAT) should be exempt from potential estate taxation under § 2036 where the actuarial value of the qualified annuity interest equaled the value of the property transferred in trust,[5] the Service explained that the transaction was not the product of a bona fide sale:

> There is a significant difference between the bona fide sale of property to a third party in exchange for an annuity, and the retention of an annuity interest in property transferred from a third party. In the bona fide sale, there is a negotiation and agreement between two parties, each of whom is the owner of a property interest before the sale; each uses his or her own property to provide consideration to the other in exchange for the property interest to be received from the other in the sale. When the transferor retains an annuity or similar interest in the transferred property (as in the case of a GRAT . . .), the transferor is not selling the transferred property to a third party in exchange for an annuity because there is no other owner of property negotiating or engaging in a sale transaction with the transferor.

T.D. 9414, 2008-2 C.B. 454. The Service's emphasis on the necessity of a "sale" for consideration that has an independent existence apart from the transferred property effectively precludes application of the statutory exception where the consideration received is derived principally from the transferred property itself. In other words, in order to implicate the statutory exception, the consideration received must have existed prior to the transaction.

[C] Summary

Based on the statutory text, the regulatory guidance, and the function of the statutory exception as explained by courts, the exception will be satisfied where the decedent participated in a non-illusory transaction (*bona fide* sale) through which the decedent received consideration having an existence distinct from the transferred property (bona fide *sale*) having an equivalent value to the property transferred by the decedent determined under objective valuation principles (adequate and full consideration *in money or money's worth*) so that the transaction served to fully augment the decedent's future gross estate. Based on the judicial requirement that "adequate and full consideration in money or money's worth" be interpreted in a like manner under the estate and gift taxes, a deficiency in the objective value of the consideration received presumably will be excused if the transfer occurs in the "ordinary course of business" as described in Reg. § 25.2512-8. Outside of this safe harbor, if the consideration received through a bona fide sale fails to fully augment the decedent's gross estate, then the date-of-transfer value of the consideration received will be excluded from the gross estate under § 2043(a).

---

[5] This planning technique, referred to as a "zeroed-out" GRAT, is described in § 10.05[B][2].

The framework described above is fairly easy to apply when the decedent conveys fee title to property. However, the statutory exception to the retained interest provisions becomes more complicated when evaluating transfers of temporal interests in property.

§ 13.02   SALES OF LIFE ESTATES

Recall that § 2035(a) seeks to prevent easy avoidance of the retained-interest and retained-power provisions of §§ 2036 through 2038 by effectively disregarding any transfer of an interest in property or relinquishment of a power over property that occurs within three years of the decedent's death. However, the three-year rule of § 2035(a) is not implicated if the transfer constitutes a "bona fide sale for an adequate and full consideration in money or money's worth." IRC § 2035(d).

Assume that a decedent contributes property to an irrevocable trust and reserves a lifetime income interest in his favor. The decedent later sells his income interest for its actuarial value, and he dies one year after the sale. Does the subsequent sale of the income interest for its fair market value invoke the adequate and full consideration exception under § 2035(d), thereby precluding the application of §§ 2035(a) and 2036? If so, note that the sale of the life estate for its commuted value—in effect, an acceleration of the income payments the decedent otherwise would have received over time—will have the effect of removing the post-funding appreciation in the trust property from the transfer tax base.

The Tenth Circuit addressed a scenario similar to that sketched above in *United States v. Allen*, 293 F.2d 916 (10th Cir. 1961), but the case was decided prior to the enactment of present-day § 2035. The decedent in *Allen* had transferred property in trust, reserving a partial life estate in her favor. Upon being advised of looming estate tax consequences under the predecessor of § 2036, the decedent sold her retained life estate to her son for a figure slightly greater than its actuarial value. The estate argued that the predecessor to § 2036 could not apply because the decedent had disposed of her retained life interest for adequate and full consideration. Although noting that it would have been practically impossible for the decedent to sell her life estate for a greater value, the court nonetheless rejected the estate's argument. Essentially, the court refused to believe that the predecessor of § 2036 could be so easily circumvented:

> It does not seem plausible, however, that Congress intended to allow such an easy avoidance of the taxable incidence befalling reserved life estates. This result would allow a taxpayer to reap the benefits of property for his lifetime and, in contemplation of death, sell only the interest entitling him to the income, thereby removing all of the property which he has enjoyed from his gross estate. Giving the statute a reasonable interpretation, we cannot believe this to be its intendment. It seems certain that in a situation like this, Congress meant the estate to include the corpus of the trust or, in its stead, an amount equal in value.

Id. at 918; *see also* Estate of D'Ambrosio v. Commissioner, 101 F.3d 309, 312 (3d Cir. 1996) (referring to the scenario in *Allen* as a "testamentary transaction with a palpable tax evasion motive").

Assuming that the rationale of the *Allen* decision was not displaced by the enactment of § 2035(d), the sufficiency of consideration under § 2035(d) will be measured *not* against the value of the property interest actually transferred *but instead* against the value that would have been included in the decedent's gross estate absent the subsequent sale. Under this approach of measuring consideration received based on its effect on the transferor's future gross estate, it is difficult to imagine when the statutory exception under § 2035(d) would be satisfied in this context. Simply put, a purchaser acting at arm's length would not pay an amount equal to the value of the property in which he receives only a temporal interest.[6] Therefore, in cases such as *Allen* where the transferee paid the actuarial value for the transferred temporal interest in property, § 2035(a) will continue to apply, but § 2043(a) will provide an offset from the gross estate for the consideration received.

§ 13.03 SALES OF REMAINDER INTERESTS

If the sufficiency of consideration for a transfer of an interest in property that otherwise would implicate § 2035(a) must be measured against the amount that otherwise would be included in the decedent's gross estate absent the transfer, does the same approach apply for purposes of determining whether the sale of a remainder interest in property is exempt from § 2036(a)(1)? Presumably the same analysis should apply, as the effect of precluding the application of § 2036 by invoking the statutory exception would be to permit the decedent to retain the lifetime beneficial enjoyment of the property while removing post-transfer appreciation from the transfer tax base.[7] However, this issue has created a split at the Circuit Court of Appeals level, with the majority holding that payment of the actuarial value for the remainder interest satisfies the statutory exception to § 2036.

The application of the statutory exception to § 2036 in this context first arose in the context of so-called "widow's election" trusts. For instance, in *Gregory v. Commissioner*, 39 T.C. 1012 (1963), the decedent's husband devised his interest in the couple's community property to a testamentary trust benefiting the decedent for her lifetime, but the devise was conditioned upon the decedent contributing her share of the community property to the same trust. The decedent did so, thereby transferring the remainder interest in her share of the community property in exchange for a lifetime interest in the share of such property owned by her husband. The decedent's estate took the position that half of the trust property attributable to the decedent's contribution was not included in her gross estate under § 2036(a)(1) on the basis that her transfer was one for consideration that satisfied the statutory exception.

In analyzing whether the transfer provided the decedent with adequate and full consideration, the court compared the actuarial value of the decedent's life estate in the property devised by her husband (roughly $12,000) to the full value of the property she contributed to the trust (approximately $66,000). The comparison of the consideration against the full value of the transferred property is consistent with the *Allen* decision and was intentional on the part of the Tax Court: "The statute excepts only those bona fide sales where the consideration received was of a comparable value which would be includable in the gross estate." *Id.* at 1016. In short, the sufficiency of consideration is to be judged against what would be included in the decedent's gross estate—not against the narrow property interest transferred. Consistent with the Tax Court's decision in *Gregory*, the Court of Claims in *Gradow v. United States*, 11 Cl. Ct.

---

[6] Indeed, if the transferee for some reason did overpay for the interest in this manner, the transaction would have gift tax consequences for the transferee.

[7] If the statutory exception to § 2036(a) were not satisfied, the decedent's gross estate would include the full fair market value of the property less the value of the consideration received (as measured when paid) through the application of §§ 2036(a)(1) and 2043. On the other hand, if the statutory exception is satisfied, then the decedent's gross estate would include only the consideration received for the transfer under § 2033, which, if the actuarial tables hold true, will have grown to the value of the full property at the time the decedent sold the remainder.

808 (1987), determined that the transferred "property" against which the consideration received must be measured referred to the entire trust principal attributable to the surviving spouse's contributions. The Federal Circuit affirmed, incorporating the analysis provided by the Court of Claims. *See* Gradow v. United States, 897 F.2d 516 (Fed. Cir. 1990).

Despite a string of successes in *Allen, Gregory,* and *Gradow,* the estate-preservation approach to evaluating the application of the statutory exception to § 2036 to transfers of partial interests in property has fallen into disfavor. In *Estate of D'Ambrosio v. Commissioner,* 101 F.3d 309 (3d Cir. 1996), the Third Circuit determined that a transfer of a remainder interest in corporate stock for its actuarial value satisfied the statutory exception to § 2036(a)(1)—precluding the application of § 2036 to property in which the decedent retained a lifetime interest. The court pointed first to the statutory text, noting that § 2036 captures property "to the extent of any interest therein" of which the decedent has made a transfer other than a transfer satisfying the statutory exception. The court concluded that the statute thereby contemplates its application to transfers of temporal interests in property.[8] *Id.* at 315. Additionally, the Third Circuit reasoned that its holding did not threaten the purpose of § 2036. The court determined that the sale of a remainder interest in property for actuarial value would produce the same gross estate as if no such transfer had occurred, so long as the consideration received for the sale was properly invested.[9] *Id.* at 316. As a final matter, the court noted that if the sufficiency of consideration for the transfer of a remainder in property were to be measured against the fee interest in evaluating the statutory exception to § 2036(a), no buyers could be found to purchase the remainder interest on those terms.

The holding of the Third Circuit in *Estate of D'Ambrosio* has gained substantial momentum, as it has been followed by both the Fifth Circuit and the Ninth Circuit. *See* Wheeler v. United States, 116 F.3d 749 (5th Cir. 1997); Estate of Magnin v. Commissioner, 184 F.3d 1074 (9th Cir. 1999). Hence, the sale of a remainder interest appears to provide an effective means of freezing the transfer tax value of property without relinquishing beneficial ownership. Yet due to the enactment of § 2702, this estate-tax freeze is available only where the purchaser is not a member of the decedent's family as defined in that statute.[10]

§ 13.04 FAMILY LIMITED PARTNERSHIP FORMATIONS

The statutory exception to § 2036 has re-emerged at the forefront of the estate tax arena through its potential to shield assets contributed to family limited partnerships from the statute's reach. Taxpayers take the position that a transfer of property to a closely owned business entity in exchange for a pro-rata beneficial interest in the entity supplies adequate and full consideration for the transfer, primarily because no value is transferred to another. On the other hand, beneficial interests in family limited partnerships are typically valued at substantial discounts from the pro-rata value of the transferred property—a position that seemingly precludes the receipt of adequate and full consideration in "money or money's

---

[8] Yet, as the Service argued in *Estate of D'Ambrosio,* the application of § 2036(a)(1) to a remainder interest in property as opposed to the fee interest suffers from structural shortcomings, as it is impossible to retain a lifetime interest in a transferred remainder.

[9] Note that this comparison is logically flawed, as it ignores appreciation in the underlying property under scenario (a) while presuming appreciation in the consideration received under scenario (b).

[10] If § 2702 applies, the sale of the remainder for its actuarial value will be treated as a transfer of the entire property for gift tax purposes. The application of § 2702 is addressed in § 10.05[B].

worth." As described below, courts have articulated their own tests for satisfying the statutory exception in this context, tests that grow farther afield from the statutory text and regulatory guidance as they develop.

[A] Early Tax Court Approach

[1] *Estate of Reichardt v. Commissioner*

One of the first Tax Court cases to invoke the statutory exception to § 2036 to transfers of property to a family limited partnership (which the transferor continued to beneficially enjoy) was *Estate of Reichardt v. Commissioner*, 114 T.C. 144 (2000). The estate argued that the decedent's transfer of property to the entity constituted a sale for adequate and full consideration for the beneficial interests in the entity. The Tax Court rejected this position in short order: "[The decedent] did not sell the transferred property to the partnership." *Id.* at 156. Hence, the statutory exception failed for want of a sale.[11]

[2] *Estate of Harper v. Commissioner*

The Tax Court undertook a more thorough explanation of why the statutory exception to § 2036 was not satisfied in the context of a particular family limited partnership in *Estate of Harper v. Commissioner*, T.C. Memo. 2002-121, 83 T.C.M. (CCH) 1641. The decedent in *Estate of Harper* transferred marketable securities and a note receivable to a limited partnership in exchange for a 99 percent interest as limited partner. The court first held that the transfer to the entity implicated § 2036(a)(1) on the basis of an implied agreement among the parties that the decedent had retained the economic benefit of the transferred property. The court then addressed the estate's claim that the capitalization of the partnership satisfied the statutory exception to § 2036(a), a claim the court rejected on two fronts. The court interpreted the "bona fide sale" aspect of the exception as requiring an arm's-length transaction. Noting that the decedent controlled all aspects of the partnership formation, the court dryly concluded that "[i]t would be an oxymoron to say that one can engage in an arm's-length transaction with oneself." *Id.* at 1653.

Whereas the court's treatment of the bona fide sale aspect of the statutory exception was brief, its discussion of the adequate and full consideration component was more elaborate. The court did not focus on the entity-related discounts to determine that the partnership formation did not provide the decedent with adequate and full consideration in money or money's worth; it concluded that the transaction did not provide the decedent with consideration separate from the property transferred whatsoever. In the court's view, the transaction simply constituted a change in the form of ownership:

> In actuality, all decedent did was to change the form in which he held his beneficial interest in the contributed property. We see little practical difference in whether [decedent] held the property directly or as a 99-percent partner (and entitled to a commensurate 99-percent share of profits) in a partnership holding the property. Essentially, the value of the partnership interest [decedent] received derived solely from the assets [decedent] had just contributed. Without any change whatsoever in the underlying pool of assets or prospect for profit, as, for example, where others make

---

[11] Note that this brief approach is consistent with the preamble of the § 2036 regulations issued in 2008. *See* § 13.01[B].

contributions of property or services in the interest of true joint ownership or enterprise, there exists nothing but a circuitous "recycling" of value. We are satisfied that such instances of pure recycling do not rise to the level of a payment of consideration. To hold otherwise would open section 2036 to a myriad of abuses engendered by unilateral paper transformations.

Id. The "recycling of value" theory for rejecting the statutory exception to § 2036 in the partnership context proved influential in future Tax Court cases. *See* Estate of Strangi v. Commissioner, T.C. Memo. 2003-145, 85 T.C.M. (CCH) 1331; Estate of Thompson v. Commissioner, T.C. Memo. 2002-246, 84 T.C.M. (CCH) 374.

[B]   Conflicting Circuit Court Decisions

[1]   *Kimbell v. United States*

The Fifth Circuit in *Kimbell v. United States*, 371 F.3d 257 (5th Cir. 2004), adopted an entirely different approach to evaluating the statutory exception to § 2036(a) in the context of partnership formations, one far more favorable to taxpayers. The court first concluded that a partnership formation will provide the contributing partners with adequate and full consideration for their transfers when the following conditions are satisfied: (1) the partnership interest credited to each partner is proportionate to the fair market value of the property contributed by the parties; (2) the property contributed is credited to each partner's capital account balance; and (3) each partner is entitled to distribution of the balance of his capital account upon the partnership dissolution. *See id.* at 266. Given that these requirements will be satisfied in any partnership that complies with the substantial economic effect safe harbor for respecting partnership income allocations under § 704(b),[12] the Fifth Circuit's test effectively amounted to a pass on the consideration front.

The court was not overly concerned that the estate valued the partnership interests received at roughly half of the value of the property contributed to the entity; it rejected the government's argument that the valuation deficiency precluded application of the statutory exception as "a classic mixing of apples and oranges." *Id.* at 266. Although the Fifth Circuit previously had instructed in *Wheeler v. United States*, 116 F.3d 749, 762 (5th Cir. 1997), that the statutory exception to § 2036(a) would not be satisfied unless the transfer of property "is joined with a transfer that augments the estate by a commensurate (monetary) amount," the court in *Kimbell* relaxed this requirement considerably by restating it as follows: "In other words, the asset the estate receives must be roughly equivalent to the asset it gave up." *Kimbell*, 371 F.3d at 262.

The Fifth Circuit was equally forgiving in its interpretation of the bona fide sale component of the statutory exception in this context. The court explained that, as a general rule, the transaction would satisfy the bona fide sale qualifier so long as the transferor parted with the property and the partnership actually issued the resulting partnership interest. *See id.* at 265. However, the court noted that the intra-family nature of the transaction—while not precluding the presence of a bona fide sale—necessitated application of heightened scrutiny. Under the facts of the case, the court determined that the transaction survived this heightened level of

---

[12] *See* Treas. Reg. § 1.704-1(b)(2)(ii)(*b*), (*d*) (providing the basic test and alternate test for economic effect, each of which contain as the first requirement the maintenance of capital accounts in accordance with the provisions of Reg. § 1.704-1(b)(2)(iv)).

scrutiny because the parties respected the partnership as an entity separate from the decedent's personal affairs, and because the transaction was motivated by substantial considerations apart from transfer tax savings. *See id.* at 269.

[2] *Estate of Thompson v. Commissioner*

Not long after the Fifth Circuit's decision in *Kimbell*, the Third Circuit addressed the statutory exception to § 2036 in *Estate of Thompson v. Commissioner*, 382 F.3d 367 (3d Cir. 2004). Whereas the Fifth Circuit was not troubled by the discrepancy between the transfer-tax value of the property transferred and that of the partnership interests received, the Third Circuit in *Estate of Thompson* suggested that the invocation of entity-related discounts in valuing the partnership interests received alone should preclude a finding of adequate and full consideration in money or money's worth.[13] *See id.* at 381. However, the Third Circuit declined to adopt an absolute rule in this area, noting that the Tax Court had held that the dissipation of estate-tax value in this context did not preclude application of the statutory exception to § 2036 in appropriate circumstances. That said, the court noted that the discrepancy in the transfer-tax value of the property transferred and the consideration received warranted the application of heightened scrutiny, which the transaction could not survive: "Where, as here, the transferee partnership does not operate a legitimate business, and the record demonstrates the valuation discount provides the sole benefit for converting liquid, marketable assets into illiquid partnership interests, there is no transfer for consideration within the meaning of § 2036(a)." *Id.* Given the lack of business activity, the court was comfortable treating the partnership formation as simply a change in the form through which the property was beneficially owned.

The absence of business activity also proved relevant to the Third Circuit's analysis of the bona fide sale component of the statutory exception. Here, the court rejected the Tax Court's equation of a bona fide sale with an arm's-length transaction, noting this definition did not appear in the statute or regulations. Instead, the court focused on the requirement under Reg. § 20.2043-1(a) that the transaction be one entered into in good faith. In this regard, the court noted that a transfer in good faith to a family limited partnership "must provide the transferor some potential for benefit other than the potential estate tax advantages that might result from holding assets in the partnership form." *Id.* at 383. Citing the absence of "legitimate business operations" or any other potential non-tax benefits from the transaction, the court found the necessary good faith element lacking.

As a technical matter, the decisions in *Kimbell* and *Estate of Thompson* can be reconciled on the basis that each case ultimately turned on the judicial determination of whether sufficient non-tax motivations for the partnership formation were present. In substance, however, the decisions embody sharply opposing views on the proper application of the statutory exception to § 2036 in this partnership formation context. The *Kimbell* court approached the issue from a standpoint of almost presumed consideration, whereas the *Estate of Thompson* court was skeptical that discounted partnership interests could ever provide sufficient consideration for the transfer. Additionally, the activities of the partnerships that the *Estate of Thompson* court

---

[13] A concurring opinion expressed this point more emphatically: "To me nothing could be clearer than a conclusion that if the discount was justified (even if in a lesser percentage than the estate claimed) in a valuation sense then the decedent could not have received an adequate and full consideration for his transfers in terms of 'money's worth.' " *Id.* at 384 (Greenberg, J., concurring). Given that the concurrence was joined by another judge on the panel, it could be construed as constituting the majority opinion.

found inadequate appeared more favorable than those the court in *Kimbell* determined were indicative of a non-tax motive.

[C]   *Estate of Bongard*

Following the conflicting guidance from the Circuit Courts of Appeals in *Kimbell* and *Estate of Thompson*, the Tax Court finally addressed the application of the statutory exception to § 2036 in the context of partnership formations through a court-reviewed decision in *Estate of Bongard v. Commissioner*, 124 T.C. 95 (2005). After noting that the statutory exception in this context had been the frequent "grist of judicial interpretation," *id.* at 114, the Tax Court proceeded to offer yet another judicial test determining when partnership formations would fall outside the potential reach of § 2036(a):

> In the context of family limited partnerships, the bona fide sale for adequate and full consideration exception is met where the record establishes [(1)] the existence of a legitimate and significant nontax reason for creating the family limited partnership, and [(2)] the transferors received partnership interests proportionate to the value of the property transferred.

Id. at 118. Noticeably absent from this test is any concern about the consideration received fully augmenting the transferor's estate "in money or money's worth." Rather than determining application of the statutory exception in this objective manner, the Tax Court instead endorsed an inquiry into the genuineness and legitimacy of the parties' professed non-tax motivations for forming the partnership. Under the Tax Court's standard, a single legitimate and significant non-tax reason will suffice.

The *Estate of Bongard* standard for interpreting the statutory exception to § 2036 in the partnership formation context is not well suited for producing a uniform application of the law, as the scope and legitimacy of a non-tax standard lies in the eye of the reviewing judge. Some cases have proven extraordinarily sympathetic to the taxpayer's professed non-tax motivations. *See* Estate of Schutt v. Commissioner, T.C. Memo. 2005-126, 89 T.C.M. (CCH) 1353 (desire to prevent descendants from selling stock after decedent's death provided sufficient non-tax motive for partnership formation); Estate of Anna Mirowski v. Commissioner, T.C. Memo. 2008-74, 95 T.C.M. (CCH) 1277 (desire for daughters to work together and promote "family cohesiveness" provided sufficient non-tax motivation for partnership formation). However, other cases have proven far more skeptical that the purpose for the entity formation was anything other than transfer tax savings. *See, e.g.,* Estate of Rector v. Commissioner, T.C. Memo. 2007-367, 94 T.C.M. (CCH) 567; Estate of Rosen v. Commissioner, T.C. Memo. 2006-115, 91 T.C.M. (CCH) 1220; Estate of Bigelow v. Commissioner, T.C. Memo. 2005-65, 89 T.C.M. (CCH) 954, *aff'd,* 503 F.3d 955 (9th Cir. 2007). In many respects, application of the statutory exception to § 2036(a) to partnership formations has been reduced to something of a haphazard exercise that turns on a combination of the contemporaneous documentation of the non-tax motivations for forming the entity as well as the receptiveness of the reviewing court to such purposes.

§ 13.05   STUDY PROBLEMS

1.   Jacob owns a modest house on a large, ocean-front lot in a region where development is booming. Seeking to cap his estate-tax exposure, Jacob transfers a remainder interest in the property to Alice—Jacob's committed partner to whom he is not

married—for its actuarial value. Jacob continues to reside in the property pursuant to his retained life estate for the remainder of his lifetime. At the time of the sale of the remainder, the fee interest was valued at $3 million, and the remainder was valued at $1 million. Upon Jacob's death five years later, the value of the property had increased to $5 million. Discuss the estate tax consequences to Jacob's estate.

2.   Assume that Jacob did not sell the remainder interest to Alice but instead conveyed it to her gratuitously. Several years thereafter, Jacob and Alice parted ways. As part of their separation agreement, Jacob sold his life estate in the property to Alice for its remaining actuarial value and moved out. Roughly a year after this transaction, Jacob died in a car accident. Discuss the estate tax consequences to Jacob's estate.

3.   At the encouragement of her estate-planner, Rita contributes $40 million of marketable securities to a limited partnership. She takes back a 99 percent interest as limited partner, and a 50 percent interest in an LLC that is formed to serve as the general partner. The other 50 percent interest of the LLC is held by her two children in equal shares. The partnership agreement calls for the net investment income of the entity to be distributed on an annual basis. The estate planner documents the following purposes for forming the entity: (1) creation of a vehicle for joint investment of family assets; (2) protection of family assets from potential claims of spouses of descendants and other would-be creditors; and (3) transfer tax savings. Upon Rita's death four years later, the estate values her partnership interests at 55 percent of net asset value, based on discounts for lack of marketability and lack of control. Discuss the prospects of the partnership assets being included in Rita's gross estate under § 2036(a).

Chapter 14

POWERS OF APPOINTMENT

Internal Revenue Code:	§§ 2041, 2514
Treasury Regulations:	§§ 20.2041-1 (skip -1(c)(3) and (4)), 20.2041-3, 25.2514-1(a) to (c)(2), (d), 25.2514-3(a) to (c)(1), (4)–(5), (d)

Perhaps the single most salient attribute of property ownership is the ability to currently enjoy or otherwise benefit from property to the exclusion of others. A less significant but nonetheless important aspect of property ownership is the ability to direct its gratuitous disposition, whether through inter vivos transfer or devise. *See* Hodel v. Irving, 481 U.S. 704, 715 (1987) ("There is no question . . . that the right to pass on valuable property to one's heirs is itself a valuable right. Depending on the age of the owner, much or most of the value of the parcel may inhere in this 'remainder' interest.").[1]

Suppose then that the ability to direct the beneficial enjoyment of property—either on a temporal basis or through the ability to transfer the underlying property itself—were separated from ownership of the underlying property. Should the possession of such power alone be regarded as tantamount to ownership for federal transfer tax purposes?

The Supreme Court in *Helvering v. Safe Deposit & Trust Co.*, 316 U.S. 56 (1942), declined to equate the two. The decedent in *Safe Deposit & Trust* was the sole income beneficiary of trusts that were to be distributed at the decedent's death as directed by his will, but the decedent failed to exercise this distribution power. Interpreting the predecessor of § 2033, the Court concluded that mere possession of the ability to dispose of trust property by testamentary direction did not rise to the level of an "interest" in property that would support the imposition of the estate tax. *Id.* at 58–63. The estate in *Safe Deposit & Trust* was aided significantly by the existence of legislation that captured in the gross estate only property subject to certain powers of appointment that the decedent in fact exercised.[2] As the Court explained, if mere possession of the power of appointment constituted an interest in property under the predecessor to § 2033, the statute specifically addressing powers of appointment would have been superfluous. *See* 316 U.S. at 61–62.

The federal transfer tax consequences of powers of appointment currently are addressed by §§ 2041 and 2514. As compared to the broad net of inclusion cast by Congress for retained powers over the beneficial enjoyment of property once owned by the decedent under §§ 2036(a)

---

[1] The Supreme Court in *Hodel* held that a federal law directing that certain fractional interests in trusts owning Indian land escheat in favor of the larger tribe—which, in the Court's words, amounted to a complete abolition of descent and devise of those property rights—constituted a taking under the Fifth Amendment of the U.S. Constitution without the payment of just compensation. *See* 481 U.S. at 712–18.

[2] *See* Revenue Act of 1918, Pub. L. No. 65-254, § 402(e), 40 Stat. 1057, 1097.

and 2038(a),[3] the estate tax is far more circumspect in its application to powers over the beneficial enjoyment of property originally owned by another. For the most part, only property subject to a "general power of appointment" is subject to federal transfer tax consequences. As discussed below, a general power of appointment is limited to a subset of powers that can be exercised to or for the benefit of the holder. Hence, the broad array of powers of appointment that fall outside of this definition allow transferors to provide others with significant amounts of discretion over the use and ultimate disposition of property without generating adverse transfer tax consequences for the power holder.

Both §§ 2041 and 2514 distinguish between powers created on or before October 21, 1942, and those created thereafter. Powers of appointment created on or before October 21, 1942, generally are subject to taxation only to the extent they are exercised. Congress expanded the power of appointment statute in 1942 to base taxation on the possession of a general power of appointment alone,[4] which is consistent with the application of the estate tax on the basis of control over the economic benefit of property. Given the significant passage of time since the October 21, 1942, dividing date, this chapter will address only post-1942 powers.

§ 14.01 SCOPE OF POWER OF APPOINTMENT CONTEMPLATED BY STATUTE

The most familiar example of a power of appointment is a power provided to a lifetime beneficiary of a trust to direct the disposition of trust property at his death by will. Typical drafting renders the existence of the power explicit: "Upon *Beneficiary's* death, the trust property shall be distributed to such one or more of *Beneficiary's* issue in such amounts and proportions as *Beneficiary* may direct through a provision in his will specifically referencing this power; in default thereof, the trust property shall be distributed to *Beneficiary's* then living issue, *per stirpes*." The scope of a power of appointment for federal transfer tax purposes is not limited to the realm of the express, however. As a general rule, the term "power of appointment" extends to any power to affect the beneficial enjoyment of property or the income it generates, regardless of the nomenclature employed. Treas. Reg. § 20.2041-1(b)(1). Hence, a beneficiary's power to consume all or a portion of the trust principal constitutes a power of appointment. *Id.* Similarly, a power of appointment exists in a beneficiary's right to compel a trustee to sell trust assets and distribute the proceeds. *See* Ewing v. Rountree, 346 F.2d 471 (6th Cir. 1965); Maytag v. United States, 493 F.2d 995 (10th Cir. 1974).

Perhaps the most significant context in which powers of appointment arise is the fiduciary setting. A trustee's discretionary power to distribute income or principal among beneficiaries constitutes a power of appointment. Treas. Reg. § 20.2041-1(b)(1). Discretionary powers held by an individual serving as trustee therefore must be closely scrutinized for possible transfer tax consequences. So too must powers to remove and replace trustees, as powers of appointment in the fiduciary context can exist by attribution:

> A power in a donee to remove or discharge a trustee and appoint himself may be a power of appointment. For example, if under the terms of a trust instrument, the trustee or his successor has the power to appoint the principal of the trust for the

---

[3] Retained powers over beneficial enjoyment of property that trigger application of §§ 2036 or 2038 are expressly excluded from the scope of a power of appointment contemplated by § 2041. *See* Treas. Reg. § 20.2041-1(b)(2).

[4] *See* Revenue Act of 1942, Pub. L. No. 77-753, § 403, 56 Stat. 798, 942.

benefit of individuals including himself, and the decedent has the unrestricted power to remove or discharge the trustee at any time and appoint any other person including himself, the decedent is considered as having a power of appointment.

Treas. Reg. § 20.2041-1(b)(1). However, similar to § 2038, a decedent's power to appoint a successor trustee under conditions that did not exist at the time of his death will not cause the trustee's powers to be attributed to him.[5] *Id.*

Given the breadth of a power of appointment governed by § 2041, it is worth clarifying the interaction of this section with other inclusionary provisions of the estate tax. While the general definition of a power of appointment would cover retained powers over transferred property, the regulations avoid any such statutory overlap by excluding reserved powers governed by §§ 2036 to 2038. Treas. Reg. § 20.2041-1(b)(2). Hence, powers of appointment are limited to property transferred by one other than the individual possessing the power.

The breadth of a power of appointment also presents the possibility of equating a power of appointment with any ability to direct the disposition of property. As an initial matter, a power of appointment assumes a separation of title. That is, an individual cannot possess a power of appointment over property that he owns as a matter of state law. Treas. Reg. § 20.2041-1(b)(2); *see also* Treas. Reg. § 25.2514-3(e), Ex. 1 (assignment by income beneficiary of income stream to another does not constitute an exercise of a power of appointment; rather, the transaction constitutes a disposition of the beneficiary's income interest). Instead, an individual's exercise of the power to dispose of property he owns will give rise to a taxable gift under the general rule of § 2501 or, if occurring at death, will result in estate tax inclusion under § 2033.

However, if an individual can dispose of property that he does not own at the time of death through the terms of his will, a power of appointment exists. For example, consider a trust created by another for the lifetime benefit of *A*, remainder to *A*'s estate. Section 2033 likely will not capture the trust property in *A*'s estate due to *A*'s inability to dispose of the property during life. *See* Second Nat'l Bank v. Dallman, 209 F.2d 321 (7th Cir. 1954). *But see* Treas. Reg. § 20.2041-1(b)(2) (finding § 2033 applicable in this context notwithstanding the potential application of § 2041). Yet regardless of the applicability of § 2033, *A*'s ability to dispose of the property through the terms of his will provides *A* with a testamentary power of appointment. If this power is not restricted, the trust property will be captured in *A*'s gross estate under § 2041(a)(2). *See* Keeter v. United States, 461 F.2d 714, 719 (5th Cir. 1972) (explaining that "the substance of the settlement option [calling for the payment of insurance proceeds to the decedent's executor] was to grant an absolute power of appointment of the insurance principal and interest to [the decedent], exercisable at her death by her will").

§ 14.02 GENERAL POWERS OF APPOINTMENT

While the determination of whether a power of appointment exists for federal transfer tax purposes is important as a threshold matter, not all powers carry transfer tax consequences. In fact, the range of powers of appointment that implicate the estate tax and gift tax regimes is fairly limited. Outside of one narrow instance,[6] only a "general power of appointment" will

---

[5] *See* Treas. Reg. § 20.2038-1(a)(3), (b) (disregarding powers subject to conditions beyond the decedent's control that were not satisfied as of decedent's death). *But see* Treas. Reg. § 20.2036-1(b)(3) (stating that the failure of a condition to an exercise of a power is immaterial for § 2036 purposes).

[6] The exception relating to the exercise of any power of appointment to delay vesting is addressed in § 14.05, *infra.*

cause the subject property to be included in the transfer tax base of the holder.

Section 2041(b) defines a general power of appointment as one exercisable "in favor of the decedent, his estate, his creditors, or the creditors of his estate," and § 2514(c) employs the same definition with reference to the individual possessing the power. Note that the statutory definition is phrased in the disjunctive. Thus, the ability to appoint property to any one of the four enumerated objects will cause the power to be classified as general. *See* Edelman v. Commissioner, 38 T.C. 972 (1962).

Whether a power of appointment is in fact exercisable in favor of one of the four objects ultimately turns on the interpretation of the power under state law. *See* Rev. Rul. 76-502, 1976-2 C.B. 273 (stating that the breadth and scope of a power of appointment is a matter of state law); Jenkins v. United States, 428 F.2d 538 (5th Cir. 1970) (noting the possibility of state law to impose a restriction on the exercise of an otherwise general power of appointment). Nonetheless, the regulations under § 2041 provide a few noteworthy clarifications. First, a power that is exercisable in favor of individuals who also happen to be beneficiaries of the decedent's probate estate does not render the power exercisable in favor of the estate. Rather, for a power to be exercisable in favor of the decedent's estate under §§ 2041(b) and 2514(c), the appointed property must be available for the payment of administrative expenses and claims. Treas. Reg. § 20.2041-1(c)(1).

Additionally, the mere fact that a permissible appointee of the power is owed money by the power holder alone is not sufficient to render the power of appointment general in nature. *Id.* Instead, the grounds for exercise must relate to the satisfaction of a legal obligation of the power holder or of his estate for the power to be viewed as exercisable in favor of the power holder or his creditors. *Id.* As is the case in retained-interest transfers, particular attention must be paid to the existence and potential effect of support obligations. In Revenue Ruling 79-154, 1979-1 C.B. 301, the decedent possessed the ability to appoint insurance proceeds for the health, education, support, and maintenance of the decedent's children. Noting that the children were adults, the Service determined that the power was nongeneral. However, the ruling observed that the decedent would have possessed a general power of appointment had the decedent owed the children a duty of support that could have been satisfied through appointment of the property.

[A]　Ascertainable-Standard Exclusion

While a general power of appointment can be broadly conceived as one capable of being exercised to or for the benefit of the holder, an important and broad exception exists within this category. If a power capable of being exercised in favor of the decedent is limited by "an ascertainable standard relating to the health, education, support, or maintenance of the decedent," the power is not general in nature. IRC § 2041(b)(1)(A); *see also* IRC § 2514(c)(1). The exception has two distinct prongs: (1) the standard for exercise of the power must be "ascertainable" in the sense of its capability of being enforced by a court of equity, and (2) the standard must be expressed in terms of the holder's "health, education, support, or maintenance." *See* Hyde v. United States, 950 F. Supp. 418, 419 (D.N.H. 1996).

The regulations adopt a liberal view of the second requirement of the ascertainable-standard exception. The synonymous standards of "support" and "maintenance" are not limited to the "bare necessities of life." Treas. Reg. § 20.2041-1(c)(2). Accordingly, expressions of the standard of exercise phrased in terms of the power holder's "support in reasonable comfort," "maintenance in health and reasonable comfort," and "support in his accustomed manner of living" are administratively sanctioned. *Id.* Thus, as a practical matter, the ascertainable-standard exception is remarkably broad. The only items not covered by a well-crafted ascertainable standard would be extraordinary expenditures that fall outside the typical consumption pattern of the power holder.

Perhaps to no surprise, a wealth of litigation exists concerning whether certain expressions of standards for distribution satisfy the ascertainable-standard exception to the definition of a general power under §§ 2041 and 2514. In particular, the "happiness" of the power holder as a basis for exercise has proven problematic. *See* Rev. Rul. 82-63, 1982-1 C.B. 135 (holding that "happiness" provided the decedent with a power to consume outside the statutory ascertainable-standard exception, rejecting the contrary holding of *Brantingham v. United States*, 631 F.2d 542 (7th Cir. 1980)). Yet given the broad range of discretion afforded by the safe-harbor standards expressed in the statute and regulations, little benefit exists from drafting outside of these bounds.

[B]　Treatment of Joint Powers

Recall that in the context of retained-power transfers, the necessity of exercising a power in conjunction with another is irrelevant to the tax consequences of the power—even if the other party possesses an interest adverse to the exercise of the power.[7] The same dismissive treatment of joint powers does not apply to powers of appointment under §§ 2041 and 2514. Rather, the definition of a general power of appointment for these purposes recognizes the potentially limiting nature of jointly held powers.

[1]　Powers Exercisable with Creator

As a starting point, a power of appointment that can be exercised only in conjunction with the creator of the power is deemed nongeneral regardless of the objects of the power. IRC §§ 2041(b)(1)(C)(i); 2514(c)(3)(A). In that case, the estate or gift tax consequences of the power will be resolved with respect to the creator.

[2]　Powers Exercisable with Adverse Party

Subjecting the exercise of a power of appointment to the consent of another will negate general power classification if the co-holder of the power possesses a substantial interest in the property that is adverse to its exercise. IRC §§ 2041(b)(1)(C)(ii), 2514(c)(3)(B). The regulations attempt to clarify the meaning of a "substantial" interest for this purpose, although the attempt is unavailing: "An interest adverse to the exercise of a power is considered as substantial if its value in relation to the total value of the property subject to the power is not insignificant." Treas. Reg. §§ 20.2041-3(c)(2); 25.2514-3(b)(2). Instead, the heart of this exception turns on whether the co-holder possesses an interest in the property adverse to the exercise of the power.

As a starting point, mere possession of the power by a co-holder does not give rise to an adverse interest in the property. *Id.* Rather, the adverse-party rule "at the very least [requires] that the third person have a present or future chance to obtain a personal benefit from the property itself." Estate of Towle v. Commissioner, 54 T.C. 368, 372 (1970). The interest of a

---

[7] *See* Treas. Reg. §§ 20.2036-1(b)(3)(i), 20.2038-1(a).

trustee in preserving the principal of the trust so as to maximize fiduciary compensation does not constitute an adverse interest for purposes of the exception. *Id.*; *see also* Miller v. United States, 387 F.2d 866 (3d Cir. 1968). Rather, the adverse interest must relate to a beneficial interest in the property. Consistent with this approach, the regulations provide that the inclusion of the co-holder among the potential objects of the power does not alone constitute an adverse interest. Treas. Reg. §§ 20.2041-3(c)(2), 25.2514-3(b)(2). However, the statute overrides this rule in one instance: If the co-holder of the power will possess a general power of appointment in the property following the death of the holder whose power is being analyzed, the co-holder possesses an adverse interest under the rule. IRC §§ 2041(b)(1)(C)(ii), 2514(c)(3)(B). This exception is consistent with the theory that sole possession of a general power of appointment over property is tantamount to ownership for transfer tax purposes.

The regulations provide straightforward examples of beneficial interests in trusts that are adverse to the exercise of a lifetime general power of appointment in favor of the holder. *See* Treas. Reg. §§ 20.2041-3(c)(2), 25.2514-3(b)(2). As a general rule, a beneficiary's status as a taker in default of exercise of the power supplies the requisite adverse interest, *id.*, which recognizes that the taker in default essentially possesses a remainder interest in the property. In applying the adverse-interest exception, each power held by the decedent must be considered. For example, in Revenue Ruling 79-63, 1979-1 C.B. 302, the decedent held two powers of appointment. As trustee, he could appoint principal to himself with the consent of one of his children. Upon the decedent's death, the remainder was to be distributed to those of the decedent's children as he appointed by will and, in default thereof, to the decedent's children equally. Even though the child whose consent was required for the decedent to exercise the lifetime power was a taker in default of the remainder, the child's status as such did not constitute an adverse interest with respect to the lifetime power. The decedent could have eliminated the consenting child's interest in the trust remainder through the exercise of his testamentary power, which he held alone. Accordingly, a power holder's beneficial interest in property will not be adverse to the exercise of the power if such interest can be unilaterally defeated by the co-holder.

[3] Powers Held by Permissible Appointees

While the inclusion of the co-holder of a power among the permissible objects of the power's exercise does not provide an absolute exception for the power under the adverse-interest rule, a limited exception from the definition of a general power exists in this setting. The power will constitute a general power of appointment only to the extent of a fractional portion of the underlying property, with the fraction being determined by the number of co-holders in whose favor the power could be exercised. IRC §§ 2041(b)(1)(C)(iii), 2514(c)(3)(C). The effect of this treatment is to assume a degree of self-interested side contracting among the co-holders of the power, with one consenting to the exercise of the power in favor of the other only if the favor is returned.

[C] Nongeneral Powers

Powers of appointment that do not satisfy the definition of a power of appointment go by a number of labels. While "nongeneral" suffices, these powers often are described as "limited" or "special" powers of appointment. As discussed below, these powers can be possessed and, for the most part, exercised without triggering the gift tax or estate tax. Given the limited scope of a general power of appointment—particularly in light of the ascertainable-standard exception—nongeneral powers afford individuals the ability to confer significant discretion to a beneficiary over the use and ultimate disposition of property without subjecting the beneficiary to adverse transfer tax consequences.

§ 14.03 POSSESSION OF GENERAL POWER OF APPOINTMENT AT DEATH

The most common basis for the estate taxation of powers of appointment is the mere possession of a general power of appointment at the time of death. In that case, the value of the property over which the decedent could have exercised the general power will be included in the gross estate under § 2041(a)(2). As discussed below, the concept of the "possession" of a power of appointment for this purpose is based on the instrument granting the power rather than the unique circumstances relating to the power holder.

[A] Capacity to Exercise

An individual can possess a general power of appointment at death under § 2041(a)(2) even though he is incapable of exercising it as a matter of law. *See* Rev. Rul. 75-350, 1975-2 C.B. 366 (holder legally incompetent under state law due to mental disability); Rev. Rul. 75-351, 1975-2 C.B. 368 (holder legally incapable of exercising power through will due to minority). Numerous Circuit Courts of Appeals have addressed the issue, and all have upheld the Service's position that legal incompetency does not serve to defeat the application of § 2041(a)(2). *See, e.g.*, Boeving v. United States, 650 F.2d 493 (8th Cir. 1981) (citing other circuit decisions in accord).

If the absence of legal capacity is insufficient to avoid inclusion based on the existence of a general power of appointment, the same treatment must follow for the absence of the practical ability to exercise the power. In *Estate of Bagley v. United States*, 443 F.2d 1266 (5th Cir. 1971), a husband and wife died in a common accident. The terms of the husband's will created a trust for the wife's benefit in which she was granted a testamentary general power of appointment, and the husband's will further provided that the wife would be presumed to have survived him in the event of a common disaster. The court determined that the wife possessed a general power of appointment for purposes of § 2041(a)(2) over the assets that would have been used to fund the trust for her benefit—even though the couple died simultaneously.

In addition to capacity to exercise, knowledge of the existence of the power also is irrelevant for purposes of § 2041(a)(2). In *Estate of Freeman v. Commissioner*, 67 T.C. 202 (1976), the decedent was the income beneficiary of a trust his parents established for his benefit while he was a minor. In order to qualify contributions for the gift tax annual exclusion, the trust provided the decedent with an unlimited lifetime power to invade the trust corpus. However, the decedent was never provided with a copy of the trust instrument, and he was unaware of the withdrawal right provided to him. The Tax Court included the trust assets in his estate under § 2041(a)(2), viewing knowledge of the power merely as an aspect of the practical ability to exercise it.

[B] Conditions to Exercise

If the general power of appointment is exercisable only upon the occurrence of a contingency that did not occur prior to the decedent's death, the decedent will not be considered to have possessed the power for purposes of § 2041(a)(2). Treas. Reg. § 20.2041-3(b). Examples of conditions precedent sufficient to preclude existence of the power at the time of the decedent's death relate to matters beyond the decedent's unilateral control, such as attainment of a certain age, survival of another person, or death without surviving descendants. *Id.* However, the statute makes clear that subjecting an exercise of the power to a notice condition or delaying the effective date of an exercise of the power will not prevent the power from being considered in existence at the time of the decedent's death. IRC § 2041(a)(2).

In *Estate of Kurz v. Commissioner*, 101 T.C. 44 (1993), the decedent was a surviving spouse whose husband had created two testamentary trusts in her favor, the "Marital Trust" and the "Family Trust." The decedent possessed an unlimited general power of appointment over the assets of the Marital Trust. Additionally, the decedent could withdraw up to five percent of the value of the Family Trust annually—but only in the event the principal of the Marital Trust was completely exhausted. When the decedent died, that condition had not occurred. Accordingly, the estate argued that the decedent's general power of appointment over five percent of the Family Trust did not exist at the time of her death for purposes of § 2041(a)(2). The Tax Court rejected the government's assertion that only conditions that remain outside the decedent's control are effective to avoid application of § 2041(a)(2). Nonetheless, the court ruled for the government on the basis that the contingency was illusory for § 2041(a)(2) purposes:

> We do not think that, where the general power of appointment is the right to withdraw principal from a trust, Congress intended that application of section 2041(a)(2) could be avoided by stacking or ordering the withdrawal powers; i.e., exercising the power to withdraw a certain number of dollars before the power to withdraw the next portion comes into operation. A condition that has no significant non tax consequence independent of a decedent's power to appoint the property for her own benefit does not prevent practical ownership; it is illusory and should be ignored. We conclude that for purposes of section 2041, although the condition does not have to be beyond the decedent's control, it must have some significant non tax consequence independent of the decedent's power to appoint the property. Petitioner has not demonstrated that withdrawing principal from the Marital Trust Fund has any significant non tax consequence independent of decedent's power to withdraw principal from the Family Trust Fund. Such condition is illusory and, thus, is not an event or a contingency contemplated by the section 20.2041-3(b), Estate Tax Regs.

Id. at 60–61. On appeal, the Seventh Circuit was leery of distinguishing among conditions based on the presence of non-tax motives to justify them. *See* Estate of Kurz v. Commissioner, 68 F.3d 1027 (7th Cir. 1995). Instead, the court simply determined that the decedent possessed the power of appointment over the Family Trust through her ability to deplete the Marital Trust:

> Section 2041 is designed to include in the taxable estate all assets that the decedent possessed or effectively controlled. If only a lever must be pulled to dispense money, then the power is exercisable. The funds are effectively under the control of the beneficiary, which is enough to put them into the gross estate. Whether the lever is a

single-clutch or double-clutch mechanism can't matter. Imagine a trust divided into 1,000 equal funds numbered 1 to 1,000, Fund 1 of which may be invaded at any time, and Fund n of which may be reached if and only if Fund n-1 has been exhausted. Suppose the beneficiary depletes Funds 1 through 9 and dies when $10 remains in Fund 10. Under the Kurz Estate's view, only $10 is included in the gross estate, because Funds 11 through 1,000 could not have been touched until that $10 had been withdrawn. But that would be a ridiculously artificial way of looking at things. Tax often is all about form, see *Howell v. United States*, 775 F.2d 887 (7th Cir. 1985), but § 2041 is an anti-formal rule. It looks through the trust to ask how much wealth the decedent actually controlled at death. The decedent's real wealth in our hypothetical is $10 plus the balance of Funds 11 through 1,000; the decedent could have withdrawn and spent the entire amount in a trice. Whether this series of trusts has spendthrift features (as the Kurz trusts did) or is invested in illiquid instruments (as the Kurz trusts were) would not matter. The Estate does not deny that Kurz had a general power of appointment over the entire Marital Trust, despite these features. If the costs of removing wealth from the trust do not prevent including in the gross estate the entire corpus of the first trust in a sequence (they don't), then the rest of the sequence also is includable.

Id. at 1029.

§ 14.04 EXERCISE OR RELEASE OF GENERAL POWER OF APPOINTMENT

[A] Exercise

If possession of a general power of appointment over property is tantamount to ownership for transfer tax purposes, then the holder's exercise of the power should be regarded as a transfer of property. Section 2514(b) supplies this rule. That is not to say that every exercise of a general power of appointment results in a taxable gift. Rather, gift tax principles take over once the exercise is deemed a transfer of property. For example, an individual's exercise of a power to withdraw corpus from a trust does not constitute a taxable gift, as one cannot make a gift to oneself. Furthermore, an exercise of a general power of appointment in favor of a trust of which the power holder serves as trustee may constitute an incomplete gift, if the interests of the trust beneficiaries can be altered through the exercise of the trustee's discretion. *See* Treas. Reg. § 25.2511-2(b), (c).

The exercise of a power of appointment can occur indirectly. For instance, suppose that an individual possesses a general power of appointment over trust property (such as a right of withdrawal) as well as a nongeneral power (such as the discretionary ability to distribute trust assets to children). If the scope of the right of withdrawal is defined as a percentage of the trust estate, an exercise of the nongeneral power will diminish the amount of property over which the general power extends. In that case, the diminishment of the value of the property subject to the general power constitutes an exercise of the general power. *See* Treas. Reg. § 25.2514-1(d).

[B] Release

A release of a general power of appointment can be conceptualized as an exercise of the power in favor of the takers in default. Section 2514(b) therefore places an exercise and release of a general power on the same footing. Both are regarded as transfers of property by the power holder.

A release of a power of appointment need not be formal or express in character. Treas. Reg. § 25.2514-3(c)(4); *see also* Treas. Reg. § 20.2041-3(d)(1). Revenue Ruling 86-39, 1986-1 C.B. 301, provides an interesting example of an indirect release of a power of appointment. The ruling concerned an individual who was an income beneficiary of two trusts, Trust A and Trust B. The beneficiary possessed a general power over Trust A, but not Trust B. Each trust held stock in a corporation which undertook a recapitalization with the consent of the trustees. While the combined value of the recapitalized stock held by Trust A and Trust B remained constant, the recapitalization had the effect of decreasing the value of stock held by Trust A and increasing the value of the stock held by Trust B. The ruling held that the beneficiary, by signing an agreement releasing the trustee of Trust A from liability for consenting to the depletion of trust assets, effectively released the power of appointment over Trust A to the extent of the decrease in value. Accordingly, the beneficiary was treated as making a contribution to Trust B to the extent of its increased value.

While Revenue Ruling 86-39 addressed a partial release of a general power of appointment in the sense of a complete termination of the power over a portion of the subject property, releases of general powers can be partial in terms of the objects of the power. For example, suppose *Parent* serves as trustee of a trust created for the lifetime benefit of his only children, *A* and *B*. Income payments are to be made equally to *A* and *B* for their joint lifetimes, and then all to the survivor. Upon the death of *A* and *B*, the trust is to be distributed to *Parent's* then-living issue, *per stirpes*. Additionally, *Parent* as trustee may distribute the trust corpus to himself, *A*, or *B* in such amounts as he deems appropriate. Several years after the trust is created, *Parent* renounces the ability to distribute principal to himself. While *Parent* will no longer possess a general power of appointment, the partial release nonetheless does not give rise to a taxable gift because *Parent* retains the ability to alter the interests of *A* and *B*. *See* Treas. Reg. § 25.2514-3(c)(1). However, if *Parent* thereafter resigns as trustee (together with the ability to serve in the future), his resignation completes the gift because his ability to alter the beneficial interests of others terminates.

[C] Disclaimer of Power

A qualified disclaimer of a general power of appointment within the meaning of § 2518 does not constitute a release of the power for gift tax purposes. *See* Treas. Reg. § 25.2514-3(c)(5). While the transfer tax treatment of disclaimers is addressed in Chapter 16, a primary requirement for a disclaimer to be qualified under § 2518 is that it take place within nine months of the transfer creating the interest. *See* IRC § 2518(b)(2). This requirement can prove problematic in cases such as *Estate of Freeman* where the power holder is not made aware of existence of the power.

[D]   Exercise or Release to Accomplish Testamentary Transfer

Recall that the retained-interest and retained-power provisions of §§ 2036 through 2038 are conditioned upon a transfer of property by the decedent. Because the exercise of a general power of appointment literally does not constitute a transfer by the donor, quasi-testamentary transfers of this sort that are funded through the exercise of a general power could escape the estate tax base. Section 2041(a)(2) forecloses this possibility. If the exercise or release of a general power of appointment results in a disposition that would have been included in the decedent's gross estate under §§ 2035-2038 had the disposition been a transfer of property owned by the decedent, then § 2041(a)(2) captures in the gross estate the property over which the power was exercised or released. This aspect of § 2041(a)(2) effectively treats the exercise or release of a general power in this context as a transfer of property by the power holder.

Returning to the hypothetical trust involving *Parent* in § 14.04[B] above, note that *Parent's* release of the ability to appoint principal to himself is not sufficient to avoid subjecting the trust assets to estate taxation. Rather, the trust property would be included in *Parent's* gross estate under § 2041(a)(2) through the would-be application of § 2036(a)(2).

§ 14.05   LAPSE OF A GENERAL POWER OF APPOINTMENT

A lapse of a power of appointment occurs when the power expires unexercised. As a general rule, a lapse of a general power of appointment is treated in the same manner as a release—that is, as the equivalent of exercise. IRC § 2041(b)(2), § 2514(e). Yet the general rule applies only after a generous exclusion is surpassed. Specifically, the lapse of a general power is treated as a release only to the extent the property which could have been appointed through the exercise of all such powers that lapsed during a given calendar year exceeds the greater of: (a) $5,000 or (b) five percent of the aggregate value of the assets (determined at the time of the lapse) out of which the exercise of the lapsed powers could have been satisfied. Note that, much like the gift tax annual exclusion, the so-called "Five or Five" exception to the general treatment of a lapse of a general power of appointment as a release is renewed on an annual basis.

As a result of the Five or Five exception, general powers of appointment that are designed to lapse within the limits of the Five or Five limitation—most commonly, *Crummey* rights of withdrawal provided to beneficiaries of an irrevocable trust[8]—are exempt from transfer tax consequences altogether. As an example, suppose that a trust is funded for the lifetime benefit of an individual, with the remainder being distributed to the individual's then-living issue upon his death. The trust is funded with $400,000, and the trust principal earns a positive rate of return each year. If the trust provides the beneficiary with a non-cumulative right to withdraw $13,000 each year, the annual lapse of the general power will not trigger gift or estate tax consequences. While the $5,000 limitation obviously is exceeded, the five percent limitation equals at least $20,000 in this case. Thus, the Five or Five exception fully shields the lapse from transfer tax consequences.

Suppose now that the beneficiary is afforded the right to withdraw an amount greater than $13,000 each year, say $30,000. In order to avoid possible gift or estate tax consequences from the lapse of the power, the extent the power lapses must be defined by reference to the Five

---

[8] For a discussion of the use of *Crummey* rights of withdrawal to avoid the future-interest prohibition on the gift tax annual exclusion, see § 5.01[B].

or Five formula. That is, the annual lapse of the power must be limited to the greater of $5,000 or five percent of the trust assets (valued at the time of lapse), with any withdrawal rights in excess of that amount remaining in effect and carrying over to the next year. The five percent threshold will prove sufficient to fully exempt each year's $30,000 withdrawal right when the trust principal grows to $600,000. As the trust principal exceeds the $600,000 level, the five percent threshold will permit portions of withdrawal rights carrying over from prior years to lapse under the Five or Five exception. Rights of withdrawal over trust contributions that are designed to lapse in this manner are often used in the context of irrevocable trusts that own life insurance policies, and they are commonly referred to as "hanging powers."

In situations where the hanging-power technique is not employed and the lapse is not fully shielded by the Five or Five exception, calculating the precise estate tax consequences of the lapse can be complicated. Taking the example above concerning a $30,000 withdrawal right over a trust initially funded with $400,000 and assuming that the withdrawal right lapses in full each year, the lapse will exceed the initial five percent threshold by $10,000. Because the trust beneficiary possesses an income interest in the trust, the deemed $10,000 release of the power eventually will result in a portion of the trust assets being included in the power holder's gross estate under § 2041(a)(2) (because an outright transfer of property to the trust would have been captured under § 2036(a)(1)).[9] The difficulty arises in transferring the $10,000 release to the date-of-death value of the trust assets. A sensible approach for determining the inclusion amount is to measure the amount of the "excess lapse" each year as a percentage of the then-prevailing value of the trust assets, and then to apply that percentage to the date-of-death value of the trust. Treas. Reg. § 20.2041-3(d)(4). In this case, the $10,000 lapse would result in inclusion of 2.5 percent of the date-of-death value of the trust property under § 2041(a)(2). Of course, the combined percentage of the trust assets subject to inclusion under this approach cannot exceed 100 percent.

§ 14.06 EXERCISE OF ANY POWER OF APPOINTMENT TO POSTPONE VESTING

While powers of appointment generally carry transfer tax consequences only if they are general in nature, the exercise of a nongeneral power can trigger gift or estate tax consequences in one narrow context. Under § 2514(d), if *any* power of appointment is exercised by creating another power of appointment that can be validly exercised to postpone the vesting of the subject property for a period that is that can be ascertained without reference to the date of the first power, then the exercise of the first power is treated as a transfer of property. Section 2041(a)(3) provides a corollary rule for powers that are exercised in this manner (a) by will or (b) during life through a disposition that accomplishes a transfer that would trigger inclusion under §§ 2035 through 2037 had the disposition been a transfer of the decedent's own property.

While these rules may be a bit cumbersome, the concept is straightforward. If the exercise of a nongeneral power to create a nongeneral power in another escaped transfer tax consequences, this act could be replicated indefinitely to pass property through generations

---

[9] In addition, the $10,000 release would be treated as a transfer of property by the beneficiary to the trust. IRC § 2514(b). Assuming the beneficiary's lifetime interest in the trust is not a qualified interest under § 2702(b), the transfer will result in a gift to the beneficiary's issue (for which no annual exclusion is available) of the full $10,000 transfer. *See* § 10.05[B].

without triggering gift or estate tax. The GST tax would supply the only transfer tax obstacle, and it will not apply in all instances.[10] However, as a practical matter, perpetuities restrictions under local law significantly limit the potential application of § 2041(a)(3) and § 2514(d). These provisions therefore are potentially relevant only in jurisdictions that have either abolished or significantly relaxed the Rule Against Perpetuities.

§ 14.07 ESTATE TAX APPORTIONMENT

Liability for the estate tax rests on the executor of the estate. IRC § 2002. Thus, the beneficiaries of the decedent's probate estate could be forced to shoulder the burden of the estate tax resulting from the inclusion of appointive property in the gross estate under § 2041. Section 2207 addresses this possibility by providing the executor with a federal right of recovery of the average (as opposed to marginal) estate tax liability attributable to the amounts included in the gross estate under § 2041 from the person receiving the property by way of exercise, nonexercise, or release of the power.[11]

The § 2207 right of recovery is not absolute. Rather, it can be waived by the decedent through a contrary provision in the decedent's will. Thus, as is the case in other contexts, careful attention must be paid to the drafting of the tax apportionment clause contained in the decedent's will. In particular, drafters should be aware of the consequences of directing that all tax obligations be paid from the residue of the decedent's probate estate.

§ 14.08 STUDY PROBLEMS

1. A client wants to create a trust for her daughter under the terms of her will. She not only wants to give the daughter as much control and access to the trust assets as possible, she also would like any trust property that the daughter does not need to pass to the daughter's surviving children without subjecting the trust assets to future estate or gift taxation. What suggestions do you have?

2. A client wishes to place assets in trust for the lifetime benefit of her son, but she desires to restrict her son's access to the trust principal to the greatest extent possible. Yet, because the client has already exhausted her GST exemption and because she does not anticipate that her son will have a taxable estate of his own, it would be advantageous to cause the trust assets to be included in the son's gross estate at the time of his death. How can § 2041 be used to accomplish the client's goals?

3. David, a client of yours, is the trustee of a trust created under the terms of his father's will. The trust provides that the trustee shall distribute the net income of the trust to David at least annually. Additionally, the trustee has discretion to distribute trust principal to any of David and his children in such amounts and proportions as the trustee determines appropriate. Upon David's death, the trust assets are to be distributed among those of David's then-living issue as David shall direct by will or, in

---

[10] For instance, a trust could have been established prior to the enactment of the GST tax, or a trust could be fully exempt from the GST tax through application of the GST tax exemption. The GST tax is addressed in Chapters 21 and 22.

[11] However, in order to prevent reduction of the marital deduction under § 2056 through this method of apportionment, the § 2207 right of recovery does not exist against property received by a surviving spouse for which a marital deduction is available.

default thereof, to David's then-living issue, *per stirpes*.

    a.   David has requested your advice concerning the potential estate tax consequences to him stemming from the trust.

    b.   Suppose David exercises his discretion as trustee to distribute principal to his children. What are the gift tax consequences, if any, of the distribution?

    c.   After hearing your advice, David says, "You know what, I should just resign as trustee." What gift tax consequences and future estate tax consequences would be triggered by David's resignation?

    d.   What changes would you have suggested to the trust if you had the opportunity to review the will prior to its execution?

4.   Steve creates a trust for the benefit of his son, Spalding, a bachelor with a record of spending family funds improvidently. Steve therefore names Spalding's more responsible brother, Wilson, to serve as a co-trustee along with Spalding. The trustees have complete discretion to distribute income or principal to Spalding as the trustees see fit. Upon Spalding's death, the trust will be distributed to his issue, otherwise to Wilson or to Wilson's issue if he is not then living. Currently, Spalding has no children.

    a.   Does Spalding possess a general power of appointment over the trust property?

    b.   Would your answer change if Spalding had a living child?

5.   Katherine has created an irrevocable trust to take title to life insurance policies on her life. Her daughters, Ella and Emma, are designated as co-trustees. During Katherine's lifetime, the trustees possess discretion to distribute trust assets to Katherine to the extent the trustees see fit. Upon Katherine's death, the proceeds of the life insurance policies will remain in trust, and the trustees will have discretion to distribute trust principal to any of Katherine's descendants as they determine appropriate. Upon the death of the second of Ella and Emma, the trust assets will be distributed to Katherine's then-living descendants, *per stirpes*.

    a.   During Katherine's lifetime, the insurance premiums contributed by Katherine to the trust are in the neighborhood of $20,000 annually. The trust agreement provides that Ella and Emma each possess a non-cumulative right to withdraw one-half of any contributions made to the trust in a given year. The insurance policy has no cash value at the outset, and the cash value slowly grows to $100,000 at the time of Katherine's death.

        i.   What are the transfer tax consequences of the withdrawal powers to Ella and Emma?

        ii.   What revisions would you suggest be made to the trust instrument?

    b.   Apart from the transfer tax consequences stemming from their withdrawal rights, would Ella and Emma face any transfer tax exposure by reason of their service as trustees following Katherine's death?

Chapter 15

ANNUITIES AND SURVIVOR BENEFITS

Internal Revenue Code:	§ 2039
	see also §§ 2033, 2036(a)(1), 2038(a)(1), 7520(a)
Treasury Regulations:	§§ 20.2039-1, 20.2036-1(c)(2)(i), 25.2511-1(h)(10)
	see also §§ 20.2031-7 & -8(a), 20.7520-1 & -3(b)(3)

One of the more elusive goals of the Service has been to subject survivor benefits provided by the decedent's employer to federal transfer taxation. Recall that attempts to include employer-provided death benefits in the decedent's gross estate under § 2033 failed on the basis that the decedent did not possess a sufficient interest in the benefit payments at the time of his death.[1] On the gift tax front, the government's attempt to tax survivor payments (valued at the time of the decedent's death) failed for want of a lifetime transfer by the decedent.[2] In addition, courts at one point were of the view that an employer-provided death benefit for which the employee did not explicitly negotiate in lieu of additional salary precluded the application of § 2038 for want of a transfer of property by the employee.[3] Thus, after rounds of litigation, the carefully crafted employer-provided death benefit plan emerged as a means of supplying wealth to beneficiaries without transfer tax consequence.

Citing the lack of clarity surrounding the estate tax treatment of employer-provided survivor benefits,[4] Congress enacted § 2039 as part of the Internal Revenue Code of 1954 to remove existing ambiguities in this area. Section 2039 includes in the decedent's gross estate the value of any annuity or other payment receivable by a beneficiary by reason of surviving the decedent under any contract or arrangement (other than insurance) if the annuity or other payment was payable to the decedent or if the decedent possessed the right to receive such annuity or payment for his life, for any period not ascertainable without reference to his death, or for any period which does not in fact end before his death. Although enacted for the purpose of addressing employer-provided death benefits, § 2039 extends to survivor benefits provided under commercial annuity contracts purchased by the decedent.

---

[1] See discussion in § 2.04[B].

[2] See discussion in § 3.02[C].

[3] As discussed in *infra* § 15.01[E], however, the transfer requirement of § 2038(a)(1) no longer serves as an obstacle to the application of that statute to employer-provided death benefits.

[4] In its report accompanying the enactment of § 2039, the Senate recognized that "[i]t is not clear under existing law whether [a joint-and-survivor annuity] purchased by the decedent's employer, or an annuity to which both the decedent and his employer made contributions is includible in the decedent's gross estate." S. Rep. No. 83-1622, at 123 (1954).

Although § 2039 provides a basis for including annuity or other survivor benefits in the decedent's gross estate, it does not operate on an exclusive basis. To the extent § 2039 does not apply, such benefits can be included under other sections. *See* Treas. Reg. § 20.2039-1(a); *see also* S. Rep. No. 83-1622, at 472 (1954) ("The provisions of this section shall not prevent the application of any other provision of law relating to the estate tax."). In that regard, §§ 2033, 2036, and 2038 continue to have potential application in the annuity context. These other more general inclusionary provisions will be addressed prior to delving into the specifics of § 2039.

§ 15.01   ESTATE TAX CONSEQUENCES OUTSIDE OF § 2039

[A]   Single-Life Annuities

Suppose an individual purchases a single-life annuity in order to ensure a steady stream of cash for the remainder of his life. Because the annuity payments will terminate upon his death, § 2033 has no application to the arrangement.[5] The recapture provisions of the estate tax similarly have no application to a single-life annuity. While it is possible that a portion of the annuity purchase price will remain undistributed as of the annuitant's death, the retention of that amount by the annuity issuer does not result from a gratuitous transfer. Rather, the annuity purchase price represented the fair market value of the future payment stream the annuity issuer was obligated to provide. Hence, the straightforward single-life annuity triggers no estate tax consequence. That stands to reason, as the transaction simply represents an investment of the individual's funds. Although the purchase of a single-life annuity may affect the size of the decedent's gross estate in a specific case—that is, the gross estate may be augmented if the decedent surpasses his life expectancy and diminished if the decedent dies prematurely—the arrangements should pose no revenue loss to the government in the aggregate.

While standard single-life annuities do not trigger estate tax consequences, § 2033 can be implicated by common variations to the standard arrangement. For instance, an individual who does not wish to bear the investment risk of dying prematurely may opt for a contract that provides a refund of premiums paid in excess of annuity payments received. Such a refund, generally payable into the decedent's probate estate, would be captured in the gross estate under § 2033. In a similar vein, a single-life annuity can be modified to provide for a minimum number of payments, with the minimum payments remaining as of the decedent's death being paid to his probate estate. In that event, the present value of the remaining annuity stream will be included in the decedent's gross estate under § 2033. State lottery winnings provide an example of such an arrangement. Suppose that an individual wins a lottery that advertises a $20 million jackpot, the proceeds of which are to be paid to the winner in 20 annual installments of $1 million. However, the winner dies after receiving the first 12 installments. The remaining eight annuity payments will be paid to the decedent's estate as they become due. In this instance, § 2033 will capture the fair market value of the remaining annuity stream in the lottery winner's gross estate.[6]

---

[5] Note that to the extent the individual does not consume the periodic annuity payments he receives, his gross estate will be augmented by the saved amounts.

[6] As a general rule, the value of the future payment stream will be determined under tables prescribed by § 7520, which presume a statutory discount rate. *See* Treas. Reg. §§ 20.7520-1(a); 20.2031-7(a), (d). A prominent split has emerged among courts concerning whether valuation under the § 7520 tables can be abandoned by reason of the

[B] Private Annuities

The failure of a standard single-life annuity to trigger estate tax consequences offers an opportunity for tax planning. In the context of commercially issued annuities, an annuitant essentially loses his bet with the insurance company if he does not reach his actuarial life expectancy. This investment loss, however, can represent a tax-free gratuitous transfer of wealth when the counterparty to the contract is a family member or other intended beneficiary of the annuitant. Taxpayers have employed the so-called "private annuity" to exploit the valuation method prescribed by § 7520. The purchase of the annuity cannot constitute a gift to the issuer if purchased for its fair market value, and § 7520 mandates, as a general rule, that annuities be valued under actuarial tables published by the Secretary based on a statutory discount rate. *See* Treas. Reg. §§ 25.7520-1(a); 20.2031-7(a), (d). If the fair market value of the annuity prescribed by the tables effectively over-values the future payment stream—either because the statutory discount rate is too low or, as is more likely the case, the annuitant does not anticipate reaching his actuarial life expectancy—the difference between the § 7520 value and the true fair market value of the annuity passes to the annuity issuer free of federal transfer tax. Of course, the ability to exploit the § 7520 valuation tables in this manner has its limits. Namely, if the annuitant suffers from a terminal illness at the time of the annuity purchase, use of the actuarial tables is precluded. *See* Treas. Reg. § 25.7520-3(b)(3). For this purpose, an individual known to have an incurable illness or other deteriorating condition is considered terminally ill if there is at least a 50 percent chance that he will die within one year.[7] *Id.*

Note that the private annuity technique has some downside risk to the parties. If the annuitant lives past his presumed life expectancy, the arrangement could lead to a transfer of wealth from the family member or other beneficiary to the annuitant—exactly the opposite of the intended result.[8] Hence, private annuities are most appropriate in situations where the annuitant's health condition makes it unlikely that he will reach his actuarial life expectancy, but not so certain to preclude use of the § 7520 tables.

---

estate's inability to make a present transfer of the future payment rights. *See* Estate of Gribauskas v. Commissioner, 342 F.3d 85 (2d Cir. 2003) (finding that the taxpayer met its burden of establishing that the tabular valuation produced a substantially unreasonable or unrealistic result); Shackleford v. United States, 262 F.3d 1028 (9th Cir. 2001) (permitting departure from actuarial tables on the basis that the inability to market the annuity payments prevented the tabular valuation from reasonably approximating fair market value). *But see* Negron v. United States, 553 F.3d 1013 (6th Cir. 2009) (finding that lack of marketability did not render use of valuation tables unreasonable, reasoning that non-marketability of a private annuity constitutes an underlying assumption of the tables); Cook v. Commissioner, 349 F.3d 850 (5th Cir. 2003) (same). The circuits upholding the use of the § 7520 tables in this context have the more reasoned position. *See* Wendy C. Gerzog, *Actuarial Tables Versus Factually Based Estate Tax Valuation: Ithaca Trust Re-Visited*, 38 Real Prop. Prob. & Tr. J. 745 (2004).

[7] However, if the individual survives 18 months after the date of the transaction, he will be presumed to not have been terminally ill at the time of the transaction unless clear and convincing evidence exists to the contrary. *See* Treas. Reg. § 25.7520-3(b)(3).

[8] The private annuity technique is subject to other estate tax challenges depending on the circumstances. In particular, the prospect of inclusion under § 2036 is raised if the annuity issuer is contractually or practically obligated to look to the property used to purchase the annuity or the income such property generates to fund the annuity payments.

[C] Survivor Annuities

Annuity contracts are often purchased not only to provide a stream of cash flow for the purchaser, but also for the lifetime of another—typically a spouse. For example, suppose *Wife* purchased a "self-and-survivor" annuity contract that required payments to be made to her for the balance of her lifetime, with payments continuing to *Husband* for his lifetime in the event *Husband* survives *Wife*. Note that if *Wife* were to predecease *Husband*, the value of the continuing annuity payments to *Husband* would be included in *Wife's* gross estate under § 2039. Yet, prior to the enactment of § 2039, the government achieved the same result by invoking § 2036. The theory behind the application of § 2036 was that *Wife*, through the retention of annuity payments for her lifetime, retained the economic enjoyment of the transferred property. As explained by the Ninth Circuit in *Commissioner v. Clise*, 122 F.2d 998 (9th Cir. 1941), such an annuity arrangement was akin to a transfer in trust under which the transferor retained an annual payment to be satisfied out of trust income and principal, with the trust remainder being paid to intended beneficiaries. *See also* Forster v. Sauber, 249 F.2d 379 (7th Cir. 1957) (following *Clise*, and analogizing the annuity arrangement to the retention of a life interest in the transferred property).

The analogy to a § 2036(a)(1) trust arrangement is less than perfect. The annuity payment to the transferor need not equal the income generated from the transferred property. Rather, the annuity payment could be less than the entire income or the payment could exhaust all income while requiring invasion of principal.[9] Yet courts have found the analogy to a retained income interest in a trust sufficient, and have rejected taxpayer arguments that no shifting of property occurred by reason of the primary annuitant's death. *See, e.g., Clise*, 122 F.2d at 1003. The predecessor to § 2036(a)(1) was determined to apply not only to survivor benefits under self-and-survivor annuity contracts, but also to such benefits under "joint-and-survivor" contracts where the initial payments are made to both annuitants jointly. *See* Estate of Mearkle v. Commissioner, 129 F.2d 386 (3d Cir. 1942). Thus, while § 2039 removes any doubt regarding the estate tax consequences of these arrangements, the enactment of § 2039 was not necessary to bring survivor annuity benefits of this sort within the scope of the estate tax.[10]

[D] Grantor Retained Annuity Trusts

While § 2039 may have eclipsed § 2036 as it applies to survivor annuity payments, § 2036 remains the exclusive source of inclusion for one prominent estate-planning technique: the grantor retained annuity trust (GRAT). Recall that under § 2702(b), a grantor's right to receive a fixed amount each year from property transferred in trust constitutes a "qualified interest" that will not be disregarded in valuing the gift of the remainder.[11] In order to

---

[9] In fact, all that can be said is that the parties anticipated that the transferred property and the income it generates would be expended by the annuity issuer over the course of the lifetime of the primary annuitant and the surviving annuitant (commercial profit aside).

[10] In enacting § 2039, the Senate noted that "[u]nder present law the value at the decedent's death of a joint and survivor annuity purchased by him is includible in his gross estate." S. Rep. No. 83-1622, at 123 (1954). The primary purpose of § 2039 was to extend this treatment to similar annuities that were purchased by the decedent's employer. *Id.*

[11] Such fixed amount can be expressed as a percentage of the fair market value of the transferred property, as finally determined for federal transfer tax purposes. *See* Treas. Reg. § 25.2702-3(b)(1)(ii).

minimize the value of this gift, if not reduce it to zero,[12] grantors commonly retain an annuity for a term of years that will continue to be paid to the grantor's probate estate if the grantor does not survive the annuity term. While the amount and basis of inclusion in the grantor's gross estate if the grantor failed to survive the annuity term was somewhat unclear, the Service issued regulations addressing the matter in 2008. The regulations under § 2039 clarify that the estate tax treatment of GRATs and similar retained-interest trusts in both the charitable and non-charitable contexts is governed exclusively by § 2036. *See* Treas. Reg. § 20.2039-1(e). The regulations under § 2036, in turn, provide that the retention of a right to an annuity from property transferred in trust for the decedent's life, for any period not ascertainable without reference to his death, or for any period that does not in fact end before the decedent's death, "constitutes the retention of the possession or enjoyment of, or the right to the income from, the property for purposes of section 2036." Treas. Reg. § 20.2036-1(c)(2)(i). The portion of the GRAT principal that is included in the grantor's gross estate under § 2036 is that portion necessary to pay the annuity amount without invading principal, capped at the fair market value of the trust principal. *Id.* In the vast majority of cases—particularly those concerning short-term GRATs—the inclusion formula will capture the entire trust principal as of the decedent's death. Hence, a GRAT is an effective tax planning tool only if the grantor survives the annuity term.

[E]   Employer-Provided Death Benefits Capable of Designation

Prior to the enactment of § 2039, it appeared that employer-provided death benefits fell outside the scope of § 2038 based on the absence of a lifetime transfer by the decedent-employee. *See* Saxton v. Commissioner, 12 T.C. 569 (1949); Hanner v. Glenn, 111 F. Supp. 52 (W.D. Ky. 1953). However, that is no longer the prevailing view. *See* Estate of Tully, 528 F.2d 1401 (Ct. Cl. 1976); Estate of Siegel v. Commissioner, 74 T.C. 613 (1980). In Revenue Ruling 76-304, 1976-2 C.B. 269, the Service held that the transfer requirement of § 2038(a)(1) was satisfied where the decedent, through the performance of services during the course of employment, "procured the transfer by the decedent's employer" of the relevant death benefit.

The removal of the "transfer" obstacle to the application of § 2038(a)(1) to employer-provided death benefits alone does not ensure that the statute will be implicated in this context. Rather, the decedent-employee must have possessed the power to alter, amend, revoke, or terminate the death benefit. This retained power must have been "demonstrable, real, apparent and evident, not speculative." *Estate of Tully*, 528 F.2d at 1404. While the right to designate the beneficiary of the death benefit constitutes such a power, see Rev. Rul. 76-304,[13] the mere practical ability to alter or amend the death benefit alone is insufficient. For instance, the practical ability to terminate the death benefit through voluntary cessation of employment does not constitute a § 2038(a)(1) retained power. *See* Estate of Whitworth v. Commissioner, T.C. Memo. 1963-41, 22 T.C.M. (CCH) 177. Furthermore, the ability to revoke a death benefit payable to a surviving spouse through the procurement of a divorce does not implicate the statute. *See Estate of Tully*, 528 F.2d at 1406. Hence, a naked survivor's benefit paid by the decedent's employer will escape inclusion under § 2038 as long as the decedent-

---

[12] The use of a fixed term annuity payable to the grantor's estate in the event of death during the annuity term to actuarially zero-out the value of the transferred remainder (a "zeroed-out GRAT") is illustrated in *Walton v. Commissioner*, 115 T.C. 589 (2000).

[13] Furthermore, an express contractual provision permitting an employee to individually modify a death benefit with the consent of his employer implicates § 2038(a)(1). *See* Estate of Siegel v. Commissioner, 74 T.C. 613 (1980).

employee does not retain an express, contractual power relating to the benefit.

§ 15.02   SECTION 2039

Despite the limited application of §§ 2033, 2036, and 2038 to annuity arrangements, § 2039 serves as the primary authority concerning the inclusion of survivor payments in a decedent's gross estate. Drafted with a self-and-survivor or joint-and-survivor annuity in mind, the statute captures the fair market value of the payment stream to the survivor to the extent of the decedent's proportional contributions to the purchase price of the arrangement. IRC § 2039(a), (b). The primary contribution of the statute is its treatment of employer-funded benefits. Any portion of the purchase price of the annuity contract or other agreement that was provided by an employer of the decedent for any reason connected with his employment is considered to have been provided by the decedent himself. IRC § 2039(b); Treas. Reg. § 20.2039-1(c).

While the general rule of § 2039(a) appears straightforward at first glance, the host of prerequisites renders the statute more complicated in practice. In order for survivor payments to be included under § 2039, three conditions must be satisfied: (1) the decedent must have been receiving "an annuity or other payment" or must have possessed the right to receive such annuity or payment for his life, for any period not ascertainable without reference to his death, or for any period which does not in fact end before his death,[14] either alone or in conjunction with another person; (2) an annuity or other payment must have been receivable by any beneficiary by reason of surviving the decedent; and (3) the payments to both the decedent and the beneficiary must have been pursuant to a contract or other agreement other than life insurance on the life of the decedent. The specifics of these three conditions are explored below, with an emphasis on employer-provided benefits.

[A]   Necessity of Contract or Agreement

Both the payments to the decedent and the payments to the beneficiary by reason of surviving the decedent under § 2039 must be paid pursuant to a "contract or agreement." The regulations elaborate on this requirement, defining the phrase broadly to include "any arrangement, understanding or plan, or any combination of arrangements, understandings, or plans arising by reason of the decedent's employment." Treas. Reg. § 20.2039-1(b)(1). Hence, the statute extends beyond the realm of enforceable arrangements to capture informal arrangements that may exist in the employment context. Furthermore, all employer-provided benefits must be considered together in determining whether the decedent and beneficiary payment conditions of the statute are satisfied. Simply segregating payment streams under different benefit programs is not a sufficient means of avoiding the reach of § 2039.[15] This aggregation approach presumably applies outside the employment context as well. In other words, a decedent's purchase of a single-life annuity followed by the purchase of an annuity contract providing for payments to a designated beneficiary only upon the decedent's death most likely would be combined for purposes of determining the application of § 2039 to the beneficiary's payment stream.

---

[14]   The period for which the decedent must possess future payment rights is identical to the language used in § 2036, and is to be interpreted in the same manner. *See* Treas. Reg. § 20.2039-1(b)(1).

[15]   As the regulations to § 2039 state, the scope of the statute "cannot be limited by indirection." Treas. Reg. § 20.2039-1(b), Ex. 6.

Despite the breadth of the contract or agreement required under § 2039, it does not include payments that are paid by statute. Hence, if a decedent were receiving Social Security payments at the time of his death and survivor benefits continued in favor of his spouse, the survivor benefits would not be subject to inclusion under § 2039. *See* Rev. Rul. 81-182, 1981-2 C.B. 179; *see also* Rev. Rul. 76-102, 1976-1 C.B. 272 (benefits paid under Federal Coal Mine Health and Safety Act); Rev. Rul. 79-397, 1979-2 C.B. 322 (benefits paid under Public Safety Officers' Benefit Act).

Furthermore, by way of parenthetical exclusion, § 2039 does not apply to payments made to a surviving beneficiary that constitute insurance under a policy insuring the life to the decedent. Instead, the estate tax consequences of such payments are left to § 2042. The life insurance exception to § 2039 becomes problematic in the context of a retirement annuity that is coupled with a death benefit. The key to resolving the all-or-nothing characterization of the contract in this context is determining whether the contract issuer retained any risk of the decedent's premature death as of the decedent's death. In doing so, the regulations focus on the reserve assigned to the contract. If the decedent died when the reserve value was less than the death benefit, an element of insurance remains that removes § 2039 from consideration. Treas. Reg. § 20.2039-1(d). However, if the policy reserve value equaled the death benefit as of the decedent's death, the contract would contain no insurance component and the survivor benefit would remain subject to § 2039. Apart from considerations of the policy reserve value, a contract fails to constitute insurance in cases where the death benefit can never exceed premium payments received.[16] *Id.*

[B]   Annuity or Other Payment to the Decedent

[1]   Qualitative Nature of Payment

Before any survivor benefits will be included in the decedent's gross estate under § 2039, there must first be a predicate "annuity or other payment" that was payable to the decedent or that the decedent possessed the right to receive for the requisite period. Note that the literal breadth of this predicate applies beyond traditional annuities payable to the decedent; it also applies if the decedent was entitled to receive a single, lump-sum payment in the future. The Senate added the "other payment" language to the statute to ensure its application when the decedent possessed the right to receive a lump-sum payment in lieu of an annuity. S. Rep. No. 83-1622, at 470 (1954). The regulations under § 2039, however, do not reference this "in lieu of" qualifier. Rather, they provide that an "annuity or other payment" as used in § 2039 refers to "one or more payments extending over any period of time." Treas. Reg. § 20.2039-1(b)(1). Furthermore, such payments may be "equal or unequal, conditional or unconditional, periodic or sporadic." *Id.* The regulations therefore define the term in the broadest sense possible.

---

[16] For cases in which the annuity-versus-insurance issue has been litigated, see *Estate of Keller v. Commissioner*, 312 U.S. 543 (1941); *Estate of Montgomery v. Commissioner*, 56 T.C. 489 (1971), *aff'd per curiam*, 458 F.2d 616 (5th Cir. 1972).

[a]   Exclusion for Compensation Payments

In the context of employer-provided survivor benefits, the predicate payment to the decedent literally could be satisfied through the payment of wages or salary. If that were a proper interpretation of the statute, then the predicate payment to the decedent would be satisfied automatically for any decedent who died prior to retirement. Not surprisingly, courts have rejected such a broad interpretation of the statute. In *Fusz v. Commissioner*, 46 T.C. 214 (1966), the decedent's employment contract called for his wife to receive a monthly stipend for her lifetime if the decedent died while employed, which he did. The Service contended that the decedent's salary constituted the "other payment" sufficient to warrant including the present value of the wife's payment stream in his gross estate under § 2039. The Tax Court was unpersuaded. It refused to interpret the phrase "annuity or other payment" as *any* payment payable to the decedent, and instead held that the "other payment" contemplated by the statute was "qualitatively limited to post-employment benefits which, at the very least, are paid or payable during decedent's lifetime." *Id.* at 217–18. The Service acquiesced to the decision in *Fusz*, 1967-2 C.B. 2, and later expanded it by providing that payments under a compensation replacement plan in the event of sickness or accident would benefit from the same treatment. *See* Rev. Rul. 77-183, 1977-1 C.B. 274. However, payments to a retiring employee that are only nominally related to the provision of services—such as a retiring employee's agreement to remain available for consulting—will not be excluded from consideration under § 2039 on the basis that they constitute compensation. *See In re* Estate of Wadewitz, 339 F.2d 980 (7th Cir. 1964) (post-retirement payments primarily in exchange for agreement not to compete sufficient to implicate § 2039); *see also* Kramer v. United States, 406 F.2d 1363 (Ct. Cl. 1969) (noting the distinction between compensatory payments and those only nominally related to consulting services of a retired employee).

[b]   Treatment of Disability Benefits

Perhaps the most complicated aspect of § 2039 is determining its application based on the decedent's future rights to benefits under a disability plan. On one hand, such payments could represent retirement income to which § 2039 applies, with the basis for the decedent's retirement being his inability to continue work. On the other hand, disability benefits could be seen as a replacement for compensation that generally fails to implicate the statute. As described below, this dichotomy has lead to conflicting judicial decisions.

In *Estate of Bahen v. United States*, 305 F.2d 827 (Ct. Cl. 1962), the decedent died while employed as an officer of a railroad company. Under its "Death Benefit Plan," which covered employees with more than 10 years of service who died while employed, the company paid his widow an amount equal to three months of his salary. In addition, the employer paid the decedent's widow $100,000 in 60 monthly installments pursuant to its "Deferred Compensation Plan." While the benefit of the Deferred Compensation Plan was to be paid following the employee's death in the ordinary case, the plan provided a limited opportunity for the employee to receive such payments: if the employee became totally incapacitated prior to retirement. For the reasons set forth in the excerpt below, the Court of Claims found that § 2039 applied to both sets of payments to the decedent's widow.

ESTATE OF BAHEN v. UNITED STATES
United States Court of Claims
305 F.2d 827 (1962)

Section 2039 was a development of the earlier provisions of the estate tax which spoke of the decedent's "property" and of "transfers" by the decedent in contemplation of or taking effect at death. See Section 811 of the Internal Revenue Code of 1939, 26 U.S.C.A. § 811. The new section does not use that phraseology but frames its operative requirements more directly in terms of particular types of transactions or arrangements involving the decedent. This change is significant. We must pay heed to the precise new form in which Congress cast its net and not become entangled in the older meshes.

A. The Deferred Compensation Plan: We first consider the application of Section 2039 (and the Regulations) to the C. & O.'s major plan, the Deferred Compensation Plan (of 1953) under which $100,000 was paid to Mrs. Bahen in a five-year span. As we read the section and the Regulations, they demand inclusion in the estate of the proceeds of this Plan. Every requirement is squarely met, not only in literal terms but in harmony with the legislative aim.

* * *

3. The next problem is whether at Mr. Bahen's death there was payable to him or he possessed the right to receive "an annuity or other payment." The Deferred Compensation Plan provided that, if Mr. Bahen became totally incapacitated for further performance of duty before retirement, the C. & O. would pay him the $100,000 in 60 equal monthly installments. Under both the normal understanding of the statutory words "annuity or other payment" and the broad definition given them by the Regulations (referred to above), these sums must be characterized as at least an "other payment." Stressing Congress's use of the singular ("payment") and a reference in the Senate Committee report to a lump-sum payment in lieu of an annuity, plaintiff appears to urge that the only "payment" to a decedent covered by Section 2039 is a lump sum paid or payable in the place of a strict lifetime annuity (i.e., an annuity paid in the form of a lump sum). But we cannot confine the general language of Section 2039, as interpreted by the Regulations, within the limits of one illustration given by the Committee as a reason for adding the all-inclusive words "other payment" to "annuity". As we point out more in detail below, the history and pattern of Section 2039 fail to indicate that it deals only with true lifetime annuities (in installment form or in a commuted lump sum). The statute covers—as an "other payment", at least—disability compensation benefits of the type involved here.

* * *

8. Finally, we note briefly that Section 2039, as we construe it, is harmonious with the general objective of the federal estate tax to include in the decedent's estate (with designated exceptions) the valuable interests belonging to, accumulated by, or created by or for him, which pass to others at his death. Many such benefits promised, given, and paid for by an employer were specifically brought within this framework by the new section in 1954. In subsection (b), quoted above, Congress provides that contributions by the employer "shall be considered to be contributed by the decedent if made by reason of his employment." Phrased in terms of the earlier concepts of a decedent's "property" "transferred" at his death, Section 2039 declares that annuities or other payments payable by an employer to his employee, and

on his death to a beneficiary, constitute his property—created by him through his employer as part of the employment arrangement and in consideration of his continued services—which is transferred to another at his death. See the discussion in Lehman v. Commissioner, 109 F.2d 99, 100 (C.A.2); and Worthen v. United States, 192 F. Supp. 727, 733-4 (D. Mass.). A new provision of the estate tax which attempts to apply these fundamental concepts to a fairly well understood set of concrete situations should not be grudgingly read so as to chip away at the specific rule and to continue (as in the past) to leave as much as possible to the ambiguities of the general sections.

* * *

B. The Death Benefit Plan: It is a more difficult question whether the Death Benefit Plan-under which the C. & O. paid Mrs. Bahen a sum equal to Mr. Bahen's salary for three months-is covered by Section 2039. Under that arrangement no benefits were payable to the decedent during his life, and if the Plan were to be judged by itself it would fall outside the ambit of the section for lack of "an annuity or other payment" to the decedent. The defendant contends that this factor is present because the words "or other payment" can include the decedent-employee's regular salary; the Death Benefit Plan must be taken, defendant says, together with Mr. Bahen's entire employment arrangement including his ordinary compensation. We cannot agree. Since employees normally receive salary or wages, defendant's interpretation would effectively obliterate, for almost all employees, the express requirement in Section 2039 of "an annuity or other payment" to the decedent. If Congress had intended that strange result, it would certainly have mentioned or referred to it. The Government's argument also runs counter to the theory and examples of the Regulations (Sec. 20.2039-1) which impliedly exclude ordinary salary from consideration.

But the Government makes another point which we do accept as bringing the Death Benefit Plan under Section 2039. The suggestion is that this Plan should not be viewed in isolation but must be considered together with the Deferred Compensation Plan—as if both arrangements were combined into one plan, providing two types of benefits for beneficiaries after the employee's death but only one type of benefit (disability compensation) to the employee himself. There is some factual support, if that be necessary, for looking at the two plans together, since the Death Benefit Plan was adopted in January 1952 and the Deferred Compensation Plan only a year later in February 1953. There appears to be a common genesis and a unifying thread.

The firmer legal basis is provided by the Regulations (Sec. 20.2039-1(b)(2), Example (6)) which provide: "All rights and benefits accruing to an employee and to others by reason of the employment (except rights and benefits accruing under certain plans meeting the requirements of section 401(a) (see § 20.2039-2)) are considered together in determining whether or not section 2039 (a) and (b) applies. The scope of Section 2039(a) and (b) cannot be limited by indirection." Effect must be given to this declaration, adopted pursuant to the Treasury's recognized power to issue regulations and not challenged by plaintiff, since it does not violate the terms or the spirit of Section 2039. In view of the general purpose of the statute to cover a large share of employer-contributed payments to an employee's survivors, it is not unreasonable to lump together all of the employer's various benefit plans taking account of the employee's death (except those qualified under Section 401(a), which are excepted by the statute, * * *) in order to decide whether and to what extent Section 2039 applies to his estate. There is no immutable requirement in the legislation that each plan separately adopted by a company must be considered alone. One good ground for rejecting that position is to prevent attempts to avoid the reach of the statute by a series of contrived plans none of which, in itself, would fall under the section.

This directive in the Regulations that all rights and benefits "are to be considered together"—read with another part of the same Regulation which defines "contract or agreement" under Section 2039 to cover "any combination of arrangements, understandings, or plans arising by reason of the decedent's employment"—requires the two plans of the C. & O. to be deemed a coordinated whole for the purposes of Section 2039. On that view the payments under the Death Benefit Plan were includable in the decedent's gross estate for the reasons given above with respect to the Deferred Compensation Plan. If the two Plans are integrated into one, each element required for coverage of all payments is present.

———

Whereas the Court of Claims relied on the breadth of the text of § 2039 and its expansive interpretation in the regulations, the Second Circuit in *Estate of Schelberg v. Commissioner*, 612 F.2d 25 (2d Cir. 1979), endorsed a more circumscribed application of § 2039 to disability benefits. The decedent in *Schelberg* died while employed as an executive at IBM. The decedent participated in a number of employee benefit plans, one of which provided a survivor's income benefit to be paid in installments to his surviving spouse. The decedent also was covered by a "Sickness and Accident Plan" that would have provided him with his full salary for 52 weeks had he been absent from work on account of sickness or accident. Following the expiration of the 52-week period, the decedent could have received benefits under a "Disability Plan" upon a determination that he was permanently disabled. The Disability Plan essentially would have provided the decedent with his salary until he reached retirement age, at which time he would have qualified for retirement benefits.

The Service already had ruled that the potential to receive payments under the "Sickness and Accident" plan could not serve as the payment to the decedent that implicates § 2039 in Revenue Ruling 77-183, 1977-1 C.B. 274. The Service, however, cited the prospect of the decedent receiving benefits under the Disability Plan as the predicate payment necessary to capture the survivor's income benefit under § 2039. For reasons reflected in the excerpted opinion, the Second Circuit was not moved by this argument—the *Bahen* decision notwithstanding.

ESTATE OF SCHELBERG v. COMMISSIONER
United States Court of Appeals, Second Circuit
612 F.2d 25 (1979)

As recognized by a learned commentator shortly after § 2039 was enacted, the statute was aimed at "annuity contracts under which the purchaser (alone or with a joint annuitant) was entitled to payments for his life, with payments to continue after his death, at either the same or a reduced rate, to a survivor." Bittker, Estate and Gift Taxation under the 1954 Code: The Principal Changes, 29 Tul. L. Rev. 453, 469 (1955). While inclusion of the survivor's rights in the estate had been generally sustained, courts had differed as to the reason. Some courts had proceeded on the theory that purchase of the contract was in effect a transfer of property with the reservation of a life estate and thus taxable under the predecessors of I.R.C. § 2036. Others had proceeded on the theory that the transfer was intended to take effect at death. *Id.* A fundamental purpose of § 2039 was to supply an affirmative answer to the question of inclusion in such cases without further need to debate the theory.

A further purpose, as revealed by the relevant House and Senate Committee reports on what became § 2039 of the revised I.R.C. of 1954, H.R. Rep. No. 1337, 83d Cong. 2d Sess. 90–91, A 314–6 (1954); S.Rep. No.1622, 83d Cong. 2d Sess. 123–24, 469–72 (1954); H.R. Rep. No. 2543 (Conference Report), 83d Cong. 2d Sess. 74 (1954), U.S. Code Cong. & Admin. News 1954, p. 4017, was to settle the question of includibility of a joint and survivor annuity where the annuity was purchased by the decedent's employer or both the decedent and the employer made contributions. Congress decided that such an annuity should be included except when the employer's contributions were made pursuant to "an approved trust, pension or retirement plan."

Both text and context show that § 2039 was conceived as dealing only with the problem of what in substance was a joint annuity, although to be sure in all its various ramifications, not with the whole gamut of arrangements under which an employee, his employer or both may create benefits for the employee's survivors. The new section applied only "if, under such contract or agreement, an annuity or other payment was payable to the decedent, or the decedent possessed the right to receive such annuity or payment, either alone or in conjunction with another for his life or for any period not ascertainable without reference to his death or for any period which does not in fact end before his death." If Congress had wished to legislate more broadly, it would have eliminated this clause or chosen more general language for it. The intended sphere of application is made quite clear by the illustrations given in the House and Senate reports "as examples of contracts, but . . . not necessarily the only forms of contracts to which this section applies." Under all of these the decedent was receiving or entitled to receive at death what anyone would consider an "annuity or other payment" for the duration of his life or for a stipulated term. Furthermore, in each case the beneficiary succeeded to the interest of the decedent, as in the classic instance of a joint and survivor annuity, quite unlike the present case. Although the term "other payment" is literally broad, Congress was clearly thinking of payments in the nature of annuities the same types of payments which, if made to the survivor, would be includible in the estate. See *Fusz v. Commissioner, supra*, 46 T.C. at 217. None of the examples is even close to payments receivable only if the deceased employee might have become totally and permanently disabled had he lived.

We do not consider the case to be altered in the Government's favor by the Treasury Regulations. While these contain some broad language, there is nothing to indicate that their framers addressed the problem here presented. The closest of the illustrations is example (6). While we have no quarrel with this, it is inapposite since the payments both to the employee and to the beneficiary were life annuities. Without endeavoring to be too precise, we deem it plain that, in framing the condition on § 2039(a), Congress was not going beyond benefits the employee was sure to get as a result of his prior employment if he lived long enough. Even more plainly Congress was not thinking of disability payments which an employee would have had only a remote chance of ever collecting had he lived. Not only are the disability payments in this case extremely hypothetical, they are also far from the "annuity or other payment" contemplated by Congress. Courts have, consistent with basic principles of statutory construction, recognized that "annuity or other payment" does not mean "annuity or any payment," but that the phrase is qualitatively limited by the context in which it appears. See *Fusz v. Commissioner, supra*, 46 T.C. at 217–18. The Service itself has acquiesced in and furthered this view. See Rev. Rul. 77-183, *supra*. Thus, it seems clear to us that Congress did not intend the phrase to embrace wages, *Fusz v. Commissioner, supra*, 46 T.C. at 217;

Kramer v. United States, supra, 406 F.2d 1363, 186 Ct. Cl. 684; *Eichstedt v. United States,* 354 F. Supp. 484, 491 (N.D.Cal.1972); possible sickness and accident payments, which were a substitute for wages, Rev. Rul. 77-183, *supra;* or the disability payments involved in this case, which likewise were a partial continuation of wages when an employee's physical health deteriorated even further. The disability payments theoretically achievable here by the decedent in his lifetime are closer to the sickness benefits which he would have received at an early stage of his illness than they are to post-retirement benefits. The Tax Court's treatment of possible disability benefits as presupposing a post-retirement status linked to the widow's ultimate succession thereto seems to us to be unsupported in fact. * * *

The most influential decision on what the decedent must receive or be entitled to receive in order to trigger application of § 2039 is *Estate of Bahen v. United States,* 305 F.2d 827, 158 Ct. Cl. 141 (1962) (Davis, J.). The opinion is indeed a virtuoso performance which has tended to dominate the field to the extent that, with the significant exception of Judge Aldisert's dissent in Gray v. United States, 410 F.2d 1094 at 1112–14 (3d Cir. 1969), courts seem to look to the *Bahen* opinion rather than to the statute and the committee reports as indicative of the legislative intent. Beyond all this it is of peculiar importance here since it involved a sum payable only in the event of disability, and the Commissioner quite properly relies heavily upon it.

* * *

While, as indicated, the case bears some resemblance to ours, there is a different flavor about it, at least so far as concerns the payments under the Deferred Compensation Plan. There was in fact a unitary right to receive deferred compensation of $100,000 in 60 equal monthly payments, this to be paid to Mrs. Bahen if Bahen died or to him if he became totally disabled prior to retirement. There was no question of grouping separate plans together, since both Mr. and Mrs. Bahen's rights were pursuant to the same Deferred Compensation Plan. Even more to the point, if payments were being made to Mr. Bahen due to his disability and he died prior to exhausting the fund, the remaining payments would be made to Mrs. Bahen. In this respect the Deferred Compensation Plan was much like the joint and survivor annuity at which § 2039 was aimed. Here, of course, Mrs. Schelberg had no rights to any payments under the Disability Plan. The possible payments to Mr. Bahen were not, as under IBM's Disability Plan, true disability payments intended to cover a portion of previous salary; they were deferred compensation, as the plan's title indicates, payable by the railway in any event, to be made available to Mr. Bahen at a date earlier than death if his needs so required. They thus met the test laid down in *Fusz v. Commissioner, supra,* 46 T.C. at 217–18, as IBM's disability benefits do not, of being of the same nature as the payments to the beneficiary. We are not sure that the distinction is sufficient or what is more or less the same thing that we would have decided *Bahen* as the Court of Claims did. For the moment we shall leave the matter that way.

———————

While the conflicting holdings in *Bahen* and *Schelberg* perhaps can be reconciled on the retirement-like nature of the disability benefits at issue, the cases reflect disparate interpretations of the scope of § 2039. In that regard, the less expansive approach of *Schelberg* seems to be the prevailing view, as it has been followed in *Estate of Siegel v. Commissioner,* 74 T.C. 613 (1980), and *Estate of Van Wye v. United States,* 686 F.2d 425 (6th Cir. 1982). Thus, while § 2039 was enacted primarily to resolve ambiguities concerning the estate tax treatment of employer-provided survivor benefits, the statute by no means subjects all payments resulting from the decedent's employment to taxation.

[c] Treatment of Qualified Plan Benefits

When § 2039 was enacted, it excluded survivor benefits paid under certain qualified retirement plans. The exclusion applied not only for purposes of § 2039, it also trumped any other inclusionary statute. Congress capped the exclusion at $100,000 in 1982 and, shortly thereafter, eliminated the exclusion altogether through the Deficit Reduction Act of 1984. Benefits paid under traditional Individual Retirement Accounts or employer-sponsored 401(k) plans therefore are subject to inclusion under § 2039.

The regulations under § 2039, promulgated at a time when survivor benefits paid under qualified retirement plans were exempt from § 2039, provided further that the decedent's future rights to such payments could not serve as the predicate for subjecting survivor benefits paid under non-qualified plans to inclusion under the statute. They provide that: (1) the decedent must have been receiving "an annuity or other payment" or must have possessed the right to receive such annuity or payment for his life, for any period not ascertainable without reference to his death, or for any period which does not in fact end before his death,[17] either alone or in conjunction with another person; (2) an annuity or other payment must have been receivable by any beneficiary by reason of surviving the decedent; and (3) the payments to both the decedent and the beneficiary must have been pursuant to a contract or other agreement other than life insurance on the life of the decedent. The Service reinforced this point in Revenue Ruling 76-380, 1976-2 C.B. 270. Thus, qualified plans were not subject to the aggregation rule of all contracts, understandings, or plans relating to the decedent's employment.

Although the exclusion of qualified plan survivor benefits has been repealed, the ability of qualified plan benefits to serve as the predicate payment subjecting other benefits to inclusion remains in doubt. Through Revenue Ruling 88-85, 1988-2 C.B. 333, the Service declared a host of rulings obsolete "to the extent" they referred to § 2039(c)–(g) prior to the repeal of those provisions. Revenue Ruling 76-380 was among those designated. However, Revenue Ruling 76-380 never referred to § 2039(a)–(g) but instead relied exclusively on Example 6 of Reg. § 20.2039-1(b)(2). Hence, it is possible to interpret Revenue Ruling 76-380 as surviving the repeal of the qualified plan exclusion unscathed.[18] On the other hand, the regulation on which Revenue Ruling 76-380 relies itself was assuredly based on the statutory exclusion, and there would be no basis for the Service's designation of the ruling as obsolete unless it intended for that designation to have some effect. In the authors' view, the congressional decision to treat qualified plans and non-qualified plans equally for purposes of subjecting survivor benefits to taxation under § 2039 also eliminated any basis for exempting qualified plans from the aggregation rule of Reg. § 20.2039-1(b)(1).

---

[17] The period for which the decedent must possess future payment rights is identical to the language used in § 2036, and is to be interpreted in the same manner. *See* Treas. Reg. § 20.2039-1(b)(1).

[18] This interpretation, coupled with the Service's failure to repeal Reg. § 20.2039-1(b)(2), Ex. 6, could be reasonably interpreted as retention of the anti-aggregation treatment for qualified plans. *See* McDaniel, Repetti, & Caron, Federal Wealth Transfer Taxation: Cases and Materials, 347 & n.12 (5th ed. 2003). However, reliance on the Service's failure to repeal obsolete regulations may be misplaced. In that regard, none of the regulations providing for the complex treatment of qualified plans under prior provisions of § 2039 have been repealed. *See* Treas. Reg. § 20.2039-2 to -5.

[2]   Requisite Entitlement to Payment

One source of potential confusion regarding the predicate payment to the decedent under § 2039 is the level of legal entitlement necessary for a payment to be taken into consideration. If the decedent was actually receiving an "annuity or other payment" as of the time of his death, the predicate is automatically satisfied. It is immaterial whether the decedent possessed an enforceable right to continued payments. *See* Treas. Reg. § 20.2039-1(b)(1), -1(b)(2), Ex. 2. Yet if the statute is applied based not on payments the decedent was receiving as of his death but instead on payments the decedent "possessed the right to receive" in the future, the right must have been enforceable. *See* Treas. Reg. § 20.2039-1(b)(1). However, enforceable should not be equated with unconditional. If the decedent's rights to future payments were subject to his continued services or some other condition, he will be considered to possess an enforceable right to those payments so long as he has complied with his obligations under the contract as of his death. *See id.* Hence, payments subject to forfeiture can supply the predicate for § 2039 as long as the decedent was in control of the forfeiture conditions. The following examples, based on those contained in the regulations, help illustrate when rights to future payment will implicate § 2039.

> Example 1: *Decedent* was employed at *X Corp.* Pursuant to his employment contract, *X Corp.* agreed to pay $5,000 per month to *Decedent* if and when he retired after the age of 65. No retirement benefit would be paid, however, if *Decedent* ended his employment for any reason other than death or disability prior to age 60. The contract also provided that if *Decedent* qualified for the retirement annuity, *X Corp.* would pay $4,000 per month to his surviving spouse, if any, at the time of his death. *Decedent* died at the age of 58 while still employed at *X Corp.*, survived by his wife.

> The fair market value of the spouse's annuity is included in the *Decedent's* gross estate under § 2039. *Decedent* possessed an enforceable right to payments when he attained age 65. Although those payments could be forfeited had he not remained employed until age 60, *Decedent* in fact complied with his obligations under the contract up to the point of his death. Hence, the condition is irrelevant for purposes of applying § 2039.

> Example 2: Assume the basic facts of Example 1, with some minor additions. The employment contract provided that *Decedent* could take a lump-sum payment of $300,000 in lieu of his monthly payment. If the Decedent elected the lump-sum option, his spouse would receive a $100,000 lump-sum payment upon his death in lieu of the survivor's annuity. *Decedent* retired at age 65 and elected to receive the $300,000 payment. *Decedent* then died at the age of 66.

> The $100,000 payment to *Decedent's* spouse will not be included in his gross estate under § 2039 because, as of *Decedent's* death, he had received all payments to which he was entitled. As no payments remained outstanding, the statute's predicate of an "annuity or other payment" payable to the decedent or to which the decedent possessed a right to receive in the future is not satisfied.

[C]   Payment to Surviving Beneficiary

Most of the cumbersome interpretive issues under § 2039 relate to whether payments to the decedent or the decedent's rights to future payments are sufficient to implicate the statute. Usually, the circumstances make clear whether a beneficiary receives an annuity or other payment by reason of surviving the decedent. For completeness, it is worth noting that the regulations define the term "annuity or other payment" under § 2039 identically as it relates to the decedent's payment and the payment to the beneficiary—that is, in an extremely broad manner. Furthermore, as with the predicate payment to the decedent, the survivor benefit must be paid pursuant to a contract or agreement. Yet the application of this requirement differs in the context of payments to beneficiaries. Recall that payment which the decedent was receiving at the time of his death can satisfy the § 2039 predicate even where the decedent's right to receive the payment was not legally enforceable. The same rule does not apply, however, to the survivor benefit. The regulations provide that where a decedent-employee had not met the conditions for a survivor benefit to be paid to his designated beneficiary but the employer nonetheless paid the beneficiary a reduced amount, the survivor benefits fell outside the scope of § 2039. Treas. Reg. § 20.2039-1(b)(2), Ex. 4; *see also* Estate of Barr v. Commissioner, 40 T.C. 227 (1963) (survivor wage dividend paid at option of employer not subject to § 2039 because it was not paid pursuant to contract or agreement). Hence, payments made out of employer benevolence do not satisfy the contract or agreement requirement.[19]

[D] Amount Included

The approach for determining the amount to be included in the decedent's gross estate under § 2039 depends on the context in which the annuity or other payment arose. If the annuity was commercially issued, the inclusion amount is determined by reference to the cost of comparable contracts sold by the annuity issuer that provide the same payment stream that is payable to the beneficiary. *See* Treas. Reg. § 20.2031-8(a). This approach has the benefit of implicitly accounting for the solvency of the company obligated to make the future payments. However, this replacement-cost approach to valuation is not available when the survivor benefits are not paid by a company regularly engaged in such activity. In that case, § 7520 requires that the payments to the surviving beneficiary be valued under tables promulgated by the Secretary of Treasury, using a discount rate equal to 120 percent of the Federal midterm rate in effect for the month in which the valuation is made (generally the decedent's death). IRC § 7520(a). For valuation dates after April 30, 1999, the appropriate tables are contained in Reg. § 20.2031-7. However, if the beneficiary is terminally ill, the actuarial values cannot be used for measuring an annuity payable with reference to the beneficiary's life. Treas. Reg. § 20.7520-3(b)(3).

After the value of the survivor's payment stream is determined, § 2039(b) includes in the gross estate only that portion of such value attributable to the portion of the annuity purchase price provided by the decedent. Thus, § 2039 operates in a manner similar to the general rule for including jointly-held property in the decedent's gross estate under § 2040 (without the specific rule pertaining to spousal-owned property). While this approach makes sense in the context of commercial annuities, the general rule standing alone is ill-suited for employer-provided benefits that are not explicitly purchased. In the absence of further guidance, a decedent's estate could contend that no portion of the survivor benefits is included under § 2039, as the benefits were purchased by the decedent's employer rather than the decedent. However, § 2039(b) avoids this absurd result by treating any amounts contributed by an

---

[19] The lack of enforceability of the payment to the beneficiary may be disregarded, however, when the obligor of such payments is a closely held corporation controlled by the decedent's family. *See* Neely v. United States, 613 F.2d 802 (Ct. Cl. 1980).

employer of the decedent by reason of the decedent's employment as having been supplied by the decedent himself.[20] As explained in the Senate Report accompanying the enactment of § 2039, contributions provided by the decedent's employer shall be considered to have been made by reason of the decedent's employment if the annuity or other payment is offered as an inducement to accept or continue employment or if the contributions are made in lieu of additional compensation to the employee (if so understood by the parties even if not reduced to writing). S. Rep. No. 83-1622, at 471. Hence, the scope of employer-provided benefits that will be treated as having been purchased by the decedent is afforded a broad interpretation.

§ 15.03 GIFT TAX CONSEQUENCES OF ANNUITY ARRANGEMENTS

The gift tax consequences of annuities are not nearly as involved as the estate tax treatment of such arrangements. No context-specific statutory regime exists, leaving general principles to govern. If an individual purchases a commercial annuity that provides survivor benefits and irrevocably designates a beneficiary, the designation constitutes a present gift of a future interest. However, in the usual case where the beneficiary designation can be revoked, no present transfer of property takes place.

As described in Chapter 3, employer-provided annuity benefits generally do not implicate the gift tax due to the absence of a lifetime transfer of property by the employee.[21] However, if the employer provides the employee with an option of receiving a single-life annuity or a reduced joint-and-survivor annuity, the employee's irrevocable election to forgo the greater benefits under the single-life annuity in favor of one supplying survivor benefits satisfies the transfer requirement. *See* Treas. Reg. § 25.2511-1(h)(10). Considering that most such elections are made to provide the employee's spouse with an income stream, the resulting gift is typically offset by the marital deduction.[22] *See* IRC § 2523(f)(6).

§ 15.04 STUDY PROBLEMS

1. Tony recently won the mega-lotto jackpot. Pursuant to the terms of the lottery, his winnings are to be paid in 10 annual installments of $5 million. If the winner dies prior to receiving all annual installments, the remaining amounts are to be paid to the winner's surviving spouse, if any, otherwise to the winner's descendants *per stirpes*.

    If Tony dies prior to expiration of the 10-year period, will any portion of the remaining payments be included in his gross estate under § 2033? Under § 2039?

2. Anna is employed as an off-shore oil rig engineer. Due to the hazardous nature of the job, her employer has a policy that will provide a payment equal to five times her annual salary to her surviving spouse (if any) in the event she is killed on the job.

    Anna, who is currently married, asks you if the death benefit will be subject to estate

---

[20] Presumably, unfunded plans for which the employer literally makes no prior contribution shall be treated as having been provided in full by the employer, whose presumed contribution will then be attributed to the decedent. *See* Beal v. Commissioner, 47 T.C. 269 (1966), *acq.* 1967-2 C.B. 1 (applying § 2039 to benefits provided under unfunded employer plan).

[21] See discussion in § 3.02[C].

[22] The marital deduction allowed under the gift tax is addressed in § 19.06.

tax.

3. Taking the same facts as problem (2), assume that Anna's employer also provides a nonqualified deferred compensation plan under which it contractually agrees to pay Anna 50 percent of her annual salary if and when she retires from the company after age 45. If she dies while employed but prior to retirement, the payment will be made to her surviving spouse, if any, otherwise to her surviving descendants.

   a. If Anna were to die at age 40 while employed, would the death benefit paid under the nonqualified deferred compensation plan be included in her gross estate?

   b. What effect, if any, will the existence of the deferred compensation plan have on the estate tax consequences of the hazard plan described in problem (2)?

4. As an alternative to the nonqualified deferred compensation plan described in problem (3), assume that Anna's employer has established a 401(k) plan for the benefit of its employees. For every $2 an employee contributes to the plan, the employer contributes $1. The current balance in Anna's 401(k) plan is $200,000. Anna has designated her husband as the primary beneficiary of her account, and she has named her children as contingent beneficiaries.

   a. Will the balance in Anna's 401(k) plan be included in her gross estate at her death?

   b. What effect, if any, will the existence of the 401(k) plan have on the estate tax consequences of the hazard plan described in problem (2)?

5. John transfers stock in his closely held company to a grantor trust (disregarded as an entity separate from the grantor under subchapter J). The terms of the trust provide that John will receive an amount equal to 40 percent of the initial value of the stock (as finally determined for estate and gift tax purposes) in each of the next three years. If John were to die within the trust term, the remaining payments would be made to his estate. Any property remaining in the trust after the trust term is to be held for the benefit of John's issue until the youngest child attains age 21, at which time the trust will be distributed to his issue then living, *per stirpes*.

   Assume John dies after receiving only the first annuity payment. In general terms, discuss how much will be included in John's estate under (a) § 2033, (b) § 2039, and (c) § 2036.

Chapter 16

DISCLAIMERS

Internal Revenue Code: § 2518
Treasury Regulations: § 25.2518-1, -2, -3
    see also § 25.2511-1(c)(2)

Suppose one of your estate-planning clients calls you with the following news: His mother recently passed away, and her will leaves her estate in equal shares to your client and his sister. Even though his mother's probate estate is of modest size, your client already possesses significant wealth that will place his future estate well above the prevailing effective estate tax exemption. Your client asks if there is any way he can simply refuse the devise in his favor in hopes that such amounts will pass to his children without first passing through him. In effect, your client would like to revise the terms of his mother's will.

Recall that the gift tax under § 2501(a) applies to the "transfer of property by gift." Does the mere refusal to accept property constitute a "transfer" for this purpose? From a state-law perspective, a disclaimer generally does not constitute a transfer on the part of the disclaimant. *See* Unif. Probate Code § 2-1105(f), 8 U.L.A. 140 (Supp. 1999) ("A disclaimer . . . is not a transfer, assignment or release."). Early tax cases were willing to import the no-transfer characterization into the federal transfer tax regime. *See* Brown v. Routzahn, 63 F.2d 914, 917 (6th Cir. 1933) (distinguishing between a "transfer of . . . property" and the "exercise of a right to refuse a gift of property"). Yet disclaimed property must pass somewhere, and one can imagine that most would-be disclaimants iron out this detail before irrevocably rejecting a transfer of property in their favor.[1] The entire transaction therefore can be conceptualized as an intentional transfer of the disclaimed property to the default recipient. The Supreme Court endorsed this approach in *Jewett v. Commissioner*, 455 U.S. 305 (1982), noting that the scope of the gift tax "unquestionably encompasses an indirect transfer, effected by means of a disclaimer, of a contingent future interest in a trust." *Id.* at 310. Because the practical effect of the disclaimer in that case was to confer a gratuitous benefit on the natural objects of the taxpayer's bounty, the Court concluded that "the treatment of disclaimers as taxable gifts is fully consistent with the basic purpose of the statutory scheme." *Id.*

While the indirect transfer that occurs as a result of a disclaimer would be included in the gift tax base as a default matter, cases incorporating the no-transfer rationale of state law eventually led to a regulatory exception for disclaimers. Under those regulations, an unequivocal refusal to accept ownership of property did not "constitute the making of a gift" so long as the refusal occurred "within a reasonable time" after knowledge of the existence of

---

[1] If the governing instrument does not expressly provide for an alternative disposition, a disclaimed devise generally passes as if the disclaimant predeceased the decedent. *See* Unif. Probate Code § 2-1106(b)(3)(B), 8 U.L.A. 142 (Supp. 1999).

the transfer. *See* Treas. Reg. § 25.2511-1(c)(2). This vague standard applies only to disclaimers occurring prior to 1977, as Congress addressed the tax treatment of disclaimers legislatively through the enactment of § 2518 in 1976.[2] Under § 2518(a), a person who makes a "qualified disclaimer" of any interest in property is treated "as if the interest had never been transferred to such person." Exclusion from the gift tax base therefore turns on compliance with the statute, irrespective of how the transaction is characterized under state law.

§ 16.01   STATUTORY REQUIREMENTS OF A QUALIFIED DISCLAIMER

Section 2518(b) enumerates the host of conditions that a disclaimer must satisfy in order to be excluded from the gift tax base as a qualified disclaimer. The report of the House Ways and Means Committee that accompanied the enactment of § 2518 summarizes these requirements as follows:

> Under the bill, a "qualified disclaimer" means an irrevocable and unqualified refusal to accept an interest in property that satisfies four conditions. First, the refusal must be in writing. Second, the written refusal must be received by the transferor of the interest, his legal representative, or the holder of the legal title to the property not later than 9 months after the day on which the transfer creating the interest is made. However, if later, the period for making the disclaimer is not to expire in any case until 9 months after the day on which the person making the disclaimer has attained age 21. For purposes of this requirement, a transfer is considered to be made when it is treated as a completed transfer for gift tax purposes with respect to inter vivos transfers or upon the date of the decedent's death with respect to testamentary transfers. Third, the person must not have accepted the interest or any of its benefits before making the disclaimer. . . . [T]he acceptance of any consideration in return for making the disclaimer is to be treated as an acceptance of the benefits of the interest disclaimed. Fourth, the interest must pass to a person other than the person making the disclaimer as a result of the refusal to accept the property.[3] For purposes of this requirement, the person making the disclaimer cannot have the authority to direct the redistribution or transfer of the property to another person and be treated as making a "qualified" disclaimer.

H.R. Rep. No. 94-1380, at 67 (1976), available at 1976-3 C.B. (vol. 3) 735, 801. Noting that the statute provides an exception to the normal tax treatment of indirect gratuitous transfers, the Eighth Circuit reasoned that the scope of § 2518 is to be interpreted narrowly. *See* Walshire v. United States, 288 F.3d 342, 346–47 (8th Cir. 2002). The conditions on qualified disclaimers therefore require careful compliance.

----

[2] *See* Tax Reform Act of 1976, Pub. L. No. 94-455, §§ 2009(b)(1), 2009(e)(2), 90 Stat. 1520, 1893, 1896.

[3] [Ed. Note: Shortly after the enactment of the disclaimer statute, this condition was liberalized to permit the disclaimed property to pass to the surviving spouse of the decedent, so that property disclaimed by a surviving spouse could pass to a trust for the spouse's benefit. *See* Revenue Act of 1978, Pub. L. No. 95-600, § 702(m), 92 Stat. 2763, 2935.]

[A]   Temporal Limitation

As a general rule, a qualified disclaimer must be filed with the appropriate party within nine months of the date on which the transfer creating the interest in the disclaimant was made.[4] IRC § 2518(b)(2); Treas. Reg. § 25.2518-2(c)(1). The time frame is firm; it does not depend on when the would-be disclaimant became aware of his interest in the transferred property. The heart of the temporal limitation on qualified disclaimers therefore lies in determining when the clock starts running—that is, when the transfer creating the subject property interest takes place.

The regulations provide two primary guidelines for determining when an interest in property is created for purposes of evaluating the timeliness of a disclaimer. A lifetime transfer of property is treated as occurring for purposes of § 2518 on the date the transfer constitutes a completed gift. Treas. Reg. § 25.2518-2(c)(3). This is the case even if the gift is excluded by reason of the annual exclusion under § 2503(b). A decedent's death serves as the effective date for transfers made at death as well as for transfers that become irrevocable by reason of death. *Id.*

[1]   Future Interests

The commencement of the nine-month disclaimer period does not always coincide with vesting in possession or, for that matter, vesting in interest. For example, assume that a settlor funds a revocable inter vivos trust for his lifetime benefit, designating his wife as the succeeding lifetime beneficiary. Upon the death of the settlor and his wife, the trust is to be distributed to the settlor's then-living issue or, if none, to the settlor's then-living siblings. At the time the trust is created, the settlor has three adult children and two siblings. Focusing on the interests of the settlor's siblings, their interests in the trust are subject to a host of contingencies: (1) the settlor not revoking the trust during his lifetime, (2) the failure of the settlor's issue to survive the settlor and his wife, and (3) the siblings surviving both the settlor and his wife. Only the first contingency operates to delay commencement of the disclaimer period. Because of the settlor's revocation right, the transfer does not constitute a completed gift. However, when the revocation right is extinguished (likely by reason of the settlor's death), the transfer of the beneficial interests in the trust will become effective at that point for purposes of measuring the disclaimer period. *Id.* Hence, even though the siblings do not know if they will ever receive a distribution from the trust, a disclaimer of their interests must be made within nine months after the trust becomes irrevocable. *See* Jewett v. Commissioner, 455 U.S. 305 (1982) (holding that the interest of a contingent remainderman was created for disclaimer purposes when the trust was created, despite the presence of an unresolved survivorship condition).

---

[4] An exception exists for individuals who have not attained age 21 at the time of the transfer creating their interest. In that case, the general nine-month filing requirement is extended to the date nine months after the disclaimant attained age 21. IRC § 2518(b)(2)(B). The extension is available even though it is possible for a guardian appointed on behalf of the individual to exercise the disclaimer on his behalf while the individual is a minor. *See* Treas. Reg. § 25.2518-2(b)(1).

[2] Lifetime Transfers Recaptured in Gross Estate

Completed lifetime gifts that are recaptured in the decedent's gross estate can prove problematic for determining when the disclaimer period begins. Does inclusion of the transferred property in the decedent's gross estate give rise to a new nine-month period following the decedent's death? The regulations address this circumstance by reiterating that there exists only one disclaimer period and that this period commences from the time the transfer becomes complete for gift tax purposes. Treas. Reg. § 25.2518-2(c)(3). Note that nothing in Reg. § 25.2518-2(c)(3) treats the decedent's death as the effective date of the transfer for § 2518 purposes for any transfer that is included in the decedent's gross estate. Rather, the general rule providing that the decedent's date of death commences the disclaimer period only for transfers that are made by the decedent at death or become irrevocable by reason of the decedent's death.

[3] Joint Tenancy Interests

At one point, the Service took the position that the interest received by a surviving joint tenant as a result of the right of survivorship was created not at the death of the predeceasing joint tenant, but instead when the joint tenancy was created. The theory was that the enhancement of the surviving joint tenant's interest was not the product of an independent transfer, but instead a mere ripening of the right of survivorship inherent in the joint tenancy title. As a practical matter, the Service's position precluded surviving joint tenants from making qualified disclaimers of portions of property received by way of the right of survivorship.

Several courts rebuffed the Service's application of the disclaimer statute in the context of survivorship rights of joint tenants. Stressing the predeceasing joint tenant's right to partition the property until the moment of death (in which case, the right of survivorship inherent in the tenancy would have been eliminated), courts reasoned that the right of survivorship did not become irrevocable until the death of the predeceasing joint tenant without partition. In this manner, the enhancement of the surviving joint tenant's title was viewed as the product of a second transfer for purposes of measuring the disclaimer period. *See, e.g.*, Kennedy v. Commissioner, 804 F.2d 1332, 1336 (7th Cir. 1986) ("[T]he gift of a joint tenancy with right of survivorship should be treated as more than one transfer in states that allow any tenant to partition the property at will."); *see also* McDonald v. Commissioner, 853 F.2d 1494 (8th Cir. 1988); Estate of Dancy v. Commissioner, 872 F.2d 84 (4th Cir. 1989). This series of judicial setbacks led the Service to reconsider its position. In 1997, the Service amended its regulations to provide that a surviving joint tenant may disclaim the interest received by right of survivorship within nine months of the death of the predeceasing joint tenant—without regard to whether the tenancy was severable at will under local law. Treas. Reg. § 25.2518-2(c)(4)(i).

As a general rule, the interest passing by right of survivorship is half of the property, regardless of the consideration provided by the surviving joint tenant and regardless of the amount included in the decedent's gross estate under § 2040. *Id.* However, with respect to joint bank, brokerage, or other accounts the creation of which does not give rise to a taxable gift (due to the transferor's unilateral ability to withdraw contributions to the account[5]), the interest passing by right of survivorship capable of being disclaimed will extend to the entire portion attributable to the contributions of the deceased co-tenant. Treas. Reg. § 25.2518-2(c)(4)(iii).

---

[5] *See* Treas. Reg. § 25.2511-1(h)(4), discussed in § 7.01[B].

[B] Acceptance of Disclaimed Interest or Its Benefits

It is not possible for a transferee to make a qualified disclaimer of property once the transferee accepts the transferred property or any of its benefits. IRC § 2518(b)(3). The regulations provide the following guidance on what constitutes acceptance for this purpose:

> Acceptance is manifested by an affirmative act which is consistent with ownership of the interest in the property. Acts indicative of acceptance include using the property or the interest in property; accepting dividends, interest, or rents from the property; and directing others to act with respect to the property or interest in property. However, merely taking delivery of an instrument of title, without more, does not constitute acceptance. Moreover, a disclaimant is not considered to have accepted property merely because under applicable local law title to the property vests immediately in the disclaimant upon the death of a decedent.

Treas. Reg. § 25.2518-2(d)(1). Special care therefore must be taken with respect to a brokerage or other bank accounts. If the ability to disclaim such property under § 2518 is to be preserved, interest and dividends must not be withdrawn from the account. Additionally, the transferee or surviving joint tenant cannot issue investment directives. However, if the individual who disclaims a beneficial interest in a trust also serves as a fiduciary, actions taken by the individual in a fiduciary capacity "to preserve or maintain the disclaimed property" will not be treated as acceptance. Treas. Reg. § 25.2518-2(d)(2). Investment decisions made to preserve the value of a trust portfolio appear to fall within this safe harbor.

[1] Continued Occupancy by Co-Tenant

Continued possession of personal use property by a devisee or surviving joint tenant who owns an interest in the property as co-tenant or joint tenant in his own right could, in theory, raise complications as to whether continued possession constitutes "acceptance" of the transferred interest. For instance, would a surviving spouse's occupation of a residence that the couple owned as tenants by the entirety constitute acceptance of the interest he receives by right of survivorship? If so, then a surviving joint tenant's survivorship interest in residential property effectively would be rendered ineligible to be disclaimed on a tax-free basis. The regulations adopt a sensible approach in the context of residential real estate, stating that mere continued possession of the residence by a surviving joint tenant does not constitute acceptance. Treas. Reg. § 25.2518-2(d)(1). The same treatment applies to a devise of a community property interest in residential property. *See* Treas. Reg. § 25.2518-2(d)(4), Ex. 8. Presumably, this treatment would extend to other types of personal use property owned in co-tenancy, where one co-tenant is permitted to occupy or use the entire property under state law.

[2] Receipt of Consideration

The receipt of consideration in return for making the disclaimer constitutes an acceptance of the benefits of the disclaimed interest. Treas. Reg. § 25.2518-2(d)(1). Of course, what rises to the level of consideration for this purpose is not immediately clear. In *Estate of Monroe v. Commissioner*, 124 F.3d 699 (5th Cir. 1997), a surviving spouse was troubled by the estate tax consequences of various bequests made by his predeceased wife. The husband requested that the legatees disclaim their bequests so that such amounts would pass to him and thereby qualify for the marital deduction. While the husband intimated that the disclaimants would be taken care of, he made no definitive promise that they would be compensated for acceding to his request. Yet shortly after the disclaimers were filed, the husband followed up with gifts to the disclaimants that equaled or exceeded the amounts they disclaimed.

The government took the position that the disclaimers did not constitute unqualified refusals to accept property as required under § 2518. Accordingly, the Service disallowed the marital deduction attributable to the predeceased spouse's estate for the amounts passing to the husband by way of disclaimer. The Tax Court upheld the deficiency and even sustained the government's imposition of a negligence penalty. 104 T.C. 352 (1995). However, the Fifth Circuit took a drastically different view of the case. It reversed in favor of the estate on the underlying deficiency, reasoning that treating a disclaimer as unqualified on grounds that the disclaimant was motivated by an expected future benefit or implied promise would introduce "an incomprehensible subjective standard" into the statute. 124 F.3d at 709. Based on the *Estate of Monroe* case, consideration sufficient to disqualify a disclaimer under § 2518 therefore appears limited to the bargained-for, enforceable variety.

[C] Passage Without Direction of Disclaimant

Qualified disclaimers must proceed on a hands-off basis. That is, the only discretion to be exercised is whether to refuse to accept the transferred property. As described by the Eighth Circuit, the disclaimer statute negates the imposition of the gift tax "where the disclaimant effectively steps back and permits transfer of the property to the next person in line." Walshire v. United States, 288 F.3d 342, 346 (8th Cir. 2002). If the disclaimant attempts to combine the refusal with a direction to whom the disclaimed interest will pass, the disclaimer is not qualified. IRC § 2518(b)(4). While disclaimers that flirt with disqualification under this rule can be saved on grounds that the naming of alternate transferees by the disclaimant constituted mere precatory language that was unenforceable under state law, *see* Treas. Reg. § 25.2518-2(e)(4), the preferable approach is simply to include nothing in the disclaimer instrument that relates to the ultimate disposition of the property.[6]

The disqualification of a disclaimer under § 2518(b)(4) applies not only when the disclaimant attempts to direct the disposition in connection with the disclaimer, but also when the disclaimant possesses the power to direct distribution of the property after the disclaimer becomes effective. Treas. Reg. § 25.2518-2(e)(1)(i). For example, assume a decedent establishes a trust under his will that will terminate upon the death of the decedent's last surviving child. The trust provides for income to be distributed to each of the decedent's children (or to any such deceased child's issue) in equal shares, and the trust authorizes the trustee to distribute principal to any of the decedent's issue in its discretion. The trust will be distributed to the decedent's then-living issue upon termination. All of the decedent's children, *C1*, *C2*, and *C3*, are named as co-trustees. An attempted disclaimer by any of the decedent's children of his beneficial interest in the trust will not be qualified because each child retains the ability to direct the disposition of the trust principal in his capacity as co-trustee. *See* Treas. Reg. § 25.2518-2(d)(2), -2(e)(5), Ex. 11. However, as is the case in a variety of other contexts, the imposition of an ascertainable standard on the exercise of discretion negates the possession of a power for this purpose. Thus, if the hypothetical trust above had restricted

---

[6] Section 2518(c)(3) provides one exception to the no-direction rule. Where the attempted disclaimer is not effective to transfer property under local law, a written transfer of the disclaimant's interest to the person or persons who would receive the property interest if the disclaimer were qualified shall be treated as a qualified disclaimer, so long as the disclaimer occurs within the nine-month period and the disclaimant has not accepted the property or its benefits.

discretionary distributions of principal to the "health, education, support or maintenance" of the recipient, a child's continued service as trustee would not render the disclaimer of his beneficial interest in the trust non-qualified. *See* Treas. Reg. § 25.2518-2(e)(i), -2(e)(5), Ex. 12.

[D] Passage to Person Other Than Disclaimant

Section 2518(b)(4) not only precludes the disclaimant from directing the disposition of trust property, it also requires that the disclaimed property pass to someone other than the disclaimant. In other words, the disclaimant cannot receive or otherwise benefit from the disclaimed property interest. *See* Treas. Reg. § 25.2518-2(e)(1)(ii). Would-be disclaimants therefore must consider the alternate dispositions of disclaimed property (e.g., specific devise dropping into residuary estate; residuary devise passing by partial intestacy; non-probate transfer becoming part of the probate estate) and ensure that they have rejected the receipt of the disclaimed property in all such capacities. *See* Treas. Reg. § 25.2518-2(e)(3), -2(e)(5), Exs. 1–3. In that sense, § 2518(b)(4) simply requires that the disclaimant be thorough in the drafting of the disclaimer. The more substantive restriction imposed by § 2518(b)(4) is the inability of a transferee to disclaim an outright interest in property but still benefit from the disclaimed interest in another capacity. For instance, if a beneficiary rejects a specific devise of property that consequently passes to a residuary trust of which the disclaimant is but one of several discretionary beneficiaries, the disclaimer is not qualified. *See* Estate of Christiansen v. Commissioner, 130 T.C. 1 (2008) (holding that disclaimer of devise that passed to a charitable lead trust of which the disclaimant was a remainder beneficiary was not qualified by reason of § 2518(b)(4)). Subjecting distributions to an ascertainable-standard limitation does not serve as a shield in this context. Rather, the mere ability to benefit from the disclaimed property interest in any form is prohibited.

Section 2518(b)(4) excludes one class of beneficiaries from the requirement that disclaimed property pass to one other than the disclaimant: surviving spouses. IRC § 2518(b)(4)(A). This exception permits fine-tuning of the use of the marital deduction in the estate of the first spouse to die. For instance, a will containing a devise to a trust that qualifies for the marital deduction may direct that any disclaimed portion of the devise pass to a so-called "non-marital trust," the assets of which will not be captured in the gross estate of the surviving spouse. *See, e.g.*, Treas. Reg. § 25.2518-2(e)(5), Exs. 4 & 7. By allowing the surviving spouse to be a beneficiary of the non-marital trust that receives disclaimed property, the statute permits the spouse to engage in post-mortem tax planning (i.e., full use of predeceased spouse's unified credit, equalizing of estates, etc.) without having to relinquish the ability to benefit from the devise altogether. However, note that surviving spouses are not exempt from the § 2518(b)(4) requirement that disclaimed property pass without direction from the disclaimant. Accordingly, if the surviving spouse is to serve as trustee of the non-marital trust to which disclaimed property passes, any discretion over distributions from the trust must be limited to an ascertainable standard.

§ 16.02 DISCLAIMER OF POWER OF APPOINTMENT

A power of appointment is treated as a separate interest in property for disclaimer purposes. IRC § 2518(c)(2). Hence, an income beneficiary of a trust who is provided a general power of appointment over the trust remainder may make a qualified disclaimer of the power without relinquishing his income interest. *See* Treas. Reg. § 25.2518-3(a)(1)(iii). Like other property interests, the holder of a general power must disclaim within nine months of the date of the transfer creating the power. Treas. Reg. § 25.2518-2(c)(3)(i). A qualified disclaimer of a general power of appointment is not treated as a release of the power for purposes of §§ 2514 and 2041. Treas. Reg. § 20.2041-3(d)(6)(i). In that case, the effective transfer of property that occurs by reason of the qualified disclaimer is viewed as emanating from the original transfer that created the power. Treas. Reg. § 25.2518-2(c)(3)(i). As such, any party receiving property by way of a qualified disclaimer of a power of appointment must disclaim, if at all, within the same nine-month period. *Id.* ("A person who receives an interest in property as the result of a qualified disclaimer of the interest must disclaim the previously disclaimed interest no later than nine months after the date of the transfer creating the interest in the preceding disclaimant.").

Turning to the transfer of property that occurs by reason of the exercise, release, or lapse of a power of appointment, the prevailing rules turn on whether the underlying power was a general power of appointment. If the power that was exercised, released, or permitted to lapse was a general power, the transferee of the property interest has nine months from the date of such event to disclaim. Treas. Reg. § 25.2518-2(c)(3)(i). This rule applies regardless of whether the exercise, release, or lapse was subject to estate or gift tax. *Id.* However, if the underlying power of appointment did not constitute a general power of appointment, the disclaimer period starts from the date the power is *created* rather than the date on which the power is exercised, released, or permitted to lapse. *Id.* Note that the potential objects or takers in default of a non-general power likely will be required to disclaim their interests well before those interests become possessory in order to satisfy § 2518, similar to beneficiaries holding contingent future interests in irrevocable trusts.

§ 16.03 DISCLAIMER OF LESS THAN ENTIRE INTEREST IN PROPERTY

Section 2518(c)(1) sanctions a disclaimer of an "undivided portion" of an interest in property. In effect, the provision clarifies that receipt of the non-disclaimed undivided portion of the property will not constitute acceptance of the entire transfer under § 2518(b)(3).

[A] Separate and Severable Property

Before examining the limits of an undivided portion of property under § 2518(c)(1), it is important to note that the disclaimer provisions of § 2518 apply independently to each separate interest in property. *See* Treas. Reg. § 25.2518-2(d)(1) ("The acceptance of one interest in property will not, by itself, constitute an acceptance of any other separate interests created by the transferor and held by the disclaimant in the same property."). For instance, suppose a decedent creates a testamentary trust that requires the income to be distributed equally to his children until the death of the last child, with the remainder to be paid in equal shares to each child's estate. The decedent's children each would possess two separate interests in the devise—one as a lifetime income beneficiary and the other as a remainderman. Each child can make a qualified disclaimer of either interest while retaining the other. *See* Treas. Reg. § 25.2518-3(a)(1).

To the extent a transfer is made of "severable" property, a disclaimer of a portion of the transfer will be treated as a disclaimer of separate property. Severable property for this purpose is property that, after its division into separate parts, "maintains a complete and independent existence." Treas. Reg. § 25.2518-3(a)(1)(ii). However, previously unified temporal interests in an item of property do not constitute severable interests. Accordingly, a disclaimer of a certain number of devised corporate shares can be qualified under the severable property rule, while a disclaimer of the lifetime income generated by the devised corporate stock cannot. *See* Treas. Reg. § 25.2518-3(d), Exs. 1–3.

[B]   Undivided Portions of Property

With respect to a single interest in non-severable property, a partial disclaimer will be qualified only to the extent it relates to an "undivided portion" of the property. As a general rule, an undivided portion consists of a fraction or percentage of each property right of the disclaimant in the property. Treas. Reg. § 25.2518-3(b). A division of property into temporal interests—so-called "horizontal slices"—does not give rise to undivided portions under § 2518(c)(1). Rather, the division must constitute a "vertical slice" of the property that extends to the entire term of the disclaimant's interest. *Id.* Hence, a beneficiary's disclaimer of a 25 percent interest in 100 acres of real property devised to him can constitute a qualified disclaimer under the undivided-interest rule of § 2518(c)(1).[7] Yet, just as previously unified temporal interests in property do not constitute severable interests in property, they do not constitute undivided portions in the same property. Hence, a disclaimer of the beneficiary's interest in the 100 acres that follows a retained life estate cannot be qualified under the undivided-interest rule. *See* Walshire v. United States, 288 F.3d 342 (8th Cir. 2002) (upholding validity of Reg. § 25.2518-3(b) against challenge).

While defining disclaimed portions of property in terms of fractions or percentages is the conservative approach to complying with the undivided-portion rule of § 2518(c)(1), it is possible for the disclaimer of a pecuniary amount to satisfy the rule. To do so, no income or other benefit from the disclaimed amount can inure to the benefit of the disclaimant. Treas. Reg. § 25.2518-3(c). For instance, if a devisee disclaims $25,000 of a $100,000 devise, the $25,000 amount and the income it generates must be segregated from the $75,000 non-disclaimed portion while the estate is being administered.[8] *Id.*

[C]   Formula Disclaimers

In *Estate of Christiansen v. Commissioner*, 130 T.C. 1 (2008), the Tax Court addressed the use of disclaimers that are defined by reference to the final estate tax value placed on the property. The decedent in *Estate of Christiansen* devised her entire estate to her daughter. However, the decedent's will anticipated a disclaimer by the daughter, providing that any disclaimed property would pass 75 percent to a charitable lead trust and 25 percent to a charitable foundation. The decedent's daughter executed a disclaimer by which she disclaimed a fractional portion of her devise. Simplifying the facts somewhat, the disclaimer instrument defined the fraction as having a numerator equal to the value of the devise less $6.35 million and a denominator equal to the value of the devise. Importantly, the value of the devise for this

---

[7] A disclaimer of a particular 25 acres of the property, however, would not need the undivided-interest rule to render it qualified; rather, such a disclaimer would relate to severable property.

[8] If the disclaimer of a pecuniary amount does not relate to a pecuniary devise (such as a devise of corporate stock), the division and segregation of the devise into disclaimed and non-disclaimed portions must be based on the fair market value of the assets at the time of the disclaimer or in a manner that is otherwise fairly representative of the changes in fair market value from the date of transfer to the date of the disclaimer. Treas. Reg. § 25.2518-3(c). This requirement would prevent a surviving spouse, for example, from using pecuniary disclaimers to transfer all post-death appreciation in property to a credit shelter trust.

purpose was that "as . . . finally determined for estate tax purposes." *Id.* at 5. While defining the fraction in this manner may seem a bit cumbersome, note the intended effect: If the Service proved successful in challenging the estate's valuation of the decedent's probate estate (which consisted primarily of family limited partnership interests), the sought-after revenue benefit would be largely offset by the resulting increase in the estate's charitable deduction.

As it turns out, the Service in *Estate of Christiansen* was successful in increasing the valuation of the decedent's partnership interests. The estate countered the increase in the gross estate by increasing its charitable deduction under § 2055. The Service was successful in rejecting the increased charitable deduction for additional amounts passing to the charitable trust on the basis that the daughter impermissibly retained an interest in the disclaimed property. *See id.* at 12–13 (citing Treas. Reg. § 25.2518-2(e)(3)).

As for the increased charitable deduction claimed by the estate for additional amounts that pass to the charitable foundation, the Service disallowed the increased deduction on public policy grounds. In essence, the government argued that to permit an increased charitable deduction under these circumstances would undermine the financial incentive for the Service to challenge property values as reported by taxpayers—in effect, providing taxpayers with an audit-proof means of undervaluing property.

The Tax Court was not moved by the government's public policy argument. The court noted that, to be successful, the technique would depend on the parties deliberately undervaluing the estate property. The court cited a number of safeguards against such chicanery, including the fiduciary duties placed on executors and administrators, the enforcement of charitable gifts by the attorneys general, and even the prospect of a charitable organization losing its tax-exempt status. *Id.* at 17–18. The Eight Circuit affirmed, finding "no evidence of a clear Congressional intent suggesting a policy to maximize incentives for the Commissioner to challenge or audit returns." Estate of Christiansen v. Commissioner, 586 F.3d 1061, 1065 (8th Cir. 2009). While formulaic transfers defined in terms of property values as finally determined for federal transfer tax purposes have been sanctioned under the regulations defining a qualified interest under § 2702,[9] the *Estate of Christiansen* case indicates that the technique is viable outside the express regulatory safe harbors.

§ 16.04 STUDY PROBLEMS

1. Sandra's mother established three brokerage accounts that she caused to be titled in her and Sandra's names as joint tenants with right of survivorship. Sandra's mother also left a will creating a residual trust of which Sandra and her brother were designated as beneficiaries.

    Two months after her mother's death, Sandra purchased stock on margin and posted the securities in one of the brokerage accounts as collateral. Six months after her mother's death, Sandra executed a written disclaimer "of any interest passing to her in the brokerage accounts by right of survivorship." Assume that under state law the disclaimed interest passes as if Sandra had predeceased her mother.

    Will Sandra's disclaimer of her survivorship interest in the brokerage accounts

---

[9] *See* Treas. Reg. § 25.2702-3(b)(1)(ii)(B) (permitting a fixed amount to be paid to a grantor of a grantor retained annuity trust to be defined as a fractional value of the transferred property "as finally determined for federal tax purposes").

constitute a qualified disclaimer under § 2518(a)?

2. Mike's mother established an inter vivos revocable trust that permitted the trustee to make discretionary distributions to his mother and members of her family. Upon his mother's death, the trust assets are to continue to be held in trust, whereby Mike (as successor trustee) would have discretion to distribute the trust property to his mother's descendants as he saw fit.

    On January 18 of this year, Mike's mother caused the trust to distribute $100,000 to each of Mike and his siblings. Mike's mother died on May 10 of the same year. It is now October 1. Because Mike is independently wealthy, he comes to seek your advice on possibly disclaiming everything he has received from his mother. However, he would like to stay on as trustee of the trust. On that note, he still has not cashed the $100,000 check.

    a. What is your advice?

    b. Is there anything you would have preferred to revise in the trust instrument?

3. In light of Congress' propensity to significantly alter the estate tax exemption, your supervising attorney has proposed that his client devise her entire estate to her husband outright, but then provide that any portion of such devise that the husband disclaims will pass to a non-marital trust for his benefit. The terms of the trust, which are set forth in the draft of the will, provide that (a) the husband will serve as trustee; (b) the trustee can make distributions of trust principal to such one or more of the husband and the testator's children for the recipient's "health, education, support and maintenance"; and (c) the trust assets will be distributed upon the husband's death to those of the testator's issue as the husband shall appoint by will, or in default thereof, to the testator's then-living issue.

    Your supervising attorney asks you to review the plan to ensure that any disclaimer by the husband will qualify under § 2518(a). Advise.

4. Jim devises to his daughter, Ellie, 100 acres of timberland and 100 shares of X Corp. In addition, Jim names Ellie as lifetime income beneficiary of a trust funded with 100 shares of Y Corp. The trust remainder passes upon Ellie's death to her surviving issue.

    Ellie executes a disclaimer within nine months of Jim's death, through which she disclaims the following items:

    -   40 shares of X Corp.;

    -   the remaining 60 shares of X Corp. stock, provided that she retains the dividend stream from the stock for her lifetime;

    -   20 identified acres of timberland;

    -   a 25 percent interest in the remaining 80 acres of timberland;

    -   30 percent of her beneficial interest in the trust; and

    -   the right to receive income distributions for 10 years from the 70 percent interest in the trust that she has not disclaimed.

    Which of the above items can be the subject of a qualified disclaimer?

Chapter 17

DETERMINING THE NET TRANSFER

Internal Revenue Code:	§§ 2053, 2054, 2058
	see also § 642(g)(1)
Treasury Regulations:	§§ 20.2053-1 to -8, 20.2054-1

The estate tax is not imposed on the amount of wealth possessed by a decedent; rather, the tax constitutes an excise on the transmission of wealth by reason of death. *See* New York Trust Co. v. Eisner, 256 U.S. 345 (1921). Hence, the estate tax allows certain deductions from the decedent's gross estate to properly determine the value that "passes from the dead to the living." Jacobs v. Commissioner, 34 B.T.A. 594 (1936). Section 2053 carries the primary load in this area, providing a deduction for the following expenses and charges: funeral expenses, costs of administration, claims against the decedent's estate, and other enforceable obligations of the decedent. The more limited § 2054 provides a deduction for casualty losses sustained by the estate during the administration process. Broadly speaking, the "net transfer" oriented deductions of §§ 2053 and 2054 can be divided into three primary categories: (1) obligations of the decedent outstanding at the time of his death; (2) expenses incurred by the decedent's estate during the course of administration; and (3) losses sustained through the destruction or theft of estate property.

§ 17.01 OBLIGATIONS OF THE DECEDENT

While the inclusionary provisions of §§ 2033 through 2044 make up what can be conceived as the asset side of the decedent's balance sheet, the decedent's liabilities are accounted for through § 2053(a)(3) and (a)(4). Section 2053(a)(3) allows a deduction from the decedent's gross estate for claims against the estate. Such claims are limited to personal obligations of the decedent that existed as of the decedent's death. Treas. Reg. § 20.2053-4(a)(1). Section 2053(a)(4) authorizes a deduction for unpaid mortgages or other indebtedness relating to property, provided that the value of the decedent's interest in the subject property, undiminished by the amount of the encumbering debt, is included in the decedent's gross estate. Both categories of deductions extend to interest accrued on the underlying obligation as of the decedent's death.[1] Treas. Reg. §§ 20.2053-4(e)(1), 20.2053-7.

As a general rule, the total deductions under § 2053(a)(3) and (a)(4) are limited to the amount of property included in the decedent's probate estate. *See* IRC § 2053(c)(2). However, deductions in excess of this amount are allowed to the extent attributable to debts and claims

---

[1] Interest accruing after the decedent's death may be deductible by the estate if it constitutes an administration expense under § 2053(a)(2). *See* Treas. Reg. § 20.2053-4(e)(2).

that were actually paid prior to the date for filing the estate tax return.[2] *Id.*

[A]   Claims Against the Estate

Not all claims paid by an estate will give rise to a deduction under § 2053(a)(3). While this perhaps goes without saying, the claim must be attributable to a personal obligation *of the decedent* that was enforceable as of the decedent's death. Treas. Reg. § 20.2053-4(a)(1). In *Lindberg v. United States*, 164 F.3d 1312 (10th Cir. 1999), the estate settled a claim of tortious interference with inheritance that was asserted against the individual named as personal representative of the decedent's estate and as trustee of trusts created under the decedent's will. Pointing out the obvious—that the decedent was not the alleged tortfeasor—the Tenth Circuit upheld the disallowance of a deduction.

Furthermore, a deduction under § 2053(a)(3) is warranted only for claims asserted by the claimant in the capacity of a creditor—that is, claims made *against* an estate that take priority over distributions to beneficiaries. The deduction does not extend to claims that are asserted *to* a distributive share of the estate. *See* Estate of Lazar v. Commissioner, 58 T.C. 543 (1972) (distinguishing the two). Hence, a surviving spouse's election to take a statutorily guaranteed portion of the decedent's estate does not give rise to a deductible claim. *See* Briscoe v. Craig, 32 F.2d 40 (6th Cir. 1929).

[1]   Relevance of Post-Death Events

The deduction for a claim against the estate under § 2053(a) is most straightforward in the following circumstances: the amount of the obligation is fixed as of the date of the decedent's death, the decedent's liability for the obligation is not questioned, and the obligation is subsequently paid in the course of the estate administration. Routine expenses incurred by the decedent, such as monthly utility bills, fall within this category.

Not all claims will be so cleanly presented. For example, suppose a decedent died as a result of injuries sustained in a car accident that appears to be the product of his negligence. The accident left others severely injured as well. Several months after the decedent's death, suits were filed against the estate seeking damages of $5 million. Looking forward from the date of the decedent's death, the best estimate of the decedent's tort liability was $1.5 million. Approximately two years after the decedent's death, the estate settled the claims through a total payment of $1 million. Under these facts, what would be the amount of the estate's deduction under § 2053(a)(3)?

One of the more difficult interpretative questions under the estate tax has been the relevance of post-death events in determining the value of a claim against the estate under § 2053(a)(3). In the absence of clear statutory or regulatory guidance, a pronounced split in judicial authority developed over whether claims against the estate were to be valued prospectively as of the decedent's death or instead through the application of hindsight. For the most part, a given court's position on the issue turned on its interpretation of the Supreme Court's decision in *Ithaca Trust Co. v. United States*, 279 U.S. 151 (1929).

The decedent in *Ithaca Trust* devised property in trust for the lifetime benefit of his wife, with the remainder passing to charity. The decedent's wife survived him by less than six

---

[2]   The due date for filing the estate tax return includes not only the nine-month period provided by § 6075(a), but also any extension (up to six months) granted by the Service under § 6081. *See* Treas. Reg. § 20.2053-1(c)(2).

months. In calculating the estate's charitable deduction for the remainder interest under § 2055, the Court was forced to determine whether the wife's intervening life interest should be valued according to the wife's projected life expectancy as of the decedent's death or instead by reference to her much shorter actual lifetime. The Court resolved the matter as follows:

> The first impression is that it is absurd to resort to statistical probabilities when you know the fact. But this is due to inaccurate thinking. The estate so far as may be is settled as of the date of the testator's death. The tax is on the act of the testator not on the receipt of property by the legatees. Therefore the value of the thing to be taxed must be estimated as of the time when the act is done. But the value of property at a given time depends upon the relative intensity of the social desire for it at that time, expressed in the money that it would bring in the market. Like all values, . . . it depends largely on more or less certain prophecies of the future; and the value is no less real at that time if later the prophecy turns out false than when it comes out true. Tempting as it is to correct uncertain probabilities by the now certain fact, we are of the opinion that it cannot be done, but that the value of the wife's life interest must be estimated by the mortality tables.

Id. at 155 (citations omitted).

Despite the Court's reasoning in *Ithaca Trust*, several courts have favored consideration of post-death events in valuing claims against the estate under § 2053(a)(3), refusing to apply *Ithaca Trust* outside of the § 2055 context in which it arose. *See* Estate of Sachs v. Commissioner, 856 F.2d 1158 (8th Cir. 1988); Gowetz v. Commissioner, 320 F.2d 874 (1st Cir. 1963); Commissioner v. Estate of Shively, 276 F.2d 372 (2d Cir. 1960); Jacobs v. Commissioner, 34 F.2d 233 (8th Cir. 1929); Estate of Kyle v. Commissioner, 94 T.C. 829 (1990). In short, these courts contended that ignoring such events was to "prefer fiction to reality." *Estate of Shively,* 276 F.2d at 375. However, Circuit Courts of Appeals increasingly took the position that *Ithaca Trust* supplied a broader directive that all valuation determinations under the estate tax were to be made from the reference point of the decedent's death. Under that view, post-death events could not be considered in valuing the claim. *See* Estate of O'Neal v. United States, 258 F.3d 1265 (11th Cir. 2001); Estate of McMorris v. Commissioner, 243 F.3d 1254 (10th Cir. 2001); Smith v. Commissioner, 198 F.3d 515 (5th Cir. 1999); Propstra v. United States, 680 F.2d 1248 (9th Cir. 1982).

[a]   General Regulatory Guidance

In light of the prevailing disparate treatment of similarly situated estates, the Service amended the § 2053 regulations to address the relevance of events occurring after the decedent's death. *See* T.D. 9468, 74 Fed. Reg. 53,652, 53,653 (Oct. 20, 2009). Consistent with its prior litigating position, the Service came down on the side of requiring post-death events to be considered in determining the value of deductions under § 2053.

As a general rule, the amount of any deduction under § 2053 is limited to the total amount actually paid in settlement or satisfaction of the claim. Treas. Reg. § 20.2053-1(d)(1). In determining this amount, events occurring within the applicable period of limitations on assessment of the estate tax must be taken into account.[3] Treas. Reg. § 20.2053-1(d)(2)(i). If

---

[3] Note that the statute of limitations on assessment is tolled during the course of any deficiency litigation.

the estate sues for a refund, then events occurring after the period of limitations on assessment must be taken into consideration as well. Treas. Reg. § 20.2053-1(d)(2)(ii).

The regulations provide one exception to the general rule that § 2053 deductions are limited to the amounts paid: A deduction will be permitted for a claim or expense that satisfies every other requirement other than payment, provided the amount is "ascertainable with reasonable certainty and will be paid." Treas. Reg. § 20.2053-1(d)(4)(i). Amounts that are contested or contingent will not be treated as ascertainable with reasonable certainty for this purpose. *Id.* If a claim or expense to be paid in the future initially fails the "ascertainable with reasonable certainty" condition but is later paid or later satisfies that standard, the estate may seek relief through a refund claim. Treas. Reg. § 20.2053-1(d)(4)(ii). In order to avoid the preclusion of a deduction by the statute of limitations on refund claims, the regulations provide for the filing of a protective refund claim. *See* Treas. Reg. § 20.2053-1(d)(5).

[b] Specific Guidance on Claims Against Estate

To be deductible under § 2053(a)(3), a claim against the decedent's estate must represent a personal obligation of the decedent existing at the time of the decedent's death. Treas. Reg. § 20.2053-4(a)(1). Additionally, the claim must be bona fide, enforceable against the decedent's estate at the time of the decedent's death, and not unenforceable at the time it is paid. *Id.* If these prerequisites are satisfied, the amount of the deduction will equal the total of (1) the amount paid in satisfaction of the claim, and (2) amounts that will be paid in the future that can be ascertained with reasonable certainty.[4] *Id.* The regulations provide a generous exception to this otherwise strict general rule: Aggregate claims not in excess of $500,000 may be presently deducted before payment even if not capable of reasonably certain approximation, so long as they are valued through a "qualified appraisal" issued by a "qualified appraiser." Treas. Reg. § 20.2053-4(c)(1).

As long as the decedent's estate contests its liability for a claim against the estate, no deduction may be taken with respect to the claim.[5] Treas. Reg. § 20.2053-4(d)(2). Similarly, a claim against the estate that has not yet matured may not be deducted. Treas. Reg. § 20.2053-4(d)(1). Claims that later mature or for which the estate later concedes liability may be deducted through a refund claim, with protective refund claims being permitted to prevent a future deduction from being effectively negated by the statute of limitations. Note that a protective claim would be necessary only for amounts that may not be deducted under the $500,000 exemption available under Reg. § 20.2053-4(c).

Applying this regulatory guidance to the example introduced at the beginning of this

---

[4] A decedent's liability for future, recurring payments that are not contingent in nature is considered to be ascertainable with reasonable certainty. Treas. Reg. § 20.2053-4(d)(6)(i). The requirement that such recurring payments not be contingent is relaxed where the contingency relates to the death or remarriage of the claimant. *Id.* Hence, the actuarial value of the decedent's liability for support payments to a former spouse may be deducted under § 2053(a)(3).

[5] The regulations provide an exception to this rule, allowing a deduction for a contested claim in certain circumstances where the claim relates to one or more causes of action that are included in the decedent's gross estate or if the claim is "integrally related" to an asset that is included in the decedent's gross estate. Treas. Reg. § 20.2053-4(b). [The exception applies only if the aggregate value of the related claims or assets represents more than 10 percent of the decedent's gross estate. Treas. Reg. § 20.2053-4(b)(1)(iv).] The basis for this exception is to avoid the decedent's estate from being whipsawed by having to include an asset that may be subject to a contingency while not being able to deduct an associated claim due to its contingent nature.

discussion, the decedent's estate contested the plaintiffs' claims for $5 million of tort damages. Hence, the estate could not claim a deduction under § 2053(a)(3) for this amount. Even though the best estimate of the decedent's liability was set at $1.5 million, it is doubtful that this estimate of the decedent's tort exposure would satisfy the "ascertainable with reasonable certainty" requirement for current deductibility. Hence, the estate would not be entitled to a deduction on account of the claim at the point of filing the estate tax return. When the $1 million settlement was paid approximately two years after decedent's death, the requirements for deductibility under Reg. § 20.2053-4(a) are then satisfied. At that point, the estate could claim the $1 million deduction through the filing of an amended return.[6] If the litigation were not settled within the period of limitations on assessment for refund claims, the estate would need to file a protective refund claim to preserve the ability to claim the deduction in the future.

[2]   Joint Obligations

If the decedent was joint and severally liable on an obligation, the estate is entitled to deduct only the decedent's pro-rata share of the liability. *See* Atkins v. Commissioner, 2 T.C. 332 (1943). This is the case even though the decedent's estate could be held accountable for the full amount of the liability due to the estate's right of contribution from the other joint obligors. The right of contribution is presumed to be collectible, although the presumption may be rebutted by evidence showing the contribution right to be worthless. *See* McCue v. Commissioner, 5 T.C.M. (CCH) 141 (1946) (contribution right presumed collectible absent contrary evidence); Estate of Belzer v. Commissioner, 1 T.C.M. (CCH) 539 (1943) (establishing that right of contribution was worthless).

Regulations issued under § 2053(a)(3) in 2009 conform to this approach. If a claim is asserted against the decedent's estate *and* one or more other parties, the estate is entitled to deduct only the portion of the total claim that is due from and actually paid by the estate. Treas. Reg. § 20.2053-4(d)(3). Hence, if the decedent were joint and severally liable for the obligation and the estate paid the full amount of the liability, the amount paid by the estate would be the starting point for the deduction under § 2053(a)(3). However, this amount will be reduced by the total reimbursements to which the estate is entitled. *Id.* If the estate can establish that only a partial reimbursement can be collected, then the estate's deduction will be reduced only by this lower amount. *See* Treas. Reg. § 20.2053-1(d)(3) (discussing reimbursements in general). Yet the estate will be charged with the amount of any contribution from other parties that it could have collected but which it declined or otherwise failed to pursue. Treas. Reg. § 20.2053-4(d)(3).

[3]   Taxes

Taxes attributable to a period prior to the decedent's death may be deducted as claims against the estate.[7] *See* Treas. Reg. § 20.2053-6(a)(1)(i). The deduction is subject to the general limitations imposed under Reg. § 20.2053-1, meaning that the taxes either must be actually paid by the estate or must be ascertainable with reasonable certainty with payment to follow

---

[6] Note that the amount of the deduction must be reduced by any amounts paid by the decedent's automobile insurance carrier. *See* Treas. Reg. § 20.2053-4(d)(3).

[7] There exists one exception: Excise taxes incurred on the sale of estate property may be deducted as administration expenses under § 2053(a)(2). *See* Treas. Reg. § 20.2053-6(e) (stating grounds for deductibility).

in the future. *See* Treas. Reg. § 20.2053-6(a)(1)(iii).

[a]　Property Taxes

State and local property taxes may be deducted only to the extent they accrued prior to the decedent's death. IRC § 2053(c)(1)(B). "Accrued" for this purpose is not synonymous with the income tax accounting concept. Rather, taxes are accrued under this provision if they constitute an enforceable obligation of the decedent at the time of his death. Treas. Reg. § 20.2053-6(b). This determination will depend on local law. In certain jurisdictions, property taxes never arise to the level of a personal liability but instead constitute encumbrances on the assessed property. In that case, the taxes will constitute indebtedness against property that are deductible under § 2053(a)(4) as opposed to § 2053(a)(3).

[b]　Income Taxes

A decedent's outstanding income tax liability may be deducted as a claim against the estate, provided the tax relates only to income received prior to the decedent's death. IRC § 2053(c)(1)(B); Treas. Reg. § 20.2053-6(f). If the decedent's estate is entitled to a refund for income taxes paid by the decedent attributable to this period, the refund constitutes an asset includible in the gross estate under § 2033.

Determining the decedent's income tax liability for a period prior to his death can become complicated when the decedent and his surviving spouse file a joint return. As a general rule, the decedent's share of the joint liability is the amount for which the decedent's estate would be liable under local law after accounting for any reimbursement right. Treas. Reg. § 20.2053-6(f). However, the regulations supply a default allocation that applies absent contrary evidence. The default allocation is a pro-rata one based on the would-be income tax liabilities of each spouse for the relevant period had the spouses filed separately. *Id.* The estate generally is entitled to deduct only the decedent's share of the tax liability, even if the estate pays the entire amount. In that case, the estate would have a right of reimbursement from the surviving spouse. *See* Treas. Reg. § 20.2053-1(d)(3); *see also* Estate of McClure v. United States, 288 F.2d 190 (Ct. Cl. 1961). However, the estate may be able to deduct the full amount paid if the surviving spouse does not possess adequate resources to satisfy the contribution right. *See* Johnson v. United States, 742 F.2d 137 (4th Cir. 1984).

[c]　Gift Taxes

Unpaid gift taxes attributable to gifts made by the decedent prior to his death may be deducted by the decedent's estate. Treas. Reg. § 20.2053-6(d). The mere filing of a split-gift election by the decedent (or his estate) and the decedent's spouse does not change this result. That is, the decedent's estate may still deduct the full amount of the gift tax attributable to gifts of which the decedent was the actual donor. *Id.* However, recall the general rule that a deduction for expenses and claims may be taken only to the extent they are paid or will be paid by the decedent's estate, taking into account post-death events. *See* Treas. Reg. § 20.2053-1(d)(1). Hence, if the surviving spouse pays a portion of the gift tax attributable to a gift from the decedent for which a § 2513 split-gift election was made, the decedent's estate can deduct only the portion of the liability it actually paid. *See* T.A.M. 8837004 (Sept. 16, 1988) (taking this approach prior to 2009 revisions to regulations under § 2053). If the decedent was not the actual donor but made a § 2513 election during his life to be treated as a donor of one-half of the property, the decedent's estate may deduct the decedent's outstanding gift tax liability.

See Rev. Rul. 70-600, 1970-2 C.B. 194. However, the split-gift election must have been made during the decedent's lifetime. While a decedent's estate is permitted to make a split-gift election on the decedent's behalf, a post-mortem election will not retroactively give rise to a liability existing on the date of the decedent's death necessary to support the deduction. *See id.*

[d]   Post-Death Adjustments in Tax Liability

Suppose that a decedent's final income tax return is selected for audit, and the Service determines a $50,000 deficiency attributable to income received prior to the decedent's death. Can the decedent's estate deduct the asserted deficiency as a claim against the estate? Initially, no. Recall that no deduction is allowed for a claim that is contested by the decedent's estate. *See* Treas. Reg. § 20.2053-4(d)(2). However, if the deficiency is ultimately sustained and paid by the decedent's estate, an increased deduction may be asserted through a refund claim. Treas. Reg. § 20.2053-6(g). Protective refund claims are permitted to preserve deductions attributable to future potential tax payments. *Id.*

[B]   Mortgages and Other Obligations Relating to Property

The decedent's estate may deduct the amount of any outstanding mortgage or other indebtedness relating to property included in the gross estate, so long as the subject property is included in the gross estate at its undiminished value. IRC § 2053(a)(4). Accordingly, if a husband dies owning property with his wife as joint tenants with right of survivorship, only one-half of any mortgage encumbering the property can be deducted under § 2053(a)(4). *See* Estate of Courtney v. Commissioner, 62 T.C. 317 (1974). However, that is not to say that the amount of the deduction is limited to the value of the property so included. Suppose the residence, valued at $500,000, was encumbered by a $600,000 mortgage for which the husband bore joint and several liability. Because the excess debt could be satisfied from the husband's other property if necessary, the husband's estate may deduct his $300,000 share of the mortgage. *See* Rev. Rul. 83-81, 1983-1 C.B. 230 (reaching this result where the lower value was the product of special-use valuation under § 2032A).

If a decedent does not bear personal liability for the debt that encumbers the property included in the gross estate, the estate may elect to report only the equity in the property (that is, the value of the property net of the debt) in the gross estate. Treas. Reg. § 20.2053-7. The ability to include only the net value of the property in the gross estate can prove beneficial to non-resident decedents who are taxed only on property situated in the United States, as deductions attributable to recourse obligations must be pro-rated between domestic and foreign assets.[8] *See* Estate of Fung v. Commissioner, 117 T.C. 247 (2001).

[C]   Necessity of Consideration Received

Deductions on account of claims against the estate, mortgages, or any other indebtedness that are based on a promise or agreement are available only to the extent that the underlying claim or obligation was contracted bona fide for an adequate and full consideration in money or money's worth. IRC § 2053(c)(1). The purpose of this requirement is to prevent an individual from undertaking obligations in favor of intended beneficiaries that do not augment

---

[8] The application of the transfer tax system to non-resident aliens is addressed in Chapter 26.

his future taxable estate, thereby turning transfers of taxable property into deductible payments. *See* United States v. Stapf, 375 U.S. 118 (1963). The requirement of adequate consideration does not apply to liability for tort claims or other obligations imposed by law, as these claims are not subject to the same degree of manipulation. Furthermore, the statutory requirement that the decedent receive adequate and full consideration for contractual obligations does not apply when the claim is premised upon the decedent's promise or agreement to make a charitable contribution. In that case, the deduction will be allowed to the extent a bequest to the recipient would be deductible under § 2055.[9]

The First Circuit addressed the scope of consideration sufficient to sustain a claim against an estate based on a promise or agreement in *Estate of Huntington v. Commissioner*, 16 F.3d 462 (1st Cir. 1994). The decedent and her husband had entered into an agreement that their combined estates would pass in equal shares to her daughter and her husband's two sons. The decedent's husband died first, leaving a will that complied with their agreement. The decedent, however, died intestate. The step-sons filed a claim against the decedent's estate, which the decedent's executor settled for $425,000. The estate claimed a deduction for this amount under § 2053(a)(3), which the Service disallowed. After identifying the proper issue as whether the mutual promises between the decedent and her husband constituted the "bona fide" consideration required under § 2053(a)(3), the First Circuit sustained the disallowance of the deduction with "little difficulty." *Id.* at 466. The court reasoned as follows:

> The estate, of course, insists that there *was* a debt . . . once [the decedent] made her promise and received a financial benefit, but then reneged on the deal. It may be that, under state law, the reciprocal will agreement was an enforceable contract that, when violated, created a debt in favor of [the step-sons] against the estate. A valid contract is not necessarily enough, however, to establish a deductible claim for purposes of section 2053. A claim derived solely from [the husband's] desire to share some portion of his estate with his sons, carried out through cooperative estate planning, is precisely the sort of "debt" section 2053(c)(1)(A) was designed to exclude.

Id. at 468 (citations omitted).

[1] Consideration Received Through Services

The *Estate of Huntington* decision explains that an enforceable contractual obligation of the decedent to devise a portion of his estate will give rise to a deduction under § 2053(a)(3) only when the consideration received by the decedent in connection with the agreement served to augment the decedent's estate. Contractual claims to a portion of the decedent's estate often are based on services provided by the claimant for the decedent—typically of a caretaking nature. Can services rendered constitute adequate and full consideration in money or money's worth for purposes of § 2053(c)(1)(A)?

In *Estate of Wilson v. Commissioner*, T.C. Memo. 1998-309, 76 T.C.M. (CCH) 350, two cousins of the decedent's predeceased husband assisted the decedent in various personal and financial matters. Each cousin asserted that the decedent had orally agreed to devise one-third of her estate to him in exchange for his agreement to assist her. The decedent died with an estate of $4.5 million, but she devised only $100,000 to each cousin. The cousins sued for breach of contract and ultimately settled their claims for $400,000 and $550,000, respectively. The jury

---

[9] The deduction for transfers to charitable organizations is addressed in Chapter 18.

estimated the value of the services each cousin provided to the decedent to be $75,000, and the Service sought to limit the estate's deduction under § 2053(a)(3) to this amount. The Tax Court disagreed. While the differences between the services provided by the cousins and the amounts they received as compensation were stark in hindsight, the court viewed the bargain as fair at the time it was entered. In particular, the court noted that the value of the services provided by the cousins would depend on the decedent's longevity and her needs, as would the size of the estate she ultimately would leave. This observation, combined with the fact that the cousins were not natural objects of the decedent's bounty, led the court to determine that the mutual promises exchanged between the cousins and the decedent at the time their agreements were entered into provided adequate and full consideration in money or money's worth for purposes of § 2053.

[2] Claims of Family Members

As explained by the Third Circuit in *Bank of New York v. United States*, 526 F.2d 1012 (3d Cir. 1975), claims asserted by members of the decedent's family are subject to particular scrutiny given the likelihood of converting a taxable devise into a deductible payment. The Second Circuit in *Estate of Flandreau v. Commissioner*, 994 F.2d 91 (2d Cir. 1993), passed on an attempt to utilize § 2053(a)(3) to effectively preserve forgone annual exclusions under § 2503(b) for the decedent's estate. In *Estate of Flandreau*, the decedent first made gifts to her sons and daughters-in-law. For the most part, these gifts were fully sheltered by the annual exclusion. Each recipient then made an interest-free loan of an identical amount to the decedent. Fourteen such transactions took place over a 3-year period. Viewed in isolation, the decedent received monetary consideration for each loan she undertook. The Tax Court, however, determined that the transactions were "merely circular transfers of money" that amounted to "unenforceable gratuitous promises to make a gift" in the future. *Estate of Flandreau*, T.C. Memo. 1992-173, 63 T.C.M. (CCH) 2512. The Second Circuit affirmed, concluding that the transactions were not contracted bona fide for an adequate and full consideration in money or money's worth for purposes of § 2053. *Estate of Flandreau*, 994 F.2d at 93.

[a] Requirement of a "Bona Fide" Claim

The regulations under § 2053 issued in 2009 reiterate the special scrutiny to be afforded to claims asserted by family members. After considering a regulatory presumption that all claims against the estate made by a member of the decedent's family and other related parties were not legitimate and bona fide,[10] the Treasury instead inserted a broad requirement that all claims and expenses for which a deduction is sought under § 2053 must be "bona fide in nature." Treas. Reg. § 20.2053-1(b)(2)(i). The regulations then provide a non-exhaustive list of factors that are indicative of when a claim asserted by a family member of the decedent, a related entity, or a beneficiary of the decedent's estate or revocable trust will satisfy the bona fide requirement. The first two positive factors appear the most significant: (1) the transaction giving rise to the claim or expense occurred in the ordinary course of business, was negotiated at arm's length, and was free from donative intent;[11] and (2) the nature of the claim or expense is not related to an expectation or claim of inheritance. Treas. Reg. § 20.2053-1(b)(2)(ii)(A)–(B).

---

[10] *See* Prop. Treas. Reg. § 20.2053-4(b)(4), 72 Fed. Reg. 20,080, 20,081 (Apr. 23, 2007).

[11] Note the similarities between this factor and the presumption of adequate and full consideration provided for transactions occurring in the ordinary course of business under Reg. § 25.2512-8.

In effect, the regulations seek to identify a narrow window in which transactions between family members bargaining at arm's length will be respected for § 2053 purposes.

[b]   Marital Property Rights as Consideration

In the divorce setting, it is not uncommon for a spouse to contractually agree to name a former spouse as a beneficiary of a life insurance policy or retirement account. In that case, can compliance with the agreement give rise to a deductible claim? Recall that, as a general rule, the release of marital rights in a decedent's property does not constitute adequate and full consideration in money or money's worth to any extent.[12] IRC § 2043(b)(1). However, transfers of property to a spouse in settlement of marital or property rights that satisfy the conditions of § 2516(1) are deemed to have been made for adequate and full consideration for purposes of § 2053. IRC § 2043(b)(2). Accordingly, if the proceeds of a life insurance policy are included in the decedent's gross estate under § 2042, payment of the proceeds to a former spouse as required by a property settlement agreement gives rise to a deduction under § 2053(a)(4). *See* Estate of Robinson v. Commissioner, 63 T.C. 717 (1975).

[c]   Support Rights as Consideration

In *Leopold v. United States*, 510 F.2d 617 (9th Cir. 1974), the decedent had contractually agreed to make a stated devise to the child of his second marriage as part of a property settlement agreement with that spouse. After the estate settled the child's claim to the contracted portion of the decedent's estate, the estate deducted the claim under § 2053(a)(3). Although a deduction under § 2053 is intended to guard against converting a testamentary devise to family members into a deductible claim, the Ninth Circuit affirmed the determination that the decedent's promise was contracted bona fide for an adequate and full consideration under § 2053(c)(1)(A). The facts indicated that the decedent's former spouse relinquished a portion of the support payments to which she was entitled to secure the devise to the couple's daughter, and the court determined that the reduced alimony obligation provided the requisite estate augmentation to the decedent. *Id.* at 624. *See also* Estate of Kosow v. Commissioner, 45 F.3d 1524 (11th Cir. 1995) (finding that reduced alimony payments supplied consideration for decedent's testamentary devise to children).

§ 17.02   POST-MORTEM EXPENSES AND LOSSES

[A]   Funeral Expenses

Section 2053(a)(1) provides a deduction from the gross estate for expenses of the decedent's funeral that are permitted under local law. In addition to the traditional costs associated with the decedent's interment, the regulations provide that funeral expenses can include a reasonable expenditure for a tombstone, monument, mausoleum, or burial lot for the decedent or his family, including amounts paid for future care of same. Treas. Reg. § 20.2053-2.

However, for the costs of perpetual care of burial lots of the decedent's family to be deductible, the decedent must be interred in the same area. *See* Estate of Gillespie v. Commissioner, 8 T.C. 838 (1947) (disallowing deduction for costs of care of burial plots for family members where decedent was buried in another cemetery); *see also* Rev. Rul. 57-530,

---

[12] Transfers made in satisfaction of marital rights or support rights are the subject of Chapter 6.

1957-2 C.B. 621 (perpetual care of burial lots in which decedent was not interred were not deductible, even though in same cemetery).

An expenditure relating to the decedent's funeral is not considered to be a deductible expense under § 2053(a)(1) to the extent the decedent's estate receives a reimbursement. The theory is that such amounts were not "actually expended" as required by Reg. § 20.2053-2. *See* Rev. Rul. 66-234, 1966-2 C.B. 436 (payments by Veterans Administration or Social Security Administration earmarked for funeral expenses reduce deduction under § 2053(a)(1)); Rev. Rul. 77-274, 1977-2 C.B. 326 (same result for wrongful death recoveries dedicated to funeral costs). While the recovery right standing alone would not have been included in the decedent's gross estate under § 2033, this treatment has the effect of subjecting the reimbursed funds to taxation.

[B]   Administration Expenses

Section 2053(a)(2) provides a deduction for expenses incurred in the administration of the decedent's estate to the extent permitted under the law of the jurisdiction in which the estate is administered. Such expenses include executor's commissions, attorney's fees, and other "miscellaneous" expenses, including those relating to the preservation, sale, or distribution of estate property. *See* Treas. Reg. § 20.2053-3(a). By way of implication from IRC § 2053(b), § 2053(a)(2) expenses are limited to those incurred in administering property "subject to claims," which essentially encompasses the decedent's probate estate. The deduction under § 2053(a)(2), when added to the other deductible expenses and claims under § 2053(a), is limited to the value of the decedent's probate estate plus any amounts paid from other sources before the due date of the decedent's estate tax return. IRC § 2053(c)(2).

While the deduction under § 2053(a)(2) is limited to the expenses of administering the decedent's probate estate, § 2053(b) provides a concomitant deduction for the expenses of administering the decedent's non-probate assets that are included in the decedent's gross estate for estate tax purposes. Deductible expenses under § 2053(b) must meet the conditions otherwise imposed by § 2053(a)(2); hence, the expenses must be occasioned by reason of the decedent's death, and they must relate to settling the decedent's interest in the subject property or vesting title to the property in the beneficiaries. Treas. Reg. § 20.2053-8(a). Additionally, such expenses must be paid within the period of limitations of assessment of the estate tax (generally three years following the filing of the return, tolled for any period in which a deficiency in estate tax is litigated). *Id.*

The deduction for administration expenses under § 2053(a)(2) and (b) generally is limited to amounts actually paid. Treas. Reg. § 20.2053-1(d)(1). However, a deduction for administration expenses that will be paid in the future may be taken currently provided that the amount of the future payment is ascertainable with reasonable certainty. Vague or uncertain estimates are insufficient for this purpose. Treas. Reg. § 20.2053-1(d)(4)(i).

[1]   Relevance of Allowance Under State Law

The allowance of a deduction for an administration expense under § 2053(a)(2) is conditioned upon the allowance of such expense under local law. Taxpayers have contended that allowance of the expense under local law constitutes not only a necessary but a sufficient condition to deductibility.[13] Yet the regulations supply a federal law condition to the deductibility of administration expenses by limiting the deduction to expenses that are "actually and necessarily incurred in the administration of the decedent's estate." Treas. Reg. § 20.2053-3(a). The regulations distinguish between expenses paid and incurred "in the collection of assets, payment of debts, and distribution of property to the persons entitled to it" and "[e]xpenditures not essential to the proper settlement of the estate, but incurred for the individual benefit of the heirs, legatees, or devisees." *Id.* Taxpayers have challenged the validity of any condition to deductibility apart from allowance under local law, but to little success. *See* Estate of Love v. Commissioner, 923 F.2d 335 (4th Cir. 1991); United States v. White, 853 F.2d 107 (2d Cir. 1988); Marcus v. De Witt, 704 F.2d 1227 (11th Cir. 1983); Hibernia Bank v. United States, 581 F.2d 741 (9th Cir. 1978); Pitner v. United States, 388 F.2d 651 (5th Cir. 1967). The Sixth Circuit at one point accepted the taxpayer argument that the deductibility of administration expenses was governed solely by state law, *see* Estate of Park v. Commissioner, 475 F.2d 673 (6th Cir. 1973), but reversed its position through a later decision. *See* Estate of Millikin v. Commissioner, 125 F.3d 339 (6th Cir. 1997) (en banc). The Seventh Circuit is the only court to hold that allowance of an expense under local law ensures deductibility under § 2053(a)(2). *See* Estate of Jenner v. Commissioner, 577 F.2d 1100 (7th Cir. 1978).

[2] Executor Commissions

Commissions paid to the personal representative of a decedent's estate are the first and most common example of an administration expense. To be deductible, the commissions must be consistent with the usually accepted standards and practices concerning the allowance of commissions in estates of similar size and character in the relevant jurisdiction. *See* Treas. Reg. § 20.2053-3(b)(2). If the decedent made a bequest to the named executor in lieu of compensation, the amount of the bequest is not deductible.[14] Treas. Reg. § 20.2053-3(b)(2). If the decedent went to the other extreme of stipulating the executor's remuneration in the terms of his will, the deduction nonetheless is limited to the amount allowable by local law or practice. *Id.*

[3] Attorney Fees

Legal fees paid by the estate are deductible to the extent they relate to the administration of the decedent's estate. However, deductible fees cannot exceed a "reasonable remuneration" for the attorney's services, taking into account the size and complexity of the estate, the typical practice in the jurisdiction in which the estate is being administered, and the expertise of the attorney. Treas. Reg. § 20.2053-3(c)(1).

Legal fees incurred by the estate to construe a will constitute deductible administration expenses, as such proceedings are necessary to determine the proper distribution of the

---

[13] The argument of taxpayers in this regard was bolstered by the § 2053 regulations prior to their amendment in 2009, which provided that a decision of a local court as to "the amount and allowability under local law of a claim or administration expense ordinarily will be accepted if the court passes upon the facts upon which the deductibility depends." *See* Treas. Reg. § 20.2053-1(b)(2) (prior to amendment by T.D. 9468). Any such support has been blunted by the current regulations, which provide that a final judicial decision of a court that reviews and approves expenditures for administration expenses "may be relied upon to establish the amount of a claim or expense that is *otherwise deductible* under section 2053 . . . provided that the court actually passes upon the facts on which deductibility depends." Treas. Reg. § 20.2053-1(b)(3)(i) (emphasis added).

[14] On the other hand, the bequest would be excluded from the beneficiary-executor's gross income under § 102(a).

decedent's estate. *See* Rev. Rul. 74-509, 1974-2 C.B. 302 (proceeding to clarify ambiguous provision in will held to be "necessary in effecting the distribution of the estate assets"). However, legal fees incurred by beneficiaries or would-be beneficiaries of the decedent's estate are a different matter. The regulations provide that fees incurred by beneficiaries concerning their respective interests in the estate are not deductible if the underlying litigation is not essential to the settlement of the estate. Treas. Reg. § 20.2053-3(c)(3). Legal fees incurred by parties in will contest proceedings therefore are not deductible simply because the estate is required to reimburse the parties for their fees under local law. Yet given that an estate cannot be distributed until the respective interests of the beneficiaries are settled, it is difficult to meaningfully distinguish between legal fees that primarily serve the interests of the beneficiaries (nondeductible) and fees that are essential to the settlement of the estate (deductible). For instance, in *Pitner v. United States*, 388 F.2d 651 (5th Cir 1967), the Fifth Circuit allowed a deduction for legal fees incurred by beneficiaries under a prior will of the decedent to establish the invalidity of a subsequent will. The court reasoned as follows: "We agree that the plaintiffs were acting in their own self-interest but we reject the conclusion that the litigation they undertook was not at the same time essential to the proper settlement of the estate." *Id.* at 660; *see also* Sussman v. United States, 236 F. Supp. 507 (E.D.N.Y. 1962) (fees incurred by disinherited daughter to contest father's will in a case that settled were held deductible where paid by estate pursuant to court order).

Legal fees incurred in defending against the assertion of an estate tax deficiency or in prosecuting a claim for a refund action necessarily will arise only after the filing of an estate tax return. These expenses fall squarely within the scope of deductible administration expenses, and the regulations provide that a deduction for such fees will be allowed even though the deduction was not claimed on the estate tax return or through a refund proceeding. Treas. Reg. § 20.2053-3(c)(2). Hence, a court resolving the estate's tax liability can make an allowance for the deductible fees incurred by the estate in the course of the litigation.

[4]   Interest Expense

[a]   Interest Paid on Decedent's Obligations

While interest on an obligation of the decedent that accrued prior to the decedent's death will be deductible as a claim against the estate, interest attributable to a period after the decedent's death is not deductible by the estate as an administration expense simply because payment is required under the terms of the decedent's loan. *See* Rev. Rul. 77-461, 1977-2 C.B. 324 (disallowing deduction for post-mortem interest on decedent's installment loan). Instead, only interest incurred after the decedent's death that yields a separate advantage to the estate—such as the ability to avoid a fire sale of estate assets in order to satisfy the liability—constitutes a deductible administration expense. *See* Ballance v. United States, 347 F.2d 419 (7th Cir. 1965); Estate of Webster v. Commissioner, 65 T.C. 968 (1976). *But see* Rev. Rul. 77-461 (allowing deduction on such grounds only for *additional* interest incurred by the estate beyond that called for under decedent's original obligation).

[b]   Interest Paid on Estate Obligations

If the decedent's estate takes out a loan, the deductibility of the interest payments as administration expenses under § 2053(a)(2) will turn on whether the borrowing was necessary to the administration of the decedent's estate. For instance, if an estate borrows to avoid a forced sale of assets that otherwise would be necessary to pay the estate tax liability, the resulting interest is deductible. *See* Todd v. Commissioner, 57 T.C. 288 (1971); Estate of Thompson v. Commissioner, T.C. Memo. 1998-325, 76 T.C.M. (CCH) 426. However, where loans are not necessary to the administration of the estate due to the availability of sufficient liquid assets or where the interest expense could have been mitigated through an earlier settlement of the estate, the interest expense will not be deductible. *See, e.g.*, Hibernia Bank v. United States, 581 F.2d 741 (9th Cir. 1978) (interest expense held nondeductible because administration was prolonged unnecessarily in order to sell property that could have been distributed to beneficiaries). Additionally, the interest deduction may be disallowed if the loan was not necessary to accomplish the estate's goals. For instance, in *Estate of Black v. Commissioner*, 133 T.C. 340, 385 (2009), the decedent's estate borrowed $71 million from a family limited partnership in which the decedent had held an interest. The Tax Court determined that, as a practical matter, the estate depended on a distribution from the partnership to satisfy its obligations under the loan: "The loan structure, in effect, constituted an indirect use of . . . stock [owned by the partnership] to pay the debts of [the decedent's] estate and accomplished nothing more than a direct use of that stock for the same purpose would have accomplished, except for the substantial estate tax savings." *Id.* at 385. Accordingly, the court upheld the Commissioner's denial of the deduction for interest paid under the loan.

[c]   Interest Paid on Tax Obligations

Interest paid by the estate to contest an asserted deficiency concerning the decedent's individual tax obligations constitutes a deductible administration expense. *See Union Commerce Bank v. Commissioner*, 339 F.2d 163 (6th Cir. 1964) (deduction for interest paid on contested gift tax liability); Rev. Rul. 69-402, 1969-2 C.B. 176 (deduction for interest on federal and state income tax deficiencies contested by the estate). The rationale for permitting a deduction for such deficiency interest is that the good faith defense against claims falls within the fiduciary obligations of the personal representative.

Interest owed to the government on estate tax obligations also receives favorable treatment under § 2053(a)(2). Interest on an estate tax deficiency constitutes a deductible administration expense, without regard to whether the estate possessed sufficient liquidity to retire the estate tax obligation at an earlier point. *See* Rev. Rul. 79-252, 1979-2 C.B. 333 (conditioning deductibility on allowance under local law alone). The same treatment applies to interest resulting from the payment of the estate tax on an installment basis pursuant to § 6161. *See* Estate of Bahr v. Commissioner, 68 T.C. 74 (1977). The deduction extends to interest owing on late payments of estate tax. *See* Rev. Rul. 81-154, 1981-1 C.B. 470. However, the penalties resulting from a failure to timely pay the tax or to file a timely return are not deductible. *Id.* Section 2053(c)(1)(D) provides the rare exception to deductibility in this context. The preferred interest rate provided when payment of the estate tax is deferred under § 6166 (pertaining to interests in closely held businesses) is expressly made nondeductible, which increases the effective interest rate under § 6166.

[5]   Expenses of Sale

Expenses incurred in selling estate property are deductible as administration expenses if the sale is necessary to generate liquidity to pay the decedent's debts, tax obligations, or expenses of the administration process. Treas. Reg. § 20.2053-3(d)(2); *see also* Estate of Smith

v. Commissioner, 57 T.C. 650 (1972), *aff'd*, 510 F.2d 479 (2d Cir. 1975) (limiting deduction to pro-rata portion of expenses of sale where sale generates proceeds in excess of amounts needed to satisfy estate obligations). Additionally, expenses of sale are deductible if the sale is necessary to preserve estate property. Treas. Reg. § 20.2053-3(d)(2). For instance, in *Estate of Papson v. Commissioner*, 73 T.C. 290 (1979), the Tax Court permitted a deduction for a commission paid in obtaining a new tenant for a shopping center owned by the estate where leasing the property was necessary to maintaining its value. Lastly, expenses incurred in selling estate property may be deducted when the sale is necessary to effect a distribution of the estate. Determining the necessity of a sale for this purpose is not a precise matter. In *Estate of Vatter v. Commissioner*, 65 T.C. 633 (1975), *aff'd*, 39 A.F.T.R.2d 1582 (2d Cir. 1976), a deduction for the estate's costs of selling rental property was permitted because of the corporate trustee's refusal to accept distribution of the property. However, in *Estate of Posen v. Commissioner*, 75 T.C. 355 (1980), the Tax Court disallowed a deduction for expenses of a sale of estate property on grounds that the sale was undertaken for the sole benefit of the estate heir.

§ 17.03   CASUALTY LOSSES

Section 2054 provides a deduction for losses realized by the estate during the administration process that are the result of casualty (fire, storm, shipwreck, or other) or theft. The deduction is allowed only to the extent not compensated by insurance or otherwise.

Note the similarity between § 2054 and § 165(c)(3), which authorizes a deduction for casualty and theft losses realized by individuals for income tax purposes. The triggering events under both sections are identical. For income tax purposes, the amount of the casualty loss is limited by the taxpayer's basis in the property. IRC § 165(b). Specifically, the amount of the casualty loss is the lesser of (a) the decline in the fair market value of the property occasioned by the event or (b) the taxpayer's basis in the property. *See* Treas. Reg. § 1.165-7(b). Note that no corollary to basis exists for estate tax purposes. To highlight the issue, suppose that the decedent owned a painting worth $2 million as of the date of his death. Due to a significant decline in the economy, the painting is worth only $1.5 million several months later when the estate is still being administered. At that point, the painting is stolen. How much should the estate be entitled to deduct under § 2054: $2 million or $1.5 million? While the statute is not clear, the more reasoned approach is that the "loss" sustained under § 2054 cannot exceed the fair market value of the underlying property at the time of the casualty or theft.

§ 17.04   CORRELATION WITH INCOME TAX

Expenses or losses that are incurred in the administration of the decedent's estate that are deductible under § 2053 or § 2054 may also give rise to deductions against the estate's income tax liability. *See* IRC §§ 162(a) (trade or business expenses), 165(c)(3) (casualty losses), 212(1) (expenses in producing or collecting income). Additionally, commissions paid in the sale of estate property may reduce the amount realized to the estate on the sale. *See* Treas. Reg. § 1.263(a)-2(e).

Section 642(g) addresses the possibility of the same expense or loss being taken as a deduction both against the decedent's estate tax liability and the estate's income tax liability, and precludes a deduction from being taken twice in this manner. The statute directs that amounts allowable as deductions under § 2053 or § 2054 may not be claimed as deductions by the estate on its income tax return unless the estate (a) indicates that such amounts have not been previously deducted for estate tax purposes and (b) waives its right to claim such deductions in the future.[15] Section 642(g) therefore permits the estate to allocate expenses against the estate tax or income tax, taking the deduction where it produces the greatest tax benefit.

Section 642(g) does not extend to deductions that relate to income in respect of a decedent that are afforded to the estate or the collecting beneficiary under § 691(b). Here, the double deduction concern is inapposite. Had the decedent lived long enough and incurred the expense in collecting his income, the expense would have reduced his income tax liability as well as the size of his future gross estate. Accordingly, § 691(b) deductions may be taken by the estate on its income tax return even though such amounts may have been deducted for estate tax purposes as well.

§ 17.05 STATE DEATH TAXES

Congress fundamentally altered the revenue sharing arrangement between the federal and state governments through the Economic Growth and Tax Relief Reconciliation Act of 2001.[16] The legislation phased out the tax credit for state death taxes provided by § 2011 by reducing the amount of the credit by 25 percent each year starting in 2002. The tax credit therefore was eliminated in 2005. In its stead, Congress enacted § 2058 to provide a deduction for estate, inheritance, legacy, or succession taxes levied at the state level on property included in the decedent's gross estate. Through this legislative restructuring, Congress reduced the value of state death taxes from a dollar-for-dollar reduction of the federal estate tax liability to a proportionate reduction determined by the marginal estate tax rate faced by the decedent's estate. The imposition of death taxes at the state level therefore necessarily increases a decedent's total tax liability, rather than effecting a revenue-sharing arrangement between federal and state governments that held the decedent's combined estate tax liability constant.

§ 17.06 STUDY PROBLEMS

1. The administration of Megan's estate was fairly complicated. Address the deductibility of the following expenditures that were either paid or reimbursed by Megan's executor:

    a. Interest on a loan obtained from a commercial bank to pay estate taxes, so that the estate would not be forced to liquidate its interest in certain closely held corporations to finance the estate tax liability.

    b. Megan's estranged son contested the validity of his mother's will, under which he received only one quarter of the share provided to Megan's other children. The estate settled the son's claim for $1 million, incurred attorney's fees of $200,000, and agreed to pay the son's attorneys fees of $150,000.

    c. Megan devised certain parcels of real estate in trust, to be administered by a corporate trustee. The corporate trustee required that an environmental study

---

[15] A § 642(g) waiver of the right to take deductions for estate tax purposes is irrevocable. *See* Estate of Darby v. Wiseman, 323 F.2d 792 (10th Cir. 1963).

[16] *See* Pub. L. No. 107-16, §§ 531-532, 155 Stat. 72-75 (2001)..

be completed on several of the parcels before it would accept title. The estate spent $25,000 on these assessments.

d. Megan owned several tracts of timberland and, a year-and-a-half after Megan's death, the estate commissioned a forestry service to thin the property and replant where necessary. The estate paid $100,000 for this service (and netted $1 million in sales from the timber).

Would your answer change if the cut occurred five years after Megan's death?

e. One item included in Megan's estate was a family homestead that has been in the family for generations. Megan devised the property to certain of her children in equal shares as tenants in common. One child wants to reside in the property, which is fine with the others as long as that child compensates them for her exclusive use of the property. To smooth matters out, the estate pays to have the rental value of the property appraised. The appraisal costs $15,000.

2. During the year of Bette's death, she made gifts of family limited partnership interests to her child that her estate valued at $25 million. The Service has asserted that the partnership interests were worth $48 million (producing a deficiency of approximately $20 million). Roughly three years after Bette's death, the parties resolve the gift tax case, settling on a value of $37 million for the gift (yielding a deficiency of approximately $10 million, and interest on the deficiency of $1.5 million). The estate incurred $1 million in legal fees and $300,000 in appraisal fees as a result of the litigation. What deductions may Bette's estate take for estate tax purposes, and when may those deductions be claimed?

3. Stan promised his favorite nephew, Ned, that he would leave his farm to Ned if Ned would live with him and tend to the farm for the rest of Stan's life. Ned did so, providing services to Ned that were estimated at $250,000 over the relevant period. Stan, however, decided to leave Ned a cash devise of $200,000 under his will and to devise the farm instead to all of his nephews and nieces (Stan had no children) in equal shares. The farm was worth $1 million as of Stan's death. Ned sued the estate to enforce his contract claim, and the parties settled the litigation for an additional payment to Ned of $400,000. Discuss the ability of Stan's estate to deduct the settlement.

4. Richard died owning a residence worth $750,000, which was encumbered by a purchase money mortgage in the amount of $725,000. Assume that under the relevant state law, the creditor's remedy is against the property only; that is, the creditor cannot pursue a deficiency claim against Richard if the property is worth less than the outstanding loan balance. How should Richard's estate report these items for estate tax purposes?

5. Sid owned a shrimp boat worth $600,000 at the time of his death. Shortly after he died, the boat was destroyed when a hurricane hit the coastline. The boat was insured, but only for $400,000. To what deduction, if any, is the estate entitled by reason of the loss?

Chapter 18

TRANSFERS FOR CHARITABLE PURPOSES

Internal Revenue Code:	§ 2055(a)–(e)(2), (e)(4)–(5), (f)
	§ 2522(a), (c), (d), (e)(1)
	§ 170(f)(3)(B), (h)(1)–(4)(A)
	§§ 642(c)(5), 664(d)(1)–(2)
	§ 2031(c)
Treasury Regulations:	§ 20.2055-1
	§ 20.2055-2(a) through (e)(2)(vi)(*a*), (e)(2)(vii)(*a*)
	§ 20.2055-3
	§ 25.2522(c)-3
	§§ 1.664-2, 1.664-3

Both the estate tax and gift tax provide deductions that are designed to achieve certain policy objectives instead of being aimed at determining the net transfer of wealth. A prominent example of a deduction not aimed at base measurement is that provided by § 2055 under the estate tax and § 2522 under the gift tax for gratuitous transfers that serve charitable purposes. By forgoing the tax revenue that otherwise would be collected on these transfers, the federal government can be viewed as subsidizing the private allocation of resources to organizations that serve the public good in some manner. With the federal "match" for transfers reaching over 50 percent of the amount supplied by the donor,[1] the charitable deduction constitutes the largest tax expenditure program in the federal transfer tax regime.

§ 18.01   QUALIFYING RECIPIENTS

Notwithstanding differences in expression, the scope of beneficiaries that may receive a transfer that supports the charitable deduction is substantially similar under the estate tax and gift tax. *See* IRC §§ 2055(a), 2522(a). The primary categories of qualifying recipients are: (1) governmental agencies; (2) charitable corporations; (3) trusts or fraternal orders established for charitable purposes; and (4) veterans' organizations.[2] The Service annually publishes the Cumulative List, Publication No. 78, to notify the public of the organizations that are qualified

---

[1] Taking a decedent whose taxable estate exceeds $5 million without considering amounts transferred to charity, the relative contributions of the government and the decedent are determined by the 35 percent marginal tax rate. Hence, if the decedent gave $2 million to charity net of any estate tax that may be imposed on the transfer, the decedent can be seen as supplying $1.3 million of the transfer with the government providing the $700,000 in forgone estate tax attributable to the devise. Hence, the government's contribution equals 53.85 percent of that supplied by the donor.

[2] The estate tax charitable deduction also encompasses certain transfers to employee stock ownership plans made after August 5, 1997. *See* IRC § 2055(a)(5) (added by Pub. L. No. 105-34, § 1530(c)(7), 111 Stat. 788, 1078 (1997)). Due

to receive charitable contributions. Any revocation of an entity's status is published weekly in the Internal Revenue Bulletin.

[A]   Transfers to Governmental Agencies

Transfers to or for the use of domestic governmental entities or agencies—including the United States, any State, any political subdivision thereof, and the District of Columbia—may be deducted as long as the transfer is used exclusively for public purposes. IRC §§ 2055(a)(1), 2522(a)(1). An Indian tribal government is treated as a State for this purpose. *See* IRC § 7871(a)(1)(B). Additionally, § 2055(g) cross references to legislation providing that transfers to certain organizations are considered to be "to or for the use of the United States." The Service explored the bounds of the government agency category of charitable recipients in Revenue Ruling 79-159, 1979-1 C.B. 308, when it determined that a cemetery owned and operated by a municipality and supported by tax revenue constituted a political subdivision of the local government under § 2055(a)(1).

[B]   Corporations Organized for Charitable Purposes

The broadest and perhaps most familiar class of permissible beneficiaries of a charitable transfer are corporations organized and operated "exclusively for religious, charitable, scientific, literary, or educational purposes." IRC §§ 2055(a)(2), 2522(a)(2). These purposes specifically include the encouragement of art, the fostering of national or international amateur sports competition, and the prevention of cruelty to animals. It is not necessary that the corporation be exempt from income taxation to constitute a qualified beneficiary under this provision; conversely, a corporation's status as an exempt entity does not assure its qualification. Rather, the purposes for which the entity is organized and operated are determinative.

In Revenue Ruling 59-310, 1959-2 C.B. 146, the Service noted that the generally accepted legal concept of "charity" includes "benefits which are for an indefinite number of persons and are for the relief of the poor, the advancement of religion, the advancement of education, or 'erecting or maintaining public buildings or works or otherwise lessening the burdens of government.' " *Id.* at 148 (citation omitted). Based on this standard, the ruling held that a non-profit corporation organized for the purpose of establishing and maintaining a swimming pool and playground facilities for residents of the community supplied the requisite charitable function for purposes of the income tax exemption. *Id.* at 147. The charitable status of such entities can be negated, however, if they provide the service on a discriminatory basis. In Revenue Ruling 67-325, 1967-2 C.B. 113, the Service concluded that an entity that restricted the use of recreational facilities to members on the basis of race did not provide a charitable function, reasoning that "no sound basis has been found for concluding that there would be an adequate charitable purpose if some part of the whole community is excluded from benefiting except where the exclusion is required by the nature or size of the facility." *Id.* at 116; *see also* Bob Jones University v. Simon, 416 U.S. 725 (1974) (upholding revocation of tax-exempt status of non-profit private school that adopted racially discriminatory admissions policies and rejecting claim of First Amendment violation).

---

to the narrow scope of these transfers and the technical requirements under § 664(g) that these transfers must satisfy, these transfers will not be addressed in this chapter.

In *Dulles v. Johnson*, 273 F.2d 362 (2d Cir. 1959), the Second Circuit determined that bequests to state and local bar associations were deductible for estate tax purposes on grounds that the totality of their operations—including the facilitation of legal research and the provision of low-cost legal services—was educational and charitable. The court justified its holding in part on the observation that the cost of the associations' regulatory activities would otherwise "descend upon the public." *Id.* at 366. However, in a later decision holding that a non-profit cemetery association did not constitute a § 2055(a)(2) entity, the Second Circuit clarified that performance of a public function was not *per se* charitable:

> Our view is that relief for the public fisc is more symptomatic than evidentiary regarding whether an activity is charitable: charity often results in an absorption of a burden otherwise falling upon the state, particularly where the social welfare is a principal purpose of the state. But this does not mean that activities lessening public expense in any of a myriad of areas of public interest are perforce charitable.

Child v. United States, 540 F.2d 579, 583 (2d Cir. 1976).

[C]   Trusts and Fraternal Societies

A transfer to a trust or fraternal society (or similar organization) may qualify for the charitable deduction, but only if the transferred property is to be used exclusively for religious, charitable, scientific, literary, or educational purposes, or for the prevention of cruelty to children or animals. IRC §§ 2055(a)(3), 2522(a)(2)–(3). The restriction on the use of the transferred property must originate in the terms of the transfer; the agreement by the transferee to use the funds for the requisite charitable purpose is not sufficient. *See* Levey v. Smith, 103 F.2d 643, 646 (7th Cir. 1939) ("The right to a deduction depends upon what a testator has willed respecting the use of a legacy and not upon the use which a legatee is willing to make of it."). *But see* Davis v. Commissioner, 26 T.C. 549 (1956) (court-reviewed decision holding that trust established to provide unrestricted monetary benefit to students enrolled at nursing school qualified for charitable deduction).

Given the relative lack of formalities in creating a trust and the private nature of such devices (as compared to non-profit corporations), transfers that test the limits of a charitable purpose typically arise in the trust context. In particular, there exists the potential for the private benefit from such transfers to outweigh the benefit to the public at large—the latter being a hallmark of a charitable transfer. If a trust is established to provide educational scholarships to the public, it appears acceptable to stipulate that relatives of the transferor be preferred. *See* Commonwealth Trust Co. v. Granger, 57 F. Supp. 502 (W.D. Pa. 1944) (preference afforded to relatives of decedent in awarding scholarship funds); *see also* Sells v. Commissioner, 10 T.C. 692 (1948) (informal will providing bequest of educational funds "first to relatives or other Boys and girls"). However, a deduction will not be afforded when the benefit of an otherwise charitable transfer is restricted to members of the transferor's family. *See* Davis v. Commissioner, 55 T.C. 416 (1970) (scholarship resources limited to grandnieces and grandnephews of transferor).

[D]   Veterans' Organizations

Veterans' organizations constitute the fourth primary category of recipients of transfers giving rise to the charitable deduction. IRC §§ 2055(a)(4), 2522(a)(4). In order to qualify for the charitable deduction under the estate tax, the organization must have been incorporated by an Act of Congress.

[E] Restrictions on Charitable Recipients

With respect to charitable transfers that obtain their qualification based on the nature of the recipient organization, Congress has directed that no part of the net earnings of the organization may inure to the benefit of a private stockholder or individual. IRC §§ 2055(a)(2), (4), 2522(a)(2), (4). The mere possibility for the earnings of the recipient organization to be distributed to private persons is sufficient to disqualify the transfer for the deduction. *See* Rev. Rul. 57-574, 1957-2 C.B. 161 (charitable deduction for transfers to communal religious organization disallowed due to participation in commercial activities for the benefit of its members). However, the Tax Court rejected the Service's argument that a deduction should be disallowed for a bequest to a charitable medical clinic due to the prospect that the doctors may charge fees for their services (which could include a charge for use of the facilities). *See* Estate of Smith v. Commissioner, T.C. Memo. 1961-242, 20 T.C.M. (CCH) 1268.

Transfers to charitable corporations or to trusts or fraternal societies exclusively for charitable purposes are not deductible if the recipient participates in lobbying activities. Specifically, a charitable deduction is not allowed if the recipient would be disqualified for income tax exemption under § 501(c)(3) by reason of attempting to influence legislation, or if the recipient participates in any political campaign on behalf of or in opposition to a candidate for office. IRC §§ 2055(a)(2)–(3), 2522(a)(2), (3). However, the prohibition on lobbying activities does not extend to veterans' organizations. IRC §§ 2055(a)(4), 2522(a)(4).

§ 18.02 TRANSFER REQUIREMENT

[A] Necessity of Transfer from Decedent to Charitable Recipient

The ultimate receipt of property by a charitable entity does not alone justify the deduction. Rather, the deduction is limited to bequests, legacies, devises, or transfers made by the decedent to the charitable recipient. Hence, a transfer that is effected by operation of law does not qualify for the deduction. *See* Senft v. United States, 319 F.2d 642 (3d Cir. 1963) (charitable deduction not available for property escheating to the state under laws of intestacy). Similarly, a bequest to a relative who is obligated to surrender the subject property to a religious order does not qualify for the deduction. *See* Estate of Lamson v. United States, 338 F.2d 376, 377 (Ct. Cl. 1964) ("The testator, and he alone, must provide for the charitable bequest and the fact that the proceeds of a bequest are used by a beneficiary for charitable purposes does not bring the bequest within the statute.") In *Estate of Pickard v. Commissioner*, 60 T.C. 618 (1973), the decedent devised her estate in trust in which her stepfather possessed a vested remainder. The stepfather predeceased the decedent and left the residue of his estate to two charitable organizations. The Tax Court disallowed the deduction to the decedent's estate, explaining that the transfer to the charitable recipient "must be manifest from the provisions of the decedent's testamentary instrument." *Id.* at 621.

Suppose that the decedent does not name the charitable recipients of a transfer but instead invests an executor or trustee with the discretion to select the charitable recipients. In that case, the charitable deduction will be allowed if the terms of the transfer restrict the recipients of the property to § 2055 entities. Revenue Ruling 69-285, 1969-1 C.B. 222, addressed a bequest of property to an individual (who also was named as executor of her estate) "to be distributed to whatever charities she may deem worthy." Because the executor owed a fiduciary duty under state law to distribute the property to charities, the ruling held that the charitable deduction was allowed. However, in Revenue Ruling 71-200, 1971-1 C.B. 272, the charitable deduction was disallowed for a bequest in trust that afforded the trustees with discretion to select beneficiaries that qualified for the estate, gift, or income tax deduction on grounds that the potential recipients were not limited to § 2055(a) entities.

Suppose that a decedent appoints property over which he possesses a testamentary general power of appointment to a charitable recipient. Standing alone, the transfer requirement of § 2055(a) may prove problematic in this context, as the appointed property often is treated as passing from the individual who created the power for state law purposes. Section 2055(b) eliminates any such ambiguity by providing that property included in the decedent's gross estate under § 2041 that is received by a charitable recipient is treated as passing by bequest for purposes of the statute.

[B] Contingent Transfers

In order to sustain a charitable deduction, the value of the interest in property passing to the charitable recipient must be presently ascertainable. Treas. Reg. § 20.2055-2(a). If the effectiveness of a transfer for charitable purposes is subject to a condition, the charitable deduction will be disallowed unless the possibility of the charitable transfer not becoming effective "is so remote as to be negligible." Treas. Reg. § 20.2055-2(b)(1). In Revenue Ruling 70-452, 1970-2 C.B. 199, the Service addressed the deductibility of a transfer of a remainder interest in a trust that was subject to the invasion to make fixed payments of principal to the income beneficiary. Given the age of the income beneficiary, there existed a 7.2 percent chance that the trust principal would be exhausted during the beneficiary's lifetime, leaving nothing to pass to the charity. In determining that no deduction was available for the remainder interest left to charity, the ruling announced that a condition to a charitable transfer becoming effective would not be considered "so remote as to be negligible" for purposes of Treas. Reg. § 20.2055-2(b)(1) where the likelihood of the condition being realized exceeded five percent. Hence, five percent appears to be the maximum threshold that the Service will view as negligible in this context. The exclusion for remote conditions is most useful for transfers to charities that are subject to divestment. *See* Treas. Reg. § 20.2055-2(b)(2), Ex. 2; *see also* Rev. Rul. 67-229, 1967-2 C.B. 335 (transfer to non-profit corporation qualified for charitable deduction as long as the corporation remained located in a certain county and operated an orphanage; disqualifying events determined to be highly improbable as of the decedent's death).

[C] Disclaimers

Recall that if a transferee makes a qualified disclaimer of an interest in property as defined in § 2518, the interest is treated as having never been transferred to the disclaimant. Accordingly, if property passes to a charitable organization by reason of a qualified disclaimer, the property will be treated as being transferred from the decedent to the charitable recipient—thereby preserving the estate's eligibility for the charitable deduction.

Section 2055(a) provides a context-specific expansion of a qualified disclaimer. If an individual is provided with a power to consume or appropriate property that will otherwise pass to a charitable recipient, the complete termination of an individual's power to consume prior to its exercise and prior to the due date for filing the estate tax return is treated as a qualified disclaimer of that individual's interest in the property.

[D] Will Contests

At one point, the Service took the position that a testamentary transfer to a charity that did not qualify for the charitable deduction could not be converted into a deductible transfer through the settlement of litigation contesting the decedent's will. *See* Rev. Rul. 77-491, 1977-2 C.B. 332 (outright transfer to charity resulting from compromise agreement not entitled to charitable deduction). Rather, the availability of the charitable deduction was to be determined by reference to the form originally selected by the decedent. Yet after suffering a series of judicial defeats at the hands of courts taking a more lenient approach to the issue, the Service revisited its position in Revenue Ruling 89-31, 1989-1 C.B. 277. There, the Service held that the settlement of a bona fide will contest that reformed a partial-interest transfer to a charity (a deduction for which is disallowed as described in § 18.04 below) to an outright bequest entitled the estate to a charitable deduction for the transfer. The Service nonetheless stressed the necessity of a bona fide dispute concerning the decedent's will, and courts have affirmed this prerequisite. *See* Estate of Burdick v. Commissioner, 96 T.C. 168, 170 (1991) ("Where the only apparent reason for termination or modification of an otherwise nonqualifying split-interest charitable bequest is circumvention of [the split-interest rule], an estate tax deduction will not be allowed even for the amount of a direct payment to the charitable organization."), *aff'd*, 979 F.2d 1369 (9th Cir. 1992); *see also* Estate of La Meres v. Commissioner, 98 T.C. 294 (1992) (following *Estate of Burdick* and finding no purposes for the modification of the relevant trust agreement apart from attempting to qualify transfer for the charitable deduction).

§ 18.03 AMOUNT OF DEDUCTION

[A] Limit on Deduction

Section 2055(d) caps the charitable deduction at the amount of the transferred property that is included in the gross estate. However, it is possible that the property transferred to charity, when valued in isolation, will fall short of the value placed on the property for purposes of gross estate inclusion. For example, if a decedent who was the sole shareholder of a corporation devised a 10 percent interest in the corporation to charity, the minority interest transferred to charity would be valued at less than its pro-rata portion of the whole. The gross estate is valued with reference to what the decedent owned at death, whereas the charitable deduction is determined by reference of the value passing to charity. *See* Ahmanson Foundation v. United States, 674 F.2d 761 (9th Cir. 1981) (addressing this issue in the context of a charitable devise of non-voting stock where the decedent owned both voting and non-voting shares at the time of his death).

[B] Reduction of Taxes and Administration Expenses

Section 2055(c) mandates that the charitable deduction be reduced by estate or inheritance taxes that are imposed on the charitable devise. Whether a charitable devise is in fact burdened by such taxes is a matter of state law, taking into consideration the law of the jurisdiction in which the decedent's estate is being administered, the law of the jurisdiction imposing the tax, and the terms of the decedent's will or other governing instrument. Treas.

Reg. § 20.2055-3(a)(1). If the charitable devise is determined to bear a portion of the federal estate tax liability, the interdependency of the two figures necessitates use of a circular calculation to determine the amount of the charitable deduction. Treas. Reg. § 20.2055-3(a)(2). To avoid diminution of the charitable deduction in this manner, it often is preferable to include a direction in the decedent's will that all estate and inheritance taxes be paid from non-charitable sources.

Courts have extended the theory of § 2055(c) to reductions in amounts passing to charity by reason of administration expenses being paid from the charitable bequest. Following the Supreme Court's decision in *Commissioner v. Estate of Hubert*, 520 U.S. 93 (1997)—addressing whether the use of post-mortem income generated by assets allocated to a charitable bequest warranted a reduction in the charitable deduction—the Service promulgated new regulations to address the effect of administration expenses in this context. *See* T.D. 8846, 64 Fed. Reg. 67,763 (Dec. 3, 1999). The regulations divide administration expenses into two categories: (1) "estate management expenses" relating to the investment of estate assets or their preservation during the period of administration, and (2) "estate transmission expenses" relating to the collection of the decedent's property, payment of the decedent's debts and death taxes, and distribution of the decedent's property to the appropriate recipients. Treas. Reg. § 20.2055-3(b)(1). Any estate transmission expense that is paid from the charitable share reduces the charitable deduction. Treas. Reg. § 20.2055-3(b)(2). However, the charitable deduction is not reduced by estate management expenses that are attributable to and paid from the charitable share, unless such amounts are deducted as administration expenses under § 2053(a).[3] Treas. Reg. § 20.2055-3(b)(3).

§ 18.04 PARTIAL-INTEREST TRANSFERS

[A] Disallowance of Deduction

Perhaps the most significant planning consideration in the charitable context is the general prohibition of the charitable deduction for so-called "partial-interest" transfers. A partial-interest transfer is one in which an interest in property passes or has passed to a charitable recipient, while an interest in the same property passes or has passed to a non-charitable recipient. A classic example of a partial-interest transfer is the contribution of property in trust under which the donor reserves an income interest for life, with the remainder interest passing to charity. Congress addressed the tax treatment of partial-interest transfers as part of the Tax Reform Act of 1969 out of concern that this and similar techniques were being employed to intentionally overvalue the amount passing to charity:

> The rules of present law for determining the amount of a charitable contribution deduction in the case of gifts of remainder interests in trust do not necessarily have any relation to the value of the benefit which the charity receives. This is because the trust assets may be invested in a manner so as to maximize the income interest with the result that there is little relation between the interest assumptions used in calculating present values and the amount received by the charity. For example, the

---

[3] If for some reason estate management expenses attributable to property not included in the charitable share are nonetheless paid from the charitable share, then the value of the charitable deduction will be reduced by that amount. Treas. Reg. § 20.2055-3(b)(4).

trust corpus can be invested in high-income, high-risk assets. This enhances the value of the income interest but decreases the value of the charity's remainder interest.

S. Rep. 91-552, at 87 (1969). In addressing this potential for abuse, Congress adopted a firm default position: No charitable deduction is allowed for the transfer of a partial interest in property to charity. *See* IRC §§ 2055(e)(2), 2522(c)(2). This general rule applies even in situations where the interest of the non-charitable recipient is minimal or does not otherwise present the potential to manipulate value placed on the charitable deduction. However, the statute softens this otherwise draconian approach by allowing the charitable deduction if the transfer takes one of several sanctioned forms that provide some measure of certainty regarding the amounts to be received by charity. In this manner, the partial-interest provisions serve something of an *in terrorem* channeling function.

Before delving into the various exceptions to the partial-interest disallowance of the charitable deduction, it is worth noting the limitations of the general rule. An outright transfer of a portion of property to charity (e.g., 10 percent of the stock in the decedent's wholly owned corporation) does not constitute a partial interest, as the charitable and non-charitable beneficiaries do not possess interests in the *same property* following the transfer as required by § 2055(e)(2). *See* Rev. Rul. 75-414, 1975-2 C.B. 371 (charitable deduction allowed for payment of a 10 percent interest in each asset held in the decedent's revocable trust). Additionally, an interest in property that is acquired by the non-charitable recipient through the provision of "adequate and full consideration in money or money's worth" does not implicate the partial-interest provisions. IRC §§ 2055(e)(2), 2522(c)(2). As an example, assume that a decedent transfers real estate to charity subject to an existing arm's-length lease to a non-charitable lessee. While temporal interests in the property are shared by charitable and non-charitable parties, the non-charitable party acquired his interest by purchase as opposed to gratuitous transfer from the decedent.

[B] Qualifying Transfers

[1] Remainder Interests

If a remainder interest in property is transferred to charity, the charitable deduction will be allowed if the remainder interest is in a charitable remainder annuity trust (as defined in § 664(d)(1)), a charitable remainder unitrust (as defined in § 664(d)(2)), or a pooled income fund (as defined in § 642(c)(5)). *See* IRC §§ 2055(e)(2)(A), 2522(c)(2)(A).

[a] Charitable Remainder Trusts

A charitable remainder annuity trust is one under which a predetermined amount is paid at least annually to at least one non-charitable recipient. The annuity amount may be defined either as a fixed sum or as a percentage of the initial fair market value of the trust, but the annuity payment must be at least five percent and not greater than 50 percent of the initial value of the trust in either case.[4] IRC § 664(d)(1)(A); Treas. Reg. § 1.664-2(a)(1)(ii), (a)(2)(i). The annuity term can be defined by reference to an individual's lifetime (or the joint lifetimes of two individuals), provided the individual is living at the time the trust is created. IRC

---

[4] The 50 percent ceiling on the annual annuity payment was added by Congress in 1997 to stem the use of high-payout, short-term charitable remainder trusts to dispose of appreciated property at reduced effective capital gain rates. Taxpayer Relief Act of 1997, Pub. L. No. 105-34, § 1089, 111 Stat. 788, 960.

§ 664(d)(1)(A). Alternatively, the non-charitable annuity may extend for a term certain not in excess of 20 years. *Id.* Following the expiration of the annuity interest, the remainder must be transferred to one or more designated charities or retained for distribution to such organizations. The value of the remainder interest at the time of trust funding must equal at least 10 percent of the initial fair market value of the trust. IRC § 664(d)(1)(D). Because the annuity payment is determined at the outset, a charitable remainder annuity trust must prohibit the contribution of additional property to the trust after its initial funding. *See* Treas. Reg. § 1.664-2(b).

A charitable remainder unitrust is similar to a charitable remainder annuity trust in principal respects, with the primary difference between the two lying in the manner in which the annual payment is defined. *See* IRC § 664(d)(2). The annual payment from a unitrust is defined as a stated percentage—not greater than 50 percent and not lower than five percent—of the fair market value of the trust assets *as determined in the year of distribution.* IRC § 664(d)(2)(A). Hence, the amount of the unitrust payment will fluctuate with the investment performance of the trust as a whole. While the unitrust approach protects payments to the non-charitable beneficiary from dilution due to inflation,[5] this protection comes at the administrative expense of potential cumbersome annual valuations of the trust assets. Because the unitrust payment is determined with reference to the current value of the trust property, a charitable remainder unitrust permits additional contributions to the trust after its initial funding (unlike a charitable remainder annuity trust). *See* Treas. Reg. § 1.664-3(b).

Another principal difference between a charitable remainder annuity trust and a charitable remainder unitrust is the ability to limit annual distributions to the net income of the trust (and to thereby preserve the trust principal). The annual payment from a charitable remainder annuity trust must be made regardless of the income generated by the trust. Hence, the invasion of trust principal may be required to satisfy the annuity payment. The charitable remainder unitrust, however, offers some flexibility on this front. For instance, the annual payment under a unitrust may be capped at the income actually generated by the trust in the given year (a so-called Net Income CRUT or NICRUT). IRC § 664(d)(3)(A). A charitable remainder unitrust may augment this limitation by further providing that shortfalls attributable to the income limitation in prior years be made up in periods in which the net income of the trust exceeds the unitrust payment (a so-called Net Income Makeup CRUT or NIMCRUT). IRC § 664(d)(3)(B). The method for computing the annual payment from a charitable remainder unitrust need not be exclusive for the initial term; rather, a change in methods is permitted if the change is triggered on a specific date or by an event that is not discretionary or within the control of the trustee or others. Treas. Reg. § 1.664-3(a)(i)(1)(*c*). For example, a charitable remainder unitrust that is funded with nonmarketable assets can limit annual payments to available income until the nonmarketable assets are sold (and presumably invested in liquid form), at which point the trust can convert to a traditional unitrust payment. *See* Treas. Reg. § 1.664-3(a)(1)(i)(*e*), Ex. 1. The combination of payment methods in this manner may be useful in avoiding the annual appraisal of illiquid assets otherwise mandated by the unitrust form.

Both the charitable remainder annuity trust and the charitable remainder unitrust are the product of extensive statutory and regulatory definition, and each contains a number of

---

[5] On the other hand, the unitrust approach can be seen as protecting the value of the charitable remainder in the context of a down market.

mandatory provisions. Given the potential for technical missteps in this area that would carry drastic tax consequences, the Service has provided model trust forms for taxpayers to follow. *See, e.g.*, Rev. Proc. 2003-53, 2003-2 C.B. 230 (inter vivos charitable remainder annuity trust for one measuring life); Rev. Proc. 2005-52, 2005-2 C.B. 326 (inter vivos charitable remainder unitrust for one measuring life). Additionally, Congress has provided that non-conforming transfers may be reformed in limited circumstances to qualify for the charitable deduction. IRC §§ 2055(e)(3), 2522(c)(4).

[b]   Pooled Income Funds

A pooled income fund defined in § 642(c)(5) provides the third type of transfer for which a charitable deduction attributable to a remainder interest is preserved. As its name suggests, a pooled income fund consists of a common fund maintained by a charitable organization as a vehicle to receive contributions from donors who wish to retain an income stream for their lives or for the lives of others (who must be living at the time of the transfer). The remainder interest in the transferred property must be irrevocably assigned to the charitable organization that maintains the fund. All such contributions from donors are commingled, with the payout rate to the income beneficiaries being determined by the investment return realized by the common pool. When the income interest terminates, that portion of the pooled income fund is liquidated and the proceeds are distributed to the charity. To prevent overvaluation of the charitable remainder in an environment of low applicable federal rates, the retained income interest must be valued based on the actual investment return earned by the pooled fund—specifically, the highest rate of return earned by the fund in the three taxable years preceding the transfer. IRC § 642(c)(5) (flush paragraph). Pooled income funds provide an attractive vehicle for making partial-interest gifts to charities of modest amounts due to the lack of formalities associated with these transfers—in particular, the absence of the need to create and administer a separate trust.

[2]   Lead Interests

If the lead interest in a trust is transferred to charity with the remainder passing to non-charitable recipients, a charitable deduction is allowed only if the interest transferred to charity consists of a guaranteed annuity or unitrust payment. IRC § 2055(e)(2)(B). In many respects, charitable lead trusts represent the inverse of qualified charitable remainder trusts. However, the term of the charitable lead interest need not be limited to 20 years, and there exists no minimum payout that must be made to the charity.

Requiring the payment to the charity to take the form of a fixed annuity or unitrust payment protects the charitable interest from being undermined through an investment strategy that emphasizes future growth over current return. However, this is not to say that charitable lead trusts do not present a source of potential transfer tax savings. As a charitable lead interest will be valued based on actuarial tables, an environment of low statutory rates under § 7520 permits earnings in excess of the discount rate to pass free of federal transfer tax to the non-charitable remainderman. The payout to the charity will be structured as an annuity in this context, both to avoid the administrative hassles of annual accountings necessitated by unitrusts and to preserve the benefit of investment returns in excess of the applicable federal rate for the non-charitable recipient of the trust remainder.

[C]　Exceptions to the Partial-Interest Rule

In addition to the number of partial-interest transfers that are statutorily blessed under § 2055(e), certain transfers are statutorily exempted from application of the partial-interest rule by way of the parenthetical exclusion for transfers described in § 170(f)(3)(B). *See* IRC §§ 2055(e)(2) and 2522(c)(2). The various transfers benefitting from the § 170(f)(3)(B) exception are addressed below.

[1]　Undivided Fractional Interests in Property

The partial-interest rule does not apply to the contribution of an undivided portion of the taxpayer's entire interest in property. IRC § 170(f)(3)(B)(ii). An undivided portion of the transferor's entire interest must relate to a percentage of "each and every substantial interest or right" that the decedent owned in the property. Treas. Reg. §§ 20.2055-2(e)(2)(i), 25.2522-3(c)(2)(i). Additionally, the transferor's interest in property may not be divided on a temporal basis; rather, the transferred interest must extend over the entire term of the transferor's interest in the property.[6] *Id.* As an example, the transfer of a 10 percent tenants-in-common interest in real property to charity will qualify for the charitable deduction even if the other 90 percent tenants-in-common interest is retained by the donor or transferred to non-charitable parties. However, the statutory exception for transfers of undivided fractional interests in property does not apply to transfers in trust—even if the transfer affords the transferee with virtually identical economic rights. For instance, if a transferor had contributed the real property to a trust that entitled the charity to 10 percent of the net rental income for a term certain and then 10 percent of the trust property upon distribution, the charity would receive a nondeductible partial interest. *See* Galloway v. United States, 492 F.3d 219 (3d Cir. 2007) (denying charitable deduction where individuals and charitable organizations were provided pro-rata interests in single trust); *see also* Rev. Rul. 77-97, 1977-1 C.B. 285 (charitable deduction disallowed for transfer in trust providing spouse and charity with equal interests in income and remainder).

[2]　Personal Residences and Farms

The partial-interest rules do not apply to a contribution of a remainder interest in a personal residence or farm (including the improvements thereon). IRC § 170(f)(3)(B)(i); *see also* Treas. Reg. §§ 20.2055-2(e)(2)(ii). Again, the transfer must be of a legal remainder in the property; transfers in trust do not qualify for the exception. *See* Rev. Rul. 76-357, 1976-2 C.B. 285. As a personal residence for this purpose is not limited to the transferor's primary residence, the transfer of a legal remainder in vacation property to charity qualifies for the charitable deduction.

While the exception for remainder interests in residences and farms is fairly straightforward, taxpayers have pushed the bounds of the exception by requiring the property to be sold following the death of the life tenant (with the charity receiving the sale proceeds). The Service at one point took the position that the conversion of the property to cash negated application of the exception, which led to the charitable deduction being disallowed. *See* Rev. Rul. 77-169,

---

[6] Section 2522(e)(1) imposes an additional limitation in the context of fractional gifts of undivided interests in tangible personal property. In that case, the property must be owned by the donor or by the donor and the donee prior to its contribution. Hence, if a third party owned a fractional interest in the property prior to the fractional gift to the charity, the charitable deduction will be disallowed.

1977-1 C.B. 286. Yet after having this position rejected by the Tax Court in *Estate of Blackford v. Commissioner*, 77 T.C. 1246 (1981), the Service revised its position in Revenue Ruling 83-158, 1983-2 C.B. 159. There, the Service announced that it would apply the remainder interest exception where the property was sold as long as the charity possessed the option under state law to take distribution of the property in lieu of the sale proceeds.

[3] Transfers for Conservation Purposes

The last type of transfer that is excluded from the partial-interest rules by way of the § 170(f)(3)(B) reference is a qualified conservation contribution. IRC § 170(f)(3)(B)(iii); *see also* Treas. Reg. § 20.2055-2(e)(2)(iv). As defined in § 170(h), such an interest includes a remainder interest in real property or a perpetual restriction on the use of real property that is donated for conservation purposes. Conservation purposes include the preservation of land for recreational purposes, the protection of habitat, the preservation of open spaces, and the preservation of historically significant property.

As part of the Tax Reform Act of 1986, Congress broadened the deductibility of transfers of perpetual easements on real property to charitable organizations by eliminating the requirement that such easements satisfy the income tax definition of conservation purposes.[7] IRC §§ 2055(f), 2522(d) (each eliminating compliance with § 170(h)(4)(A)). Hence, the easement still must be donated "exclusively for conservation purposes," *see* IRC § 170(h)(1)(C), but the requisite conservation purposes are not statutorily defined (and are presumably broader) in the transfer tax context.[8]

Given that the creation of a conservation easement on real property in many cases enhances the value of the retained property interest (or, at a minimum, does not diminish the owner's enjoyment of the property), conservation easements have emerged as a popular tax-planning technique among owners of real property.[9] Note that the allowance of a charitable deduction for conservation easements is just one instance in which these partial-interest transfers receive preferable transfer tax treatment. Section 2031(c)(1) provides an exclusion from the gross estate for a percentage of the value of real property subject to a "qualified conservation easement." The percentage exclusion is set at 40 percent, with a two percentage point reduction for each percentage point by which the value of the easement is less than 30 percent of the value of the property subject to the easement, with the total dollar value of the exclusion being capped at $500,000. Section 2031(c)(9) goes further to permit the estate to take a deduction under § 2055(f) for the *post-mortem* grant of a qualified conservation easement prior to the due

---

[7] Pub. L. No. 99-514, § 1422(a), (b), 100 Stat. 2085, 2716–17 (1986). Sections 2055(f) and 2522(d) are drafted in a somewhat clumsy manner. Each requires the easement to satisfy the requirements of § 170(h) but without regard to § 170(h)(4)(A). Yet § 170(h)(1) requires that the easement be granted "exclusively for conservation purposes," while § 170(h)(4)(A) defines those purposes. The legislative history reflects the intent to drop the conservation requirement altogether to prevent liquidity burdens that could otherwise result if an easement was irrevocably conveyed but the conservation purpose was later determined not to be satisfied. *See* H.R. Rep. No. 99-841, at II-772 (1986) (describing deduction as being permitted "without regard to whether the contribution satisfies the income tax conservation purpose requirement").

[8] The Joint Committee on Taxation explained the legislation as follows: "The Act permits gift or estate tax deductions to be claimed for *qualified conservation contributions* without regard to whether the contributions satisfy the income tax conservation purpose requirement." Joint Comm. on Tax'n, General Explanation of the Tax Reform Act of 1986, at 1257 (1987) (emphasis added).

[9] *See* Josh Eagle, *Notional Generosity: Explaining Charitable Donors' High Willingness to Part with Conservation Easements*, 35 Harv. Envtl. L. Rev. 47 (2011).

date of the estate tax return, as long as no party takes a deduction for income tax purposes with respect to the contribution.

§ 18.05 DONOR ADVISED FUNDS

Congress officially recognized the concept of a "donor advised fund" through the Pension Protection Act of 2006.[10] In general terms, a donor advised fund is a fund or account (a) that is owned and maintained by a sponsoring organization, (b) that is separately identified by reference to the contribution maintained by the donor, and (c) with respect to which the donor (or a person appointed by the donor) reasonably expects to have advisory privileges over the investment and distribution of fund amounts by reason of the donor's status as donor. IRC § 4966(d)(2) (incorporated by reference through §§ 2055(e)(5) and 2522(c)(5)). A sponsoring organization is a § 170(c) organization (other than a governmental entity) that is not a private foundation. IRC § 4966(d)(1). Distributions from a donor advised fund may not be made to individuals. Rather, broadly speaking, distributions must be made to organizations for charitable purposes in order to avoid a considerable excise tax. *See* IRC § 4966(a), (c). A donor advised fund thus enables a donor to make a contribution to a charitable organization while retaining the ability to advise the organization on the timing, amount, and charitable recipients of distributions from the fund.[11] In this manner, a donor advised fund operates as a simplified private foundation that allows the donor to benefit from the investment expertise of the fund managers.

The charitable deduction under the estate tax and gift tax is limited to contributions to donor advised funds whose sponsoring organizations are not fraternal societies established for charitable purposes or veterans' organizations.[12] IRC §§ 2055(e)(5)(A)(i), 2522(c)(5)(A)(i). Additionally, availability of the deduction depends on the taxpayer receiving a contemporaneous acknowledgement from the sponsoring organization that the organization has exclusive control over the assets contributed to the fund. IRC §§ 2055(e)(5)(B), 2522(c)(5)(B).

§ 18.06 STUDY PROBLEMS

1. Margaret has made the following transfers during this calendar year:

   a. $5,000 to Harvest Hope, a non-profit community food bank;

   b. $100,000 to her alma mater, to establish a fund to award scholarships to deserving students from her city;

   c. $200,000 to a community foundation, under which Margaret retains an income stream for life with the remainder passing to the foundation upon her death;

   d. A remainder interest in undeveloped real property to her church;

   e. A remainder interest in her vacation home to her church; and

---

[10] Pub. L. No. 109-280, § 1226, 120 Stat. 780, 1094 (2006).

[11] A fund established for the exclusive benefit of a single charitable organization does not constitute a donor advised fund. IRC § 4966(d)(2)(B)(i).

[12] Additional limitations of a more technical nature concerning which parties may serve as a sponsoring organization are provided in §§ 2055(e)(5)(A)(ii) and 2522(c)(5)(A)(ii), respectively.

    f.   50 percent of the common stock in a closely held business that Margaret operated with her daughter, but, as part of the transfer, Margaret retained the right to vote the transferred stock.

Determine whether the transfers qualify for the charitable deduction.

2.   Burt made the following devises through his will:

    a.   All of the preferred stock that he owned at the time of his death in X Corp to a local non-profit organization that operates a shelter for homeless individuals (while leaving his common stock holdings to his grandchildren);

    b.   A 50 percent interest as tenants in common in a downtown office building (subject to a lease by a commercial bank) to his city's non-profit art museum;

    c. $100,000 to be distributed by his executor in her discretion to the § 2055(a) entity having the greatest positive influence on his community at the time of his death;

    d. $250,000 in trust, the terms of which require the trustee to pay Burt's daughter five percent of the value of the trust property on an annual basis for her lifetime, remainder to Burt's non-profit alma mater; and

    e.   Six months after Burt's death, his executor donates a perpetual easement on real property to the Nature Conservancy that requires the land to remain in its undeveloped natural state to protect native wildlife and to provide the public with access to an undeveloped beach front.

Determine whether the transfers qualify for the charitable deduction.

3.   Helen is the majority shareholder of a closely held business. The shareholders have turned down several unsolicited purchase offers, but Helen and others plan on selling their stock in the future at the right price. Helen would like to make a charitable remainder gift of a portion of her stock holdings. Would you suggest a charitable remainder annuity trust or a charitable remainder unitrust? Explain your recommendation.

4.   Hank is contemplating making a term gift to a charity, with the remainder following the term to pass to his descendants then living. Hank intends to fund the transfer with cash, bonds, and marketable securities. The applicable federal rate for valuing the transfer is low by historic measures. Would you suggest that Hank provide the charity with a fixed annuity, a unitrust payment, or a payment of net income for the lead term? Explain your recommendation.

Chapter 19

TREATMENT OF THE MARITAL UNIT

The treatment of gratuitous transfers between spouses is a fundamental structural aspect of the federal transfer tax system. Each spouse constitutes a separate transferor under the estate tax and gift tax, yet §§ 2056 and 2523 provide an unlimited deduction for transfers to a spouse—whether occurring during life or by reason of death—that satisfy certain conditions. Thus, broadly speaking, the unlimited marital deduction reflects congressional intent to defer imposition of the federal transfer tax until property exits the marital unit.

Congress first introduced the marital deduction to the federal transfer tax system in 1948 for the purpose of equalizing the treatment of spouses in community property and separate property states. Recall that a surviving spouse in a community property jurisdiction is effectively entitled to receive one-half of the couple's community property free of estate tax, as the surviving spouse's beneficial interest in the property arises upon its acquisition by the community rather than through a transfer from the other spouse. Accordingly, a surviving spouse's one-half interest in the community property is not included in the gross estate of the predeceasing spouse. Through the 1948 legislation, Congress sought to extend the "estate splitting" benefit enjoyed by spouses in community property states to all taxpayers through the allowance of a deduction for transfers to a surviving spouse equal to one-half of the deceased spouse's separate property.[1] Congress liberalized the deduction in 1976 by expanding the limitation to the greater of one-half of the deceased spouse's separate property or $250,000—which effectively amounted to an unlimited marital deduction for estates of modest size.[2] Not long thereafter, Congress in 1981 removed all quantitative limits on the marital deduction.[3] Congress thereby signaled a revised policy with respect to transfers within the marital unit, one that generally exempts a transfer to a spouse from transfer taxation as long as the property will be subject to taxation in the hands of the transferee spouse. *See* Estate of Clayton v. Commissioner, 976 F.2d 1486, 1489, 1491 (5th Cir. 1992) (describing taxation in the estate of the surviving spouse as "essential feature" of the marital deduction regime).

In addition to permitting transfers between spouses occurring during life or at death to be effectively disregarded for federal transfer tax purposes, Congress has recognized the commonality of interests of married individuals in determining the transferor of property for gift tax purposes. Under the "split-gift" election contained in § 2513, spouses may elect to treat

---

[1] Revenue Act of 1948, Pub. L. No. 80-471, § 361(a), 62 Stat. 110, 117–21. The same legislation introduced the joint income tax return, permitting the benefits of income-splitting to be enjoyed by spouses in separate property jurisdictions.

[2] Tax Reform Act of 1976, Pub. L. No. 94-455, § 2002, 90 Stat. 1520, 1854. With respect to inter vivos transfers between spouses, the legislation provided a deduction for lifetime gifts up to $100,000. The donor was effectively forced to disgorge the excess deduction on the next $100,000 of lifetime gifts (which were not deductible). Thereafter, the donor could deduct one-half the value of gifts to a spouse in excess of the $200,000 lifetime figure. *See id.* at § 2002(b), 90 Stat. at 1855.

[3] Economic Recovery Tax Act of 1981, Pub. L. No. 97-34, § 403, 95 Stat. 172, 301.

an actual lifetime gift by one spouse as if it were made one-half by each. Among other things, the § 2513 election allows one spouse to make use of the non-transferring spouse's gift tax annual exclusion under § 2503(b).

Lastly, Congress introduced portability into the unified credit regime commencing in 2011. In general terms, the portability feature permits a surviving spouse to increase his or her unified credit by the amount of the unified credit that was not used by the predeceased spouse. A devise of a decedent's entire estate to a surviving spouse in a form that qualifies for the marital deduction will no longer effectively waste the decedent's unified credit, as the surviving spouse will then be entitled to twice the basic exclusion amount in passing property to the next generation.

This chapter focuses on the treatment of the marital unit in the federal transfer tax system. Given the frequency of transfers to or for the benefit of spouses and the potentially detailed rules that govern such transfers, marital deduction planning is a central aspect of any estate planning practice.

§ 19.01   PRELIMINARY CONDITIONS TO THE ESTATE TAX MARITAL DEDUCTION

Internal Revenue Code: § 2056(a), (b)(4), (b)(9), (c), (d)(1)
Treasury Regulations: § 20.2056(c)-2(c) to (e), 20.2056(b)-4(b), Ex. 3

The marital deduction is granted in fairly straightforward terms. To the extent an interest in property is included in the decedent's gross estate, a deduction is permitted for the value of the interest in property that passes or has passed from the decedent to a surviving spouse. IRC § 2056(a). Although the reference to property that has already passed from the decedent to the surviving spouse may appear curious at first glance, the purpose of this language is to extend the deduction to lifetime transfers that are recaptured in the decedent's gross estate under §§ 2035 through 2042. The limitation of the deduction to interests in property included in the decedent's gross estate precludes an estate-tax windfall, and § 2056(b)(9) reinforces this concept by denying the marital deduction if the relevant interest may be deducted from the gross estate under another provision (e.g., as a deductible claim under § 2053 or as a casualty loss under § 2054).

[A]   The Surviving Spouse as Recipient

The status of an individual as the surviving spouse of a decedent is determined as of the decedent's death. Thus, property transferred to a spouse that is recaptured in the decedent's gross estate will not qualify for the marital deduction if the spouse predeceased the decedent, or if the couple subsequently divorced. *See* Rev. Rul. 79-354, 1979-2 C.B. 334. Conversely, property given to a non-spouse that is recaptured in the transferor's gross estate may qualify for the marital deduction if the individuals had subsequently wed. *Id.*

The status of a spouse assumes the existence of a valid marriage at the time of the decedent's death that had not been dissolved by the entry of a final decree of divorce. In addition to the necessity of a valid state law marriage, a marriage for purposes of federal law is limited to a state law marriage between one man and one woman.[4] Questions concerning the marital status of the decedent are to be resolved under the law of the decedent's domicile, and these questions can necessitate an examination of the decedent's prior divorce. *See* Estate of Goldwater, 539 F.2d 878 (2d Cir. 1976) (determining that decedent's first wife was his surviving spouse based on invalidity of attempted Mexican divorce from first wife). In addition to ensuring that the recipient was the decedent's spouse at the time of his death, the spouse also must have survived the decedent—a factual question that becomes complicated in the context of simultaneous death. A decedent's will or local law often will supply a presumption concerning the order of deaths in this setting, and a presumption that the decedent was survived by his spouse will be respected for marital deduction purposes as long as the property interest will be included in the surviving spouse's gross estate.[5] *See* Treas. Reg. § 20.2056(c)-2(e).

In addition to surviving the decedent, the surviving spouse must be a United States citizen in order for the transfer to qualify for the marital deduction. IRC § 2056(d)(1). The purpose of this requirement is to keep property from permanently exiting the transfer tax base via the marital deduction. Deductible transfers to a non-citizen spouse must be made through a qualified domestic trust as defined in § 2056A, which contains provisions ensuring the collection of estate tax either upon the death of the surviving spouse as well as upon any distributions made prior to that point. The specifics of a qualified domestic trust are addressed in Chapter 26.

[B]   The "Passing" Requirement

In order to ensure that the marital deduction is available for the broad variety of property interests that may be included in a decedent's gross estate, § 2056(c) defines in expansive terms when property will be considered to have "passed" from the decedent. In addition to transfers of probate property by devise or inheritance, property may pass to a surviving spouse by right of survivorship, through the exercise or lapse of a power of appointment, and through the designation of the spouse as the beneficiary of life insurance proceeds. IRC § 2056(c)(1)–(2), (5)–(7). Amounts that a spouse receives by reason of the exercise of state law rights to a portion of the decedent's estate also satisfy the passing requirement. *See* IRC § 2056(c)(3) (dower interest, or statutory interest in lieu thereof, treated as passing from decedent); Treas. Reg. § 20.2056(c)-2(c).[6] Lifetime transfers are considered to have passed from the decedent to the extent the interest in property "has been transferred . . . by the decedent at any time." IRC § 2056(c)(4).

Although property passing from the decedent is defined in broad terms, two scenarios in particular test the bounds of the "passing" requirement. First, assume that a decedent fails to make a disposition in his wife's favor under his will, instead opting to leave his entire probate estate to his children. His spouse, displeased with the decedent's devise and not assuaged by

---

[4] *See* Defense of Marriage Act, Pub. L. No. 104-199, § 3(a), 110 Stat. 2419 (1996) (codified as amended at 1 U.S.C. § 7).

[5] Note that if it appears more advantageous for the surviving spouse to have predeceased the decedent, that result can be accomplished by the estate of the surviving spouse through the use of a qualified disclaimer.

[6] The marital deduction would be allowed in this case even if the spouse immediately transferred to the decedent's intended devisees the amounts received through the exercise of elective share rights. *See* Harter v. Commissioner, 39 T.C. 511 (1962). The combination of these two steps effectively amounts to the surviving spouse's post-mortem assignment of her unified credit for gift tax purposes to the predeceasing spouse.

her elective share rights, challenges the validity of the decedent's will on a number of state law theories. The parties ultimately agree to a settlement calling for the spouse to receive three-fourths of the decedent's estate. Do these amounts "pass" from the decedent to the surviving spouse, or should they be viewed as passing from the decedent's intended devisees? Reflecting a concern over familial participation in post-mortem tax planning, the regulations dictate that the amounts paid to the spouse will be treated as passing from the decedent only if the transfer was "a bona fide recognition of enforceable rights of the surviving spouse in the decedent's estate." Treas. Reg. § 20.2056(c)-2(d)(2). In making this determination, the federal authorities generally must make an independent determination of relevant state law. *See* Commissioner v. Estate of Bosch, 387 U.S. 456, 465 (1967) (explaining that where federal estate tax liability turns on application of state law on which highest court of the state has not passed, federal authorities must independently apply state law "after giving 'proper regard' to relevant rulings of other courts of the State"). Thus, neither an adjudication of the matter by a lower state court nor a good faith settlement of a state law claim is conclusive for this purpose. *See* Ahmanson Foundation v. United States, 674 F.2d 761, 774 (9th Cir. 1981) ("We cannot conclude that Congress's concern that the availability of the marital deduction be cautiously guarded, as recognized by the Court in *Bosch*, would apply any less to cases of settlement than to cases of lower state court adjudication.").

In situations where a decedent's beneficiaries would like to revise the dispositions made by the decedent (or those made for him by the relevant intestacy regime), qualified disclaimers may be employed to change the recipient of the decedent's property. Under § 2518(a), the federal transfer tax regime applies as if the disclaimed property "had never been transferred" to the disclaimant. Thus, in the hypothetical above, it may have been possible for the decedent's children to employ qualified disclaimers to substitute the surviving spouse as the transferee of the requisite portion of the decedent's estate.[7] The use of qualified disclaimers to make unabashed post-mortem revisions to the decedent's estate plan is limited, however, by the various definitional requirements set forth in § 2518(b).[8]

The so-called "widow's election" devise provides another scenario that indirectly tests the passing requirement to the marital deduction. The technique, previously discussed in the context of retained-interest transfers,[9] involves a conditional bequest of the decedent's interest in the couple's community property to a trust benefitting the surviving spouse, but only if the surviving spouse also contributes her community property interest to the trust. Assuming the surviving spouse complies with the conditional devise, what amounts are viewed as passing from the decedent for marital deduction purposes: the actual amount of the decedent's devise to the trust, or that amount reduced by the surviving spouse's required contribution? Section 2056(b)(4) addresses the valuation issue in somewhat cryptic fashion:

> In determining . . . the value of any interest in property passing to the surviving spouse for which a deduction is allowed by this section —

---

[7] Because property passing by way of a qualified disclaimer must do so without direction on the part of the disclaimant, a careful examination of the passage of the disclaimed property must be undertaken to ensure that the disclaimed property will pass to the intended recipient. For instance, if the decedent's children had issue of their own, a series of cascading disclaimers may be necessary for the property to pass by way of partial intestacy to the decedent's surviving spouse.

[8] Qualified disclaimers are the subject of Chapter 16.

[9] *See* § 10.01[C][2].

. . . (B) where such interest or property is encumbered in any manner, or where the surviving spouse incurs any obligation imposed by the decedent with respect to the passing of such interest, such encumbrance or obligation shall be taken into account in the same manner as if the amount of a gift to such spouse of such interest were being determined.

Based on this statutory formulation, the valuation question turns on whether the transfer of the surviving spouse's community property interest as a condition to the devise in her favor constitutes an "obligation imposed by the decedent with respect to the passing of such interest." The Supreme Court in *United States v. Stapf*, 375 U.S. 118 (1963), rejected the taxpayer's argument that the obligations contemplated by the statute were limited to those to be satisfied only from the property transferred by the decedent. Instead, the Court determined that the required transfer by the surviving spouse of her own community property interest to the trust constituted an obligation imposed on the transfer in her favor. Hence, in determining the amount of the marital deduction, the value of the transfer from the deceased spouse to the surviving spouse had to be reduced by the value of the surviving spouse's transfer. In so holding, the Court confirmed the approach taken by the regulations. *See* Treas. Reg. § 20.2056-4(b), Ex. 3.

§ 19.02   THE TERMINABLE INTEREST RULE

Internal Revenue Code: § 2056(b)(1)–(2)
Treasury Regulations: § 20.2056(b)-1(a) to (c), (e) to (g)

The apparent simplicity of the conditions to the marital deduction provided by § 2056(a) is belied by the terminable interest exception contained in § 2056(b)(1). Under the terminable interest rule, the marital deduction is not allowed for an interest in property passing to the surviving spouse if (1) the interest passing to the surviving spouse will terminate or fail upon the lapse of time or the occurrence of an event or contingency, (2) an interest in the same property passes or has passed from the decedent to a person other than the surviving spouse, and (3) by reason of such passing, the other person may possess or enjoy any part of the property after the termination or failure of the interest of the surviving spouse.[10]

A devise of property in trust in which the surviving spouse possesses a beneficial interest for her lifetime, with the remainder passing to the decedent's children, serves as a simple illustration of a transfer that implicates the terminable interest rule. The surviving spouse receives an interest in the transferred property (her lifetime beneficial interest in the trust property); an interest in the same property passes from the decedent to one other than the surviving spouse (the vested remainder of the decedent's children in the trust property); and, upon the occurrence of an event (the death of the surviving spouse), the children's remainder interest in the trust property will become possessory. This example also serves to highlight the purpose behind the disallowance of the marital deduction for terminable interest transfers. Because the surviving spouse's interest in the trust property terminates upon her death and the surviving spouse is not the transferor of the property, the property will not be included in her gross estate at her death. Hence, if the marital deduction were not disallowed in the estate of the predeceasing spouse, the transferred property ultimately would be distributed to the

---

[10] The terminable interest rule cannot be circumvented by avoiding the transfer of a terminable interest from the decedent. Rather, the marital deduction will be disallowed if the decedent directs that his estate use estate funds to acquire a terminable interest to be distributed to the surviving spouse. IRC § 2056(b)(1)(C).

decedent's children free of any estate tax at the parental level. *See* Novotny v. Commissioner, 93 T.C. 12, 16 (1989) ("The purpose of the [terminable interest] rule, generally speaking, is to deny eligibility for the marital deduction if the predeceasing spouse structures the surviving spouse's interest to avoid estate tax at the death of the surviving spouse.").

The terminable interest rule is a forward-looking provision: its conditions are to be evaluated as of the death of the predeceasing spouse. Yet the future inclusion of the transferred property in the surviving spouse's transfer tax base does not provide an exemption to the terminable interest rule, leading to insidious applications of the provision. In *Jackson v. United States*, 376 U.S. 503 (1964), the Supreme Court determined that amounts paid to the surviving spouse from the decedent's estate pursuant to a statutory allowance for support were non-deductible under the terminable interest rule because the spouse's right to the payments was not indefeasible as of her husband's death. Because the spouse's rights to the payments could have terminated by reason of her death or remarriage during the relevant payment period, the spouse's interest was subject to a contingency implicating the terminable interest rule. Hence, the deduction was denied even though the spouse actually received all of the scheduled support payments. The mere possibility that a third party may possess or enjoy the transferred property upon the expiration of the surviving spouse's interest is sufficient to trigger disallowance of the marital deduction under § 2056(b)(1).

[A] Necessity of Interest in Third Party

The terminable interest rule does not apply to all transfers of property that may expire in the spouse's hands. Rather, an interest in the same property must also pass from the decedent to a third party, and it must be possible for the third party to possess or enjoy the transferred property as a result of the transfer from the decedent. For example, suppose a decedent devised to his spouse rights to a pharmaceutical patent that will expire 10 years after the decedent's death. By definition, the spouse's property interest will expire upon the passage of time. Although this satisfies the first condition of the terminable interest rule, the other elements are lacking. Namely, no interest in the property passes from the decedent to a third party. The value of the patent therefore will be eligible for the marital deduction. *See also* Treas. Reg. § 20.2056(b)-1(g), Ex. 3 (joint and survivor annuity includible in decedent's gross estate and payable to surviving spouse qualified for marital deduction). This definitional means of avoiding the terminable interest rule has fueled taxpayer attempts to characterize annuities payable to the decedent's surviving spouse for a term and, thereafter, to the decedent's children as two annuities: one payable to the spouse, and one payable to the children. These attempts have met with success only when the annuity payments to the third party are not dependent on those payable to the surviving spouse. *See* Rev. Rul. 77-130, 1977-1 C.B. 289 (marital deduction allowed where annuity payable to child was independent of amounts paid to surviving spouse); Meyer v. United States, 364 U.S. 410 (1960) (marital deduction denied where child was to receive only the balance of guaranteed annuity payments not paid to spouse).

Another means of avoiding a third-party interest is to devise property in trust for the lifetime benefit of the spouse, remainder to the spouse's probate estate (without condition). *See* Rev. Rul. 68-554, 1968-2 C.B. 412. The devise circumvents the terminable interest rule for want of a third-party interest, because the surviving spouse's probate estate serves as a mere extension of the spouse. The "estate trust" technique possesses certain advantages when compared to the popular QTIP Trust exception to the terminable interest rule (discussed in

§ 19.03[D] below)—namely, the ability to accumulate trust income and to retain property that does not generate an income stream. However, the primary disadvantage of using an estate trust to qualify for the marital deduction is the absence of control over the disposition of the trust property upon the surviving spouse's death. Additionally, the estate trust approach subjects the trust assets to the claims of the surviving spouse's creditors.

[B] Ordering of Respective Interests

The mere passage of an interest in property to both a surviving spouse and a third party does not automatically trigger the disallowance of the marital deduction on terminable interest grounds. Suppose that a decedent devised property in trust for the lifetime benefit of his parents, remainder to his surviving spouse. While the spouse receives an interest in property, no party receives an interest in the same property that arises upon the failure of a condition relating to the spouse's interest. In that regard, consider the result if the trust distributed to the surviving spouse only if she survived the decedent's parents, otherwise to the decedent's issue.

[C] Scope of Prohibited Contingencies

A terminable interest in property is one that will terminate or fail as a result of the passage of time or upon the future resolution of a contingency. *See* Treas. Reg. § 20.2056(b)-1(b). A "contingency" for this purpose pertains to the nature of the spouse's interest, not to any procedural requirements that the spouse must satisfy in order to receive the interest. Hence, amounts paid to a surviving spouse under a state's elective share regime are deductible even though the spouse's interest is contingent upon the proper exercise of the statutory rights. *See* Rev. Rul. 72-8, 1972-1 C.B. 309. In that regard, suppose a decedent's will provides that the surviving spouse may elect to receive distribution of certain assets outright; otherwise, the decedent's property will be left in trust for the surviving spouse's lifetime benefit. If the spouse elects to receive property outright, does the mere existence of the election constitute a contingency that triggers the terminable interest rule? In *Estate of Mackie v. Commissioner*, 545 F.2d 883 (4th Cir. 1976), the court determined that the marital deduction was available for properties the spouse elected to receive outright pursuant to the terms of the decedent's will, analogizing the situation to a spouse who exercised statutory rights to receive an elective share of the decedent's estate. Thus, a spouse's ability to select between an outright devise and a terminable interest in property alone does not preclude the marital deduction where the spouse chooses the deductible devise. However, if the conditions on the spouse's receipt of an outright distribution are more substantive, the marital deduction may be disallowed. For example, in *Estate of Edmonds v. Commissioner*, 72 T.C. 970 (1979), the surviving spouse exercised her right to receive $100,000 from a trust established by the decedent for the benefit of his descendants if she purchased a residence, which she did three years following his death. The court disallowed the marital deduction for the $100,000 amount due to the "substantial condition" that the spouse purchase a new residence. *Id.* at 996; *see also* Rev. Rul. 82-184, 1982-2 C.B. 215 (recognizing distinction between *Estate of Mackie* and *Estate of Edmonds*).

Whereas a spouse may chose between receiving a deductible property interest and a terminable interest without jeopardizing the marital deduction, the same treatment does not extend to discretion afforded to a decedent's executor. If a devise to a surviving spouse may be satisfied out of a pool of assets that include terminable interests (e.g., a temporal interest retained by the decedent in property transferred to someone other than the spouse), then the marital deduction must be reduced by the aggregate value of such interests—regardless of whether the terminable interest property ultimately is distributed to the surviving spouse. IRC § 2056(b)(2). In effect, the provision adopts a draconian presumption that the executor will satisfy the marital devise with any available terminable interest property. Disallowance of the marital deduction under § 2056(b)(2) can be avoided by a specific devise of any terminable interest property to one other than the surviving spouse (thereby removing the property from the relevant pool of assets), or through a direction in the decedent's will that only assets qualifying for the marital deduction be used to fund the marital devise (thereby eliminating the executor's discretion).

§ 19.03   STATUTORY EXCEPTIONS TO THE TERMINABLE INTEREST RULE

[A]   Survivorship Conditions

Internal Revenue Code: § 2056(b)(3)
Treasury Regulations: § 20.2056(b)-3

To avoid the distribution of property from one probate estate into another, it is common for a decedent to require the beneficiary to survive the decedent by a defined period of time. Even if a decedent fails to impose such a condition by will, state law may supply a period of required survivorship. *See* Uniform Simultaneous Death Act § 2, 8B U.L.A. 148 (1993) (requiring clear and convincing evidence that a beneficiary survived the decedent by 120 hours). Section 2056(b)(3) is intended to exempt such conditions from triggering disallowance of the marital deduction on terminable interest grounds. In particular, § 2056(b)(3) provides that an interest passing to a surviving spouse will not be considered to terminate or fail upon the death of the spouse even though the spouse's death (a) within a period not exceeding six months from the date of the decedent's death, or (b) resulting from a common disaster that caused the death of the decedent would, in fact, terminate the spouse's interest. Yet if the survivorship condition on the spouse's interest could be resolved more than six months after the decedent's death, the § 2056(b)(3) exemption from the terminable interest rule will not apply unless the condition relates to death resulting from a common disaster. Treas. Reg. § 20.2056(b)-3(b). Thus, if a devise to a surviving spouse is conditioned upon the spouse surviving to the point of distribution of the probate estate or the completion of the administration process, the marital deduction will be disallowed. *See* United States v. Mappes, 318 F.2d 508 (10th Cir. 1963) (disallowing marital deduction where will directed that spouse's interest would fail if she died "before my estate has been administered"); Estate of Bond v. Commissioner, 104 T.C. 652 (1995) (disallowing devise of personal property to spouse requiring spouse to "survive distribution," but allowing deduction for same devise of real property because the transfer vested as of the decedent's death under state law).

[B]   The Power of Appointment Trust

Internal Revenue Code: § 2056(b)(5), (b)(10)
Treasury Regulations: § 20.2056(b)-5(a) to (c)(2), (f), (g), (j)

Section 2056(b)(5) provides an exception to the terminable interest rule for certain transfers for the lifetime benefit of the surviving spouse over which the spouse possesses the power to appoint the trust property to herself or to her estate. The theory behind this exception is that the transferred property will be included in the estate or gift tax base of the surviving spouse to the extent not consumed. *See* S. Rep. No. 80-1013, 28 (1948). If the conditions to § 2056(b)(5) are satisfied, no part of the transferred interest in property is considered as passing to any person other than the surviving spouse (which, in turn, precludes application of the terminable interest rule).

Section 2056(b)(5) at one point served as a preferred means of qualifying spousal transfers in trust for the marital deduction. Yet following the introduction of the exception provided under § 2056(b)(7) for qualified terminable interest property in 1981 (which, as discussed below, permits the predeceasing spouse to control disposition of the trust remainder),[11] section 2056(b)(5) largely has taken a back seat in the marital deduction arena. Yet because § 2056(b)(5) and (b)(7) share common elements—in particular, the spouse's entitlement to income from the transferred property—the study of § 2056(b)(5) provides more than mere historic perspective.

[1]   Income Requirement

The first condition to qualification for the marital deduction under § 2056(b)(5) is that the spouse be entitled to receive all the income from the transferred property for life, payable annually or on a more frequent basis. The regulations substantially augment the relatively scant statutory directive. In general terms, a spouse will be entitled to all of the income from the transferred property if the transfer provides "substantially that degree of beneficial enjoyment of the trust property during her life which the principles of the law of trusts accord to a person who is unqualifiedly designated as the life beneficiary of a trust." Treas. Reg. § 20.2056(b)-5(f)(1). It is immaterial whether the spouse's enforceable rights to beneficial enjoyment of the property emanate from the trust instrument or state law. Treas. Reg. § 20.2056(b)-5(f)(2). Additionally, a transfer satisfying the § 2056(b)(5) income requirement need not be made in trust; legal life estates in property are sufficient (albeit impracticable). *See* Treas. Reg. § 20.2056(b)-5(a) (describing application of provision to transfers "whether or not in trust").

[a]   Effect of Administrative Powers

A trustee may exert considerable influence over the income stream produced by trust assets through the exercise of administrative powers, whether pertaining to the manner in which the trust property is invested or through the discretionary allocation of receipts and disbursements between income and principal. For the most part, the regulations confirm that the reasonable exercise of such administrative powers will not jeopardize compliance with § 2056(b)(5). In particular, the grant of administrative discretion will not violate the income requirement of § 2056(b)(5) unless the grant "evidences the intention to deprive the surviving spouse of the beneficial enjoyment required by the statute." Treas. Reg. § 20.2056(b)-5(f)(4). This prohibited intent will not be imputed to the decedent if the relevant powers are subject to reasonable limitations that may be enforced by local courts. *Id.* In particular, the power to determine the allocation of receipts and disbursements between income and principal will not disqualify a transfer from satisfying § 2056(b)(5) if subject to reasonable conditions. *Id.* The Service addressed a wide range of administrative powers in Revenue Ruling 69-56, 1969-1 C.B. 224, holding that none violated the requirement that the spouse be entitled to all of the income from the transferred property. The favorable treatment of the administrative powers provided in the ruling was based on (a) the existence of a fiduciary obligation to fairly balance the

---

[11]   The § 2056(b)(7) exception to the terminable interest rule is discussed in § 19.03[D].

respective interests of the beneficiaries in exercising the power, or (b) the ability of local courts to impose reasonable limitations on the exercise of the power to protect the interest passing to the spouse.

Perhaps the most troublesome administrative power in the § 2056(b)(5) setting is an authorization of the trustee to retain assets that are not productive of income. Examples of property that is not productive of income include unimproved land, equity interests in closely held entities with history of retaining earnings, and life insurance. If the trust consists of such unproductive assets, the spouse would appear to have no enforceable right to beneficially enjoy the property for her lifetime (outside the context of personal-use property). The regulations protect the spouse in this context, providing that the trustee's retention of unproductive assets will not disqualify the interest from the marital deduction as long as the relevant administrative provisions require, or permit the spouse to require, the trustee to make the property productive or to convert the property within a reasonable time. Treas. Reg. § 20.2056(b)-5(f)(4); *see also* Treas. Reg. § 20.2056(b)-5(f)(5) (income condition not satisfied "if the primary purpose of the trust is to safeguard property without providing the spouse with the required beneficial enjoyment"). However, no such qualification on the retention power is necessary with respect to residential property or other property retained for the personal use of the surviving spouse. Treas. Reg. § 20.2056(b)-5(f)(4).

[b]   Total Return Trusts

A modern trend in fiduciary administration is to move away from the traditional income/principal means of delineating the respective interests of lifetime and remainder trust beneficiaries and instead to determine the beneficiaries' respective interests based on the total investment return realized by the trust. In that regard, a 2004 revision to the regulations accommodates the total return approach in the marital deduction context. The income condition under § 2056(b)(5) is satisfied if the spouse is entitled to income as determined by applicable local law that provides for a "reasonable apportionment" between the income and remainder beneficiaries of the total return of the trust and that satisfies the requirements of Reg. § 1.643(b)-1. Treas. Reg. § 20.2056(b)-5(f)(1) (as modified by T.D. 9102, 69 Fed. Reg. 12 (effective for taxable years ending after January 2, 2004)). The fiduciary accounting definition of income under Reg. § 1.643(b)-1, in turn, provides that a state statute defining income as a unitrust amount of no less than three percent and no more than five percent of the fair market value of the trust assets constitutes a reasonable apportionment of the total return of the trust. The preamble to the 2004 regulations stressed the need for a state law definition of income as including a unitrust amount, rejecting a comment that a trust providing a unitrust payment to the surviving spouse should satisfy the income condition even if the relevant state had not enacted relevant legislation.

[c]   Frequency of Payments

Although § 2056(b)(5) requires that the surviving spouse be entitled to income payments on an annual or more frequent basis, the failure of a trust instrument to address the timing of income distributions is not necessarily fatal to marital deduction qualification. The income requirement is violated in this context only if local law permits distributions to the surviving spouse to be made less frequently than annually. Treas. Reg. § 20.2056(b)-5(e). Courts often will go to painstaking lengths to interpret a trust as satisfying the annual income requirement. The decision in *Estate of Mittleman v. Commissioner*, 522 F.2d 132 (D.C. Cir. 1975), provides an extreme example. The trust at issue in *Estate of Mittleman* permitted the trustees to make discretionary distributions of corpus for the "proper support, maintenance, welfare and comfort" of the surviving spouse. However, the trust not only failed to address the timing of income distributions, it made no provision for income distributions whatsoever. Nonetheless, the Court of Appeals interpreted the trust as requiring an annual income distribution based on other provisions of the decedent's will and extrinsic evidence, including the testimony of the drafting attorney.

Although the statute addresses the frequency with which income distributions must be made, the statute does not address when the recurring income payments must commence. The regulations provide a measure of leeway on this issue, stating that the income requirement of § 2056(b)(5) will not be failed merely because the spouse is not entitled to the income from estate assets prior to their distribution from the executor. Treas. Reg. § 20.2056(b)-5(f)(9). However, this protection is not available if the terms of the decedent's will require or even authorize the executor to delay distribution beyond a reasonable period of administration. *Id.*

[d]   Power to Withdraw Income

The income requirement of § 2056(b)(5) does not turn on the actual distribution of income to the spouse, but rather on the spouse's entitlement to the income. It is sufficient that the spouse have "such command over the income that it is virtually hers." Treas. Reg. § 20.2056(b)-5(f)(8). Thus, a transfer in trust may comply with § 2056(b)(5) even if trust income is accumulated, provided the surviving spouse has the right, exercisable at least annually, to require the distribution of the trust income.

[e]   Prohibited Limitations on Income Interest

Section 2056(b)(5) requires that the spouse's entitlement to the income generated by the transferred property be unqualified. Hence, the income requirement of § 2056(b)(5) is failed if a third-party trustee possesses discretion to accumulate trust income, or if distribution of trust income requires the consent of one other than the spouse. Treas. Reg. § 20.2056(b)-5(f)(7). Similarly, if the spouse's entitlement to the distribution of trust income can terminate—whether expressly upon the occurrence of a condition (such as remarriage) or implicitly through the distribution of trust principal to another—the income requirement is failed. However, insulating the trust from claims of the spouse's creditors through the inclusion of "spendthrift" provisions (prohibiting the voluntary or involuntary assignment of the spouse's beneficial interest) does not undermine the spouse's entitlement to trust income. *Id.*

[2]   Power of Appointment Requirement

Section 2056(b)(5) requires that the surviving spouse possess the power to appoint the property to herself or to her estate, regardless of whether the spouse may exercise the power in favor of another. A power of appointment for this purpose is not limited to express powers; it encompasses the right to invade trust principal as well as the unilateral right of a joint tenant to receive fee ownership through severance. Treas. Reg. § 20.2056(b)-5(g)(1), (2). On the other hand, nominal powers of appointment in favor of the spouse or her estate do not suffice. If the surviving spouse entered into a binding agreement with the decedent to exercise the power only in favor of their issue, the spouse does not possess a § 2056(b)(5) power notwithstanding its terms. Treas. Reg. § 20.2056(b)-5(g)(2).

A § 2056(b)(5) power may be exercisable by the spouse either during life or by will. Treas. Reg. § 20.2056(b)-5(g)(1). In either case, the power must be exercisable by the spouse "alone and in all events." IRC § 2056(b)(5) (flush paragraph). Conditioning the exercise of the power on the joinder or consent of a third party therefore is prohibited. Treas. Reg. § 20.2056(b)-5(g)(3). Although no person other than the spouse may possess the power to appoint the property to one other than the spouse, a third party may possess the power to distribute property to the spouse as this would not undermine the spouse's interest. Treas. Reg. § 20.2056(b)-5(j). A trustee therefore may be afforded discretion to distribute trust corpus to the spouse, as long as the spouse possesses the requisite power of appointment over any remaining trust assets.

The requirement that the spouse's power of appointment be exercisable "in all events" precludes the imposition of any conditions to the exercise of the power, however benign the conditions may appear. A lifetime power of invasion is exercisable in all events only if the spouse is afforded the unrestricted power to use or dispose of the subject property in any manner, including the power to dispose of the property by gift. Treas. Reg. § 20.2056(b)-5(g)(3). Additionally, the power may not be subject to termination for any reason other than exercise or release by the spouse. A power that may terminate upon the occurrence of a contingent event (such as the spouse's remarriage) therefore falls outside the scope of § 2056(b)(5). *Id.*; *see also* Estate of Walsh v. Commissioner, 110 T.C. 393 (1998) (holding that power of appointment that would lapse upon spouse's incompetency does not satisfy § 2056(b)(5)).

The power of appointment condition of § 2056(b)(5) has generated a wealth of litigation, which generally confirms the restrictive scope of the qualifying powers. For example, the Second Circuit in *Estate of Foster v. Commissioner*, 725 F.2d 201 (2d Cir. 1984), determined that a spouse's power to invade principal "for her needs and the needs of [the decedent's] children as she in her discretion may deem necessary" failed to satisfy § 2056(b)(5). Under applicable state law, the invasion power was subject to a standard of good faith in favor of the remaindermen, and this standard violated the all events condition. *Id.* at 203. The importance of these decisions has diminished considerably, however, as any attempted § 2056(b)(5) transfer that fails on power of appointment grounds may qualify for the marital deduction under § 2056(b)(7).[12]

[3] Application to "Specific Portion" of Trust Property

Qualification for the marital deduction under § 2056(b)(5) is not an all-or-nothing inquiry. The statute provides that the income and power of appointment requirements may be met with respect to the entire transferred interest or a "specific portion thereof." A "specific portion" for purposes of § 2056(b)(5) contemplates a fractional or percentage share of the underlying property, so that the spouse's interest will realize a ratable share of the appreciation or depreciation in the transferred property. Treas. Reg. § 20.2056(b)-5(c)(2). Despite this directive, courts have determined the "specific portion" requirement to be satisfied through the payment of fixed pecuniary amounts to the spouse. *See, e.g.,* Northeastern Pennsylvania Nat'l Bank & Trust Co. v. United States, 387 U.S. 213 (1967). Following continued litigation in this area, Congress statutorily confirmed the regulatory insistence on a ratable division of shares through the enactment of § 2056(b)(10).

---

[12] The § 2056(b)(7) exception to the terminable interest rule is discussed in § 19.03[D] below.

[C]   Insurance Proceeds or Annuity Payments Retained by Issuer

Internal Revenue Code: § 2056(b)(6)

Life insurance proceeds paid to the spouse will qualify for the marital deduction, as will a joint and survivor annuity that continues for the spouse's lifetime. Neither transfer implicates the terminable interest rule. However, what if the agreement between the decedent and the issuer requires the proceeds of such contracts to be retained by the issuer and held for the spouse's lifetime benefit? In that case, the terminable interest rule will preclude a marital deduction for the spouse's interest provided there exists a possibility that the funds will be paid to another following the spouse's death.

Section 2056(b)(6) provides an exception to the terminable interest rule that is narrowly targeted to this instance. As the scenario closely resembles a trust arrangement, the requirements of § 2056(b)(6) largely mirror those of § 2056(b)(5). In particular, § 2056(b)(6) establishes the following requirements for the arrangement to be exempt from the terminable interest rule:

1. The proceeds of the relevant contract must be held by the insurer subject to an agreement to pay the proceeds to the spouse in installments or to pay interest thereon, and all such amounts payable during the life of the surviving spouse must be paid to the spouse alone;

2. The required payments to the spouse must be made on an annual or more frequent basis, and the payments must commence not later than 13 months after the decedent's death;

3. The spouse must possess the power to appoint the amounts payable under the contract either to herself or to her estate, regardless of whether the power may be exercised in favor of another;

4. The spouse's power must be exercisable by her alone and in all events; and

5. No party other than the spouse may possess the power to appoint the proceeds to one other than the spouse.

As with § 2056(b)(5), the exception provided by § 2056(b)(6) may apply to a specific portion of the proceeds payable to the spouse.

[D]   Qualified Terminable Interest Property

Internal Revenue Code: § 2056(b)(7), 2044, 2519, 2207A(a), (b)
Treasury Regulations: § 20.2056(b)-7(a) to (d)(3)(i), (d)(4)–(6),
                           § 20.2056(b)-7(g), (h) Exs. 1, 2, 4
                           § 25.2519-1

In addition to removing the quantitative limits on the marital deduction, Congress fundamentally altered the marital deduction regime in 1981 through the introduction of the "qualified terminable interest property" (QTIP) exception to the terminable interest rule. In general terms, the QTIP exception under § 2056(b)(7) permits the decedent's executor to elect to override the application of the terminable interest rule if the surviving spouse receives a "qualifying income interest for life" in the transferred property. IRC § 2056(b)(7)(B)(i)(II). As QTIP qualification focuses on the spouse's income interest, the QTIP exception to the terminable interest rule allows a decedent to obtain the marital deduction without relinquishing control over the disposition of the trust remainder. In enacting § 2056(b)(7), Congress did not see any inherent inconsistency between the allowance of the marital deduction and the decedent's retention of control over the trust remainder; instead, Congress viewed the pre-existing requirement that the decedent relinquish control over the transferred property as generating deadweight loss:

> Under present law, the marital deduction is available only with respect to property passing outright to the spouse or in specified forms which give the spouse control over the transferred property. Because the surviving spouse must be given control over the property, the decedent cannot insure that the spouse will subsequently pass the property to his children. . . . [U]nless certain interests which do not grant the spouse total control are eligible for the unlimited marital deduction, a decedent would be forced to choose between surrendering control of the entire estate to avoid imposition of estate tax at his death or reducing his tax benefits at his death to insure inheritance by the children. The committee believes that the tax laws should be neutral and that tax consequences should not control an individual's disposition of property. Accordingly, the committee believes that a deduction should be permitted for certain terminable interests.

H.R. Rep. No. 97-201, 159–60 (1981).

Note that because the spouse's income interest in the QTIP property[13] expires upon the spouse's death, the QTIP property will not be captured in her gross estate under § 2033. Additionally, because the spouse is not the transferor of property to the QTIP trust, none of the retained-interest provisions will operate to subject the trust assets to estate taxation in the spouse's estate. Section 2044 steps in to protect the estate tax base in this context, requiring that any property for which a QTIP election has been made in the predeceasing spouse's estate be included in the surviving spouse's gross estate at her death. Section 2207A, in turn, provides the surviving spouse's probate estate with a right to recover the marginal estate tax attributable to the inclusion of the QTIP property in her gross estate under § 2044 from the person receiving the property.[14] Taken together, §§ 2056(b)(7) and 2044 can be conceptualized as a deferred estate tax on the predeceasing spouse. Section 2519 backstops this regime by treating the spouse's lifetime release or assignment of all or a portion of her income interest in the QTIP property as a transfer of the entire remainder interest in trust.

The marital deduction under § 2056(b)(7) turns on the definition of "qualified terminable interest property." This term encompasses property (1) which passes from the decedent, (2) in which the spouse has a "qualifying income interest for life," and (3) to which the decedent's executor has made a proper election. IRC § 2056(b)(7)(B)(i). The "passing" requirement is familiar from the discussion of the general terminable interest rule. The remaining requirements are addressed below.

---

[13] Even though the "property" aspect of the reference to "QTIP property" is redundant, the authors use this phrase because "QTIP" reads more naturally as an adjective (e.g., "QTIP trust").

[14] The surviving spouse may waive the statutory right of contribution through a specific direction in her will or revocable trust agreement. IRC § 2207A(a)(2).

[1]   Qualifying Income Interest for Life

[a]   Income Requirement

For a surviving spouse to possess a qualifying income interest for life, the spouse must be entitled to all the income from the transferred property payable on an annual or more frequent basis. IRC § 2056(b)(7)(B)(ii)(I). Alternatively, the spouse must possess a usufruct interest for life in the property—permitting legal life estates to satisfy the requirement. *Id.*; *see also* Treas. Reg. § 20.2056(b)-7(h), Ex. 1 (legal life estate provided to spouse in personal residence). Although the statutory language differs somewhat from that of § 2056(b)(5), the principles outlined in the regulations defining the income requirements of a § 2056(b)(5) trust apply in determining whether the income component of a qualifying income interest for life is satisfied. *See* Treas. Reg. § 20.2056(b)-7(d)(2). These requirements have been discussed in detail in the context of § 2056(b)(5) above, but a few principles are worth repeating. To start, the spouse's entitlement to the income payments cannot be subject to a standard for distribution or otherwise conditioned in any manner. *See* Estate of Nicholson v. Commissioner, 94 T.C. 666 (1990) (direction to distribute so much of trust income as spouse may require "to maintain [her] usual and customary standard of living" did not satisfy QTIP income requirement). Additionally, the surviving spouse's entitlement to income payments may not terminate upon the occurrence of a contingency. *See* Treas. Reg. § 20.2056(b)-7(d)(3)(i) (noting specifically the condition of remarriage). Although the trustee's ability to accumulate trust income generally is antithetical to the spouse's income rights, the trust may direct that income be accumulated as long as the spouse possesses the power, exercisable annually, to require the income to be distributed. *See* Treas. Reg. § 20.2056(b)-7(h), Ex. 2.

Entitlement to the payment of "stub income"—that is, income accumulating from the date of the last distribution to the date of the surviving spouse's death—at one point presented a thorny issue concerning the QTIP income requirement. In *Estate of Shelfer v. Commissioner*, 86 F.3d 1045 (11th Cir. 1996), and *Estate of Howard v. Commissioner*, 910 F.2d 633 (9th Cir. 1990), the estate of the surviving spouse sought to avoid inclusion of trust assets in the gross estate under § 2044 on the basis that the failure of the trust instrument to require distribution of the stub income to the spouse's estate prevented the spouse from possessing a qualifying income interest for life (which, in turn, prevented the trust assets from constituting qualified terminable interest property).[15] In both cases, the Court of Appeals determined that the payment of stub income to the remainder beneficiaries did not preclude QTIP treatment. The regulations under § 2056(b)(7) now confirm that a spouse's income interest in property does not fail to constitute a qualifying income interest for life merely because the stub income is not required to be paid to the spouse or the spouse's probate estate. Treas. Reg. § 20.2056(b)-7(d)(4).

[b]   Power to Appoint Principal

Apart from the surviving spouse's income rights, a qualifying income interest for life under § 2056(b)(7) mandates that no person—not even the surviving spouse—possess a power to appoint any part of the property to one other than the surviving spouse.[16] *See* Estate of

---

[15] In both cases, the estate of the predeceasing spouse had made the QTIP election and claimed the marital deduction under § 2056(b)(7).

[16] The regulations indicate that a fiduciary power under local law to adjust between income and principal to fairly

Bowling v. Commissioner, 93 T.C. 286 (1989) (trustee power to invade corpus for emergency needs of surviving spouse as well as those of her son and decedent's brother precluded spouse from possessing a qualifying income interest for life); *see also* Treas. Reg. § 20.2056(b)-7(h), Ex. 4 (confirming that a power held by the surviving spouse to appoint property to others is impermissible). The purpose of the prohibition on the potential to appoint property to one other than the surviving spouse is to ensure that the QTIP property not consumed by the spouse will be included in her future transfer tax base under either § 2044 or § 2519. While no person may possess the power to appoint property to others during the spouse's lifetime, a power which takes effect only at or after the death of the surviving spouse is permissible. Hence, a surviving spouse may be provided with a testamentary limited power of appointment over the assets of a QTIP trust.

[2] The QTIP Election

The QTIP exception to the terminable interest rule requires an affirmative election on the part of the decedent's executor on the decedent's estate tax return. IRC § 2056(b)(7)(B)(v). Qualification for the marital deduction under § 2056(b)(7) therefore is not automatic, and the decedent's executor may determine whether qualification for the marital deduction is desirable with the benefit of hindsight.

The QTIP election need not be made on an all-or-nothing basis. Rather, the election can be made with respect to a "specific portion" of the property, which § 2056(b)(10) defines as a fractional or percentage share. IRC § 2056(b)(7)(B)(iv). Thus, if a spouse is entitled to the income from only a fractional share of the transferred property or if the trustee is authorized to distribute a fractional portion of the trust principal to one other than the spouse, a QTIP election may be made with respect to the remaining fractional share that constitutes a qualifying income interest for life. In addition, limiting the QTIP election to a fractional portion of the trust property may provide a method of utilizing the unified credit in the estate of the first spouse to die. *See* Treas. Reg. § 20.2056(b)-7(h), Exs. 7 & 8 (permitting formula partial QTIP elections designed to reduce federal estate tax to zero based on final estate tax values).

The QTIP election is irrevocable. However, if the election is made prior to the due date of the estate tax return, the election may be modified or revoked on a subsequent timely-filed return (considering any extensions granted for filing). Treas. Reg. § 20.2056(b)-7(b)(4)(ii). Additionally, improvident QTIP elections may be treated as a nullity by the Service. For example, suppose a decedent leaves the balance of his estate in trust for the lifetime benefit of his wife, and the entire taxable estate falls below the $5 million applicable credit amount under § 2010(c) without regard to the marital deduction. Nonetheless, the decedent's executor makes a QTIP election. The Service in Revenue Procedure 2001-38, 2001-2 C.B. 124, announced a rule of mercy in such cases. If the QTIP election was not needed to reduce the estate tax liability of the predeceasing spouse to zero, the Service will treat the QTIP election as a nullity.[17] Thus, the trust property will not be included in the surviving spouse's gross estate under § 2044, nor

---

balance the interests of the beneficiaries that satisfies the conditions of Reg. § 1.643(b)-1 will not be considered to provide the fiduciary with the power to appoint trust property to one other than the spouse. Treas. Reg. § 20.2056(b)-7(d)(1).

[17] With the advent of portability of the estate tax unified credit, an estate may desire QTIP treatment for a trust even where the QTIP election is not necessary to reduce the estate tax to zero. Making the QTIP election even though the devise does not exceed the decedent's applicable exclusion amount would permit the trust assets to receive a second step-up in basis under § 1014 at the surviving spouse's death (as a result of the inclusion of the trust assets in the surviving spouse's gross estate under § 2044) while affording the deceased spouse control over the disposition of the

will § 2519 apply if the spouse makes a transfer of her income interest. However, no leeway is afforded for mere calculation errors. If a QTIP election was necessary to reduce the predeceasing spouse's estate tax liability to zero but was made with respect to more property than was necessary, no portion of the QTIP election will be disregarded. *Id.*

[3] QTIP Treatment for Annuities

Section 2056(b)(7)(C) extends QTIP treatment to certain survivorship annuities that are included in the decedent's gross estate pursuant to § 2039 (or under § 2033 if the annuity constitutes a community property asset). This provision is of considerable importance, as IRAs and other qualified retirement plans often comprise a significant portion of a decedent's gross estate. There exists only one requirement for the annuity to qualify for QTIP treatment: the right to receive the annuity payments must be limited to the surviving spouse during the spouse's lifetime.[18] If that condition is satisfied, the executor is treated as having made the QTIP election with respect to the annuity. An affirmative election is required to negate QTIP treatment.

The Service addressed the application of § 2056(b)(7) to an IRA that passed to a trust created under the decedent's will in Revenue Ruling 2000-2, 2000-1 C.B. 305. The ruling reasoned that, in order for the IRA and the trust to provide the surviving spouse with a qualifying income interest for life, the spouse must be entitled to receive the income from both at least annually. The trust instrument provided that all income would be distributed to the spouse on an annual or more frequent basis. Additionally, the trust provided the surviving spouse with a right, exercisable annually, to compel the trustee to withdraw the income generated by the assets in the IRA (if greater than the required minimum distribution) and to distribute that amount to the spouse. As a result of this power to compel the trustee to withdraw the IRA income, the Service determined that both the IRA and the trust qualified for QTIP treatment.[19]

[4] Subsequent Inclusion in Transfer Tax Base of Spouse

[a]   Section 2044

To ensure that QTIP property does not escape taxation altogether in both spouse's estates, § 2044(a) includes in the surviving spouse's gross estate any property with respect to which the spouse possessed a qualifying income interest for life and with respect to which a QTIP election was made by or on behalf of the predeceasing spouse. The surviving spouse is treated as the transferor of any property included in her gross estate under § 2044 for purposes of the estate tax and the GST tax.[20] *See* IRC § 2044(c).

---

trust remainder. This approach no longer would waste the deceased spouse's unified credit, as the unused portion would carry over to the surviving spouse. Portability of the estate tax unified credit is discussed in § 19.05.

[18] Note that if the surviving spouse is the sole beneficiary of the annuity, the spouse does not receive a terminable interest, and the § 2056(b)(7)(C) exception is not necessary.

[19] Revenue Ruling 2000-2 was modified and superseded by Revenue Ruling 2006-26, 2006-1 C.B. 939, which addresses the potential effect of fiduciary adjustments between income and principal in this context. Nonetheless, the basic reasoning of Revenue Ruling 2000-2 is incorporated into and serves as the foundation for the analysis in Revenue Ruling 2006-26.

[20] However, § 2652(a)(3) permits the estate of the predeceasing spouse to elect to treat property for which a QTIP election was made for estate tax purposes (in order to qualify the transfer for the marital deduction) as if the election

Property included in the gross estate under § 2044 is not to be aggregated with property included in the spouse's gross estate under other sections. *See* Estate of Mellinger v. Commissioner, 112 T.C. 26, 37 (1999) ("There is . . . no indication that section 2044 mandated identical tax consequences as an outright transfer to the surviving spouse.").[21] Hence, if a surviving spouse owned 40 percent of the stock of a corporation in her individual name and a QTIP trust for her benefit held another 40 percent interest, the spouse's estate presumably would be entitled to value both interests through the application of a minority-interest discount.

Oftentimes, there will not be a unity of interest among the remainder beneficiaries of a QTIP trust and the devisees of the surviving spouse's residual estate—particularly in the context of second marriages. Section 2207A therefore provides the surviving spouse's estate with a right to recover the marginal estate tax attributable to the inclusion of QTIP property in the spouse's gross estate under § 2044. The surviving spouse may waive this right of recovery on behalf of her estate through a provision in her will or revocable trust, but an effective waiver must "specifically indicate[] an intent to waive any right of recovery under this subchapter" with respect to the QTIP property. IRC § 2207A(a)(2). Congress amended § 2207A in 1997 to require a specific indication of the intent to waive the recovery right, out of concern that a decedent may inadvertently waive the recovery right through a standard provision directing the payment of taxes from the residuary estate. *See* H.R. Rep. No. 105-148, at 613–14, 1997-4 C.B. (vol. 1) 319, 935–36 (suggesting a reference to "QTIP, the QTIP trust, section 2044, or section 2207A"). If the surviving spouse does not validly waive the § 2207A right of recovery on behalf of her estate, the failure to exercise the right of recovery constitutes a gift under § 2501 from those who would have benefitted from the recovery to those from whom the recovery would have been obtained. Treas. Reg. § 20.2207A-1(a)(2).

[b]　　Section 2519

Just as the gift tax can be envisioned as a backstop to the federal estate tax, § 2519 can be conceived as a backstop to the inclusion of QTIP property in the surviving spouse's gross estate under § 2044. Pursuant to § 2519(a), a spouse's disposition of all or any part of her qualifying income interest for life in QTIP property is treated as a transfer of all interests in the property other than the qualifying income interest. In other words, if the spouse disposes of *any* portion of her income interest in QTIP property, she is treated as having made a gift of the entire remainder interest in the property. If the spouse disposes of only a portion of the qualifying income interest, § 2702 may apply to assign a zero value to the portion of the spouse's income interest that is not transferred (provided a member of the spouse's family possesses an interest in the property). In that case, the combined gifts will equal the entire value of the QTIP property. The actual transfer of the portion of the income interest will constitute a gift under § 2501, while the deemed gift of all other interests in the property under § 2519(a) will be valued by assigning a zero value to the spouse's retained income interest. *See* IRC § 2702(a)(2)(B); Treas. Reg. § 25.2519-1(g), Ex. 4. Additionally, the portion of

---

had not been made for GST tax purposes. The effect of this provision is to allow the predeceasing spouse to override the application of § 2044(c) for GST tax purposes only, which, in turn, allows the predeceasing spouse to allocate his available GST exemption to the QTIP trust.

[21]　The spouse's lack of control over both holdings provides the justification for not aggregating § 2044 property with other assets. In *Estate of Fontana v. Commissioner*, 118 T.C. 318 (2002), the Tax Court determined that stock over which the surviving spouse possessed a general power of appointment (under a § 2056(b)(5) trust) had to be aggregated with stock owned by the spouse outright due to the spouse's control over both portions.

the trust principal attributable to the portion of the income interest actually retained by the spouse will be included in the spouse's gross estate under § 2036(a)(1), as the spouse retained the income stream attributable to the portion of the trust principal deemed transferred by her under § 2519(a).[22] *See* Treas. Reg. § 25.2519-1(a).

Section 2519 adopts a broad definition of a "disposition" that triggers the deemed transfer of the remainder interest in QTIP property. The term is not limited to a gratuitous transfer of the spouse's income interest, but also encompasses sales of the income interest to third parties for value and commutations of the spouse's income interest. While the receipt of consideration for the transfer may shield the transfer of income rights from gift taxation, the deemed transfer of the remainder interest in the QTIP property under § 2519 will not be offset by consideration.

One potentially clever way to minimize the future transfer tax consequences to the surviving spouse with respect to a QTIP trust established for her benefit is for the spouse to purchase the remainder interest in the trust for its actuarial value. Literally, the spouse makes no disposition of her income interest, which serves as the predicate to the application of § 2519. Although the full value of the QTIP property will be subsequently included in the spouse's gross estate under § 2033 (assuming the possession of the income interest and remainder effects a merger into fee title), the spouse will have removed the actuarial value of the remainder from her gross estate through the payment of consideration. However, the transaction does not successfully avoid the reach of § 2519. Because the net effect is to leave the spouse with property equal to the commuted value of her income interest in the trust, the Service treats the purchase of the remainder interest as a commutation of the spouse's income interest. The deemed commutation, in turn, triggers the deemed transfer of the remainder interest under § 2519. *See* Rev. Rul. 98-8, 1998-1 C.B. 541.

Just as a surviving spouse's estate is entitled to recover the marginal estate tax attributable to the inclusion of QTIP property in the surviving spouse's gross estate under § 2207A(a), § 2207A(b) permits the spouse to recover any marginal gift tax from the person receiving the property. The right of recovery, in turn, reduces the amount of the deemed gift under § 2519. *See* Treas. Reg. § 25.2519-1(c)(4). Yet even if the gift tax is paid by the recipients of the QTIP property, the gift tax is treated as having been paid by the surviving spouse for all other purposes. For instance, if the surviving spouse dies within three years of the § 2519 transfer, the gift tax paid by the recipients of the QTIP property will be included in the spouse's gross estate under § 2035(b). *See* Estate of Morgens v. Commissioner, 133 T.C. 402 (2009).

[E]   Charitable Remainder Trusts

Internal Revenue Code: § 2056(b)(8)

Note that a lead interest provided to the surviving spouse in a charitable remainder trust constitutes a terminable interest for which a marital deduction generally would be disallowed. Section 2056(b)(8) exempts these transfers from the terminable interest rule, provided the surviving spouse is the only non-charitable beneficiary. Hence, if the lead interest in a charitable remainder trust were paid to a surviving spouse for life and then to a child for life, § 2056(b)(8) would not apply. In that case, the decedent's estate would have to rely on the QTIP provisions of § 2056(b)(7) to qualify the transfer for the marital deduction—meaning that the

---

[22] In that case—where the same property that was the subject of a gift by the spouse is captured in the spouse's gross estate—an adjustment to the spouse's adjustable taxable gifts is required under § 2001(b)(1)(B).

spouse must be entitled to at least the income from the transferred property for her lifetime.

§ 19.04   VALUING THE MARITAL DEDUCTION

Internal Revenue Code: § 2056(b)(4)
Treasury Regulations: § 20.2056(b)-4(a) to (d)(4)

As a general matter, the amount of the marital deduction is limited to the value of property which passes or has passed to the surviving spouse. IRC § 2056(a). Only the net value of the property passing to the spouse may be deducted, and this value is to be determined prospectively as of the decedent's date of death.[23] Treas. Reg. § 20.2056(b)-4(a). Questions concerning the value to be placed on the marital deduction arise in three primary contexts: (1) the effect of estate administration expenses; (2) the effect of estate, inheritance, or other death taxes paid from the marital share; and (3) the effect of encumbrances or other obligations relating to the marital devise.

[A]   Reduction on Account of Administration Expenses

Historically, the effect of estate administration expenses on the value of the marital deduction was anything but a model of clarity. Although the payment of administration expenses from the principal of a marital devise reduced the value of the marital deduction, considerable uncertainty surrounded the issue of whether the same reduction was required for administration expenses that were satisfied from the income generated by the marital devise during the period of administration. The Supreme Court addressed this issue in *Commissioner v. Estate of Hubert*, 520 U.S. 93 (1997), but the plurality opinion interpreting when the payment of administration expenses from income generated by assets allocable to the marital share constituted a "material limitation" (the prevailing regulatory standard) on the spouse's income interest did little to clear the air.

Following the *Estate of Hubert* decision, Treasury promulgated new regulations in this area that eschewed the principal-versus-income distinction. Instead, the regulations now divide estate administration expenses into two categories for determining the effect on the marital deduction: (1) estate management expenses and (2) estate transmission expenses. Treas. Reg. § 20.2056(b)-4(d)(1). Estate management expenses are those incurred with investment of the estate assets or with the preservation and maintenance of estate property for a reasonable period of administration; examples include investment advisory fees, brokerage commissions, insurance, and interest. Treas. Reg. § 20.2056(b)-4(d)(1)(i). Estate transmission expenses, on the other hand, technically include any administration expense that is not an estate management expense. This latter category can be conceived as expenses that are attendant to the collection of the decedent's property, the administration of the decedent's estate, and the transmission of property to the decedent's beneficiaries or heirs. Treas. Reg. § 20.2056(b)-4(d)(1)(ii).

The revised regulatory regime takes a benign approach to estate management expenses. Estate management expenses attributable to the marital share of the decedent's estate and

---

[23] The marital deduction is to be valued as of the decedent's date of death. But if the decedent's estate elects to employ alternate valuation under § 2032, the value of the property passing to the surviving spouse is adjusted for any difference in value that is not attributable to the mere lapse of time as of the date six months after the decedent's death or the date the property is distributed or disposed of, whichever occurs first. Treas. Reg. § 20.2056(b)-4(a) (incorporating Treas. Reg. § 20.2032-1(a)(3)).

paid from such share do not reduce the value of the marital deduction.[24] Treas. Reg. § 20.2056(b)-4(d)(3). Although § 2056(b)(9) prevents those same expenses from being deducted from the gross estate under § 2053, nothing prevents estate management expenses that fail to reduce the marital deduction under § 2056 from being deducted for fiduciary income tax purposes.

The potential to obtain an effective double deduction for estate management expenses does not extend to estate transmission expenses. Rather, the value of the marital deduction must be reduced by the amount of estate transmission expenses that are paid from the marital share. Treas. Reg. § 20.2056(b)-4(d)(2). Although those expenses may still be deducted from the gross estate pursuant to § 2053(a)(2), such a deduction comes at the expense of a deduction for fiduciary income tax purposes. *See* IRC § 642(g).

[B] Reduction on Account of Estate or Inheritance Taxes

The value of the interest passing to the surviving spouse must take into account the federal estate tax that is charged against the transfer, as well as any estate or inheritance taxes that are assessed at the state or local level. IRC § 2056(b)(4). Accordingly, if the decedent devises all or a portion of the residuary estate to his surviving spouse while directing all estate and inheritance taxes to be paid from the residue, the value of the marital deduction must be reduced by the portion of the taxes attributable to the spousal devise. Treas. Reg. § 20.2056(b)-4(c)(4). The same goes for estate and inheritance taxes that are apportioned to the residue pursuant to local law. *Id.* This result is unfortunate in taxable estates, as the allocation of estate taxes to a marital devise reduces the marital deduction, which, in turn, increases the resulting tax to be allocated to the marital share. Well drafted tax apportionment provisions therefore will exempt a devise to a surviving spouse that qualifies for the marital deduction from bearing any portion of estate or inheritance taxes due in the decedent's estate. Default state law following the equitable apportionment approach (of charging the tax liability to the transfers that generate the resulting tax) accomplishes the same result. Even in the absence of an equitable apportionment of the tax liability contained in the decedent's will or supplied by state law, courts at times will endeavor to interpret the decedent's will as exempting the spousal devise from bearing a portion of the tax liability. *See, e.g.*, Dodd v. United States, 345 F.2d 715 (3d Cir. 1965) (exempting portion of residuary devise to spouse from estate tax based on decedent's likely intention to maximize marital deduction). However, express tax apportionment provisions may prove too much to overcome. *See, e.g.*, Estate of Lurie v. Commissioner, T.C. Memo. 2004-19, 87 T.C.M. (CCH) 830 (decedent's revocable trust called for payment of estate taxes from the trust—which included marital devises—to the extent decedent's probate estate was not sufficient).

[C] Effect of Encumbrances or Other Obligations

As the marital deduction is allowed only for the net value transferred to the surviving spouse, the value of any property transferred to the spouse must be reduced by the amount of any encumbrances on the property. IRC § 2056(b)(4)(B). This rule is not limited to obligations that give rise to formal liens on the transferred property; rather, the rule extends to "any obligation imposed by the decedent with respect to the passing of such interest." *Id.*

---

[24] As one might expect, the marital deduction must be reduced to the extent the marital share is used to satisfy estate management expenses attributable to other portions of the decedent's estate. Treas. Reg. § 20.2056(b)-4(d)(4).

Substance-over-form principles apply in this context. If a surviving spouse is obligated to make a transfer of her own funds to a third party as a condition to receiving a devise from the deceased spouse, the marital deduction is reduced by the amount of the transfer from the spouse. *See* Treas. Reg. § 20.2056(b)-4(b), Ex. 1; United States v. Stapf, 375 U.S. 118 (1963). Because the transfer from the spouse would reduce the amounts subject to taxation at her subsequent death, reduction of the marital deduction for the decedent's initial transfer is necessary to ensure that the transfer is subject to estate tax in at least one spouse's estate.

§ 19.05 PORTABILITY OF THE UNIFIED CREDIT

Internal Revenue Code: §§ 2010(c), 2505(a)

The existence of the estate tax marital deduction provides married individuals with a ready means of postponing federal estate taxation until the death of the surviving spouse. If the predeceasing spouse devises his entire estate to the surviving spouse in a deductible form, no estate tax will be assessed in the estate of the predeceasing spouse—regardless of the size of the gross estate. Prior to 2011, this basic estate plan effectively wasted the predeceasing spouse's unified credit. The couple's combined assets ended up in the hands of the surviving spouse, and the surviving spouse's transfer of this property to future generations would be shielded from taxation by that spouse's unified credit only. Hence, for couples whose combined estates exceeded the value of an amount shielded from taxation by a single unified credit, this straightforward estate plan imposed an additional federal transfer tax burden.

As part of the Tax Relief, Unemployment Insurance Reauthorization, and Job Creation Act of 2010 (Tax Relief Act of 2010),[25] Congress finally heeded the repeated calls of professional organizations to make the unified credit portable among spouses. Congress did so by expanding the applicable exclusion amount of the credit to include not only the "basic exclusion amount" of $5 million (as adjusted for cost of living from 2010 starting in 2012) but also the "deceased spousal unused exclusion amount." IRC § 2010(c)(2). In general terms, this additional exclusion is the amount of the unified credit that was not used by the individual's predeceased spouse to offset gift tax or estate tax on taxable transfers. *See* IRC § 2010(c)(4)(B) (defining the deceased spousal unused exclusion amount as the excess of the basic exclusion over the amount with respect to which the tentative tax under § 2001(b)(1) is determined in the predeceasing spouse's estate). For a surviving spouse to benefit from the deceased spouse's unused credit, the executor of the deceased spouse must file a timely estate tax return on which the executor irrevocably elects that no portion of the unused exclusion may be taken on behalf of the deceased spouse.[26] IRC § 2010(c)(5)(A).

To illustrate the operation of the portability feature of the unified credit now provided in § 2010(c), assume that *Husband* dies with a $10 million gross estate. *Husband* had made taxable gifts to his two children totaling $1 million, and his will provides for specific bequests of an additional $1 million to each child. *Husband* leaves the balance of his estate to a QTIP trust for the lifetime benefit of *Wife* for which his executor makes the QTIP election.

---

[25] Pub. L. No. 111-312, 124 Stat. 3296 (2010).

[26] As a practical matter, this condition to preserving the predeceasing spouse's unused exclusion amount expands considerably the range of estates for which estate tax returns will be filed. Prior to portability, if a predeceasing spouse's gross estate did not exceed the applicable exclusion amount of the unified credit, no estate tax return needed to be filed. While that rule remains the same following portability (substituting the basic exclusion amount for the filing threshold, *see* IRC § 6018(a)(1)), the failure to file an estate tax return in this range operates to effectively extinguish the predeceasing spouse's unused exclusion amount.

Husband's taxable estate is thereby reduced to $2 million. The tentative tax under § 2001(b)(1) in *Husband's* estate is computed on $3 million, consisting of *Husband's* $2 million taxable estate and $1 million of adjusted taxable gifts. *Husband's* estate therefore uses only $3 million of his $5 million applicable exclusion amount to offset the estate tax otherwise due in his estate. Assuming *Husband's* estate files a timely tax return electing to not take the remaining $2 million exclusion amount, the unified credit available to *Wife* under § 2505 and § 2010 following *Husband's* death will exempt $7 million from taxation, consisting of *Wife's* $5 million basic exclusion amount plus a deceased spousal unused exclusion amount of $2 million. *See* IRC § 2010(c)(4)(B).

Portability of the unified credit is subject to a host of limitations. First, the unified credit is not portable among spouses during their lifetimes.[27] As the name suggests, the deceased spousal unused exclusion amount arises only upon the death of an individual's spouse. On that note, an individual cannot collect multiple additions to the basic exclusion amount by surviving multiple spouses. The additional exclusion is available with respect to the unused basic exclusion amount of the "last such deceased spouse of such surviving spouse" only. IRC § 2010(c)(4)(B)(i). Hence, at any given time, an individual cannot possess an applicable exclusion amount that exceeds twice the basic exclusion amount.[28]

Second, the portability feature of § 2010(c) is not retroactive. Instead, the deceased spousal unused exclusion amount benefits only those surviving spouses whose spouse died after December 31, 2010. *See* IRC § 2010(c)(4). Portability is not necessarily prospective either. Because the transfer tax amendments made by the Tax Relief Act of 2010 expire on December 31, 2012, there is no statutory guarantee that a surviving spouse dying after such date will be entitled to the additional exclusion amount.[29]

Third, whereas the basic exclusion amount is indexed for inflation from 2010, the deceased spousal unused exclusion amount is not similarly adjusted for increases in the cost of living. Thus, assuming that *Wife* in the illustration above survives *Husband* for a significant period, the addition to her inflation-adjusted basic exclusion amount will remain at $2 million. Accordingly, it may have been preferable for the executor of *Husband's* estate to have made a partial QTIP election, so that $2 million of the trust would have been included in *Husband's* taxable estate and shielded from taxation by the remaining portion of his unified credit. Assuming positive rates of return, the increased principal balance remaining in the non-QTIP

---

[27] As a practical matter, the basic exclusion amount may be shared by spouses during their lifetimes either through employing the split-gift election or by taking advantage of the ability to make initial transfers between spouses that qualify for the gift tax marital deduction.

[28] However, a multiple widow may utilize more than one spousal addition to the applicable exclusion amount with proper planning. For example, assume *Wife* survives *Husband 1* and benefits from his $5 million unused exclusion amount. *Wife* remarries *Husband 2* who has not used any portion of his basic exclusion amount. To prevent the elimination of the unused exclusion amount from *Husband 1* that would occur if *Husband 2* were to predecease her, *Wife* can make taxable gifts to utilize the unused exclusion amount from *Husband 1*. The portion against which *Wife's* taxable gifts will be first charged—that is, against her basic exclusion amount or the deceased spousal unused exclusion amount from *Husband 1*—presumably will be addressed in future administrative guidance. On that note, in an example addressing use of the surviving spouse's applicable exclusion amount by reason of her death, the Joint Committee on Taxation explained that the deceased spousal unused exclusion amount would be applied before the surviving spouse's basic exclusion amount. *See* Joint Committee on Taxation, Technical Explanation of the Revenue Provisions Contained in the "Tax Relief, Unemployment Insurance Reauthorization, and Job Creation Act of 2010" Scheduled for Consideration in the United States Senate, JCX 55-10, at 53 (Dec. 10, 2010).

[29] If it appears that the benefit of portability will not be extended in the future, one can expect surviving spouses to make considerable taxable gifts to capture the benefit of portability prior to its expiration.

portion of the trust would have passed (presumably to *Husband's* children) free of estate tax in *Wife's* estate.[30]

Fourth, portability of the unified credit does not extend to the GST exemption. Hence, the estate plan adopted by *Husband* does not allow him to make effective use of his GST exemption. If *Husband's* executor makes the QTIP election for the entire trust, any allocation of the GST exemption to the trust will be effectively wasted given that *Wife* will become the GST transferor upon her death. Accordingly, *Husband's* estate plan should divide the trust created for *Wife* into two portions, one of which being equal to the amount of *Husband's* remaining GST exemption to be allocated to the trust (and for which *Husband's* executor could make a reverse QTIP election under § 2652(a)(3) to the extent necessary).

Due to the various limitations on the benefits of portability of the unified credit detailed above,[31] married couples having a combined net worth in excess of a single basic exclusion amount may be well advised not to rely on portability of the unified credit by simply having the entire estate of the predeceased spouse pass to the survivor. Instead, these couples should consider traditional credit shelter trust planning of the variety discussed in § 19.06 below. However, this is not to suggest that portability of the unified credit represents a hollow gesture on the part of Congress. The feature eliminates what had been a significant transfer tax penalty for married couples who failed to undertake the sometimes complicated estate planning necessary to ensure effective use of the predeceasing spouse's unified credit. Based on a $5 million applicable exclusion amount and a 35 percent marginal tax rate, the penalty for wasting a spouse's unified credit would have totaled $1.75 million.

§ 19.06 A NOTE ON MARITAL DEDUCTION PLANNING

Prior to the introduction of portability of the unified credit in 2011, a staple of estate planning for couples whose projected combined wealth exceeded the basic exclusion amount of the unified credit involved ensuring effective use of the unified credit available to the predeceasing spouse. Even though this concern is mitigated considerably now that a predeceasing spouse can effectively leave his unused unified credit to his surviving spouse, for reasons described in § 19.05 above, creating a taxable devise in the predeceasing spouse's estate that exhausts his unified credit may still be preferred.

An extremely simple method of exhausting the unified credit available to the predeceasing spouse is for such spouse to devise property to his children or other intended beneficiaries other than his spouse. Yet for perhaps obvious reasons, a typical client prefers to leave the bulk of his property for the benefit of his surviving spouse. To do so without wasting the predeceasing spouse's unified credit through an outright devise to the surviving spouse, planners typically employ a trust (commonly referred to as a "credit shelter trust") that benefits the surviving spouse and potentially other family members.

Successful use of the predeceasing spouse's unified credit through a credit shelter devise depends on the assets of the trust not subsequently being included in the surviving spouse's

---

[30] Note that the benefit of insulating the appreciation of the trust assets in the non-QTIP portion of the trust from being subject to tax in *Wife's* estate comes at the expense of a later step-up in basis under § 1014 at *Wife's* death.

[31] In addition, leaving property in trust for the surviving spouse rather than through an outright devise may offer creditor protection for the trust property that would not be available to the spouse if she self-settled a trust for her benefit.

gross estate. Yet avoiding inclusion in the surviving spouse's gross estate does not pose a major obstacle. For instance, a well designed credit shelter trust can (a) name the spouse as trustee; (b) designate the spouse as a mandatory or discretionary distributee of trust income; (c) enable the spouse to withdraw (or to distribute to herself in her capacity as trustee) amounts for her health, education, support in her accustomed manner of living, or maintenance; (d) provide the spouse with a non-cumulative annual right to withdraw the greater of $5,000 or five percent of the value of the trust assets; and (e) provide the spouse with a limited power of appointment over the trust principal, exercisable inter vivos, by will, or both. Because the surviving spouse is not the transferor of property to the trust, none of these rights or powers will cause the assets of the credit shelter trust to be included in the surviving spouse's gross estate for estate tax purposes. Hence, all or a combination of the above provisions could be incorporated into the credit shelter devise, depending on the client's goals.

Including a credit shelter trust in an individual's estate plan gives rise to a potentially cumbersome practical issue: How to define the devise qualifying for the marital deduction and the devise to the credit shelter trust. The first determination is whether to require the division of the predeceasing spouse's estate between the two devises, or to permit the division to be made post-mortem. For instance, a decedent could devise his entire estate to his surviving spouse while creating a credit shelter trust under his will to receive any amounts disclaimed by the surviving spouse.[32] This approach provides the surviving spouse with the benefit of hindsight in making determinations concerning the funding of the credit shelter trust, yet the technique depends on the spouse satisfying the various conditions on qualified disclaimers provided in § 2518.[33]

Alternatively, it is possible to provide the decedent's executor with the ability to divide the decedent's estate between the marital deduction devise and the credit shelter devise. If the decedent were to leave his entire estate in a trust satisfying the conditions of a QTIP trust, the decedent's executor can make a partial QTIP election with respect to the transfer. The unelected portion of the devise would constitute the credit shelter devise. However, this approach eliminates much of the flexibility otherwise available in crafting the terms of the credit shelter trust. In order to render the trust eligible for QTIP treatment, the trust must provide the surviving spouse with annual income distributions while precluding the distribution of principal to others. Hence, the decedent's children could not benefit from the credit shelter trust during the surviving spouse's lifetime.

For individuals who wish to direct the terms by which their estates will be divided between the marital devise and the credit shelter devise, formulaic devises generally are used to accomplish this goal. Although numerous options exist for this purpose, the formulaic devises fall into two general categories: "pecuniary" devises of a specific dollar amount, and "fractional share" devises of a portion of the decedent's residuary estate. A sample pecuniary devise of the marital share could read as follows:

[32] In the event a surviving spouse is designated to serve as trustee of the credit shelter trust to be funded through the spouse's disclaimer, any discretionary distributions from the trust must be subject to an ascertainable standard. If no such limitation exists, the attempted disclaimer will not be qualified unless the spouse also disclaims the discretionary power. *See* IRC § 2518(b)(4); Treas. Reg. § 25.2518-2(e)(2).

[33] Additionally, the disclaimer-funded credit shelter technique depends on the surviving spouse resisting the natural urge to shun the perceived complexity of trusts and to simply accept all of the outright devise.

I give [to the surviving spouse or a marital deduction trust] an amount equal to the minimum amount which, if allowed as a federal estate tax marital deduction, would result in the least possible federal estate tax being payable by reason of my death.[34]

The residual amount would then be used to fund the credit shelter devise. Alternatively, the decedent's residuary estate could be divided between the marital devise and the credit shelter devise on a fractional basis, as in the following example:

I give [to the surviving spouse or a marital deduction trust] a fractional share of my residuary estate having a numerator equal to the smallest amount that, if allowed as a marital deduction under the federal estate tax, would result in the least possible federal estate tax being payable by reason of my death, and a denominator equal to the value of my residuary estate as finally determined for federal estate tax purposes.[35]

Variations exist on each of these formulaic devises, with the variations addressing primarily the terms on which the respective shares of the decedent's estate will be funded. Issues to be considered in crafting a formula devise include, among others, (a) the ease of administering the devise (including the possible necessity of revaluing the estate property at the point of distribution); (b) the flexibility afforded to the decedent's executor in selecting the assets to fund the respective shares; (c) the potential income tax consequences of funding the shares with distributions of property in-kind (including the potential acceleration of income in respect of a decedent); and (d) the likelihood of fluctuation in the value of estate property between the decedent's date of death and the point of distribution.[36]

In crafting a formula devise to or for the benefit of the surviving spouse, care must be taken to ensure that the spouse's devise is not rendered sufficiently indefinite so as to jeopardize the availability of the marital deduction in the first place. For instance, in Revenue Procedure 64-19, 1964-1 C.B.682, the Service addressed a pecuniary devise of the marital share that the executor could satisfy through the distribution of property valued at its federal estate tax value. Note that if the executor's discretion in this regard were uninhibited, the executor could fund the marital devise with property that had depreciated since the date of the decedent's death. The Service held that the property passing to the surviving spouse under such an arrangement would not be ascertainable as of the decedent's death (and therefore would not qualify for the marital deduction) unless fiduciary obligations under state law or the terms of the governing instrument obligated the executor (1) to fund the marital devise with property having a value determined at the date of distribution that was no less than the pecuniary devise, or (2) to distribute assets in satisfaction of the devise that were "fairly representative of appreciation or depreciation" in the property available for distribution. *Id.* at 683. The issues addressed by the Service in Revenue Procedure 64-19 do not exist where the executor lacks discretion in funding the marital devise—such as where the executor must fund the devise in cash or fund the devise with a pro-rata portion of all estate property.[37]

---

[34] *See* Jeffrey N. Pennell, *Estate Tax Marital Deduction*, 843-2nd Tax Management Portfolio (BNA) at A-121 (2004) (providing a sample devise on which this illustration is based).

[35] *See id.* (providing a sample devise on which this illustration is based).

[36] The relative merits of various formula devise options serves as the subject of separate treatise discussion. *See* Richard B. Covey, Marital Deduction and Credit Shelter Dispositions and the Use of Formula Provisions (4th ed. 1997); Jeffrey N. Pennell, *Estate Tax Marital Deduction*, 843-2nd Tax Management Portfolio (BNA) at A-121 to A-158 (2004).

[37] However, each of these more conservative approaches has its own drawbacks. Liquidating estate property to

§ 19.07   THE GIFT TAX MARITAL DEDUCTION

Internal Revenue Code: § 2523

The ability to make tax-free transfers to one's spouse is not limited to those made by descent and devise. Rather, § 2523 provides a deduction for inter vivos transfers to a spouse that largely parallels the provisions of § 2056 under the estate tax. The primary differences are those necessary to accommodate a living donor as opposed to a decedent. For instance, the terminable interest rule provided in § 2523(b) covers not only the transfer of an interest in property by the donor to another (which may become possessory after the termination or failure of the spouse's interest), but also the donor's retention of an interest in the transferred property. *See* IRC § 2523(b)(1). Although this broadened terminable interest rule would capture a donor's contingent survivorship interest in property transferred by the donor to himself and his spouse as joint tenants with right of survivorship (or as tenants by the entirety), the terminable interest rule does not apply to such common transfers. Pursuant to § 2523(d), the donor's contingent survivorship interest in the property is disregarded as a retained interest for purposes of § 2523(b). In addition to broadening the terminable interest rule to accommodate retained interests by the donor, § 2523(b)(2) expands the rule to instances in which the donor-spouse can convert the spouse's interest into a terminable interest after the transfer takes place through the exercise of a power of appointment over the transferred property.

Section 2523 contains a number of familiar exceptions to the broadened terminable interest rule of § 2523(b)(1). Section 2523(e) treats the spouse as receiving the entire interest in property if she is entitled to all of the income generated by the property at least annually together with a power to appoint the property to herself or her estate (exercisable by the spouse alone and in all events). Additionally, § 2523(f) ensures the availability of the marital deduction for lifetime transfers of QTIP property (for which the donor-spouse must make the QTIP election on a timely filed gift tax return).

Pursuant to § 2523(f)(5), any interest retained by the donor-spouse in the QTIP property is effectively disregarded for estate and gift tax purposes until the transferred property is included in the donee-spouse's transfer tax base. That is, until the QTIP property is included in the donee-spouse's gross estate under § 2044 or deemed to be transferred inter vivos by the donee-spouse through the operation of § 2519, the donor's retained interest cannot generate additional gift or estate tax consequences to the donor-spouse. However, these rules do not apply once the donee-spouse becomes the transferor of the QTIP property, either through the application of § 2044 or § 2519. *See* IRC § 2056(f)(5)(B).

As an example, assume that *Wife* transfers property in trust that requires income to be distributed at least annually to *Husband*. Upon *Husband's* death, income payments are to continue to *Wife* for her lifetime if she survives *Husband*, otherwise the trust property will be distributed to *Wife's* then-living issue. If *Wife* predeceases *Husband*, § 2523(f)(5)(A) prevents the QTIP property from being captured in her gross estate under § 2036(a)(1).[38] However, if *Wife* survives *Husband*, the QTIP property will be included in *Husband's* gross estate under

---

fund a cash bequest may not be desirable if the goal is to preserve family-owned assets, and the forced sale of property may run counter to the preservation of wealth. Opting for a pro-rata allocation eliminates the possibility of strategic allocation of the decedent's assets among the respective shares, and the pro-rata division of all of the decedent's property may prove cumbersome as an administrative matter.

[38] Recall that § 2036(a)(1) otherwise would be triggered based on *Wife's* retention of a secondary income interest in the transferred property. *See* Treas. Reg. § 20.2036-1(b)(1)(ii).

§ 2044. If *Husband's* estate then makes the QTIP election under § 2056(b)(7) to obtain the marital deduction for estate tax purposes, the property will be included in *Wife's* gross estate at her death under § 2044. *See* IRC § 2523(f)(5)(B).

§ 19.08   THE SPLIT-GIFT ELECTION

| *Internal Revenue Code*: | §§ 2513, 2001(b), (d), (e) |
| *Treasury Regulations*: | § 25.2513-1(a) to (b) |

Apart from the exemption of most inter-spousal transfers from transfer tax offered by the marital deduction, married individuals also may be treated as a single unit for purposes of determining the identity of the transferor of gifts to non-spouses. Section 2513(a) provides spouses with the election to treat an actual transfer from one spouse as if the transfer was made one-half by each spouse. Although the original motivation behind § 2513 was to achieve gift tax parity between spouses in community property states and those in separate property jurisdictions, the ability of spouses to "split" their gifts under § 2513 can be conceived as a natural byproduct of the gift tax marital deduction itself. If one spouse may transfer property outright to another on a tax-free basis and that spouse could then transfer such property to a third party (thereby becoming the transferor for purposes of § 2501), § 2513 obviates the need for the intermediate spousal transfer. The statute also eliminates any concern that would exist in its absence regarding the application of the step-transaction doctrine to the integrated transfers.

Both spouses must consent to the application of § 2513(a), generally through a timely filed gift tax return. The election does not operate on a gift-by-gift basis; rather, the election applies to all transfers by either spouse during the calendar year that take place while the spouses are married. *See* Treas. Reg. § 25.2513-1(b). The split-gift election can be made for a calendar year even if the marriage dissolves during that period (whether by reason of death or divorce), but the election extends only to gifts made while the individuals were married.[39] However, if the marriage dissolves and either spouse remarries during the calendar year, the election under § 2513 is unavailable even for transfers made while the first marriage was intact. *See* IRC § 2513(a). To prevent property from escaping the transfer tax base altogether, the split-gift election is further limited to transfers made while both spouses were citizens or residents of the United States. *Id.*

The most common use of the election is to permit one spouse to benefit from both spouse's annual exclusions in determining the amount of the taxable transfer. With respect to larger transfers, the election may also make available each spouse's unified credit against the gift tax under § 2505. The operation of § 2513, however, is limited to the gift tax. For purposes of determining whether the transferred property will be captured in the gross estate of either spouse at death, the donor spouse constitutes the transferor of the entire property interest. Consequently, the consenting spouse is not a transferor of any portion of the property for estate tax purposes.

As an example, assume that *Husband* transferred ownership of a life insurance policy on his life to *Child*. *Husband* and *Wife* made the split-gift election under § 2513(a), resulting in a gift tax liability of $50,000 for *Husband* and $10,000 for *Wife* (due to differences in available unified

---

[39] The split-gift election can be made on behalf of a deceased spouse by the personal representative of the decedent's estate. Treas. Reg. § 25.2513-2(c).

credit). *Husband* died in the year following the transfer, causing the insurance proceeds to be included in his gross estate under § 2035(a). Although *Husband* is treated as having made the entire gift of the policy for estate tax purposes, the value of that gift is excluded from his "adjusted taxable gifts" under § 2001(b)(1)(B) due to the inclusion of the proceeds in his gross estate. Additionally, the reduction from the estate tax liability under § 2001(b)(2) for gift tax payable on the gift made by *Husband* will include not only his $50,000 gift tax payment but also the $10,000 gift tax payment by *Wife*. IRC § 2001(d). Note that the portion of *Wife's* unified credit that was absorbed by treating her as the transferor of one-half of the gift was essentially wasted in hindsight, as the policy proceeds were taxed in *Husband's* estate. Nothing in the statutory structure entitles *Wife* to a restoration of that portion of her unified credit for gift tax purposes in this unfortunate circumstance. *See* Ingalls v. Commissioner, 336 F.2d 874 (4th Cir. 1964) (consenting spouse not entitled to restoration of pre-1977 gift tax exemption due to inclusion of transferred property in donor spouse's gross estate).

As an additional fact, assume that *Wife* died in the year following *Husband's* death. In that case, the $10,000 gift tax liability resulting from the transfer of the life insurance policy paid by *Wife* will be brought back into *Wife's* gross estate under § 2035(b). The estate tax consequences to *Wife's* estate end there.[40] Section 2001(e) provides that no portion of the gift will be included as an adjusted taxable gift in *Wife's* estate, and *Wife* will not be entitled to a reduction under § 2001(b)(2) on account of her $10,000 payment.[41] By excluding the portion of the gift attributable to *Wife* from her tentative estate tax base under § 2001(b)(1)(B), § 2001(e) effectively allows *Wife* to recoup under the estate tax that portion of her unified credit that was applied toward the taxable gift.

§ 19.09   STUDY PROBLEMS

1.   Francine devised 12,000 acres of timberland in trust for the lifetime benefit of her husband, Mitch. While Mitch is alive, the Trustee is authorized to make distributions of trust income and, if necessary, principal to Mitch. In addition, discretionary distributions of income and principal may be made to Francine's then-living issue. Upon Mitch's death, the trust is to be distributed to Francine's then-living issue, *per stirpes*.

     a.   As drafted, the trust does not qualify for the marital deduction. Explain.

     b.   Would it matter if all of Francine's issue executed qualified disclaimers of their interests in the trust within the meaning of § 2518?

     c.   Would it matter if Francine's estate, Mitch, and Francine's issue entered into a settlement agreement by which Mitch received distribution of a 1/3 tenants in common interest in the timberland for his relinquishment of his trust interest? Suppose the family settlement agreement stems from a legal challenge to the validity of Francine's will commenced by Mitch.

---

[40] However, if *Husband* had paid the $10,000 liability on behalf of *Wife*, no amount would be captured in *Wife's* estate under § 2035(b) because *Wife's* estate would not have been depleted by the payment. Furthermore, because liability for payment of the combined gift tax generated by split gifts is joint and several under § 2513(d), *Husband's* payment of *Wife's* gift tax liability would not have given rise to a separate gift. Treas. Reg. § 25.2511-1(d). [And even if it were a gift, the gift would have been offset by the gift tax marital deduction.]

[41] *Wife's* estate would have been entitled to the benefit offered by § 2001(e) even if *Wife* had predeceased *Husband*. *See* Rev. Rul. 81-85, 1981-1 C.B.452 (providing that a predeceasing consenting spouse is entitled to recompute her estate tax liability following the death of the donor spouse).

    d. Would it matter if Mitch received a distribution of 4,000 acres outright as a result of the exercise of his elective share rights under state law?

    e. What if Mitch had the right to elect to receive distribution of 2,000 acres outright in lieu of his interest in the trust and, during the administration of Francine's estate, Mitch elected to receive the outright devise?

2. Malcom's will provides that his estate is to be distributed to his wife, Helen, if she survives to the point of his estate being distributed. Otherwise, the estate is to be distributed to Malcom's children in equal shares. Helen survives Malcom, and the administration of Malcom's probate estate is hastily concluded within five months. Does the devise to Helen qualify for the marital deduction?

3. Bonnie devised the residue of her estate in trust for the benefit of her husband, Otis. The relevant provisions of the trust read as follows:

> *During my husband's lifetime, the Trustee shall distribute the net income of the trust to my husband on an annual or more frequent basis. In addition, the Trustee may distribute to my husband as much of the principal of the trust as the Trustee determines necessary for my husband's health, education, support in his accustomed manner of living, or maintenance. During my husband's lifetime, my husband shall have the power to appoint the trust principal to those of my children, upon such terms and conditions, as my husband shall direct in a signed writing delivered to the Trustee. Upon my husband's death, the trust property shall be distributed to my husband's estate if he so appoints by Will through a provision specifically referring to this power. In default thereof, the property shall be distributed to my then-living issue, per stirpes.*

    a. Does Bonnie's devise of property to the trust qualify for the marital deduction?

    b. Does the result change if, instead of requiring the Trustee to distribute the net income of the trust directly, the trust provided Otis with the annual right to withdraw trust income?

    c. Suppose the residue of Bonnie's estate consists primarily of undeveloped real property held for investment. Does this present an issue concerning qualification of the devise for the marital deduction?

    d. Suppose the trust instrument further provided that the Trustee possessed discretion to allocate receipts and disbursements between income and principal in order to fairly balance the respective interests of the income and remainder beneficiaries. Would this power jeopardize allowance of the marital deduction?

    e. Following Bonnie's death, Otis makes a discretionary distribution to his children. What are the tax consequences of the distribution to Otis?

    f. Suppose the trust instrument did not permit Otis to appoint the trust principal to his probate estate by way of his will. Would the marital deduction still be available?

4. Tina, an estate planning client of yours, would like her husband to benefit from her property for his lifetime if he survives her. However, Tina is adamant that her husband not benefit from her property if he remarries or otherwise cohabitates with another woman following Tina's death. Is there any way to structure a devise for the benefit of

Tina's husband that meets these objectives and qualifies for the marital deduction?

5.   Howard's will devises his entire probate estate in trust for the benefit of his wife, Constance. The trust contains the following provisions:

> During the lifetime of my wife, the Trustee shall distribute the net income to my wife on a regular, but not less frequent than annual, basis. Additionally, the Trustee, in its sole discretion, may distribute as much of the trust principal to my wife as the Trustee determines necessary or appropriate for her health, support in her accustomed manner of living, or maintenance. Upon my wife's death, the trust assets shall be distributed to my issue then living, by representation.

Howard died with a gross estate in the $8 million range, without having used any portion of his unified credit during his lifetime. Constance has approximately $10 million of assets in her individual name.

Does the devise in favor of Constance qualify for the marital deduction? What advice do you have for Howard's executor?

6.   Zach was the beneficiary of a QTIP trust established by his predeceased wife, Rita. Rita had three children from a prior marriage, and they were designated as the remainder beneficiaries of the QTIP trust. As of Zach's death, the QTIP trust held assets valued at $7 million.

Zach's brother (who is designated as personal representative) seeks your assistance in the administration of Zach's estate. Zach's will devises his entire estate to Zach's brother and sister in equal shares. Additionally, Zach's will contains the following provision:

> I direct that all estate, inheritance, or succession taxes, whether resulting from property passing under this Will or by non-probate transfer, be paid from the residue of my estate.

What are the estate tax consequences of the QTIP trust in Zach's estate, if any? Also, explain the potential importance of the tax allocation provision in Zach's will.

7.   Taking the same facts as in problem 6, suppose that Zach decided to sell his income interest in the QTIP trust to Rita's children because he needed current access to cash. Zach received $3 million on the transaction, representing the actuarial value of Zach's income interest. Does the transaction have any transfer tax consequences for Zach?

8.   Donald transferred stock in his closely held corporation to his daughter valued at $3 million. Donald and his wife, Alexis, elected to split the gift pursuant to § 2513. The transfer generated a gift tax liability of $700,000 for Donald and $300,000 for Alexis, but Donald paid the entire $1 million gift tax liability out of his funds. Donald died two years after the gift.

   a.   Are there any gift tax consequences to Donald from paying the portion of the gift tax liability owed by Alexis?

   b.   What are the estate tax consequences of the transaction, if any, to Donald?

Chapter 20

TAX LIABILITY, TAX CREDITS, AND TAX PAYMENTS

§ 20.01 ESTATE TAX LIABILITY AND TAX CREDITS

Internal Revenue Code: §§ 2001(b), 2010 to 2014
Treasury Regulations: §§ 20.2013-1, -2(a) to (c)(1), -3(a)

As discussed in the opening chapter of this text, the estate tax liability of a decedent's estate is determined by calculating a tentative tax on the sum of the decedent's taxable estate plus the amount of the decedent's adjusted taxable gifts (defined as total gifts made by the decedent other than those that are recaptured in the decedent's gross estate) and subtracting from this amount the gift tax that would have been imposed on post-1976 gifts at the current tax rate schedule. *See* IRC § 2001(b). Once this amount has been established, the estate is entitled to subtract a host of tax credits in determining the ultimate tax liability.

[A] The Unified Credit

[1] Base Amount of Credit

The most significant credit against the estate tax is the unified credit provided under § 2010. The credit operates to permit an individual to make a certain amount of gratuitous transfers, whether during life or by reason of death, without incurring federal gift or estate tax. As discussed in Chapter 1,[1] Congress has provided for considerable increases in the amount exempted from taxation by the unified credit. As a result of the Tax Relief, Unemployment Insurance Reauthorization, and Job Creation Act of 2010 (Tax Relief Act of 2010),[2] the basic exclusion amount of the unified credit now stands at $5 million per person, to be adjusted for cost of living starting in 2012. Compared to the $675,000 exclusion amount that prevailed in 2001, the recent increases in the unified credit represent a significant contraction of the scope of the federal transfer tax system.

For historical perspective, the amounts exempted from taxation by way of the unified credit for roughly the past two decades combined with a look into the legislated future are reproduced below:

Year	Applicable Exclusion Amount of the Unified Credit	
	Gift Tax	*Estate Tax*
1987–1997	$600,000	$600,000
1998	625,000	625,000
1999	650,000	650,000

---

[1] *See* § 1.07.

[2] Pub. L. No. 111-312, 124 Stat. 3296 (2010).

Year	Applicable Exclusion Amount of the Unified Credit	
	Gift Tax	*Estate Tax*
2000	675,000	675,000
2001	675,000	675,000
2002 to 2003	1,000,000	1,000,000
2004 to 2005	1,000,000	1,500,000
2006 to 2008	1,000,000	2,000,000
2009	1,000,000	3,500,000
2010	1,000,000	5,000,000*
2011	5,000,000	5,000,000
2012	5,000,000	5,000,000
2103	1,000,000	1,000,000

* This assumes the decedent's executor does not elect to apply the provisions of EGTRRA calling for repeal of the estate tax in 2010 at the expense of a modified carry-over basis regime under § 1022.

[2] Portability of Unused Credit of Predeceased Spouse

In addition to considerably increasing the amount exempted by the unified credit, Congress through the Tax Relief Act of 2010 for the first time rendered the credit portable between spouses. *See* IRC § 2010(c)(2), (4)–(5). While the details of the portability regime are examined in § 19.05 in the context of transfers between spouses, portability generally allows a surviving spouse to the unused portion of her most recent deceased spouse's unified credit. As a result, if a predeceasing spouse died after 2010 having made no taxable gifts and having left his entire estate to his surviving spouse, the applicable exclusion amount of the surviving spouse's unified credit under § 2010(c) and § 2505 will be increased to $10 million (ignoring any inflation adjustments to the basic exclusion amount).

[B] The State Death Tax Credit

Prior to the enactment of the Economic Growth and Tax Relief Reconciliation Act of 2001 (EGTRRA),[3] Congress provided a tax credit against the federal estate tax for estate, inheritance, legacy, or succession taxes imposed at the state level on property included in the decedent's gross estate under § 2011(a) subject to limits provided in § 2011(b). Allowance of the credit led many states to enact their own estate or inheritance taxes equal to the credit limitation (so-called sponge or pick-up taxes) as a means of accepting the federal government's effective offer to share a portion of its estate tax revenue.

The state death tax credit under § 2011 survived the enactment of EGTRRA for a limited time, albeit in reduced form. The legislation phased out the credit through annual 25 percent reductions commencing in 2002, so that the credit was eliminated entirely by 2005. In place of the credit, Congress supplied a deduction for state death taxes under § 2058. EGTRRA thereby effectively eliminated the estate tax revenue sharing arrangement between the federal and state governments. Due to the sunset provision contained in EGTRRA legislation (which Congress deferred through the Tax Relief Act of 2010), the state death tax credit is scheduled to be reinstated at pre-2002 levels on January 1, 2013.

---

[3] *See* Pub. L. No. 107-16, 115 Stat. 38 (2001).

[C]　Credit for Gift Taxes Paid

Section 2012 provides a credit for gift taxes paid on prior transfers in fairly narrow circumstances. First, the value of the decedent's prior gift must be included in the decedent's gross estate. Hence, one of the estate tax recapture provisions must apply to the lifetime gift. IRC § 2012(a). Additionally, the prior gift must have been made before 1977. IRC § 2012(e). Because gift taxes attributable to post-1976 gifts are addressed under § 2001(b)(2) in the computation of the tentative estate,[4] the purpose of the § 2012 credit is to prevent pre-1977 gifts from being subject to two separate transfer taxes. Consistent with this purpose, the credit is equal to the lesser of the gift tax paid with respect to the prior gift or the estate tax attributable to inclusion of the gift in the decedent's gross estate (reduced by allowable marital and charitable deductions). *See* IRC § 2012(a).

[D]　Credit for Estate Tax on Prior Transfers

Section 2013 seeks to mitigate the rapid depletion of wealth that otherwise would occur if the same property were subject to estate tax in multiple decedents' estates within a relatively short time frame. The statute does so by providing an estate tax credit to a decedent's estate determined with reference to the estate tax paid by another decedent (who the statute designates as the "transferor") with respect to property the transferor transferred to the decedent, provided the transferor died within the period 10 years before or 2 years after the decedent's death. IRC § 2013(a).

[1]　First Limitation

The base amount of the § 2013 credit is subject to two independent limitations. First, the credit may not exceed that portion of the estate tax paid in the transferor's estate (as adjusted) as the value of the property transferred to the decedent bears to the taxable estate of the transferor (as adjusted). IRC § 2013(b). Employing the terminology of the regulations, the first limitation on the amount of the § 2013 credit can be expressed as follows:

$$\text{First Limitation} = \frac{\text{Value of Transferred Property}}{\text{``Transferor's Adjusted Taxable Estate''}} \times \text{``Transferor's Adjusted Federal Estate Tax''}$$

Treas. Reg. § 20.2013-2(a). The "transferor's adjusted Federal estate tax" is determined by adding to the transferor's ultimate estate tax liability any credit allowed under § 2012 and any credit allowed under § 2013, provided the transferor acquired property from a prior transferor who died within 10 years before the decedent's death. Treas. Reg. § 20.2013-2(b). The "transferor's adjusted taxable estate" is determined by reducing the transferor's taxable estate by the amount of any federal, state, or local estate, inheritance, or similar taxes. Treas. Reg. § 20.2013-2(c)(1).

---

[4] Section 2001(b)(2) reduces the tentative estate tax by the gift tax that would be imposed on post-1976 gifts at the current tax rates under § 2001(c). In this manner, § 2001(b) ensures that the decedent's post-1976 gifts are used to subject the decedent's taxable estate to higher marginal estate tax brackets while eliminating any estate tax resulting from inclusion of post-1976 gifts in the tentative tax base.

[2] Second Limitation

The second limitation on the § 2013 credit is imposed by § 2013(c) and is designed to limit the credit to the amount of federal estate tax attributable to the transferred property in the decedent's estate.[5] *See* Treas. Reg. § 20.2013-3(a). To determine the marginal estate tax attributable to the previously transferred property, the federal estate tax that would result if the decedent's gross estate were reduced by the value of the transferred property is subtracted from the amount of the decedent's total estate tax liability. IRC § 2013(c)(1). The value of the transferred assets to be subtracted from the decedent's gross estate in computing the § 2013(c) limitation is the value at which the property was included in the gross estate of the transferor, reduced by any encumbrances on the property. IRC § 2013(d).

Somewhat surprisingly, § 2013 does not require that the property transferred to the decedent be included in the decedent's gross estate. As explained in the regulations,

> There is no requirement that the transferred property be identified in the estate of the present decedent or that the property be in existence at the time of the decedent's death. It is sufficient that the transfer of the property was subjected to Federal estate tax in the estate of the transferor and that the transferor died within the prescribed period of time.

Treas. Reg. § 20.2013-1(a). Accordingly, if the transferor established a trust providing the decedent with a mandatory income interest in property for life, the § 2013 credit will be computed based on the value of the life estate (determined based on the actuarial value of the life estate at the transferor's death) even though no portion of the remaining trust assets is included in the decedent's gross estate. *See* Treas. Reg. § 20.2013-4(a), Ex. 2; *see also* Rev. Rul. 59-9, 1959-1 C.B. 232 (holding that the value of a life estate transferred to the decedent qualifies for the § 2013 credit).

[3] Percentage Reduction

The base amount of the § 2013 credit is determined by the lower of the limitations imposed by § 2013(b) and (c). Once this base amount is determined, it is subject to further reduction by § 2013(a). Signaling the importance of the proximity of the imposition of two separate estate taxes with respect to one item of property, the base amount of the credit is available only if the transferor dies within two years before or after the decedent. Where the transferor dies more than two years before the decedent, the amount of the § 2013 credit is reduced by 20 percent for every prior 2-year period. IRC § 2013(a). Hence, if the transferor died 9 or 10 years prior to the decedent, the § 2013 credit in the decedent's estate equals only 20 percent of the base amount.

[4] Illustration

The application of § 2013 is potentially complex. The following example illustrates a straightforward application of the statute.

Assume that *Transferor*, who died on June 1, 2005, specifically devised stock in X Corp. to his brother, *Decedent*. *Transferor's* taxable estate totaled $3 million, of which $1 million was attributable to the X Corp. stock. The estate tax attributable to the specifically devised X Corp.

---

[5] The § 2013 credit does not extend to gift tax or GST tax paid with respect to prior transfers to the decedent.

stock was paid from the residue of *Transferor's* probate estate. *Decedent* died on May 1, 2011, leaving the X Corp. stock he received from *Transferor's* estate to *Decedent's* son. *Decedent's* taxable estate totaled $9 million, of which $2 million was attributable to the value of the X Corp. stock he received from *Transferor*.

In determining the amount of the § 2013 credit to which *Decedent's* estate is entitled, the first step is to determine the total estate tax paid in *Transferor's* estate. Assuming a taxable estate of $3 million, a unified credit in 2005 that shielded $1.5 million from estate taxation, and a maximum marginal estate tax rate of 47 percent, *Transferor's* estate tax liability would have totaled $695,000. With this amount in hand, the first limitation on the § 2013 credit imposed by § 2013(b) can be determined. The base amount of the credit equals the portion of *Transferor's* $695,000 estate tax liability that the property transferred to *Decedent* ($1 million of X Corp. stock) bears to the value of *Transferor's* $3 million taxable estate reduced by the estate's $695,000 estate tax liability. In this manner, the amount of the credit determined under § 2013(b) is $301,518.

The limitation on the base amount of the § 2013 credit imposed by § 2013(c) equals the difference between the amount of *Decedent's* estate tax liability and *Decedent's* estate tax liability calculated by subtracting the value at which the X Corp. stock was included in *Transferor's* estate (that is, $1 million instead of $2 million). Because *Decedent* died in 2011, the unified credit shielded tax on an applicable exclusion amount of $5 million. Additionally, the maximum marginal rate was 35 percent. Accordingly, *Decedent's* normal estate tax liability was $1.4 million, and *Decedent's* estate tax liability computed by subtracting the $1 million value of the X Corp. stock from his gross estate would have been $1.05 million. The $350,000 difference between these figures serves as the second limitation on the § 2013 credit.

The lower of the two limitations, $301,518, serves as the base amount of the § 2013 credit available to *Decedent's* estate. Yet because *Transferor* died within six years of *Decedent*, § 2013(a) reduces the amount of the base credit by 40 percent. Hence, *Decedent's* estate is entitled to a § 2013 credit of $180,911.

[E] The Foreign Death Tax Credit

For a decedent who was a U.S. citizen or resident at the time of death, the estate tax applies on a worldwide basis. That is, property is included in the decedent's gross estate regardless of where the property is situated. Recognizing that the jurisdiction in which the decedent's property is situated possesses a priority claim to subject the property to estate or inheritance taxation, Congress provides an estate tax credit under § 2014 for death taxes that are paid to a foreign country with respect to property situated in such country and included in the decedent's U.S. gross estate. The specifics of the foreign death tax credit are addressed in Chapter 26, which examines international aspects of the U.S. transfer tax system.

§ 20.02 PAYMENT OF ESTATE TAX

Internal Revenue Code: §§ 2002, 6075(a), 6161(a), 6163(a)–(b), 6166(a), (b)(1), (b)(4), (b)(9), 6601(a), (b)(1), (j)

Treasury Regulations: §§ 20.6161-1(a)(1), (2), 20.6163-1(a)(2)

[A] Responsible Party

Liability for payment of the estate tax rests on the executor of the decedent's estate.[6] IRC § 2002. As the executor may not have control over nonprobate assets that are included in the decedent's gross estate, Congress has provided the executor with the following rights of recovery: (1) against beneficiaries of life insurance policies whose proceeds are included in the decedent's estate, see IRC § 2206; (2) against recipients of property included in the decedent's gross estate based on the decedent's general power of appointment, see IRC § 2207; (3) against persons receiving QTIP property included in the decedent's gross estate under § 2044, see IRC § 2207A; and (4) against the persons receiving property that was included in the decedent's gross estate under § 2036 based on the decedent's retention of lifetime beneficial ownership of or control over property, see IRC § 2207B.

[B] Due Date for Payment

Payment of the decedent's estate tax liability is due nine months following the date of the decedent's death. See IRC §§ 6151(a), 6075(a). However, a number of remedial provisions exist to defer payment of the estate tax liability.

[1] Section 6161

Pursuant to § 6161(a), the Service is authorized to extend the time period for paying the estate tax for reasonable cause, provided the extension is for a reasonable period not in excess of 10 years. Regulatory guidance establishes two grounds for the § 6161(a) extension. An extension for payment of up to 12 months may be granted by the Service if the request by the decedent's executor is supported by "reasonable cause." Treas. Reg. § 20.6161-1(a)(1). As indicated in the regulatory examples, reasonable cause for an extension generally exists if the estate faces liquidity burdens in making a timely payment of the tax. Treas. Reg. § 20.6161-1(a)(1), Exs. 1–4.

The permissible length of the extension increases significantly if the executor can establish that timely payment of the estate tax would impose an "undue hardship." Treas. Reg. § 20.6161-1(a)(2)(i). In that case, the Service may extend the due date of any payment of estate tax for one year, with the total extension not exceeding 10 years. An undue hardship for this purpose requires more than a mere inconvenience to the estate. Rather, the concept includes the necessity of selling a farm or family-owned business that the estate wishes to retain and the necessity of selling estate assets at below market, fire sale prices to generate the requisite liquidity to pay the tax. See Treas. Reg. § 20.6161-1(a)(2)(ii), Exs. 1 & 2.

Even if the date for paying the tax liability is extended under § 6161(a), interest on the tax liability accrues from the date payment of the tax liability was originally due. Section 6601 imposes interest at statutory rates from the last date prescribed for payment, and for this purpose the last date prescribed for payment of the tax liability is determined without regard to any granted extensions. IRC § 6601(b)(1).

---

[6] If no executor or administrator is appointed to administer the decedent's probate estate, then the "executor" for purposes of the estate tax includes any person in actual or constructive possession of any of the decedent's property. See IRC § 2203.

[2]   Section 6163

The inclusion of a reversionary or remainder interest in property in the decedent's gross estate under § 2033 presents a particular liquidity concern. The value of the future interest increases the decedent's estate tax liability, but no additional funds exist from which to satisfy the resulting increase. For this reason, a decedent's executor may elect under § 6163(a) to defer payment of the estate tax attributable to a reversionary or remainder interest in property until six months following termination of the prior possessory interest in the property. The Service is permitted to extend this deferral period for an additional three years for reasonable cause. IRC § 6163(b). As indicated in the regulations, this additional extension requires the executor to establish that payment of the tax attributable to the future interest would result in "undue hardship," which generally entails the inability of the decedent's heirs or beneficiaries to convert the decedent's future interest in the property to possession. *See* Treas. Reg. § 20.6163-1(a)(2). Interest on the estate tax liability accrues during the § 6163 extension period pursuant to § 6601.

[3]   Section 6166

Section 6166(a) provides a decedent's estate with the opportunity to elect to pay the estate tax attributable to the inclusion of an "interest in a closely held business" in 10 annual installments, with the executor having the option of deferring the first installment payment until five years after the estate tax is regularly due. IRC § 6166(a). To qualify for this preferential payment plan, the value of the closely held business interest must exceed 35 percent of the value of the decedent's "adjusted gross estate," defined as the decedent's gross estate reduced by the deductions under §§ 2053 and 2054. An interest in a closely held business encompasses ownership of an entity through which a trade or business is carried on, but the value of the interest must be reduced by the value of the interest that is attributable to passive assets owned by the entity. IRC § 6166(b)(1), (9). If the estate is entitled to defer payment of a portion of the estate tax liability pursuant to § 6166, the interest rate on the deferred liability can run as low as two percent. IRC §§ 6166(k)(4), 6601(j).

§ 20.03   GIFT TAX LIABILITY AND TAX CREDITS

Internal Revenue Code: §§ 2501(a), 2502(a), 2505

A donor's gift tax liability is determined and imposed on an annual basis. IRC § 2501(a). To ensure that a donor enjoys only one progression through the progressive marginal rate schedule for gifts made over the donor's lifetime, a donor's gift tax liability for a given year is calculated by first determining the gift tax resulting from the donor's current year gifts *plus* gifts made by the donor in prior calendar years and then subtracting from this amount the gift tax attributable to gifts made in prior years. IRC § 2502(a).

While numerous credits are available to reduce a decedent's estate tax liability, only one credit is available to offset a donor's gift tax—the unified credit under § 2505. As discussed in § 20.01 above, the amount excluded by the unified credit currently stands at $5 million (to be adjusted for cost of living from 2010 commencing in 2012) plus "the deceased spousal unused exclusion amount." *See* IRC § 2505(a) (providing for the applicable exclusion amount to be determined by reference to the amount that would be excluded under § 2010 "if the donor died as of the end of the calendar year"). Thus, if an individual is a surviving spouse, the amount of lifetime transfers shielded from gift taxation is increased by the unused portion of the predeceasing spouse's unified credit. To the extent it appears that portability of the unified credit will expire at the end of 2012 in accord with the temporary legislation currently in effect,[7] surviving spouses whose applicable exclusion amounts have been increased by portability could capture its benefits by making taxable gifts before the end of 2012.

§ 20.04   PAYMENT OF THE GIFT TAX

Internal Revenue Code: §§ 2502(c), 6075(b)(1), 6151(a), 6161(a)

Gift tax attributable for gifts made within a given calendar year must be paid by April 15 of the following year. IRC §§ 6151(a), 6075(b)(1). Liability for payment of the gift tax rests with the donor, see IRC § 2502(c), although assignments of that obligation to the donee can be used to reduce the value of the taxable transfer.[8]

An extension for payment of the tax may be granted by the Service pursuant to § 6161, although the grounds for obtaining the extension in this context are more restrictive than in the estate tax setting. This stands to reason, as a taxable gift presumably has a voluntary origin. As explained in the regulations, an extension for payment of up to six months may be granted if payment of the tax in a timely manner would effect an undue hardship on the donor, such as substantial financial loss resulting from the sale of property at a sacrifice price. *See* Treas. Reg. § 25.6161-1(a)(1), (b).

§ 20.05   STUDY PROBLEMS

1.   *Husband* died survived by *Wife*, and *Husband's* will divides his residuary estate into the following two shares: One share equal to the amount that can pass free of estate tax taking into account Husband's unified credit under § 2010 passes to a credit shelter trust (of which the spouse is a discretionary beneficiary of income and principal); the remaining share passes to a QTIP trust. Four months following *Husband's* death, *Wife* died unexpectedly as a result of a heart attack. Assume that *Wife's* life expectancy under the relevant actuarial tables was approximately 20 years at the time of *Husband's* death.

      What steps should the executor of *Husband's* estate consider with respect to the QTIP trust to save total estate taxes?

2.   What difference could it make if the credit shelter trust established under *Husband's* will designated *Wife* as the sole mandatory recipient of income distributions for her life? *Compare* Tech. Adv. Mem. 8512004, *with* Tech. Adv. Mem. 8944005.

---

[7] Portability of the unified credit was introduced as part of the Tax Relief, Unemployment Insurance Reauthorization, and Job Creation Act of 2010, Pub. L. No. 111-312, 124 Stat. 3296. This legislation currently is scheduled to expire on December 31, 2012.

[8] The "net gift" technique, in which the donee assumes responsibility for payment of the gift tax, is discussed in § 3.06.

Chapter 21

THE GENERATION SKIPPING TRANSFER TAX BASE

Internal Revenue Code:	§§ 2601–2603, 2611–2613, 2621–2623, 2651–2653
Treasury Regulations:	§§ 26.2612-1(d)(2)(ii), (e)(2)(i), 26.2652-1(a)(1)–(2)

Because the federal estate and gift taxes are predicated on the transfer of property owned by the transferor (whether actually or constructively through the possession of a general power of appointment), the two-tax regime, standing alone, would provide transferors the opportunity to insulate property from future transfer taxation at lower generation levels. The key to doing so rests in the creation of beneficial interests in property that do not rise to the level of ownership for estate and gift tax purposes.

As an example, assume that a testator (*T*) devises property in trust for the lifetime benefit of her child (*C*). The trust, of which *C* is designated to serve as trustee, provides that the net income of the trust is to be distributed to *C* on an annual basis. Additionally, the trustee is authorized to make discretionary distributions of trust principal to *C* for her health, education, support in her accustomed manner of living, or maintenance. Upon *C's* death, the trust property will distribute in favor of *C's* then-living issue.

While the funding of the trust will be subject to estate tax at *T's* death, any property remaining in the trust at *C's* death will not be included in *C's* estate tax base. Section 2033 does not operate to include the trust property in *C's* gross estate because *C's* interest in the property is extinguished by reason of her death. While *C* possesses a right to the income from the trust property, § 2036(a)(1) has no application because *C* was not the transferor to the trust. Finally, although *C* possesses the ability to access the trust principal, *C's* access is limited by an ascertainable standard. Hence, *C's* power of appointment over the property does not rise to the level of a general power of appointment, and *C's* possession of the power at death therefore does not trigger inclusion under § 2041(a)(2).[1] The trust property will be distributed to *C's* issue undiminished by an intermediate estate tax levy, which would have been imposed had *T* devised the property to *C* outright. While the property thereafter will be subject to gift or estate taxation in the hands of *C's* issue, this levy also could have been avoided had the property simply remained in trust along similar terms. Accordingly, only perpetuities restrictions under state law prevent the estate and gift tax regime from amounting to a one-time transfer tax levy.

Congress first responded to the use of multi-generational transfers in trust to undermine the estate and gift tax regime through the enactment of the generation-skipping transfer tax

---

[1] Similarly, any exercise of the power of appointment by *C* during her lifetime would not trigger gift tax consequences under § 2514(b).

("GST tax") in 1976.[2] The purpose of this supplementary tax was to ensure that wealth transfer taxes were imposed at "reasonably uniform intervals." H.R. Rep. No. 94-1380, at 46 (1976). The tax focused on shifts in beneficial ownership in property, subjecting them to a separate tax that was intended to achieve parity with the estate and gift tax consequences that would have resulted had the property been transferred outright rather than in trust. However, the tax proved overly cumbersome in application. The tax also was underinclusive, because it failed to address outright transfers that simply bypassed generations entirely (such as a devise to a grandchild).

As part of the Tax Reform Act of 1986, Congress repealed its first attempt at the GST tax and enacted a wholesale revision now contained in chapter 13 of the Code (§§ 2601–2664). See Pub. L. No. 99-514, § 1431, 100 Stat. 2085, 2717–29 (1986). In addition to shifts of beneficial interests in property occurring from one generation to the next, the current GST tax addresses direct transfers of property that skip intervening generations altogether. Hence, a devise from a testator to her grandchild now is captured in the GST tax base. Each transferor is afforded a GST tax exemption equal to the prevailing basic exclusion amount of the estate tax unified credit under § 2010(c), and any non-exempt transfers are subject to tax at the highest marginal estate tax rate.[3] See IRC §§ 2631, 2641. This chapter focuses on the composition of the GST tax base; issues relating to the GST tax exemption and the determination of GST tax liability are addressed in Chapter 22.

§ 21.01 FOUNDATIONAL CONCEPTS

The GST tax base consists of three types of transfers, all of which depend in some manner on the definition of a "skip person." The most straightforward type of generation-skipping transfer, a direct skip, is a transfer to a skip person that is subject to estate or gift tax. IRC § 2612(c). The other two generation-skipping transfers—a taxable distribution and a taxable termination—arise in the trust context. A taxable distribution is a transfer from a trust to a skip person. IRC § 2612(b). A taxable termination occurs when an individual's interest in a trust terminates unless a non-skip person continues to possess an interest in the trust.[4] IRC § 2612(a). The definition of a skip person therefore serves as a prerequisite to examination of the GST tax base.

---

[2] See Tax Reform Act of 1976, Pub. L. No. 94-455, § 2006, 90 Stat. 1520, 1879–90.

[3] As part of the Economic Growth and Tax Relief Reconciliation Act of 2001 (EGTRRA), Congress enacted § 2664 repealing the GST tax for transfers occurring after December 31, 2009. See Pub. L. No. 107-16, § 501(b), 115 Stat. 38, 69 (2001). However, repeal of the GST tax was effective for one year only, as EGTRRA contains a sunset provision providing that the legislation shall not apply to generation-skipping transfers made after December 31, 2010. Id. § 901(a), 115 Stat. at 150. As part of the Tax Relief, Unemployment Insurance Reauthorization, and Job Creation Act of 2010, Congress extended the term of EGTRRA for an additional two years. See Pub. L. No. 111-312, § 101(a), 124 Stat. 3296, 3298 (2010). However, Congress also retroactively repealed § 2664 (which itself would have repealed the GST tax for years after 2009). In its place, Congress assigned an applicable rate of zero to all generation skipping transfers that occurred in 2010. See id. § 302(c), 124 Stat. at 3302. As a result, 2010 offered a one-year opportunity for individuals to make direct skip transfers to grandchildren or to cause taxable terminations or taxable distributions from non-GST exempt trusts without incurring this additional level of federal transfer tax.

[4] As discussed in § 21.02[B], a taxable termination also occurs in limited situations where no person possesses an interest in the trust (meaning that no party may receive a current distribution of income or principal) following the termination of an individual's interest. See IRC § 2612(a)(1)(B).

[A] The Skip Person

[1] Individuals

An individual's status as a skip person depends on her generational relationship to the transferor. Specifically, an individual constitutes a skip person if she is assigned to a generation that is two or more generations below the generation assigned to the transferor. IRC § 2613(a)(1).

[a] Relatives

For individuals who are descendants of (a) a grandparent of the transferor or (b) a grandparent of the transferor's current or former spouse,[5] generation assignments are determined by relative positions on the family tree. With the relevant grandparent serving as the reference point, the individual is assigned to the generation that results from comparing the number of generations between the grandparent and the individual to the number of generations between the grandparent and the transferor. IRC § 2651(b)(1), (2). As an illustration, consider the relationship between the transferor, T, and the grandchild of the transferor's brother, GN, in the family represented below:

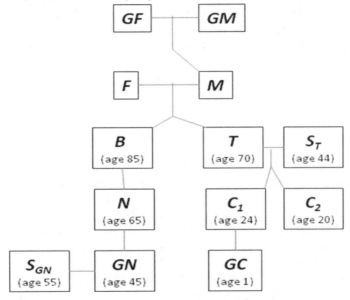

Because T is two generations below his grandparent and GN is four generations below the transferor's grandparent, GN is two generations below T. Hence, GN is a skip person in reference to T, even though T has a child who is much younger than GN. See IRC § 2651(b)(1). Similarly, GN constitutes a skip person with respect to T's spouse, S_t, even though S_t is younger than GN. See IRC § 2651(b)(2). Although the age discrepancies among the parties in

---

[5] In determining whether an individual is related to the transferor or the transferor's current or former spouse in this manner, adopted individuals are treated as blood relatives, and a relationship by half-blood is treated as a relationship by whole blood. IRC § 2651(b)(3).

this hypothetical may be atypical, the hypothetical illustrates that the ages of the individuals are not relevant in this context.

[b]   Spouses

A current or former spouse of a transferor is assigned to the same generation as the transferor. IRC § 2651(c)(1). Similarly, if an individual is related to the transferor or the transferor's spouse within the meaning of § 2651(b), then the spouse of any such individual is assigned to that individual's generation. Accordingly, S_{GN} is a skip person with respect to S_T, even though S_{GN} is the older of the two.

[c]   Predeceased-Parent Rule

Section 2651(e) addresses generation assignments when the parent of the transferee has predeceased the transfer. To illustrate the application of the "predeceased-parent rule," assume T transfers $100,000 to GC following the death of C_1. Because both C_1 and GC are lineal descendants of T's parent and C_1 predeceased the transfer that gave rise to GC's interest (in this case, the outright gift), GC is assigned to one generation below that of T. IRC § 2651(e)(1). Accordingly, the gift from T to GC does not constitute a direct skip.

For the most part, the predeceased-parent rule is limited to lineal descendants of the transferor. For example, suppose T made a similar $100,000 transfer to GN following the death of B. Even though all of the conditions to the reassignment of GN's generation level under § 2651(e)(1) are satisfied, that provision applies to collateral relatives only in the event the transferor has no living descendants at the time of the transfer. IRC § 2651(e)(2). Accordingly, the predeceased-parent rule would not apply to GN unless C_1, C_2, and GC all had predeceased the date of the gift.

[d]   Other Individuals

If the transferee is not (a) a lineal descendant of a grandparent of the transferor, (b) a lineal descendant of a grandparent of the transferor's spouse (current or former), or (c) a spouse of any individual in groups (a) and (b), the transferee's generation assignment is determined based on the age discrepancy between the transferee and the transferor. An individual born not more than 12½ years after the birth of the transferor is assigned to the transferor's generation, while an individual born more than 12½ years but not more than 37½ years after the transferor is assigned to the first generation below the transferor. IRC § 2651(d). Subsequent generation assignments are made based on the same 25-year interval. Thus, if B and T were friends rather than brothers, then a transfer from B to C_1 would constitute a direct skip. A transfer from T to GN would not.

[e]   Entities

For the most part, the GST tax does not respect legal entities as separate transferees of property. Instead, the GST tax adopts a look-through rule: If an estate, trust, partnership, corporation, or other entity possesses an interest in property, each individual possessing a beneficial interest in the entity is treated as holding an interest in the property itself. IRC § 2651(f). A gratuitous transfer from an individual to a corporation therefore will be treated as a transfer to the corporation's shareholders, and the generation assignment of the shareholders will determine whether the gift carries GST tax consequences. Similarly, a distribution from one trust to another is treated as a distribution to those holding beneficial interests in the transferee trust.

There exists one significant exception to the look-through rule that generally applies to entities under the GST tax. As discussed below, a trust, as a separate entity, may constitute a skip person under the GST tax. IRC § 2612(c)(1). Consequently, solely for purposes of determining whether a transfer to a trust constitutes a direct skip, the look-through rule of § 2651(f)(2) does not apply. IRC § 2612(c)(2).

[2] Trusts

Whether a trust constitutes a skip person initially turns on whether a person holds an interest in the trust. An "interest" in a trust for this purpose exists (1) if a person possesses a present right to receive a distribution of income or principal, or (2) if a person is a permissible current recipient of trust income or principal.[6] IRC § 2652(c)(1)(A), (B). To the extent a person makes a qualified disclaimer of an interest in a trust pursuant to § 2518, the person at no point possesses an interest in the trust. Treas. Reg. § 26.2612-1(e)(3).

Instances in which a person possesses a present "right to receive" trust income or principal for GST tax purposes requires some elaboration. In addition to being the recipient of distributions of trust income or principal that are required by the terms of the trust instrument, a person possesses a right to receive trust income and principal through the possession of a general power of appointment over those portions of the trust. Furthermore, an individual may possess a right to receive trust income or principal constructively through the potential use of such amounts to satisfy the individual's support obligations. *See* Treas. Reg. § 26.2612-1(e)(2)(i). However, this attribution rule does not apply to the extent distributions that satisfy an individual's support obligations are made either at the discretion of the trustee or pursuant to state law modeled on the Uniform Gifts (Transfers) to Minors Act. *See* IRC § 2652(c)(3).

To illustrate these rules, assume that *Decedent*, who dies survived by *Spouse*, *Child*, and *Grandchild*, devises the residue of his estate to a QTIP trust. Upon *Spouse's* death, the property is to remain in trust, with the trustee having discretion to distribute trust income or principal to *Child* or *Grandchild* for the recipient's health, education, support, or maintenance. Upon *Child's* death, all trust income is accumulated (with no distributions of principal permitted) until *Grandchild* attains age 40, at which point *Grandchild* will receive the trust property outright. If *Grandchild* dies before attaining age 40, the trust assets will be distributed to his probate estate.

When the trust is funded at *Decedent's* death, only *Spouse* possesses an interest in the trust through her right to receive annual distributions of income. Neither *Child* nor *Grandchild* is a permissible recipient of trust income or principal during *Spouse's* lifetime. Because *Spouse* is a "non-skip person" in reference to *Decedent*, the QTIP trust does not constitute a skip person. Upon *Spouse's* death, both *Child* and *Grandchild* possess an interest in the trust because they are permissible recipients of income or principal.[7] Following *Child's* death, no

---

[6] Special rules apply to charitable organizations. The possession of an interest in a trust by reason of being a permissible distributee of trust income or principal does not extend to charitable organizations. However, a charitable organization possesses an interest in a trust if the trust is a charitable remainder annuity trust, charitable remainder unitrust, or a pooled income fund. Treas. Reg. § 26.2612-1(e)(1)(iii).

[7] Even if *Child* were not a permissible distributee of trust income or principal, *Child* would not be treated as

person possesses an interest in the trust until *Grandchild* attains age 40. At that point, *Grandchild* will possess an interest in the trust due to his entitlement to receive a distribution of the trust property.

If any person possesses an interest in a trust, then all persons holding an interest must be skip persons in order for the trust, as a separate entity, to constitute a skip person.[8] A trust in which no person holds a chapter 13 interest also may constitute a skip person. For the trust to constitute a skip person in this setting, there must exist no possibility for a distribution to be made to a non-skip person. IRC § 2613(a)(2). In making this factual determination, a potential distribution is to be disregarded if the probability of its occurring is so remote as to be negligible. *See* Treas. Reg. § 26.2612-1(d)(2)(ii). Returning to the example above, if *Decedent* had devised amounts directly to the accumulation trust that would distribute to *Grandchild* upon his attaining age 40 or to *Grandchild's* estate upon his earlier death, the trust would constitute a skip person. Consequently, the devise would constitute a direct skip.

[B] The Transferor

Although the concept of a skip person serves as the foundation for the GST tax regime, the concept itself is relational. That is, an individual's status as a skip person turns on her relationship to the transferor. Any GST tax inquiry therefore starts with the identification of the relevant transferor.

[1] Necessity of Inclusion in Estate or Gift Tax Base

Section 2652 defines the transferor for GST tax purposes in a roundabout manner by focusing on the potential inclusion of property in the tax base of the estate tax or gift tax. Specifically, the decedent constitutes the transferor for any property that is subject to the estate tax, and the donor constitutes the transferor for any property that is subject to the gift tax. IRC § 2652(a)(1). Property is "subject to" the estate tax if it is included in the decedent's gross estate; similarly, property is "subject to" the gift tax if the property was transferred by gift under § 2501(a). Treas. Reg. § 26.2652-1(a)(2). In determining whether a transfer is subject to the gift tax for this purpose, any exemption, exclusion, deduction, or credit is to be disregarded. *Id.* Hence, a transfer shielded from the gift tax by operation of the annual exclusion under § 2503(b) nonetheless can render the donor a transferor for GST tax purposes.

If property is subject to either the estate tax or gift tax, the person designated as the transferor will be treated as having transferred the subject property at the time of inclusion—even if the person was not the literal transferor of the property at that point. *See* IRC § 2652(a)(1) (flush language). An individual retains his status as the transferor of property under § 2652(a) until there is an intervening party for whom the property is subject to gift or estate taxation. *See* Treas. Reg. § 26.2652-1(a)(1) (identifying the transferor as the party "with respect to whom property was most recently subject to Federal estate or gift tax").

---

possessing an interest in the trust due to the trustee's ability to make distributions in support of *Grandchild* (to whom *Child* may owe an obligation of support) because those distributions rest in the discretion of the trustee. *See* IRC § 2652(c)(3).

  8 Because all interests in a trust must be held by skip persons in order for the trust to constitute a skip person, it is not difficult to envision the creation of a nominal interest in a trust in favor of a non-skip person in order to defer imposition of the GST tax. Yet any interest created primarily to postpone or delay imposition of the GST tax is to be disregarded. IRC § 2652(c)(2).

As an example, take a testamentary trust created under *Decedent's* will for the benefit of *Child*. During his lifetime, *Child* possesses a non-cumulative annual right to withdraw the greater of $5,000 or five percent of the value of the trust property. Upon *Child's* death, the trust shall be distributed to those of *Child's* issue as *Child* shall appoint by will, otherwise to *Child's* then-living issue.

Decedent serves as the initial transferor of the trust property for GST tax purposes, as the property used to fund the trust was included in his gross estate under § 2033. In fact, *Decedent's* status as transferor does not change until the trust is completely distributed. The annual lapse of *Child's* withdrawal right does not render *Child* the transferor, as the lapse does not constitute the release of a general power of appointment under § 2514(b). *See* Treas. Reg. § 26.2652-1(a)(5), Ex. 5. Similarly, because *Child* holds only a limited testamentary power of appointment over the trust principal, the trust assets are not captured in his gross estate under § 2041.

Changing the facts somewhat, had *Child* possessed a testamentary power to appoint the trust assets to his estate, the power would have triggered inclusion of the trust property in *Child's* gross estate under § 2041(a)(2). Consequently, *Child* would have become the transferor of the trust property for GST tax purposes at his death.

[2] Effect of Estate and Gift Tax Elections

Elections made with respect to transfers of property under the estate and gift taxes are binding for GST tax purposes as well. For instance, if spouses make a split-gift election under § 2513, each spouse is treated as a transferor of one-half of the gift for GST tax purposes. Similarly, if a decedent's executor makes a QTIP election in order to qualify a devise for the marital deduction under § 2056(b)(7), that election creates a qualified income interest for life in the surviving spouse. This interest will trigger inclusion of the trust property in the spouse's gross estate at her death under § 2044, which, in turn, causes the surviving spouse to become the transferor of property to the trust for GST tax purposes at her death. Hence, under these general principles, a deceased spouse seeking a marital deduction under § 2056(b)(7) cannot constitute the final transferor to the QTIP trust for GST tax purposes.

Section 2652(a)(3) provides a special rule with respect to QTIP transfers. If property is transferred to a QTIP trust so the transfer qualifies for the estate tax marital deduction under § 2056(b)(7) or for the gift tax marital deduction under § 2523(f), the executor or the donor spouse may additionally elect to treat the trust, for GST tax purposes, as if the underlying QTIP election had not been made. This additional election, commonly referred to as a "reverse QTIP election," would prevent the surviving spouse from assuming chapter 13 transferor status with respect to the trust. Accordingly, the reverse QTIP election offers the predeceasing spouse the potential to be the last transferor to the trust for purposes of determining the GST tax consequences of future distributions of the trust property. Unlike the QTIP election for marital deduction purposes, the reverse QTIP election cannot be made on a fractional basis; rather, the reverse QTIP election applies on an all-or-nothing basis.[9]

Reverse QTIP elections were most prevalent when the GST exemption exceeded the available unified credit. To the extent the predeceasing spouse allocated all of his GST

---

[9] However, as a practical matter, a partial reverse QTIP election can be obtained through the creation of two separate QTIP trusts under the decedent's will (or through a subsequent severance of a single QTIP trust), with the shares of the QTIP trusts being determined on a formulaic basis.

exemption to the credit-shelter devise, the predeceasing spouse would want to create a separate QTIP trust to which he could allocate the remaining exemption. [Otherwise, allocating the predeceasing spouse's remaining GST exemption to a single QTIP devise would effectively waste that portion of the exemption because the surviving spouse would later become the transferor by operation of § 2044.] Now that the GST exemption is set at an amount equal to the basic exclusion amount of the § 2010 unified credit,[10] reverse QTIP elections presumably are less prevalent.[11]

§ 21.02   GENERATION-SKIPPING TRANSFERS

The rules governing the identification of skip persons and non-skip persons in relation to the transferor for GST purposes set the stage for an examination of the GST tax base. Section 2611(a) identifies the three generation-skipping transfers, and each transfer is defined in § 2612.

[A]   Direct Skip

A direct skip is a transfer of an interest in property to a skip person that is subject to estate or gift taxation when made. IRC § 2612(c). By definition, a direct skip therefore implicates two transfer taxes at once. The simplest form of a direct skip is a lifetime transfer of property from a grandparent to a grandchild. The transfer is subject to the gift tax (notwithstanding any application of the gift tax annual exclusion), and the grandchild constitutes a skip person. The result would be the same if the grandparent had funded a discretionary trust for the exclusive benefit of the grandchild, as the trust would constitute a skip person in that case. However, if the grandparent had funded a trust for the lifetime benefit of her child, with the remainder passing to the grandchild upon the child's death, the funding of the trust would not constitute a direct skip. The trust would not separately constitute a skip person because the child, a non-skip person, would possess an interest in the trust immediately after its funding. The GST tax consequences in this later case would await a termination of the child's interest in the trust.

[1]   ETIP Deferral

In determining whether lifetime transfers constitute direct skips, a special rule applies when the transferred property could be captured in the gross estate of the transferor. Specifically, if the value of the transferred property would be included in the transferor's gross estate if the individual died immediately after making the transfer (other than by reason of § 2035), the direct skip is treated as not occurring until the close of the "estate tax inclusion period" (ETIP). IRC § 2642(f). As an example, suppose *Grandparent* funds an irrevocable trust

---

[10] For a decedent dying in 2010 whose estate exercised the irrevocable election provided by the Tax Relief, Unemployment Insurance Reauthorization, and Job Creation Act of 2010 to apply the provisions of EGTRRA that repealed the estate tax, *see* Pub. L. No. 111-312, § 301(c), 124 Stat. 3296, 3300 (2010), the unified credit for estate tax purposes will not exist for 2010. As a result, there would be no need to make a QTIP election for a devise to a surviving spouse occurring that year, which obviates the need for a reverse QTIP election to render the decedent the transferor.

[11] However, the reverse QTIP election will remain useful where (a) the decedent has used all or a portion of his unified credit by making non-GST lifetime gifts, or (b) the decedent creates a credit shelter devise that is not intended to generate GST consequences. Examples of the latter include devises to the testator's children outright, to a trust that will distribute in favor of the testator's children upon the death of the surviving spouse, or to a trust over which the testator's children possess a general power of appointment.

for the exclusive benefit of *Grandchild* while retaining, in his capacity as trustee, discretionary authority over the timing and amount of distributions to *Grandchild*. The funding of the trust satisfies both elements of a direct skip. *Grandparent* makes a completed gift by transferring property to the trust because he has relinquished the ability to change the identity of the beneficiaries. *See* Treas. Reg. § 25.2511-2(b). *Grandchild* is the only person possessing a current interest in the trust; hence, the trust constitutes a skip person. IRC § 2613(a)(2)(A). However, note that if *Grandparent* died after funding the trust, the trust assets will be captured in his gross estate under § 2036(a)(2) due to his retained discretionary authority over income distributions. *See* Estate of O'Connor v. Commissioner, 54 T.C. 969 (1970) (discretion over timing and amount of income distributions to single beneficiary sufficient to implicate § 2036(a)(2)). Accordingly, the direct skip is deferred under § 2642(f) until the ETIP closes, whether through *Grandparent's* lifetime relinquishment of the discretionary power or upon *Grandparent's* death. Assuming increasing property values, § 2642(f) therefore operates to include in the GST tax base any appreciation in the transferred property that occurs during the ETIP.

[2] Multi-Generational Direct Skip

Although the overarching goal of the GST tax is to subject property to federal transfer taxation at each generation, opportunities remain under the GST tax to bypass generation levels at no additional transfer tax cost. For example, assume a grandparent makes an outright transfer of property to her great-grandchild. The transfer is subject to both gift tax and GST tax as a direct skip, but the property has passed down to the third generation.[12] Similarly, if the grandparent funds a trust for the benefit of his descendants (which includes at least one non-skip person) to remain in effect for the maximum period permitted by perpetuities restrictions, any distribution of trust property to a great-grandchild will constitute a taxable distribution. Avoiding federal transfer taxation in this manner is not painless, however, as it requires eliminating the potential for a generation to benefit from the transferred property.

[B] Taxable Termination

If a person possesses an interest in a trust for GST tax purposes, the termination of the person's interest in the trust (whether by reason of death, lapse of time, release of a power of appointment, or otherwise) may trigger imposition of the GST tax. Indeed, as a default matter, a taxable termination occurs any time an interest in a trust terminates, unless one of two exceptions applies: (1) immediately after the termination, a non-skip person possesses an interest in the trust, or (2) following the termination, no distribution from the trust may be made to a skip person. IRC § 2612(a)(1).

To illustrate these rules, assume an individual, P, funds a trust for the benefit of his descendants. The trustee is authorized to make discretionary distributions of income or principal to the P's children, C_1 and C_2, and grandchildren, GC_1 and GC_2, until the death of P's last surviving child, at which point the trust property will be distributed to those of P's grandchildren who are then living. Several years after the funding of the trust, C_1 dies. Although his interest in the trust terminates, C_1's death does not constitute a taxable

---

[12] In comparison, had the property been left in trust for the benefit of the grandchild with a distribution to the great-grandchild upon the grandchild's death, the GST tax would have been imposed twice. The funding of the trust would constitute a direct skip, and the termination of the grandchild's interest in the trust would constitute a taxable termination.

termination for GST tax purposes because C_2, a non-skip person, continues to hold an interest in the trust. However, upon the death of C_2, only GC_1 and GC_2 hold interests in the trust. Because the trust property is not included in C_2's gross estate for estate tax purposes, P remains the transferor of the trust property, and GC_1 and GC_2 retain their status as skip persons. Hence, only skip persons hold an interest in the trust following the death of C_2. Because the skip persons may (in fact, will) receive future distributions from the trust, the death of C_2 constitutes a taxable termination with respect to the trust.

[1] Partial Terminations

Pursuant to § 2612(a)(2), the termination of an interest in a trust occurring by reason of the death of a beneficiary may constitute a taxable termination even though a non-skip person continues to possess an interest in the trust. The exception applies only if the deceased beneficiary is a lineal descendant of the transferor. In that case, if a specified portion of the trust assets are to be distributed to one or more skip persons (or a trust established for the exclusive benefit of skip persons), the termination constitutes a taxable termination with respect to that portion of the trust property. As an example, suppose the trust above required that one-half of the trust property be distributed upon the death of the predeceasing child, C_1, to his then-living issue, GC_1, with the remainder of the trust property continuing to be held for the benefit of C_2 and GC_2. The termination of C_1's interest will constitute a taxable termination as to one-half of the trust property.

[2] Exclusion for Terminations Included in Gift or Estate Tax Base

Note that the statutory definitions of a taxable termination and a direct skip potentially overlap. For example, if a grantor funds a trust for the benefit of his grandchildren but retains the right to receive income payments for his lifetime, the grantor's death constitutes a taxable termination. The grantor possesses an interest in the trust through his right to receive income payments and, following the termination of his interest, the only interests in the trust are held by skip persons. Yet, at the same time, the termination of the trust constitutes a direct skip. The trust property is included in the grantor's gross estate under § 2036(a)(1), and the trust itself constitutes a skip person at that point.

The regulations resolve this discrepancy in favor of the direct skip. If the trust property is subject to federal estate or gift taxation at the time of the termination (a condition to a direct skip), then the termination of the interest is excluded from the definition of a taxable termination. Treas. Reg. § 26.2612-1(b)(1)(i).

[C] Taxable Distribution

The third type of generation-skipping transfer, a taxable distribution, occurs when a distribution is made from a trust to a skip person. IRC § 2612(b). The taxable distribution occupies a subordinate role within the GST tax base, because the definition specifically excludes a distribution that constitutes a direct skip or a taxable termination. *Id.*

Taking the hypothetical trust created by P for the benefit of his children, C_1 and C_2, and grandchildren, GC_1 and GC_2, discussed above in its original form, discretionary distributions from the trust to GC_1 or GC_2 would constitute taxable distributions. However, when the trust terminates as a result of the death of C_2, the resulting distribution of the trust property to GC_1

and GC_2 would not constitute taxable distributions. Rather, the death of C_2 constitutes a taxable termination with respect to the property remaining in the trust.

§ 21.03 GENERATION REASSIGNMENTS FOLLOWING GST TRANSFER

Suppose a testator devised property in trust to be held for the benefit of the testator's descendants until the death of the last descendant living at the testator's death, at which point the trust property will be distributed to those of the testator's descendants who are then living. The testator was survived by several children and grandchildren. Note that the death of the testator's last surviving child will implicate the GST tax as a taxable termination. Yet because the property will remain in trust for the testator's remaining issue, subsequent discretionary distributions to the testator's grandchildren would constitute taxable distributions, barring any corrective measures. Application of the GST tax in this manner would operate as a transfer tax penalty on the use of multi-generational trusts.

Section 2653(a) provides the corrective measure that prevents the GST tax from being duplicated with respect to property that skips only one generation. The correction occurs through a reassignment of the generation level of the transferor. If there is a generation-skipping transfer with respect to property and the property is held in trust immediately after the transfer, the transferor is assigned to one generation above the highest generation of any person then possessing an interest in the trust. IRC § 2653(a). In the context of the trust created for testator's descendants above, the taxable termination occurring by reason of the death of the last surviving child would move the generation assignment of the testator to one above that of the testator's grandchildren. Accordingly, any later distributions in favor of the grandchildren would not constitute taxable distributions. However, the testator's great-grandchildren would continue to be skip persons, and any discretionary distributions in their favor would constitute taxable distributions subject to an additional round of GST taxation.

§ 21.04 COMPARISON OF GST TRANSFERS

The GST tax is levied at the same 35 percent rate on all three types of generation-skipping transfers. *See* IRC § 2641(a), (b). Nonetheless, the three types of generation-skipping transfers do not carry the same GST tax burden.

The GST tax is levied on a tax-exclusive basis in the context of a direct skip. Liability for the GST tax in this context is imposed on the transferor, and the taxable amount of a direct skip is the amount received by the transferee. *See* IRC §§ 2603(a)(3), 2623. While § 2515 includes the GST tax resulting from lifetime direct skips in the transferor's gift tax base,[13] this provision operates to subject the GST tax to only one of two potential federal transfer taxes.

By contrast, the GST tax resulting from taxable terminations and taxable distributions is levied on a tax-inclusive basis. The taxable amount of a taxable termination is the value of the trust property with respect to which the termination occurred (net of administration expenses related to the transfer). IRC § 2622. Liability for the GST tax rests on the trustee in this context; accordingly, the funds that will be used to pay the GST tax are included in the GST

---

[13] Note that, in the context of direct skips occurring by reason of death, the GST tax imposed on the estate will be paid from estate property presumably included in the decedent's gross estate under § 2033.

tax base. IRC § 2603(a)(2). Because the trust was previously subject to estate or gift tax upon funding, the amount used to pay the GST tax will have been subjected to two levels of federal transfer taxation. Taxable distributions share the same unfortunate tax-inclusive characterization. The taxable amount of a taxable distribution is the value of the property received by the transferee (reduced by associated administration expenses), and liability for the resulting tax is imposed on the transferee.[14] IRC §§ 2603(a)(1), 2621. Hence, the GST tax on the distributed amount—which would have been previously subject to estate or gift tax—itself is included in the GST tax base in this setting.

The differences in the combined federal transfer tax burden imposed on various generation-skipping transfers may be highlighted by calculating the taxes levied on the following transfers: (1) a lifetime direct skip; (2) a direct skip occurring by reason of death; (3) a taxable termination of a trust created by a lifetime transfer; and (4) a taxable termination of a trust funded at death.[15] Each of the scenarios below assumes an initial amount of $10 million from which the transfer and all associated transfer taxes must be satisfied. Additionally, the transferor has exhausted any unified credit and GST exemption, so that the transfer is subject to the full weight of the transfer tax system.[16]

Lifetime Direct Skip:

Amount received by skip person (X)	=	$10 million	−	GST tax on X	−	Gift tax on $[X + $ (GST tax on $X)]$
	=	$10 million	−	$.35X$	−	$.35[X + .35X]$
	=	$10 million	−	1,920,439	−	2,592,593
	=	**$5,486,968**				

Direct Skip Occurring by Reason of Death:

Amount received by skip person (X)	=	$10 million	−	Estate tax on $10 million	−	GST tax on X
	=	$10 million	−	$3.5 million	−	$.35X$
	=	$6,500,000			−	1,685,185
	=	**$4,814,815**				

Taxable Termination of Trust Funded During Life:

Amount received by skip person (X)	=	Funding of trust net of gift tax (Y)	−	GST tax on Y
	=	$[Y = ($10 million − $.35Y)]$	−	$.35Y$
	=	$7,407,407	−	$2,592,593
	=	**$4,814,815**		

---

[14] To prevent parties from circumventing the tax-inclusive nature of the GST tax in the context of taxable distributions by having the trustee pay the GST tax liability on behalf of the transferee, any such payment by the trustee is treated as an additional taxable distribution. IRC § 2612(b).

[15] No separate calculations are made for taxable distributions from trusts, because the combined tax burden will match those of taxable terminations (as both are subject to GST tax on a tax-inclusive basis).

[16] As a final parameter, the examples predicated on the creation and termination of a non-exempt GST trust provide for no change in the value of trust assets between funding and termination.

Taxable Termination of Trust Funded at Death:

$$\begin{aligned}
\text{Amount received by skip person } (X) &= \text{Funding of trust net of estate tax } (Z) \quad - \quad \text{GST tax on } Z \\
&= [Z = \$10 \text{ million} - .35(\$10 \text{ million})] \quad - \quad .35Z \\
&= \$6{,}500{,}000 \quad - \quad \$2{,}275{,}000 \\
&= \mathbf{\$4{,}225{,}000}
\end{aligned}$$

The differences among these scenarios are attributable to (a) the tax-exclusive nature of the gift tax versus the tax-inclusive nature of the estate tax and (b) the tax-exclusive nature of a direct skip versus the tax-inclusive nature of a taxable termination. The lifetime direct skip yields the lowest combined effective tax rate, as the two transfer taxes to which it is subject are levied on a tax-exclusive basis. The taxable termination of a trust funded at death lies at the other extreme, because the two transfer taxes it implicates are levied on a tax-inclusive basis.

§ 21.05 EXCLUDED TRANSFERS

[A] Section 2503(e) Expenses

Section 2611(b)(1) provides an exclusion from the GST tax base for transfers that, "if made inter vivos by an individual, would not be treated as a taxable gift" by reason of the exclusion under § 2503(e) for direct payments of tuition or medical care expenses paid on behalf of an individual. Hence, while lifetime payments of § 2503(e) expenses that are made by an individual on behalf of a skip person are effectively excluded from the GST tax base through the assignment of a zero tax rate,[17] payments of such amounts by a trustee on behalf of a skip person are literally excluded from the GST tax base.

[B] Prior Transfers Subject to GST

Section 2611(b)(2) supplies a narrow exclusion for transferred property that was previously subjected to GST tax as a result of a prior transfer to a transferee who is assigned to the same (or lower) generation than the transferee of the second transfer. Hence, due to an intervening upstream transfer of the property, the second transfer does not deliver the property to a generation lower than that obtained by way of the first transfer.

As an example, suppose a grandparent devises the family homestead to his granddaughter. As a testamentary direct skip, the transfer is subject to both estate and GST tax. The granddaughter then makes a lifetime gift of the property to her great aunt (sister of her grandfather), who wishes to reside in the home until her death. At her death, the great aunt devises the property to the granddaughter's husband. The exclusion under § 2611(b)(2) applies to exclude what otherwise would be a testamentary direct skip from the great aunt. The property was subject to GST tax in the prior transfer to the granddaughter, the granddaughter is assigned to the same generation as the transferee in the later transfer (her husband), and there appears to be no tax avoidance effect from the transfers. Thus, in this limited context, § 2611(b)(2) spares the parties from an unfortunate duplication of the GST tax burden.

---

[17] As discussed in Chapter 22, § 2642(c)(3)(B) assigns a zero inclusion ratio to any lifetime direct skip that is excluded from the gift tax base pursuant to § 2503(e). Hence, a § 2503(e) transfer from an individual literally is included in the GST tax base, but it is effectively exempt from GST taxation by being taxed at a zero rate.

§ 21.06   GRANDFATHERED TRUSTS

While the legislation that would enact the current GST tax was pending, Congress sought to prevent taxpayers from avoiding the imposition of the looming GST tax by making irrevocable transfers in advance of the October 23, 1986, effective date. Congress therefore provided that inter vivos transfers subject to the gift tax made after September 25, 1985, but before October 23, 1986, were to be treated as if they were made on October 23, 1986.[18] On the bright side, transfers from a trust that became irrevocable on or before September 25, 1985, are exempt from the imposition of GST tax. *See* Treas. Reg. § 26.2601-1(b)(1)(i).

The status of a "grandfathered" trust that is exempt from GST tax consequences should be cautiously guarded. In that vein, the regulations contain detailed guidance on when a modification, judicial construction, settlement agreement, or trustee action with respect to a GST exempt trust will cause the trust to forfeit its exempt status. *See* Treas. Reg. § 26.2601-1(b)(4). As a general matter, modifications that threaten a trust's exempt status are those that shift a beneficial interest in the trust to a beneficiary who occupies a lower generation than the existing trust beneficiaries, and those that extend the time for vesting of a beneficial interest in the trust beyond the period provided in the original trust. Additionally, if a power of appointment over assets of a grandfathered trust is released, exercised, or allowed to lapse after the September 25, 1985 operative date of the GST tax in a manner that is subject to the estate tax or gift tax, the property subject to the power is treated as added to the trust at the time of the lapse, release, or exercise. *See* Treas. Reg. § 26.2601-1(b)(1)(v)(A). As a result, the property subject to the power will forfeit its exempt status. *See* Estate of Timken v. United States, 601 F.3d 431 (6th Cir. 2010) (upholding the validity of Reg. § 26.2601-1(b)(1)(v)(A) as applied to a post-GST lapse of a general power of appointment over what previously had been a grandfathered GST trust).

§ 21.07   STUDY PROBLEMS

1.   Having recently won the lottery, Joe (age 65) decides to share his wealth by making a series of $50,000 gifts to the following individuals:

   -   GC_1 and GC_2 (children of Joe's child, C_1) and their spouses;

   -   GC_3 (child of Joe's child, C_2, who died several years before the transfer) and his spouse;

   -   GN_1 and GN_2 (children of Joe's nephew, N_1, who predeceased the transfer); and

   -   F_1 and F_2 (children of Joe's long time neighbor). F_1 is age 32 at the time of the transfer, and F_2 is 26.

   Which of these transfers are included in the GST tax base as direct skips?

2.   Seeking to avoid probate, Danielle transfers title to her beach house to herself and her three grandchildren as joint tenants with right of survivorship. The initial transfer occurs in Year 1, when the property is valued at $1.2 million. Danielle dies in Year 10, when the property is valued at $1.8 million. Assuming Danielle had already exhausted her GST tax exemption, what are the GST tax consequences of these transfers?

---

[18]   *See* Tax Reform Act of 1986, Pub. L. No. 99-514, § 1433(b)(2)(A), 100 Stat. 2085, 2731.

3. Harold funds a trust through a devise in his will that contains the following dispositive provisions:

    If my wife survives me, the trustee shall distribute the net income of the trust to her on a regular, but not more infrequent than annual, basis. Upon my wife's death, the trust property shall continue to be held in trust for the benefit of my issue. The trustee, in its sole discretion, may distribute trust income or principal for the benefit of my then-living children and grandchildren; any income not so distributed shall be accumulated and added to principal. Upon the death of any child, or upon my wife's death if a child predeceases my wife, a fraction of the trust property (with the denominator equaling the number of my children who survived me) shall be distributed to that child's then-living issue, per stirpes. If a child dies without then-living issue, the portion of the trust that otherwise would have been distributed to that child's then-living issue shall be distributed to my then-living issue, per stirpes.

    Harold dies survived by his wife (W), two children (C_1, C_2), and four grandchildren (GC_1, GC_2, GC_3, who are children of C_1; GC_4, child of C_2). Following Harold's death, his family members die in the following order: W, C_1, and C_2.

    a. Assuming that Harold's executor makes a QTIP election, identify all the possible transferors to the trust for GST tax purposes. Can Harold's executor do anything to change these results?

    b. Describe the GST tax consequences, if any, when W dies.

    c. Following W's death, the trustee makes a discretionary distribution of $20,000 to each of GC_1, GC_2, GC_3, and GC_4. What are the GST tax consequences, if any, of these distributions?

    d. Following W's death, the trustee pays GC_1's college tuition bill of $40,000. Discuss the GST tax consequences of this payment.

    e. Discuss the GST tax consequences to the trust when C_1 dies.

4. Ellen devises stock to her grandson, Nathan. Nathan, who is independently wealthy, seeks to avoid the transfer tax burden by making a qualified disclaimer of the devise. Under state law, Nathan's disclaimer causes the devise to pass to his two children. How has Nathan's disclaimer saved federal transfer taxes?

5. Patricia devises her property in trust for the benefit of her children and grandchildren. The trust contains the following terms:

    Until the death of my last living child, the trustee shall divide the net income of the trust in equal shares, creating a share for each child of mine who is then living and a share for the issue of any child who is then deceased. The trustee shall distribute the net income to those for whom a share was created. Upon the death of my last surviving child, the trustee shall accumulate the net income of the trust until my youngest living grandchild attains age 21. At that point, the trust shall be distributed to my then-living grandchildren in equal shares.

    Assume that Patricia is survived by four children, each of whom has two children of their own.

    a.   Upon Patricia's death, who possesses an interest in the trust for GST tax purposes?

    b.   How does your answer to (a) change, if at all, when Patricia's first child dies?

    c.   Patricia's last child dies when the youngest living grandchild is age 15. Who possesses an interest in the trust for GST tax purposes at that point?

    d.   Continuing with the facts of problem (c), what are the GST tax consequences of the trust termination that occurs when the youngest of Patricia's grandchildren attains age 21?

6.   Gary establishes a charitable remainder annuity trust for the benefit of his granddaughter.

    a.   Does the establishment of the trust constitute a direct skip? *See* IRC §§ 2651(f)(3), 2652(c)(1)(C).

    b.   Describe the GST tax consequences of the annuity payments to the granddaughter.

Chapter 22

THE GST EXEMPTION AND APPLICABLE RATE

Internal Revenue Code: §§ 2631, 2632, 2641, 2642, 2652(a)
Treasury Regulations: § 26.2612-1(f)
                          § 26.2632-1(a) to (b)(2)(ii), (c)(1) to (4), (d)
                          § 26.2642-2(a) to (b)

§ 22.01 THE APPLICABLE RATE

The rate of GST tax is determined by navigating something of a definitional gauntlet. The starting point for determining the GST tax rate is the maximum federal estate tax rate, presently 35 percent. This rate is multiplied by the "inclusion ratio" that applies to the transferred property to produce the "applicable rate" at which the GST tax will be levied. IRC § 2641(a). The inclusion ratio is defined as the excess of the number one over the "applicable fraction." IRC § 2642(a). As a general matter, the value of the transferred property supplies the denominator of the applicable fraction,[1] and the numerator of the fraction equals the amount of "GST exemption" allocated to the transfer.

If the transferor allocates GST exemption in an amount equal to the value of the transferred property, the applicable fraction will be one. This yields an inclusion ratio of zero, which, in turn, produces an applicable rate of zero. In that case, as long as there is no intervening transferor with respect to the property, any future generation-skipping transfers emanating from the original transfer will be immune from GST tax. At the other end of the spectrum, the failure to allocate any GST exemption to a transfer will result in an applicable fraction of zero and an inclusion ratio of one. In that case, any current or future generation-skipping transfers attributable to that transfer of property will be subject to the highest possible applicable rate of 35 percent. Estate planning with respect to planned or potential generation-skipping transfers therefore centers on the allocation of the transferor's GST exemption.

---

[1] For transfers in trust, the denominator of the applicable fraction starts with the value of the property transferred in trust but is reduced by the sum of (a) the amount of any federal estate tax or state death tax attributable to the transferred property and recovered from the trust and (b) any charitable deduction allowed with respect to the property. *See* IRC § 2642(a)(2)(B)(ii).

§ 22.02 THE GST EXEMPTION

Each individual is afforded a GST exemption equal to the basic exclusion amount of the unified credit under § 2010(c). IRC § 2631(c). Although Congress recently introduced portability into the unified credit regime,[2] it did not extend portability to the GST exemption. Thus, for 2011, an individual's GST exemption equals $5 million. The GST exemption is scheduled to be increased based on the cost-of-living adjustments to the basic exclusion amount that commence in 2012.[3]

In order to allocate GST exemption to transferred property, an individual must serve as the chapter 13 transferor of the property. *See* IRC § 2631(a). In other words, the transferred property must be subject to inclusion in the individual's gift tax or estate tax base, determined without regard to any available deduction, exclusion, exemption, or credit. *See* IRC § 2652(a); Treas. Reg. § 26.2652-1(a)(2). An individual's GST exemption is allocated on a cumulative basis to lifetime transfers. Any portion of the exemption not allocated during a transferor's lifetime remains to be allocated by the individual's executor, whether to prior inter vivos transfers or to transfers occurring by reason of individual's death. An allocation of GST exemption, once made, may not be revoked.[4] IRC § 2631(b). To protect the unwitting or apathetic transferor, § 2632 prescribes a regime by which an individual's GST exemption is automatically allocated to transfers absent a contrary election, the details of which are discussed below. With respect to transfers in trust, the allocation of GST exemption is made to the trust property as a whole; allocation of GST exemption to particular trust assets is not permitted. *See* Treas. Reg. § 26.2632-1(a).

[A] Longevity of Exemption Allocation

Once a transferor has allocated GST exemption to transferred property, the resulting applicable fraction under § 2642(a) will apply to all future generation-skipping transfers associated with the transferred property as long as there is no intervening chapter 13 transferor. As an example, assume that a testator devises property worth $2 million in trust, to which the testator's executor timely allocates $2 million of the testator's remaining GST exemption. The trust permits the testator's only child to withdraw the net income of the trust during the child's lifetime on an annual basis. The trust further authorizes the trustee to make discretionary distributions of principal to any of the testator's descendants during the child's lifetime. Upon the child's death, the property will continue to be held in trust until the death of the testator's last surviving grandchild, at which point the trust will distribute in favor of the testator's then-living descendants.

The allocation of GST exemption to the trust produces an inclusion ratio of zero. This inclusion ratio applies to any discretionary distributions of principal to the testator's

---

[2] Portability of the unified credit is discussed in § 19.05.

[3] As described at the outset of the text, current law provides for the entire federal transfer tax system to revert to its pre-EGTRRA state on January 1, 2013. If this unlikely event occurs, the GST exemption will return to a $1 million base amount indexed for inflation from 1997, which would leave the exemption in the neighborhood of $1.4 million. *See* § 1.07. For purposes of simplicity, this chapter assumes that Congress will take future action to extend the GST exemption levels contained in the 2010 temporary legislation.

[4] For this purpose, an allocation of GST exemption does not become final until the due date of the gift tax return for the year in which the transfer constituted a completed gift. Hence, if an allocation of GST exemption is made on a gift tax return filed before its due date, the allocation may be revised ay an amended return provided the amended return is timely filed. *See* Treas. Reg. § 26.2632-1(b)(4)(i).

grandchildren during the child's lifetime. Additionally, the zero inclusion ratio eliminates any GST tax that otherwise would result from the taxable termination of the trust occurring at the child's death. These results in no way depend on the value of the future generation-skipping transfer. Because the inclusion ratio produces a GST tax rate of zero, the GST exemption effectively extends to any future appreciation in the transferred property.

Now suppose that the trust had provided the child with a testamentary power to appoint the trust assets to her probate estate. Even if the child fails to exercise the power, its mere existence causes the trust assets to be included in the child's gross estate under § 2041(a)(2). The child therefore would become the chapter 13 transferor to the trust upon her death, rendering the testator's allocation of GST exemption to the trust meaningless from that point on. While any future distributions to the testator's grandchildren will no longer constitute taxable distributions, *see* IRC § 2653(a), a distribution to a great-grandchild of the testator will be exempt from GST tax only if the child were to allocate a sufficient amount of her GST exemption to the trust. If the trust had provided the child with a general power of appointment over the trust property in this manner, the testator's GST exemption would have been effective to shield from GST tax only discretionary distributions to the testator's grandchildren made during the child's lifetime. Use of the testator's GST exemption in this manner would have been less than optimal, to put it mildly.

Recall that to avoid the problem of the intervening transferor with respect to QTIP transfers, § 2652(a)(3) permits a transferor-spouse to treat the property in the QTIP trust as if the deduction-qualifying election under § 2056(b)(7) or § 2523(f) had not been made. As a result of the "reverse QTIP" election, a transferor-spouse may make a meaningful allocation of GST exemption to the QTIP trust that will not be negated by the subsequent inclusion of the QTIP property in the surviving spouse's gift tax or estate tax base.

[B] Protection Against Wasteful Allocations

An attempted allocation of GST exemption to a trust that will not yield a future generation-skipping transfer is void. *See* Treas. Reg. § 26.2632-1(d)(1). Returning to the hypothetical trust above in which the child possessed a general testamentary power over the trust property, note that the future inclusion of the trust property in the child's gross estate does not eliminate the possibility of a generation-skipping transfer from occurring. Rather, the trustee possessed discretion to distribute trust principal to the testator's grandchildren and great-grandchildren during the child's lifetime. While the likelihood of these taxable distributions may be remote, the probability of the generation-skipping transfer occurring is not relevant. *Id.* However, had discretionary distributions of principal been limited to the child during her lifetime, the possibility of a generation-skipping transfer with respect to the testator would have been eliminated. Distributions to the testator's grandchildren or great-grandchildren could occur only after the child's death, at which point the child would become the chapter 13 transferor to the trust. In that case, the regulations would save the testator's executor from improvidently allocating GST exemption to a transfer where it could never be used.

§ 22.03 ALLOCATION OF GST EXEMPTION TO LIFETIME TRANSFERS

[A] Express Allocations

As a general rule, an individual who makes a transfer that has current or potential future GST consequence may allocate any unused GST exemption to the transfer once the transfer becomes a completed gift. IRC § 2632(a)(1). An allocation may thereafter be made by or on behalf of the individual until the due date for filing the individual's federal estate tax return. *Id.* While the window for making a lifetime allocation of GST exemption is remarkably broad, that is not to suggest that the timing of the allocation lacks importance. As discussed below, the timing of the allocation of GST exemption carries significant practical ramifications.

For an allocation of GST exemption to become effective as of the date of the original transfer, the allocation must be made on a timely filed gift tax return for the year in which the gift became complete.[5] IRC § 2642(b)(1)(B). Section 6075(b) designates April 15 of the year following the calendar year in which the gift became complete as the general due date for filing the gift tax return, but the due date for this purpose includes any extensions for filing that are actually granted. Because individuals may apply for an automatic six-month extension of time to file, transferors effectively have until October 15 of the year after the transfer to make an allocation of GST exemption that is effective as of the date of the transfer. An allocation of GST exemption that is not made on a timely filed gift tax return is effective only as of the date of the allocation. IRC § 2642(b)(3).

To illustrate the importance of the timeliness of an allocation of GST exemption, assume that an individual transfers stock in a closely held corporation worth $2 million to a trust benefitting her descendants. The transfer occurs on March 1 of Year 1. Prior to April 15 of Year 2, the individual applies for an automatic extension for filing the gift tax return for Year 1. On July 1 of Year 2, a private equity firm acquires the stock of the corporation and pays the trust $10 million for its shares. If the individual allocates $2 million of GST exemption to the transfer through a gift tax return filed on or before the extended due date of October 15 of Year 2, the entire trust property will be exempt from future GST tax. However, if the allocation of GST exemption were made on a return that was not timely filed, the allocation would not relate back to the date of the original transfer. Instead, the allocation would be effective only as of the date the gift tax return is filed. Given the significantly increased value of the trust corpus, the individual would not have sufficient GST exemption to render the trust fully exempt.

[B] Deferral of Allocation During ETIP

Although GST exemption generally may be allocated to a transfer once the transfer becomes a completed gift, an exception applies for transfers that may have potential estate tax consequences to the transferor. Specifically, if an inter vivos gift may be included in the gross estate of the donor or the donor's spouse other than by reason of § 2035, an allocation of GST

---

[5] Section 2642(e) provides a special rule for determining when a timely allocation of GST exemption to a charitable lead trust will be effective. In general terms, the inclusion ratio for the transfer is not determined until the termination of the charitable lead interest, and the ratio is based on the then-prevailing value of the trust assets. The GST exemption originally allocated to the transfer will be adjusted for inflation (the "adjusted GST exemption") in determining the inclusion ratio that will apply to the remainder interest.

exemption to the transferred property will not become effective until the close of the "estate tax inclusion period" (ETIP).[6] IRC § 2642(f)(1), (4). The ETIP encompasses the period during which the transferred property would be included in the gross estate of the donor or the donor's spouse if either died. IRC § 2642(f)(3). However, in no event will the ETIP extend beyond the date on which there is a generation-skipping transfer with respect to the property or the date of the death of the donor or donor's spouse. *Id.* For purposes of calculating the inclusion ratio, the transferred property is valued as of the close of the ETIP. IRC § 2642(f)(2).

To illustrate the potential application of the ETIP rules, assume that a grantor transfers property valued at $1 million to himself as trustee of a trust benefitting his grandchild. The terms of the trust permit the trustee to distribute income to the grandchild in the trustee's sole discretion until the grandchild attains age 25, at which point the grandchild will be entitled to receive the entire net income of the trust. The trust assets will be distributed to the grandchild's then-living issue upon the grandchild's death.

The transfer in trust constitutes a completed gift to a skip person. Cognizant of the GST tax but unaware of the ETIP provisions, the grantor allocates $1 million of GST exemption to the transfer on a timely filed gift tax return. Even though the allocation is irrevocable, it does not have immediate effect. Rather, the allocation is held in abeyance until the close of the ETIP. *See* Treas. Reg. § 26.2632-1(c)(5), Ex. 1. The ETIP will not close with respect to property remaining in the trust[7] until the grandchild attains age 25 or dies beforehand.[8] Assuming the grandchild reaches age 25, the grantor's prior allocation of GST exemption would then become effective. If the trust property were valued at $1.5 million at that point, the grantor would have to allocate an additional $500,000 of GST exemption to the transfer to fully shield the delayed direct skip from GST tax. However, had the grantor not retained the right to accumulate income in his fiduciary capacity until the grandchild attained age 25, the original allocation of GST exemption to the trust would have been sufficient to insulate any distributions from the trust from GST tax consequences.

[C] Deemed Allocations

[1] Direct Skips

Suppose an individual gave $50,000 to each of his three grandchildren. Unaware of the GST tax, the individual fails to make an allocation of his GST exemption to the transfers. While the individual otherwise would owe GST tax on the amount of the transfers, § 2632(b) prevents this result by automatically allocating a transferor's unused GST exemption to any lifetime direct skip to the extent necessary to generate an inclusion ratio of zero.[9] If the transferor does not

---

[6] The possibility of the transferred property being included in the estate of the donor's spouse is disregarded in this context if the transferor made a reverse QTIP election under § 2652(a)(3). *See* Treas. Reg. § 26.2632-1(c)(2)(ii)(C).

[7] Had the grantor-trustee made a discretionary distribution, the ETIP would have closed as to the distributed funds. *See* Treas. Reg. § 26.2632-1(c)(3)(iii).

[8] The ETIP would close when the grandchild attained age 25 because the grantor's § 2036(a)(2) right to accumulate income would cease at that point. The ETIP would close upon the grandchild's death prior to attaining age 25 because that event would trigger a direct skip with respect to the property to the grandchild's issue.

[9] Due to the operation of § 2642(c), the amount of the transfer that is excluded from the gift tax base under § 2503(b) is treated as a separate transfer having a statutorily assigned inclusion ratio of zero. *See* § 22.05[A]. Accordingly, the automatic allocation of GST exemption to each direct skip would equal the amount of the transfer in excess of the annual exclusion amount.

possess sufficient remaining exemption to fully shield the transfer from GST tax, the deemed allocation consumes the remaining exemption. In this manner, § 2632(b) prevents the individual from unintentionally incurring GST tax liability to the extent possible.

A deemed allocation of GST exemption under § 2632 may be prevented through an express contrary election made on a timely filed gift tax return for the calendar year in which the direct skip occurs.[10] IRC § 2632(b)(3). Alternatively, a transferor may avoid the deemed allocation of GST exemption by paying the GST tax triggered by the direct skip. Treas. Reg. § 26.2632-1(b)(1)(i). If the deemed allocation of GST exemption is not negated in either manner, the deemed allocation becomes irrevocable as of the due date of the transferor's gift tax return. *See* Treas. Reg. § 26.2632-1(b)(1)(ii).

[2] Indirect Skips

As part of the Economic Growth and Tax Relief Reconciliation Act of 2001, Congress expanded the scope of deemed allocations to lifetime transfers having potential GST tax consequences beyond direct skips.[11] Similar to the deemed allocation of GST exemption to direct skips, the expanded deemed allocation rules under § 2632(c) are intended to protect the unsuspecting transferor from incurring GST tax liability unnecessarily. Yet the attempt to envision the intent of a typical transferor in the context of completed gifts that may or may not ultimately yield generation-skipping transfers leads to a considerable deal of complexity.

The deemed allocation regime of § 2632(c) starts off with a simple directive: If an individual makes an inter vivos gift that constitutes an "indirect skip," the "unused portion" of the individual's GST exemption is allocated to the transfer to the extent necessary to produce an inclusion ratio of zero. IRC § 2632(c)(1). If the indirect skip cannot be rendered fully exempt from GST tax, then the entire unused GST exemption will be allocated to the transfer. *Id.* An indirect skip for this purpose is any inter vivos transfer that is subject to gift tax, other than a direct skip, to a "GST trust." IRC § 2632(c)(3)(A). As a general rule, a GST trust is any trust that could yield a generation-skipping transfer with respect to the transferor. IRC § 2632(c)(3)(B). However, the definition of a GST trust includes a number of exceptions that are designed to remove transfers from the deemed allocation regime when the prospect of distributions to non-skip persons would significantly dilute the benefit of the exemption allocation.[12]

[a] Exceptions to GST Trust

[i] Significant Planned Distributions to Non-Skip Persons

If more than 25 percent of the trust corpus must be distributed or may be withdrawn by one or more individuals who are non-skip persons before the individual attains age 46 or

---

[10] If property transferred in a direct skip could subsequently be included in the estate of the transferor or the transferor's spouse other than by reason of § 2035, the direct skip is treated as not occurring until the close of the ETIP. *See* IRC § 2642(f)(1).

[11] *See* Pub. L. No. 107-16, § 561(a), 115 Stat. 38, 86–89 (2001). As discussed in § 1.07, the amendments to the federal transfer tax system made by EGTRRA are scheduled to expire on December 31, 2012.

[12] If any of the foregoing exceptions apply, the transferor nonetheless may elect to treat the trust as a GST trust for a particular transfer or all transfers made to the trust so that the automatic allocation regime will apply. IRC § 2632(c)(5)(A)(ii).

before a designated event that will occur before the individual attains age 46, the trust does not constitute a GST trust. IRC § 2632(c)(3)(B)(i). Additionally, if more than 25 percent of the trust corpus must be distributed or may be withdrawn by non-skip persons who are living on the date of death of another person named in the trust instrument who is more than 10 years older than the non-skip persons, the trust is excluded from the definition of a GST trust. IRC § 2632(c)(3)(B)(ii).

A few presumptions apply in determining whether the 25-percent exceptions to the definition of a GST trust are satisfied. First, rights of withdrawal for this purpose do not include withdrawal rights that do not exceed the amount of the annual gift tax exclusion under § 2503(b). IRC § 2632(c)(3)(B) (flush paragraph). Hence, a beneficiary's *Crummey* right of withdrawal[13] is disregarded in determining the portion of a trust an individual may withdraw under § 2632(c). Second, it is presumed that all powers of appointment held by non-skip persons will not be exercised. *Id.* The second presumption is designed to eliminate questions regarding the total value of the trust corpus that serves as the reference point for determining whether the 25 percent test is satisfied. Any discretionary powers of invasion held by non-skip persons therefore will not operate to reduce the denominator of the fraction, but will be considered only for purposes of determining whether more than 25 percent of the trust corpus may be withdrawn by non-skip persons.[14]

The exceptions to the definition of a GST trust in this context are perhaps best explained through illustration. Suppose a parent established a trust for the benefit of his child, with any property remaining in the trust at the child's death to be distributed to the child's issue. The child is entitled to receive the net income of the trust on an annual basis, and the trustee possesses the ability to distribute trust principal to the child for his health, support, or maintenance. In addition, the child may withdraw 10 percent of the trust corpus upon attaining age 30, an additional 20 percent upon attaining age 35, and an additional 30 percent upon attaining age 50. Because the child, a non-skip person, possesses the right to withdraw more than 25 percent of the trust corpus prior to attaining age 46, the trust is not a GST trust warranting a deemed allocation of parent's GST exemption. *See* IRC § 2632(c)(3)(B)(i).

Alternatively, assume that a grantor establishes a discretionary trust for the benefit of his wife for her lifetime. Upon the wife's death, the trustee is directed to distribute an amount equal to 10 percent of the trust principal to each of the grantor's four children who are then living. The balance of the trust assets will continue to be held in trust for the benefit of the grantor's descendants. Assuming the grantor's wife is more than 10 years older than the grantor's children, the trust does not constitute a GST trust because more than 25 percent of the trust corpus will be distributed to those of the grantor's children who survive her. *See* IRC § 2632(c)(3)(B)(ii).

---

[13] The use of rights of withdrawal to qualify transfers in trust for the gift tax annual exclusion pursuant to the case of *Crummey v. Commissioner*, 397 F.2d 82 (9th Cir. 1968), is discussed in § 5.01[B].

[14] The breadth of the second statutory presumption is problematic. Because a right of withdrawal possessed by a beneficiary constitutes a power of appointment, a literal application of the statutory presumption would eliminate the 25 percent exception to the definition of a GST trust based on rights of withdrawal possessed by non-skip persons. Accordingly, the statutory presumption is sensible only if applied in determining the denominator—and not the numerator—of the portion of the trust that will be distributed to or may be withdrawn by non-skip persons.

[ii] Inclusion in Non-Skip Person's Gross Estate

The exceptions to the definition of a GST trust discussed above address the prospect of significant trust distributions to non-skip persons, which would dilute the benefit of any GST exemption allocated to the trust. The allocation of GST exemption would be similarly diluted if the trust assets will or may be subject to inclusion in the gross estate of a skip person.

Starting with the clearest case, if all or any portion of the trust assets would be included in the gross estate of a non-skip person if the non-skip person were to die immediately after the transfer, the trust is not a GST trust.[15] IRC § 2632(c)(3)(B)(iv). Returning to the example of a trust established by a parent for the lifetime benefit of his child with the remainder passing to the child's issue, suppose the child is age 40 when the trust is funded. If the child were to die immediately after the funding of the trust, approximately 32 percent of the trust principal would be included in the child's gross estate under § 2042(a)(2). Accordingly, the trust does not constitute a GST trust.

Because § 2632(c)(3)(B)(iv) applies if *any portion* of the trust assets would be included in the gross estate of a non-skip person, this exception to the definition of a GST trust would apply any time the trust provided a non-skip person with a *Crummey* right of withdrawal. To avoid this result, the statutory exception later provides that transferred property will not be considered to be includible in the gross estate of a non-skip person by reason of the possession of a power of withdrawal that does not exceed the amount of the gift tax annual exclusion under § 2503(b).

In addition to situations where a portion of the trust assets will be included in the gross estate of a non-skip person, exceptions to the definition of a GST trust exist for situations where a significant portion of the trust assets may be subject to estate tax in the hands of a non-skip person. Section 2632(c)(3)(B)(iii) supplies another 25 percent text in this context. The exception focuses on what would happen if a non-skip person were to die before attaining age 46 or before the death of an individual more than 10 years older than the non-skip person. If, in either event, more than 25 percent of the trust corpus would be paid to the probate estate of the non-skip person or subject to the non-skip person's general power of appointment, the trust will not be considered a GST trust. For example, if a trust established by a parent for his child provides the child with a power to appoint 30 percent of the trust property to his estate if the child dies prior to age 45, the trust is not a GST trust for § 2632(c) purposes.

[iii] Charitable Trusts

Because charitable organizations generally are assigned to the transferor's generation under § 2651(f)(3), it is not likely that an individual would want to automatically allocate GST exemption to a charitable trust. Accordingly, a GST trust for purposes of § 2632(c) does not include charitable lead annuity trusts, charitable remainder annuity trusts, or charitable remainder unitrusts. IRC § 2632(c)(3)(B)(v). Furthermore, a charitable lead unitrust is excepted from the definition of a GST trust if the principal of the trust will be paid to a non-skip person upon the termination of the charitable interest. IRC § 2632(c)(3)(B)(vi).

---

[15] Presumably this exception will not be triggered in the context of a lifetime QTIP trust solely by reason of the potential inclusion in the done-spouse's gross estate under § 2044 where the done-spouse has made a reverse QTIP election under § 2652(a)(3).

[3]   Specifics of Deemed Allocation

If an individual makes a transfer to a trust that constitutes an indirect skip during life, the individual's "unused portion" of his GST exemption is allocated to the transfer to the extent necessary to produce an inclusion ratio of zero. IRC § 2632(c)(1). The unused portion of the GST exemption is the portion remaining after express allocations, deemed allocations to direct skips, and prior deemed allocations to indirect skips. IRC § 2632(c)(2). If property transferred in an indirect skip is subject to being recaptured in the gross estate of the transferor or the transferor's spouse, the deemed allocation does not take place until the close of the estate tax inclusion period. IRC § 2632(c)(4). To the extent a transferor wishes to preclude a deemed allocation of GST exemption to an indirect skip, the transferor may so elect on a timely filed gift tax return for the year in which the deemed allocation would become effective. IRC § 2632(c)(5)(B)(i).

[D]   Retroactive Allocations

Suppose an individual creates a trust for the benefit of his child, the assets of which will be distributed to the child when the child attains age 35. If the child were to die before reaching the age of distribution, the trust assets will be distributed to the child's then-living issue, if any. No deemed allocation would be made under the provisions applicable to indirect skips, given the prospect of distribution to a non-skip person. See IRC § 2632(c)(3)(B)(i). One would not expect the individual to make an express allocation of GST exemption to the trust, given the slim prospects of the trust yielding a generation-skipping transfer. Yet what if those slim prospects were realized? In other words, what if the child were to die prior to the age of distribution, with the trust assets therefore being distributed to the child's issue? Under the regular GST tax regime, the child's death would constitute a taxable termination that could be shielded from GST tax consequences only if the transferor made a late allocation of GST exemption to the trust. Yet for the taxable termination to be fully exempt, the GST exemption allocated to the trust would have to equal the value of the trust assets as of the child's death. See IRC § 2642(b)(3). In certain situations, § 2632(d) will mitigate the otherwise harsh GST tax consequences that result from the untimely death of a non-skip person.

Section 2632(d) applies if the following conditions are satisfied: (1) a non-skip person who is assigned to a generation below the generation assignment of the transferor holds a chapter 13 interest in a trust or possesses a future interest in a trust to which a transfer has been made; (2) the non-skip person is a lineal descendant of a grandparent of the transferor or of a grandparent of the transferor's current or former spouse; and (3) the non-skip person predeceases the transferor. IRC § 2632(d)(1). By requiring the transferor to be predeceased by a relative assigned to a lower generation, the statute generally presumes an unnatural order of death. If these prerequisites are satisfied, the transferor may make an allocation of the transferor's unused GST exemption (determined as of the date immediately before the non-skip person's death) that will apply to any prior transfers to the trust on a chronological basis. *Id.* So long as this "retroactive allocation" is made on a timely filed gift tax return for the calendar year in which the non-skip person died, the value of the transfer to the trust is determined as if the allocation had been made on a timely-filed gift tax return *for the year in which the original transfer took place.* IRC § 2632(d)(2)(A). Assuming the trust assets have appreciated in value since funding, a retroactive allocation of an amount equal to the original contribution to the trust will shield the trust from future GST tax consequences. As a technical matter, the retroactive allocation becomes effective immediately prior to the non-skip person's death, *see* IRC § 2632(d)(2)(B), so that the allocation will operate to minimize, and possibly negate, the GST tax consequences resulting from the taxable termination.

In practice, § 2632(d) allows transferors to take a wait-and-see approach to transfers in trust that may, but likely will not, yield generation-skipping transfers. The transferor can wait to see if a non-skip person experiences an untimely death and, if so, make a late allocation of GST exemption to the trust that effectively will be treated as a timely allocation. In this manner, the transferor does not lose the opportunity to shield post-transfer appreciation in the trust property from GST tax consequences. The wait-and-see approach has its limits, however. If the untimely death of the non-skip person occurs after the death of the transferor, no retroactive allocation of GST exemption to the trust is possible. *See* IRC § 2632(d)(1)(C).

§ 22.04 ALLOCATION OF GST EXEMPTION TO PROPERTY INCLUDED IN GROSS ESTATE

Any GST exemption not consumed through an express or deemed allocation during an individual's lifetime remains available for allocation by the executor of the individual's estate. *See* IRC § 2631(a). An allocation of GST exemption by an individual's executor must be made by the due date for filing the estate tax return for the individual's estate (determined with regard to any extensions actually granted), regardless of whether an estate tax return is otherwise required. IRC § 2632(a); Treas. Reg. § 26.2632-1(d)(1).

While an executor may allocate GST exemption to lifetime transfers made by the decedent (which may be timely or late, based on the date the lifetime transfer took place), the executor also may allocate remaining GST exemption to property included in the decedent's estate for estate tax purposes. An allocation of GST exemption to property included in the gross estate is effective as of the date of the decedent's death, and the inclusion ratio with respect to such transfers is determined based on the estate tax value of the transferred property. IRC § 2642(b). Additionally, allocations of GST exemption may be made on a formulaic basis. *See* Treas. Reg. § 26.2632-1(d)(1). Hence, an allocation of an individual's unused GST exemption to a transfer equal to "the minimum amount necessary to produce an inclusion ratio of zero with respect to the transfer based on the value of the transferred property as finally determined for estate tax purposes" would be a permissible means of ensuring that the transfer would be exempt from current or future GST tax consequences, provided the value of the transfer does not exceed the available exemption. The value of a transfer itself often is defined in similar formulaic terms to ensure the ability to render the transfer fully exempt.

§ 22.05 RESIDUAL ALLOCATIONS

Any GST exemption that remains unallocated as of the due date for filing a decedent's estate tax return is allocated pursuant to the residual allocation regime of § 2632(e). The remaining GST exemption is allocated first to property that is the subject of a direct skip occurring at the decedent's death. IRC § 2632(e)(1)(A). A lifetime direct skip that was deferred as a result of an estate tax inclusion period that terminated by reason of the transferor's death is treated as a direct skip occurring at death for this purpose. IRC § 2642(f). If the amount of direct skips occurring at the transferor's death exceeds the amount of the unused GST exemption, the exemption will be prorated among the direct skips based on the relative nonexempt portions of each transfer. IRC § 2632(e)(2)(A). The nonexempt portion of each transfer is determined by multiplying the estate tax value of the transferred property by the inclusion ratio of the property (determined prior to the deemed allocation of exemption). IRC § 2632(e)(2)(B).

After allocating the unused GST exemption to direct skips occurring at death, any remaining exemption is allocated to transfers in trust with respect to which the decedent was the transferor and from which a taxable distribution or taxable termination may occur at or after the decedent's death. IRC § 2632(e)(1)(B). Again, to the extent the remaining GST exemption is not sufficient to cover all such transfers in trust, the remaining exemption is prorated among the transfers based on the relative values of their nonexempt portions.

§ 22.06   TRANSFERS ASSIGNED A ZERO INCLUSION RATIO

Certain lifetime direct skips are assigned an inclusion ratio of zero by statute, without the need to consume any portion of the transferor's GST exemption. As a general matter, these transfers are designed to extend the exclusions from the gift tax base to the GST tax.

[A]   Annual Exclusion Transfers

If an outright transfer by a donor to a skip person qualifies for the annual gift tax exclusion under § 2503(b), the transfer is statutorily assigned an inclusion ratio of zero. IRC § 2642(c)(1), (3). Hence, the transfer is effectively exempt from the GST tax as well as the gift tax. If the amount of the transfer to the skip person exceeds the prevailing amount of the annual gift tax exclusion, the transfer is divided into two portions: one being equal to the annual exclusion amount having a zero inclusion ratio, and the other being equal to the excess of the transfer over the annual exclusion amount. *See* Treas. Reg. § 26.2642-1(d), Ex. 3. The second portion of the transfer will have an inclusion ratio of zero only if sufficient GST exemption is allocated to that portion.

If an annual exclusion gift for the benefit of a skip person is made in trust, the direct skip will be assigned a zero inclusion ratio only if the trust meets certain conditions. First, the trust must be established for the lifetime benefit of only one individual. During the life of the individual, no portion of the trust income or principal may be distributed to any person other than the individual for whose benefit the trust was created. IRC § 2642(c)(2)(A). Additionally, if the trust remains in existence at the individual's death, the trust assets must be included in the individual's gross estate. IRC § 2642(c)(2)(B). The second requirement could be satisfied by causing the trust assets to be distributed to the beneficiary's estate, or by providing the beneficiary with a general power of appointment over the trust property. In essence, for a direct skip transfer in trust to qualify for the statutory inclusion ratio of zero, the beneficiary must be afforded the equivalent of ownership of the trust property for estate tax purposes.

Providing a trust beneficiary with a lapsing power to withdraw a contribution to a trust (that is, a *Crummey* power) serves as the most common means of qualifying transfers in trust for the annual gift tax exclusion.[16] The justification for not treating the transfer as one of a future interest is that the right of withdrawal renders the power holder the constructive initial transferee of the gift. This substance-over-form characterization, however, does not apply for § 2642(c) purposes. Rather, for GST tax purposes, a transfer in trust subject to a right of withdrawal is treated as a transfer in trust as opposed to a transfer to the trust beneficiary. *See* Treas. Reg. § 26.2612-1(f), Ex. 3. Accordingly, a lifetime direct skip to a discretionary trust

---

[16] The use of rights of withdrawal to qualify transfers in trust for the gift tax annual exclusion pursuant to the case of *Crummey v. Commissioner*, 397 F.2d 82 (9th Cir. 1968), is discussed in § 5.01[B].

for the benefit of the transferor's grandchildren will not qualify for a zero inclusion rate under § 2642(c), even if the transfer is shielded from gift tax by the powers of withdrawal afforded to the trust beneficiaries. Additionally, providing a grandchild who constitutes the sole lifetime beneficiary of a trust with a power to withdraw the trust contribution will not qualify the transfer for a statutory zero inclusion ratio under § 2642(c) unless the trust assets will be included in the grandchild's gross estate at death.

[B] Transfers for Tuition and Medical Expenses

In addition to transfers excluded from the gift tax base by reason of the annual exclusion under § 2503(b), payments for tuition or medical expenses made for the benefit of a skip person that are excluded from the gift tax base under § 2503(e) are statutorily assigned an inclusion ratio of zero. IRC § 2642(c)(1), (3). Accordingly, a grandparent's direct payment of a grandchild's college tuition will not carry GST tax consequences.

§ 22.07 PLANNING CONSIDERATIONS

Tax planning with respect to the GST exemption generally focuses on two primary goals: (1) leveraging the exemption to shield future appreciation in transferred property from GST tax consequences, and (2) ensuring that the exemption is not wasted through an allocation to property that likely will be included in the gift tax or estate tax base of a non-skip person. The first goal is achieved through the creation of trusts designed to have an inclusion ratio of zero. The second goal is achieved through the creation of trusts that have skip persons as the primary if not exclusive beneficiaries.

To illustrate, assume a client asks you to review her existing estate plan. Her will leaves the residue of her estate (estimated in the $15 million range) to a trust benefiting her descendants. The trust directs the trustee to distribute the net income of the trust to her children in equal shares (with the share of any deceased child being paid to that child's issue, if any) until the death of her last surviving child, at which point the trust will be distributed to her then-living issue, *per stirpes*. The trust also permits the trustee to make discretionary distributions of trust principal to the client's children or grandchildren for the recipient's health, education, support, or maintenance, with preference being afforded to the needs of her children.

Note the GST tax consequences if the client's estate plan were implemented without revision. First, it would not be possible to render the trust fully exempt from GST tax consequences. Assuming a $5 million remaining GST exemption and a $15 million transfer, the trust would have an inclusion ratio of 2/3. Hence, if the property were to appreciate in value after the client's death, only 1/3 of the future appreciation would be effectively shielded from GST tax consequences. Additionally, the GST exemption that is allocated to the trust will not be maximized for the benefit of skip persons. The trust accumulations will be depleted through annual income distributions to the client's children, and the trustee is directed to prefer the interests of the children in making any discretionary distributions of principal.

With these drawbacks in mind, what alterations could be made to maximize the benefit of the client's GST exemption? At a minimum, the single trust should be divided into two. The first trust would be funded with an amount equal to the client's remaining GST exemption, with the excess being used to fund the second trust.[17] By design, the division will allow the client's executor to allocate the GST exemption to the first trust to create an inclusion ratio of zero (with the second trust having an inclusion ratio of one). While exempting 100 percent of the appreciation in 1/3 of the transferred property from GST tax consequences alone is not an improvement over exempting 1/3 percent of the appreciation of the whole, the division would permit the trustee to make discretionary distributions of principal to children from the non-exempt portion of the trust. Additionally, the investment portfolio of the exempt trust may emphasize capital appreciation, with the investment strategy of the non-exempt trust making an offsetting allocation in favor of current return.

To achieve the second goal of GST exemption planning, the client should consider eliminating the mandatory income payment to her children from the GST exempt trust and, perhaps, altering the dispositive provisions of the non-exempt trust to make up any shortfall (perhaps through an annual right of withdrawal over a portion of trust principal). While the client's children could remain as discretionary beneficiaries of the GST exempt trust, the trust instruments should state a preference the discretionary distributions to a child be made from the non-exempt trust to the extent possible. In this manner, the assets of the GST exempt trust will be preserved for ultimate distribution to the client's grandchildren.

As a final matter, the client should weigh the GST tax consequences of the taxable termination of the non-exempt trust that occur upon the death of her last surviving child with the estate tax consequences to her children if each child's portion of the trust assets were subject to estate tax at the child's estate. Depending on the anticipated net wealth of her children, it may be preferable to expose the trust assets to estate taxation at the child level (perhaps through the creation of testamentary general powers of appointment over each child's share of the non-exempt trust). Doing so may subject the trust property to lower effective estate tax rates through the use of each child's unified credit, as opposed to exposing the trust assets to the maximum GST tax rate of 35 percent when the death of the last child yields a taxable termination.

§ 22.08 STUDY PROBLEMS

1. Gerald has two children, Ellen and Evan. Ellen has one son, Frank, and Evan has one daughter, Fran. Gerald makes the following transfers to or for the benefit of his grandchildren:

   - On February 1, Year 1, Gerald transfers 1,000 shares of stock in X Corp. to Fran. On the date of the transfer, the X Corp. stock is valued at $80 per share.

   - On August 1, Year 1, Gerald pays $45,000 to the college where Fran is enrolled to cover that year's tuition.

   - On September 1, Year 1, Gerald transfers 3,000 shares of stock in Y Corp. to

---

[17] If this change were not made prior to the client's death, § 2642(a)(3) provides a mechanism by which a single trust may be divided into two or more trusts for chapter 13 purposes through a "qualified severance." For the division to constitute a qualified severance, the division must be permitted by the trust instrument or by local law; the trust must be divided on a fractional basis; and the new trusts must, in the aggregate, provide for the same succession of beneficial interests as provided under the original trust. IRC § 2642(a)(3)(B)(i). If a trust to be divided has an inclusion ratio between one and zero, the trust must be divided into two portions on a fractional basis, with the portion of the first trust equaling the applicable fraction of the initial trust (which therefore can be rendered fully exempt). The second trust resulting from the division will have an inclusion ratio of one. IRC § 2642(a)(3)(B)(ii).

Frank. On the date of the transfer, the Y Corp. stock is valued at $40 per share.

- On October 1, Year 1, Gerald pays $25,000 to Frank's orthopaedic surgeon, representing charges stemming from Frank's knee surgery.

- On January 15, Year 2, X Corp. announces that one of its promising pharmaceutical drugs has passed FDA approval. Following the announcement, the stock trades for around $200 per share for the remainder of the year.

- On May 1, Year 2, the Y Corp. stock plummets to $10 per share after the corporation disclosed that past irregularities in its financial statement reporting. The stock hovers near this level for the remainder of the year.

a.   Assuming that Gerald has never heard of the GST tax and therefore takes no steps to allocate GST exemption, discuss the default GST tax consequences of the above transfers. Further assume that Gerald has not made any prior generation-skipping transfers.

b.   If you could have provided Gerald with timely advice to improve his GST tax exposure, what would you have suggested?

2.   Assume that, in addition to the above transfers, Gerald makes the following lifetime transfers to or for the benefit of his children and grandchildren during Year 2:

- $1.5 million in trust (Trust 1) for the primary benefit of Ellen. The trustee is authorized to distribute the net income to Ellen on an annual basis, and the trustee further possesses discretion to distribute principal to Ellen or her children as the trustee determines necessary or appropriate. Upon Ellen's death, the trust principal is to be distributed to those of Ellen's issue as she shall direct by will; in default thereof, the trust principal shall be distributed to Ellen's then-living issue, *per stirpes*. Gerald designates himself as the initial trustee. Gerald allocates $1.5 million of his GST exemption to the trust on a timely-filed gift tax return.

- $1.3 million in trust (Trust 2) for the primary benefit of Evan. The trustee is authorized to distribute as much of the trust income and principal to Evan during his lifetime as the trustee deems necessary and appropriate. Any income not so distributed is to be accumulated and added to principal. When Evan attains age 40, he is entitled to withdraw one-third of the trust principal. When he attains age 50, he is permitted to withdraw the balance. If Evan dies prior attaining age 50, the trust is to be distributed to his then-living issue, *per stirpes*. A third party is designated to serve as trustee. Gerald fails to allocate any portion of his GST exemption to the trust.

a.   Discuss the GST tax consequences of the transfers made by Gerald.

b.   Assume that Gerald resigns as trustee of Trust 1 in Year 4, when the trust property is worth $2 million. What are the GST tax consequences of his resignation?

c.   Assume that, in Year 10, Evan predeceases Gerald at the age of 38 when the trust is valued at $4 million. Per the trust instrument, the trust principal is to be distributed to Evan's children in equal shares. Can Gerald minimize the GST tax consequences of these events?

3. Kelly makes the following dispositions in her will, having made no lifetime gratuitous transfers:

    -   $100,000 to each of her ten grandchildren who survive her;

    -   $2 million in trust for the benefit of her grandchildren. The trustee is directed to distribute the net income of the trust to her grandchildren in equal shares (with any share of a deceased grandchild being paid to his or her issue) until the death of the last surviving grandchild, at which point the trust property will be distributed to Kelly's then-living issue, *per stirpes*.

    -   The residue of her estate (estimated at $6 million) passes in a single trust for the benefit of her descendants. The trust provides the trustee with discretion to distribute income and, to the extent necessary, principal to any of Kelly's children or grandchildren for the recipient's health, education, support, or maintenance. Upon the death of Kelly's last surviving child, the trust assets are to be distributed to Kelly's then-living issue, *per stirpes*.

    a. Discuss the GST tax consequences of these transfers, assuming Kelly's executor makes no express allocation of GST exemption.

    b. What recommendations do you have to improve the use of the GST exemption afforded to Kelly?

Chapter 23

THE BUSINESS ENTITY ESTATE FREEZE

In 1990, Congress enacted four valuation provisions (§§ 2701–2704) that comprise chapter 14 of the Code.[1] These "special valuation rules" address planning techniques that permitted taxpayers to exploit general valuation principles to undervalue lifetime transfers or to otherwise depress the transfer tax value of retained property. One such provision, § 2702, has been addressed in the context of retained-interest transfers in trust.[2] Recall that § 2702 targets the potential for transferors to exploit the assumptions underlying the § 7520 valuation tables to overvalue a donor's retained interest in transferred property. Section 2702 addresses this prospect in a heavy-handed manner, assigning a zero value to the retained interest unless the interest takes a statutorily sanctioned form that protects the integrity of the actuarial valuation.

In many respects, § 2701 can be conceived as the business-entity corollary to § 2702. Section 2701 targets the potential to undervalue the transfer of a residual equity interest in a corporation or partnership where the transferor's retained preferred interest is valued by reference to discretionary rights that may not (and likely will not) be maximized by the transferor. Section 2701 follows the approach of § 2702 by assigning a zero value to certain discretionary rights relating to a senior equity interest retained by the transferor unless those rights fall within a statutory safe harbor that ensures a payment stream to the transferor.

Section 2701 potentially applies to any recapitalization or contribution of property to a closely held entity that has more than one class of equity. Because the statute can rear its head in a variety of transactions that are not driven by federal transfers tax considerations, § 2701 presents a significant trap for the unwary—one that carries potentially dire gift tax consequences depending on the value of the entity. Most of the planning associated § 2701 therefore centers on avoiding its application altogether. With that in mind, this chapter focuses primarily on the conditions to and exceptions from the statute's application.

§ 23.01 THE PROTOTYPICAL TRANSACTION

Given the considerable level of detail and complexity surrounding § 2701, it is helpful to first approach the statute from the standpoint of a prototypical transaction the statute was designed to address. Suppose an individual who owns the only class of stock of a closely held corporation seeks to transfer future appreciation in the entity to her children at minimal transfer tax cost. To accomplish this goal, the individual recapitalizes the corporation into two classes of stock: (1) preferred stock that she will retain, and (2) common stock that she will transfer to her

---

[1] Omnibus Budget Reconciliation Act of 1990, Pub. L. No. 101-508, § 11602, 104 Stat. 1388, 1388-491 to -501.

[2] *See* § 10.05[B].

children.[3] In an attempt to minimize the value of the transferred common stock, the preferred stock is adorned with a variety of non-mandatory economic rights, such as a non-cumulative preference to dividend distributions and a right to put the stock to the corporation at a substantial per-share price. While the parent is not likely to maximize the economic rights relating to the preferred stock, a hypothetical willing purchaser of the common stock transferred to the children certainly would take those rights into consideration in making a purchase offer. In this manner, the value of the preferred stock could be tailored to equal the entire present value of the entity, allowing the parent to "freeze" her transfer tax base at the current value of her equity holdings. The transfer of the right to future appreciation in the entity would be accomplished free of transfer tax.

The corporate estate freeze technique described above was employed in *Snyder v. Commissioner*, 93 T.C. 529 (1989). The taxpayer transferred publicly traded stock worth approximately $2,592,000 to a corporation in exchange for 2,591 shares of preferred stock that could be called at the election of the preferred shareholders at $1,000 per share. The preferred stock therefore was valued at $2,591,000, leaving just $1,000 of value allocated to the common stock that the taxpayer transferred to her grandchildren. Any future appreciation in the assets contributed to the corporation therefore would inure to the holders of the common stock, and any appreciation in the value of the common stock would escape the taxpayer's transfer tax base.

Congress first attempted to address the preferred stock estate freeze through an expansion of the estate tax base. Section 2036(c), added in 1987, treated the retention of a "substantial interest" in an enterprise by any person who transferred a "disproportionately large" share of the future appreciation in such interest as retaining the enjoyment of the transferred property under § 2036(a)(1).[4] Responding to complaints concerning the vagueness and potential over-breadth of this approach, Congress retroactively repealed § 2036(c) when it introduced the chapter 14 valuation regime.[5] As discussed below, § 2701 addresses the business entity estate freeze technique primarily through an expansion of the gift tax base. However, the scope of § 2701 remains broad, and its provisions should be consulted anytime there is a transfer of a residual equity interest in an entity to a family member even if the transfer is not motivated by transfer tax considerations.

§ 23.02   SCOPE OF SECTION 2701

Internal Revenue Code:	§ 2701(a)–(c), (e)(1)–(5)
Treasury Regulations:	§§ 25.2701-1(a) to (b), 25.2701-2(b)(1) to (5), 25.2701-6

---

[3] Note that this recapitalization can be accomplished on a nonrecognition basis for income tax purposes. *See* IRC § 368(a)(1)(E).

[4] *See* Omnibus Budget Reconciliation Act of 1987, Pub. L. No. 100-203, § 10402(a), 100 Stat. 1330, 1330-431 to -432, *as amended by* Technical and Miscellaneous Revenue Act of 1988, Pub. L. No. 100-647, § 3031, 102 Stat. 3342, 3634–40.

[5] Omnibus Budget Reconciliation Act of 1990, Pub. L. No. 101-508, § 11601, 104 Stat. 1388, 1388-490 to -491.

[A]   General Prerequisites

[1]   Transfer of Equity Interest to Member of Family

Section 2701 applies only to the transfer of an interest in a corporation or partnership[6] to or for the benefit of a member of the transferor's family. IRC § 2701(a)(1). While the scope of the transferor's family for this purpose includes the transferor's spouse, the definition generally focuses on younger generations by including lineal descendants of the transferor or the transferor's spouse, as well as spouses of any such lineal descendants. IRC § 2701(e). Thus, upstream transfers of beneficial interests to the transferor's parents and lateral transfers of beneficial interests to the transferor's siblings do not implicate the statute.

Because § 2701 applies to determine both the existence and amount of any gift of an equity interest, application of the statute depends on the existence of a completed gift. Hence, if the transferor retains sufficient control over the transferred equity interest to render the transfer incomplete for gift tax purposes,[7] § 2701 will not apply. *See* Treas. Reg. § 25.2701-1(b)(1). However, this is not to say that § 2701 is conditioned upon the existence of a taxable gift. If the transfer of the equity interest would not otherwise constitute a gift because the transferee supplied adequate and full consideration (as determined under general valuation principles) for the property, the transfer nonetheless will remain subject to § 2701. In that case, the adequacy of the consideration supplied by the transferee must be determined by reference to the value of the transferred equity interest as determined under the special valuation rules supplied by § 2701.

[2]   Retention of Applicable Retained Interest by Transferor or Applicable Family Member

The transfer of an equity interest to a member of the transferor's family does not alone trigger the valuation regime of § 2701. In addition, the transferor or an "applicable family member" must hold an "applicable retained interest" in the entity. IRC § 2701(a)(1)(B). The scope of applicable family members for purposes of § 2701 can be conceived as the corollary to the definition of the transferor's family. In addition to the transferor's spouse, applicable family members include ancestors of the transferor or the transferor's spouse, as well as spouses of any such ancestors. IRC § 2701(e)(2). Hence, the applicable retained interest must reside in a generation equivalent to or higher than that of the transferor.

[B]   Scope of Applicable Retained Interest

The heart of § 2701 lies in the definition of an "applicable retained interest." Such an interest can take one of two general forms: (1) a "distribution right" with respect to a controlled entity, or (2) a liquidation, put, call, or conversion right in any entity (which the regulations refer to collectively as an "extraordinary payment right"). IRC § 2701(b)(1); Treas. Reg. § 25.2701-2(b)(1).

---

[6] A limited liability company (LLC) that has two or more members is treated as a partnership for federal transfer tax purposes unless the LLC elects to be classified as an association (and therefore taxed as a corporation). *See* Treas. Reg. § 301.7701-3(a), (b).

[7] For discussion of when the retention of control over transferred property will render a gift incomplete, see § 11.08.

[1] Extraordinary Payment Rights

Extraordinary payment rights include any (a) put right (a right to require the entity to purchase equity), (b) call right (a right to acquire one or more classes of equity in the entity), (c) conversion right (a right to convert one class of equity to another), (d) right to compel liquidation of the entity, and (e) similar right the exercise or nonexercise of which affects the value of the transferred equity interest. IRC § 2701(c)(2); Treas. Reg. § 25.2701-2(b)(2). Because possession of these rights provides the holder with the unilateral ability to enhance the value of the retained equity interest, extraordinary payment rights do not require the holder to possess control over the entity.

[2] Distribution Rights

As a general rule, a distribution right in an entity is the right to receive distributions with respect to an equity interest. IRC § 2701(c)(1); Treas. Reg. § 25.2701-2(b)(3). Because the economic benefit attributable to distribution rights depends on the entity declaring an operating distribution, distribution rights implicate § 2701 only if the transferor and "applicable family members" possess control of the entity immediately after the transfer of the beneficial interest to a member of the transferor's family. IRC § 2701(b)(1)(A).

Adding to the complexity of § 2701, the definition of "applicable family members" for purposes of determining whether a distribution right constitutes an applicable retained interest differs from the meaning of that term for purposes of the § 2701 general rule. Solely for purposes of determining whether the transferor and applicable family members possess control over an entity so as to render a distribution right an applicable retained interest, applicable family members also include any lineal descendant of a parent of the transferor or the transferor's spouse. IRC § 2701(b)(2)(C). "Control" of an entity necessitates (a) the possession of at least 50 percent of the stock of a corporation (determined by voting power or value), (b) the possession of at least 50 percent of the capital or profits interests in any partnership, or (c) the possession of an interest as a general partner in a limited partnership.[8] IRC § 2701(b)(2). This threshold for control will be easily satisfied in the context of most family-owned entities.

Notwithstanding the above, a distribution right does not constitute an applicable retained interest sufficient to trigger application of § 2701 if the distribution right relates to a class of equity that is equal to or subordinate to the transferred equity interest. IRC § 2701(c)(1)(B)(i); Treas. Reg. § 25.2701-2(b)(3)(i). In short, the distribution right must relate to a senior equity interest. Additionally, if a distribution right can be characterized as an extraordinary payment right, the latter characterization takes precedence. IRC § 2701(c)(1)(B)(ii); Treas. Reg. § 25.2701-2(b)(3)(ii). This resolution operates to maximize the reach of the § 2701 valuation rules, as an extraordinary payment right does not depend on the transferor and applicable family members possessing control of the entity.

---

[8] By analogy, presumably any interest in an manager-managed LLC held by a manager would constitute control for purposes of § 2701(b)(2). A member-managed LLC, on the other hand, presumably would be treated as a general partnership for purposes of § 2701(b)(2), so that a determination of control would depend on the possession of the requisite percentage interest in the LLC's capital or profits.

[3]   Exclusion for Nondiscretionary Rights

Recall that the statutory purpose of § 2701 is to prevent the overvaluation of retained equity interests that embody economic rights that may (or may not) be maximized at the discretion of the transferor. With this purpose in mind, the otherwise broad scope of applicable retained interests under § 2701 must be narrowed to exclude what may be characterized as mandatory economic rights—that is, economic rights whose exercise or maximization are not subject to the discretion of the holder.

[a]   Mandatory Payment Rights

The first exclusion from the scope of an extraordinary payment right or a distribution right applies to "mandatory payment rights." Treas. Reg. § 25.2701-2(b)(4)(i). A mandatory payment right is fairly self explanatory, encompassing a right to receive a payment that is required to be made at a specific time for a specific amount. A redemption right with respect to preferred stock that requires the entity to purchase the stock at par value on a date certain therefore does not constitute an extraordinary payment right or a distribution right for purposes of § 2701. *Id.* Similarly, the obligation of an entity to purchase an interest at a defined price upon the occurrence of an ascertainable event—such as the death of the owner of the interest—does not give rise to an applicable retained interest. *Id.* Such mandatory buy-sell provisions are common in the context of closely held entities, and their existence does not present the holder with an opportunity to shift value to the owners of the residual equity.[9] If the payment must take place, the holder of the right cannot deflect that value to another through a failure to exercise.

[b]   Liquidation Participation Rights

A common aspect of equity interests in business-related entities is a right to participate in the liquidation of an entity. If this right alone constituted an applicable retained interest, then the retention of any senior equity interest would trigger application of § 2701. Hence, the regulations exclude the right to participate in a liquidating distribution from the definition of an extraordinary payment right. Treas. Reg. § 25.2701-2(b)(4)(ii). This treatment does not change even if the transferor, members of the transferor's family, or applicable family members possess the ability to compel liquidation of the entity. Rather, the liquidation participation right in this setting generally is valued as if the right to compel liquidation did not exist. Treas. Reg. § 25.2701-2(b)(4)(ii)(A).

[c]   Rights to Guaranteed Payments

The right of a corporate shareholder to receive compensation for services rendered to the entity does not constitute a distribution right, because the distribution is not made with respect to the shareholder-employee's stock ownership. To maintain parity in the partnership setting, a § 2701 distribution right does not include a partner's right to receive a § 707(c) guaranteed payment, provided the guaranteed payment is of a fixed amount. IRC § 2701(c)(1)(B)(iii). To ensure that the payment right is in no way discretionary, the regulations require that the payment not be contingent as to time or amount to be considered fixed. Treas. Reg. § 25.2701-2(b)(4)(iii).

---

[9] Whether rights to acquire property pursuant to buy-sell provisions in shareholder agreements or partnership agreements are binding for federal transfer tax purposes is addressed by § 2703. *See* § 24.02.

[d]   Non-Lapsing Conversion Rights

A right to convert a retained equity interest in a corporation does not constitute an extraordinary payment right if the conversion right does not lapse and is not subject to dilution. Specifically, the non-lapsing right to convert (a) must relate to a fixed number of shares or a fixed percentage of the transferred class of stock (without regard to non-lapsing differences in voting power); (b) must provide for adjustment to account for stock splits, class combinations, and other similar changes in the corporate capital structure; and (c) must provide for adjustment to account for accumulated but unpaid distributions with respect to the retained interest. IRC § 2701(c)(2)(C). The regulations provide a similar exception for partnerships, and this exception clarifies that the conversion right may not relate to a specified interest in a partnership that is limited by a fixed dollar amount. Treas. Reg. § 25.2701-2(b)(4)(iv)(B). While the conversion right must be related to an equity interest in the partnership of the same class as the equity interest initially transferred, non-lapsing differences in management rights or limitations on liability are permitted. *Id.* Because these rights to convert are non-lapsing and not subject to dilution, they do not present the discretionary ability to shift value from the retained equity interest to the holders of the transferred residual equity.

[C]   Indirect Transfers

The first prerequisite to the application of § 2701 is the transfer of an equity interest from the transferor to a member of the transferor's family. The statute could be easily avoided if it were limited to express transfers. The application of § 2701 therefore extends to indirect transfers that have the effect of (a) providing the transferor or an applicable family with an applicable retained interest in the entity, or (b) enhancing the value of an applicable retained interest held by the taxpayer or an applicable family member immediately after the transaction. IRC § 2701(e)(5). Generally speaking, the indirect transfers to which § 2701 applies are those that offer the potential for taxpayers to freeze the transfer tax value of their holdings.

[1]   Contributions to Capital

A contribution of capital to a new or existing entity constitutes a transfer for purposes of § 2701. Treas. Reg. § 25.2701-1(b)(2)(i)(A). For instance, if a taxpayer who owns the preferred stock of a corporation transfers property to the corporation for no consideration other than any enhancement in the value of her stock interest attributable to the contribution, the transaction constitutes an indirect transfer of an equity interest to the owner of the common stock. Accordingly, if the owner of the common stock is a member of the taxpayer's family, § 2701 applies to determine the existence and amount of the gift.

[2]   Capital Structure Transactions

Section 2701 can be implicated by indirect transfers of equity interests that occur as the result of a redemption, recapitalization, or other change in the capital structure of the entity. Treas. Reg. § 25.2701-1(b)(2)(i)(B). These capital structure transactions may trigger application of § 2701 in one of three ways.

The first avenue is the most straightforward. If the transferor or an applicable family member receives an applicable retained interest as a result of the transaction, the transaction constitutes a § 2701 transfer. Treas. Reg. § 25.2701-1(b)(2)(i)(B)(*1*). For example, if a single class of corporate stock is held by a parent and her children, a redemption of the parent's stock holdings in exchange for preferred stock in the entity implicates § 2701. This transaction is functionally equivalent to the contribution of property in exchange for all classes of equity that were enhanced by the contribution, followed by a transfer of the residual interest.

The second capital structure transaction that may implicate § 2701 involves the exchange of a junior equity interest for value. If the transferor or an applicable family member transfers an equity interest that is subordinate to the applicable retained interest and receives property other than an applicable retained interest, the transaction constitutes a transfer for § 2701 purposes. Treas. Reg. § 25.2701-1(b)(2)(i)(B)(*2*). The theory is that the termination of a preferred equity holder's interest in the residual class of equity increases the percentage of the residual equity class held by members of the transferor's family, thereby accomplishing the same result as a direct transfer of a transferor's residual equity interest.

The third capital structure transaction that may implicate § 2701 involves the surrender of a preferred interest by one who continues to hold an applicable retained interest following the transfer. If the transferor or an applicable family member holds an applicable retained interest prior to the transaction and surrenders an equity interest in the entity other than a subordinate or residual interest, the transaction constitutes an indirect transfer for purposes of § 2701 when the transaction operates to increase the value of the applicable retained interest. Treas. Reg. § 25.2701-1(b)(2)(i)(B)(*3*). This transaction therefore contemplates at least three classes of equity, with a relinquishment of one class of preferred equity that increases the value of the remaining preferred class. In this manner, the transaction is functionally equivalent to the transfer of property in exchange for an applicable retained interest in the entity.

As a general rule, none of the capital structure transactions will constitute indirect transfers for § 2701 purposes if the interests in the entity held by the transferor, applicable family members, and members of the transferor's family before and after the transaction are substantially identical. IRC § 2701(e)(5) (flush paragraph). However, this exception does not apply to an indirect transfer occurring by way of a contribution to capital, *see id.*, as the indirect transfer occurs in that event *because* the relative equity interests remain the same following the contribution of property.

[3] Transactions Concerning Equity Interests Held Indirectly

The transactions that implicate § 2701 described above assume that an applicable retained interest in the entity is held by the transferor or applicable family members immediately after the transfer. Yet, as a practical matter, the same transactions can be accomplished through the imposition of an intervening business entity, trust, or estate. Section 2701 therefore envisions indirect ownership of equity interests, *see* IRC § 2701(e)(3), and the relevant attribution rules are supplied by Reg. § 25.2701-6.

The ownership attribution rules for corporations and partnerships are based on proportionate fair market value of the transferor's holdings of the intervening entity. Treas. Reg. § 25.2701-6(a)(1)–(3). Hence, if the corporation or partnership holding the relevant equity interest itself has only one class of equity, the entity's holdings are attributed to its owners on a pro-rata basis. As an example, assume *Parent* owns all of the stock of X Corp. X Corp., in turn, owns the Class A preferred stock and Class B preferred stock in Y Corp. The common stock of Y Corp. is held by *Parent* and *Child* in equal shares. Under this scenario, the transfer of *Parent's* common stock in Y Corp. to *Child* would constitute a § 2701 transfer, because *Parent* holds an applicable retained interest in Y Corp. through X Corp. *See* Treas. Reg. 25.2701-6(a)(2). For similar reasons, a contribution to the capital of Y Corp. by X Corp. would constitute an indirect transfer under § 2701, as would the retirement of the Class B preferred stock in Y Corp. if the value of the Class A preferred stock were thereby enhanced.

The attribution rules that apply to equity interests held by estates and trusts are more complicated. As a general rule, an individual is considered to own an equity interest actually held by an estate or trust to the extent the individual's beneficial interest could be satisfied by a distribution of the equity interest (or the income it generates), assuming the maximum exercise of discretion by the fiduciary. Treas. Reg. § 25.2701-6(a)(4). As the same equity interest could be attributed to multiple beneficiaries under this rule, the regulations prioritize the attribution of interests among multiple beneficiaries. The prescribed prioritization is designed to maximize the reach of § 2701. In particular, subordinate equity interests are allocated to members of the transferor's family before being allocated to the transferor or applicable family members. *See* Treas. Reg. § 25.2701-6(a)(5).

§ 23.03 TRANSACTIONS EXCLUDED FROM APPLICATION OF § 2701

Internal Revenue Code: § 2701(a)(2)
Treasury Regulations: § 25.2701-1(c)

Section 2701(a)(2) details a number of instances in which the special valuation rules of the statute will not apply to a right pertaining to an applicable retained interest held by the transferor or an applicable family member.

[A] Marketable Securities

If market quotations are readily available with respect to the applicable retained interest, § 2701 does not apply to value any right relating to the interest. IRC § 2701(a)(2)(A). In this context, there exists no opportunity for the transferor to overstate the value of the applicable retained interest. The value of the retained interest will be determined objectively by the market.

[B] Retention of Same Class as Transferred Equity Interest

If the applicable retained interest is of the same class as the transferred equity interest, there exists no potential to freeze the value of the retained interest by shifting the benefit of future appreciation in the value of the entity to members of the transferor's family. Rather than dividing economic rights temporally between present economic benefit and future appreciation, a transfer of the same class of equity merely transfers a portion of the same bundle of economic rights. Because the opportunity to effect an estate freeze is not possible with respect to a proportionate transfer, § 2701 does not apply to the valuation of the applicable retained interest. IRC § 2701(a)(2)(B).

Uniformity in voting rights is not required for equity to be treated as being of the same class for purposes of this exception. Treas. Reg. 25.2701-1(c)(3). Hence, the recapitalization of an S corporation into voting and non-voting common stock, followed by a parent's transfer of non-voting common stock to her children, would not implicate § 2701(a)(1). In the partnership setting, non-lapsing differences in management rights or limitations on liability will not cause equity interests to be of different classes.[10] *Id.* For example, suppose a member of an LLC who also serves as the entity's manager transfers a portion of her beneficial interest to a family member who is not a manager. So long as the transferred beneficial interest shares the same economic rights as the interest retained by the transferor (which would be the case if there existed only one class of beneficial interest), the transfer is excepted from the application of § 2701(a)(1).

[C] Retention of Interest Proportional to Transferred Interest

If the transferred interest is not of the same class as the applicable retained interest but the two interests nonetheless share economic rights in the entity in the same proportion, § 2701 does not apply in valuing the retained interest. IRC § 2701(a)(2)(C). As is the case in determining whether equity interests are of the same class, non-lapsing differences in voting rights and limitations on liability are disregarded in determining whether equity classes are proportionate to one another. As an example, assume that Class A stock and Class B stock share liquidating and operating distributions in a fixed ratio. The two classes are proportionate for purposes of § 2701(a)(2)(C), and thus a transfer of one class and a retention of the other does not trigger application of the § 2701 valuation rules. Note that, in substance, two classes of equity that share economic rights in a fixed ratio amount to nothing more than an elaborate division of a single class of equity.

[D] Proportionate Transfers

The regulations offer an additional exception to the application of § 2701, one that applies to proportionate transfers of the collective holdings of the transferor and applicable family members. *See* Treas. Reg. § 25.2701-1(c)(4). As a simple example, assume that a parent owns all of the preferred stock and common stock of a corporation, and transfers 25 percent of her holdings of each equity class to her children. While the transfer of the common stock may otherwise implicate § 2701 because the parent has retained the preferred stock, the transfer is sensibly exempted from the application of the statute because, taken as a whole, the parent has transferred a proportionate amount of her entire holdings in the entity.

The exception for proportionate transfers takes into account the holdings of applicable family members as well as those of the transferor. For example, assume that the preferred stock of a corporation is owned 60 percent by *Husband* and 40 percent by *Wife*, while the common stock is held 20 percent by *Husband* and 80 percent by *Wife*. As part of an integrated transaction, *Husband* and *Wife* transfer the following interests to their children: (1) a 20 percent interest in the preferred stock from *Husband*; (2) a 10 percent interest in the preferred stock from *Wife*; (3) a 25 percent interest in the common stock from *Wife*; and (4) a 5 percent interest in the common stock from *Husband*. While the transfers of common stock, viewed in isolation, would trigger application § 2701, the entire transaction results in a 30 percent reduction of *Husband* and *Wife's* ownership of the preferred stock and common stock. Because Reg. § 25.2701-1(c)(4) determines proportionate reductions based on the holdings of

---

[10] Non-lapsing provisions in a partnership agreement that are necessary to ensure compliance with the § 704(b) substantial economic effect safe harbor for allocation of tax items among the partners are treated as non-lapsing differences with respect to limitations on liability. Treas. Reg. § 25.2701-1(c)(3).

the transferor and applicable family members as a whole, the transfers are exempt from the application of § 2701.

§ 23.04   THE VALUATION REGIME OF § 2701

Internal Revenue Code: § 2701(a)(3)–(4), (d)
Treasury Regulations: §§ 25.2701-2, 25.2701-3

[A]   Assignment of Zero Value to Certain Retained Rights

The discussion thus far has centered on the predicates and exceptions to the application of the special valuation rules of § 2701, which accounts for the bulk of the statute's complexity. Once the application of the statute to the transfer of a subordinate equity interest in a partnership or corporation has been determined, the resulting gift tax valuation presumptions of the statute are fairly straightforward. As a general rule, rights relating to an applicable retained interest that trigger the application of § 2701—that is, distribution rights in a family-controlled entity and extraordinary payment rights—generally are assigned a zero value. IRC § 2701(a)(3)(A). In this manner, the statute effectively presumes that the discretionary economic entitlements inherent in these retained rights will not be maximized by the transferor, but instead will go unexercised so as to enhance the value of the transferred subordinate equity interest.

[B]   Exception for Qualified Payments

Not all distribution rights in family-controlled entities are subject to the zero-valuation presumption of § 2701(a)(3)(A). Rather, if a distribution right consists of a right to receive a qualified payment, the distribution right generally will be valued at its fair market value as determined under general valuation principles. *See* IRC § 2701(a)(3)(C). A qualified payment refers to a dividend on cumulative preferred stock or a comparable payment with respect to a partnership interest that is determined at a fixed rate.[11] IRC § 2701(c)(3)(A). Dividends or similar payments with respect to partnership interests that fluctuate based on market interest rates are considered to be fixed as to rate so long as there exists a fixed relationship between the payment and a specified market rate of interest. IRC § 2701(c)(3)(B).

Qualified payments are exempted from the zero-valuation presumption of § 2701(a)(3)(A) because they do not present the opportunity to shift value to other classes of equity. If the dividend payment or other operating distribution is not made, the economic right relating to the payment stream does not lapse. Rather, the payment right is preserved for the holders of the preferred equity interest. If the entity fails to meet its obligation to make qualified payments within a four-year grace period, the transferor's estate tax or gift tax base will be increased on account of the accumulated payment rights when the applicable retained interest is transferred.[12] *See* IRC § 2701(d). Because qualified payments may not be used to inflate the

---

[11] If the qualified payment right is held by an applicable family member as opposed to the transferor, the distribution right constitutes a qualified payment right only if the applicable family member makes an election to treat the distribution right as a qualified payment. *See* IRC § 2701(c)(3)(C)(i). While this election seems unnecessary, the possession of qualified payment rights can trigger future transfer tax consequences to the holder of the distribution rights. *See* IRC § 2701(d). The election therefore effectively reflects the consent of the applicable family member to the future application of the § 2701(d) regime.

[12] The additional transfer tax consequences relating to outstanding qualified payments are discussed in § 23.05.

value of a retained equity interest, a transferor or applicable family member may irrevocably elect to treat otherwise nonqualifying distribution rights as qualified payments to avoid the zero-value presumption.[13] IRC § 2701(c)(3)(C)(ii), (iii).

The treatment of qualified payments under § 2701 can be complicated if an applicable retained interest provides not only a distribution right that constitutes a qualified payment (generally exempt from the zero-value presumption) but also an extraordinary payment right (for which no exception exists). As an example, suppose that an individual transfers common stock to a member of his family while retaining cumulative preferred stock that may be redeemed at the option of the holder at a fixed price. In that case, the "lower of" rule of § 2701(a)(3)(B) applies, directing that the extraordinary payment right is presumed to be exercised in the manner that produces the lowest value for all of the retained rights, determined collectively. *See* Treas. Reg. § 25.2701-2(a)(3). Accordingly, if the present value of future rights to qualified payments exceeds the price at which the preferred stock may be put to the corporation, the transferor's preferred stock will be valued as if the put right were immediately exercised. *See* Treas. Reg. § 25.2701-2(a)(5), Ex.

[C] Application of Subtraction Method to Value Transferred Interest

By its terms, the special valuation regime of § 2701 does not value the transferred subordinate equity interest directly. Instead, the statute only supplies valuation assumptions for rights relating to the equity interests retained by the transferor or applicable family members. The regulations under § 2701 fill the gap by providing a step-by-step formula for determining the amount of the gift of the transferred equity interest. *See* Treas. Reg. § 25.2701-3. The regulatory framework employs its own terminology: (1) "family-held" refers to ownership by the transferor, applicable family members, lineal descendants of the transferor's parents, and lineal descendants of the parents of the transferor's spouse; (2) "senior equity interest" refers to any equity interest that carries a right to distributions of income or capital that is preferred to the rights of the transferred equity interest; and (3) "subordinate equity interest" refers to an equity interest in an entity in which a senior equity interest constitutes an applicable retained interest. Treas. Reg. § 25.2701-3(a)(2).

[1] General Approach

The subtraction method of valuing the transferred equity interest proceeds in four steps, each of which is detailed below:

Step 1: Determination of Starting Value. The starting point of the subtraction method of valuation is to determine the fair market value of all family-held equity interests immediately after the transfer. Although these interests may be held by multiple parties, the fair market value of the holdings for this purpose is determined by assuming that all interests are held by a single individual. Treas. Reg. § 25.2701-3(b)(1)(i). Hence, a control premium may be appropriate in determining the initial value of the family-held interests, even though no one person possesses voting control over the entity.

---

[13] Conversely, if the transferor desires to face the current gift tax consequence that would result from the zero-value presumption of § 2701(a)(3)(A), the transferor may irrevocably elect to treat a distribution right that constitutes a qualified payment as if the right were not a qualified payment. IRC § 2701(c)(3)(C)(i).

Step 2: Isolate Value of Subordinate Equity Interests. From the combined value of the family-held equity interests, the first amount to be subtracted is the value of the family-held senior equity interests other than applicable retained interests held by the transferor or applicable family members. Treas. Reg. § 25.2701-3(b)(2)(i)(A). Because these interests are not subject to the zero-value presumption of § 2701(a)(3)(A), these interests are valued at their fair market value. Additionally, any equity interest of an equivalent or lesser class than the transferred equity interests held by persons other than the transferor, members of the transferor's family, and applicable family members (the remaining group including collateral relatives such as siblings, nieces, and nephews) are subtracted at their fair market value. *Id.*

After making the subtractions above, the value of any applicable retained interests held by the transferor or applicable family members (other than an applicable retained interest received as consideration for the transfer) is addressed. Any such interest is valued at its § 2701 value. Treas. Reg. § 25.2701-3(b)(2)(i)(B). Hence, extraordinary payment rights are valued at zero, as are distribution rights that do not constitute qualified payments.[14] Additionally, a qualified payment distribution right that is coupled with an extraordinary payment right is valued pursuant to the "lower of" rule of § 2701(a)(3)(B).

Step 3. Apportionment of Subordinate Equity Interest. Following Step 2, the remaining value is attributable to the subordinate equity interests held by the transferor, applicable family members, and members of the transferor's family. The purpose of Step 3 is to isolate the amount of this residual value allocable to the subordinate equity interests transferred to members of the transferor's family. If there exists only one class of subordinate equity interest, the allocation among the parties is made on a pro-rata basis.[15] *See* Treas. Reg. § 25.2701-3(d), Ex. 4.

Step 4. Final Adjustments in Determining Amount of Gift. The value of the transferred subordinate equity interest determined at the conclusion of Step 3 is subject to three possible reductions.

First, if the transferred interest would have been valued through application of a minority-interest discount had § 2701 not applied, a minority-interest discount is permitted in determining the value of the gift under § 2701. The discount is equal to the excess of the pro-rata portion of the family-held interests of the same class (determined without reference to § 2701 and as if all voting power relating to the interests were consolidated in one person) over the value of the transferred interest (determined without reference to § 2701). Treas. Reg. § 25.2701-3(b)(4)(ii).

---

[14] For this purpose, the percentage of applicable retained interests that are held by the transferor and applicable family members is capped at the "family interest percentage," which is set at the highest percentage of family-owned interests in any class of subordinate equity, or all subordinate equity interests (valued in the aggregate). *Id.*; Treas. Reg. § 25.2701-3(b)(5). Any percentage of applicable retained interests held by the transferor and applicable family members that exceeds the family interest percentage is treated as if it were family-held by individuals other than the transferor and applicable family members (and therefore valued at its fair market value). Treas. Reg. § 25.2701-3(b)(5).

[15] If there exists more than one class of subordinate equity interest, the remaining value is allocated in order of the seniority of the equity class, in a manner that approximates the value of the class as if all § 2701 rights valued at zero did not exist. Treas. Reg. § 25.2701-3(b)(3). To the extent this allocation is not possible or is not complete, the residual value is allocated among the classes based on their relative fair market values determined without regard to § 2701. *Id.* Once residual value has been allocated among the classes of subordinate equity interests in this manner, the allocation of value to interests transferred to members of the transferor's family presumably is undertaken on a pro-rata basis.

Second, if the transferor retained a temporal interest in the transferred subordinate equity interest, the value of the § 2701 gift is reduced by the value of the transferor's temporal interest under § 2702. Treas. Reg. § 25.2701-3(b)(4)(iii). Note that this reduction would be warranted only if the transferor's retained temporal interest took the form of a qualified interest under § 2702—otherwise, the transferor's retained interest would be valued at zero under that statute. *See* IRC § 2702(a)(2)(A).

Third, the amount of the transfer determined under § 2701 is reduced by the amount of consideration received by the transferor in money or money's worth. Treas. Reg. § 25.2701-3(b)(4)(iv). If the consideration received by the transferor takes the form of an applicable retained interest, the amount of the consideration is determined through the application of § 2701.

[2] Modified Approach for Contributions to Capital

If the § 2701 transfer is accomplished indirectly through a contribution to capital, a simplified version of the subtraction method applies. The initial value of the transfer under Step 1 is equal to the value of the property contributed to the entity. Treas. Reg. § 25.2701-3(b)(1)(ii). Under Step 2, the § 2701 value of any applicable retained interest received as consideration for the transfer is subtracted from the amount contributed to the entity. Treas. Reg. § 25.2701-3(b)(2)(ii). The resulting value is then allocated to the subordinate equity interest held by members of the transferor's family, as adjusted pursuant to Step 4. However, in this context, the value of any consideration received for the transfer in the form of an applicable retained interest in the entity is valued at zero. Treas. Reg. § 25.2701-3(b)(4)(iv).

[3] Minimum Value Assigned to Subordinate Equity Interest

Notwithstanding the results under the subtraction method detailed in Reg. § 25.2701-3, a floor exists on the value of the residual class of equity interest in the entity. Pursuant to § 2701(a)(4), the combined value of the "junior equity interest" in the entity—that is, the interest whose rights to distributions of income and capital are junior to the rights of all other classes of equity—cannot be valued at an amount less than 10 percent of the total value of all classes of equity plus the amount of the entity's indebtedness to the transferor or an applicable family member.[16] The justification for this valuation floor is that the right of the residual class of equity to share in future appreciation in the value of the entity has some "option" value.

[D] Examples

The subtraction method of valuing subordinate equity interests under § 2701 can appear daunting. The mechanics of the valuation regime will become more accessible through illustration.

Example 1: *Parent* transfers a 20 percent interest in the common stock of X Corp. to *Child*. Prior to the transfer, the capital stock of X Corp. is held as follows:

---

[16] Indebtedness of the entity to the transferor or an applicable family member does not include short-term operating obligations or amounts permanently set aside in deferred compensation plans. Treas. Reg. § 25.2701-3(c)(3).

Shareholder	Non-Voting, Non-Cumulative Preferred Stock	Common Stock
Grandparent (*Parent's* mother)	200 shs	100 shs
Parent	300 shs	300 shs
Spouse (*Parent's* wife)	300 shs	300 shs
Brother (of *Parent*)	200 shs	200 shs
Child	0	100 shs

The pro-rata fair market value of the preferred stock, valued as a whole, is $3,000 per share. Of this amount, $2,000 per share is attributable to the non-cumulative right to preferred dividend distributions. The pro-rata fair market value of the common stock, again valued as a whole, is $2,000 per share.

Under Step 1, all interests in the entity are family-held. Because each shareholder falls within this group, the starting value under the subtraction method is $5 million.

Under Step 2, the senior equity interests other than applicable retained interests held by the transferor or applicable family members are subtracted at their fair market value, determined without reference to § 2701. Pursuant to this step, the $600,000 value of *Brother's* preferred stock is subtracted. Additionally, the value of any equity interest of the same class as the class of the transferred equity held by persons other than the transferor, applicable family members, or members of the transferor's family (leaving *Brother* alone) is subtracted. This step yields a $400,000 subtraction. The last amount subtracted under Step 2 is the § 2701 value of any applicable retained interest held by the transferor or applicable family members. This includes the preferred stock of *Parent*, *Spouse*, and *Grandparent*. Because the distribution right is non-cumulative, the distribution preference is valued at zero for § 2701 purposes. Hence, only $800,000 is subtracted on account of the applicable retained interests held by *Parent* and applicable family members (as opposed to the $2.4 million fair market value of such stock).

Under Step 3, $3.2 million remains to be allocated among the subordinate equity interests held by *Parent*, *Grandparent*, *Spouse*, and *Child*. Allocating this amount on a pro-rata basis, the 200 shares of common stock transferred from *Parent* to *Child* is valued at $640,000.

Step 4 provides for adjustments to the residual value of the transferred equity interest. Because the family-held common stock represents voting control of the entity whereas the transferred 200 shares do not, a minority-interest discount is appropriate. Assuming a 10 percent discount for this purpose, the resulting amount of the gift from *Parent* to *Child* would be $576,000. Note that, even if *Child* had paid $400,000 for the 200 shares of common stock (the fair market value of the common stock determined without regard to § 2701 and without regard to a minority-interest discount), a gift of $176,000 would have remained.

Example 2: Assume that *Parent* contributes property worth $5 million to a newly formed corporation. In return, *Parent* receives 1,000 shares of $5,000 par value preferred stock that pays a cumulative 6 percent dividend. The preferred stock may be redeemed at par value at the election of the holder. *Child1* and *Child2* receive 700 shares and 300 shares of common stock, respectively.

Shareholder	Non-Voting, Non-Cumulative Preferred Stock	Common Stock
Parent	1,000 shs	0 shs

Shareholder	Non-Voting, Non-Cumulative Preferred Stock	Common Stock
Child1	0 shs	700 shs
Child2	0 shs	300 shs

Step 1 starts with the value of the property transferred to the entity, $5 million. Under Step 2, the § 2701 value of *Parent's* preferred stock is subtracted. Because the cumulative dividend stream constitutes a qualified payment right, the preferred stock is valued under the "lower of" rule of § 2701(a)(3)(B). If the present value of the cumulative dividend stream is $3 million, the redemption right will be presumed to go unexercised so as to value *Parent's* preferred stock at $3 million. The amount to be allocated to the common stock transferred to *Child1* and *Child2* totals $2 million, allocated $2,000 per share. Under Step 4, the otherwise $600,000 gift to *Child2* may be reduced by a minority-interest discount.

§ 23.05   SUBSEQUENT TRANSFER TAX TREATMENT OF DELINQUENT QUALIFIED PAYMENT RIGHTS

Internal Revenue Code: § 2701(d)
Treasury Regulations: § 25.2701-4

Recall that distribution rights in family-controlled entities that satisfy the definition of a qualified payment (that is, cumulative dividend payments determined at a fixed rate) are not subject to the valuation presumptions of § 2701 on the theory that the guaranteed payment stream precludes the ability of the holder of such rights to deflect value to others through nonexercise. This theory breaks down, however, if the entity does not live up to its obligation to make the qualified payments. Accordingly, § 2701(d) provides a transfer tax backstop designed to increase the gift tax or estate tax base of the holder of the qualified payment right by the grossed-up value of the delinquent payments.

[A]   Triggering Events

The increase in the transfer tax base occasioned by § 2701(d) generally awaits the transfer of an applicable retained interest that contains a distribution right previously valued as a qualified payment right (in the terms of the regulations, a "qualified payment interest") by the transferor or applicable family member. *See* IRC § 2701(d)(3)(A), (d)(4)(A); *see also* Treas. Reg. § 25.2701-4(a). For example, if a qualified payment interest is included in the transferor's gross estate at death, the transferor's gross estate will include an amount attributable to the delinquent qualified payments as well as the prevailing value of the qualified payment interest itself. IRC § 2701(d)(1)(A), (d)(3)(A)(i). Similarly, a lifetime transfer of the qualified payment interest will increase the transferor's taxable gifts for the calendar year in which the transfer takes place by an amount attributable to the delinquent qualified payments.[17] IRC § 2701(d)(1)(B), (d)(3)(A)(ii). A termination of the qualified payment interest (e.g., through a redemption) is treated as a transfer of the interest for this purpose. IRC § 2701(d)(5).

---

[17] If the transferred qualified payment interest would be includible in the transferor's gross estate other than by reason of § 2035, the initial transfer does not trigger the application of § 2701(d). Rather, the transfer will be deemed to occur when the prospect of gross estate inclusion terminates. *See* Treas. Reg. § 25.2701-4(b)(2).

[B] Amount of Increase

If a triggering event occurs under § 2701(d), the transferor's gift tax or estate tax base is increased by an amount designed to replicate the transfer tax consequences that would have occurred had the qualified payments been paid in a timely fashion. The tax base increase therefore is defined as (a) the value of all qualified payments grossed up from the date the payments were scheduled to be made (using the discount rate used to initially value the qualified payment stream), over (b) the value of the qualified payments as grossed up from the date of actual payment. IRC § 2701(d)(2)(A). In this manner, the increase is designed to capture not only the nominal amount of qualified payments that remain outstanding, but also the forgone investment yield on outstanding and delinquent payments.

Given the overall purpose of § 2701 to guard against a tax-free shift of future appreciation in the entity to holders of residual equity interests, the transfer tax base increase provided by § 2701(d) is subject to a ceiling to prevent the backstop from exceeding its function. Generally speaking, the § 2701(d) increase is limited to the actual appreciation in the value of the transferred subordinate equity interest. See IRC § 2701(d)(2)(B).

[C] Grace Period for Making Qualified Payments

Recognizing that dividend payments may be deferred as a result of business-related exigencies, § 2701(d) provides a liberal grace period before qualified payments will be considered delinquent. The payment of a distribution within four years of its due date is treated as having been timely paid. IRC § 2701(d)(2)(C).

Upon receiving a delinquent qualified payment (that is, a payment that is more than 4 years overdue), the holder of the qualified payment right may elect to treat the receipt of the qualified payment as the event triggering application of § 2701(d). See IRC § 2701(d)(3)(A)(iii). In that case, the gift tax base of the holder of the payment right will be increased by the would-be investment yield on the qualified payment between the due date of the payment and the date on which the payment actually was made. IRC § 2701(d)(2)(A). Because any delinquent payments for which the election is made are treated as having been paid on their due dates for purposes of subsequent taxable events, see Treas. Reg. § 25.2701-4(d)(1), acceleration of the taxable event under § 2701(d) is designed to limit future compounding of the forgone investment yield.

[D] Transfers Between Spouses and Other Applicable Family Members

If a transfer of a qualified payment interest to a spouse—whether during life or by reason of death—qualifies for the marital deduction, the transfer does not trigger application of § 2701(d). See IRC § 2701(d)(3)(B). Instead, the spouse steps into the shoes of the transferor for § 2701(d) purposes, meaning that the grossed-up value of delinquent qualified payments will be subject to additional gift taxation or estate taxation in the spouse's hands. IRC § 2701(d)(3)(B)(iii).

If a qualified payment interest is transferred during life by the original transferor to an applicable family member other than the transferor's spouse, the transferee is treated in the same manner as the transferor for purposes of § 2701(d). IRC § 2701(d)(4)(B). Hence, not only will the transferor's gift tax base be increased on account of the delinquent qualified payments, the transfer tax base of the applicable family member will be subject to increase on account of future delinquencies in qualified payments. Section 2701(d) therefore cannot be avoided or minimized through a transfer of the qualified payment interest to an applicable family member. Similarly, while a transfer of a qualified payment interest by an applicable family member to the transferor will trigger application of § 2701(d) with respect to any unpaid qualified payments, *see* IRC § 2701(d)(4)(A), the potential application of § 2701(d) is not extinguished by such a transfer. Rather, § 2701(d) will continue to apply to the transferor for any period during which the transferor holds the qualified payment interest. IRC § 2701(d)(4)(C).

§ 23.06   TRANSFER TAX RELIEF FOR FUTURE TRANSFERS OF APPLICABLE RETAINED INTERESTS

Internal Revenue Code: § 2701(e)
Treasury Regulations: § 25.2701-5

If an applicable retained interest that was valued under § 2701(a) is subsequently transferred or included in the gross estate of the transferor, § 2701(e)(6) provides for "appropriate adjustments" to be made in the transferor's gift tax, estate tax, or GST tax base to reflect the increase in gift tax value occasioned by the § 2701 valuation rules. These adjustments, designed to mitigate the potential for excessive taxation of the applicable retained interest, are detailed in Reg. § 25.2701-5.

[A]   Subsequent Transfers During Lifetime of Initial Transferor

The "initial transferor" of a "section 2701 interest" (the latter being an applicable retained interest originally valued through application of the § 2701 valuation presumptions) is entitled to a reduction in his gift tax base if the section 2701 interest is subject to gift taxation or estate taxation—either in the hands of the transferor or an applicable family member—by reason of a transfer of the interest to one other than the initial transferor or applicable family member during the initial transferor's lifetime. Treas. Reg. § 25.2701-5(a)(1), (2). The reduction in the initial transferor's taxable gifts under § 2502(a) generally is equal to the lesser of (a) the increase in the initial transferor's gift tax base occasioned by application of the § 2701 valuation rules to the initial transfer, or (b) the "duplicated amount," which equals the excess of the transfer tax value of the section 2701 interest determined at the time of the subsequent transfer over the § 2701 value of such interest at the time of the initial transfer. Treas. Reg. § 25.2701-5(b), (c). This reduction to the gift tax base of the initial transferor takes place in the year of the subsequent transfer, with any reduction in excess of the amount necessary to eliminate that year's gift tax base carrying over to future years and, if necessary, to the determination of the initial transferor's adjusted taxable gifts for estate tax purposes. Treas. Reg. § 25.2701-5(a)(3).

[B]   Subsequent Transfers Included in Gross Estate of Initial Transferor

If a section 2701 interest is included in the gross estate of the initial transferor, the executor of the initial transferor's estate is entitled to reduce the initial transferor's adjusted taxable gifts under § 2001(b). In this context, the amount of the reduction is equal to the lesser of (a) the increase in the initial transferor's gift tax base occasioned by application of the

§ 2701 valuation rules to the initial transfer, or (b) the estate tax value of the section 2701 interest over the § 2701 value of such interest at the time of the initial transfer. Treas. Reg. § 25.2701-5(a)(3).

[C] Deemed Transfer of Section 2701 Interest by Applicable Family Member

The gift tax or estate tax mitigation provisions of § 2701(e)(6) apply only to the initial transferor of the section 2701 interest. Hence, if a section 2701 interest is held by an applicable family member of the initial transferor at the time of the initial transferor's death, the ability to mitigate the potential double taxation of the section 2701 interest would be eliminated absent a special rule. Accordingly, any section 2701 interest held by an applicable family member of the initial transferor as of the initial transferor's date of death is treated as being then transferred to one other than the initial transferor or an applicable family member of the initial transferor. Treas. Reg. § 25.2701-5(c)(3)(ii). This hypothetical transfer will trigger a reduction in the adjusted taxable gifts of the initial transferor, with the amount of the reduction being determined with reference to the value of the section 2701 interest immediately prior to the initial transferor's death.

§ 23.07 STUDY PROBLEMS

1. For purposes of this problem, assume the equity interests in X Corp. are held in the following manner immediately prior to the transactions alternatively described below:

Shareholder	Non-Voting, Non-Cumulative Preferred Stock	Common Stock
Grandparent (*Parent's* mother)	400 shs	200 shs
Parent	200 shs	300 shs
Spouse (*Parent's* wife)	100 shs	100 shs
Brother (of *Parent*)	300 shs	300 shs
Child	0	100 shs

Assume that the preferred stock is valued collectively at $2 million, with the common stock being valued collectively at $1 million. Evaluate whether the transfers described in the alternative scenarios below implicate the special valuation rules of § 2701:

a. *Parent* gives *Child* his 200 shares of preferred stock.

b. *Parent* gives *Child* his 300 shares of common stock.

c. *Parent* gives *Child* his 300 shares of common stock. In conjunction with this transfer, *Grandparent* gives *Child* 350 shares of her preferred stock.

d. *Parent* sells 200 shares of common stock to *Child* for its fair market value of $1,000 per share.

2. *Parent* owns real property valued at $1 million. He contributes the property to an LLC in exchange for 1,000 Class A LLC units and 500 Class B LLC units. The remaining 500 Class B LLC units are issued to *Child*. The Class A LLC units may be redeemed at the option of the holder for $1,000 per unit. Otherwise, the Class A units and Class B units possess the same rights to operating and liquidating distributions. Address the gift tax

consequences to *Parent*.

3. For purposes of this problem, assume the following capital structure of Y Corp.:

Shareholder	Class A Stock	Class B Stock
Parent	400 shs	400 shs
Spouse (*Parent's* wife)	200 shs	0 shs
Brother (of *Parent*)	600 shs	600 shs

Parent transfers his 400 shares of Class B stock to *Child*. In the alternative scenarios below, determine whether there exists an applicable retained interest sufficient to trigger § 2701 and, if so, how the rights relating to the interest described below will be valued:

   a. Holders of the Class A stock are entitled to a 5 percent annual dividend on its $1,000 per-share par value before any dividends are paid on the Class B stock. Any dividend that is not paid in a given year lapses.

   b. Same as (a), except that any annual dividend on Class A stock that is not paid in a given year remains outstanding and is added to the dividend preference in the next succeeding year.

   c. Same as (b), with the addition that the Class A stock is redeemable at the election of the holder at par value.

   d. Same as (b), with the addition that the Class A stock must be purchased by the corporation at par value upon the holder's death.

   e. Class A and Class B share rights to operating and liquidating distributions in a 4:1 ratio.

   f. Class A and Class B have the same per-share rights to operating and liquidating distributions; however, Class A stock is voting while Class B stock is non-voting.

4. *Mother* organizes her operating business, formerly a sole proprietorship, as an LLC. Shortly after this capitalizing transfer, *Mother* gratuitously assigns a 60 percent membership interest to *Daughter*.

   a. Assume that the LLC operating agreement provides that *Mother* is entitled to a guaranteed payment of $100,000 per year for services that she renders to the entity. Has mother retained an applicable retained interest for purposes of § 2701?

   b. Alternatively, assume that the LLC operating agreement provides that all operating and liquidating distributions will be made first to *Mother* until she has received $500,000 in the aggregate. Afterward, distributions will be made based on pro-rata ownership of LLC units.

   c. In scenario (b) above, is there any way for *Mother* to increase the value of her retained equity interest on account of the distribution preference?

5. For purposes of this problem, assume the following capital structure of Z Corp.:

Shareholder	Cumulative Preferred Stock	Common Stock
Parent	200 shs	1,000 shs

Shareholder	Cumulative Preferred Stock	Common Stock
Grandparent	800 shs	0 shs

Parent transfers all of his common stock to *Child*. Although the corporation is obligated to pay a five percent cumulative dividend on the preferred stock, the corporation has not paid a dividend since the transfer. Describe the transfer tax consequences in the alternative scenarios.

a. Six years after *Parent's* transfer of the common stock to *Child, Parent* transfers his preferred stock to *Child*. Describe the gift tax consequences of the transfer.

b. *Parent* dies six years following the initial transfer while still owning the preferred shares. Describe the estate tax consequences to *Parent*.

c. *Parent* transfers his preferred stock to *Spouse* three years after the transfer of the common stock to *Child*. Two years later, *Spouse* dies. Describe the gift tax consequences to *Parent* and the estate tax consequences to *Spouse*.

d. *Grandparent* dies six years after *Parent's* transfer to *Child*.

Chapter 24

CONTRACTUAL AGREEMENTS CONCERNING THE TRANSFER OR USE OF PROPERTY

The special valuation rules of §§ 2701 and 2702 address the potential to undervalue a transferred interest in property by exploiting general valuation principles to overvalue the transferor's retained interest. Generally speaking, each of those provisions requires a present transfer of property that is intended to shift future appreciation to the donee outside the transferor's tax base. However, estate freeze techniques need not be that elaborate.

For example, suppose an individual sells an option to purchase property that he owns, with the exercise price of the option set at the then-prevailing $1 million value of the property. Years later, the individual dies when the property is worth $1.5 million. Assuming the option remains outstanding and enforceable, a hypothetical willing buyer would not pay more for the property than the $1 million proceeds due upon exercise of the option. In this manner, the $500,000 of appreciation in the property following the grant of the option would be excluded from the individual's transfer tax base.

Note that the above transaction is not per se objectionable from a transfer tax standpoint. The grantor of the option presumably would demand fair market consideration for its issuance, and the invested proceeds of the option would preserve the grantor's transfer tax base.[1] However, the transaction appears suspect when the grantee of the option is a member of the grantor's family or another intended beneficiary of the grantor's estate. In that case, the primary purpose of the arrangement may be to minimize the tax consequences of gratuitous transfers by locking in an artificially low valuation of the transferred property. The potential for transfer tax avoidance is heightened when the consideration received for the option takes the form of a cross-option that expires upon the grantor's death.

While transfer agreements among family members raise the prospect of a disguised gift, owners of closely held businesses frequently employ these arrangements for legitimate, non-tax reasons. Governing documents often provide shareholders or partners with a right of first refusal if a fellow owner attempts to transfer an equity interest, to prevent outsiders from acquiring a stake in the business. Additionally, mandatory redemption or cross-purchase agreements are common in the event of an owner's withdrawal or death, as means of providing a source of liquidity to a retiring owner or his probate estate. The purchase price under these agreements often is governed by a predetermined formula, which avoids the need for expensive appraisals and the costs of resolving valuation disputes among the parties.

As discussed in this chapter, options to acquire property and restrictions on the transfer or use of property present challenging issues in the administration of the transfer tax system. Identifying a reasonable demarcation between (a) a value-depressing restriction that should be

---

[1] Any discrepancy between the invested proceeds of the option and the post-grant appreciation in the property would be attributable to the overall success of the initial financial transaction.

taken at face value in recognition of the non-tax motivations supporting the arrangement and (b) a restriction employed to deliberately suppress the transfer tax value of a gratuitous transfer is no simple task.

§ 24.01   REGULATORY STANDARD FOR ESTATE TAX VALUATION

Treasury Regulations: § 20.2031-2(h)

Prior to the enactment of § 2703, the regulations on estate tax valuation supplied the primary authority on the transfer tax consequences of a contractual agreement to acquire property. By its terms, Reg. § 20.2031-2(h) is limited to determining the effect of a binding option or other contract to acquire securities held by the decedent at death for estate tax valuation purposes. The regulation provides in relevant part as follows:

> The effect, if any, that is given to the option or contract price in determining the value of the securities for estate tax purposes depends upon the circumstances of the particular case. Little weight will be accorded a price contained in an option or contract under which the decedent is free to dispose of the underlying securities at any price he chooses during his lifetime. . . . Even if the decedent is not free to dispose of the underlying securities at other than the option or contract price, such price will be disregarded in determining the value of the securities unless it is determined under the circumstances of the particular case that the agreement represents a bona fide business arrangement and not a device to pass the decedent's shares to the natural objects of his bounty for less than an adequate and full consideration in money or money's worth.

As noted in *Estate of True v. Commissioner*, 390 F.3d 1210 (10th Cir. 2004), courts have interpreted Reg. § 20.2031-2(h) as imposing the following conditions for the price determined under a buy-sell agreement to govern estate tax valuation: (1) the price must be determinable from the agreement; (2) the agreement must bind the parties both during the decedent's life and at the decedent's death; (3) the agreement must be legally enforceable; and (4) the agreement must have been entered into for bona fide business reasons and not as a testamentary substitute intended to pass on the decedent's property for less than adequate and full consideration. *Id.* at 1218 (citing a collection of prior cases).

The terms of Reg. § 20.2031-2(h) provide the foundation for § 2703, which Congress enacted in 1990 to address the effect of rights and restrictions relating to the transfer and use of property for all federal transfer tax purposes—not just the estate tax.[2] To the extent § 2703 employs the same or similar terms as Reg. § 20.2031-2(h), case law applying the regulation remains relevant in interpreting its statutory successor. Yet this is not to suggest that Reg. § 20.2031-2(h) has been rendered a historic relic. Legislative history indicates that § 2703 was intended to supplement the conditions provided in Reg. § 20.2031-2(h), not to supersede the regulation altogether:

> The bill does not otherwise alter the requirements for giving weight to a buy-sell agreement. For example, it leaves intact present law rules requiring that an agreement have lifetime restrictions in order to be binding on death.

---

[2] *See* Omnibus Budget Reconciliation Act of 1990, Pub. L. No. 101-508, § 11602(a), 104 Stat. 1388, 1388–491. Section 2703, examined below, applies to agreements created or substantially modified after October 8, 1990. *Id.* at § 11602(e), 104 Stat. 1388-500; *see also* Treas. Reg. § 25.2703-2.

136 Cong. Rec. 30,541 (1990). Accordingly, for a purchase price supplied in a buy-sell agreement to be binding for estate tax purposes, the conditions of § 2703 and Reg. § 20.2031-2(h) must be satisfied. *See* Estate of Blount v. Commissioner, T.C. Memo. 2004-116, 87 T.C.M. (CCH) 1303.

§ 24.02 SECTION 2703

Internal Revenue Code: § 2703
Treasury Regulations: §§ 25.2703-1, 25.2703-2

[A] General Rule

Section 2703 takes an unsympathetic default posture concerning the valuation implications of options to acquire or use property and restrictions on the sale or use of property. As a general rule, the transfer tax value of property is to be determined without regard to any option, agreement, or other right to acquire or use property at an amount less than the property's fair market value (determined in the absence of such contractual provisions).[3] IRC § 2703(a)(1). Pursuant to this general rule, the property referenced in the opening hypothetical of this chapter would be included in the individual's estate at its $1.5 million unencumbered value, notwithstanding the existence of the outstanding option to acquire the property at $1 million. Additionally, a restriction on the right to sell or use property generally is to be disregarded in determining the transfer tax value of the property. IRC § 2703(a)(2). Hence, a right of first refusal on property—which has a depressing effect on value because it hinders marketability—would not be taken into account for valuation purposes.

[B] Scope of Right or Restriction

The regulations interpreting § 2703 collectively refer to a "right or restriction," which include (1) options, agreements, or rights to use or acquire property and (2) restrictions on the right to use or sell property. Treas. Reg. § 25.2703-1(a)(2). This same term is used below for the sake of brevity. The regulations note that a right or restriction frequently can be found in partnership agreements, shareholder agreements, corporate bylaws, and similar agreements. Treas. Reg. § 25.2703-1(a)(3). Additionally, the right or restriction may exist implicitly in the capital structure of the entity. *Id.* As an example, preferred stock that provides the issuing corporation with a call option presumably contains a right or restriction for § 2703 purposes.

[C] The Section 2703(b) Exception

Recognizing that not all rights or restrictions represent an attempt to depress the value of gratuitous transfers, § 2703 contains an exception for business-motivated contractual provisions. A right or restriction will be respected for valuation purposes if the following requirements are satisfied: (1) the provision represents a "bona fide business arrangement"; (2) the provision does not constitute a "device" to transfer property to natural objects of the transferor's bounty for less than full and adequate consideration in money or money's worth;

---

[3] Conservation easements are not subject to being disregarded for valuation purposes under the general rule, as such easements are not treated as a right or restriction under § 2703(a). *See* Treas. Reg. § 25.2703-1(a)(4) (excluding perpetual restrictions on the use of real property that qualify for the charitable deduction under either § 2055(f) or § 2522(d)).

and (3) the terms of the provision "are comparable to similar arrangements entered into by persons in an arm's length transaction." IRC § 2703(b); Treas. Reg. § 25.2703-1(b)(1). The first two requirements of the § 2703(b) exception are drawn from Reg. § 20.2031-2(h), while the third requirement represents an innovation of the 1990 legislation. The elements of the statutory exception are conjunctive; each must be independently established. *See* Treas. Reg. § 25.2703-1(b)(2).

[1] Bona Fide Business Arrangement

Neither the statute nor the regulations provide guidance on when a contractual provision relating to the use or transfer of property will constitute a bona fide business arrangement under § 2703(b)(1). However, the legislative history accompanying the enactment of § 2703 highlights certain motivations that fall within the umbrella of "legitimate business reasons" that presumably satisfy this statutory condition:

> The committee believes that buy-sell agreements are common business planning arrangements and that buy-sell agreements generally are entered into for legitimate business reasons that are not related to transfer tax consequences. Buy-sell agreements are commonly used to control the transfer of ownership in a closely held business, to avoid expensive appraisals in determining purchase price, to prevent the transfer to an unrelated party, to provide a market for the equity interest, and to allow owners to plan for future liquidity needs in advance.

136 Cong. Rec. 30,539 (1990). In interpreting Reg. § 20.2031-2(h), courts have held that the use of buy-sell agreements to maintain family ownership and control of a business constitutes a legitimate business motivation. *See, e.g.*, St. Louis County Bank v. United States, 674 F.2d 1207 (8th Cir. 1982); Estate of Bischoff v. Commissioner, 69 T.C. 32 (1977); Estate of Reynolds v. Commissioner, 55 T.C. 172 (1970).

The scope of the "bona fide business arrangement" contemplated by § 2703(b)(1) served as a central issue in *Holman v. Commissioner*, 130 T.C. 170 (2008). The donors in *Holman* capitalized a limited partnership with stock of a publicly traded company. The partnership restricted withdrawal from the partnership and the scope of permissible transferees of a partnership interest, while providing the partnership with a right of first refusal with respect to an attempted transfer of a partnership interested to a non-permitted transferee. The donors in *Holman* contended that these transfer restrictions were imposed to ensure family control of the entity, and that this goal constituted a bona fide business purpose. The Service, on the other hand, argued that the bona fide business arrangement inquiry depended on the nature of the entity's activities. Specifically, the Service contended that simply holding title to securities and maintaining records did not rise to the level of a "business," and the absence of a business precluded a finding of a bona fide business arrangement.

The Tax Court rejected the Service's broader argument, noting that the subject of the restrictive agreement "need not *directly* involve an actively managed business." *Id.* at 192 (emphasis added). On this point, the court discussed its prior decision in *Estate of Amlie v. Commissioner*, T.C. Memo. 2006-76, 91 T.C.M. (CCH) 1017, concerning value-fixing arrangements relating to a minority stock interest in a closely held bank. There, the court determined that the goals of mitigating the investment risk of owning a minority interest and ensuring a source of future liquidity served valid business justifications. Hence, an investment-related motivation for a restrictive agreement can serve as the basis for a bona fide business arrangement condition.

Having rejected the Service's broader argument, the court nonetheless went on to rule in the government's favor. Acknowledging case law and legislative history establishing that buy-sell agreements serve a legitimate goal of maintaining control of a closely held business, the court concluded that the requisite closely held business did not exist at any level. *See Holman*, 130 T.C. at 194. The assets of the partnership in *Holman* consisted of publicly traded securities. Hence, traditional business justifications for restricting the transfer of beneficial interests in an entity couched in terms of maintaining ownership and control of a business within a family were inapposite. Rather than maintaining control of a business, the court determined that the principal motivation behind the formation of the partnership and the restriction on the transfer of partnership interests was to prevent the taxpayers' children from dissipating the wealth the taxpayers were transferring to them. In not so many terms, the court in *Holman* reasoned that concerns regarding the beneficial use of property—as opposed to motivations relating to the operation of a business or the investment performance of an asset—did not fall within the scope of business purposes required by § 2703(b)(1). *See id.* at 195. The Eighth Circuit Court of Appeals affirmed the Tax Court's holding on this issue. *See* Holman v. Commissioner, 601 F.3d 763, 770 (8th Cir. 2010) ("We and other courts have held that 'maintenance of family ownership and control of [a] business' may be a bona fide business purpose. . . . We have not so held, however, in the absence of a business.").

[2] Not a Device to Gratuitously Transfer Property

The second element of the § 2703(b) exception requires that the contractual provision not constitute a device for the transfer of property "to members of the decedent's family" for less than adequate and full consideration. IRC § 2703(b)(2). The regulations sensibly interpret the statute more broadly. Because § 2703 applies for all transfer tax purposes, "the decedent" is dropped in favor of "the transferor." Treas. Reg. § 25.2703-1(b)(1)(ii). Additionally, the regulations broaden the scope of the suspect transferees beyond just family members to "natural objects of the transferor's bounty." *Id.* The regulations do not attempt to define the scope of the natural objects of the transferor's bounty, but they do indicate that the term is not limited to relatives by blood or marriage. *See* Treas. Reg. § 25.2703-1(b)(3); *see also* Estate of Blount v. Commissioner, 1314, T.C. Memo. 2004-116, 87 T.C.M. (CCH) 1303 (determining that ESOP shareholders, with whom decedent had no personal relationship outside of work, were not natural objects of decedent's bounty); Estate of Gloeckner v. Commissioner, 152 F.3d 208 (2d Cir. 1998) (finding that employee of decedent whom decedent named in his will was not a natural object of decedent's bounty). The more expansive class of recipients is consistent with the purpose of § 2703(b)(2) to guard against arrangements designed to suppress the value of gratuitous transfers.

Note that § 2703(b)(2) does not require that a buy-sell agreement provide the transferor with consideration equal to the unrestricted fair market value of property at the time of its transfer. If that were the case, the § 2703(b) exception would be of no avail. Rather, § 2703(b)(2) presumably assumes the existence of a contract price below the unrestricted fair market value of the property, with the insufficiency of consideration inuring to the benefit of the natural objects of the transferor's bounty. In this manner, § 2703(b)(2) amounts to a subjective inquiry concerning whether the favorable tax result was deliberate or fortuitous.

[a]   Application to Transfers at Death

While no single factor is determinative in resolving the "device" inquiry under § 2703(b)(2), an overall lack of seriousness concerning the terms of the relevant agreement and its ramifications provides circumstantial evidence that the indirect transfer of value was purposeful. Two cases interpreting the device standard under Reg. § 20.2031-2(h), *St. Louis County Bank v. United States*, 674 F.2d 1207 (8th Cir. 1982), and *Estate of Lauder v. Commissioner*, T.C. Memo. 1992-736, 64 T.C.M. (CCH) 1643, demonstrate how circumstances surrounding the pricing mechanism employed in a stock-purchase agreement can support a finding that the arrangement was a device to effectuate a testamentary disposition.

In *St. Louis County Bank*, the owners of a closely held operating business had entered into a stock-purchase agreement for the purpose of maintaining family control over the enterprise. The agreement employed a formula for valuing the stock that was based on the earning history of the business, net of gains and losses on investments in real estate. Several years after the agreement was executed, the company sold its operating assets and engaged primarily in the rental of real estate. As a result, the formula valuation was reduced to zero. Although the corporation did not enforce the agreement upon the prior death of another shareholder, the corporation in this instance exercised its option to acquire the decedent's stock for zero consideration. The redemption had the effect of enhancing the holdings of the decedent's daughter and granddaughters. *See* 674 F.2d at 1209. After conceding that the terms of the stock-purchase agreement were reasonable at the time it was executed, the Eight Circuit rejected the estate's argument that the device inquiry was restricted to that time frame. Noting that the decedent as the majority shareholder voluntarily transformed the nature of the corporation's business in a manner that would have a profound effect on the valuation formula, the court determined that a jury could reasonably view the agreement as a testamentary tax-avoidance device. *Id.* at 1211.

In *Estate of Lauder v. Commissioner*, the Tax Court similarly focused on the formula employed for determining the value of stock to be sold pursuant to a stock-purchase agreement in resolving the device inquiry. After first conceding that the agreement served a legitimate business purpose of preserving family ownership and control of a business, the court noted that the agreement nonetheless may achieve testamentary objectives if the agreement facilitated the sale of stock to younger generations at bargain prices. 64 T.C.M. (CCH) at 1657. The stock-purchase agreement valued the decedent's stock based on the corporation's adjusted book value, which had the effect of excluding consideration of valuable intangible assets such as trademarks, trade names, and goodwill. Noting that this formula was selected arbitrarily in the absence of negotiation and without the input of professional advice, the court determined that the formula "appears to have been adopted in order to minimize or mask the true value of the stock in question." *Id.* at 1659.

[b]   Application to Lifetime Transfers

The Tax Court in *Holman v. Commissioner*, 130 T.C. 170 (2008), undertook the device inquiry in the context of inter vivos assignments of transfer-restricted partnership interests. Pursuant to the partnership agreement, if a partner attempted to transfer his interest to one other than a permitted transferee (generally, family members or trusts created for their benefit), the partnership could acquire the interest for an amount equal to the value of an assignee's right to receive distributions with respect to the interest. *Id.* at 176–77. The court noted that this option would permit the partnership to capture the difference in value between

(a) the net-asset value of the subject partnership interest and (b) the present value of the distribution rights relating to such interest. This captured value would be effectively redistributed among the remaining partners, a group that included the taxpayers' children. Finding that the taxpayers fully understood the potential redistributive ramifications of the transfer restrictions, the court determined that the restrictions constituted a device to transfer partnership units to natural objects of the taxpayers' bounty for less than adequate and full consideration. *Id.* at 197.

[3] Comparability to Similar Arrangements in Arm's Length Transactions

Section 2703 augmented the preexisting regulatory guidance on options and transfer restrictions on property by requiring that the relevant contractual provision be comparable to similar arrangements entered into by parties acting at arm's length. *See* IRC § 2703(b)(3). To satisfy this condition, the right or restriction must have been one that could have been obtained "in a fair bargain among unrelated parties in the same business dealing with each other at arm's length."[4] Treas. Reg. § 25.2703-1(b)(4)(i). This regulatory formulation of the test, in turn, is satisfied if the right or restriction conforms "with the general practice of unrelated parties under negotiated agreements in the same business." *Id.* Relevant factors to be considered include the prevailing fair market value of the property subject to the right or restriction, the expected term of the agreement, the adequacy of consideration received for the rights conferred, and anticipated changes in the value of the subject property. *Id.*

[a] Practical Obstacles

The "similar arrangements" condition of § 2703(b)(3), as expanded in the regulations, raises a natural question: How many comparables are enough? The regulations warn that "isolated comparables" do not supply evidence of a general business practice. *See* Treas. Reg. § 25.2703-1(b)(4)(ii). On the other hand, the regulations concede that it is not necessary that the right or restriction parallel the terms of any particular agreement. *Id.* Combining this guidance, the relevant right or restriction must be consistent with practices of the relevant business community, but not necessarily identical to any particular comparable arrangement.

The requirements of § 2703(b)(3) raise another practical matter: How does a taxpayer go about carrying his burden of proof on the issue? As noted by the Tax Court in *Estate of Blount v. Commissioner*, T.C. Memo. 2004-116, 87 T.C.M. (CCH) 1303, the statute "appears to contemplate a taxpayer's production of evidence of agreements actually negotiated by persons at arm's length under similar circumstances and in similar businesses that are comparable to the terms of the challenged agreement." *Id.* at 1314. However, comparable arrangements, such as shareholder agreements or partnership agreements, rarely are a matter of public record. The legislative history accompanying § 2703 suggests that expert testimony can be employed to establish the general practice of unrelated parties. *See* 136 Cong. Rec. 30,541 (daily ed. Oct. 18, 1990) ("Expert testimony would be evidence of such practice."). Perhaps a transactional attorney could provide expert testimony concerning the standard practice in the

---

[4] This determination is to be made at the time the right or restriction is created. Treas. Reg. § 25.2703-1(b)(1)(iii). A substantial modification of an existing right or restriction is treated as the creation of a new right or restriction for this purpose. *See* Treas. Reg. § 25.2703-1(c)(1). The failure to periodically update the right or restriction as required by its terms is presumed to be a substantial modification, as is the addition of any family member in a lower generation as a party to the arrangement. *Id.*

field, but the attorney's obligation to maintain client confidences would preclude the introduction of comparable agreements absent consent. Additionally, the attorney may not be considered an expert in any one type of business.

[b]   *Estate of Blount v. Commissioner*

The Tax Court opinion in *Estate of Blount* illustrates the extent of the practical hurdle imposed by § 2703(b)(3). The decedent in *Estate of Blount* operated a construction company with his brother-in-law through a corporation they owned equally. Upon the brother-in-law's death, the corporation redeemed his stock pursuant to a mandatory redemption agreement. The redemption left the decedent with a controlling 83 percent interest in the corporation. An ESOP established for the benefit of employees in the interim held the remaining shares. Concerned about the effect of the corporation's obligation to redeem his stock at his death (shortly after being diagnosed with cancer), the decedent and the corporation modified the redemption agreement to set a firm $4 million purchase price for his shares.[5] The modification represented a substantial concession on the decedent's part. The most recent appraisal valued the corporation at $155 per share; the $4 million redemption price equated to $93 per share.

Following the decedent's death, the corporation used $3 million of insurance proceeds along with its cash reserves to fulfill its $4 million redemption obligation.[6] The decedent's estate reported the shares on the estate tax return at this amount. The government, on the other hand, determined that § 2703(a) required the shares to be valued without regard to the redemption agreement. The Tax Court's analysis of § 2703 largely focused on the § 2703(b)(3) requirement that the agreement be comparable to similar arrangements entered into by persons in arm's length transactions. Following a review of the statute, its legislative history, and the interpretive regulations, the court assessed the estate's obligation as follows:

> In the instant case, the estate must demonstrate that the terms of the [modified agreement] are similar to terms in agreements entered into by unrelated parties in businesses similar to that of [the construction company].

87 T.C.M. (CCH) at 1315.

The decedent's estate attempted to meet its evidentiary burden by offering an expert witness to opine on this issue. The witness concluded that the redemption agreement was comparable to similar arrangements entered into at arm's length under § 2703(b)(3) because the agreement provided for a fair market value price. The expert reached this conclusion because the price called for by the agreement was equivalent to a multiple of four times earnings, and the witness claimed this multiple was commonplace in the construction industry. In addition to rejecting the expert's methodology for determining fair market value, the court noted that the witness did not present evidence of other buy-sell agreements or similar

---

[5] The modification changed the original formula redemption price to a fixed payment that could not be adjusted, while eliminating the corporation's option of paying the redemption price in installments. These changes were determined to constitute a "substantial modification" to the preexisting agreement, so as to implicate § 2703. *See Estate of Blount*, 87 T.C.M. (CCH) at 1314.

[6] While the appellate court affirmed the Tax Court's application of § 2703, the court reversed the Tax Court's determination that the insurance proceeds used to fund the corporation's agreement should be taken into consideration in valuing the corporation as a whole (as a starting point for determining the estate tax value of the decedent's stock ownership). *See* Estate of Blount v. Commissioner, 428 F.3d 1338 (11th Cir. 2005). On this latter point, the Tax Court had the more reasoned view. *See* Adam S. Chodorow, *Valuing Corporations for Estate Tax Purposes: A Blount Reappraisal*, 3 Hastings Bus. L.J. 1 (2006).

arrangements that were actually entered into by persons at arm's length. Instead, the court found that the only comparable arrangement was the original buy-sell agreement entered into by the decedent with his brother-in-law, which the decedent later unilaterally modified:

> The best evidence we have on this record of an arm's-length arrangement involving the [construction company's] stock is the unmodified [agreement], which was negotiated between decedent and his brother-in-law when both were 50-percent shareholders and neither knew who would survive the other. The redemption price set in that agreement was (i) book value or (ii) whatever price these two shareholders, in relatively equal bargaining positions, could annually agree upon. Given the disparity in the prices dictated in the [original agreement] versus the [modified agreement], we have no confidence that the [modified agreement] was comparable to an arm's-length bargain.

Id. at 1316. The *Estate of Blount* decision indicates that § 2703(b)(3) imposes a considerable obstacle in qualifying for the § 2703(b) exception. This third condition penalizes not only originality in buy-sell provisions, but also the relative obscurity of these agreements.

[4] Presumed Qualification

Neither an option to use or acquire property nor a restriction on the transfer or use of property is likely to constitute a means of suppressing the transfer tax value of a gratuitous transfer where the option or restriction relates to property owned by unrelated third parties. Rather, those options and restrictions presumably result from arm's length transactions. Accordingly, the regulations presume that all three elements of the § 2703(b) exception are satisfied when more than 50 percent of the property subject to the right or restriction is owned by individuals other than members of the transferors family. Members of the transferor's family for this purpose include those individuals referenced in Reg. § 25.2701-2(b)(5) as well as any other natural objects of the decedent's bounty. Treas. Reg. § 25.2701-3(b)(3).

[D] Effect of Right or Restriction That Qualifies for Section 2703(b) Exception

A right or restriction that satisfies the three conditions of § 2703(b) does not automatically set the value of the subject property for transfer tax purposes. To start, the right or restriction must satisfy the other conditions of Reg. § 20.2031-2(h), at least where the issue concerns estate tax valuation. This requires that the right or restriction be binding both during the transferor's lifetime and at the transferor's death. If the decedent were free to transfer the subject property without restriction during life, acquiescence to the operation of the right or restriction at death has the appearance of a *de facto* testamentary transfer. Additionally, for the stated price to fix estate tax valuation, the estate must be obligated to sell the subject property rather than merely being obligated to first offer the interest to the counterparty prior to transferring. A right of first refusal may reduce value due to its effect on marketability, but a right of first refusal does not lock in a deprivation of value to the one holding the property interest. The owner can avoid the loss of value simply by retaining ownership of the property. Only where the owner is obligated to sell and the counterparty is obligated to purchase will the agreement price essentially dictate transfer tax valuation.

§ 24.03   ATTEMPTED USE OF SECTION 2703 TO COMBAT VALUATION DISCOUNTS

The Service has attempted to employ § 2703 as a means of combating the intentional use of family-owned partnerships to generate considerable tax savings through valuation discounts (that is, discounts for lack of control and for lack of marketability).[7] To apply § 2703 in this manner, the "property" to which the statute applies must be the property contributed to and held by the partnership. In that case, the practical limitations imposed under governing partnership law would constitute the right or restriction to be disregarded by way of § 2703(a). *See* Tech. Adv. Mem. 9842003 (Oct. 16, 1998).

The government advanced this expansive theory of § 2703 in *Estate of Church v. United States*, 85 A.F.T.R.2d 2000-804 (W.D. Tex. 2000). As reflected in the excerpt below, the government's intended application of § 2703 was not well received:

> The Government makes two contentions with respect to the application of I.R.C. section 2703 to this case. It first suggests that the term "property" refers to the assets Mrs. Church contributed to the Partnership prior to death, rather than her Partnership interest. There is no statutory basis for this contention. Mrs. Church did not own the assets she contributed to the Partnership on the date of her death; she owned a Partnership interest. The estate tax is imposed on that which a decedent transfers at death without regard to the nature of the property interest before or after death. I.R.C. section 2033 provides that the gross estate shall include any partnership interest owned by a decedent as defined by I.R.C. section 7701(a)(2). I.R.C. section 2703 does not define the term "property" in any manner inconsistent with these provisions, or indeed at all, and ["property"] cannot have a meaning attributed to it without Congressional authorization that would make it unique in the estate tax provisions of the Code.

> The Government alternatively contends that if I.R.C. section 2703 does require taxation of Mrs. Church's Partnership interest, it may nonetheless disregard the term restriction, and restrictions on sale in the Partnership Agreement that serve to reduce its market value. No case supports the Government's position, and nothing in the legislative history, or the regulations adopted by the IRS itself, convince this Court to read into Section 2703 something that is not there. By its very nature, a partnership is a voluntary association of those who wish to engage in business together, and upon whom the law imposes fiduciary duties. Term restrictions, or those on the sale or assignment of a partnership interest that preclude partnership status for a buyer, are part and parcel of the property interest created by state law. These are not the agreements or restrictions Congress intended to reach in passing I.R.C. section 2703. Reviewing the legislative history, and construing I.R.C. section 2703 with its companion statute, I.R.C. section 2704, it is clear that the former was intended to deal with below-market buy-sell agreements and options that artificially depress the fair market value of property subject to tax, and are not inherent components of the property interest itself.

Id. at 2000-810 to 2000-811 (citations omitted).

---

[7] *See* § 7.07[B].

Note that the district court's rejection of the government's argument in *Estate of Church* may have gone too far. If the governing partnership agreement imposes a restriction on the transfer of beneficial interests in the entity in excess of any limitation existing under default state law, the contractual restriction on transfer is subject to § 2703. *See* Holman v. Commissioner, 130 T.C. 170 (2008) (holding that transfer restrictions imposed by partnership agreement were disregarded under § 2703).

§ 24.04   GIFT TAX CONSEQUENCES OF CREATION OF RIGHT OR RESTRICTION

The discussion thus far has focused on the effect of an option to acquire property or a restriction on the use of property on the transfer tax valuation of the underlying property when it is transferred. Yet the creation of the right or restriction itself may constitute a taxable transfer. For instance, the grant of a binding and enforceable option to acquire property will constitute a gift to the extent the grantor does not receive adequate and full consideration for its issuance. *See* Rev. Rul. 80-186, 1980-2 C.B. 280. Note that an option to acquire property at its value on the date of the option grant has value, due to the option holder's right to benefit from future appreciation in the subject property.

With respect to buy-sell agreements that obligate the survivor to purchase the equity interest of the first to die, differences in the relative probability of survival do not appear to give rise to a present gift. Addressing such an arrangement, the Tax Court in *Estate of Littick v. Commissioner*, 31 T.C. 181 (1958), refused to treat the buy-sell agreement as constituting a retained-interest transfer for estate tax purposes. The court justified its holding in part by finding that the mutual promises exchanged by the parties constituted adequate and full consideration:

> The agreement was by its clear terms enforceable in favor of and against the estate of the first copartner to die and the two surviving copartners, whether the first to die was the decedent or one of the sons. It was specifically enforceable regardless of which copartner should die first. It was not known whether the decedent would outlive one or both of the sons. And it was supported by an adequate and full consideration, within the intent and meaning of the statute. . . .

> We recognize that here it was likely that [the decedent] would die before his brothers, but that was not a foregone conclusion and it is not such fact as should destroy the validity of his agreement with his brothers. Had either brother predeceased him we think the agreement to purchase the stock at the [redemption price] would clearly have been enforceable.

Id. at 188. If the mutual promises supplied adequate and full consideration to preclude application of the retained-interest estate tax provisions, the mutual promises likewise should provide adequate and full consideration under § 2512(b), thereby precluding the existence of a gift.

Adding a measure of comfort to the result of *Estate of Littick*, the Service internally has reasoned that a binding agreement between two shareholders that requires the surviving party to purchase the stock from the decedent's estate does not rise to the level of a grant of an option on the holder's stock. *See* Tech. Adv. Mem. 8140016 (June 30, 1981). Accordingly, the Service reasoned that Revenue Ruling 80-186 did not apply in this context due to the absence of a present transfer of an interest in property. If this internal memorandum represents the Service's position on the matter, then transfer provisions contained in shareholder agreements or similar documents appear to be immune from application of the gift tax.

§ 24.05 STUDY PROBLEMS

1. Jan owns a residential building in a hip, downtown district. The bottom floor is leased out for retail, and the prime location of the building allows Jan to command top-of-the-market rent. Jan's son, Stuart, recently finished graduate school and now wants to open an eclectic bookstore. To help get Stuart up and running, Jan rents the retail space to him for $1,000 a month, even though her prior tenant had been paying 10 times that amount. The lease has a 10-year term. Jan dies two years into the lease. Absent the lease, the building is valued at $3 million. With the lease, the building is valued at $2.7 million. What is the estate tax value of the property?

2. Mel has operated a local steakhouse for 25 years. He would really like to see his son, Tim, continue the operation following his death. Accordingly, Mel gives Tim an option to purchase his ownership of the LLC (through which the steakhouse is operated) at the book value of the restaurant's tangible assets on Mel's death or disability. When Mel dies, the book value is estimated at $200,000. Given the steady patronage of the steakhouse, the fair market value of the business is $500,000. Shortly after Mel's death, Tim exercises the option.

    a. Discuss the gift tax consequences, if any, of the option grant.

    b. Discuss the estate tax consequences of the option to Mel's estate.

3. Assume the same scenario as in problem 2, except that Mel and Tim operate the steakhouse together as 60/40 owners when the option is created. The option permits either party to purchase a deceased owner's interest at the proportionate date-of-death book value.

    a. Discuss the gift tax consequences, if any, of the option grant.

    b. Discuss the estate tax consequences of the option to Tim's estate.

4. Hank and Ron are brothers who operate a successful printing company through an LLC that they own equally. The brothers have executed a contract whereby, upon either brother's (a) death or (b) withdrawal from the business, the remaining party has the option to purchase the other's LLC units. The per-unit strike price on the option is set at an amount equal to 60 percent of the fair market value of the optioned LLC units, as determined by a qualified appraiser at the time of the triggering event.

    When asked why they each would agree to such a low option price, Ron responds, "[a] couple reasons. One, we don't want any outsiders mucking things up. Two, we want to provide an incentive for each of us to remain committed to the business. Three, the agreement gives us an incentive to stay in shape—to outlive the other. Believe it or not, Hank started to lay off the donuts after we signed the agreement." Each brother is married with children, and each brother's will devises his estate to his immediate family.

    a. Would the agreement be respected under Reg. § 20.2031-2(h)?

     b.   Would the agreement be respected under § 2703?

5.   Wayne contracted to sell a vacant beachfront lot for $2 million, with the transaction to close three months from the contract date.

     a.   A few weeks after the contract is executed, the State announces a major beach renourishment project to be undertaken at the State's expense. This immediately increases the value of the lot to $3 million. After the announcement and well before closing, Wayne deeds the property to his daughter. What is the value of the gift?

     b.   Alternatively, a massive storm devastates the region a few weeks after the contract is executed. Due to the damage to the local infrastructure, real estate values plummet. Wayne dies in the storm, and the fair market value of the lot without regard to the contract of sale is estimated at $800,000. The contract remains outstanding, and the purchaser is capable of performing. What is the estate tax value of the property?

Chapter 25

VOTING AND LIQUIDATION RIGHTS IN CLOSELY HELD ENTITIES

Closely held business entities have gained prominence as vehicles for the transfer of wealth for a variety of reasons, not the least of which is the ability to exploit valuation discounts traditionally associated with valuing equity interests in this context (namely, minority-interest discounts and discounts for lack of marketability[1]). Although the discount-driven use of business entities as estate planning vehicles poses a significant threat to the integrity of the federal transfer tax base, congressional action on this front generally has been wanting. The limited response of Congress to the matter is contained in § 2704. The legislation does not limit entity-related discounts categorically;[2] rather, the statute targets certain arrangements that are designed to maximize the extent of such discounts.

Section 2704 addresses valuation discounts in closely held entities on two fronts. Section 2704(a) applies to voting rights and liquidation rights in a closely held entity that lapse. These lapsing rights, if respected for valuation purposes, would allow an individual to enjoy a beneficial interest in an entity of a greater extent than he is capable of transferring. Section 2704(a) addresses this technique by treating the lapse of the relevant right as a constructive transfer equal to the difference in the value of the interest prior to and following the lapse of the right. Section 2704(b) has a somewhat broader application, addressing any restriction limiting the ability of a family-controlled entity to liquidate. In a manner reminiscent of § 2703, § 2704(b) provides that the liquidation restriction is to be disregarded for valuation purposes to the extent the restriction exceeds the limitations imposed by default state law.

§ 25.01 LAPSING VOTING RIGHTS AND LIQUIDATION RIGHTS—SECTION 2704(a)

Internal Revenue Code: § 2704(a), (c)
Treasury Regulations: § 25.2704-1

[A] Origins of Legislation

The origins of § 2704(a) lie in the seminal valuation case of *United States v. Land*, 303 F.2d 170 (5th Cir. 1962). The decedent in *Land* owned a partnership interest that could be purchased for two-thirds of its value by the remaining partners if he withdrew during his life. However, if the decedent remained a partner until his death (which he did), the surviving partners were obligated to purchase the interest at its full fair market value to avoid dissolution of the entity. The Fifth Circuit concluded that the decedent's partnership interest

---

[1] Discounts traditionally recognized in valuing equity interests in closely held entities are addressed in § 7.07[B].

[2] *See* H.R. Rep. No. 101-964, at 1137 (1990) ("These rules do not affect minority discounts or other discounts available under present law.").

should be valued free of the lifetime restriction for estate tax purposes, reasoning that "value looks ahead." *Id.* at 173. Specifically, the court noted that a willing buyer of the property interest "attributes full value to any right that vests or matures at death, and he reduces his valuation to account for any risk or deprivation that death brings into effect." *Id.*

While the government benefitted from the Fifth Circuit's framing of the valuation inquiry in *Land*, the case provided a roadmap for taxpayers seeking to obtain a valuation advantage: structure a transaction to provide for a "deprivation [of value] that death brings into effect." Cue the Tax Court case of *Estate of Harrison v. Commissioner*, T.C. Memo. 1987-8, 52 T.C.M. (CCH) 1306. The decedent in *Estate of Harrison* owned an approximate 80 percent economic interest in a limited partnership, 1 percent as general partner and 79 percent as limited partner. The decedent's sons owned the remaining limited partnership interests equally, roughly 10 percent each.

As general partner, the decedent possessed the right to liquidate the entity during his lifetime. The limited partnership interest, however, did not provide this right. The case therefore focused on the valuation of the decedent's 79 percent limited partnership interest. Valued in conjunction with the general partner's right to liquidate the entity, the limited partnership interest was worth $59 million. However, the limited partnership interest was determined to be worth only $33 million when valued in isolation (that is, without consideration of the general partner's liquidation right).

Following the Fifth Circuit's directive in *Land*, the Tax Court focused on the property interest that was transferred by the decedent at the moment of death. Because the decedent's right as general partner to liquidate the entity expired upon his death and did not pass to his estate,[3] the court upheld the $33 million valuation advanced by the estate. *Id.* at 1309. Adamant that $26 million of value did not simply disappear, the Service argued that "something of value" passed to the decedent's sons when the decedent's liquidation right lapsed. *Id.* The court rejected this argument, noting that the value of the sons' limited partnership interests was not affected by the decedent's death. However, the Service's argument foreshadowed the statutory remedy provided in § 2704(a).

[B] Lapsing Rights as Constructive Transfers

Seeking "to prevent results similar to that of *Estate of Harrison v. Commissioner*," Congress enacted § 2704(a) to address the use of lapsing rights in family-owned entities to reduce transfer tax value.[4] The legislation treats an individual who holds either a voting right or a liquidation right in a family-controlled entity as making a constructive transfer when the right lapses.[5] *See* IRC § 2704(a)(1). The statute does not attempt to identify the transferee; rather, the statute simply increases the individual's gift tax base or estate tax base, depending on when the lapse occurs.[6] The amount of the constructive transfer equals the value of all

---

[3] The parties had stipulated that, pursuant to the partnership agreement and relevant state law, the decedent's right as general partner to liquidate the entity did not pass to his probate estate. Estate of Harrison v. Commissioner, 1308, T.C. Memo. 1987-8, 52 T.C.M. (CCH) 1306.

[4] H.R. Rep. No. 101-964, at 1137 (1990).

[5] Congress has authorized the Treasury Department to promulgate regulations extending application of § 2704 to rights similar to voting rights and liquidation rights, *see* IRC § 2704(a)(3), but the Treasury Department has yet to do so.

[6] The absence of an actual transferee of the constructive transfer under § 2704(a) precludes the availability of any

interests owned by the individual immediately prior to the lapse of the relevant right over the value of those interests immediately after the lapse. IRC § 2704(a)(2). In this manner, any diminution in the transfer tax value of the equity interest that results from the lapse of the voting or liquidation right is offset by the amount of the constructive transfer.

[1]   Meaning of Voting Rights and Liquidation Rights

The scope of the voting rights addressed by § 2704(a) is broad. A voting right includes a right to vote on any matter of the entity. Treas. Reg. § 25.2704-1(a)(2)(iv). This would include a shareholder's right to elect members of the board and a limited partner's right to elect a general partner. The regulations also note that a general partner's right to participate in the management of the entity constitutes a voting right. *Id.* However, to the extent the voting right can be exercised to cause the entity to redeem an owner's interest, the right is treated as a liquidation right under the statute as opposed to a voting right. *Id.*

A liquidation right is not limited to a right to force the entity to dissolve. Rather, a liquidation right extends to a right or ability to compel the entity to redeem all or a portion of the holder's equity interest, regardless of whether the transaction would effect a complete liquidation. Treas. Reg. § 25.2704-1(a)(2)(v). Hence, a "liquidation" in this context refers to the holder's equity interest, not the entity as a whole.

[2]   Scope of Lapse

A lapse of a voting right or liquidation right occurs when a presently exercisable right is restricted or eliminated. Treas. Reg. § 25.2704-1(b), (c). A lapse may occur by reason of the entity's charter documents, agreements among owners, or other means. Treas. Reg. § 25.2704-1(a)(4). However, § 2704(a) does not apply to the lapse of a liquidation right that occurs solely by reason of a change in state law.[7] Treas. Reg. § 25.2704-1(c)(2)(iii).

The lapse of a liquidation right occurring by reason of a transfer of an equity interest does not constitute a lapse for purposes of § 2704(a) as long as the rights relating to the transferred interest are not restricted or eliminated. Treas. Reg. § 25.2704-1(c)(1). For example, suppose an LLC requires a vote of 75 percent of the membership interests to liquidate. If an individual who owns a 90 percent interest in the entity makes gifts of a collective 20 percent interest, the transfers eliminate the individual's ability to liquidate the entity. Yet the transfers do not implicate § 2704(a) because the right to vote in favor of liquidation follows the transferred interests. However, if a transfer of an interest results in the loss of the transferor's ability to liquidate a retained interest that is subordinate to the transferred interest, the transfer results in the lapse of a liquidation right with respect to the subordinate interest. *Id.* This exception ensures that the result in *Estate of Harrison* cannot be achieved through a lifetime transfer of the general partnership interest.

If the lapsed liquidation right does not effectively re-emerge in the hands of the former holder of the right and members of his family, then no disguised transfer of the value attributable to the lapsed right takes place and § 2704(a) should have no application. Consistent

---

transferee-dependent deductions, such as the marital deduction or the charitable deduction. On the other hand, the absence of a transferee can prove beneficial, as any enhancement in the value of equity owned by a grandchild of the individual or by any other skip person will not constitute a generation-skipping transfer.

[7] This limitation is sensible, as an individual taxpayer's fervor in maximizing entity-related valuation discounts presumably would not extend to obtaining changes in default state law.

with this theory, the regulations instruct that § 2704(a) does not apply if the holder of the right and his family cannot liquidate an interest immediately after the lapse of a right that, prior to its lapse, would have permitted the holder to liquidate an interest. Treas. Reg. § 25.2704-1(c)(2)(i). In that case, the diminution of value attributable to the lapse of the right is truly lost to the individual and his family members—a result that the individual presumably would avoid unless adequately compensated.

[3] Family-Controlled Entity

The constructive transfer regime of § 2704(a) applies only if the entity in which the voting right or liquidation right lapses is controlled by the transferor and members of his family both immediately before and immediately after the lapse. The members of an individual's family for this purpose include the individual's spouse, the ancestors and lineal descendants of the individual or the individual's spouse, the spouse of any such ancestor or descendant, a sibling of the individual, and a spouse of any such sibling.[8] IRC § 2704(c)(2). As for the requisite level of control, § 2704 incorporates standard employed by § 2701. IRC § 2704(c)(1). For a corporation, control is established through the holding of at least 50 percent of the corporation's stock, measured by vote or value. See IRC § 2701(b)(2)(A). For a partnership, control is established through the holding of at least 50 percent of the capital or profits interests in the entity. However, in the case of a limited partnership interest, the holding of an interest as general partner alone establishes control.[9] See IRC § 2701(b)(2)(B).

§ 25.02 RESTRICTIONS ON LIQUIDATION—SECTION 2704(b)

Internal Revenue Code: § 2704(b), (c)
Treasury Regulations: § 25.2704-2

Recall that § 2703 is designed to limit the valuation-depressing effect of contractual provisions relating to the transfer or use of property. The rights or restrictions addressed by § 2703 are external to the property interest whose value is being determined, rather than features of the underlying property interest itself.[10] Section 2704(b) therefore can be envisioned as extending the approach of § 2703 to restrictions on the ability to liquidate an entity that are inherent in the equity interest being valued.

---

[8] Recall that this definition of an individual's family applies for purposes of § 2702 as well.

[9] While an LLC has no direct counterpart to a general partner, the general-partner specific rule of § 2701(b)(2)(B)(ii) presumably is based on the general partner's right to participate in the management of the partnership. Accordingly, the status of an LLC member as a manager of a manager-managed entity likely will constitute control under the same provision.

[10] The government in *Church v. United States*, 85 A.F.T.R.2d 804 (W.D. Tex. 2000), attempted to treat the restrictions on the ability to liquidate a partnership interest contained in the partnership agreement and default state law as a "right or restriction" to be disregarded under § 2703(a). See § 22.03. This theory of § 2703 depended on the relevant property being the property contributed to the partnership as opposed to the partnership interest owned by the decedent. The district court rejected the government's expansive reading of § 2703, reasoning in part that Congress intended to address any reduction in value attributable to the disabilities associated with a partnership interest through § 2704 as opposed to § 2703. See *Estate of Church*, 85 A.F.T.R.2d at 811.

[A] General Rule

Section 2704(b) applies to the transfer of an interest in a partnership or corporation to or for the benefit of a member of the transferor's family (within the meaning of § 2704(c)(2)), where the transferor and members of his family hold control of the entity (within the meaning of § 2704(c)(1)) immediately after the transfer. IRC § 2704(b)(1). In this context, the statute directs that any "applicable restriction" is to be disregarded in determining the transfer tax value of the transferred interest. *Id.* The heart of § 2704(b) therefore lies in the scope of an applicable restriction.

[B] Applicable Restriction

An applicable restriction for purposes of § 2704(b) encompasses any restriction that effectively limits the ability of the corporation or partnership to liquidate, if (1) the restriction lapses after the transfer of the beneficial interest, or (2) the transferor and members of the transferor's family, either alone or collectively, possess the right to remove the restriction following the transfer.[11] IRC § 2704(b)(2). The determination of whether the transferor and members of his family possess the ability to remove the restriction immediately after the transfer is to be made with reference to state law that would apply in the absence of a more restrictive rule in the entity's governing instrument. *See* Treas. Reg. § 25.2704-2(b) & (d), Ex. 3.

Note that the description of a liquidation right under § 2704(b) differs significantly from the description employed in § 2704(a). A liquidation right for purposes of § 2704(a) extends to the ability to compel an entity to redeem the equity interest of the party possessing the right. *See* Treas. Reg. § 25.2704-1(a)(2)(v). In contrast, a liquidation right for purposes of § 2704(b) refers to the ability to liquidate the entity, in whole or in part. *See* Treas. Reg. § 25.2704-2(b).

[1] Commercially Reasonable Restrictions Associated with Financing

The definition of an applicable restriction contains two important exclusions. First, a commercially reasonable restriction that arises in connection with any financing undertaken by the entity with a person who is not related to the transferor or transferee, or a member of the family of either, does not constitute an applicable restriction for purposes of § 2704(b). IRC § 2704(b)(3)(A). This exception permits an unrelated party providing capital to an entity—whether in the form of equity or debt—to restrict the ability of the entity to undertake major capital transactions. *See* Treas. Reg. § 25.2704-2(b). This exception shares the same spirit as § 2703(b), as it respects restrictions on liquidation that are not motivated by tax considerations.

---

[11] Congress has authorized the Treasury Department to promulgate regulations designating other restrictions that will be disregarded for valuation purposes under § 2704(b), where the restriction has the effect of reducing the value of the transferred interest for transfer tax purposes but does not ultimately reduce the value of the transferred interest to the transferee. *See* IRC § 2704(b)(4). The Treasury Department has yet to exercise this authority.

[2] Relevance of Default State Law

The second exception to the definition of an applicable restriction has far greater breadth. An applicable restriction does not include any restriction imposed by operation of law, whether federal or state. IRC § 2704(b)(3)(B). The regulations clarify the exception somewhat, defining an applicable restriction as a limitation on the ability to liquidate an entity that is more restrictive than the limitations that would be imposed under state law in the absence of the restriction. Treas. Reg. § 25.2704-2(b). In effect, § 2704(b) presumes that any limitation on the ability to liquidate an entity above that imposed by state law is motivated by the desire to enhance the minority-interest discount. Consistent with this presumption, § 2704(b) disregards the additional liquidation restriction in valuing the transferred equity interest.

Because § 2704(b) essentially treats restrictions on liquidation imposed by state law as permissible, the specifics of the relevant partnership or LLC statute that otherwise would govern the transferred interest assume central importance in the § 2704(b) setting. This interdependence has led to a considerable amount of forum shopping among those who employ family limited partnerships or similar entities for wealth-transfer purposes. Not surprisingly, a number of states have amended their partnership or LLC statutes to impose greater restrictions on the ability to liquidate entities in an effort to make their jurisdictions more estate-planning friendly.

[3] *Kerr v. Commissioner*

The Tax Court first examined application of § 2704(b) in the family limited partnership context in *Kerr v. Commissioner*, 113 T.C. 449 (1999). The taxpayers, husband and wife, made substantial capitalizing transfers to two limited partnerships they had formed with their children. The taxpayers initially held the general partnership interests in both entities, but assigned portions of their general partnership interests to their children shortly after formation. The taxpayers thereafter made a variety of assignments of limited partnership interests in the entities to their children and to grantor retained annuity trusts. In addition, the transferors assigned a portion of their limited partnership interests in each entity to their university alma mater.

In valuing these transfers, petitioners claimed considerable discounts from the proportionate net-asset value attributable to the transferred interest on the basis that the transferred interests did not supply voting control over the entity and were not readily marketable. The Service, in turn, claimed that the restrictions on liquidation contained in the partnership agreements should be disregarded for valuation purposes pursuant to § 2704(b).

The partnership agreements governing each entity shared the same principal terms. The entities would dissolve and liquidate on the earlier of (1) the expiration of a 50-year term for the entity; (2) the agreement of all of the partners; or (3) the occurrence of narrowly defined acts of dissolution. The relevant state law provided that a limited partnership would dissolve on the earlier of (1) the occurrence of events specified in the partnership agreement to trigger dissolution; (2) the consent of all partners; (3) the withdrawal of a general partner; or (4) the entry of a decree of judicial dissolution. In comparing the restrictions on liquidation contained in the partnership agreements to those supplied by state law, the Tax Court determined that restrictions contained in the partnership agreements were no more restrictive than the restrictions that would exist in their absence. Accordingly, the court determined that § 2704(b) did not apply due to the absence of an applicable restriction. *Id.* at 473 (citing IRC

§ 2704(b)(3)(B) and Treas. Reg. § 25.2704-2(b)).

The Service contended that the relevant comparison to state law was not to the instances in which an entity could be liquidated, but rather to the right of a partner to withdraw from the partnership and receive payment for his interest. The court rejected this argument as well, noting that a "limitation on the ability to liquidate the entity" for purposes of § 2704(b)(2)(A) refers to a liquidation of the entity as a whole—not to the redemption of a particular partner's interest. *Id.*

The Fifth Circuit affirmed the result of the Tax Court's decision in *Kerr*, but on a different theory. The appellate court focused on the § 2704(b)(2)(B) requirement that the transferor and members of the transferor's family possess the right to remove any nonlapsing limitation on the entity's ability to liquidate for the limitation to constitute an applicable restriction. Recall that the taxpayers had made transfers of limited partnership interests in both entities to their university alma mater. Because removal of the restriction on liquidation required the consent of all of the partners, the restriction could not be removed by the collective action of the transferors and their family members. Hence, the definition of an applicable restriction was not satisfied under the facts of the case. *See* Kerr v. Comm'r, 292 F.3d 490, 494 (5th Cir. 2002). Although the parties stipulated that the university would convert its limited partnership interests to cash as soon as possible and, therefore, likely would not oppose removal of the limitation on liquidation contained in the partnership agreement, the Fifth Circuit found the university's likely compliance irrelevant. The statute requires that the transferor and members of his family hold the right to remove the limitation immediately after the transfer, and the school's status as a partner precluded this finding.

After holding for the taxpayer under § 2704(b)(2)(B), the Fifth Circuit noted that it need not address the issue of whether the restriction on a partner's right to withdraw from the entity and receive fair value for his interest constituted a limitation on the ability to liquidate within the meaning of § 2704(b)(2)(A). *Id.* at 494. The Fifth Circuit thereby left the Tax Court's interpretation of § 2704(b) in this context in limbo. However, the Tax Court has reaffirmed its reasoning in *Kerr* that a § 2704(b) liquidation restriction encompasses rights to liquidate the entity as a whole rather than the right of an individual partner to have his interest redeemed. *See* Estate of Jones v. Commissioner, 116 T.C. 121 (2001); Knight v. Commissioner, 115 T.C. 506 (2000).

The lasting validity of the Tax Court's reasoning in *Kerr* is important, as it is not uncommon for state law to permit a partner to withdraw and receive fair value for his interest shortly thereafter. If the Tax Court's analysis is correct, any provision in a partnership agreement restricting or even eliminating a partner's right to withdraw from the entity would not constitute an applicable restriction for purposes of § 2704(b).

§ 25.03 STUDY PROBLEMS

1. Explain how § 2704 would reverse the result in *Estate of Harrison v. Commissioner*, T.C. Memo. 1987-8, 52 T.C.M. (CCH) 1306.

2. Edward forms a family limited partnership with his two daughters. Edward contributes land worth $3 million and marketable securities worth $5.9 million; his daughters each contribute $500,000 in marketable securities. Edward also forms a wholly owned S corporation, which contributes another $100,000 in cash. In connection with the capitalization, the S corporation receives a 1 percent interest as general partner;

Edward receives an 89 percent interest as limited partner; and each of Edward's daughters receives a 5 percent interest as limited partner. Under state law, the general partner possesses managerial authority over the partnership, and the withdrawal of a general partner will cause the entity to dissolve unless the remaining partners vote to continue the entity.

After the partnership formation, Edward makes periodic gifts of his limited partnership interest to his daughters. Edward dies owning a 10 percent interest as limited partner, while retaining ownership of the S corporation that holds the 1 percent general partnership interest. Edward's will devises the remaining portion of his limited partnership interest and his S corporation stock in equal shares to his daughters.

Discuss the application, if any, of § 2704(a) to the inter vivos assignment of limited partnership interests, as well as to the transfers that occur by reason of Edward's death.

3. Assume that Maya forms an LLC to hold family assets in a jurisdiction whose LLC statute provides the following: (1) The LLC may be liquidated upon the vote of at least 80 percent of the members in interest; and (2) any LLC member may withdraw by providing 6 months notice, and the LLC member will be entitled to receive the fair value of the interest upon withdrawal.

The operating agreement of the LLC formed by Maya contains the following provisions: (1) no member may withdraw from the entity before the expiration of the entity's 40-year term; and (2) a liquidation of the entity requires the unanimous approval of all members.

After initially capitalizing the entity as a single-member LLC, Maya assigned a 10 percent membership interest to her son. The following year, Maya died owning a 90 percent interest in the LLC.

Does § 2704(b) limit the valuation discounts that are otherwise available in valuing these transfers?

Chapter 26

INTERNATIONAL CONSIDERATIONS IN FEDERAL TRANSFER TAXATION

The text thus far has addressed the federal transfer tax regime through the lens of a single state. That is, the discussion essentially has assumed that the transfer tax trilogy applies to transfers of all property made by any individual. While these assumptions are largely accurate with respect to transfers made by individuals who are citizens of the United States or non-citizen residents of the country, the federal transfer tax regime is far more circumscribed in its application to transfers by individuals who are neither citizens nor residents. As an initial matter, considerations of national sovereignty limit application of the federal transfer tax system to nonresident non-citizens to transfers of property having a domestic situs.[1] Additionally, the desire to attract foreign investment has led Congress to enact additional exclusions from the transfer tax base for nonresident non-citizens and to tolerate fairly simple planning that circumvents the transfer tax system in this context.

The porous transfer tax base applicable to nonresident non-citizen transferors creates an incentive for individuals of substantial means to expatriate to avoid the estate tax. Congress formerly addressed this prospect through an expansion of the estate and gift tax bases applicable to expatriates, but Congress revised its approach to this issue through the enactment of § 2801. Under this new approach, transfer tax is imposed at the highest marginal rate on the recipient of gifts and bequests from certain expatriated transferors.

Although issues concerning the reach of the federal transfer tax regime to nonresident non-citizens tend to dominate the international transfer tax field, the tax treatment of transfers to surviving spouses who are not citizens of the United States provides another central topic. Recall that the marital deduction implements the congressional determination to defer imposition of the federal transfer taxes until property gratuitously exits the marital unit. Yet if a transferor subject to the U.S. transfer tax system were afforded a marital deduction for

---

[1] In *Burnet v. Brooks*, 288 U.S. 378 (1933), the Supreme Court addressed whether Congress could impose an estate tax on the transfer of property of a nonresident non-citizen decedent situated in the United States. The property at issue in *Brooks* consisted primarily of securities—including stock in a foreign corporation, bonds in domestic and foreign corporations, bonds issued by foreign governments, and bonds issued by a domestic municipality—that were physically located in New York City at the time of the decedent's death. The Court upheld the application of the estate tax to this property on national sovereignty grounds:

> So far as our relation to other nations is concerned, and apart from any self-imposed constitutional restriction, we cannot fail to regard the property in question as being within the jurisdiction of the United States;—that is, it was property within the reach of the power which the United States by virtue of its sovereignty could exercise as against other nations and their subjects without violating any established principle of international law. This view of the scope of the sovereign power in the matter of the taxation of securities physically within the territorial limits of the sovereign is sustained by high authority and is a postulate of legislative action in other countries.

Id. at 396. By implication, property of a nonresident non-citizen decedent not situated in the United States would fall outside of the congressional taxing power.

transfers to a non-citizen spouse, the intended deferral of the transfer tax could amount to a permanent exclusion. To prevent this result, Congress has enacted special provisions to ensure that deductible transfers to nonresident non-citizen spouses will later be included in the federal transfer tax base.

As a final matter, the reach of the federal estate tax to property owned by citizens and residents located abroad creates the possibility for property to be subjected to transfer taxation in multiple jurisdictions. Recognizing that the country in which the transferred property is situated possesses the primary claim to taxation, Congress has provided an estate tax credit for foreign death taxes in § 2014. Additionally, the United States has entered into bilateral transfer tax treaties to resolve conflicting assertions of taxing authority.

§ 26.01 APPLICATION OF FEDERAL TRANSFER TAX REGIME TO CITIZENS AND NON-CITIZEN RESIDENTS

The federal estate tax is levied on the value of property included in a decedent's gross estate under §§ 2033 through 2044, regardless of where the property is situated. IRC § 2031(a). These provisions apply to the taxation of the estate of an individual who was a citizen of the United States or a non-citizen resident of the country at the time of death. IRC § 2001(a); Treas. Reg. § 20.0-1(b)(1). Similarly, the gift tax applies to the gratuitous transfer of property by a citizen or non-citizen resident, regardless of the location of the transferred property. *See* IRC § 2501(a); Treas. Reg. § 25.2501-1(a)(1). The GST tax follows the same path. Generation-skipping transfers of property by citizens and non-citizen residents are subject to GST tax, with the determination of citizenship or residency being made at the time of the initial inclusion of the transferred property in the transferor's gift tax or estate tax base. IRC § 2601; Treas. Reg. § 26.2663-2(a). Thus, if a transferor is determined to be a citizen of the United States or a non-citizen resident, the federal transfer tax regime applies on a worldwide basis.

[A]   Citizenship

The determination of whether an individual is a United States citizen will be straightforward in the vast majority of cases. The Constitution sets a minimum floor on citizenship, conferring that status upon any individual who is born or naturalized within the United States. U.S. Const. amend. XIV, § 1. Congress has expanded the scope of citizenship beyond the categories mandated by the Constitution, with statutory citizenship applying primarily to children born abroad if both parents are U.S. citizens or one parent is a U.S. citizen who satisfies certain residency requirements.[2]

[B]   Residency

Internal Revenue Code: §§ 2208, 2209, 2501(b), (c)
Treasury Regulations: §§ 20.0-1(b)(1), 25.2501-1(b)

While Congress has provided statutory tests for determining when an individual is a resident of the United States for federal income tax purposes, *see* IRC § 7701(b), residency for purposes of the federal transfer tax regime is determined according to an individual's

---

[2] *See* 8 U.S.C. § 1401.

domicile.[3] *See* Treas. Reg. § 20.0-1(b)(1). The regulatory definition of domicile provides as follows:

> A person acquires a domicile in a place by living there, for even a brief period of time, with no definite present intention of later removing therefrom. Residence without the requisite intention to remain indefinitely will not suffice to constitute domicile, nor will intention to change domicile effect such a change unless accompanied by actual removal.

Id. (domicile for estate tax purposes); *see also* Treas. Reg. § 25.2501-1(b) (nearly identical definition of domicile for gift tax purposes). The definition of domicile thus amounts to a two-part conjunctive test: (1) physical residence in the United States for any period of time, coupled with (2) an intention to remain in the United States indefinitely.[4] Once a domicile in the United States has been established, an individual's domicile is presumed to continue until superseded by the establishment of a domicile in another jurisdiction. *See* Rev. Rul. 80-209, 1980-2 C.B. 248, 249 (citing Mitchell v. United States, 88 U.S. (21 Wall.) 350 (1875)). Because a new domicile requires a new physical residence, a mere change in the individual's intention to remain indefinitely is not sufficient to alter the individual's domicile.

[1]   Totality of Evidence Determinations

Given that a decedent's physical residence in the United States can be readily determined, determinations of domicile generally amount to fact-intensive inquiries concerning the decedent's subjective intent to remain in the country on an indefinite basis. Because circumstantial evidence in these cases rarely points in a single direction, decisions of domicile frequently are based on the relative weight of conflicting factors. The Tax Court's decision in *Estate of Khan v. Commissioner*, T.C. Memo. 1998-22, 75 T.C.M. (CCH) 1597, provides an illustrative case.

The decedent in *Estate of Khan* was born and raised in Pakistan, where he also died. Yet the decedent had several connections to the United States. The decedent's father had immigrated to California and started a farming operation, and the decedent's son later immigrated to work in the family business. While the decedent previously had entered the country to visit his son on a temporary visa, the decedent later entered the country pursuant to a permanent resident visa (facilitated by his son's naturalization) to reside with his son and to assist his son with the family's business operations. The son expanded his residence to accommodate the decedent, adding a bedroom and bathroom for his use. During this second trip the decedent obtained a green card and a Social Security number. Roughly two years later, the decedent returned to Pakistan to visit his wife and other children, and to tend to family business affairs there. Although the decedent obtained a permit to re-enter the United States on his departure, he never returned. His health began to fail two years after his return to Pakistan, and he died in his native country a few years later.

---

[3] Because of the differing standards, an individual could be a resident of the United States for federal transfer tax purposes while not being treated as a resident alien under the federal income tax, and vice versa.

[4] Whereas birth in the "United States" for purposes of establishing citizenship includes not only the 50 states and the District of Columbia but also Puerto Rico, Guam, and the U.S. Virgin Islands, *see* 8 U.S.C. § 1101(a)(38), the "United States" for purposes of rendering an individual a resident under the federal transfer tax regime includes only the 50 states and the District of Columbia. Treas. Reg. §§ 20.0-1(b), 25.2501-1(b).

In an attempt to obtain a full unified credit under § 2010 (as opposed to the meager $13,000 credit provided to estates of nonresident non-citizen decedents under § 2102), the decedent's estate claimed that the decedent had established a U.S. domicile during his second trip and that the decedent did not establish a new domicile in Pakistan thereafter. The Tax Court agreed. In addition to citing the factors mentioned above that supported his intention to remain in the country indefinitely, the court placed considerable emphasis on the relative value of the decedent's assets that were located in the United States. *See id.* at 1604. However, as is often the case in domicile determinations, the decision was by no means clear cut. In reaching its holding, the court had to discount evidence contrary to the decedent's establishment of a U.S. domicile, including his filing of income tax returns as a nonresident alien and the fact that his wife at all times remained in Pakistan. The case demonstrates that a continued absence from a jurisdiction is not enough to alter domicile, provided the individual maintains an intention to return.

[2] Relevance of Legal Residency

Suppose an individual resides in the United States without the legal entitlement to do so. Does the absence of legal residency preclude the establishment of domicile? In Revenue Ruling 80-209, 1980-2 C.B. 248, the Service addressed the issue of whether an individual who entered the United States illegally and who continued to reside in the United States until death was a resident for purposes of the federal estate tax. Noting that the legal capacity to acquire a domicile had been found to exist even when an individual was subject to transfer to another jurisdiction at the direction of others, the ruling concluded that the decedent acquired domicile in the United States even though the decedent was subject to deportation. *Id.* at 249. The ruling noted that the result would be the same if an individual entered the United States legally pursuant to a temporary visa but overstayed the visa term. *Id.* Hence, the legal status of an individual's presence in the United States is not dispositive in the determination of residency for transfer tax purposes.

[3] Relevance of Visa Status

In *Estate of Jack v. United States*, 54 Fed. Cl. 590 (2002), the Federal Court of Claims addressed the residency status of a Canadian citizen who entered the country on a one-year nonimmigrant professional visa that he extended until his death four years later. Seeking to protect the decedent's Canadian assets from U.S. estate taxation, the decedent's estate argued that the terms of the decedent's temporary visa precluded him from establishing a domicile in the United States. Noting that the terms of a decedent's visa did not prevent the decedent from forming a subjective intent to remain in the United States indefinitely, the court denied the estate's motion for summary judgment on the residency issue. *Id.* at 599. In short, the terms of the decedent's visa were relevant but not dispositive. This holding is consistent with the articulated standard for determining domicile, which turns on the decedent's subjective intent. *See also* Rev. Rul. 80-363, 1980-2 C.B. 249 (nature of visa permitting entry into the United States did not preclude formation of intent to remain indefinitely in country). However, the Ninth Circuit took a different approach in *Carlson v. Reed*, 249 F.3d 876 (9th Cir. 2001). Noting that Congress expressly conditioned the grant of a temporary nonimmigrant visa on an individual's intent not to establish a permanent domestic residence, the Court reasoned that

Congress precluded holders of such visas from establishing domicile in the United States.[5] *Id.* at 880.

[C]   Effect of U.S. Citizenship Based on Citizenship or Birth in U.S. Possessions

An individual who is a citizen of the United States and a resident of a U.S. possession (e.g., Puerto Rico, Guam, Northern Mariana Islands, U.S. Virgin Islands, American Samoa) at the time of death or at the time a gift is made is considered a citizen of the United States subject to the U.S. estate tax and gift tax in full, unless the individual acquired U.S. citizenship solely by reason of (a) being a citizen of the U.S. possession, or (2) his birth or residence in the U.S. possession. IRC §§ 2208, 2501(b). If these latter exceptions are satisfied, the individual is treated as a nonresident non-citizen transferor for U.S. transfer tax purposes. IRC §§ 2209, 2501(c).

§ 26.02   PROPERTY SITUATED IN THE UNITED STATES

Internal Revenue Code: §§ 2104, 2105; *see also* §§ 861(a)(1)(A), 871(i), (h)

Treasury Regulations: §§ 20.2104-1, 20.2105-1, 25.2511-3

The estate of a decedent who was neither a citizen nor a resident of the United States at the time of his death is subject to U.S. estate tax only on the portion of his gross estate (determined under § 2031) that is "situated in the United States." IRC § 2103. Application of the U.S. gift tax to lifetime gratuitous transfers made by nonresident non-citizens is further circumscribed. Not only is the tax base limited to transfers of property situated in the United States, *see* IRC § 2511(a), the tax base excludes intangible property in this context regardless of its would-be situs. IRC § 2501(a)(2). The generation-skipping transfer tax as it applies to nonresident non-citizens piggy backs on these situs provisions, as the tax requires an initial transfer that was subject to either estate tax or gift tax. *See* Treas. Reg. § 26.2663-2(b). The application of the U.S. transfer tax system to transfers by individuals who are neither citizens nor residents therefore largely turns on the determination of whether property has a U.S. situs.

Sections 2104 and 2105 address when property will be considered to be situated in the United States for purposes of subjecting property of a nonresident non-citizen decedent to U.S. estate taxation. These situs provisions are generally mirrored under the regulations interpreting the gift tax. *See* Treas. Reg. § 25.2511-3.

[A]   Real Property

The quintessential example of an asset situated in the United States is domestic real property. Treas. Reg. § 20.2104-1(a)(1). Situs is based on physical location; hence, foreign realty owned by a nonresident non-citizen decedent is exempt from U.S. estate taxation. Treas. Reg. § 20.2105-1(a)(1). The determination of whether an asset constitutes real property for this purpose presumably will be determined under local law, and it is likely that a long-term lease on real property will be treated as realty for this purpose. *See* De Perigny v. Commissioner, 9 T.C. 782 (1947) (holding that 99-year leasehold interests in property located

---

[5] Accordingly, the court rejected the non-citizen's claim of state residency for purposes of obtaining lower in-state tuition.

in Kenya to be real property located outside of the United States).

Suppose a nonresident non-citizen decedent owned domestic realty encumbered by a mortgage. What amount should be included in the decedent's gross estate: the net equity of the property, or the full unencumbered fair market value of the property? The Tax Court in *Estate of Fung v. Commissioner*, 117 T.C. 247 (2001), determined that an estate must include the unencumbered fair market value of real property in the decedent's gross estate in instances where the decedent is personally liable for repayment of the debt secured by the property. However, if the debt obligation is nonrecourse as to the decedent, the estate may elect to include in the gross estate only the net equity of the property. Treas. Reg. § 20.2053-7; *see also* Johnstone v. Commissioner, 19 T.C. 44 (1952). While this point may prove academic in the purely domestic setting given the § 2053(a)(4) deduction for indebtedness attributable to property included in the gross estate, the estate of a nonresident non-citizen decedent is limited to a pro-rated § 2053 deduction based on the relative value of the gross estate having a U.S. situs in relation to the value of the entire gross estate, wherever situated. IRC § 2106(a)(1). Hence, the absence of personal liability for the debt obligation secured by the domestic real property effectively provides an undiluted deduction for the secured debt.

[B] Tangible Personal Property

Like real property, the determination of whether tangible personal property is situated within or without the United States is based on physical location. Treas. Reg. §§ 20.2104-1(a)(2), 20.2105-1(a)(2). An exception to this general rule exists for works of art that are located in the United States for purposes of exhibition at a nonprofit museum or gallery. IRC § 2105(c). Additionally, tangible personal property located within the United States because it is in the possession of a nonresident non-citizen visiting the country will not be considered to be "situated" in the United States for estate tax purposes, as the requisite degree of permanency is lacking. *See* Delaney v. Murchie, 177 F.2d 444, 448 (1st Cir. 1949) (reasoning that the situs of a chattel "involves some degree of permanence").

While tangible personal property typically encompasses movable physical objects that have intrinsic value (as opposed to representative value), the line between tangible and intangible personal property at times is not clear. Take United States currency for example. Technically, a dollar bill represents a debt obligation of the United States. Yet, as a practical matter, the use of currency as a medium of exchange yields intrinsic value to the paper. Consistent with this view, the regulations governing debt obligations exclude currency from their reach. Treas. Reg. § 20.2104-1(a)(7). Both domestic and foreign currencies therefore are regarded as tangible personal property for purposes of the situs rules. Currency that is physically located in the United States therefore is subject to U.S. estate taxation, even if the cash is located in a safe deposit box. *See* Rev. Rul. 55-143, 1955-1 C.B. 465 (cash in safe deposit box not treated as a bank deposit under situs rules due to absence of debtor-creditor relationship). Additionally, lifetime gifts of cash by a nonresident non-citizen donor that have a physical connection to the United States—either because the gifts are drawn on a U.S. bank or deposited to a U.S. account—run the risk of being subject to U.S. gift taxation.

[C] Intangible Personal Property

The regulations provide a general rule for determining the situs of intangible personal property, provided that the written evidence of the property is not treated as being the property itself. In that case, the intangible personal property is situated in the United States if it is issued by or enforceable against a United States resident, a domestic corporation, or a governmental unit. Treas. Reg. § 20.2104-1(a)(4); *see also* Treas. Reg. § 20.2105-1(e) (intangible personal property not meeting these conditions considered to have non-U.S. situs). Yet due to the presence of specific statutory treatment of corporate stock, debt instruments, and life insurance, the general rule may have only a limited, residual application. *See* Treas. Reg. § 20.2104-1(a)(4) (noting that the statutory exceptions "cause this subparagraph to have relatively limited applicability").

Application of the general rule concerning the situs intangible property appears clear in certain instances. Under the "issued by" prong, any intangible property right that is conferred by a U.S. government agency would have a U.S. situs. Additionally, a license issued by a U.S. individual or corporation to use or exploit intangible property rights (e.g., software, music) would have a U.S. situs. Under the "enforceable against" prong, a cause of action against a U.S. individual or corporation would be regarded as situated in the United States. Yet the awkward wording of the general provision may preclude it from serving a true catch-all function for intangible property. For instance, suppose a nonresident non-citizen owns a restaurant located in the United States that is operated as a sole proprietorship. The restaurant has a loyal following, and one of its most valuable assets is the goodwill of the business. Yet goodwill is not issued by a given party, it arises as a result of operations. Additionally, goodwill cannot be enforced against a party; rather, it simply represents the prospect of continued patronage. Hence, goodwill and other vaguely defined intangible assets may fall outside the intended default rule on definitional grounds.

[D]   Corporate Stock

Corporate stock constitutes property situated in the United States only if the stock is issued by a domestic corporation. IRC § 2104(a). Accordingly, stock in a corporation incorporated under the laws of a foreign jurisdiction is situated outside of the United States. The regulations make no reference to the location of the corporation's assets or the jurisdiction in which the corporation operates its business, suggesting that these considerations are irrelevant. Instead, the regulations state that the physical location of the stock certificates in the subject corporation are not relevant to the determination of situs, a statement that essentially clarifies that corporate stock will not be treated as tangible personal property for situs purposes. Treas. Reg. §§ 20.2104-1(a)(5), 20.2105-1(f).

The situs provisions applicable to corporate stock provide the primary means of insulating property owned by a nonresident non-citizen from U.S. transfer taxation. Capitalizing a foreign corporation with property that would have a U.S. situs if owned by the contributing shareholder renders the situs of the corporate assets irrelevant for transfer tax purposes. For example, a nonresident non-citizen could capitalize a foreign corporation with real estate located in the United States and thereby insulate the realty from U.S. estate taxation.

The key to this relatively straightforward planning technique is to ensure that the foreign corporation is not viewed as the alter ego of the decedent, which would permit a court to look-through the entity in determining the transfer tax situs of the corporate assets. For example, in *Fillman v. United States*, 355 F.2d 632 (Ct. Cl. 1966), a Swiss national transferred securities in United States and foreign entities to two Argentinean corporations in an attempt to prevent the property from being confiscated by the German army. The corporations opened custodial accounts with a brokerage firm in New York. Finding that the corporations acted as a mere depositor and custodian for the decedent, the court determined that the decedent owned the underlying securities for purposes of subjecting them to U.S. estate taxation. Accordingly, if a foreign corporation is employed as a holding company to circumvent U.S. transfer taxation on its assets, care should be taken to ensure that the parties comply with corporate formalities and respect the corporation as an entity separate and distinct from the personal affairs of the shareholders.[6] *See* Moline Properties, Inc. v. Commissioner, 319 U.S. 436 (1943) (recognizing a corporation as a separate taxable entity so long as the corporation has a business purpose or carries on a business).

Additionally, it is imperative that the entity employed constitute a corporation to benefit from the § 2104(a) corollary safe harbor. *See, e.g.*, Estate of Swan v. Commissioner, 247 F.2d 144 (2d Cir. 1957) (determining that family foundations established in Liechtenstein and Switzerland more closely resembled revocable trusts than foreign corporations). Presumably much of the uncertainty on this front has been eliminated through promulgation of the entity-classification regulations under § 7701, which treat certain foreign business entities as corporations for federal tax purposes. *See* Treas. Reg. § 301.7701-2(b)(8).

[E]   Partnership Interests

If a non-corporate entity is not automatically treated as a corporation pursuant to Reg. § 301.7701-2, an entity having multiple members may elect to be treated as a corporation or a partnership for federal tax purposes, with a partnership serving as the default classification. Treas. Reg. § 301.7701-3(a), (b). However, unlike corporate stock, the situs treatment of beneficial interests in partnerships is not addressed by statute or specific regulation. Due to the lack of clarity, use of non-corporate entities for international estate planning purposes is generally viewed as undesirable.

A preliminary inquiry in determining the U.S. tax treatment of a transfer of a beneficial interest in a partnership by a nonresident non-citizen is whether the partnership will be analyzed under an aggregate or entity theory. If the partnership is viewed simply as an aggregation of the partners' direct ownership interests, the entity is irrelevant in determining situs for U.S. transfer tax purposes. Instead, the owner of the beneficial interest is treated as owning a pro-rata portion of the partnership assets, requiring a situs determination with respect to each asset of the partnership.

The Service has indicated that it will not follow the aggregate theory when making situs determinations concerning the transfer of a partnership interest by a nonresident non-citizen. In Revenue Ruling 55-701, 1955-2 C.B. 836, the Service addressed the U.S. estate tax treatment of a partnership interest of a British subject and domiciliary under the existing U.S.-U.K. estate tax convention, which at that time allocated taxing rights based on the situs

---

[6] In that regard, the volume of litigation concerning the application of § 2036(a)(1) to property contributed to family limited partnerships based on a contributing partner's continued beneficial enjoyment of the partnership property would appear relevant to the foreign corporation holding company technique. *See* § 10.01[E]. Even if the separate existence of the corporation is respected, it remains possible for the government to assert that § 2036(a)(1) and (a)(2) apply to property contributed to the foreign corporation based on the contributing shareholder's ability to control the timing and amount of corporate distributions to himself and others. *See, e.g.*, Estate of Strangi v. Commissioner, T.C. Memo. 2003-145, 85 T.C.M. (CCH) 1331, discussed in § 11.06. However, this argument for treating the capitalization of a foreign corporation as an incomplete transfer of the corporate assets for U.S. estate tax purposes has been largely eliminated by the forgiving interpretation of the § 2036(a) exception for transfers that constitute a bona fide sale for an adequate and full consideration in money or money's worth. *See* Estate of Bongard v. Commissioner, 124 T.C. 95 (2005), discussed in § 13.04[C].

of property. In examining the various options for determining situs, at no point did the ruling consider disregarding the entity and making an asset-by-asset situs determination. After rejecting the option of determining situs of the partnership interest by treating it as a debt obligation, the ruling addressed whether the situs of the partnership interest (as a separate asset) should be determined by (1) the location of the partnership assets or (2) the location where the partnership's business is carried on. Evidently viewing the first option as an extension of the aggregate theory that had been rejected in the context of interstate taxation, the ruling determined that the situs of the partnership interest should be determined by the location of its business operations.

Although Revenue Ruling 55-701 suggests that the Service will view a beneficial interest in a partnership as separate item of intangible property (consistent with the entity theory of partnerships), the Service continues to refuse to issue advance rulings on whether a partnership interest constitutes intangible personal property for gift tax purposes. *See* Rev. Proc. 2010-7, 2010-1 I.R.B. 231. Assuming that a beneficial interest in a partnership is appropriately viewed as an intangible asset for purposes of determining the situs of the property, the situs of a partnership interest would be determined under the general provision of Reg. § 20.2104-1(a)(4).

Under Reg. § 20.2104-1(a)(4), a partnership interest would have a U.S. situs if it were issued by or enforceable against a U.S. resident, a domestic corporation, or a governmental unit. Given that unincorporated business entities generally are organized pursuant to state statutory authority, a partnership interest can be viewed as having been issued—at least in part—by a domestic governmental unit. In that case, a partnership formed under domestic state law would constitute property situated in the United States, regardless of the location of the entity's assets or the location of its business operations. As a corollary, a partnership or other entity organized in a foreign jurisdiction would have a non-U.S. situs under this interpretation of Reg. § 20.2104-1(a)(4).

On the other hand, Reg. § 20.2104-1(a)(4) may be more appropriately applied to a partnership interest based on the "enforceable against" prong of the regulation. Presumably, the party against whom the interest would be enforced would be the partnership itself—a somewhat question-begging inquiry. Yet the entity classification regulations speak to this latter issue. A business entity is classified as domestic if it is created or organized in the United States or pursuant to any federal or state law. Treas. Reg. § 301.7701-5(a). Any business entity that is not a domestic entity is treated as foreign. *Id.* Application of the "enforceable against" prong of Reg. § 20.2104-1(a)(4) therefore appears to yield the same result as the "issued by" prong, with the situs of a partnership interest being determined by the jurisdiction in which the partnership is organized.

[F]　Debt Obligations

As a general rule, a debt obligation has a U.S. situs if it constitutes an obligation of (1) a United States resident, (2) the United States government, (3) any political subdivision of the United States, or (4) the District of Columbia. IRC § 2104(c). This general rule applies regardless of whether the debt instrument is regarded as the property interest itself, and regardless of whether the decedent is engaged in business in the United States at the time of death. Treas. Reg. § 20.2104-1(a)(7).

The situs rule for general debt obligations is subordinate to § 2105(b), which primarily treats certain bank deposits as situated outside of the United States. However, one provision of § 2105(b) applies to nondepository debt obligations. If the interest on the debt obligation would be excluded from the gross income of the nonresident non-citizen pursuant to the portfolio-interest exclusion of § 871(h), the debt obligation is treated as situated outside of the United States. IRC § 2105(b)(3). The exception for debt obligations that generate portfolio interest generally applies to debt obligations that are issued in registered form. Hence, publicly traded bonds of a U.S. corporation held by a nonresident non-citizen decedent will be treated as situated outside of the United States and thereby exempt from U.S. estate taxation, provided the numerous requirements for the portfolio-interest income exclusion of § 871(h) are satisfied.

Additionally, the § 2104(c) general rule for determining the situs of a debt obligation does not apply to an obligation of a U.S. corporation if the interest on such obligation would be treated as income from sources outside the United States under § 861(a)(1)(A). Generally, this exception is satisfied if the corporate obligor realizes more than 80 percent of its gross income from active foreign businesses.

[G] Bank Deposits

By providing that certain bank deposits and debt obligations will be considered to be situated outside the United States, § 2105(b) represents a broad exception to the general debt situs provision contained in § 2104(c). So long as the deposit is not effectively connected with the operation of a trade or business within the United States, the balance of the account will be considered to be situated outside the United States. IRC §§ 2105(b)(1), 871(i). Accordingly, a nonresident non-citizen does not face exposure to the U.S. estate tax by making deposits with domestic banking institutions.[7] Bank deposits made with a foreign branch of a domestic bank are similarly considered to be situated outside the United States, provided the foreign branch is engaged in the commercial banking business. IRC § 2105(b)(2).

The generous treatment of bank deposits for situs purposes requires a depository relationship between the nonresident non-citizen decedent and the banking institution. Amounts held by an institution in a fiduciary capacity do not constitute a deposit with a person carrying on a banking business, due to the restrictions placed on the beneficiary's right to the funds. Rev. Rul. 69-596, 1969-2 C.B. 179. Similarly, amounts held by a brokerage firm as an agent of a decedent following the sale of property on decedent's behalf—even if deposited in the brokerage firm's bank account—do not provide the decedent with the requisite direct and enforceable claim against a deposit. Rather, the decedent must be the depositor. See Estate of Ogarrio v. Commissioner, 40 T.C. 242 (1963), aff'd per curiam, 337 F.2d 108 (D.C. Cir. 1964); see also Rev. Rul. 65-245, 1965-2 C.B. 379. However, the Tax Court took a more forgiving approach in Estate of Worthington v. Commissioner, 18 T.C. 796 (1952). The decedent in Estate of Worthington was a nonresident non-citizen who died possessing the right to receive a distribution from her grandfather's estate. An investment advisory firm, as an agent of the grandfather's estate, had deposited funds with two New York banks in the firm's name. Notwithstanding the decedent's inability to withdraw the account proceeds, the court determined that the funds constituted amounts on deposit on behalf of the decedent that,

---

[7] Although § 2104(c) treats amounts on deposit with a domestic branch of a foreign bank as situated in the United States provided the branch is engaged in the commercial banking business, the exception under § 2105(b) overrides this situs determination for most depository accounts.

accordingly, were treated as situated outside of the United States. *Id.* at 800–01.

[H] Life Insurance

Amounts received as insurance on the life of an individual who is a nonresident non-citizen are deemed to be property located outside of the United States. IRC § 2105(a). Presumably this statutory situs exclusion represents a nod to domestic insurance companies, as it eliminates any estate tax barrier to the purchase of an insurance policy by a nonresident non-citizen. However, it is worth noting that the exclusion does not apply to life insurance policies across the board. If a nonresident non-citizen decedent owned an insurance policy on the life of another, the situs of that asset would be determined under the general rules applicable to intangible property.

[I] Incomplete Lifetime Transfers

Because the incomplete-transfer provisions of §§ 2035 to 2038 apply in determining the gross estate of a nonresident non-citizen decedent, it is important to ascertain at which point the situs of the transferred property will be determined—that is, at the time the decedent transferred the property, or at the time of the decedent's death. From a policy perspective, it makes more sense to determine the situs of the transferred property for purposes of determining inclusion in the gross estate at the time of the decedent's death. Because a decedent who retained ownership of property could avoid U.S. taxation by ensuring the property had a foreign situs at the time of death, individuals who make incomplete lifetime transfers of property should be afforded the same flexibility. Yet § 2104(b) adopts a harsher approach. Property captured in the gross estate under §§ 2035 through 2038 will be treated as situated in the United States for estate tax purposes if the property had a U.S. situs *either* at the time of the transfer *or* at the time of the decedent's death. Hence, if a nonresident non-citizen individual transfers U.S. real estate and stocks in U.S. corporations while retaining the right to receive the income from the transferred property, the trust assets will be subject to U.S. estate taxation even if the trust assets had been reinvested in property having a foreign situs.

§ 26.03 APPLICATION OF FEDERAL TRANSFER TAX REGIME TO NONRESIDENT NON-CITIZENS

[A] Estate Tax

Internal Revenue Code: §§ 2101–2104, 2106, 2056(d)(1), (2)(A).
Treasury Regulations: §§ 20.2106-1, -2

[1] The Taxable Estate

The heart of the application of the U.S. estate tax to decedents who are neither citizens nor residents of the United States at the time of death lies in determining whether the decedent's property was situated in the United States, as § 2103 limits the decedent's gross estate to property having a domestic situs in this context. Once the decedent's gross estate has been determined, § 2106(a) provides for certain deductions in computing the decedent's taxable estate.

Section 2106(a)(1) provides for a proportionate deduction of expenses under §§ 2053 and 2054 based on the ratio of the gross estate comprised of property situated in the United States to the value of the decedent's gross estate, wherever situated. In calculating this proportionate deduction, whether the amounts deducted were incurred or expended in the United States or abroad is immaterial. Treas. Reg. § 20.2106-2(a)(2). Pursuant to § 2106(a)(2), a charitable deduction is allowed on the terms provided in § 2055, provided the charitable recipient constitutes a domestic governmental unit, a charitable corporation or association created or organized in the United States, or a trust whose assets must be used for charitable purposes within the United States. IRC § 2106(a)(2); Treas. Reg. § 20.2106-1(a)(2). Additionally, the amount of the deductible transfer may not exceed the amount of the transferred property that is required to be included in the gross estate under § 2103. IRC § 2106(a)(2)(D). Hence, transfers of foreign situs property to U.S. charitable organizations are not deductible against the U.S. estate tax. Because the extent of the deduction for expenses or losses under § 2106(a)(1) and the charitable deduction under § 2106(a)(2) depend in some part on the portion of the decedent's gross estate that is not situated in the United States, these deductions are allowed only if the estate files an estate tax return that discloses the extent of the decedent's gross estate that has a foreign situs. IRC § 2106(b).

Following the retirement of the state death tax credit under § 2011 and the advent of the deduction for state death taxes under § 2058, § 2106(a)(4) provides a proportionate deduction for state death taxes in the estate of a nonresident non-citizen decedent. The proportion is based on the ratio that the value of the property included in the decedent's gross estate under § 2103 and subject to the relevant state death taxes bears to the total value of the decedent's gross estate under § 2103.

As a final matter, § 2106(a)(3) allows a marital deduction with respect to transfers of property included in the decedent's gross estate under § 2103 to the decedent's spouse under the principles of § 2056. However, if the decedent's surviving spouse is not a U.S. citizen, the marital deduction is allowed only if the property transferred to the surviving spouse is held in a qualified domestic trust. IRC § 2056(d)(1), (2)(A).[8]

[2]   Computation of Tax Liability

Once the taxable estate is determined, a tentative tax is computed on the combined amount of the taxable estate plus the adjusted taxable gifts (post-1976 gifts that are not captured in the gross estate) of the decedent under the rates imposed by § 2001(c), less the amount of the tentative tax computed on the decedent's adjusted taxable gifts alone. IRC § 2101(b), (c). Various credits are available to reduce the gross estate tax liability. Section 2102(a) makes available the full credit under § 2012 for gift tax paid on pre-1977 gifts and the full credit under § 2013 for tax paid on property included in the gross estate that was subject to a recently imposed estate tax. However, unless modified by an existing tax treaty, the unified credit otherwise provided under § 2010 is severely limited in the estate of a nonresident non-citizen decedent. Instead of the regular unified credit of $1,730,800 (shielding $5 million from taxation), § 2102(b)(1) provides a meager unified credit in this context of only $13,000.[9] This

---

[8] These additional limitations are the subject of § 26.05.

[9] If a tax treaty affords the estate of a nonresident non-citizen decedent a full unified credit under § 2010, the credit is allowed only on a pro-rated basis. The portion of the credit allowable is based on the ratio of the value of the decedent's gross estate having a U.S. situs to the value of the decedent's gross estate, wherever situated. IRC § 2102(c)(3). Additionally, decedents who are treated as nonresident non-citizens pursuant to § 2209 are offered a

credit exempts only $60,000 from taxation. Given the minimal amount of the unified credit, the marginal rate that applies to the estate of a nonresident non-citizen decedent starts at 26 percent. *See* IRC § 2001(c).

[B]   Gift Tax

Internal Revenue Code: §§ 2501(a)(2), 2511(a), 2522(b), 2523(i), 2513(a)

[1]   Taxable Transfers

The U.S. gift tax is far less reaching in its application to nonresident non-citizen transferors than the estate tax. Pursuant to § 2501(a)(2), the gift tax does not apply to the gratuitous transfer of intangible property by a nonresident non-citizen transferor. The gift tax therefore is limited to transfers of tangible property, real or personal. Section 2511(a) confirms that gifts of real property or tangible personal property by a nonresident non-citizen transferor are subject to U.S. gift taxation only if the transferred property is situated in the United States.

Given the limited application of the U.S. gift tax to nonresident non-citizen transferors, the tax may amount to little more than a trap for the unwary. For example, suppose a nonresident non-citizen desires to make a gift of U.S. real property to a family member. With no planning, a transfer of the property would trigger U.S. gift taxation. However, if the transferor were to restructure ownership of the real property through a foreign corporation or partnership, the transferor would then hold an intangible asset. The subsequent transfer of that intangible asset then would be exempt from U.S. gift taxation.

The technique of converting tangible property into an intangible asset yields some exposure to the step transaction doctrine, particularly when the conversion occurs shortly before the gift. For example, in *De Goldschmidt-Rothschild v. Commissioner*, 168 F.2d 975 (2d Cir. 1948), the transferor converted domestic stocks and bonds (which, at the time, would have subjected the transferor to gift tax) to government bonds, and transferred those bonds to trusts established for her children. Half of the bonds were sold a week after the gifts were made, while the remaining half were sold within eight months. Based on this record, the Second Circuit affirmed the Tax Court's determination that the asset conversion resulted from a pre-arranged plan to avoid the gift tax. Accordingly, the transferred property was considered to have a U.S. situs. *Id.* at 979.

Additionally, potential substance-over-form arguments must be considered in structuring gratuitous transactions by nonresident non-citizen transferors to avoid the gift tax. In *Davies v. Commissioner*, 40 T.C. 525 (1963), the donor sold real estate in Hawaii to his son for a cash down payment and a promissory note for the balance of the purchase price. The donor supplied his son with the funds necessary to make the down payment prior to the completion of the transfer. Although the transaction was structured as sale for adequate and full consideration, the Tax Court concluded that father had made a gift of the U.S. realty to his son equal to the difference between the value of the property and the amount of the son's promissory note, disregarding the circular flow of the cash down payment because it was required to be used for that purpose. *Id.* at 530–31. However, even though the father made subsequent gifts to his son to enable the son to satisfy his obligations under the note, these later gifts were not similarly disregarded because the son's use of the transferred funds was not restricted. *Id.* at 531.

---

slightly increased unified credit, which is capped at $46,800. IRC § 2102(b)(2).

[2] Exclusions and Deductions

Given the ease with which the U.S. gift tax base can be circumvented in this context, the ancillary aspects of the gift tax as applied to a nonresident non-citizen transferor warrant only cursory discussion. The inflation-adjusted annual exclusion under § 2503(b) is available on the same basis afforded to U.S. citizens or residents. Gifts to charitable organizations are deductible, but only to the extent the charitable recipient is a U.S. governmental unit, a domestic charitable corporation, a veterans' organization organized in the United States, or a charitable trust the property of which will be used within the United States. IRC § 2522(b).

A marital deduction is permitted under § 2523 if the transferor's spouse is a United States citizen. IRC § 2523(i)(1). However, not only is a deduction disallowed for a transfer to a non-citizen spouse, the exception for transfers to a qualified domestic trust under the estate tax is not available under the gift tax. Instead, the § 2503(b) annual exclusion for otherwise deductible lifetime transfers to a non-citizen spouse is increased to a generous level of $100,000, as adjusted for inflation.[10] IRC § 2523(i)(2). This enhanced annual exclusion amount stands at $136,000 for 2011. The absence of a marital deduction therefore does not preclude meaningful transfers to non-citizen spouses from occurring free of gift tax.

[3] Rates and Credits

The gift tax rates applicable to transfers by U.S. citizens or residents imposed by § 2501(a) (which incorporates the estate tax schedule under § 2001(c)) apply to gifts made by nonresident non-citizen transferors as well. However, the unified credit provided by § 2505 is not available to a nonresident non-citizen transferor. Accordingly, the gift tax commences on taxable gifts at a marginal rate of 18 percent.

[4] Determination of Transferor

Section 2513(a) generally treats a married couple as a single unit for gift tax purposes by permitting spouses to elect for a transfer from one spouse to be considered as having been made by both spouses in equal shares. The primary benefit of the so-called "split-gift" election is to allow each spouse's annual exclusion to reduce the amount of the taxable gift. However, the election is available only if both spouses are citizens or residents of the United States. *See* IRC § 2513(a). Converting a single transfer from one spouse into two transfers of equal portions from both spouses in this context therefore requires a preliminary transfer from one spouse to another that is not disregarded under the step-transaction. Due to the disallowance of the marital deduction to lifetime transfers to a non-citizen spouse under § 2523(i)(1), this preliminary transfer must be structured to take advantage of the increased annual exclusion for transfers to such spouses provided by § 2523(i)(2).[11]

[C] Generation-Skipping Transfer Tax

Internal Revenue Code: § 2663(2)
Treasury Regulations: § 26.2663-2(a), (b)

---

[10] Additionally, special rules apply to the creation of joint interests in property between spouses where one spouse is a non-citizen. *See* § 26.05[C].

[11] For a discussion of lifetime transfers to non-citizen spouses, see § 26.05.

Section 2663(2) authorizes the Treasury Department to promulgate regulations that apply the generation-skipping transfer tax to transfers made by a nonresident non-citizen transferor. Treasury has done so through Reg. § 26.2663-2. In short, imposition of GST tax in this context is predicated on the nonresident non-citizen transferor having made a transfer that is subject to either the estate tax or the gift tax. Treas. Reg. § 26.2663-2(b). Accordingly, if a transfer in trust does not constitute a direct skip (so that the imposition of the GST tax is separated from the imposition of the gift or estate taxes), the situs of the transferred property at the time of its initial transfer to the trust determines whether the GST tax will apply in the future.

Pursuant to the regulations, each nonresident non-citizen transferor is allowed a GST exemption of $1 million. Treas. Reg. § 26.2663-2(a). This regulation was issued in 1995, before the GST exemption was indexed for inflation and before the base amount of the GST exemption was increased. The regulation presumably should be interpreted as affording a nonresident non-citizen transferor the full amount of the current $5 million GST exemption under § 2631. The rules concerning allocation of the GST exemption in this context are the same as those applicable to transfers by U.S. citizens or residents. Treas. Reg. § 26.2663-2(a).

§ 26.04   EXPATRIATION AS A MEANS OF AVOIDING FEDERAL TRANSFER TAXATION

Internal Revenue Code: §§ 2801, 877A, 877(a)(2)(A)–(C)
                              skim §§ 2701, 2501(a)(3), (5), 2511(b)

[A]   Prior Expansion of Transfer Tax Base of Expatriates

Given the limited application of the U.S. estate tax and gift tax to nonresident non-citizens, it would be tempting for individuals of substantial means to move abroad, renounce their citizenship, and structure their holdings to have a foreign situs. Congress previously addressed this prospect through an expansion of the estate and gift tax bases applicable to expatriated transferors for a 10-year period following expatriation.[12] Specifically, §§ 2107 and 2501(a)(5) broadened the estate tax base and gift tax base, respectively, of a transferor to include a portion of the value of the transferor's stock in a closely held foreign corporation based on the portion of the corporation's assets having a U.S. situs. IRC §§ 2701(b), 2501(a)(5). Additionally, § 2501(a)(3) eliminated the exclusion of all intangible property from the gift tax base of a nonresident non-citizen transferor. Accordingly, transfers of intangible property by an expatriate during the 10-year period following expatriation would be subject to gift tax if the intangible property was considered to be situated in the United States. *See* IRC § 2511(b) (providing situs rules for intangible property in this context).

Congress fundamentally altered the tax treatment of expatriation through the enactment of the Heroes Earnings Assistance and Relief Tax Act of 2008.[13] *See* Notice 2009-85, 2009-2 C.B. 598 (explaining provisions of legislation addressing tax consequences of expatriation).

---

[12]   Sections 2107(a) and 2501(a)(3), (5) applied to expatriates who were subject to the alternative income tax regime of § 877. As a general rule, the alternative income tax regime of § 877 applied to expatriates who met certain income or wealth thresholds and for whom limited exceptions for individuals possessing dual citizenship and for minors having limited contact with the United States did not apply. The alternative income tax regime under § 877 applied for 10 years following the date of expatriation; hence, §§ 2107(a), 2503(a)(3), and 2501(a)(5) had the same 10-year shelf life.

[13]   Pub. L. No. 110-245, 122 Stat. 1624 (2008). The legislation applies to transfers made by individuals who expatriated on or after June 17, 2008.

The primary feature of the legislation was the introduction of § 877A,[14] under which all property owned by a "covered expatriate" is deemed to have been sold for fair market value on the date prior to the date of expatriation. IRC § 877A(a)(1)–(2). Any resulting net gain is included in the individual's gross income to the extent it exceeds an inflation-adjusted $600,000 exemption. IRC § 877A(a)(3). The exit tax imposed by § 877A superseded and replaced the alternative income tax regime imposed by § 877 for those whose expatriation date was on or after June 17, 2008, the date the legislation became effective. *See* IRC § 877(h). Because the base-expanding provisions of §§ 2701, 2501(a)(3), and 2501(a)(5) are all predicated on the transferor being subject to the alternative income tax regime of § 877, these provisions similarly have limited future application.

[B] Section 2801

In addition to imposing mark-to-market income taxation on certain expatriates, the 2008 legislation introduced chapter 15 into the U.S. transfer tax system, entitled "Gifts and Bequests from Expatriates."[15] This chapter consists of a single statute, § 2801. Instead of focusing on the transfer tax base of an expatriated individual, § 2801 imposes a transfer tax on the recipient of a gratuitous transfer from a covered expatriate. Section 2801 is apparently based on the belief that, while the expatriation of one member of a wealthy U.S. family may be worth the transfer tax savings, the savings likely will not be sufficient to cause the entire family to relinquish U.S. citizenship or residency. Accordingly, when property is subsequently transferred to a U.S. citizen or resident from an expatriated family member, the property will then be subject to U.S. transfer tax.

[1] Tax Imposed on Recipient of Covered Gift or Bequest

Section 2801 imposes a transfer tax at the highest marginal rate provided in § 2001(c) on the receipt of any "covered gift or bequest" by a U.S. citizen or resident, to the extent the transfer is not included in the estate tax or gift tax base of the transferor. IRC § 2801(a), (e)(2). Whereas primary liability for U.S. transfer taxes generally is imposed on the transferor, liability for the § 2801 tax rests on the recipient. IRC § 2801(b). If a covered gift or bequest is made to a domestic trust, the trust is treated as a recipient for purposes of § 2801(a) and the resulting tax must be paid by the trust. IRC § 2801(e)(4)(A). On the other hand, a foreign trust is not treated as a recipient under § 2801(a). Instead, if a covered gift or bequest is made to a foreign trust, any subsequent distribution from such trust to a U.S. citizen or resident is treated as a covered gift or bequest that triggers the § 2801(a) tax. IRC § 2801(e)(4)(B).

A number of offsets or exclusions are available in computing the § 2801(a) tax. To start, the recipient is entitled to the benefit of the § 2503(b) annual exclusion. IRC § 2801(c). Additionally, a covered gift or bequest that serves as the base of the § 2801(a) tax does not include any property with respect to which a charitable deduction or marital deduction would have been allowed if the transferor were a U.S. person. IRC § 2801(e)(3). Finally, the amount of the § 2801(a) tax imposed on the recipient is reduced by any estate tax or gift tax imposed on the transfer by a foreign jurisdiction. IRC § 2801(d).

---

[14] *See id.*, § 301(a), 122 Stat. at 1638–44.

[15] *See id.* § 301(b), 122 Stat. at 1644–46.

[2] Covered Expatriates

A "covered gift or bequest" for purposes of § 2801 encompasses any property acquired by gift, either directly or indirectly, from an individual who was a "covered expatriate" immediately prior to the transfer, as well as property acquired by reason of the death of a covered expatriate. IRC § 2801(e)(1). Section 2801 incorporates the definition of a covered expatriate employed under § 877A, *see* IRC § 2801(f), and that term is defined in § 877A(g)(1).

The starting point of a covered expatriate under § 877A(g)(1) is the definition of an expatriate. Under § 877A(g)(2), an expatriate includes not only a U.S. citizen who relinquishes citizenship, but also a long-term resident of the United States who ceases to be a lawful permanent resident of the country within the meaning of § 7701(b)(6) (generally, termination of green card status). An individual is a long-term resident of the United States if the individual was a lawful permanent resident of the United States for 8 out of the past 15 taxable years prior to the termination of lawful permanent residence status. IRC §§ 877A(g)(5), 877(e)(2).

In determining whether an expatriate constitutes a covered expatriate, § 877A incorporates the tests employed by § 877. IRC §§ 877A(g)(1)(A), 877(a)(2)(A)–(C). Under these provisions, an expatriate is a covered expatriate if (a) the individual's average income tax liability exceeded an inflation-adjusted floor of $124,000 (which amounted to $147,000 in 2011 for the 5-year period preceding expatriation, (b) the individual's net worth exceeded $2 million on the date of expatriation, or (c) the individual failed to certify under penalties of perjury compliance with U.S. federal tax obligations for the 5-year period preceding expatriation or failed to supply evidence of such compliance requested by the Service. Given the importance of the expatriation date under these provisions, § 877A defines the expatriation date in § 877A(g)(3). In particular, the statute clarifies that an individual will not be treated as losing U.S. citizenship based on a renunciation or voluntarily relinquishment of nationality until a statement of such renunciation or relinquishment is approved by the U.S. State Department. IRC § 877A(g)(4) (flush paragraph).

The statute provides exceptions to an individual's status as a covered expatriate based on the income tax liability and net worth tests described in § 877(a)(2)(A) and (B). The first exception applies to individuals who possessed dual citizenship with the United States and another country from birth. In that case, the individual is not a covered expatriate (a) if he continues to be a citizen of, and is taxed as a resident of, such other country as of the date of expatriation, and (b) the individual has not been a resident of the United States for more than 10 taxable years during the 15-taxable-year period ending with the year of expatriation. IRC § 877A(g)(1)(B)(i). The second exception applies to minors who have limited contact with the United States. An individual is not a covered expatriate if (a) the individual relinquishes U.S. citizenship prior to attaining age 18½ and (b) the individual has not been a resident of the United States for more than 10 years. IRC § 877A(g)(1)(B)(ii).

If an individual who satisfies the test for a covered expatriate again becomes subject to U.S. taxation either as a citizen or resident during a period following expatriation, § 2801 does not apply to the individual during any such period. IRC § 877A(g)(1)(C). Accordingly, transfers from an individual during this period will be taxed at their actual rate under § 2001(c) as opposed to the maximum marginal rate required by § 2801(a), and the resulting tax will be paid by the transferor as opposed to the recipient.

§ 26.05 TRANSFERS TO NON-CITIZEN SPOUSES

Internal Revenue Code: §§ 2056(d), 2056A(a), (b)(1)–(4), (10)–(12), 2523(i), 2040(a), (b)

Treasury Regulations: §§ 20.2056A-2(a), (b)(1), 20.2056A-5(b)(3), (c)(2)

skim § 20.2056A-2(d)(1)(i), (ii), (d)(3)

[A] General Disallowance of the Marital Deduction

The unlimited marital deduction is premised on the view that U.S. transfer taxation should be deferred until property gratuitously exits the marital unit, which effectively treats a married couple as a single unit for transfer tax purposes. Yet if a donor or decedent's spouse is not a U.S. citizen, there exists a meaningful prospect that the intended deferral of the transfer tax burden will amount to a permanent exclusion. If the non-citizen surviving spouse was not a resident of the United States or subsequently moved to a foreign country, no subsequent transfer tax burden would be imposed on property having a foreign situs. Due to this possibility, the marital deduction is not allowed for gratuitous transfers to non-citizen spouses as a general rule.[16] IRC §§ 2056(d)(1), 2523(i)(1). If the estate tax marital deduction is denied solely because the surviving spouse is not a U.S. citizen but the disallowance of the deduction is not warranted in hindsight (because the estate of the surviving spouse is subject to U.S. estate taxation because the surviving spouse is a U.S. citizen or resident at death), the estate of the surviving spouse is entitled to a credit under § 2013 for the estate tax paid on property that passed to the surviving spouse. IRC § 2056(d)(3).

[B] Qualified Domestic Trust

The general rule disallowing the marital deduction for transfers to a non-citizen spouse primarily serves as a channeling provision under the estate tax, as an exception exists for transfers to a "qualified domestic trust." IRC § 2056(d)(2)(A). Because § 2056(d)(2)(A) operates only as an exception to the disallowance of the marital deduction for transfers to non-citizen surviving spouses (as opposed to a deduction conferring provision), the general requirements of § 2056(a) must be satisfied. Transfers in trust for the benefit of a surviving spouse generally are structured to qualify for the marital deduction as a QTIP trust under § 2056(b)(7), which, among other things, requires the trust income to be distributed to the spouse at least annually and prohibits the distribution of trust principal to anyone other than the surviving spouse for the spouse's lifetime.[17]

---

[16] A limited exception to the general rule of disallowance exists for a spouse who becomes a citizen of the United States before the decedent's estate tax return is filed, provided the spouse was a resident of the United States at all times following the death of the decedent and until the date citizenship was obtained. *See* IRC § 2056(d)(4).

[17] The QTIP provisions of § 2056(b)(7) do not constitute the exclusive means of qualifying a transfer in trust for the marital deduction, only the most common. The QDOT also may qualify for the marital deduction under § 2056(b)(5) (power of appointment trusts), § 2056(b)(8) (charitable remainder trust of which spouse is sole noncharitable beneficiary), and the estate trust provisions of Reg. § 20.2056(c)-2(b)(1). *See* Treas. Reg. § 20.2056A-2(b)(1).

[1]　Statutory Conditions

The additional requirements of a qualified domestic trust—commonly referred to by the "QDOT" acronym—are addressed separately in § 2056A. First, at least one trustee of the trust must be an individual U.S. citizen or a domestic corporation. IRC § 2056A(a)(1)(A). Second, the trust must prohibit distributions of principal unless the trustee who is a U.S. citizen or domestic corporation possesses the right to withhold the tax imposed by the statute. IRC § 2056A(a)(1)(B); *see also* IRC § 2056A(b). Third, the trust must comply with any additional restrictions imposed by the regulations to ensure collection of the tax on distributions of principal. IRC § 2056A(a)(2). Fourth, the executor of the decedent's estate must elect to have the provisions of § 2056A apply to the trust. IRC § 2056A(a)(3).

[2]　Imposition of Deferred Estate Tax

The hallmark of the QDOT regime under § 2056A is the imposition of a deferred estate tax on the trust under § 2056A(b). The tax is imposed on distributions from the trust made during the surviving spouse's lifetime, other than distributions of income.[18] IRC § 2056A(b)(1)(A), (b)(3)(A). The value of any property remaining in the trust as of the death of the surviving spouse is subject to the deferred estate tax at that time. IRC § 2056A(b)(1)(B). Additionally, if the trust ceases to satisfy the conditions of a QDOT (e.g., because the trust no longer has at least one U.S. trustee), the deferred estate tax is imposed as if the surviving spouse died on the date the trust ceased to qualify as a QDOT. IRC § 2056A(b)(4); *see also* Treas. Reg. § 20.2056A-5(b)(3).

For each triggering event, the amount of the estate tax imposed under § 2056A is designed to replicate the marginal estate tax that would have resulted from the inclusion of such property in the taxable estate of the decedent spouse (taking into account any prior inclusions under § 2056A). IRC § 2056A(b)(2). Liability for the deferred estate tax is imposed on the trustees, IRC § 2056A(b)(6), and any tax paid on account of a lifetime distribution is treated as an additional distribution. IRC § 2056A(b)(11). In computing the estate tax imposed on the QDOT upon the death of the surviving spouse, the marital deduction, charitable deduction, and other estate tax benefits will be allowed provided the conditions for those benefits are otherwise satisfied. *See* IRC § 2056A(b)(10).

[3]　Hardship Exception

Section 2056A(b)(3)(B) provides an exception from the imposition of the deferred estate tax for any distribution to the surviving spouse on account of a hardship. A distribution of principal is treated as being made on account of a hardship if it is made in response to an "immediate and substantial" need relating to the health, education, support, or maintenance of the surviving spouse or any person the surviving spouse is obligated to support. Treas. Reg. § 20.2056A-5(c)(1). However, the hardship exception is not available if the distributed amount could have been obtained from resources that are reasonably available to the surviving spouse, such as publicly traded stock or certificates of deposit. *See id.* Illiquid assets such as closely

---

[18] For purposes of this exclusion, "income" has the same meaning as provided in § 643(b) in the income tax context, except that income will not include capital gains under any circumstance. Treas. Reg. § 20.2056A-5(c)(2). Additionally, income will not include any other item that otherwise would be allocable to corpus under local law notwithstanding an express provision in the trust to the contrary. *Id.*

held stock, real estate, and tangible personal property are not considered to be "reasonably available" for this purpose. *Id.*

[4]   Security Requirements

As contemplated by § 2056A(a)(2), the regulations impose additional conditions on a QDOT that are designed to ensure collection of the deferred estate tax imposed under § 2056(A)(b). To ensure domestic jurisdiction over the trust, the trust must be maintained under the laws of a state of the United States or the District of Columbia, and such laws must govern the trust administration. Treas. Reg. § 20.2056A-2(a). If the value of the property passing to the trust exceeds $2 million, then (a) one of the U.S. trustees must be a domestic bank, or (b) the U.S. trustee must furnish a bond or letter of credit in favor of the Service in an amount equal to 65 percent of the fair market value of the trust assets. *See* Treas. Reg. § 20.2056A-2(d)(1)(i). The value of the property in the QDOT for these purposes is determined by reference to values as of the decedent's date of death (or the alternate valuation date, if applicable), without reduction on account of indebtedness relating to the trust property. If the value of QDOT property (determined by aggregating all QDOTs) falls below the $2 million threshold, the QDOT is prohibited from owning more than 35 percent of its assets in the form of real estate located outside the United States unless the security requirements imposed on trusts in excess of $2 million are satisfied.[19] *See* Treas. Reg. § 20.2056A-2(d)(1)(ii). Annual reporting requirements imposed by Reg. § 20.2056A-2(d)(3) assist the Service in enforcing these conditions.

[5]   Post-Mortem Planning to Obtain QDOT Treatment

Even if the decedent-spouse did not create a QDOT to receive property devised on behalf of the non-citizen surviving spouse, the ability to obtain a deduction under the QDOT exception is not lost. For instance, if the decedent simply left property to the surviving spouse outright, the spouse may obtain the deduction for the estate either by transferring the property to a QDOT or by making an enforceable and irrevocable assignment of the property to a QDOT prior to the filing of the decedent's estate tax return. IRC § 2056(d)(2)(B). Additionally, the statute contemplates post-mortem revisions to a trust receiving property on behalf of the surviving spouse that does not originally satisfy the terms of a QDOT. The determination of whether a trust is a QDOT is made as of the date the decedent's estate tax return is filed or, if a judicial reformation proceeding is commenced prior to such date, the date on which any resulting changes to the trust are made. IRC § 2056(d)(5).

[C]   Increased Annual Exclusion for Lifetime Transfers

The disallowance of the marital deduction under the gift tax for transfers to non-citizen spouses carries more sting than the disallowance of the estate tax marital deduction in this context, as the gift tax does not provide a corollary QDOT exception. However, the sting of the marital deduction disallowance under the gift tax is significantly mitigated by the treatment of lifetime marital deductions to non-citizen spouses under the annual gift tax exclusion. If a transfer to a spouse otherwise would qualify for the gift tax marital deduction but for the donee-spouse's lack of U.S. citizenship, the base amount of the § 2503(b) exclusion (to be

---

[19] For purposes of determining whether the QDOT holds more than 35 percent of its assets in foreign real estate, the regulations contain look-through provisions for real estate owned by certain closely held entities. *See* Treas. Reg. § 20.2056A-2(d)(1)(ii)(B).

adjusted for inflation) is increased substantially from $10,000 to $100,000. IRC § 2523(i)(2). The inflation-adjusted figure for 2011 stands at $136,000. Given the liberal annual exclusion in this context, substantial transfers can be made to a non-citizen spouse over time without automatically subjecting the transfers to any form of deferred U.S. transfer taxation.

[D]　Jointly Held Property

In addition to the increased annual gift tax exclusion, special rules concerning the gift of a joint interest in property exist in this context. The creation of a joint tenancy with right of survivorship in real property between spouses is not considered a transfer of property by gift; rather, the transfer occurs only upon termination of the joint tenancy. IRC § 2523(i)(3) (incorporating § 2515 prior to its repeal in 1981). On the other hand, the creation of a joint tenancy with right of survivorship in personal property is not subject to this delayed-transfer rule. Instead, each spouse is treated as receiving one-half of the value of the property, regardless of their relative life expectancies. IRC § 2523(i)(3) (incorporating § 2515A prior to its repeal in 1981).

Recall that division of beneficial ownership of jointly held property in the estate tax setting is presumed to be equal, regardless of the spouses' relative contributions to the acquisition or improvement of the property. See IRC § 2040(b). However, if the surviving spouse is not a U.S. citizen, the presumption of equal contributions no longer applies. IRC § 2056(d)(1)(B). As a result, the amount of the jointly held property that will be included in the decedent-spouse's estate will be the full date-of-death value of the property, less any portion of the acquisition price the decedent's estate can establish was supplied by the surviving spouse. See IRC § 2040(a).

§ 26.06　THE FOREIGN DEATH TAX CREDIT

Because the U.S. transfer tax regime applies to the transfer of property by a U.S. citizen or resident on a worldwide basis, the potential exists for the transfer of property located abroad to be subject to transfer tax by multiple jurisdictions. To mitigate the potential for excessive estate taxation in this context, § 2014(a) provides a credit for any estate or inheritance tax paid to a foreign country with respect to property included in the decedent's gross estate that is situated in such foreign country. The existence of the foreign death tax credit under § 2014(a) recognizes that the country in which property is situated possesses a priority claim to tax the transfer of that property by reason of death.

The foreign death tax credit is limited in two respects. First, to be creditable, the foreign tax must be levied on a proportionate basis. That is, the amount of foreign tax that may be credited against the U.S. estate tax under § 2014(a) may not exceed the portion of the total tax paid to the foreign country that (a) the value of property situated in the foreign country, subject to the foreign tax, and included in the decedent's gross estate bears to (b) the value of all property subject to the foreign tax. IRC § 2014(b)(1). Additionally, the foreign death tax credit may not exceed the amount of U.S. estate tax attributable to the property that generated the foreign tax. Specifically, the amount of the credit may not exceed an amount which bears the same ratio to the gross U.S. estate tax liability (determined by deducting only the credit for prior gift taxes under § 2012) as (a) the value of property situated in such foreign country, subject to the foreign death tax, and included in the decedent's gross estate bears to (b) the value of the decedent's gross estate reduced by the marital and charitable deductions. IRC § 2014(b)(2).

Pursuant to this second limitation, the United States guarantees only that it will not add its estate tax burden to that imposed by the country in which the transferred property is situated; the credit is not designed to hold a U.S. citizen or resident harmless from a higher rate of estate taxation imposed by the foreign jurisdiction. These two limitations on the foreign death tax credit under § 2014(b) apply independently, such that the allowable credit is the lower of the two.

The credit for foreign death taxes under § 2014(a) is provided only against the U.S. estate tax. No corollary credit exists under the U.S. gift tax. Any foreign tax credit in the gift tax setting will be provided by treaty only.

§ 26.07   TRANSFER TAX TREATIES

The United States has entered into bilateral transfer tax treaties with 17 countries: Australia, Austria, Canada, Denmark, Finland, France, Germany, Greece, Ireland, Italy, Japan, the Netherlands, Norway, South Africa, Sweden, Switzerland, and the United Kingdom. While all of these treaties address transfer taxes imposed by reason of death, several cover taxes imposed on gifts and generation-skipping transfers as well. These treaties are designed to prevent the same property from being subject to transfer taxation by the United States and another country, either because (a) one country bases transfer taxation on the situs of property and the other on the transferor's domicile, (b) each country imposes transfer taxation on the basis of the situs of property but the countries' situs rules are not consistent, or (c) each country bases transfer taxation on the basis of citizenship or residency, but the tests for residency are not mutually exclusive.

The transfer tax treaties to which the United States is a party fall into two general camps. One type of treaty resolves competing claims to transfer taxation by assigning priority to the country in which the transferred property is situated, based on situs provisions set out in the treaty. *See* Treas. Reg. § 20.2104-1(c) (noting the potential for the U.S. situs rules to be overridden by death tax convention).[20] The other type of treaty focuses on resolving conflicting determinations of domicile. These treaties employ a number of tie-breaking provisions aimed at determining which country possesses the superior claim to treat the transferor as a resident, which in turn provides that country with the primary right to impose transfer taxation on the transferor's property.

Because an estate tax can be envisioned as a deferred income tax, problems can arise in attempting to resolve one country's treatment of death as an event triggering realization of gain on appreciated property under an income tax with another country's treatment of death as an event triggering transfer taxation. For example, the Tax Court in *Estate of Ballard v. Commissioner*, 85 T.C. 300 (1985), held that Canadian income taxes resulting from a deemed disposition of property occurring upon a decedent's death could not be credited against the U.S. estate tax imposed on such property, because the foreign death tax credit under § 2014 is available only for estate, inheritance, or succession taxes. *See* Treas. Reg. § 20.2014-1(a)(1). The two countries later resolved this inconsistency by amending the U.S.-Canada Income Tax Treaty to permit the Canadian income tax imposed in this setting to be credited against the U.S. estate tax, subject to the normal limitations on the amount of the credit. *See* Protocol to

---

[20] Note that the foreign death tax credit provided by § 2014 provides a default means of assigning priority in transfer taxation based on the situs of property in the absence of a transfer tax treaty.

the U.S.-Canada Income Tax Treaty, art. 19 (Mar. 17, 1995) (art. XXIX B, para. 7, of the Treaty as amended).

If a U.S. citizen or resident owns property in a treaty country, or if an individual owning property situated in the United States is a citizen or resident of a treaty country, the terms of the treaty must be consulted in determining the individual's total transfer tax exposure. The terms of these treaties are beyond the scope of this text, but a thorough analysis can be found in Jeffrey A. Schoenblum, *Bilateral Transfer Tax Treaties*, 851 Tax Mgmt. Port. (BNA) (2007).

§ 26.08 STUDY PROBLEMS

1. George, a citizen of Mexico, has a sizeable estate that includes the following assets:

    - A condominium in Vail, Colorado;

    - A house in Mexico City;

    - Cash and diamonds located in a safe deposit box in a Houston, Texas bank;

    - $2 million of stock in U.S. corporations and $10 million of stock in foreign corporations, held through a brokerage firm located in New York City;

    - $500,000 of publicly traded bonds issued by U.S. corporations;

    - A $10 million promissory note issued by a Mexican corporation;

    - A cause of action for securities fraud and related claims against a U.S. investment advisor;

    - A limited partnership interest in a Cayman Islands partnership that owns, among other things, a dog track located in Florida;

    - A $20 million policy on his life issued by a U.S. insurance company;

    - A $5 million policy insuring the life of his wife issued by a U.S insurance company;

    - Certificates of deposit and savings accounts at a bank in Miami, Florida, having a combined balance of $1 million.

    a. George occasionally spends time in the United States attending to his domestic business interests and vacationing with his family. Each trip lasts only a matter of weeks, after which he returns to his home in Mexico City.

        George gave all of the above-described assets to his children. To what extent, if any, does he owe U.S. gift tax?

    b. Same as (a), except that George retained all of his assets until his death, which occurred during a trip to the United States. Assuming all of the assets pass to his children, to what extent is George's estate liable for U.S. estate tax?

    c. In light of your answer to (b), how could George have minimized his estate's exposure to U.S. estate tax?

    d. For purposes of this question, assume that George possessed a temporary work visa to perform work in the Houston, Texas division of his employer. Even though the visa expired after three years, George remained in Houston in an apartment he rented on a year-to-year basis where he lived with his girlfriend. George occasionally returned to Mexico City prior to his visa expiration, but has not left Houston since. How do these facts change the answers to (a) and (b) above, if at all?

2. Lora, a Canadian citizen, is a lawful permanent resident of the United States who lives with her husband Robb in the United States.

    a. The two purchased a residence for $500,000 with funds supplied by Robb. What are the gift tax consequences, if any, from the purchase?

    b. The two purchased a car for $40,000 titled in their names as joint tenants with right of survivorship. Robb supplied the consideration for the car. Additionally, Robb transferred securities worth $1 million to an account established in Lora's individual name. What are the gift tax consequences, if any, of these events?

    c. Robb predeceases Lora and devises his entire probate estate worth $10 million to Lora outright. Additionally, Lora acquires fee ownership of the residence pursuant to the right of survivorship. What are the estate tax consequences to Robb's estate?

    d. In light of your answer to (c), what steps can Lora take following Robb's death to minimize the estate tax due in his estate?

3. Nicola is a citizen and resident of Sweden who recently purchased a $10 million condominium in New York City, financing $4 million of the purchase price through a loan for which she bears personal liability. Nicola owns substantial property in her native country worth approximately $90 million. If she dies owning the New York condominium, what would be the U.S. estate tax consequences to her estate? How could her loan be restructured to improve the result?

4. Assume that Nicola in problem (3) transfers the condominium to an irrevocable trust of which she is a lifetime beneficiary. The terms of the trust specifically permit Nicola to use the condominium as a vacation residence for the remainder of her lifetime. Three years after transferring the condominium to the trust, the trust sells the property and uses the net proceeds to purchase a villa in the Greek Isles for $8 million. Nicola dies 10 years later, when the villa is worth $10 million. To what extent will the villa be subject to U.S. estate taxation?

5. Jack recently sold his technology company for $250 million. A rabid critic of the U.S. estate tax, Jack is considering renouncing his U.S. citizenship and moving to the Cayman Islands, where he will happily spend his remaining days playing golf and snorkeling. He has two adult children and several grandchildren who will remain in the United States. Jack asks you for your advice on whether such a move will be effective at avoiding the U.S. estate tax.

TABLE OF CASES

[References are to pages.]

TC-1

[References are to pages.]

[References are to pages.]

[References are to pages.]

[References are to pages.]

TABLE OF STATUTES

[References are to sections.]

[References are to sections.]

[References are to sections.]

[References are to sections.]

[References are to sections.]

[References are to sections.]

OMNIBUS BUDGET RECONCILIATION ACT OF 1987

OMNIBUS BUDGET RECONCILIATION ACT OF 1990

PENSION PROTECTION ACT OF 2006

REVENUE ACT OF 1916

REVENUE ACT OF 1918

REVENUE ACT OF 1942

[References are to sections.]

[References are to sections.]

[References are to sections.]

[References are to sections.]

[References are to sections.]

PROPOSED TREASURY REGULATIONS

UNIFIED LIMITED PARTNERSHIP ACT

UNIFORM PROBATE CODE

UNIFORM SIMULATENOUS DEATH ACT

UNIFORM TRANSFERS TO MINORS ACT

UNIFORM TRUST CODE

UNITED STATES CODE (U.S.C.)

TABLE OF SECONDARY AUTHORITIES

[References are to sections.]

[References are to sections.]

SENATE REPORTS

T.C. MEMO

TABLE OF SECONDARY AUTHORITIES

[References are to sections.]

TECHNICAL ADVICE MEMO

INDEX

[References are to sections.]

[References are to sections.]

[References are to sections.]

[References are to sections.]

[References are to sections.]